D1615283

Islam in Liberalism

Islam in Liberalism

JOSEPH A. MASSAD

The University of Chicago Press   Chicago and London

JOSEPH A. MASSAD is professor of modern Arab politics and intellectual history in the Department of Middle Eastern, South Asian, and African Studies at Columbia University. He is the author of *Desiring Arabs* (2007), *The Persistence of the Palestinian Question: Essays on Zionism and the Palestinian Question* (2006), and *Colonial Effects: The Making of National Identity in Jordan* (2001).

The University of Chicago Press, Chicago 60637
The University of Chicago Press, Ltd., London
© 2015 by The University of Chicago
All rights reserved. Published 2015.
Printed in the United States of America

24 23 22 21 20 19 18 17 16 15   1 2 3 4 5

ISBN-13: 978-0-226-20622-6 (cloth)
ISBN-13: 978-0-226-20636-3 (e-book)
DOI: 10.7208/chicago/9780226206363.001.0001

Library of Congress Cataloging-in-Publication Data

Massad, Joseph Andoni. 1963– author.
    Islam in liberalism / Joseph A. Massad.
        pages   cm
    Includes bibliographical references and index.
    ISBN 978-0-226-20622-6 (hardcover : alkaline paper)—
ISBN 978-0-226-20636-3 (e-book)   1. Orientalism. 2. Liberalism—Moral
and ethical aspects. 3. Islam—Relations. 4. Middle East—Foreign public
opinion, Western. 5. East and West.   I. Title.
    DS61.85.M37 2015
    306.6'97—dc23

                                                2014021594

♾ This paper meets the requirements of ANSI/NISO Z39.48-1992
(Permanence of Paper).

For Neville Hoad

Contents

Acknowledgments

I have been thinking about the modern intellectual and semantic history of the term "Islam" for a few years and began my work on the "Genealogies of Islam" in 2008, soon after my last book, *Desiring Arabs*, had come out. As soon as I began to research the book, however, I realized that I needed to explain my point of departure for this endeavor, namely the uses to which the term "Islam" has been put by European and Euro-American liberalism (and increasingly by Arab and Muslim liberals) since the eighteenth century. I initially decided to do so in a long introduction to the project but quickly realized that an introduction would not suffice as the issues multiplied and needed a more extensive scholarly treatment. This is when I decided that I had to write a book on the topic to contextualize my forthcoming project. This is how *Islam in Liberalism* was born.

The book was written over a protracted period of time. The first drafts of chapters 3, 4, and 5 were written in the fall of 2008 and the spring of 2009 in Cairo, while I was on a research sabbatical, and were expanded in subsequent years in New York, Amman, and Cairo. I thank Tim Sullivan for facilitating my affiliation with the American University in Cairo during my sabbatical. Parts of chapter 1 were also written in Cairo in the fall of 2010 during a one-semester sabbatical I had that year. The rest of chapter 1 and chapter 2 were written mostly in New York between 2011 and 2013, but redrafted in Cairo and Amman in the summers of 2012 and 2013. The introduction was written during the summer of 2013 in Amman when the book was finalized.

I am grateful to a number of friends and colleagues who took the time to read drafts of chapters and provided me with advice and recommendations. Asʿad Abukhalil, Ahmad Atif Ahmad, Judith Butler, Kaoukab Chebaro, Marwa Elshakry, Ahmed Issawi, Islah Jad, Samia Mehrez, Alan Mikhail, Rosalind Morris, Lecia Rosenthal, Leticia Sabsay, Mayssoun Sukarrieh, and Alexis Wick read earlier drafts of at least one chapter, and in some cases two or three chapters. Their insights were crucial to improving the arguments and the research for these chapters. I also thank Joan Copjek for her comments and suggestions on an earlier version of chapter 4. Ali Abunimah and Wael Hallaq read most of the manuscript and were generous with their time and comments, providing me with important suggestions, critiques, and recommendations. I am grateful for their efforts and exemplary friendship and collegiality. Talal Asad and Anne Norton provided meticulously detailed critiques, insights, and suggestions that have improved the book immeasurably. I cannot begin to express my appreciation and gratitude for their serious engagement with my work.

At Columbia, my students in my seminars "Psychoanalysis, Identity, and Culture" and "Universalizing Sexuality" also provided important suggestions for chapters 3, 4, and 5. I thank especially Nasser Abourahmeh, Ahmed Dardir, Emily Ming Yao, and Stephanie Skier. Ahmed Dardir was gracious enough to also read chapter 1 and provided important suggestions. I am grateful to all of them.

Neville Hoad read the manuscript since its early infancy and in several of its metamorphoses and reread its final form at least twice. I am indebted to him forever! The book, like all my previous books, bears the mark of his numerous suggestions and insights. Neville has been my main intellectual interlocutor since we met in 1991 at a party at the apartment of our common friend Aamir Mufti, a few weeks after we had both started graduate school at Columbia University. Ever since then our intellectual and political concerns have defined our friendship and scholarly and political alliance. His support and love have sustained me ever since. I dedicate this book to him as a token of my friendship and appreciation.

I was invited to give a number of lectures based on the book and/ or its constituent chapters at a number of universities. I thank Ussama Makdisi for inviting me to give a lecture at the James A. Baker III Institute for Public Policy at Rice University, Alejandro Paz for inviting me to the University of Toronto, Abdel Razzaq Takriti for inviting me to St Antony's College at Oxford University, Dana Sajdi for inviting me to Boston College, Nimer Sultany for inviting me to Harvard Law School,

Sara Roy and Roger Owen for inviting me to the Center for Middle Eastern Studies at Harvard University, Suad Joseph for inviting me to give a lecture at the "Rights Talk and Rights Work in the Middle East and South Asia" symposium sponsored by The Middle East/South Asia Studies Program at the University of California at Davis, Nahla Abdo for inviting me to deliver the keynote address at the "Counterpoints: Edward Said's Legacy" conference at the University of Ottawa and the University of Carleton, Gil Anidjar and Stathis Gourgouris for inviting me to deliver the keynote address at the "Orientalism from the Standpoint of Its Victims" conference at Columbia University, Mohammed Tabishat for inviting me to the Wissenschaftkolleg seminar on "Islam, the Qur'an, and Late Secularism," Caroline Rooney for inviting me to deliver the keynote address at the University of Kent's conference "Cultural Memory," Julia Borossa for inviting me to deliver the keynote address at the conference "Psychoanalysis, Fascism, Fundamentalism" at the Freud Museum in London, Samia Mehrez for inviting me to deliver the keynote lecture at the Magda al-Nowaihi Award ceremony and for inviting me to deliver a lecture at the Center for Translation Studies, both at the American University in Cairo, Islah Jad for inviting me to deliver a lecture via video link at Birzeit University, Ramón Gutiérrez for inviting me to deliver the keynote address at the "Islam and Sexuality" conference at the University of Chicago, Lisa Wedeen for inviting me to present at the Comparative Politics Workshop at the Department of Political Science at the University of Chicago, Shaden Tageldin for inviting me to deliver two lectures at the Institute for Global Studies at the University of Minnesota, 'Ismat Husu for inviting me to deliver a guest lecture at the Institute of Social Service at the University of Amman al-Ahliyyah and the National Jordanian Committee for Women's Affairs, Faris Hilmi for inviting me to lecture at the Department of Psychology at the University of Jordan, Jayesh (Jay) Needham for inviting me to deliver the keynote address at the "The Sexualized Other: A Symposium on Asian Sexuality and Gender Identity" as well as another separate lecture at Oberlin College, Michael Warner for inviting me to the conference "Why Homosexuality: Religion, Globalization, and the Anglican Schism" at Yale University, Amy Aisen Elouafi for inviting me to lecture at Syracuse University's Departments of History and of Women and Gender Studies, Susan Slymovich for inviting me to lecture at the Center for Near Eastern Studies at the University of California, Los Angeles, Jeffrey Sacks for inviting me to lecture at the University of California Riverside, Katherine Franke for inviting me to give a seminar at the Gender and Sexuality Law Colloquium at the Columbia University Law School,

Gabriëlle Schleijpen and Nat Muller for inviting me to deliver the keynote address at the "Becoming Nation" conference held at the Gerrit Rietveld Academie, Amsterdam, Edda Manga for inviting me to deliver two lectures at the University of Gothenberg and the Clandestino Institute in Sweden, and Mikela Lundahl for inviting me to deliver a lecture at the Symposium on "Disidentification" at the University of Gothenberg and to give a lecture at the Department of Gender Studies also at the University of Gothenberg, Alberto Toscano for inviting me to lecture at the University of London's Goldsmiths College, Mouannes Hojairi for inviting me to lecture at the Department of Africana Studies at Vassar College, Jeff Handmaker for inviting me to lecture at the International Institute of Social Studies at Erasmus University in The Hague, Michael Salvatore for inviting me to deliver a lecture the University of Southern California, Khaled Ziyadah and Sumantra Bose for inviting me to give a lecture at the London School of Economics, Thomas Waugh for inviting me to lecture at Concordia University in Montreal, Ahmad al-Mallah for inviting me to lecture at Middlebury College, Alexis Wick for inviting me to the Department of History and the American Studies Center at the American University of Beirut, Tarik Sabry for inviting me to give the keynote address at the conference "Arab Subcultures" at the University of Westminster's Communication and Media Research Institute, Sonja Hegasy for inviting me to give a series of lectures at the Zentrum Moderner Orient and Humboldt University in Berlin, Beth Baron for inviting me to give a paper at "The Dissections Seminar: New Directions in Research on the Middle East and North Africa," cosponsored by the Middle East and Middle Eastern-American Center and the Center for the Humanities at the City University of New York, Graduate Center, Camila Pastor de Maria y Campos, Gilberto Conde, and Shadi Rohana for inviting me to deliver the keynote address at the Semana Árabe conference at the Colegio de Mexico and the Centro de Investigación y Docencia Económica in Mexico City, Stella Magliani Belkasem of the March 20 Front for inviting me to give a lecture at Columbia University's Reid Hall in Paris, Burcak Keskin-Kozat for inviting me to present a paper at the Winter Workshop of the Sohaib and Sara Abbasi Program in Islamic Studies at Stanford University, Robbert Woltering for inviting me to deliver the keynote address at the opening of the Amsterdam Centre for Middle Eastern Studies (ACMES) at the University of Amsterdam, and Marcela Zedán for inviting me to give a series of lectures at the University of Chile's Center for Arab Studies in Santiago.

I thank my research assistant Isaac Park for his tireless procuring of books and other documentary sources, which I requested almost daily.

He also kindly put the Works Cited list together. I am grateful to him for his efforts. This book would not have seen the light were it not for my editor Douglas Mitchell, whose unflinching support and hard work made it possible. I owe him much appreciation and gratitude.

An earlier version of the last section of chapter 2 was previously published in Arabic as "Kayfa ʿalayna alla nadrus al-nawʿ al-ijtimaʿi (al-jindar) fi al-ʿalam al-ʿarabi" (How Not to Study Gender in the Arab World), *Majallat al-Adab*, Beirut, June 2009. An earlier shorter version of chapter 4, "Pschoanalysis, Islam, and the Other of Liberalism," was first published in the special "Islam" issue of *Umbr(a): A Journal of the Unconscious* (SUNY Buffalo, 2009): 43–68, and another yet shorter version in *Psychoanalysis and History* 11, no. 2 (2009): 193–208. It is reproduced here (in expanded form) with permission. An Arabic translation of an earlier version of the chapter was published as "Al-Islam: Ishkaliyyat al-Mustalah," *Wujuhat Nazar* 11, no. 127 (September 2009): 17–27. An earlier version of chapter 5, "Forget Semitism!" was published in my book *La persistance de la question palestinienne* (Paris: La Fabrique, 2009), and another version in *Living Together: Jacques Derrida's Communities of Peace and Violence*, ed. Elisabeth Weber (New York: Fordham University Press, 2013), 59–79. It is reproduced here with permission.

The Choice of Liberalism

Islam is at the heart of liberalism, at the heart of Europe; it was there at the moment of the birth of liberalism and the birth of Europe. Islam is indeed one of the conditions of their emergence as the identities they claim to be. Islam, as I will show, resides inside liberalism, defining its identity and its very claims of difference. It is an internal constituent of liberalism, not merely an external other, though liberalism often projects it as the latter. The establishment of differing forms of liberalism as the reigning political, social, and/or economic system in parts of Western Europe and the United States since the late eighteenth century and its main deployment thenceforward as the ideological weapon of choice against the "internal" and "external" others of Europe, is what marks its current legitimation as a global ideological system.

Europe's external others have historically been defined as Orientals and the Orient, Muslims and Islam, Africans and Africa, Native Americans and Aboriginal Australians and New Zealanders, Oriental despotisms of various kinds extending from East to West Asia and everything in between. Europe's internal others, in contrast, have been identified as Orthodox and Catholic Christians (and Mormons in the case of Protestant Anglo-Americans) and their forms of Christianity, Jews and Judaism, socialism, fascism, anarchism and communism. Like Europe, liberalism's external others turn out to be internal to it, though the ruse of externalizing them as outsiders intends to hide the operation of projecting them as an outside so that liberalism's inside can be defined as their opposite, as their superior. Edward

Said understood this well. "The Orient," he declared, "is an integral part of European *material* civilization and culture."[1]

The situation following the collapse of the Soviet Union as the last state-sponsored threat to liberalism within Europe is astutely described by Toula Nicolacopoulos in these terms: "Today Anglophone political philosophy is generally conducted in the light of the perceived triumph of liberalism. That is, it typically proceeds on the assumption that it is unreasonable, if not irrational or pathological, to resist liberalism, whether as a mode of thought or as a social order."[2] This is hardly a condition confined to Anglophone political philosophy but encompasses the dominant political discourse across Western and Northern Europe and beyond. The hegemony of liberalism is such that "to resist" it "would be unreasonably to deny the moral and/or political superiority of (the values governing) liberal societies as compared with their historical and contemporary social alternatives."[3]

Alasdair MacIntyre, writes Gerald Gauss, poses the question: "'Nietzsche or Aristotle?' If *I* am right, the question is 'Nietzsche or Liberalism?'; and, unless one is a psychopath . . . the answer must be the latter."[4] In its constitution of an "Islam" that it names and wants to oppose, contemporary Western liberalism offers the more detrimental "choice": Islam or liberalism, or variations therein, totalitarian Islamism or liberalism, Islamofascism or liberalism, Islamic despotism or liberalism, etc. The correlate to Gauss's reply here would be that *unless one is a barbarian, a despot, an irrational psychopath, a neurotic, a totalitarian, an intolerant brute, a misogynist, a homophobe*, in short, a Muslim, *the answer must be the latter.*

In this vein, Paul Kahn paraphrases Americans' view of themselves and the world at large as follows:

Our contemporary missionaries preach democracy, free markets, and the rule of law— all institutions founded on our belief in the equality and liberty of every person. This dogged commitment to a universal community is a product of both our Christian and Enlightenment traditions. We experience this commitment simultaneously as a kind of open-ended love and as a faith in the capacity of each individual to enter a rational debate that will result in mutual agreement. No one, we believe, is beyond conversion

1. Edward W. Said, *Orientalism* (New York: Pantheon Books, 1978), 2.
2. Toula Nicolacopoulos, *The Radical Critique of Liberalism: In Memory of a Vision* (Melbourne: re.press, 2008), 3.
3. Ibid., 4.
4. Gerald Gauss, *Value and Justifications: The Foundations of Liberal Theory* (Cambridge: Cambridge University Press, 1990), 457n, cited in ibid., 3.

to our values. When we dream of a global order, we project our own values onto it. We do not imagine that the global community of the future will be led by an Islamic cleric.[5]

We will see, throughout this book, how American and European missionaries of liberalism, that is, those who imagine that the global community of the future will be led by a *secular* cleric, will seek to proselytize their value system and model of social and political order to all Muslims whom they seek to *save and rescue* from their despotic system of rule, failing which, the missionaries would at least want to rescue Muslim women and increasingly male (and female, though less attention is paid to the latter) Muslim "homosexuals" from Islam's misogyny, homophobia, and intolerance. This act of proselytization aims to convert *Muslims and Islam* to Western liberalism and its value system as the only just and sane system to which the entire planet must be converted. As Talal Asad put it, the liberal mission is to have the Islamic tradition "remade in the image of liberal Protestant Christianity."[6] Muslim resistance to this benevolent mission is represented as a rejection of modernity and the liberal values of freedom, liberty, equality, the right-bearing individual, democratic citizenship, women's rights, sexual rights, freedom of belief, secularism, rationality, etc., in short as a pathology and a form of neurosis that must not only be vanquished, but also, and as we will see, psychoanalyzed. Thus if Muslims refuse to convert willingly to liberalism or at least to forms of Islam that liberalism finds tolerable, then they must be forced to convert using military power, as their resistance threatens a core value of liberalism, namely its universality and the necessity of its universalization as globalization. Talal Asad understands this project thus: if the European Enlightenment's "secular redemptive politics" condemns religious forms of violence, pain, and suffering as non-emancipatory of sinners, "there is a readiness [on its part] to cause pain to those who are to be saved by being humanized."[7]

Naming Islam

The more robust recent campaign to identify Islam as the last holdout resisting Western liberalism is significant on a number of fronts, not

---

5. Paul W. Kahn, *Putting Liberalism in Its Place* (Princeton, NJ: Princeton University Press, 2008), 6–7.

6. Talal Asad, "Europe against Islam: Islam in Europe," *Muslim World* 87, no. 2 (April 1997): 189.

7. Talal Asad, *Formations of the Secular: Christianity, Islam, Modernity* (Stanford, CA: Stanford University Press, 2003), 61–62.

least of which is the deployment of the referent "Islam." The very naming of that which resists liberalism's universalization as "Islam" has been
fraught with political and definitional problems that are not easily surmountable. One of the difficulties in analyzing what Islam has come
to *mean* and to refer to since the nineteenth century is the absence of
agreement on what Islam actually *is*. Does *Islam* name a religion, a geographical site, a communal identity; is it a concept, a technical term, a
sign, or taxonomy? The lack of clarity on whether it could be all these
things at the same time is compounded by the fact that Islam has acquired referents and significations it did not formerly possess. European
Orientalists and Muslim and Arab thinkers have begun to use "Islam" in
numerous ways while seemingly convinced that it possesses an immediate intelligibility that requires no specification or definition. "Islam,"
for these thinkers, is not only the *name* the Qur'an attributes to the
din—often (mis)translated as "religion," though there is some disagreement about this—that entails a faith (*iman*) in God disseminated by the
Prophet Muhammad, but can also refer to the history of Muslim states
and empires, the different bodies of philosophical, theological, jurisprudential, medical, literary, and scientific works, as well as to culinary,
sexual, social, economic, religious, ritualistic, scholarly, agricultural, and
urban practices engaged in by Muslims from the seventh to the nineteenth century and beyond, as well as much, much more.

Some of the new meanings and referents of Islam had a significant
impact on political and social thought as well as on national and international politics in the nineteenth and twentieth centuries, and may
have even more of an impact in the twenty-first. The implication of
these meanings for politics and society results from their transformation
of "Islam" into a "culture" and a "civilization" or a "cultural tradition,"[8]
a "system,"[9] a "*manhaj*" (way of life, method),[10] a "programme,"[11] an ethics, a code of public conduct, a gendered sartorial code, a set of banking
principles, a type of governance. Moreover, "Islam" has also come to be
deployed as a metonym: *fiqh* (problematically rendered "jurisprudence")

8. See G. E. von Grunebaum, *Islam: Essays in the Nature and Growth of a Cultural Tradition*
(London: Routledge & Kegan Paul, 1955).

9. D. S. Margoliouth referred to Islam as a "system," in his *Mohammedanism* (London: Williams
and Norgate, 1896), 42.

10. Sayyid Qutb uses the term "manhaj" throughout his writings, especially in *Al-Islam wa
Mushkilat al-Hadarah* (Islam and the Problems of Civilization) (Cairo: Dar al-Shuruq, 2005), as does
Mahmud Muhammad Shakir in his *Risalah fi al-Tariq ila Thaqafatina* (A Message on the Path to Our
Culture) (Cairo: Mu'assassat al-Risalah, 1992).

11. On the use of "programme," see Muhammad Asad, *Islam at the Crossroads* (Lahore: Arafat
Publications, 1947), 5, 14, 152, *inter alia*. The book was first published in 1934.

and *kalam* ("theology," again, problematically)—which were traditionally sciences established by Muslim thinkers—or *Shariʿa* ("sacred law,"
also problematically)—a term loaded with different connotations and
trajectories, often referring to a body of opinions and interpretations—
come to be conceived as constituent parts of "Islam," for which it can
metonymically substitute.[12]

While the easiest transformation to identify is the one that makes
Islam over into a "culture" and a "civilization," given the centrality of
this meaning among Orientalist thinkers and their Muslim and Arab
counterparts since the nineteenth century, the production of Islam's
many other new meanings and referents may not be as clear. Yet a history of the multiplication of the meanings of Islam is necessary for
understanding what Islam has become in today's world, both in those
parts of the world where peoples as well as political and social forces
claim to uphold one kind of Islam or another, and in those parts of the
world where peoples as well as political and social forces see "Islam" as
"other," whether or not they "oppose" it. Indeed, the current ongoing
war among the many forces that claim to speak in the name of Islam
and in the name of anti-Islam is itself not only part of the productive
process of endowing Islam with new meanings and referents, but also
part of the related process of controlling the slippage of the term toward
specific and particular meanings and referents and away from others. In
this way, "Islam" is being opposed to certain antonyms ("Christianity,"
"the West," "liberalism," "individualism," "democracy," "freedom,"
"citizenship," "secularism," "rationality," "tolerance," "human rights,"
"women's rights," "sexual rights") and decidedly not to others with
which it is often identified ("oppression," "repression," "despotism,"
"totalitarianism," "subjection," "injustice," "intolerance," "irrationalism," "cruelty," "misogyny," or "homophobia").

Two central religious and intellectual strands emerged in the nineteenth century among Arab, Muslim, and European Orientalist thinkers who argued for the compatibility or incompatibility of "Islam" with
Western modernity and progress. The word—or, more precisely, the
name—"Islam" itself began to conjure up immediate comprehension
and significance in ways assumed to have always been the case. This
project of thinking (about) "Islam" in new ways, while often passing

12. Dale F. Eickelman and James Piscatori have written perceptively about the "systematization" of Islam and its "objectification" and how the latter "reconfigures the symbolic production
of Muslim politics." For them, however, Islam denotes a "religion" and not multiple referents. See
Dale F. Eickelman and James Piscatori, *Muslim Politics* (Princeton, NJ: Princeton University Press,
1996), 38.

itself off as a return to old or original ways of thinking, was situated in the political context of the rise of European imperial thought and territorial expansion as well as in the corresponding decline of Ottoman political and imperial power. Yet the "Islam" to which these European and non-European thinkers referred was a more expansive concept, encompassing phenomena that had hitherto been seen as extraneous to it. Indeed, "Islam" had never been the catchall term the eighteenth and especially the nineteenth century would make of it, but was, rather, something more specific, more particular.

Additionally, one of the more interesting aspects of post-nineteenth century uses of the term "Islam" is not just its accretion of referents, nor that the accreted meanings were deployed by different thinkers or different intellectual or political trends, but that they were employed differently by each thinker and each trend. European Orientalists, Arab secularists (Muslim and Christian), pious (and later Islamist) thinkers, postcolonial states defining themselves as "Muslim" or "Islamic," and their "Western" and "secular" opponents—all seem to use the term "Islam" in a variety of ways to refer to a whole range of things. The productive multiplication of referents that Islam would begin to acquire would ultimately destabilize whatever meaning it had had before or even *after* this transformation, in that in modern writing about Islam it is not always clear which referent it has in a given text. Rather, it often seems that all of them are in play interchangeably *in the same text*, as well as across texts, thus rendering "Islam" a catachresis that always stands in for the *wrong* referent. In my next book, tentatively titled *Genealogies of Islam*, for which *Islam in Liberalism* is intended to serve as a prolegomenon, I will study the intellectual and semantic history of the multiplication of the meanings of Islam since the eighteenth century. In this book, I will investigate the role of Western liberalism in producing these referents and meanings, as well as what Western liberalism produces as Islam's synonyms and antonyms. It is at the site of translation that this becomes significant for the Western liberal project.

Translating Islam

One often thinks of translation as opening up access to texts in other languages, a process by which one produces literal copies of an original text, albeit rendered through a different communicative medium. This optimistic, one would say vernacular, view of translation as linguistic equivalence has been complicated by myriad theories of language, linguistics, or even earlier on in philological approaches. Still, translation in the publishing industry remains mostly seen as opening doors for one language group to another, universalizing a particular language beyond its structural confines, the limitations of which were explored by Pascale Casanova in her discussion of what she calls "the World Republic of Letters."[13]

I understand translation as an epistemology, a way to apprehend what lies outside the confines of one's language, which, paradoxically, can only be apprehended through one's own language. But while translation as such is an epistemology, the act of translation itself is enmeshed in a web of linguistic, political, social, economic, "cultural," in short, *power* contexts that determine that act itself, its structures, its imperatives, its effects, and its publics. In a colonial world of unequal power, languages are not equal; indeed, as Talal Asad has shown, they are so "unequal" that some languages are "stronger" than others.[14] This is not to say that Arabic is in any way more or less accessible, or more or less transparent, than English or other European, Asian, or African languages, but rather that it is equally accessible and inaccessible depending on epistemological considerations and the context of power dynamics within which the act of translation takes place.

Beyond the publishing industry and the profit motive, one of the most interesting uses of translation is ideological. The US government and subsidiary nongovernmental organizations (NGOs) and private foundations rushed to fund all kinds of translation projects from English to Arabic in the wake of September 11. This was not a new project, as US interest in translation projects in Muslim-majority countries goes back to the dawn of the Cold War. The idea is that translation would bring about a cultural transformation in Arab and Muslim countries, where al-Qaʿida-style cultures are said to prosper.

Nonetheless, these translational efforts acknowledge that there are certain conceptual limitations to the common understanding of translation as an automatic rendering of one language into another, including the dilemma presented by certain words that are judged as "untranslatable" and that must therefore be adopted in their original form in the new language to which they were intended to be translated. Examples

---

13. See Pascale Casanova, *The World Republic of Letters* (Cambridge, MA: Harvard University Press, 2007).

14. Talal Asad, *Genealogies of Religion: Discipline and Reasons of Power in Christianity and Islam* (Baltimore: Johns Hopkins University Press, 1993), 189–93. On "strong" languages, see also Talal Asad, "Ethnographic Representation, Statistics, and Modern Power," *Social Research* 61, no. 1 (Spring 1994): 78.

between English and French include idioms with culturally specific conceptual histories like "joie de vivre," "weekend," "gourmet," "leader," "femme fatale," "chic," among others. In more recent years, one observes an insistence on not translating certain Arabic words to English and on rendering them in the original. These include secular words like "intifada," words that have secular and religious resonance like "sheik" as a rendering of "shaykh" (meaning old man, elder, elderly, learned man, religious and pious man, head of tribe) but also include words identified as "Islamic," most prominently "Allah" and "jihad," and sometimes "hijab" and "Shariᶜa." "Allah," an Arabic word meaning God that was used by Arab Christians and non-Christians before the Qurʾanic revelation, is rendered in English and other European accounts as the proper name of the God of the Muslims, even though the Prophet Muhammad's father was named ᶜabd Allah, or worshipper of God, long before his son was born or became a prophet.[15] Jihad, a common name among Christian Arabs, including Lebanese Maronites, with the secular meaning of struggle, is used in the original in English and juxtaposed to the translation "Holy War." Anxiety about the meanings of words identified as "Islamic" was such that it became key to American investigators looking into the causes of the Egypt Air flight 990 crash of 1999, off the US East Coast, as the Egyptian pilot's use of the normative invocation "tawakkaltu ᶜala Allah" (often translated as "I put my trust in God") became key to attributing suspicious motives to him. Moreover, the Western media and Western officialdom expended special time in order to understand the word "hudna" and its "Islamic" implications when Hamas offered a "ceasefire" to Israel a few years ago.[16]

It seems here that the problem may lie less with comparative translations than with comparative untranslatability. Is there an essential arbitrariness to why one word versus another would be left untranslated, or is there a way in which people "understand" the word's resistance to translation—and if so, how? For something like "gourmet" or "chic" (and the latter should not be confused with "sheik"!), there is a general

15. Recently, in October 2013, and in an ironic twist, the second highest Malaysian court, in line with European and American Orientalist and anti-Muslim polemicists, has banned the use of the term "Allah" by non-Muslims, decreeing that it is the exclusive property of Muslims! See "UN Official Says Malaysia Should Reverse Allah Ban," *Reuters*, 26 November 2013, http://www.reuters.com/article/2013/11/25/us-un-malaysia-allah-idUSBRE9AO0BJ20131125 (accessed 12 February 2014).

16. See for example Katin Laub, "Hamas Hard-Liners Edge Toward Cease-Fire," *Associated Press*, 22 June 2003, which asserts that "the success of peacemaking may well hang on a legal concept dating to the birth of Islam: a 'hudna,' or a truce of a fixed duration, usually between Muslims and non-Muslims."

sense that it signifies "Frenchness" in such a way that its link to French carries over—i.e. French culture, fashion, and food—which makes it "make sense" not to be able to translate it. This is of course pure fiction. But if it were the case, then how would such a fantasy of cultural essence and linguistic rootedness compare in the case of say "intifada" or "jihad"? Again, if the more specific question is something to the effect of how to think about comparative untranslatability, then the larger question is how to think about the untranslated and the untranslatable? Is the untranslatable being acknowledged as respect for difference and as limit to narration, or is it an emphasis on othering and exoticization? What about words that have "religious" significance?

Ismaʿil Raji al-Faruqi, a committed Muslim American who immigrated to the US from Palestine, suggests that many such words are in fact not translatable. He provides the example of how the Arabic Qurʾanic word "salah," (sometimes rendered "salat") which refers to a set of rituals repeated five times a day by observant Muslims and includes a set of "recitations, genuflections, prostrations, standings and sittings with orientation towards the Kaʿbah, and should be entered into after ablutions and a solemn declaration of intention" is (mis)translated as "prayer" into English, when in fact the forms that varying Christian "prayers" take are more akin to what Muslims call *duʿaʾ* (or *ibtihal*) than to *salah*.[17] Other examples al-Faruqi provides include "zakah" which is (mis)translated as charity or almsgiving. He concludes that as such a word has no equivalent in English, "it must therefore never be translated. Rather, it must be understood as it stands in its Arabic form."[18] For al-Faruqi, whose interest is that Muslims who are native speakers of English understand their religion *correctly* and *accurately* and learn the wide range of meanings Qurʾanic words have in Arabic, giving such words English terms through translation is "to reduce, and often to ruin, those meanings."[19] In the academic realm, Wael Hallaq has argued in turn that the very (mis)translation of Shariʿa into "law" has been detrimental to the way Orientalists understood and judged it.[20] These are hardly new translational preoccupations. Orientalists themselves have

17. On translation of religious terminology from Arabic to English, see Ismaʿil Raji al Faruqi, *Toward Islamic English* (Hernden, VA: International Institute of Islamic Thought, 1986), 11. On the debate among Muslims who are native-speakers of English on the question of Islam and English, see Mucahit Bilici, *Finding Mecca in America: How Islam is Becoming an American Religion* (Chicago: University of Chicago Press, 2012), 64–89.

18. Al Faruqi, 12.

19. Ibid.

20. Wael B. Hallaq, *Shariʿa: Theory, Practice, Transformations* (Cambridge: Cambridge University Press, 2009), 1–6.

dabbled in a variety of ethnographic translations whose difficulty they identified and whose etymological implications some of them fantasized, the most infamous perhaps is Bernard Lewis's charlatanism in "excavating" the word "thawra," meaning revolution, which he linked to the rising of camels.[21]

Edward Said put it thus in his 1981 book *Covering Islam*: "the term 'Islam' as it is used today seems to mean one simple thing but in fact is part fiction, part ideological label, part minimal designation of a religion called Islam. In no really significant way is there a direct correspondence between the 'Islam' in common Western usage and the enormously varied life that goes on within the world of Islam, with its more than 800,000,000 people, its millions of square miles of territory principally in Africa and Asia, its dozens of societies, states, histories, geographies, cultures."[22] What is it then about Islam, what is at stake in translating it and (what is identified as) its subsidiary vocabulary to English and other European languages?

Some scholars argue that in the modern era, Islam, like the Orient, is another antonym for the West, while others have argued that European secularism is its proper opposite. Yet, others speak of democracy, civilization, freedom, etc., as the opposites of this Islam. Indeed, a *Washington Post* veteran journalist went as far as positing the English language itself as the antonym of "Islam," when she described the outcome of Qatari school curricular reform as "less Islam, more English."[23] It seems, therefore, that as the referents of Islam have multiplied so have its antonyms. The question then becomes whether the production of Islam's many new referents was part of the same translational process of producing its many new antonyms, from being a singular Christendom or Christianity to many more opposites. I should note here that the Western and Orientalist deployment of Christianity and Christendom themselves as singular is based on a retrospective deployment of a unitary community on what was historically disunited peoples, doctrines, and churches.

A number of scholars of religion agree that the development of the multiple significations of Islam after the colonial encounter was greatly conditioned by it. Leonard Binder sketches Western imperial liberalism's

21. See Edward Said's response to him on this count in "Orientalism: An Exchange," *New York Review of Books*, 12 August 1982.

22. Edward W. Said, *Covering Islam: How the Media and the Experts Determine How We See the World*, rev. ed. (New York: Vintage Books, 1997), l.

23. Susan Glasser, "Qatar Reshapes its Schools, Putting English over Islam," *Washington Post*, 2 February 2003.

THE CHOICE OF LIBERALISM

efforts at the conversion of Islam into a form the former can accept. He asserts that "from the time of the Napoleonic invasion, from the time of the Janissaries, from the time of the Sepoy mutiny, at least, the West has been trying to tell Islam what must be the price of progress in the coin of tradition which is to be surrendered. And from those times, despite the increasing numbers of responsive Muslims, there remains a substantial number that steadfastly argue that it is possible to progress without paying such a heavy cultural price."[24] In response, Talal Asad maintains that it is

no incidental detail that each of the "tellings" [Binder] cited—when traditional authority was successfully attacked in the name of rationalism and progress—was at the same time an act of violence. In each of them, Western political, economic, and ideological power increased its hold over non-European peoples. That power, unleashed in Enlightenment Europe, continues to restructure the lives of non-European peoples, often through the agency of non-Europeans themselves. And if "Islamic fundamentalism" is a response to that power, then certainly so, even more thoroughly, are the intellectual currents called "modernist Islam" (which is concerned to adapt theology to the models of Christian modernism) and "Muslim secularism" (which are preoccupied less with theology than with separating religion from politics in national life). And so, too, are the progressivist movements in literature and the arts, in politics and law, that have arisen in Muslim societies.[25]

Islam in Liberalism

Islam in Liberalism seeks to understand how Islam became so central to liberalism as ideology and as identity, indeed how liberalism as the antithesis of Islam became one of the key components of the very discourse through which Europe as a modern identity was conjured up. This book will analyze how in the process of identification, the emergence of "Europe" was predicated on a series of projections, disavowals, displacements, and expulsions in order to produce a coherent self cleansed of others to which this self was opposed in its very constitution. That the Orient and Orientals, Semitism and Semites, and specifically Islam and Muslims would constitute a primary other that was internal to this Europe and which had to be expelled from its emergent formation is now uniformly accepted in scholarship. Still, however, some scholars

24. Leonard Binder, *Islamic Liberalism* (Chicago: University of Chicago Press, 1988), 293.
25. Asad, *Genealogies of Religion*, 228–29.

continue to resist the links between liberalism and its derivatives and the internal and external others of Europe. While in his magisterial study of liberalism, Domenico Losurdo has comprehensively shown the links of liberalism as ideology and as political regime to slavery, colonialism, and class oppression, inside and outside Europe, Charles Taylor's monumental study of secularism presents the latter as a development internal to Europe and its Christian populations.[26] It is in this vein that Wendy Brown insists that

absent from Taylor's account is every stripe of outsider to Latin Christendom, from Jews and Muslims in Europe to colonized natives and other outsiders, as well as dissident voices, reversals and disruptions to what he calls his "story." The missing elements make it more provincially European, monolithic, colonial, than it needs to be. Above all, they make the emergence of EuroAtlantic secularism a product of tensions within Christendom rather than, in part, a feature of Christendom's encounter with others and especially with its constitutive outside. More than a problem of historiography or comprehensiveness, this omission has consequential politics; today, Western secularism is so relentlessly defined through its imagined opposite in Islamic theocracy that to render secularism as generated exclusively through Western Christian European history is to literally eschew the production of ourselves as secular through and against our imagined opposite. It is to be locked into Thomas Friedman's conceit about "our" secular modernity and "their" need for it.[27]

What I seek to understand in this book is the intellectual and political histories within which Islam operated as a category of Western liberalism, indeed, how the anxieties about what this Europe constituted and constitutes—despotism, intolerance, misogyny, homophobia—were projected onto Islam and that only through this projection could Europe emerge as democratic, tolerant, philogynist, and homophilic, in short Islam-free. My project is not one that seeks to investigate the whole range of concerns that constitute liberalism, but specifically how Islam figures in it as ideology and the policies that liberal regimes in Europe and the United States pursued and pursue vis-à-vis this Islam. I also do not intend to explore how "Islam," whatever that is, constitutes itself, but emphatically how liberalism constitutes Islam in constituting itself.

26. See Domenico Losurdo, *Liberalism: A Counter-History*, translated by Gregory Elliott (London: Verso, 2011), and Charles Taylor, *A Secular Age* (Cambridge, MA: Harvard University Press, 2007).

27. Wendy Brown, "Idealism, materialism, secularism," 22 October 2007, blog post, http://blogs .ssrc.org/tif/2007/10/22/idealism-materialism-secularism (accessed 12 February 2014). For another critique of Taylor along similar lines, see Luca Mavelli, *Europe's Encounter with Islam: The Secular and the Postsecular* (London: Routledge, 2012), 68–74.

Once Europe is produced as this paradisiacal place, it becomes incumbent on Christian and liberal Europeans not only to proselytize their "culture" and mode of living, but also to save and rescue non-Europeans from their anti- and un-European cultures and modes of life. *Islam in Liberalism* documents this Christian and liberal zealotry of missionizing democracy, women's rights, sexual rights, tolerance, and equality, indeed even of therapeutic methods, specifically psychoanalysis, to cure Muslims and Islam of their un-European, un-Christian, and illiberal ways.

The first chapter of the book will discuss the history of the production of Europe as "democratic" and of Islam as "despotic," while the second will focus on the production of European women as the "luckiest in the world" and Muslim women as the "most oppressed in the world." The third chapter addresses how US and Europe-based academics and activists and a few of their colleagues in Muslim-majority countries link Islam, liberalism, and sexuality in such a way as to produce the West as a paradise of equality and tolerance for homosexuals and the "Muslim world" as a veritable hell from which Muslim homosexuals must be saved through transforming Muslim-majority countries and nationals into copies of a fantasized West. The fourth chapter focuses on psychoanalytic approaches to Islam and/in liberalism, and how European-based psychoanalytic thinkers (many among whom are Muslim immigrants who live in Europe) summon the power of liberalism to substitute for psychoanalytic analysis in their pathologization of Islam. The fifth and last chapter situates Islam within the scholarship of Semitics and the liberal (and eirenic) idea of equalizing Islam with Judaism and Christianity as "Abrahamic" religions, and with Jewish and Christian fundamentalisms, as another form of messianism—an equalization that will be shown to be a part of the liberal ruse of inclusion that yet again sidesteps the question of imperial power.

ONE

The Democracy Offensive and the Defenses of "Islam"

This chapter assembles a range of writing around the question of democracy and Islam in an attempt to understand the deep intellectual genealogy of Western liberal claims that Islam is "culturally" un- or antidemocratic and that the major cultural achievement of Christianity (in the form of Protestantism) and the West has been their commitment to democratic governance. I will look at the liberal context in which these arguments emerged and the impact of their culturalist bent on politics and the ongoing efforts by the United States, and Britain (and France) before it, to produce an Islamic theology, if not a whole new "Islam," compatible with the colonial and imperial order they seek to impose on Muslim-majority countries under the sign of "spreading democracy and freedom." In contrast to (Protestant) Christianity, capitalism, or modernity, which are often claimed by liberal thinkers as enablers of "democracy," Islam has been said to be either fully fortified or "defenseless" against this "Western" political order. US president George W. Bush was clear on the Christian origins of freedom when he declared in 2004: "Freedom is the Almighty's gift to every man and woman in this world. And as the greatest power on the face of the earth we have an obligation to help the spread of freedom."[1] Clearly the offensive capability of democracy is organized by both

1. President George W. Bush, Press Conference, 13 April 2004.

secular *and* divine power simultaneously. Indeed, as will become clear in this chapter, democracy has in certain ways become the new name of Christianity and has been missionized to the heathens in ways that are no less deadly.

The emergence of the Eastern Question in eighteenth-century Western Europe was part and parcel of the attempt, ongoing since the Renaissance, to create "Europe" as a transcendental idea, composed of a set of Enlightened ideals differentiated from a prior historical moment that this nascent Europe would call "the dark ages," and as a unified and separate geography differentiated from "dark" lands and continents lying outside it. Indeed, as Roberto Dainotto pithily put it, "a theory of Europe, from its very outset, is a theory of Orientalism," one that differentiates Europe from the Orient, and from Islam, and sets it up as their opposite.[2] This geographic demarcation would become essential for the European project that would in the nineteenth century be called "civilization" and "culture."

Even those who would posit the origins of the European idea in the era of Charlemagne cannot ignore the role of Islam. In this regard, Henri Pirenne had declared: "The conquest of Spain and Africa by Islam had made the king of the Franks the master of the Christian Occident. . . . It is therefore strictly correct to say that without Mohammed Charlemagne would have been inconceivable."[3] This also applies to those who attribute the origins of Europe to the unifying quest of Christendom, which developed through the Crusades, and which ultimately failed to dislodge the Muslims from the "Holy Land."[4] It applies as well to those who view 1492, the year of the Conquest of the Americas and the coeval Reconquista over the remaining presence of Muslims and "Islam" in Spain, as the inaugural moment of the invention of Europe.[5] Whatever point of origin is chosen for the story of Europe to begin, "Islam" seems to have a foundational role at every turn. Indeed, the question of European origins is even more complicated when we take into consideration that, through the end of the eighteenth century, the understanding that much of "European" literature, inaugurated by Provençal poetry, was

2. Roberto M. Dainotto, *Europe (In Theory)* (Durham, NC: Duke University Press, 2007), 18–19.
3. Henri Pirenne, *Mohammed and Charlemagne*, trans. Bernard Miall (New York: Barnes and Noble Books, 1992), 234. For the French original, see *Mahomet et Charlemagne*, 3rd ed. (Paris: Librairie Félix Alcan, 1937), 210.
4. See Robert Bartlett, *The Making of Europe: Conquest, Colonization, Cultural Change, 950–1350* (London: Allen Lane, Penguin, 1993).
5. See Roger Ballard, "Islam and the Construction of Europe," in *Muslims in the Margin: Political Responses to the Presence of Islam in Western Europe*, ed. Wasif Shadid and Sjoerd von Koningsveld (Kampen, Netherlands: Kok Pharos, 1996), 15–51.

based on and derived from Arabic poetry from Muslim Spain (so much so that the very word troubadour comes from the Arabic *taraba*, meaning to sing), or what is referred to as "the Arabist theory," was a major, if controversial, claim put forth by Juan Andrés in his 1782–1822 eight-volume history of European literature titled *Dell' origine, progressi, e stato attuale d'ogni litteratura*. The anxiety that such findings would cause were such that

In the middle of the nineteenth century it would have been inconceivable or very difficult for most Europeans to imagine, let alone explore or defend, a view of the "European" as being culturally subservient to the "Arab." To imagine that France's first literary flower, one that had been cultivated and idolized for so long as the first in Europe was not only not the first, but that it might be in any way derivative of the culture of people who were now politically colonized and culturally and materially "backwards" vis-à-vis Europeans was just too much.[6]

Andrés did not only posit Arabic literature as the origin of what would become "European" literature but would also insist:

Paper, numerals, gunpowder, the compass came to us from the Arabs. Maybe also the pendulum and the law of gravity, and other recent discoveries . . . were known by them long before they came to our philosophers. Universities, astronomical observatories, academics, literary institutions do not think they have an Arab origin, and perhaps they will not be very grateful to me for having refreshed their memory with remembrance of such an old event.[7]

Andrés's views would not prevail in Enlightenment "Europe." The invention of Europe's Greek origins and the suppression of its Arabo-Islamic origins would proceed to the present, as it was and remains crucial to its invented Islam-free identity.[8]

Thus, *the Eastern Question, against which this nascent Europe measured itself, was always the Western Question*, the question of constituting the West as the West and repudiating the East, which it feared was the point

---

6. María Rosa Menocal, "Pride and Prejudice in Medieval Studies: European and Oriental," *Hispanic Review* 53, no. 1 (Winter 1985): 68. See also María Rosa Menocal, *The Arabic Role in Medieval Literary History: A Forgotten Heritage* (Philadelphia: University of Pennsylvania Press, 1987).

7. Quoted in Dainotto, *Europe (In Theory)*, 127. On the centrality of "Islamic science" to the European Renaissance, see George Saliba, *Islamic Science and the Making of the European Renaissance* (Cambridge, MA: MIT Press, 2011).

8. On this active suppression and especially the role of Madame de Staël, Sismonde de Sismondi, and Wilhelm von Schlegel, see Dainotto, *Europe (In Theory)*, 143–50, 157–65.

of origin of this West, as its antithesis. This much we have already learned from Edward Said's *Orientalism*.[9] That the Eastern Question would also become the Question of Islam and therefore the Question of (Protestant) Christianity would be germane to the European liberal project, which emerged from the Enlightenment, of presenting the West as a place with important characteristics that are always lacking in its Eastern and Islamic antitheses.

Like the emerging "West," "Muslim" countries were recognized by Orientalism as sharing a common culture. Oxford and later Harvard Orientalist Sir Harold Gibb explained in the 1960s how knowledge of all aspects of the Islamic world was organized around the recognition that it formed a cultural unity with a cultural "central core."[10] My goal in this chapter is to understand how the question of a geographically and religiously mapped notion of culture has come to be related to political arrangements of governance, how *Oriental* cultures seem to have produced "Oriental despotism" while a unitary *Occidental culture* produced "Western democracy" in a context in which religion (specifically Islam and Christianity), as a subset or often a synonym of culture, is foregrounded as that which essentializes the "East" and the "West."

It bears noting here that democracy and despotism are, despite their Greek origins, reinvented modern concepts that emerged in eighteenth-century Europe as conceptual and practical opposites. While Enlightenment figures acknowledged the Aristotelian origins of the term "despot," the word, which had fallen out of use (it was often translated from the Greek as "tyrant"), would not make an appearance until the seventeenth century and would have to wait for another century to enter common parlance.[11] Indeed, "despotism" emerged before "democracy," making an inaugural appearance in a French dictionary in 1720, while its conceptual meaning would be formed and refined as the century proceeded. Montesquieu's *The Spirit of the Laws* (published in 1748)[12] would make the term a permanent fixture in the European political vocabulary, as would its modification by the adjective "Oriental," rendering "Oriental despotism," which defined the Ottoman Empire in

9. Edward W. Said, *Orientalism* (New York: Pantheon Books, 1978).

10. H. A. R. Gibb, *Area Studies Reconsidered* (London: School of African and Oriental Studies, 1963), 15.

11. See R. Kroebner, "Despot and Despotism: Vicissitudes of a Political Term," *Journal of the Warburg and Courtauld Institutes* 14 (1951): 275–302, and Lucette Valensi, *The Birth of the Despot: Venice and the Sublime Porte* (Ithaca, NY: Cornell University Press, 1993), 92–94.

12. On Montesquieu's notion of despotism, see Alain Grosrichard, *The Sultan's Court: European Fantasies of the East*, translated by Liz Heron (London: Verso, 1998).

this literature, substantially different from other forms of despotism, including "enlightened" European forms.[13] This European incitement to discourse on despotism since the eighteenth century is identified by Michel Foucault as "an ambiguous phobia about despotism,"[14] which this chapter seeks to explain.

As for "democracy," while its Greek origins were noted as the word was often associated with negative political valences, the modern meaning of "democracy" and its common usage in English would not emerge until the time of the American and French Revolutions and would be especially linked to America's self-understanding and self-representation.[15] That despotism would be linked to Islam and the Ottomans (because Ottomans were the closest identifiable "Muslim" state to Europe) since its modern (re)birth, and democracy to a Europeanized Greek origin carried into modernity by revolutionary Europeans at home and in the North American colonies is, as we will see, more than incidentally related to contemporary representations.

The history I will review is one of continuity and rupture, dislocation and relocation within the shifts from mostly British, and sometimes French, colonialism—though Orientalism is almost pan-European—through the Cold War to the US New World Order imperialism. The uncomfortable shifts within Euro-American and European conceptions of "the Muslim world," especially in connection with the long view of the invented "West," often reflect, as Edward Said has shown, attempts by the self-constituting West to understand itself in relation to others.[16] It is also the history of the production of a despotic and antidemocratic Islam as a self-consolidating other for a "West" that likes to imagine its trajectory, if not its origins, as democratic. To do so, I will be dealing with a heterogeneous material: intellectual history and its shifting institutional locations, unevenly overlapping world historiographical periodizations (colonialism, Cold War, globalization), and the history of the culture concept and its political and colonial deployments. This varied material

---

13. Valensi, *The Birth of the Despot*, 2–4. Voltaire's linkage is explicit in his naming of Muslim rulers as "despots" in *L'A, B, C: Dialogues curieux traduits de l'Anglais de Monsieur Huet*, in *Oeuvres* (Paris: Garnier, 1879), 27:323n, cited by R. Kroebner, "Despot and Despotism," 275.

14. Michel Foucault, *The Birth of Biopolitics: Lectures at the College de France, 1978–1979*, ed. Michael Senellart (New York: Picador, 2010), 76.

15. Raymond Williams, *Culture and Society, 1780–1950* (New York: Columbia University Press, 1983), xiv. See also Raymond Williams, *Keywords: Vocabulary of Culture and Society*, rev. ed. (Oxford: Oxford University Press, 1983), 95.

16. See Said, *Orientalism*. On Europe's self-constitution in relation to Islam as other, see also Barbara Fuchs, *Mimesis and Empire: The New World, Islam, and European Identities* (Cambridge: Cambridge University Press, 2001).

shares the same ontology and epistemology as well as the same empirical data about the "West" and "Islam." I will chart the connections between epistemic genealogy and politics (especially as many academics and scholars would serve British, French, German, and US political power as consultants, officers, and advisors over the decades) in the production of a relationship that, many Western liberals insist, connects both Islam and democracy as well as democracy and the Christian West. This chapter principally argues that the assumption of democratic identity by the "West" and of despotic identity as the West's other, represented by the figure of "Islam," is both an act of self-constitution and projection *as well as* an imperial strategy that uses cultural assimilation and othering as tactics of economic and political domination. In this regard, I will not concern myself with the rich intellectual production in Muslim-majority societies since the eighteenth century, which was not always *directly* related to this European and Euro-American liberal imperial history (something I study in a forthcoming book), but will rather focus on the relationship between European and Euro-American liberalism and European and American policies and the emergence of specific forms of theological and intellectual effects and political transformations in the "Muslim world" that issue from them.

This is then a discourse about the West as a modern category, its despotism, its undemocracy, and its conjuring up of an "Ottoman despotism" and of "Islamic" undemocracy that did not exist as such before their European marking, itself a ruse for the production of "European democracy." The discourse on democracy, as we will see, is also largely a Christian religious discourse, which posits *democracy* as the *highest stage of (Protestant) Christianity*. This discourse is in short not less than what Foucault calls a coupling of a set of practices (which in our case would be local and imperial governance) and a regime of truth (which in our case would be Orientalism) from an apparatus of knowledge-power (liberalism *tout court*) "that effectively marks out in reality that which does not exist and legitimately submits it to the division between true and false," the truth of "European democracy" and of "Islamic" un-democracy.[17]

I attend mainly to the intellectual history of the liberal linkage of Christian Europe, Islam, and democracy in the first half of the chapter, while in the second half I attend mainly to the history of colonial and neocolonial policies that proceeded from this liberal linkage to clarify the intersections between the intellectual history of liberalism and the

17. Michel Foucault, *The Birth of Biopolitics*, 19.

19

diplomatic history of the US and European liberal regimes on the one hand and their induction of the category of Islam into the heart of their varied modernist projects on the other. The intellectual, the political, and the diplomatic, as readers will note, are so intricately intertwined that I make no attempt to disentangle them from one another but rather work to expose their complex and not-so-complex linkages throughout.

American Democracy

One of the cornerstones of United States nationalism has been the assertion in official discourse, media representations, and in its educational system that the United States is the "oldest democracy" in the world, an assertion that always raises eyebrows outside the United States and among many Americans at home, though the latter rarely challenge this assertion directly in any organized fashion. National wisdom has it that US democracy "evolved" to include segments of the population that were denied inclusion in citizenship. What does it mean for a country whose two-century history is divided between a century of racialized slavery and another century of racial apartheid to broadcast itself internally and externally as the oldest democracy? And what does it mean for a country where women were not allowed to vote for the first century and a half of its existence to consider itself the oldest democracy? Could white South Africans get away with describing their country, since it was founded in 1910, or at least since 1948 when Apartheid became its ruling ideology, as a "democracy" which "evolved" to include Indians and coloreds halfheartedly in 1983 with the tricameral parliament, and Blacks after 1994?

These are not just polemical questions but also conceptual ones that are central to our understanding of how the United States, presenting itself as an extension of Europe, as well as "Europe" itself, which remains an amorphous political, historical, and geographic category,[18] set themselves up as the home and originary space of democracy, something not only based on the development of a governing system that they name "democracy" but also on the claim that such development reflected the commitments of Euro-American and European *culture* and *religion*, which are compatible with democracy, and encourage and make

---

18. On the still ongoing debates around what constitutes Europe which led to the 1992 Maastricht Treaty and the doubts about whether the "PIGS" (Portugal, Italy, Greece, and Spain) are part of this Europe or not, see Dainotto, *Europe (In Theory)*, 1–9.

it possible. The association of Christianity with rationalism, science, and reason, of Protestantism with the capitalist economy and political democracy (and Catholicism and Orthodox Christianity with feudalism and dictatorship) had clearly become codified in liberal ideology long before Weber's famous intervention. While John Locke excluded Islam, Judaism, Confucianism, among others, from reasonableness which seemed to be the exclusive property of Christianity and to which he dedicated his book *The Reasonableness of Christianity* in 1695,[19] Protestant doubts about Catholic and Jewish dicta would largely disappear (though not doubts about Orthodox Christianity let alone Islam), however, in the mid twentieth century, on the eve of World War II, under the rubric of the "Judeo-Christian" tradition inaugurated in the late 1930s in the United States, which would allow Protestantism, Catholicism, and Judaism to be formalized in that country as the "religions of democracy." Here one could perhaps turn Marx's question of "why does the history of the East *appear* as a history of religions?"[20] on its head: why does the history of Western democracy *appear* as a history of Christianity?

European liberal thought, which articulated notions of political freedom and democracy since the Enlightenment, was linked to the rise of European empires that subjugated much of the globe to Europe's control. The link between European liberal thought and the rise of empire, as Uday Mehta argues, has often been denied despite its imbrication in it, an argument also advanced by Edward Said with regards to the imbrication of modern European culture more generally with imperialism.[21] Britain's view of itself as a democracy in the nineteenth century (not unlike the view the United States has always had of itself whether under slavery, Jim Crow, or in the current moment of racial criminalization and imperialism) was not weakened as far as its liberal political thinkers were concerned by its undemocratic and despotic rule over millions of natives in the Empire, and which was rationalized by many of them as just and in keeping with the natives' own traditions.[22]

John Stuart Mill expresses this aptly in *On Liberty*, understanding himself to be a democrat at home and a despot abroad.[23] Indeed, he

19. See Uday Singh Mehta's discussion of this aspect of Locke in *Liberalism and Empire: A Study in Nineteenth-Century British Liberal Thought* (Chicago: University of Chicago Press, 1999), 60n.

20. Karl Marx, Letter from Marx to Engels, 2 June 1853, in *K. Marx and F. Engels On Religion* (Moscow: Foreign Languages Publishing House, 1957), 120.

21. See ibid., and Edward W. Said, *Culture and Imperialism* (New York: Knopf, 1993).

22. Mehta, *Liberalism and Empire*, 7–8.

23. Homi Bhabha summarizes him thus in his conversation with Bhikhu Parekh in "Identities on Parade: A Conversation," in *Marxism Today*, June 1989, 27.

is clear that "despotism is a legitimate mode of government in dealing with barbarians, provided the end is their improvement, and the means justified by actually effecting that end."[24] Similarly, Alexis de Tocqueville was unrelenting in his commitment to what Domenico Losurdo refers to as "master race democracy" and to despotism for the barbarians, especially the Algerians: "It is possible and necessary that there be two sets of laws in Africa, because we are faced with two clearly separate societies. When one is dealing with Europeans, *absolutely* nothing prevents us from treating them as if they were alone; the laws enacted for them must be applied exclusively to them."[25]

It was in such a context that the notion of liberal democratic citizenship, already articulated as a cornerstone of liberal Enlightenment thinking, would be deployed in contrast to despotic subjects. Like democracy and despotism, citizenship (though of Latin etymological origins) is also of Greek conceptual provenance, resuscitated for the Enlightenment liberal project. That citizenship should be restricted to the non-laboring classes for thinkers like Locke, Mandeville, Constant, and Sieyès and would be expanded to some of them in the form of "passive citizenship" after the French Revolution is much related not only to the Athenian distinction between citizens and women, children, resident aliens, and slaves, but also as a contrast with the status of Oriental despotic subjects. This restriction of who is and is not a citizen and who is or is not an active or passive citizen is constitutive of the very notion of European liberal citizenship as a graduated system. It was enshrined in the 1792 constitution of Revolutionary France, which while eliminating the duality of active and passive citizenship and including wage-earners as citizens, still excluded vagabonds, criminals, and servants. Women of course continued to lack in full citizenship and did not obtain suffrage till 1946.[26]

In contrast with Rousseau's support for direct nonrepresentative democracy (which liberalism never took up in practice anywhere in the Western "democracies"), for Montesquieu, this would be nothing less than "popular despotism," which he, like all liberal democratic orders

24. John Stuart Mill, *On Liberty*, in *On Liberty and Other Essays* (Oxford: Oxford University Press, 1991), 14–15.

25. Alexis de Tocqueville, *Oeuvres complètes*, ed. Jacob-Peter Mayer (Paris: Gallimard, 1951), vol. 3, pt.1, 275, cited in Domenico Losurdo, *Liberalism: A Counter-History*, trans. Gregory Elliott (London: Verso, 2011), 235. On liberalism and "master race democracy," see Losurdo, *Liberalism*, 219–40.

26. On "passive citizenship," see Losurdo, *Liberalism*, 184–91. See also Charles Tilly, "The Emergence of Citizenship in France and Elsewhere," in *Citizenship, Identity and Social History*, ed. Charles Tilly (Melbourne: University of Cambridge Press Syndicate, 1996), 223.

after him, vehemently opposed.[27] But the question of citizenship would be increasingly linked to the notion of civil society, whose presence or absence was seen as essential to the nature of democratic and despotic governance. It was in this vein that, as Bryan Turner demonstrates, European liberal thought argued that "despotism presupposes a society in which 'civil society' is either absent or underdeveloped," and that "the notion of 'civil society' is not only fundamental to the definition of political life in European societies, but also a point of contrast between Occident and Orient."[28] Turner explains that although this was the problem of Asia as a whole according to Orientalism, "it has played an important role in the analysis of Islamic societies."[29] Since the 1980s and through the present, Western NGOs as well as government agencies would begin to set the building of "civil society" in Arab and Muslim countries as a primary goal of Western and NGO aid as part of their mission to spread democracy.

In his study of how citizenship itself is related to Orientalism, Engin Isin shows how the European-invented tradition of democracy and citizenship is deployed:

An occidental tradition where the origins of "city," "democracy" and "citizenship" are etymologically traced to the "Greek," "Roman" and "medieval" cities and affinities between "their" and "our" practices are established not only [to] orient toward but also assemble and reproduce such practices. An entire tradition reminds us that polis, politics and polity, civitas, citizenship and civility, and demos and democracy have "common roots."[30]

Isin quotes Weber's exceptionalization of Europe in contrast with its others, specifically the Orient: "'The modern state is the first to have the concept of the citizen of the state' according to which 'the individual, for once, is not, as he is everywhere else, considered in terms of the particular professional and family position he occupies, not in relation

27. See Baron de Montesquieu, *The Spirit of the Laws*, trans. Thomas Nugent (New York: Hafner, 1949), vol. 1, book 2, 8–18. The term "popular despotism" is Althusser's, in Louis Althusser, *Montesquieu, Rousseau, Marx* (London: Verso, 1972), 64. On Montesquieu's support for colonial slavery on climatological grounds and his injunctions of how to reform it there, while rejecting it as unsuitable on the European mainland, see Losurdo, *Liberalism*, 44–47.

28. Bryan Turner, "Orientalism and the Problem of Civil Society in Islam," in *Orientalism, Islam, and Islamists*, ed. Asaf Hussain, Robert Olson, and Jamil Qureshi (Brattleboro, VT: Amana Books, 1984), 27.

29. Ibid., 34.

30. Engin F. Isin, "Citizenship after Orientalism: Ottoman Citizenship," in *Citizenship in a Global World: European Questions and Turkish Experiences*, ed. Fuat Keyman and Ahmet Icduygu (London: Routledge, 2005), 34.

to differences of material and social situation, but purely and simply as a citizen.'"[31] Isin then summarizes the European imaginary rendering itself a superior exception compared to an inferior Orient: "For the occidental imagination some images are now such ways of seeing: that democracy was invented in the Greek polis; that Roman republican tradition bequeathed its legacy to Europe and that Europe Christianized and civilized these traditions. . . . Many representations of orientalism either rely upon or reproduce this one essential difference between the Occident and the Orient."[32] Weber, Isin argues persuasively, is the canonical figure that remains the referent of such comparisons until today.

The European liberal division between citizen and subject and between active and passive citizens would become operative in the colonies as well. In his classic study of colonial and postcolonial Africa, Mahmood Mamdani asserts that colonial "indirect rule" survived the end of European colonial rule, if in deracialized form: "What we have before us is a bifurcated world, no longer simply racially organized, but a world in which the dividing line between those human and the rest less human is a line between those who labor on the land and those who do not. This divided world is inhabited by subjects on one side and citizens on the other."[33] But if one were to go back to Enlightenment understandings of citizenship, the difference Mamdani discerns in postcolonial Africa is one *not* external to liberal citizenship, but *internal* to it, between active and passive citizenship—urban colonially educated Africans as active citizens who could in theory access liberal institutions and rural and peasant Africans without colonial education and middle class privilege as passive citizens who are relegated to the realm of "customary" institutions; this is a difference that is constitutive and foundational to European liberal citizenship, as we saw, even if posited as an antonym to the fantasized Oriental despotic subject and adapted to the racialized colonies through appeal to the "customary" which always remains subordinated to the civil institutions of the colonial and postcolonial state. Whereas Africans were transformed into passive and active citizens, they became subjects not of despotism as such but rather of European liberalism and its institutions, which first distinguished between European Enlightened despotism and Oriental despotism and then reordered and recoded European forms of despotism *as* democracy.

31. Cited in ibid.
32. Ibid., 35.
33. Mahmood Mamdani, *Citizen and Subject: Contemporary Africa and the Legacy of Late Colonialism* (Princeton, NJ: Princeton University Press, 1996), 61.

The question of the laboring and non-laboring classes is of course the question of private property. How central private property is to theories of democracy is illustrated by de Tocqueville's assertion that it is the absence of feudalism and landed property and the presence of private and personal property (which fosters trade and commerce) that led to development of "democracy" in the United States and not in France.[34] He also linked the strength of religion in American public life to its "separation" from the sphere of governance, which was lacking in France: "Religion in America takes no direct part in the government of society, but it must nevertheless be regarded as the foremost of the political institutions of that country; for if it does not impart a taste for freedom, it facilitates the use of free institutions."[35] As for societies that do not govern based on this separation, like the "Turks": "In the present age they are in rapid decay, because their religion is departing, and despotism only remains."[36] The later Weberian connection drawn between Protestant Christianity and capitalism completes the circle. It is thus that the trajectory of Protestant Christianity to capitalism to democracy gets codified in liberal thought.

The Orientalist insistence that Islam's hostility to capitalism would augur badly for economic development and for democracy would be taken up by most Orientalists (those who are sympathetic and those who are hostile to "Islam") and late nineteenth and early twentieth century Muslim intellectuals (Muhammad ʿAbduh, Rashid Rida, *inter alia*) alike. Hostile Orientalists would argue after World War II that this would doom Islam and Muslim societies "to a satanic alliance with Communism," while more sympathetic Orientalists, Louis Massignon in particular, would argue that it would predispose Islam to a more politically equitable society than Western capitalism.[37] Others like Maxime Rodinson set out to investigate precisely the relationship between capitalism and Islam and to challenge the Weberian link that Protestantism was a necessary precondition for the development of capitalism.[38]

34. Alexis De Tocqueville, *Democracy in America* (New York: Adlard and Saunders, 1838), 2 vols., especially vol. 1, chap. 3, 28–35.

35. Ibid., 286.

36. Ibid., 74.

37. Maxime Rodinson, *Islam and Capitalism*, trans. Brain Pierce (Austin: University of Texas Press, 1981), 3. The book was first published in French in 1966. For the differing responses to these claims by Orientalists and Muslim intellectuals, and for his discussion of Massignon's views, see Rodinson's extensive endnotes, 242–44.

38. Ibid., 7–9,77–78,103–6, 116–17. American historian Peter Gran would follow suit with his book *Islamic Roots of Capitalism: Egypt, 1760–1840* (Syracuse, NY: Syracuse University Press, 1998). The book was first published in 1979.

It should be stressed here that the liberal and Orientalist notion of "Oriental despotism" would act as a precursor to justify European colonial despotism in Asia and Africa. As Wael Hallaq has forcefully argued:

The concept of "Oriental despotism" . . . was given added weight by the spurious Prophetic report proclaiming that "sixty years of tyranny are better than one day of civil strife." This was taken to be evidence that "Orientals" are inherently submissive and therefore possess a natural capacity to endure tyranny and oppression (needless to say, a doctrine necessary to justify colonialism, past and present). While the Prophetic report does reflect an accurate understanding by Muslims of their own political-legal systems and practices, the Orientalist interpretation of it is entirely erroneous. The key terms here are "tyranny" and "civil strife." If "tyranny" is defined by pre-nineteenth century European standards, the period in which the concept of [Oriental despotism] was fashioned, then it becomes clear that we are dealing here with the projection of the European concept of monarch—who was absolutist and an arbitrary legislator and executor—onto the Islamic scene. But this projection is unjustified because "Oriental tyranny," at its worst, could not accomplish two goals that the European monarch successfully and easily achieved, namely, (1) sultans and kings could never penetrate the societies they came to rule, but could only govern from the "outside," and, more importantly, (2) these rulers were severely constrained by a law that they did not create and that was largely out of their control. Thus, whatever tyranny they practiced could not, as a rule, have affected the integrity of the communities they ruled, communities that were the basis and defining parameters of life. In the Orientalist definition, the meaning and range of "tyranny" has been wildly amplified, whereas the paramount significance of "civil strife," where the all-important Community is split asunder, has been dramatically de-emphasized. On the other hand, and given the nature of Islamic constitutional organization, the Muslim conception privileges the community as the cradle of life and the locus of meaningful living, deeming tyranny and its political sultanic source as comparatively far less pernicious than its European counterpart.[39]

French historian Henry Laurens echoes this irony: "while Enlightenment thought had defined the Muslim states as instances of military despotism, the [British] East India Company became in fact its most perfect incarnation."[40] The despotism expelled to and projected by European liberalism onto the Orient, while being replaced by liberal notions of democracy, would not only be posited by European colonial liberals as

39. Wael Hallaq, *The Impossible State: Islam, Politics, and Modernity's Moral Predicament* (New York: Columbia University Press, 2012), 65.

40. John Tolan, Gilles Veinstein, and Henry Laurens, *Europe and the Islamic World: A History* (Oxford: Oxford University Press, 2013), 276.

"Oriental" in character but would also be extended to Africa through the colonial appeal to "African customary traditions." Liberal forms of citizenship would be deployed in the colonies for white settler populations in contrast with the natives who became imperial "subjects" in keeping with "local" tradition. But the notion of "subjects" that colonial liberalism imposed, as we saw, was internal to its ideological framework. Mamdani argues that while the natives could have a "modicum of civil rights," they could not access "political" rights: "Citizenship would be the privilege of the civilized; the uncivilized would be subject to an all-around tutelage . . . an unmediated—centralized—despotism."[41] Indeed, the "division between the citizen and the subject, the nonnative and the native, was characteristic of all colonial situations."[42] Yet, as Mamdani explains, following George Padmore, in much of Africa the British followed an indirect form of rule of granting "local" and "native" traditions and "laws" authority alongside British colonial oversight that resulted in what Mamdani calls "decentralized despotism." The bifurcation was most clearly manifest in the law, wherein criminal law was mostly colonial, civil law "customary." This legacy would inform the experiences of postcolonial Africa, whether in countries ruled by "conservative" or "radical" regimes, which organized power despotically, leading Mamdani to conclude that "the most important legacy of colonial rule . . . may lie in the inherited impediments to democratization."[43]

One could argue, however, that introducing the notion of a bifurcated citizenship to Africa and the "Muslim world" was *itself* the introduction of a specific European opposition to "democracy," in the form of active and passive citizenship, of dividing the people into classes with differential access to the privileges of citizenship, in the form of a European despotism coded as "democracy" *tout court*. In this vein, the difference between the gradations of citizenship in postcolonial Africa or in much of the Arab and Muslim "worlds" is hardly one of kind with the gradations of classes of citizenship in liberal democratic European countries or in the United States, but rather and at most one of degree. In his important study comparing governance based on Shariʿa and the modern European liberal state form, where he demonstrates the lack of an actual separation of powers despite liberal theory's claim to the contrary, Hallaq concludes:

41. Mahmood Mamdani, *Citizen and Subject*, 17.
42. Ibid., 48.
43. Ibid., 25.

For Muslims today to seek the adoption of the modern state system of separation of powers [which is not really a separation] is to bargain for a deal inferior to the one they secured for themselves over the centuries of *their* history. The modern deal represents the power and sovereignty of the state . . . working for its own perpetuation and interests. By contrast, the Shariʿa did not—because it was not designed to—serve the ruler or any form of political power. It served the people, the masses, the poor, the downtrodden, and the wayfarer, without disadvantaging the merchant and others of his ilk.[44]

Since the Renaissance, the imagining of ancient Greece as the originary nucleus of modern Europe, whose historical relationship to its Greek origins is said to have been interrupted by medieval darkness, was deployed to provide Europe with an antediluvian "civilized" history. Positing Greek "democracy," which was based on slavery and the exclusion of women as citizens, as the basis of United States democracy (whose own democracy is deployed as a legacy of antiquity) then is not just mythical but also mimetic. It is also a philological argument, as historian of religion Tomoko Masuzawa argues, wherein modern Europeans saw that their languages and the Greek language belonged to the same family of languages, which provided them with a direct cultural legacy to their linguistic ancestors' putative achievements:

This deep division of the "races" implied, conversely, commensurability and commutability of peoples, languages, 'geniuses,' and 'spirits' belonging in the same family, even if they were separated by great distance in space or in time. Thus the nineteenth century Englishman could presume that there was an essential tie between him and an Athenian of the fourth century BCE, whereas a medieval Mohammedan from North Africa, for all his knowledge of Aristotle, presumably could not claim the same kinship.[45]

But given the co-habitation of the myth of Greek origins and Protestantism's rediscovery of the foundational Hebraism from which Europe's Christian heritage emerged, the nineteenth century continued to debate the merits of Hellenism and Hebraism as the dual "tradition" to which modern Europe was/is said to be heir (Matthew Arnold's 1869 book *Culture and Anarchy* remains the classic record of this debate).[46]

These core and often contradictory assumptions expand and contract in response to political exigencies. It is in the context of a more

---

44. Hallaq, *The Impossible State*, 72.

45. Tomoko Masuzawa, *The Invention of World Religions: Or, How European Universalism was preserved in the Language of Pluralism* (Chicago: University of Chicago Press, 2005), 168.

46. Matthew Arnold, *Culture and Anarchy*, ed. Samuel Lipman (New Haven, CT: Yale University Press, 1994).

intense mobilization of culture and religion in the interest of the liberal ideological struggle against communism and fascism that attempts were made to unify American and West European religions and cultures as cornerstones of democracy in the twentieth century. The attempt to rehabilitate Hebraism as Judaism in the America of the late 1920s and early 1930s, which would be crowned with the invention of the "Judeo-Christian" tradition, is explained by Masuzawa as coming about "when the surging tide of fascism threatened Europe, and when the Americans were about to enter the fray . . . and no doubt also in reaction to the new domestic situation where they began to see a swelling number of immigrants from Asia and other non-Christian territories." While the new immigration from outside of Europe would not increase substantially till the 1950s and the 1960s, it was this new alliance between liberal Protestants and Jews, "and some Catholics in tow," that produced the new configuration in the early 1940s of Christianity and Judaism being "religions of democracy" against the tide of secularism, Soviet Communism, and Nazism.[47] With the increasing American deployment of Muslims and "Islam" as a "threat" to the American "way of life," including American "freedoms," and "democracy," which was earnestly deployed in the wake of the Iranian Revolution, this discourse would be affirmed with renewed strength in the wake of 9/11, giving rise to what is now identified as "Islamophobia."

It is in this context that Jacques Derrida announces that unlike Christianity or Judaism, or a "mixed religious culture,"

Islam, or a certain Islam, would thus be the only religious or theocratic culture [worldwide] that can still, in fact or in principle, inspire and declare any resistance to democracy. If it does not actually resist what might be called a real or actual democratization, one whose reality may be more or less contested, it can at least resist the democratic principle, claim, or allegation, the legacy and the old name of "democracy."[48]

Derrida adds that "this Islam, this particular one and not Islam in general (if such a thing exists), would represent the only religious culture that would have resisted up until now a European (that is, Greco-Christian and globalatinizing) process of secularization, and thus of democratization, and thus, in the strict sense, of politicization."[49] While Saudi Arabia

47. Masuzawa, *The Invention of World Religions*, 301.
48. Jacques Derrida, *Rogues: Two Essays on Reason* (Stanford, CA: Stanford University Press, 2005), 29.
49. Ibid., 31.

is the only "spectacular" example that Derrida cites when he speaks of "Islam," or of "a certain Islam" (Saudi Arabia has a population of 28 million people out of 1.2 billion Muslims worldwide), it is this "Islam" that he wants to privilege against all the others, whose existence he implies by way of alibi (Derrida seems unaware of or indifferent to the existence of a huge body of "Arabic and Islamic" intellectual production and political movements that exist in "Arab and/or Islamic spaces" and in "Arab and/or Islamic lands," which call for and theorize democracy in their countries and have been doing so since the nineteenth century).[50] Indeed, he is interested in producing a new democratic Islam, and as a missionary of Judeo-Christian democracy (he names Christian countries and the Jewish settler-colony as democracies or at least as claimants to democracy), Derrida elaborates on the necessary missionary tasks and responsibilities of Judeo-Christians towards Muslims:

For whoever, by hypothesis, considers him- or herself a friend of democracy in the world and not only in his or her own country . . . the task would consist in doing every-thing possible to join forces with all those who, and first of all in the Islamic world, fight not only for the secularization of the political (however ambiguous this secularization remains), for the emergence of a laic subjectivity, but also for an interpretation of the Koranic heritage that privileges, from the inside as it were, the democratic virtualities that are probably not any more apparent and readable at first glance, and readable under this name, than they were in the Old and New Testaments.

Derrida discusses much of this under the heading "the other of democracy," which Islam has come to occupy (and which he constitutes as "a certain Arab and Islamic world," which is also "an Arab and Islamic exception").[51]

In contrast to Derrida's interest in "the other of democracy," let me turn now to the question of how Christianity, or "a certain" Christianity, Protestantism, the Judeo-Christian, Europe, and America, or, a certain Christian and European world, came to constitute and be constituted as the "self" of democracy. This is important because, as Derrida himself remarks elsewhere, "there is no political power without the control of the archive. Effective democracy can always be measured by this essential criterion: the participation in and the access to the archive,

50. Ibid., 32.

51. Ibid., 28, 41. For an important critique of Derrida, see Anne Norton, "On the Muslim Question," in Democracy, Religious Pluralism and the Liberal Dilemma of Accommodation, Studies in Global Justice 7, ed. M. Mookherjee (New York: Springer Link, 2011), 65–75.

its constitution, and its interpretation. A contrario, the breaches of democracy can be measured by what a recent . . . work entitles *Forbidden Archives*."[52] Perhaps what Derrida fails to discern in the "resistance" to Western liberal democracy that "Islam" is said to constitute is a resistance to Western liberalism's attempt to form and control the archive of its very own constitution *and* its constitution of "Islam," and a resistance on the part of "Islam" to the monopoly Western liberalism wants to establish over the archive's "interpretation."

The publication in 1941 of the book *The Religions of Democracy: Judaism, Catholicism, Protestantism in Creed and Life*[53] was part of the institutionalization of the new hyphenated connection between Judaism and Christianity.[54] Exported to post-Nazi Europe, it is this American creed that would be deployed, after the Cold War ended, against Islam as the religion of "tyranny" and "repression." In his introduction to the book, Robert Ashworth, the editorial secretary of the National Conference of Christians and Jews (under whose auspices the book was published), identified the contributors' liberal and American nationalist commitments and credentials at the outset: "In entitling the book *The Religions of Democracy*, we have in mind the belief in the worth and rights of the individual which characterizes all three of the faiths with which it deals. Based upon religion, it repudiates all forms of tyranny. This affirmation of the supreme importance of the individual lies at the foundation of all true democracy."[55] The book, Ashworth claimed, was intended to help American adherents of all three "religions" to live cooperatively "as Americans."

While supporting the American tradition (which is non-constitutionally-based) of the separation of church and state, Ashworth insists that this separation does not render America "anti-religious or what Europeans call 'laic.'"[56] Indeed, the "religious freedom" that America allegedly has does not mean that it should not forbid "the practice of 'suttee'—the burning of a widow on the funerary pyre of her dead husband—or polygamy. . . . No, for religious freedom is not license, and

---

52. Jacques Derrida, *Archive Fever: A Freudian Impression* (Chicago: University of Chicago Press, 1996), 4n.

53. Louis Finkelstein, J. Elliot Ross, and William Adams Brown, *The Religions of Democracy: Judaism, Catholicism, Protestantism in Creed and Life* (New York: Devin-Adair, 1941).

54. On the anti-Catholic campaigns of the nineteenth century and the conspiracy theories about the Catholic Church plotting to overthrow the "democratic institutions" of the American republic, see Anne Norton, *Alternative Americas: A Reading of Antebellum Political Culture* (Chicago: University of Chicago Press, 1986), 64–96.

55. Ibid., iii.

56. Ibid., vii.

individuals or groups of individuals should not be permitted, under the plea of following their consciences, to do what is offensive to the consciences of a great many others."[57] Note that "religious freedom" here is invoked not against the antidemocratic and anti-individualist beliefs of other religions, but rather (and this will be discussed in chapter 2) against their gendered and conjugal arrangements and practices and that this "freedom" is invoked at the precise moment when the limitations on it are affirmed in the strongest of terms. Non-European non-Christian culture must clearly be subordinated to Euro-Christian culture in these assertions. This axiom of power relations aside, the United States would soon begin to insist to the world that while it is one of the most youthful of countries, having only been created in 1776, that it is in effect the oldest continuous democracy on the planet.

But does the peculiar American penchant for historically designating itself as a "young" state with the "oldest" democracy betray a strange national form of insecurity, or let us call it neurosis, about the age of the US republic, which, as a nation-state, is indeed not young at all, and is arguably one of the oldest independent nation-states worldwide, especially when compared to the majority of African, Asian, and especially European nation-states (from Italy to Germany and Greece to Bulgaria, Moldavia, and Montenegro)? Whence comes then the importance of this claim of youthfulness, which is often deployed to insist on America's old age as a democracy? I am not entirely persuaded that this is solely a manifestation of a national form of group neurosis. Oscar Wilde has famously quipped: "The youth of America is their oldest tradition. It has been going on now for three hundred years. To hear them talk one would imagine they were in their first childhood. As far as civilization goes they are in their second."[58] This age contrast, or rather, this dual positioning of the United States on a temporal axis of youth and old age, seems, as we will see, to serve ideological culturalist purposes, and not only psychological and narcissistic ones, namely the not-so-implicit claim that there is something particular and fundamental about American white Christian Protestant culture that rendered the US republic a democracy from the outset. Psychologically, it might be a group neurosis caused by white Americans' sense of a narcissistic injury that nonwhite Americans and non-American others do not see the US as either "democratic" or "young," which leads to a defensive posture

57. Ibid., iv.
58. Oscar Wilde, *A Woman of No Importance*, in Oscar Wilde, *Two Plays by Oscar Wilde: "An Ideal Husband" and "A Woman of No Importance"* (New York: Signet Classics, 1997), 163-64.

that the US is indeed what it claims to be even though many Americans realize that their country has never been, and is not, what it claims to be. This narcissistic trait was recognized by the biggest fan of American democracy in the nineteenth century, namely, de Tocqueville, as "national vanity": "The Americans, in their intercourse with strangers, appear impatient of the smallest censure and insatiable of praise. . . . They unceasingly harass you to extort praise, and if you resist their entreaties they fall to praising themselves. It would seem as if, doubting their own merit, they wished to have it constantly exhibited before their eyes. Their vanity is not only greedy, but restless and jealous."[59]

Perhaps it is most ironic when an African American (of either gender) or an American woman (of whatever race) repeats the United States' nationalist presuppositions about being the oldest of democracies, when both racial and gender groupings were excluded from this alleged democracy for the longest period of the age of this republic, and in large measure, in the case of Black Americans remain so (it should be remembered here that during the Revolutionary War against British despotism, Virginia, the Carolinas, and Georgia offered their soldiers lands and slaves in recognition of their contribution to American "democracy").[60] Yet, such assertions are repeated time and again to affirm the place of the United States in the world, especially in the "non-democratic" and the "antidemocratic" parts of the world with which the United States often contrasts itself. Hence while welcoming the Chinese president Hu Jintao in January 2011, US president Barack Obama repeated this nationalist incantation: "President Hu, we have met today in a spirit of mutual respect: the United States—the oldest democracy in the world, and China—one of the oldest civilizations in the world."[61] Obama clearly did not mean that the United States has only been a democracy since the early 1970s when its manifest racial apartheid system finally ended juridically while being replaced with a new racialized criminal system immediately after to accompany its maintenance of economic apartheid.[62] Not to be outdone, Obama's secretary of state, Hillary Rodham Clinton, repeated this same formula on Egyptian television less than two

59. De Tocqueville, *Democracy in America*, 2:238.
60. See Robin Blackburn, *The Overthrow of Colonial Slavery, 1776–1848* (London: Verso, 1988), 116. See also Eric Foner, *The Story of American Freedom* (New York: W. W. Norton, 1998), 32.
61. President Barack Obama, speech delivered on 19 January 2011 in Washington, D.C. during a state dinner welcoming Chinese president Hu Jintao.
62. For the continuation of US racialism today which politically disenfranchises "more black men than in 1870" and which places more African American adults under correctional control "than were enslaved in 1850," see Michelle Alexander, *The New Jim Crow: Mass Incarceration in the Age of Colorblindness*, rev. ed. (New York: New Press, 2012), 180.

months later in Cairo, following the removal of US-backed dictator Husni Mubarak from power by a popular uprising: "We have the greatest respect for Egypt's 7,000 years of civilization. We are a young country by comparison. But we are the oldest democracy in the world. So we have some idea, having gone through these stages ourself."[63] Like Obama, Clinton did not mean to say that the US was a forty-year old limited racialized "democracy" that has seen increasingly large restrictions on civil and political rights following 9/11 and the enactment of the Patriot Act which Obama has extended and expanded.[64]

Clinton's reliance on the epistemological claims of modernization theory, which represents Westerners as adults who have gone through the "stages" of growth and can now guide Arabs and Muslims out of their childhood stage, is hardly innovative. Edward Said saw these claims as the point where "Orientalism and modernization theory dovetail nicely."[65] But given this rhetoric, the United States, indeed the entire "West," seem to have been waiting for a very long period (perhaps since the emergence of social evolutionary theory in the eighteenth century, or at least since the articulations of Social Darwinism and colonial anthropology in the nineteenth) for the time when Arabs and Muslims would grow up and begin to work for democracy and the rights of the individual and throw off the sway of undemocratic and despotic Arab cultural traditions and Islam over them. In both declarations by Obama and Clinton, civilization is being juxtaposed and compared to a political system of governance with which it seems to compete for temporal precedence and lateness. How did "civilization" and "democracy" come to inhabit a line of comparison and an imperial argument? It is within the deployment of culture that this juxtaposition is intelligible, wherein democracy and despotism are both posited as civilizational, religious, and cultural achievements and failures respectively.

I will return to the democratic precedent that the US constitutes for itself later, but in the meantime I want to draw a connection between the importance of the question of the youthfulness of the United States in a world where it is one of the oldest of nation-states and the nineteenth-century discourse on comparative world religions, which also insisted that Christianity itself was the youngest of religions and

63. Hillary Rodham Clinton, 16 March 2011, interview with Shahira Amin on Nile TV channel, also issued as a press release by the State Department on 17 March 2011.

64. Charlie Savage, "Senators Say Patriot Act is being Misinterpreted," *New York Times*, 26 May 2011.

65. Edward W. Said, *Covering Islam: How the Media and the Experts Determine How We See the Rest of the World* (New York: Pantheon, 1981), 28.

one which corrected the flaws in previous archaic faiths (both those religions that are now dead and those that survived through modernity).
Just like the counterfactual claims of the United States to youthfulness,
this nineteenth-century discourse on the youthfulness of Christianity
as the new generative "world" religion that achieves what old religions
could not had to account for the chronological lateness of Islam, which
appeared six centuries after it. To do so, Reverend James Cameron Lees,
for example, would state in 1882 that "in Mohameddanism there is no
regenerative power; it is 'of the letter, which killeth,'—unelastic, sterile,
barren. . . . To . . . progress it must prove an obstacle from its very character. . . . It has no power of adaptation, expansion, development."[66]
Masuzawa paraphrases his approach and the place of Islam in these
nineteenth-century debates: "strange as it might sound, [Islam was then]
a belated 'old religion.' "[67] Some even posited Islam not as an offshoot
of Christianity, which some early Christians understood it to be, but,
as Orientalist Ernest Renan has posited it, as an offshoot of Judaism,
hence Semitic through and through, and clearly pre-Christian in its
affiliations.[68] Here the point of the youthfulness of Christianity and
American democracy seem to be more related to a modernizationist
normative bias that always contrasts itself with a tradition of its own
invention and which it seeks to replace, if not sublate. The questions
of chronological anteriority of dictatorship to democracy, and of Islam, Judaism, "Buddhism," "Hinduism," and other "world religions" to
Christianity, inhabit a similar evolutionary temporal structure in contemporary liberal discourse, one whose origins are primitive cults and
religions and whose telos will always be American- and Western-style
democracy and Christian- and Protestant-style, or more specifically,
secular-style understandings of religion and its role in contemporary
life. What is being posited then in these comparisons and juxtapositions
is a contrast between old and primitive civilizations and cultures that
are manifestations of old cults and primitive religions whose modern
failure is exemplified in their despotic systems of rule contrasted with a
young vital and robust American civilization adhering to a younger and

---

66. James Cameron Lees, "Mohamedanism," in *The Faiths of the World*, St. Giles Lectures, (New York: Scribners, 1882), 331, cited in Masuzawa, *The Invention of World Religions*, 82–83.

67. Masuzawa, 83. See also Masuzawa's discussion of this question in ibid., 82–86.

68. I thank Tomoko Masuzawa for her clarifications on this point. Also, many German Jewish Orientalists would connect Islam to Judaism. On this, see Susannah Heschel, "German-Jewish Scholarship on Islam as a Tool for De-Orientalizing Judaism, " *New German Critique* 36, no. 1 (2012): 91–107.

more (if not most) evolved religion whose main cultural achievement has been democracy.

Indeed, when European liberal republicans would come to recognize some of the atrocities committed by European Christians, they would attribute their religious pedigree to "Islam," as did the nineteenth-century French historian Edgar Quinet who explained not only the Inquisition and the genocide of Native Americans by Spain as inspired by its Islamic legacy, but also the Crusades themselves and their atrocities, which were also blamed on the prayers of the Spaniard San Domenico de Guzmán: "In the Crusades the Catholic Church enacted the principle of Islamism: extermination."[69] In the American context as in Europe these comparisons are linked to the shifting evolutionary articulation of racial categories with cultural and religious ones.

From Orientalism to Middle East Studies

One of the earliest Cold War statements on the relationship between Islam and democracy would apply to Turkey and its government's move toward liberal secularist and democratic structures of governance in 1950. Iranologist and Harvard professor Richard N. Frye explained in 1957:

The Turkish transformation under Atatürk in the 20s and 30s is certainly one of the greatest revolutions in history. If today Turkey is a "Western" state, she has not only the many headaches of the West: "What is democracy? What is the moral basis of the state and society?" in a Western framework, but also the resurgence of the past, time-honored traditions, and the Islamic heritage. Turkey will undoubtedly remain an object of observation and study, as well as suspicion, by the *rest* of the Muslim world.[70]

But even then, Turkey was seen as an unstable exception to the rule of "Islamic" tyranny. The question of "tradition" would occupy many American commentators and political scientists in the 1950s and beyond when examining the relationship of Islam to democracy, especially as related to modern rationalism and positivism. In that vein, American social scientist Daniel Lerner (whose Orientalist method was

---

69. Edgar Quinet, *Le Christianisme et la Révolution française* (Paris: Fayard, 1984), 137, cited in Losurdo, *Liberalism*, 312.

70. Richard N. Frye, ed., *Islam and the West: Proceedings of the Harvard Summer School Conference on the Middle East, July 25–27, 1955* (The Hague: Mouton, 1956), 3.

on full display in his influential 1958 book on modernization in the Middle East) asserted predictively, and perhaps wishfully, "imply[ing] no ethnocentrism," that "whether from East or West, modernization poses the same basic challenge—the infusion of a 'rationalist and positivist spirit' against which, scholars seem agreed, 'Islam is absolutely defenseless.' "[71] Lerner's point should be contrasted with the later point of Derrida's cited above, which insists on Islam as the only contemporary force resisting the rhetoric and the name of democracy. Lerner's modernizationist political assertions are hardly original, as they are borrowed from none other than Karl Marx, who posited the economically transformative power of capital as one

draw[ing] all, even the most barbarian, nations into civilisation. The cheap prices of commodities are the heavy artillery with which it batters down all Chinese walls, with which it forces the barbarians' intensely obstinate hatred of foreigners to capitulate. It compels all nations, on pain of extinction, to adopt the bourgeois mode of production; it compels them to introduce what it calls civilisation into their midst, i.e., to become bourgeois themselves. In one word, it creates a world after its own image.[72]

It is this capitalist determinism, read as modernization by American social scientists, that will come up against a fortified "Islam" with unanticipated offensive capabilities that will take American politicians and social scientists by surprise since the triumph of the Iranian Revolution in 1979. How could Islam, which was supposed to be defenseless against the march of Western modernity, become such a challenge to it? The answer will lie in deployments of the central Enlightenment notion of "religion" and the nineteenth-century concept of "culture."

One of the truisms that the mainstream US academy disseminated until January 2011 was the proposition of Arab and Muslim exceptionalism, wherein while other cultural formations from Japan to India to Latin America have come to embrace "democracy" at various times in the twentieth century, Muslim and Arab countries have not, which left the cultural and religious argument as the main factor explaining this Muslim, or more precisely, *Islamic* failure to democratize. The journey that Orientalism traveled to become "Middle East Studies" was neither a long nor an arduous one. Indeed, as Said had noted, there was little

71. Daniel Lerner, *The Passing of Traditional Society: Modernizing the Middle East* (New York: Free Press, 1958), 45.

72. Karl Marx, *The Communist Manifesto*, in *The Marx-Engels Reader*, ed. Robert Tucker (New York: W. W. Norton, 1978), 477.

methodological or theoretical innovation in the move from European Orientalism to American Middle East Studies, except perhaps in the mode of further geographical particularism and the disappearance of proficiency in Middle East languages. There were no epistemological breaks, no scientific revolutions, no gestalt switches, and no paradigm shifts, in short, nothing that Thomas Kuhn would have recognized as even a crisis in the field.[73]

While institutional change linking US foreign policy and academic research was inaugurated in the 1950s with what came to be known as Title VI (though the connection was already made during World War II with the need for experts on countries the US had an involvement in, something which the Fulbright Program which was established in 1946 would attend to), which provided government funds for the setting up of area studies, ranging from Latin America to Africa and the Middle East, this new institutional rubric did not spur scholars of this new entity called the Middle East into a comparative or universalist mindset, which Orientalists had held on to, at least as far as the Orient was concerned as a unitary idea. Thus, for European Orientalists, the cultural logic governing China, India, and the Arab World was more or less the same "Oriental" logic.

American Middle East Studies, by definition, saw itself in much narrower terms than European Orientalism, limiting itself to a narrower object of study, which it began to posit was exceptional and noncomparative. With the rise of modernization theory and the devastating riposte to it that came to be known as dependency theory, mainstream Middle East Studies remained immune to the universalist impulse, insisting tenaciously to the particularity of its region, to its exceptionalism. This was not because mainstream Middle East Studies was aware of an assimilationist imperial gaze that subjected all that it did not know to a familiar form of "universal" knowledge, nor was it because practitioners in the field were culturally sensitive and comfortable with radical alterity as enriching human experience, anymore than the universalists' claim of cultural relativism mediated through a Social Darwinist developmentalism reflected a commitment to human equality. Indeed, the new rubric institutionalized in the United States created disciplinary divisions between Middle East Studies departments specialized in philological, theological, and literary studies and Middle East Institutes/Centers associated with social science departments concerned mainly

73. See Thomas Kuhn, *The Structure of Scientific Revolutions* (Chicago: University of Chicago Press, 1962).

with policy. This disciplinary division would dictate how social science theories could be augmented with Orientalist views of culture housed in Middle East departments. The insistence on the exceptionalism of the Middle East and Islam was then, as now, an identitarian architectural project in the strictest sense. It was, as Said has shown, an insistence on othering, and on worlding the world of Europe and Euro-America by constructing them as a recognizable self, and in the process rendering the Arabs and Muslims as a necessary "other."[74] We will see in the following how this unfolds.

This is not to say that many American scholars of the Middle East did not reject these culturalist methods; indeed, a good number of them did and some of them organized themselves as progressive groups of scholars and published their own journals and research, most notably the group associated with the Middle East Research and Information Project (MERIP), and the group of Arab and Arab-American scholars located in the United States who began rival scholarly organizations (the Arab-American University Graduates [AAUG]) and journals (*MERIP Reports* and *Arab Studies Quarterly*) to challenge the orthodoxy of the establishment Middle East scholarship organized under the umbrella of the Ford Foundation-funded Middle East Studies Association (established in 1966) and its official journal. Said's early research and conclusions about Orientalism would be first shared in the context of AAUG's annual conferences.[75]

The articulation of modernization theory and its related concepts of political and civic cultures in mainstream Middle East Studies were mediated through the filter of Orientalism. The failure of modernization theory to explain political, social, economic, and cultural processes in the Middle East and Muslim countries beyond it seemed to US establishment scholarship as less related to the theoretical fallacies of modernization theory itself and more a function of the exceptionalism of Arab or Islamic cultures more generally. While the rest of area studies and anti-establishment Middle East scholars were turning to dependency theory to understand socioeconomic and political processes unfolding in Africa, Asia, and Latin America (Samir Amin, who is primarily a

---

74. On this, see also Asad's classic, *Formations of the Secular: Christianity, Islam, Modernity* (Stanford, CA: Stanford University Press, 2003), 161–70.

75. For these details, see Said, *Orientalism*, 284–328; Said, *Covering Islam*, 135–61; and Timothy Mitchell, "The Middle East in the Past and Future of Social Science," in *The Politics of Knowledge: Area Studies and the Disciplines*, ed. David Szanton (Berkeley: University of California Press, 2002). See also Zachary Lockman, *Contending Visiovns of the Middle East: The History and Politics of Orientalism* (Cambridge: Cambridge University Press, 2004).

Middle East scholar, is a pioneer theorist of dependency, having written his dissertation in 1957 in France on the topic which was later published in English under the title *Accumulation on a World Scale*),[76] mainstream Middle East Studies was turning to Islam and culture. Ignoring the central attribute of imperial connections to the region that are primarily defined by oil, it was not the nature of US imperial interest in and control of oil production that was seen as "exceptional" about the region, regulating the types of its ruling regimes and the kinds of resistance they generated, but rather the facile notion of Islamic and Arab "culture."

British literary scholar Raymond Williams had excavated the modern term culture as emerging in the eighteenth and nineteenth centuries and historicized its emergence as a *category* in terms of which modern scholars study "a people," itself a modern invention, as well as its emergence as an *object* of study for imperial anthropology and archeology (and here Franz Boas's notion stands out, namely of culture as a bounded universe of shared ideas and customs), wherein culture refers to material production, and to imperial historiography and more recently to signifying and symbolic systems of production.[77]

Williams elaborated on the organic link between "culture" and "civilization": "Like culture . . . with which it has had a long and still difficult interaction, [civilization] referred originally to a process, and in some contexts this sense still survives." He located the modern meaning of civilization in English as having emerged in the 1830s. Its use in the plural would come about in the 1860s, when it would be contrasted with barbarism and savagery.[78] In line with such understandings, Ernest Renan, who had helped place Islam in the realm of the pre-Christian Semitic, would later in the century posit it as an enemy of all science, prompting a response from Muslim reformist Jamal al-Din al-Afghani. In a lecture that he gave at the Sorbonne in March 1883 on "Islamism and Science," Renan argued that Islam as a religion and the Arabs as a people had always been hostile to science and philosophy and that any Arab and Islamic achievement in these fields was brought about despite Islam and from mostly non-Arab and non-Muslim populations conquered by Islam and the Arabs. Once the Arabs reestablished control and

76. See Mitchell, "The Middle East in the Past . . . ," where he challenges the more common accounts of the lateness of Middle East studies in adopting dependency theory. For Samir Amin's book in English, See Amin, *Accumulation on a World Scale: A Critique of the Theory of Underdevelopment* (New York: Monthly Review Press, 1974).

77. Raymond Williams, *Keywords: Vocabulary of Culture and Society*, 87–93. See also Raymond Williams, *Culture and Society, 1780–1950*, introduction, xiii–xx.

78. Williams, *Keywords*, 57–60.

Islam strengthened itself, these achievements were crushed and the true spirit of both was made manifest, namely, their "hatred of science."[79] Here the question of the "decadence of states governed by Islam, and the intellectual nullity of the races that hold, from that religion alone, their culture and their education," were observable by Europeans as "the inferiority of Mohammedan countries."[80]

Sharing many of Renan's conclusions regarding the present (late nineteenth century) state of Muslim countries and the "responsibility" of the "Muslim religion" for "why Arab civilization . . . suddenly became extinguished . . . and why the Arab world still remains buried in profound darkness,"[81] al-Afghani universalized religious repression of science by comparing Islam's record to Christianity's, thus doing away with the exceptionalism with which Renan endowed Islam. Where al-Afghani disagreed with Renan was on the racialist premises Renan had employed to castigate Arabs as inimical to science and philosophy. Al-Afghani deployed Social Darwinism as the basis of his refutation, explaining the evolutionary basis of all societies wherein religion, and not "pure reason," emerges in their barbaric state as a transitional phase to civilization. Al-Afghani's universalism was central: "It is by this religious education, whether it be Muslim, Christian, or pagan, that all nations have emerged from barbarism and marched toward a more advanced civilization."[82] If the "Muslim religion" had become an "obstacle to the development of sciences," this was a mere evolutionary phase that would one day "disappear."[83] The motor for the evolutionary change in Europe, al-Afghani had surmised, after François Guizot, author of *L'Historie de la civilisation*, was the Protestant Reformation.[84] Positing Islam as living in the childhood stage compared to the adulthood in which Christianity found itself in the nineteenth century, al-Afghani implored Renan to be patient:

79. Ernest Renan, "Islamism and Science," reproduced in *Orientalism: Early Sources*, vol. 1, *Readings in Orientalism*, ed. Bryan S. Turner (London: Routledge, 2000), 210. Renan's lecture was delivered on 29 March 1883.

80. Ibid., 1:200.

81. See "Answer of Jamal al-Din al-Afghani to Renan," first published in the *Journal Des Débats*, 18 May 1883 and reproduced in Jamal Ad-Din al-Afghani, *Réfutation des matérialistes*, ed. and trans. A. M. Goichon (Paris: Paul Geuthner, 1942), 184, and in Nikki Keddie, *An Islamic Response to Imperialism: Political and Religious Writings of Sayyid Jamal ad-Din al-Afghani* (Berkeley: University of California Press, 1983), 187.

82. Goichon, 177, and Keddie, 183.

83. Ibid.

84. He cites Guizot in his *Réfutation des matérialistes*; see Goichon, 165. See also the Arabic translation of the book from the original Persian undertaken by Muhammad ʿAbduh, *Al-Radd ʿala al-Dahriyyin* (Cairo: Al-Salam al-ʿAlamiyyah lil-Tabʿ wa al-Nashr wa al-Tawziʿ, 1983), 101.

The Christian religion . . . has emerged from the first period [of its evolution]; thence-forth free and independent, it seems to advance rapidly on the road of progress and science, whereas Muslim society has not yet freed itself from the tutelage of religion. Realizing, however, that the Christian religion preceded the Muslim religion in the world by many centuries, I cannot keep from hoping that Muhammadan society will succeed someday in breaking its bonds and marching resolutely in the path of civiliza-tion after the manner of Western society, for which the Christian faith despite its rigors and intolerance, was not at all an invincible obstacle. No I cannot admit that this hope be denied to Islam. I plead here with M. Renan not the cause of the Muslim religion, but that of several hundreds of millions of men, who would thus be condemned to live in barbarism and ignorance.[85]

In some ways it seems that if religion was a causal factor in econom-ics, modes of thought, and political systems from the sixteenth century onwards, and culture and later civilization (and their relationship to climate and geography and later to race and genetics) became the heir to this system of causality in the nineteenth and much of the twen-tieth century, today we find that it is religion as culture, or culture as religion, that defines Islam as a causal factor determining certain po-litical systems and not others. Here it is not a juxtaposition of civiliza-tion and democracy in a temporal comparison that is being staged, but rather civilization, culture, and religion as anterior to and productive of political systems of rule, including democracy, and as a religious tradi-tion that survives in modernity and continues to promote or suppress democracy.

In a review of the political science literature, Lisa Anderson con-cluded that "what had been understood [by American academics] in the 1950s and 1960s as 'culture,' and therefore of interest only to students of exotica, had become 'tradition,' the provenance of area specialists in the 1970s."[86] Still, until the emergence of a new interest in democracy and democratization in the 1980s, opposition to the paradigm of American political science on the Middle East, which had held onto moderniza-tion theory, came from conservative corners and not from Marxists, as

85. Goichon, 177–78, Keddie, 183. On the debate between Renan and al-Afghani, see Joseph Massad, *Desiring Arabs* (Chicago: University of Chicago Press, 2007), 12–13.
86. Lisa Anderson, "Policy-Making and Theory Building: American Political Science and the Islamic Middle East," in *Theory, Politics and the Arab World: Critical Responses*, ed. Hisham Sharabi (New York: Routledge, 1990), 66. For a review of Lerner's views, see Anderson, "Policy-Making and Theory Building," 56–57. For a discussion of the prospects of democracy in the Arab world and a dismissal of the "Islam" factor, see Lisa Anderson, "Arab Democracy: Dismal Prospects," *World Policy Journal* 18, no. 3 (Fall 2001): 53–60.

had happened in Latin America for example. American modernization theorists were calling for the destruction of tradition and religious institutions and elites (which were the traditional allies of American imperialism) as part of the process of modernization, which is what prompted American conservatives to respond. As Anderson explains, the challenge to the modernizationists came "not from Huntingtonian circles, however, but from those who felt a need to explain what was to most of these theorists—and not a few of the political elites of the region—the surprising, indeed, dismaying resiliency of tradition."[87] Out of touch with the rest of the political science discipline, which had turned to the study of "political economy," US-based political scientists working on the Middle East began to study "tradition," itself a modern category that would play a central role in modernization theory (this is not to say that the study of political economy is necessarily void of culturalist arguments but rather that culture is not used as the only "independent variable" which could "explain" them comprehensively). In doing so, they would allow full admission of Orientalist theories about Islamic and Arab culture, which they had neglected in an earlier phase (when the Arab and Muslim world was not a focus of study) on account of their interest in modernizing processes and not in the remnants of the premodern.[88]

But how did culture come to be mobilized as an imperial argument for and against democracy? American social scientists Gabriel Almond and Sydney Verba were the pioneers in this regard. Their 1963 book *The Civic Culture: Political Attitudes and Democracy in Five Nations* ushered in the debate about the link of democracy and the culture defining "the political culture of a nation" as "the particular distribution of orientation toward political objects among the members of the nation"[89] They created a tripartite typology of political cultures: parochial, subject,

87. Anderson, "Policy-Making and Theory Building," 60.
88. Historian Peter Gran has argued in the same vein that it is indeed "Orientalism, as a logical and natural aspect of the dominant culture of [European] democracy and as a cultural tradition that serves to retard the development of a tradition of political economy in [Western] Middle East studies," in Peter Gran, "Studies of Anglo-American Political Economy: Democracy, Orientalism, and the Left," in *Theory and Politics and the Arab World: Critical Responses*, ed. Hisham Sharabi (New York: Routledge, 1990), 228. It would seem that it is also the culture of Western academic knowledge and media representations, indeed Western political discourse itself, that has become a persistent tradition (the limitations of this homology notwithstanding) as much as the so-called Muslim "traditions" that are said to explain Muslim and Islamic "despotism" and hostility or at least incompatibility with democracy.
89. Gabriel Almond and Sydney Verba, *The Civic Culture: Political Attitudes and Democracy in Five Nations* (Princeton, NJ: Princeton University Press, 1963), 14–15.

and participant.[90] Examples of parochial political cultures unsurprisingly include "the loosely articulated African kingdoms, and even the Ottoman Empire [which] are examples of stable mixed subject-parochial cultures."[91] Parochial political cultures indicate "the comparative absence of expectations of change initiated by the political system."[92] Thus parochial political culture is a feature of despotism and it should of course be contrasted with the participant political culture, which leads to democratic governance. Revising the findings of their book and responding to criticisms two decades later, Almond ventured an explanation for the salience of the concept of political culture. Whereas he asserted ahistorically that political culture is an ancient notion, in that the modern term simply reflects ancient concepts that went back to the Bible and the Greeks (thus reaching for Hellenism and Hebraism as origins yet again) and "has in some sense always been with us," he posed the following question:

How do we explain its sudden popularity in the 1960s and the proliferation of research dealing with it in recent decades? We suggest that the failure of enlightenment and liberal expectations as they related to political development and political culture set the explanatory problem to which political culture research was a response, and the development of social theory in the nineteenth and twentieth centuries and of social science methodology after World War II (particularly survey methodology) provided the opportunity for solving this problem. The intellectual challenge plus the theoretical developments and the methodological inventions explain the emergence of this field of inquiry.[93]

If Fascism, Nazism, and "Bolshevism," were the mark of the Enlightenment's failure to produce liberal polities through the 1940s for Almond and Verba, then the research agenda would be set for the rest of the field to explain the persistence of communist and "totalitarian" systems after the War, and, in the case of Euro-American and European specialists in countries with Muslim majorities, the persistence of Islam (with the intermittent exception of Turkey) as productive of a political culture that is inimical to democracy and partial to despotism.

90. Ibid., 17.
91. Ibid., 22.
92. Ibid., 18.
93. Gabriel A. Almond, "The Intellectual History of the Civic Culture Concept," in *The Civic Culture Revisited*, ed. Gabriel A. Almond and Sydney Verba (Boston: Little, Brown, 1980), 6.

Huntington's Interventions

But whereas modernization theory predicted democratic transformation with the advent of modernity and abandonment of "tradition," and political culture theories proposed that the limitations on stable democratic governance were related to culture as a "set of variables which may be used in the construction of theories,"[94] US interest during the Vietnam War was increasingly aimed at producing "stable" regimes that needed not be democratic at all and that would not disrupt or threaten the flow of Western capital. It was in this vein that Harvard academic (and US government consultant during the US invasion of Vietnam) Samuel P. Huntington's classic intervention, *Political Order in Changing Societies*, published in 1968, seemed more interested in questions of order and corruption than in democracy, especially when it came to Islam: "Corruption . . . should be less extensive in the modernization of feudal societies than it is in the modernization of centralized bureaucratic societies. It should have been less in Japan than in China and it should have been less in Hindu cultures than in Islamic ones. Impressionistic evidence suggests that these may well be the case."[95]

In the 1980s, after the academic demise of modernization theory (which continues to live, however, not only in many corridors of the academy but also and especially in media representations and in international policy institutionalized in Western- and UN-based development agencies and their local affiliates of nongovernmental organizations) and of dependency theory, and in the aftermath of the anti-Soviet human rights campaigns of the Jimmy Carter years, a rejuvenated discourse on liberal democracy would emerge that would inaugurate the "cultural turn," outside Middle East Studies, where, as we have seen already, it had never been dislodged at any rate. These were the years when the US government began to support, train, finance, even create Islamist groups to fight the Soviet presence in Afghanistan and the Communist

94. Ibid., 26. These methodological assumptions continue to be employed in political science research on the Middle East wherein an "Arab Democracy Barometer," financed by the State Department, measures the political orientations of the citizens of an Arab country, which would contribute to "democratization and good governance," thus assessing that country's "political culture in general, and in particular, the degree to which there is both public support for democracy and citizen values conducive to democratic governance." See Mark Tessler and Amaney Jamal, "Political Attitude Research in the Arab World: Emerging Opportunities," *PS: Political Science and Politics* (July 2006): 39, 3, 434, 435. All of this seems to continue the *academic and popular* liberal American assumptions that Arab (and Muslim) despotisms in fact reflect citizen attitudes!

95. Samuel P. Huntington, *Political Order in Changing Societies* (New Haven, CT: Yale University Press, 1968), 65.

government set up after the Afghani revolution that overthrew the monarchy. These arguments would be championed by Samuel P. Huntington himself. Huntington would begin these debates by making an argument about democracy and its relationship to the modes of governance that precede it that is related to the argument he had made above on corruption and regime type:

According to one line of argument, pluralism (even highly stratified pluralism) in traditional society enhances the probability of developing stable democracy in modern society. The caste system may be one reason why India has been able to develop and to maintain stable democratic institutions. More generally, the argument is made that societies with a highly developed feudalism, including an aristocracy capable of limiting the development of state power, are more likely to evolve into democracies than those that lack such social pluralism. The record of Western Europe versus Russia and of Japan versus China suggests that there may well be something to this theory. But the theory fails to account for differences between North America and South America. Tocqueville, Louis Hartz, and others attribute democracy in the former to the absence of feudalism. The failure of democracy in South America has, conversely, often been attributed precisely to its feudal heritage, although the feudalism that existed there was, to be sure, highly centralized.[96]

Thus, following Huntington, "Islamic" societies are more "corrupt" on account of their centralized bureaucratic systems and this is also one of the probable reasons why they remain undemocratic. This is not unrelated to Karl Wittfogel's Cold War hydraulic theory of Oriental despotism popularized by his 1957 book and extended to the Soviet Union.[97] But there are other factors too. Huntington classifies them into four separate categories: "economic, social, external, and cultural."[98] Huntington, however, would move to downplay some of these factors as indeterminant of democracy, focusing on the cultural as the most relevant element.

Arguing against the thesis that economic development and wealth fosters democracy, Huntington provided many examples of countries that were acquiring more wealth and considered by the World Bank as middle-income countries but which failed to democratize. Abandoning the Marxian notions on which modernization theory, despite its imperial

---

96. Samuel P. Huntington, "Will More Countries Become Democratic?" *Political Science Quarterly* 99, no. 2 (Summer 1984): 203.

97. Karl A. Wittfogel, *Oriental Despotism: A Comparative Study of Total Power* (New Haven, CT: Yale University Press, 1957).

98. Huntington, "Will More Countries Become Democratic?" 198.

liberal commitments, relied (that advanced capitalism will sweep away traditional elites, economic structures, and ruling ideologies, including religion), he concluded that "economic development compels the modification or abandonment of traditional political institutions; it does not determine what political system will replace them. That will be shaped by other factors, such as the underlying culture of the society, the values of the elites, and external influences."[99] It is when Huntington brings in the cultural factor that Islam rears its ugly, undemocratic face:

Islam . . . has not been hospitable to democracy. Of thirty-six countries with Moslem majorities, Freedom House in 1984 rated twenty-one as "not free," fifteen as "partially free," none as "free." The one Islamic country that sustained even intermittent democracy after World War II was Turkey, which had, under Mustapha Kemal, explicitly rejected its Islamic tradition and defined itself as a secular republic. The one Arab country that sustained democracy, albeit of the consociational variety, for any time was Lebanon, 40 to 50 percent of whose population was Christian and whose democratic institutions collapsed when the Moslem majority asserted itself in the 1970s. Somewhat similarly, both Confucianism and Buddhism have been conducive to authoritarian rule, even in those cases where, as in Korea, Taiwan, and Singapore, economic preconditions for democracy have come into being. In India and Japan, on the other hand, the traditional Hindu and Shinto cultures at the very least did not prevent the development of democratic institutions and may well have encouraged it.[100]

This interesting culturalist schema will be redeployed by Huntington a few years later to explain the factors that enable and disable the emergence of democracy in different "cultural" areas around the world in strongly deterministic terms: "In China, the obstacles to democratization are political, economic, and cultural; in Africa they are overwhelmingly economic; and in the rapidly developing countries of East Asia and in many Islamic countries, they are primarily cultural."[101]

Citing Daniel Pipes, Huntington proceeded to explain why Islam, as culture, is so hostile to democracy. Following Pipes, he argued: "In Islam . . . no distinction exists between religion and politics or between the spiritual and the secular, and political participation was historically an alien concept."[102] In the context of the Cold War and its theories

99. Ibid., 201–2.
100. Ibid., 208. He would later elaborate on the Lebanese exception and its relationship to Christianity and Islam in Huntington, "Democracy's Third Wave," *Journal of Democracy* 3 (Spring 1992): 28.
101. Huntington, "Democracy's Third Wave," 33.
102. Huntington, "Will More Countries Become Democratic?" 208.

of "totalitarian" versus "democratic" systems, Islam seemed to belong to the totalitarian category. Huntington would continue to repeat this mantra, if in a slightly altered form, in future writings: "Islam . . . rejects any distinction between the religious community and the political community,"[103] and "to the extent that governmental legitimacy and policy flow from religious doctrine and religious expertise, Islamic concepts of politics differ from and contradict the premises of democratic politics."[104] Note how "Islam" and "Islamic" concepts of politics are one and the same thing for him. Hence, the lack of separation between the political and the theological is the operative criterion distinguishing modern democratic societies and cultures from totalitarian ones (in the case of communism, ideology is seen as the counterpart to theology), and which distinguish Protestant Christianity and the secularism it gave birth to from Judaism and Islam (and Catholicism and Orthodox Christianity) which could not separate the two. Indeed, arguments about the links of Orthodox and Catholic Christianity to despotism would proceed as explanatory factors to account for the persistent "dictatorships" reigning in Greece, Spain, and Portugal through the mid to late 1970s, when all of Western Europe would finally become "democratic," and in Eastern Europe until 1990, when all of Europe would be unified under the rubric of "democracy."

But, while Islam hinders democracy, Christianity (in the form of Protestantism) can help bring it about. Huntington makes certain to add that "one can also speculate on whether the spread of Christianity in [South] Korea may create a cultural context more favorable to democracy."[105] By 1992, Huntington generalizes his argument and gives it a historical dimension: "Historically, there has been a strong correlation between Western Christianity and democracy."[106] This Western Christian link to democracy (inspired by the Weberian connections between Protestantism and capitalism) though can be trumped by race, especially in Africa, for "by 1990, sub-Saharan Africa was the only region of the world where substantial numbers of Catholics and Protestants lived under authoritarian regimes in a large number of countries."[107] In the case of the Arab and Muslim worlds, Islam as culture (which for Huntington is clearly a more expansive notion than religion) has reigned supreme: "No Arab leader comes to mind, and it is hard to identify any Islamic

103. Huntington, "Democracy's Third Wave," 28.
104. Ibid.
105. Huntington, "Will More Countries Become Democratic?" 216.
106. Huntington, "Democracy's Third Wave," 13.
107. Ibid., 14.

leader who made a reputation as an advocate and supporter of democracy while in office. Why is this? This question inevitably leads to the issue of culture."[108] Huntington finally concludes coldly:

Among Islamic countries, particularly those in the Middle East, the prospects for democratic development seem low. The Islamic revival, and particularly the rise of Shi'ite fundamentalism would seem to reduce even further the likelihood of democratic development, particularly since democracy is often identified with the very Western influences the revival strongly opposes. In addition, many of the Islamic states are very poor. Those that are rich, on the other hand, are so because of oil, which is controlled by the state and hence enhances the power of the state in general and of the bureaucracy in particular. Saudi Arabia and some of the smaller Arab oil-rich Gulf countries have from time to time made some modest gestures toward the introduction of democratic institutions, but these have not gone far and have often been reversed.[109]

Understanding the power of "culture" as so insurmountable that not even US imperial power could alter it, Huntington adds that the "ability of the United States to affect the development of democracy elsewhere is limited. There is little that the United States or any other foreign country can do to alter the basic cultural tradition and social structure of another society or to promote compromise among groups of that society that have been killing each other."[110] With this stark conclusion, Huntington seems to hold true to colonial anthropology's two major ways of understanding otherness to the European self and difference from Europe, namely developmentalism and radical alterity, identifying "Islam" and its "culture" as radically other and unsusceptible to change along a developmentalist schema, as Marx and following him the modernizationists had argued. Thus, for Huntington, in the absence of Christianity, the only possible change that such an other, as this culturally essentialist "Islam," would undergo could only be achieved (perhaps following a Rousseauian schema) through Western forceful and military means. Here again, a missionizing democracy is the most recent form of Christianity, whose only hope to influence Muslims would be nothing less than converting Islam itself to this most recent and highest stage of Christianity.

The tradition of linking antidemocracy, or more precisely, despotism to Islam and the Orient is hardly a Huntingtonian invention but

---

108. Ibid, 22.
109. Huntington, "Will More Countries Become Democratic?" 216.
110. Ibid., 218.

harks back to the seventeenth-century European representations of a menacing Ottoman Empire. By the Age of the Enlightenment, Antoine Boulanger would give such propagandistic representations scientific authority in his *Recherches sur les origines du despotisme oriental*, published in 1761, as would many others who followed in his footsteps. Though the link would become hegemonic in the rising field of Orientalism following the 1798 Napoleonic invasion of Egypt and Syria, it would not go unchallenged. It was French proto-Orientalist Anquetil-Duperron who would be the first to challenge Montesquieu and the ongoing European legitimation of colonial theft which based itself on the grounds that despotism, whether on the part of Native Americans or Orientals, was linked to the absence of private property, thus providing justification for European imperial pillage of the lands of the colonized.[111] Across the Channel, it would be conservatives like Edmund Burke, who despite his general hostility to Islam, would rebut the charge of despotism and instead link Islam to democracy, precisely to limit imperial dispossession of Muslim lands and the imposition of British tyranny.[112]

In the context of the impeachment of Warren Hastings as governor-general in Bengal, Burke, contesting Hastings' claims that the despotism he exercised was one he inherited from Muslim rule in India, declared on the fourth day of the trial that "nothing is more false than that despotism is the constitution of any country in Asia that we are acquainted with. It is certainly not true of any Mahomedan constitution." He added:

The greatest part of Asia is under Mahomedan governments. To name a Mahomedan government is to name a government by law. It is a law enforced by stronger sanctions than any law that can bind a Christian sovereign. Their law is believed to be given by God; and it has the double sanction of law and of religion, with which the prince is no more authorized to dispense than any one else. And if any man will produce the Koran to me, and will but show me one text in it that authorizes in any degree an arbitrary power in the government, I will confess that I have read that book, and been conversant in the affairs of Asia, in vain. There is not such a syllable in it; but, on the contrary, against oppressors by name every letter of that law is fulminated. There are interpreters established throughout all Asia to explain that law, an order of priesthood, whom they call *men of the law*. These men are conservators of the law; and to enable them to preserve it in its perfection, they are secured from the resentment of the sovereign:

111. Franco Venturi, "Oriental Despotism," *Journal of the History of Ideas* 24, no. 1 (January-March 1963): 133–42.

112. See Mehta's discussion of Burke's defense in *Liberalism and Empire*, 185–86.

for he cannot touch them. Even their kings are not always vested with a real supreme power, but the government is in some degree republican.[113]

The discipline of Orientalism, however, would not take these early objections on board but would indulge in representations of "Oriental despotism" and "sultanism" for which Islam was the poster religion. It is this legacy that formed the academic culture that produced Huntington and his ideas, including the historical construction of the other in Orientalism and in American political science.[114] Add to this that European anti-Ottoman propaganda (which insisted on the horror of Ottoman despotism since the seventeenth century,[115] and informed the representation of Islam as despotic by Enlightenment figures— Montesquieu and Voltaire stand out in this effort, though Rousseau and his disciples had a different view of the Ottomans as less corrupt and more decent than European despotism— and described despotism as a system that does not recognize private property, facilitating imperial dispossession by Europe, something nineteenth-century Orientalism and European liberal thought would generally legitimize) might not be that different from imperial arguments with regards to "Arab" and "Islamic" oil since World War I through the present moment, articulated under the sign of "development."

Former British governor of Nigeria and British representative to the Permanent Mandates Commission of the League of Nations (1922–36), Lord Frederick Lugard, articulated this argument in his classic guide to how British colonial officials should rule the colonized natives: the subject peoples had no right "to deny their bounties to those who need them."[116] By the conclusion of World War II, a report prepared by the Office of Strategic Services for the US State Department argued that "the

113. Edmund Burke, "Speech in Opening the Impeachment," Fourth Day, Saturday, 16 February 1788, in *Speeches in the Impeachment of Warren Hastings, Esquire, Late Governor-General of Bengal*, in *The Works of The Right Honourable Edmund Burke*, vol. 9 (London: John C. Nimmo, 1887), electronic version, http://www.gutenberg.org/files/13968/13968-h/13968-h.htm#ARTICLES_OF_CHARGE (accessed 17 February 2014).

114. On this tradition of scholarship, see Yahya Sadowski, "The New Orientalism and the Democracy Debate," in *Political Islam: Essays from Middle East Report*, ed. Joel Beinin and Joe Stork (Berkeley: University of California Press, 1997), 33–50.

115. For a review of the French debates on Ottoman "despotism," see Thomas Kaiser, "The Evil Empire: The Debate on Turkish Despotism in Eighteenth-Century French Political Culture," *Journal of Modern History* 72, no.1 (2000): 6–34.

116. Frederick Lugard, *The Dual Mandate in British Tropical Africa*, 5th ed. (Hamden, CT: Archon Books, 1965), 61, 194, cited in Timothy Mitchell, *Carbon Democracy: Political Power in the Age of Oil* (London: Verso, 2011), 86, 100–101. On Lugard's colonial role in setting up "indirect rule" in Britain's African colonies, see Mamdani, *Citizen and Subject*.

principle of equitable distribution and exploitation overrides to some extent the sovereign rights of the oil producing countries and pre-supposes a kind of trusteeship of the big Powers over the world's oil resources."[117] This is not unrelated to the arguments the Bush adminis-tration would make before and after the 2003 US invasion of Iraq, that Iraq could "pay" the US for the cost of the invasion ("liberation") from its oil revenues, thus making the venture cost-free to the US.[118]

It is this comparative grid of religion, culture, race, and society through which "Europe" and the "West" were (and are) produced. That terms like "non-Christian" or "Oriental" countries, which were used be-fore World War I, would be replaced by the "Third World" after World War II, and with more specificity the "Muslim" or Islamic world since the 1960s and increasingly since 2001 does not indicate a differing premise. Bryan Turner put it thus: "If the basic issue behind Christian theology was the uniqueness of the Christian revelation with respect to Islam, the central question behind comparative sociology was the uniqueness of the West in relation to the alleged stagnation of the East."[119] In the context of the rise of liberalism, Turner adds:

Underlying this liberal theory of the individual was, however, a profound anxiety about the problem of social order in the West. . . . Bourgeois individualism—in the theories of Locke and Mill—was challenged by the mob, the mass and the working class which was excluded from citizenship by a franchise based on property. The debate about Oriental Despotism took place in the context of uncertainty about Enlightened Despotism and monarchy in Europe. The Orientalist discourse of the absence of civil society in Islam was thus a reflection of basic political anxieties about the state of political freedom in the West. In this sense the problem of Orientalism was not the Orient but the Occident. These problems and anxieties were consequently transformed [sic] onto the Orient which became, not a representation of the East, but a caricature of the West. Oriental Despotism was simply Western monarchy writ large.[120]

Not only is the European liberal notion of civil society being opposed to an Oriental despotism that suppresses its emergence; it is rather, and in line with Engin Isin's argument discussed above, that *citizenship itself is constituted in opposition to the Orientalist production of Oriental subjec-tion*, contrasting a Western liberal democratic order (and even Western

117. Cited in Mitchell, *Carbon Democracy*, 114.
118. Gerry J. Gilmore, "Bulk of Iraq Monies 'Will come From Iraqis,' Rumsfeld Says," *American Forces Press Service*, 2 October 2003. http://www.defense.gov/News/NewsArticle.aspx?ID=28388.
119. Bryan Turner, "Orientalism and the Problem of Civil Society in Islam," 26.
120. Ibid., 39–40.

"enlightened despotism") brought about by Christian Protestantism, the Enlightenment, and later by the American and French Revolutions, with an Oriental despotic Muslim order that can only allow for subjection. This is notwithstanding that ancient "Near Eastern society," as Patricia Springborg reminds us, has "the longest recorded history of civil and private law regarding the rights and property of the trader . . . [and] it likely pioneered the contractual forms in which they are expressed."[121]

Montesquieu, Mill, Marx, Weber, and Durkheim, however, would insist that the presence and absence of civil society is what determines the difference between democracy and despotism and between enlightened European despotism (referred to by Montesquieu as "monarchy") and Oriental despotism.[122] This would be the difference between European civilization and its others. To that effect, Turner astutely argues:

The doctrines of individualism have been regarded as constitutive, if not of Western culture as such, then at least of contemporary industrial culture. . . . Individualism appears to lie at the foundations of Western society. The additional importance of individualism is that it serves to distinguish Occidental from Oriental culture, since the latter is treated as devoid of individual rights and of individuality. Individualism is the golden thread which weaves together the economic institutions of property, the religious institution of confession of conscience and the moral notion of personal autonomy; it serves to separate "us" from "them." In Orientalism, the absence of civil society in Islam entailed the absence of the autonomous individual exercising conscience and rejecting arbitrary interventions by the state.[123]

The *citizen as the civilized* became the very Western figure that always reminds Europe of the projected Oriental *subject and the primitive* because it was constitutionally linked to it. And not only Europe; in describing the system of "indirect rule" that Lord Lugard had set up in the African colonies and which established a kind of imperially sponsored local despotisms, Pan-Africanist and Communist activist and historian George Padmore asserted in stark terms: "No oriental despot ever had greater power than these black tyrants, thanks to the support which they receive from white officials who quietly keep in the

121. Patricia Springborg, *Western Republicanism and the Oriental Prince* (Cambridge: Polity Press, 1992), 20. Springborg cites Mikhail Rostovtzeff, *Caravan Cities* (Oxford: Clarendon Press, 1932), 8–9.

122. See the discussion of these authors in Bryan Turner, "Orientalism and the Problem of Civil Society in Islam."

123. Ibid., 39.

background."[124] That even a radical anticolonialist as Padmore would subscribe to "Oriental despotism" as a point of reference attests to the internalization of this othering European discourse by (intellectuals among) Europe's others. Citizenship as the antonym of subjection is not therefore only Orientalist, it is the very figuration of Orientalism, and not only in the eighteenth, nineteenth, and twentieth centuries, but as we shall see, all the way to the present. That both figures, the citizen and the subject, the civilized and the primitive, are coeval necessitates the deployment of Social Darwinism and culturalism as explanatory theories that offer the hegemonic accounts of Oriental difference from Europe, all the while rendering all non-Europeans subjects of Western liberalism.

This European and American knowledge constituted an academic cultural legacy that would be integrated into post-WWII American academia, especially area studies since the 1960s, so much so that Iraqi Jewish academic Elie Kedourie (who supported British colonialism in the Arab world and opposed local anticolonial nationalism) would declare without apology, or a Lerner-type caveat, as late as 1992 that "Democracy is alien to the mindset of Islam."[125] Diagnosing this institutionalized Western academic culture of representing Islam and Muslim societies, Said clarified that "Orientalism responded more to the culture that produced it than to its putative object, which was also produced by the West."[126] After all, US academic linking of Islam and despotism was being made while US "democracy" was declared matter-of-factly in spite of the institutionalized racial apartheid reigning in the country. Still, following the Civil Rights movement, liberal American political scientists could now sound even more self-confident than before in their culturalist judgments. We see this very clearly in the declaration made by American political scientist John Waterbury (one of the few Middle East political scientists who would write on the political economy of the Middle East in 1990,[127] a methodological turn that did not detract from his culturalist commitments) on the subject: "Whether or not Islam and Middle Eastern 'culture' are separable phenomena, the two work in ways that do not augur well for democracy. I believe that basic tendencies in regional culture and in religious practice must be

124. George Padmore, *How Britain Rules Africa* (London: Wishart Books, 1936), 317.

125. Elie Kedourie, *Democracy and Arab Political Culture* (Washington, DC: Washington Institute for Near East Policy, 1992), 1.

126. Said, *Orientalism*, 22.

127. See John Waterbury and Alan Richards, *A Political Economy of the Middle East* (Boulder, CO: Westview Press, 1990).

overcome rather than utilized in any efforts to promote pluralism and democracy."[128]

But while tradition and culture structured many of these debates, a subsidiary idea would dominate discussions of Islam since 1990, one propagated by the Orientalist and White House consultant Bernard Lewis. As the Cold War was ending and the search for new enemies starting, Lewis rushed to declare in his essay "The Roots of Muslim Rage" that "we are facing a mood and a movement far transcending the level of issues and policies and the governments that pursue them. This is no less than a clash of civilizations—the perhaps irrational but surely historic reaction of an ancient rival against our Judeo-Christian heritage, our secular present, and the worldwide expansion of both."[129] Note the way history is deployed by Lewis, wherein on the one hand the so-called Judeo-Christian heritage is not presented historically as a half-century-old notion but rather ahistorically as an ancient formation, at the very same moment that history is invoked to produce an "ancient rival" to this allegedly ancient formation. It is here where Huntington appropriates Lewis's new ideological configuration to chart out a new American and Western ontology after the end of the Cold War.

Lewis had been a major contributor at the dawn of the Cold War to the discourse on Islam and democracy. In his lecture of 1953 on Communism and "Islam" at the Royal Institute of International Affairs in London, he had already laid the foundations for the incompatibility of Islam with democracy. His article wanted to answer "the question before us . . . : in the present competition between the Western democracies and Soviet Communism for the support of the Islamic world, what factors or qualities are there in Islamic tradition, or in the present state of Islamic society and opinion, which might prepare the intellectually and politically active groups to embrace Communist principles and methods of government, and the rest to accept them?"[130] Laying out his own normative biases before proceeding to answer his question, Lewis tells us that "I believe that parliamentary democracy as practised in the West, with all its manifest faults, is still the best and most just form of government yet devised by man."[131] Lewis did add that democracy requires "certain qualities of mind and habit, of institution and tradition,

128. John Waterbury, "Democracy without Democrats: The Potential for Political Liberalization in the Middle East," in *Democracy without Democrats? The Renewal of Policy in the Muslim World*, ed. Ghassan Salamé (London: I. B. Tauris, 2001), 33.
129. Bernard Lewis, "The Roots of Muslim Rage," *Atlantic Monthly* 266 (September 1990): 60.
130. Bernard Lewis, "Communism and Islam," *International Affairs* 30, no. 1 (January 1954): 1.
131. Ibid., 1–2.

perhaps even of climate, for its effective working. It has taken firm root only among the peoples of the northern and north-western fringes of Europe, and in the territories colonized by their descendants overseas . . . [and] in a few other regions . . . but otherwise it is unknown to the rest of the human race, in most of the world, and through most of recorded history."[132] Explaining that much of the world in Asia and Africa is more familiar with autocracy than democracy, Lewis finds Islam unexceptional in its preference for the former, as "it is we who are the exception in both history and geography."[133] Lewis finds that "the present circumstances, and indeed the ancient traditions of Islam, do not wholly favour us but, on the contrary, contain much which might incline the Muslim individual, class, or nation, which is ready to abandon traditional values and beliefs, to accept the Communist rather than the democratic alternative."[134] He adumbrates the reasons why: "The first of these is the authoritarianism, perhaps we may even say the totalitarianism, of the Islamic political tradition."[135] Note that Lewis seems *not* to identify Islam with despotism. Indeed he is clear on this point: "Except for the early caliphate, when the anarchic individualism of tribal Arabia was still effective, the political history of Islam is one of almost unrelieved autocracy. I say autocracy, not despotism, since the sovereign was bound by and subject to the Holy Law, and was accepted by the people as rightful ruler, maintaining and maintained by the authority of the Holy Law. But still, it was authoritarian, often arbitrary, sometimes tyrannical."[136] Many of these ideas would influence Huntington's views on Islam.

In his 1993 essay on the "Clash of Civilizations," later expanded into a book, Huntington was most explicit: "Ideologically, the Cold War ended with the end of the Iron Curtain. As the ideological division of Europe has disappeared, the cultural division of Europe between Western Christianity, on the one hand, and Orthodox Christianity and Islam, on the other, has emerged."[137] Huntington moved on to enumerate world civilizations at present. There again he was hardly original, as his thinking bore the marks of nineteenth-century racialism. As Paul Gilroy has astutely remarked, "Gobineau's influential *Essay on the Inequality of*

132. Ibid., 2.
133. Ibid.
134. Ibid., 3.
135. Ibid., 7.
136. Ibid.
137. Samuel P. Huntington, "The Clash of Civilizations," *Foreign Affairs* 72 (Summer 1993): 29–30.

the Human Races has a disputed place in the genealogy of modern race thinking, but in 1854, he had managed to identify ten civilizations. In the early 1990s, Samuel Huntington could locate only seven."[138] Gilroy adds that if "Gobineau identified the ultimate danger to civilization in any departure from 'the homogeneity necessary to their life' and the consequent loss of what he calls 'the common logic of existence' . . . Huntington specifies the same sort of raciological and geopolitical problem aphoristically in the contemporary idiom of multiculturalism and globality,"[139] Huntington's conceding, unlike Gobineau, the possibility of an African civilization notwithstanding.

Democratizing Islam

It remains most curious though that culturalist arguments have not been posited by either liberal imperial thinkers anymore than by anti-imperialist thinkers to explain Europe's and the United States' penchant for ruling despotically in the colonies, or in the case of the United States imposing and propping up despotic rulers around its imperial domain.[140] Nor have arguments been advanced that European and American cultures are incompatible with democratic rule in their imperial domains. Indeed, when the United States and Britain denied their non-propertied classes and their female citizens suffrage, or when the US operated a colonial system of slavery, genocide, and racial apartheid, no culturalist arguments were advanced to explain this grave democratic deficit among white Euro-American property-owning Protestant Christian men either (the only exception was the use by antebellum Northern white abolitionists of culturalist arguments against Southern whites as sexually excessive and libertine—on account of having learned such traits from their Black slaves and from living in a warmer climate—and confining of women, but no arguments were offered to explain the racism of Northern whites against Blacks and Native Americans, let alone Northern intolerance of Catholics and Mormons or discrimination against women).[141]

138. Paul Gilroy, *Postcolonial Melancholia* (New York: Columbia University Press, 2006), 22.
139. Ibid., 23.
140. Perhaps the exception to this rule is Roger Ballard's argument about the intolerance of European culture being based on the ideas of St. Augustine and his followers; see Roger Ballard, "Islam and the Construction of Europe," 42–48.
141. Anne Norton, *Alternative Americas*, 155–59, 164–76. Similar arguments were and continue to be made about American Mormons since the 1830s and the ensuing "Mormon Wars," which led to the expulsion of Mormons from Illinois and Missouri and their settlement in Utah, through the 2012 presidential candidacy of Mitt Romney.

This however has not stopped the forward march of culturalist arguments about Muslim minorities living in Europe and the United States "subverting" the democratic cultures of both by their "antidemocratic" proclivities, manifested in a variety of attitudes and mechanisms, not least of which in the form of headscarves for women in social and sartorial relations and Shariʿa in the realm of the juridical, manifesting most clearly in the 9/11 attacks.[142] Indeed, measures in the US Congress and in state legislatures to ban Shariʿa law have been afoot for several years with US presidential candidate Newt Gingrich identifying Shariʿa as a "mortal threat" to the United States.[143] Jacques Rancière has more recently identified this anti-Muslim and antidemocratic discourse in the United States and Western Europe that seeks to deny Muslims equal rights as part of the Western "hatred of democracy,"[144] while Wendy Brown astutely described it as "an unwitting neo-Orientalism on the European Left, one that figures anxiety about (a) identification with the putatively fundamentalist, theocratic, ideological, unfree Other; (b) the many sources and sites of unfreedom in constitutional democracies in the age of globalization; and (c) the barbarism inside Euro-Atlantic democracy and the barbarism wreaked by democracy."[145]

Might this whole recent and rejuvenated anxiety about Islam and democracy then be a projection of the West and its own failures in establishing democratic governance in its own societies and the societies it governed and governs and not about Islam at all? Indeed the very suspension of certain citizenship rights of Muslims as individuals and

142. On the allegations that Shariʿa is being imposed on unsuspecting American and European societies, see Michael Carl, "Decorated General: Shariah is Here Now," *World Net Daily*, 13 July 2012, retrieved from http://www.wnd.com/2012/07/decorated-general-shariah-is-here-now/ (accessed 18 February 2014).

I should note here that attempts to revive the Orientalist intellectuals who theorized Oriental despotism as relevant to today's world continue apace. A recent addition to the literature is Michael Curtis' *Orientalism and Islam*, where he argues, in a Bernard Lewis fashion, that "without claiming that [the European Orientalists'] views and perceptions of Muslims and of the countries in the Orient discussed by our writers are directly relevant to the resolution of the current problems in the area, and without making explicit comparisons between the past and the present, their perceptions and diverse views are nevertheless helpful in providing a background for understanding the nature of contemporary Muslim societies and the cultural identities of the peoples in the Orient, particularly at a moment when Western countries are being challenged by groups and organizations stemming from the Middle East, and when the number of Muslims resident in Western countries has been increasing" (Michael Curtis, *Orientalism and Islam: European Thinkers on Oriental Despotism in the Middle East and India* [Cambridge: Cambridge University Press, 2009], 1–2).

143. Newt Gingrich, "I'd Support A Muslim Running For President Only If They'd Commit To Give Up Sharia" *Huffington Post*, 17 January 2012.

144. See Jacques Rancière, *Hatred of Democracy*, trans. Steve Corcoran (London: Verso, 2006).

145. Wendy Brown, "Sovereign Hesitations," in *Derrida and the Time of the Political*, ed. Cheah Pheng and Suzanne Guerlac (Durham, NC: Duke University Press, 2009), 131.

communities in Europe and the United States or the redefinition of citizenship as secular-Christian European norm that should be imposed on Muslims is essentially a reinforcement of the understanding of citizenship as a Western value that is in opposition to Muslim tradition and corrupted in the hands of Oriental Muslims, and must be withdrawn from them or imposed on them as a Western construct. This is not a new anxiety among liberal theorists. De Tocqueville seemed most concerned that the rapid increase in the number of non-Protestant immigrants to the United States from Eastern and Southern Europe, who were "alien to the English race," could corrupt the democratic political culture of the country in the middle of the nineteenth century, putting it in "the greatest danger."[146] Toward the end of his life, Huntington would echo similar concerns about the increase in the number of Mexicans and "Hispanics" more generally in the US and their "Hispanization" impact on American identity, culture, and the English language, let alone the transformation of the United States into an "unrepresentative democracy."[147]

With these entrenched notions as background, the United States began to waiver on the Huntingtonian notion of clash of civilizations and adopted a new project of pluralizing the one Islam identified by Huntington and his culturalist predecessors while maintaining Christianity as singular. This pluralization of Islam, as Islams, would allow the US to support the emergence of a new "Islam," a liberal form of Islam, that is more in tune with US imperial designs, and which would approximate modern Western notions of religions and religious subjectivities, as well as Western liberal citizenship, so as not to be incompatible with the rhetoric of democracy, while at the same time allowing the US to wage war against that other "Islam" which continues to resist the Western (neo)liberal order.

To this end the US embarked on a new project once the new millennium started and in the shadow of the 11 September attacks, one of "reforming" the "culture" of "Islam." This project was not much unlike American cultural policies since the dawn of the Cold War, except that it now had a broader cultural and religious focus on Islam than the more specific ideological focus it had before on Communism, which also failed to foster liberal citizenship.[148] The new project, like the previous

146. Quoted in Losurdo, *Liberalism*, 266.

147. Samuel P. Huntington, *Who Are We? The Challenges to American National Identity* (New York: Simon & Schuster, 2004), 221–56, 324–35.

148. On this, see Frances Stoner Saunders, *The Cultural Cold War: The CIA and the World of Arts and Letters* (New York: New Press, 2001). On the CIA production and funding of "culture" in the Arab world, see Timothy Mitchell, "The Middle East in the Past and Future of Social Science," 9–12.

one, would involve major wars but would have a much larger budget in the hundreds of billions of dollars, especially given that it was not only aiming to destroy existing regimes, religions, and ideologies but also, and equally important, to produce new ones. As I already signaled in the introduction, this is not to say that theological change and opinion among Muslims and Muslim scholars were all mortgaged to Western interventions and lacked any internal dynamic since the eighteenth century, but rather that what I am interested in elucidating in the rest of this chapter are those Islamic theological trends that were produced, mobilized, funded, and deployed by Western powers and which would become dominant forms (though not exclusively) in Muslim-majority countries since the nineteenth century.

The current US project, however, has important British and French colonial precedents of which it is merely a continuation. If in our times, the US has been concerned about identifying the strengths and weaknesses of "Islam" and "Islamism" at present and in the foreseeable future and has busied itself with coming up with the best strategies to oppose, contain, reform, transform, and co-opt "Islam" in order to neutralize its "negative" effects on American interests and mobilize different "Islams" in their favor, the British and the French showed equal concern in the second half of the nineteenth century, and certainly by the turn of the twentieth century, about the political and religious "revival" of Islam and its potential implications on European colonial interests. The question of "reform" of Islam in its entirety, or of its system of governance, or of Shariʿa itself is significant in this regard. Wael Hallaq has studied precisely how "Western-inspired 'reform' was parachuted in to rescue Shariʿa's subjects from the despotisms of the jural (if not also political) tyranny of the past and to escort them along the path of modernity and democracy."[149]

The British concern would arise in the early 1870s with regards to several developments. First, it was a concern about developments in Indonesia communicated by the Netherland's ambassador to London, Count Bylandt, to the Foreign Office in July 1873. The Dutch were very concerned that the Sultanate of Aceh in northern Sumatra was using religion in its struggle against Dutch colonial power. Indeed, the emissary of the sultan had been dispatched to Mecca and to the Ottoman capital to seek "the intervention of the Caliph, insisting especially on the religious nature of his mission." Bylandt insisted to British Foreign

---

149. Wael B. Hallaq, *Shariʿa: Theory, Practice, Transformations* (Cambridge: Cambridge University Press, 2009), 4.

Minister Granville that the Turkish-language press supported their struggle and that this Muslim "revival" would have major consequences for the "Christian 'powers' who have major interests to safeguard in this neighborhood, primarily for the Netherlands and Great Britain."[150] Then it was an investigation originating in the India office in August 1873 which took the form of a call for a report on Muslim actions in the East, monitoring Muslim actions in Najd and Lahj and Muslim insurrections in Chinese Kashgaria and Yunnan, in addition to a request to Granville for "any information which may tend to throw light upon this important subject."[151] Finally, the third factor that increased British concern originated in Aleppo, where the British consul expressed concern about the impartiality of the religiously mixed courts in handling local disputes. The "mixed courts" were imposed on the Ottomans as part of the capitulations and concessions to European powers and were instituted in 1856 in the Hatt-i Hümayun Decree (the Europeans would impose the "mixed courts" on Egypt in 1876).[152] It was these three factors that Granville would include in a confidential memo that prompted him to launch an investigation into this matter. Thus on 22 August 1873, Granville dispatched a brief circular of instructions to her Majesty's consuls in the "East" and in China:

> The proceedings of Mussulmans in Eastern countries, partaking in some degree of the character of religious and political *revival*, have lately attracted considerable attention; and I should be glad to receive from you a Report in regard to any circumstances which may come under your observation, calculated to show the existence and objects of any movement of the kind among the Mussulman population of the country in which you reside.[153]

His consuls would write back, some observing no such revival, while others observing much of it. The discrepancies were such that the

---

150. Cited in Marwan Buheiry, "Islam and the Foreign Office: An Investigation of Religious and Political Revival in 1873," in *Studia Arabica et Islamica: Festschrift for Ihsan Abbas on his Sixtieth Birthday*, ed. Wadad al-Qadi (Beirut: American University of Beirut, 1981), 48. It is important to note here that the Sultanate of Aceh had first sought Ottoman military help against Portuguese naval encroachment in Malacca in 1562. The Acehnese, who would become a powerful military force in their own right in the seventeenth century, would see their military power finally destroyed by the Portuguese in 1627. The Portuguese themselves would be defeated in 1641 by the Dutch, who would become along with the English, the Safavids, and the Mughals the new reigning powers in the Indian Ocean region. See Giancarlo Casale, *The Ottoman Age of Exploration* (Oxford: Oxford University Press, 2010), 123–25, 180–81, 200.

151. Buheiry, "Islam and the Foreign Office," 49.

152. Hallaq, *Shariʿa*, 407, 423–25.

153. Buheiry, "Islam and the Foreign Office," 47.

Alexandria consul saw a revival there while the Cairo consul saw none at all in the Egyptian capital.[154] Nine years later, in September 1882, Britain would invade and occupy Egypt.

While providing a legal basis for the Ottoman caliphate would be undertaken in the late sixteenth century by Ottoman legal scholar Ebu's Suʿud (1490–1574) in the context of the Ottoman conquest of the Hijaz in 1517 and their military confrontations with the Hapsburgs and the Safavids,[155] the Ottoman revival of the caliphate was first enshrined in their foreign relations with Christian countries as part of the capitulations and the concessions that the Ottomans were forced to make in the wake of their military defeat in the 1774 Russian-Ottoman War. This would be enshrined in the Küçük Kaynarca Treaty with Russia in which the Ottoman caliph was recognized as caliph, having "spiritual" jurisdiction over Muslims living in Russian territory in exchange for the recognition of the Russian patriarch of the Orthodox Church as a protector of all Orthodox Christians living in Ottoman territory. This new "spiritual" role of the Ottoman caliph was in fact a French innovation, proposed by the anti-Muslim, anti-Ottoman, and pro-Russian Catholic French ambassador at the Porte, François-Emmanuel Guignard, comte de Saint Priest, echoing Catholic pontifical concepts.[156] The arrangement would

154. Ibid., 54. The report can be found in Great Britain, Foreign Office 881, Confidential Print no. 2621, *Correspondence Respecting the Religious and Political Revival Among Mussulmans, 1873–1874* (London, July 1875), Item 4, "Circular Addressed to H.M. Consuls in the East and also to Mr. Wade and to Consuls and Vice-Consuls in China," Granville, 22 August 1873.

155. See Colin Imber, *Ebu's Suʿud: The Islamic Legal Tradition* (Stanford, CA: Stanford University Press, 2009), 98–111.

156. See Louis Massignon, "Introduction à l'étude des revendications musulmanes," *Revue du monde Musulman* 39 (June 1920): 3. The comte indeed went to Russia after the French Revolution as an émigré in 1791 and again in 1795, and Catherine the Great, who welcomed him as an expert on the Ottomans, Russia's enemy, gave him a monthly stipend. It is believed that his *Mémoire sur les Turcs* was written for the Empress of Russia. The comte was a practicing Catholic and believed Muhammad to be "a false prophet" and referred to the Ottoman Sultans as "despotic." See Jacob M. Landau, "Saint Priest and His *Mémoire sur les Turcs*," in *L'Empire Ottoman, la République de Turquie et la France*, ed. Hâmit Batu and Jean-Louis Bacqué-Grammont (Istanbul: L'institut Français d'études Anatoliennes d'Istanbul," 1986), 129, 132, 134. See also Jacob M. Landau, *The Politics of Pan-Islam: Ideology and Organization* (Oxford: Clarendon Press, 1990), 10. It should be noted that it would be the French who would in the mid-nineteenth century question this Russian role, which they coveted for themselves as protectors of Ottoman Christians, including the Palestinian Christian Holy Places. It would be this French attempt to undercut the Russians and increase its influence over the Ottoman Empire that would lead to the Crimean War between Russia and the Ottomans, with the French fighting on the Ottoman side, a war, which Karl Marx would call a "Holy War," and "a war of religious fanaticism on both sides," meaning the Russian and the Ottoman sides. France's involvement, not to mention Britain, which joined the war also on the side of the Ottomans, however, did not impel Marx to refer to them as "religious fanatics," a charge that seems to apply only to Islam and Eastern Orthodox Christianity. See Karl Marx, *The Eastern Question*, ed. Eleanor Marx Aveling and Edward Aveling (London: Swab Sonnenschein, 1897), 153.

prove of much benefit for the Russians who took over more territories with Muslim populations who did not seem to appeal to Ottoman caliphal authority. As the Ottoman Christian population in the Balkans began to secede from the Ottoman Empire in the nineteenth century (and to expel the Muslim population to Anatolia and other parts of the Ottoman Empire east of the Balkans, considering them not "native" even when they were native speakers of the local Balkan languages), rendering it more and more Muslim demographically, the struggle of the Ottomans shifted increasingly to legitimize their caliphal rule over Muslims within the Empire more than over Muslims without. Still it would be the Indian Muslims who would seek Ottoman caliphal patronage after the 1857 rebellion and the end of Muslim Mughal rule in India.

Within the Ottoman Empire itself and as early as 1876, supporters of the Ottoman Constitutional Movement, namely Midhat Pasha and Namik Kamal, discussed separating the caliphate from the sultanate, transferring the former to the Amir of Mecca, the Sharif ʿAbd al-Muttalib.[157] Their views, however, appear not to be widespread during this period. Indeed, this is the year when Sultan Abdülhamid II (whose reign lasted from 1876 to 1909) reaffirmed the universal caliphate in the 1876 Ottoman Constitution. Wary of European Christian attempts to weaken the universal representation of the caliphate over all Muslims, he censored all Prophetic hadiths published in the Ottoman Empire that asserted that the caliph should be a descendant of the Meccan tribe of Quraysh to which the Prophet Muhammad belonged. The fact that the Ottoman Empire remained the only major sovereign Muslim power that had not fallen under European colonial tutelage was significant for the period and accounts for why Indian and other Muslim leaders gave the Ottoman caliphate their support at the time. This situation was not lost on Abdülhamid himself, as he recognized British ambitions in this regard, of which he spoke to an Ottoman journalist: "England's aim is to transfer the Great Caliphate from Istanbul to Jidda in Arabia or to a place in Egypt and by keeping the Caliphate under her control to manage all the Muslims as she wishes."[158]

The British as early as 1877 were already engaged in unofficial debates on the question of the caliphate joined by parliamentarians, publicists, and scholars. Opponents of the Ottoman caliphate were exclusively retired civil servants of the British government in India. Their

157. See S. Tufan Buzpinar, "Opposition to the Ottoman Caliphate in the Early Years of Abdülhamid II: 1877–1882," *Die Welt des Islams* 36, no. 1 (1996): 63–65.
158. Cited in ibid., 64.

views would be published in English newspapers in which calls for the Sharif of Mecca to become caliph were issued. Legal arguments against the Ottoman caliphate were also publicized in pamphlets arguing that the caliph should be an Arab.[159] British Turcologists (J. Redhouse) and Arabists (G. P. Badger) begged to differ and defended the Ottoman claim historically and legally.

The British anti-Ottoman views would coincide with those of some Arab nationalists in reaction to the Russian-Ottoman War of 1877–78, which ended with Ottoman defeat. This would be the case in Syria, Hijaz, and Egypt, as well as among Arab exiles in France and Britain. In the Egyptian context, the questioning of the Ottoman caliphate would be sponsored by the khedive Ismail Pasha, whom the Ottoman sultan had deposed in June 1879 on the orders of France and Britain. He would launch and sponsor Arabic newspapers in Europe arguing the case against the Ottomans. In Naples, his private secretary Ibrahim al-Muwaylihi established and edited the newspaper *Al-Khilafah* (the caliphate), which argued that the caliphate should be transferred to the Egyptian khedives. In September 1880, al-Muwaylihi would move to Paris and set up *Al-Ittihad*, which attacked Abdülhamid's right to the caliphate. *Al-Ittihad* was financed by Ismail. Under Ottoman pressure, the French closed down the paper after three issues.[160] The mantle would be picked up in London by the Arab Syriac Catholic priest John Louis Sabunji (1838–1931). Sabunji, who was born in the Ottoman province of Diyarbakir, had published several newspapers in Beirut before fleeing to the United States and then England. He began to edit *Al-Nahlah* in London in 1877. From 1878 onwards, Sabunji, who was a collaborator with the Arabist Badger on some of the latter's scholarly work, switched from a pro-Ottoman to an anti-Ottoman position and began to question the Ottoman caliphate.[161] In January 1881, and after the demise of *Al-Nahlah*, Sabunji would establish another London-based newspaper called *Al-Khilafah* in which he continued to attack Abdülhamid. The Ottomans expressed dissatisfaction and prevented its circulation in the Arab provinces, and the British followed suit by instructing British post offices in Damascus and Baghdad to stop its circulation.[162]

159. On details of this debate, see ibid., 65–66.
160. Al-Muwaylihi would end up later at the Ottoman court and would ask Abdülhamid for forgiveness.
161. On Sabunji, see L. Zolondek, "Sabunji in England 1876–1891: His Role in Arabic Journalism," *Middle Eastern Studies* 14, no. 1 (January 1978): 102–15.
162. On these developments, see Buzpinar, "Opposition to the Ottoman Caliphate," 69–80.

As the unofficial British debate died down and the Ottomans were able to control the dissemination of the Arab exile press, the debate on the caliphate would be relaunched once again in 1880. European diplomatic correspondence in August 1880 alleged that there existed an Ottoman conspiracy to foment anticolonial revolts against the French in Algeria and the British in India and to unify all Muslims under the Ottoman caliph. By 1881, European diplomats began to use the term "pan-Islamism," whose invention is credited to French publicist Gabriel Charmes. In the twentieth century, it would be referred to simply as "Islamism."[163] Pan-Islamism would become the threat European powers began to use to justify occupying Ottoman territories—the French invoked it to conquer Tunisia and the British to acquire Cyprus.[164]

It is in this context that Wilfred Scawen Blunt (1840–1922), a British patriotic aristocrat, former diplomat, minor poet, and the student and employer of Sabunji, would prepare a memorandum to the Foreign office in 1880 in which he argued that much debate existed among Arabs about the Ottoman caliphate and proposed its transfer to the Arabs as being in the interests of Great Britain. He would visit Egypt and the Hijaz for a while, and would learn Arabic and meet with Muhammad ʿAbduh in Cairo.[165] Blunt would later pen a couple of articles in the summer and autumn of 1881 in the *Fortnightly Review*, which he would then bring out in book form in January 1882 under the title *The Future of Islam*.[166] Blunt maintained a home in Cairo and was a good friend of General Ahmad ʿUrabi as well as of the khedive of Egypt ʿAbbas Hilmi. He claimed to have first learned about the history and significance of the caliphate from Sabunji.

Writing a few months before the British invasion of the country and encouraged by the ʿUrabi Revolt against the French- and British-supported khedive, which established an elected parliament, Blunt tells us that he had just returned to Egypt "and has there the satisfaction of finding the ideas vaguely foreshadowed by him as the dream of some few liberal Ulema of the Azhar, already a practical reality. Cairo has now declared itself as the home of progressive thought in Islam, and its university as the once more independent seat of Arabian theology. Secured from Turkish interference by the national movement of the Arabs, the Ulema of the Azhar have joined heart and soul with the party of

---

163. John Tolan, Gilles Veinstein, and Henry Laurens, *Europe and the Islamic World*, 319.
164. Ibid.
165. On the background and details of Blunt's activities, see ibid., 80–88.
166. Wilfred Scawen Blunt, *The Future of Islam* (1882; rpt., Charleston, SC: Bibliobazaar, 2007).

reform." Blunt was excited about the probability of the establishment of "a liberal Mohameddan Government by a free Mohameddan people . . . on the Nile" and concluded that "it is beyond question that the basis of a social and political Reformation for all Islam has been laid." His enthusiasm was also on account of his expectation that "liberal thought will have a fair field for its development, and can hardly fail to extend its influence wherever the Arabic language is spoken, and among all those races which look on the Azhar as the centre of their intellectual life." He finally announced that the death of the reigning Ottoman caliph Abdülhamid or "his fall from Empire, will be the signal for the return of the Caliphate to Cairo, and a formal renewal there by the Arabian mind of its lost religious leadership."[167]

The question of who should become Caliph, Blunt tells us, is one

which ought certainly to interest Englishmen, for on its solution the whole problem of Mussulman loyalty or revolt in India most probably depends, and though it would certainly be unwise, at the present moment, for an English Government to obtrude itself violently in a religious quarrel not yet ripe, much might be done in a perfectly legitimate way to influence the natural course of events and direct it to a channel favourable to British interests.[168]

Blunt proceeds to explain that Mecca would be the most ideal place to locate the future caliphate, and that a descendant of the Prophet who belongs to the tribe of Quraysh could occupy it. Blunt even volunteers that it "is surely not beyond the flight of sane imagination to suppose, in the last overwhelming catastrophe of Constantinople, a council of Ulema assembling in Mecca, and according to the legal precedent of ancient days electing a Caliph."[169] He finally proposes that England safeguard and protect an Arabian sovereign caliphate whose authority outside Arabia would be, presumably following the papal model, "spiritual": "The Caliph of the future . . . will be chiefly a spiritual not a temporal king, and will be limited in the exercise of his authority by few conditions of the existing material kind. He will be spared the burden of despotic government."[170]

Blunt's expectations of a fast end to the Ottomans would have to wait almost four more decades. In the meantime, anti-Ottoman Arab

167. All the above quotes are from ibid., 10.
168. Ibid., 62.
169. Ibid., 80.
170. Ibid., 112.

nationalist fervor was increasing in the Ottoman provinces and internal opposition to the sultan continued to build up within the Turkish-speaking provinces themselves. The khedive ʿAbbas Hilmi, himself not of Arab let alone Qurayshi descent, would meet secretly with al-Afghani in the mid 1890s in Istanbul and would offer himself as an alternate caliph for the pan-Islamic movement. European imperial ambitions about the fate of the Ottomans would continue unabated, especially after the Berlin Conference and the expansion of European colonialism globally. It was in this context that in 1901 the French concern about the future potential of an Islamic revival, indeed what France, which "is and will become increasingly and without a doubt a great Muslim power," given its acquisition of new colonies with large Muslim populations, should expect Islam to be in the twentieth century, became so grave that a colonial "quest" for knowledge was issued.

The editor of the French colonial journal *Questions diplômatiques et coloniales*, Edmond Fazy, set out to investigate the question through an "enquête" soliciting the opinions of some fifteen (German, Dutch, British, Hungarian, Russian, French, and even a Turco-Greek Christian) Orientalists and colonial administrators and two Muslims (an Iranian and an Algerian) about "the Future of Islam" in the next century.[171] Fazy expressed concern about the increasing and underreported number of Muslims worldwide (he cited the figure of 300 million, constituting a fifth of the world's population) and the propagation of their "simple" religion to Africa.[172] The responses he solicited would be published in successive issues of the journal starting in May 1901.

Baron Carra de Vaux, a specialist on Ibn Sina at the Catholic Institute, announced that "from the point of view of its worldly destiny" and based on its political decadence and its inability to compete with "Christian nations" scientifically, "L'islamisme est une religion finie."[173] As for whether Islam was democratic, while registering objections about the lack of clarity of a term like democracy, Carra de Vaux affirmed without hesitation that "Islam, since its origins, is as democratic as we would wish it to be. . . . In principle, Islam is a democratic and imperialist republic; it is a plebiscitary democracy ruled by king elected by the

---

171. "L'Avenir de l'islam," enquête par Edmond Fazy, *Questions diplômatiques et coloniales* 11, no. 102 (15 May 1901): 579.
172. Ibid., 580. For a thorough and learned analysis of the responses to this "enquête" by the French journal, see Marwan Buheiri, "Colonial Scholarship and Muslim Revivalism in 1900," *Arab Studies Quarterly* 4, nos. 1–2 (1982): 1–16.
173. "L'Avenir de l'islam," 582, "Islam, as a religion, is over."

community."[174] In contrast with the reigning despotism in Turkey (an empire that could only die "slowly or violently"), which, he affirms, contradicts the Qur'an, "liberalism" is "not incompatible with Islam, and less so in practice. Indeed [liberalism] can take hold in Islam, and it has done so often before, taking the form of tolerance."[175] This does not mean that Muslims could have a parliamentary democracy, given that the multitude of believers are "semi-civilized, primitives." Instead of liberal values, which "Arabs" seem to have plenty of, Europeans could offer them courage, the chivalrous spirit, military talents, loyalty and generosity, traits that have always "distinguished our race" and could "seduce" a "primitive" and "noble" people like the Arabs.[176] This is not to say that Carra de Vaux was not worried about the anticolonial resistance mounted by Muslims in French colonies, which was instigated by "pan-Islamism;" he was. He asserted that "colonization is a business that requires time, and in which any abruptness could prove fatal." To proceed carefully, Carra de Vaux proposed that "we should split the Muhamaddan world, and break its moral unity, taking advantage of the political and ethnic divisions that already exist in it. . . . We should accentuate these differences among the diverse Muhamaddan races in such a way as to increase nationalist sentiments and diminish those of religious communitarianism."[177] He proposed making of Egypt a barrier between "Asian" and "African" Islam: "In a word, we must segment Islam. Then we can take advantage of its heresies and [Sufi] brotherhoods," setting the Sufi orders against one another. While he feared this could incite local troubles, as a whole they would serve to "weaken Islam, make it restless, numb it, and render it forever incapable of great awakenings."[178]

Another consultant for the journal issue, the Ottoman Greek exile M. Musurus-Ghikis Bey, who was living in Europe, insisted that he could not see how "the Arab tribes of Najd, of Hijaz, or of Yemen will feel in the year 2000, any more than they do at present, the need for taxation, military service, to have tribunals and schools, etc., or to debate in parliament budgetary issues and expenditures." Though he predicted that Slavic Muslims in Bosnia and Albania would be able to do so, as would certainly the Turks.[179]

174. Ibid., 583.
175. Ibid., 584.
176. Ibid., 586.
177. Ibid., 588.
178. Ibid.
179. Ibid., 596.

Many of the contributors saw fit to manipulate Islamic theology and transform Muslim *ulamas* to produce not only a modern Islam compatible with European modernity, but also one that, they hoped, would weaken the Ottoman Empire. Aside from the theological interventionist plan of dividing "African" and "Asian" Islam advanced by Carra de Vaux, the major Hungarian Orientalist Ignác Goldziher proposed that in the twentieth century,

Muslim theologians . . . will have to imitate the work done in Europe in the nineteenth century by scientific theology and thus raise the level of religious thinking to conform with historical knowledge. . . . In order for Islam to raise itself to the same degree [as Europe], its proper religious sciences will have to begin an analogous evolution [to Europe's]. Islam's Ulamas will have to assimilate the methods according to which we in Europe study religious phenomena. . . . There needs to emerge enlightened minds in Islam who would naturalize in its colleges our historical method for the study of religion. This method must replace the cheap apologetics and superficial rationalism. We will see then come out of this evolution an enlightened Muslim theology which will no longer be incompatible with science and which will be able to exercise a salutary influence on its institutions as well. . . . What I am asking of Muslim theologians to do therefore is not impossible.[180]

Recognizing that this would not be new, as Muslims had used the scientific method in the ninth century to examine religious sources, the role "European intervention" should play, according to Goldziher, in this "movement" must be "considerable," namely that it should "provoke it and encourage it practically in all Muslim countries where academia is under the influence of European pedagogy."[181]

The editor of *Questions diplômatiques et coloniales* was also very interested in the caliphate question, which he posed to the Dutch Orientalist (and Indonesia specialist) Christian Snouck Hurgronje and the German Orientalist M. Martin Hartmann. The Caliphate Question, as we saw, had indeed been on the minds of European colonial powers and Orientalists for a few decades, especially given its revival by the Ottoman sultan Abdülhamid II as a pan-Islamic force to unify Muslims around the world against the increasing territorial encroachment of European Christendom on his empire. While, as mentioned earlier, Ottoman sultans had designated themselves as caliphs since 1517, a pan-Islamic caliphal authority was not of primary interest to them. This

180. Ibid., 601.
181. Ibid., 602.

would change with Abdülhamid II, who, in the face of European aggression, would invoke it time and again following the British occupation of Egypt (1882) and the Berlin Conference (1884–85) in order to resist European colonial designs. As a result, Western powers became seriously concerned with the matter, as evidenced by the question the editor put to his commissioned writers.[182]

After providing a quick review summary of the history of the caliphate in Islam, Snouck Hurgronje, who was also serving as a Dutch colonial official in Aceh, cautioned his French colonial readers that "it is one thing to leave to Muslims their religious and political beliefs and quite another to adopt these beliefs in international relations. Recognizing the sultan of Turkey as the caliph by Muslim subjects of non-Muslim powers means that these subjects would consider their present political position [under European Christian rule] as an anomaly that would end one day. This is why these powers cannot recognize the Caliphate without compromising themselves in the process."[183] Snouck Hurgronje was a major player in undermining things Islamic in the Dutch Indies through his "discovery," circa 1891, of non-Islamic juridical traditions, *adat*, which had been intertwined with and complementary to Shari'a before the end of the nineteenth century, and setting them aside as an independent system of law for Indonesians, an action which "in effect opened a Pandora's box within the political and legal life of Indonesia that has not been closed to this day."[184] Snouck Hurgronje's "discovery" was part of a new Dutch imperial strategy to undermine the latest anticolonial revolt in Aceh that would last for three decades. Clearly, for Snouck Hurgronje, the fate of European colonial rule lay in the balance. Angry that Kaiser Wilhelm II had paid obeisance to the Ottoman sultan as caliph with little cost to Germany, which had few Muslim subjects (upon visiting the Ottoman Empire three years earlier in 1898 and while in Damascus, the kaiser proclaimed that "the Sultan and the three hundred million Muslims who revere him as their leader should know

182. Vladimir Lenin seemed to understand this dynamic, despite his hostility to pan-Islamism. In a speech to the second Congress of the Communist International on 5 June 1920, he asked his audience to bear in mind "the need to combat Pan-Islamism and similar trends which strive to combine the liberation movement against European and American imperialism with an attempt to strengthen the positions of the khans, landowners, mullahs, etc." Vladimir Ilyich Lenin, "Preliminary Draft of Theses on the National and Colonial Questions," in *Lenin on the National and Colonial Questions: Three Articles* (Peking: Foreign Languages Press, 1967), 18.

183. "L'Avenir de l'islam," *Questions diplômatiques et coloniales*, no. 106 (15 July 1901): 81.

184. Hallaq, *Shari'a*, 393. On the "discovery" of "adat law," see C. Fasseur, "Colonial Dilemma: Van Vallenhoven and the Struggle between Adat Law and Western Law in Indonesia," in *European Expansion and Law in 19th Century Africa and Asia*, ed. W. J. Mommsen and J. A. De Moor (Oxford: Berg, 1992), 237–356. On Hurgronje's views, see also Said, *Orientalism*, 255–56.

that the German Emperor is their friend forever"),[185] Snouck Hurgronje insisted that European colonial powers with numerous Muslim subjects must "wisely reject the theory of the Caliphate of the Sultan of Turkey by mutual agreement and unconditionally. For there is no more Caliphate, because the political unity of Muslims has ended for ever, and political unity is held not by the Caliph but by the *ulama*."[186] The question of the caliphate, as we will see, will remain of much significance to European colonial powers in the two decades to come.

The respondents to the journal's "enquête" seemed keen on strategic thinking. German Orientalist M. Martin Hartmann declared that "there is no Islamic danger [at present] but certain precautions are in order. The growing movement inside Islam should be closely monitored so that it does not become a danger." He added that while "around the year 1800, Islam, as a political power, appeared dead," it was today "on the eve of a new evolution."[187]

The most practical advice, however, came from the French school of Arabists, namely French colonial settlers (*pieds noirs*) in North Africa. One of them, Edmond Douttée, of the "école algérienne," a specialist in religion and "Islam," spoke of his encounter with Muslim fanaticism and intolerance, especially in Fez in Morocco, and would assert that had there been no indigenous Muslims in North Africa "the problem of colonization would not even arise."[188] Traditionally educated Muslims seem to have "moved away from us" in contrast with the native workers, who fraternize with the colons and learn "our habits."[189] Rather than repress "the exaggerated religious manifestations" of extant Islam, the task before Europeans was more productive: "we could, on the contrary, favor the birth of a new Islam more inclined towards compromise and tolerance of Europe; to encourage the young generation of *ulama* who are working in that direction, and to increase the number of mosques, madrasas, and Muslim universities, ensuring that we staff them with adherents of the new theories."[190] Douttée's comments ring so familiar because they could have easily been uttered by any contemporary US or West European politician or pundit.

As for M. William Marçais, the director of the Tlemcen madrasa founded by the French to train Algerian Muslim judges (qadis) on

---

185. Jacob M. Landau, *The Politics of Pan-Islam*, 47.
186. "L'Avenir de l'islam," *Questions diplômatiques et coloniales*, no. 106 (15 July 1901): 82.
187. Ibid., 84.
188. *Questions diplômatiques et coloniales*, no. 112 (1 October 1901): 391.
189. Ibid., 396.
190. Ibid.

"rationalist" bases, and an expert in Islamic "law," he was partial toward the "new" and "modern" Islam that the French were fashioning in North Africa and in which he was a participant, an Islam that "was closely tied to France's destiny."[191] It was in the new elite educated in "modern" Islam by the French that hope resided, even though Marçais was concerned that this elite was French-imposed and not organic to Muslim society.[192] Given these hopes and uncertainties, Marçais wondered "who" in 1901 "could predict the balance of these modifications for the year 2000?"[193] Marwan Buheiri, a scholar of French and British Orientalisms, concludes that, for these scholars, "manipulation was more important than scholarly detachment."[194] Indeed, it was the production of an Islam compatible with European colonial strategy that was most urgent. The French were so confident of their achievement in Algeria that they decided to exhibit it to the world at large by hosting the International Congress of Orientalists in 1905 in Algiers.[195]

Dividing Muslims, however, would be a steady colonial strategy, so much so that it rendered European Orientalists sufficiently mobile in their national allegiances as to advise different colonial powers on how to better divide colonized Muslims. It would be in this context that the Snouck Hurgronje would become a consultant to the French colonial authorities on the subject of codifying Berber customary law in 1931, which was also the year when he presided in Leiden over the International Congress of Orientalists. (Bernard Lewis, belonging to the next generation of Orientalists, would prove equally mobile, moving from his native Britain, where he served in the army and later advised the British Foreign Office on colonial policies in the Arab world, to the United States in the mid 1970s where he advised the American empire on its imperial policies towards Arabs and Muslims). French-Algerian Orientalist Jacques Berque (born to a pied noir family) will continue Hurgronje's work by codifying Berber customary law in Morocco.[196]

It is important to note this "predictive" or "prophetic" strain or problem for British (recall Blunt) and French imperial commentators, which I noted earlier, and their concern with the "future" of Islam—not the past,

191. Ibid., 400.
192. Ibid., 401–2.
193. Ibid., 403.
194. Buheiry, "Colonial Scholarship and Muslim Revivalism in 1900," 15.
195. Allan Christelow, *Muslim Law Courts and the French Colonial State in Algeria* (Princeton, NJ: Princeton University Press, 1985), 249.
196. See Mona Abaza, "ʿAda/Custom in the Middle East and Southeast Asia," in *Words in Motion: Towards a Global Lexicon*, ed. Carol Gluck and Anna Lowenhaupt Tsing (Durham, NC: Duke University Press, 2009), 75.

or even the present. From where do these commentators suggest their authority derives for such predictive (prophetic?) powers? Is it prophecy, determinism, causality, speculation, theology, or imperial strategy that justifies speaking of the "future"—the future *in* Islam, *for* Islam, *of* Islam? A discussion of later debates and policies might offer an answer.

The "Future" of Islam and Its "Present"

In the twenty-first century and in the context of the current US wars and in line with US imperial designs, many Arab and Western conservatives, liberals, and not a few Marxists opted for challenging the democratic "deficit" in the "Islamic world" as a question of religion, and not just of the culture it fosters. This led them to the conclusion that what should be undertaken in the Arab and Muslim worlds is not a colonial *mission civilisatrice* but rather a European—style secularization which would not only transform Islam into a Protestant-like religion confined to the private sphere but also would usher democracy and liberal citizenship into the public sphere unopposed by the alleged antidemocratic precepts of the one extant Islam.[197] In this sense, if Protestantism is posited as the origin (or a return to the foundational Greek origin) of a culture of democracy and liberal citizenship, Islam is posited as the origin of un-democracy, if not of antidemocracy. Much of what I have so far elucidated is a history of this very discourse.

But the scholarly part of this effort would begin a bit earlier, in the wake of the Iranian Revolution, when we began to see an increased interest in the West in "liberal" forms of Islam. US political scientist Leonard Binder would publish a discussion of Islamic "liberalism" to demonstrate its closeness and comparability with Western liberalism as well as its deviation from it. Binder presents "political liberalism" as a universal category based on rational discourse, which he defines as transcultural and as "the basis of improving the human condition through collective action." Binder insists that political liberalism is universal and "indivisible. It will either prevail worldwide, or it will have to be defended by nondiscursive action."[198]

---

197. On this, see Talal Asad, "Europe against Islam: Islam in Europe," *Muslim World* 87, no. 2 (April 1997): 183–95.

198. Leonard Binder, *Islamic Liberalism: A Critique of Development Ideologies* (Chicago: University of Chicago Press, 1988), 1.

By the 1990s, an active translation effort would begin to make available to English readers a panoply of Muslim thinkers from the nineteenth century to the present who are identified as "liberal." Charles Kurzman, who edited two volumes of translations of "liberal" and "modernist" Muslim thinkers,[199] would intervene on the side of the pluralization of the one Islam stating clearly that "the Orientalist view of Islam should not be mistaken for the whole of Islam. In historical terms, Islam has consisted of countless varied interpretations, among those a tradition that voices concerns parallel to those of Western liberalism."[200] Whereas Kurzman decides to use the adjective "liberal" to describe these thinkers, he understands that his use is an external imposition, as "the authors in this collection do not necessarily self-identify as liberals" (though he quotes one Muslim thinker as using the term), nor is his use intended to examine how much "Islamic variants of liberalism meet Western standards of liberalism," as Binder does, but rather "to examine liberal Muslims in light of Islamic tradition."[201] Nonetheless, his book is divided in accordance with Western liberal themes and categories, namely "Against Theocracy," "For Democracy," "Rights of Women," "The Rights of non-Muslims," "Freedom of Thought," and "Progress," thus recognizing these views and opinions as internal to Western liberalism rather than outside its ideological confines.[202]

The National Security Research Division of the Rand Corporation issued a report in 2003 that identified which "strains" of Islam were necessary for the US to produce. The report summarized its goal at the outset:

Islam is an important religion with enormous political and societal influence; it inspires a variety of ideologies and political actions, some of which are dangerous to global stability; and it therefore seems sensible to foster the strains within it that call for a more moderate, democratic, peaceful, and tolerant social order. The question is how best to do this.[203]

199. See Charles Kurzman, ed., *Liberal Islam: A Sourcebook* (Oxford: Oxford University Press, 1998), and Charles Kurzman, *Modernist Islam: A Sourcebook* (Oxford: Oxford University Press, 2002).

200. Kurzman, ed., *Liberal Islam*, 4.

201. Ibid., 4 and 13.

202. Ibid., 19–26. During my graduate student years I was commissioned by Kurzman to translate texts by two such authors for his important collection, namely the texts of ʿAli ʿAbd al-Raziq and Muhammad Khalafallah.

203. Cheryl Benard, *Civil Democratic Islam: Partners, Resources, and Strategies* (Santa Monica, CA: Rand, 2003), 1. Also, see Saba Mahmood's important discussion of the report in her "Secularism, Hermeneutics, and Empire: The Politics of Islamic Reformation," *Public Culture* 18, no. 2 (2006): 323–47.

To do so, the report recognizes that "it is no easy matter [for Americans] to transform a major world religion. If 'nation-building' is a daunting task, 'religion-building' is immeasurably more perilous and complex."[204] In line with many of Kurzman's Western liberal themes, the Rand report examines the position of differing Muslim groups on "key issues," namely, "democracy and human rights," "polygamy," "criminal punishment," "minorities," "women's dress," and on whether "husbands [are] allowed to beat [their] wives."[205] As for the US war on Arab and Muslim anti-imperialist nationalists and socialists throughout the Cold War, the Rand report shows retrospective regret and anxiety about the West's commitment to democracy:

We are today prepared to accept postures that include a level of hostility to the West, the United States, and Western values, aggressive language and assertive postures that go significantly beyond levels we found unacceptable when they were manifested by nationalists and quasi-socialists in that same part of the world. We can only speculate what different path history might have taken if we had shown some of the socialist Arab nationalists as much indulgence as we are prepared to show some of the fundamentalist extremists today.[206]

The report is clear that while there has been and is room for different kinds of rapprochements with Muslim "fundamentalists" and "traditionalists," it is the "modernists" whose "vision matches our own. Of all the groups, this one is most congenial to the values and the spirit of modern democratic society."[207]

This is hardly only the view of US imperial strategists, but as Saba Mahmood has astutely noted, "it has become de rigueur for leftists and liberals alike to link the fate of democracy in the Muslim world with the institutionalization of secularism both as a political doctrine and as a political ethic. This coupling is now broadly echoed within the discourse emanating from the US State Department, particularly its programmatic efforts to reshape and transform 'Islam from within.' "[208] It is with this in mind that Mahmood suggests not only that the secular state enshrines the separation between church and state and guarantees freedom of conscience and controls the exception by intervening in both when it deems it appropriate in the name of sovereign power, but also

204. Ibid., 3.
205. See Kurzman, ed., *Liberal Islam*, 14–24.
206. Ibid., 26.
207. Ibid., 37.
208. Saba Mahmood, "Secularism, Hermeneutics, and Empire," 323.

that "the political solution that secularism proffers . . . lies not so much in tolerating difference and diversity but in remaking certain kinds of religious subjectivities (even if this requires the use of violence) so as to render them compliant with liberal political rule."[209]

Mahmood affirms that "the aim of this multilayered project is singular: to foster what is now broadly called 'moderate Islam' as an antidote and prophylactic to fundamentalist interpretations of Islam. This broad-based ideological project bears obvious similarities with the State Department's Cold War policies of aiding and abetting oppositional currents in the former Soviet Union—with one important exception: the current campaign has an overt *theological* agenda."[210] What we see emerge then is a secular religion, or perhaps even a secular fundamentalism, that seeks to overthrow Islamic "fundamentalism" in its embrace of its own progressive values that are fighting the "reactionary" values of "fundamentalist Islam."[211]

Mobilizing Islam against Democracy

Mahmood cites prior US and Western support for jihadist Islamists to overthrow the Communist government of Afghanistan, but this, as we will see, is a much older imperial project. During the Cold War, the main Islamist group in the Muslim world, namely the Egyptian Society of the Muslim Brothers, and the Saudi Arabian government and its state clerics, as well as other Muslim clerics were all conscripted and abetted by an initially tacit and later express US plan to create and mobilize a jihadist Islam as a theological duty of Muslims to battle those Arabs and Muslims who were fighting American imperial forces and the local dictators that US imperialism sponsors across the Muslim world, and not only on the military battlefields. In the context of encouraging a Protestant Islam, the call for a "jihad" and for institutionalizing a Wahhabist form of Islam across the Arab and Muslim worlds and to issue edicts for jihad's permissibility and necessity against godless communists and secular nationalists in the Arab world (especially Arab nationalism and its champion Jamal ʿAbd al-Nasir), the first major venture of US imperialism in the politicization of Islamic theology was launched, long before Afghanistan.

209. Ibid., 328.
210. Ibid., 331.
211. On this, see Asad, *Formations of the Secular.*

It was under the Truman administration that US interest in Islam started with searching for a Muslim leader who could spearhead a crusade against the Soviets. Truman's Psychological Strategy Board came up with a program that would be adopted in February 1953, soon after Eisenhower took office. The program affirmed: "No consideration of the traditional Arab mind is possible without taking into consideration the all-pervading influence of the Muslim faith on Arab thinking."[212] As it is clear, modernization theory's notion of "tradition" and the more insidious notion of mentality captured by the expression "Arab mind" were already part of a powerful culturalist idiom in these reports. If Daniel Lerner thought Islam was "defenseless" against the march of modernization in 1958, the report would come to this conclusion much earlier than he: "Contrary to received wisdom in the West," the report stated, "Islam was not a natural barrier to communism. Many reformers who took power in these countries *put economics before religion*; that weakened the role of faith and made the region vulnerable to communism."[213] Here, it is clear that US policy makers were not Orientalist in their characterization of Islam as a powerful all-encompassing culture but rather recognized its limitations—in that they appear to abandon essentialist notions of Islam's alleged insurmountable fortifications that can rebuff secular ideologies—in the name of realpolitik; hence their intent of fostering its expedient use as an anticommunist weapon so as to put religion back "before" economics and strengthen "the role of faith."

Chief psychological warfare strategist for Eisenhower, Edward P. Lilly, drew up a memorandum titled "The Religious Factor" in 1953. It called on the US to use religion more explicitly in its fight against the Soviet Union and recognized that using Islam as a vehicle to reach the tens of millions of Soviet Muslims would be to the advantage of US policy. Lilly spoke of the religious revival in the Muslim world, which he likened to the great Wesleyan Christian revival in eighteenth-century England. His memorandum would circulate in different administration branches, reaching the National Security Council in 1954, which in turn would call it one of its landmark documents of the period on US policy towards the Soviets for "mobilizing the spiritual and moral resources necessary to meet the Soviet threat."[214] In the same spirit, the State Department hosted in September 1953 a major delegation of

---

212. Cited in Ian Johnson, *A Mosque in Munich: Nazis, the CIA, And the Muslim Brotherhood in the West* (New York: Houghton Mifflin Harcourt, 2010), 68.

213. Ibid., 68–69.

214. For the account on Lilly and his document, see Johnson, *A Mosque*, 69–70.

"distinguished Muslim scholars" for a colloquium on "Islamic culture" held at Princeton University. The guests included Saʿid Ramadan, then a senior member of the Egyptian Society of the Muslim Brothers (founded in 1928), and Muhammad Khalafallah, an Egyptian professor and author who had gained much notoriety in 1947 for his dissertation at Fuʾad (later Cairo) University, which was rejected due to its controversial borrowing from Orientalists, and according to some accusers, from a Christian missionary. He persisted in his views and published his dissertation in 1953, which might account for his invitation to the Princeton conference.[215] He later wrote on Islam as mandating secular and democratic governance.[216] Other guests at the colloquium included ʿAbdullah Ghosheh, a Jordanian minister (of Palestinian background) and Chief Justice for decades in that country, and an assortment of ambassadors and officials from Muslim-majority countries. It was the US ambassador to Egypt at the time who recommended that Ramadan (and presumably Khalafallah) be invited.[217] The delegation would go on to the White House and meet with President Eisenhower.

Footing the bill—to the tune of $25,000, plus additional expenses for transporting attendees from the Middle East—was the International Information Administration (IIA), a branch of the State Department that had its roots in the US intelligence community; supplementary funding was sought from US airlines and from Aramco, the US oil consortium in Saudi Arabia. Like many of the participants, Ramadan, an ideologue and not a scholar, was visiting the conference as an all-expenses-paid guest. A declassified IIA document labeled "Confidential—Security Information" sums up the purpose of the project: "On the surface, the conference looks like an exercise in pure learning. This in effect is the impression desired." The true goal, the memo notes, was to "bring together persons exerting great influence in formulating Muslim opinion in fields such as education, science, law and philosophy and inevitably, therefore, on politics. . . . Among the various results expected from the colloquium are the impetus and direction that may be given to the Renaissance movement within Islam itself."[218]

The published proceedings of the colloquium speak of the coming together of this group as a happenstance rather than design: "During

215. On the Khalafallah dissertation controversy, see Donald Malcolm Reid, *Cairo University and the Making of Modern Egypt* (Cambridge: Cambridge University Press, 1990), 155–56.
216. See his *Al-Qurʾan wa al-Dawlah* (Cairo: Maktabat al-Anjlo al-Misriyyah, 1973).
217. See Robert Dreyfus, *Devil's Game: How the United States Helped Unleash Fundamentalist Islam* (New York: Metropolitan Books, 2005), 77–78.
218. Robert Dreyfus, "Cold War, Holy Warrior," *Mother Jones*, January-February 2006.

the summer of 1953, there happened to be an unusually large number of distinguished Muslim scholars in the United States."[219]

Mobilizing Islam and Muslims would be stepped up fairly quickly thenceforward. As early as 1954, the CIA would already dispatch spy agitators to Mecca during the Muslim pilgrimage to foment anti-Soviet sentiments among Soviet pilgrims. The agents the CIA sent were Soviet Muslim collaborators with the Nazis who had previously worked with the Nazi regime to mobilize Soviet Muslims against their government during World War II.[220] The US inherited and utilized a whole Nazi team of spies and their handlers who used to work for the Reich Ministry of the Occupied Eastern Territories (*Ostministerium*). Indeed one of the same Nazi collaborator agents sent to Mecca by the CIA would be dispatched the following year to Indonesia, to the Bandung Conference, to propagandize against the Soviet Union and its treatment of Soviet Muslims, in an attempt to undermine Soviet standing among the non-aligned nations. One Eisenhower administration official identified the CIA operation at Bandung approvingly as a "Machiavellian" move.[221] Another important mission was supporting right-wing Indonesian Muslim organizations against the Indonesian Communist Party. The right-wing Indonesian Islamists were led by a former government minister who financed their anticommunist sabotage operations from a Swiss bank account. The minister's overseas contact was the same CIA agent sent to Bandung.[222]

The British had already seen fit to seek an alliance with the Egyptian Society of the Muslim Brothers since the early 1940s to defeat secular anti-imperialist nationalists and communists, a strategy that entailed a British financial offer to the Society's founder Hasan al-Banna after his release from prison in October 1941. The Society, according to the most credible accounts, rejected the offer, even though it had accepted back in 1928, the year of its founding, a £E500 donation from the British- and French-owned Suez Canal Company to finance the building of a mosque.[223] The Society also infiltrated the communist movement in 1944 and would pass information obtained by its "intelligence" after the end of World War II to the Egyptian government that helped it to

219. *Colloquium on Islamic Culture in Its Relation to the Contemporary World, September 1953* (Princeton, NJ: Princeton University Press, 1954), 7.
220. Johnson, *A Mosque*, 65.
221. Ibid., 71–73.
222. Ibid., 147–48.
223. See Richard P. Mitchell, *The Society of the Muslim Brothers* (Oxford: Oxford University Press, 1969), 28, 9.

round up communists at universities and in the unions.[224] Soon after the 1952 coup that brought the Free Officers and ʿAbd al-Nasir to power, the Society, which had alienated the British since 1946 when it began to launch attacks against the British occupation, would sit down for meetings and talks with them (namely the famed meeting in 1953 between the Society's General Guide Hasan Ismaʾil al-Hudaybi and British embassy official and Oriental Counsellor Trefor Evans),[225] which ʿAbd al-Nasir recognized as part of Hudaybi's hostility to his land-reform program.[226] It was in that context that he would dissolve the Society. The ʿAbd al-Nasir government alleged that the Society also received financial contributions from the Americans, but no clear evidence was presented.[227]

After members of the Society failed to assassinate ʿAbd al-Nasir in 1954, King Husayn's regime in Jordan would provide its leaders, including the denationalized and fugitive Ramadan, with diplomatic passports to facilitate their movements to organize against ʿAbd al-Nasir. There are also claims that the CIA approved funding by Saudi Arabia of the Society to act against ʿAbd al-Nasir, according to former CIA officer Robert Baer.[228] Indeed, British diplomats who were gathering intelligence in Egypt, and whom ʿAbd al-Nasir caught in 1956 and expelled, were said to be in contact with "student elements of a religious inclination" with the idea of "encouraging fundamentalist riots that could provide an excuse for military intervention to protect European lives."[229] Other members of the spy ring were arrested, including one James Swinburn, who ran an MI6 front organization called the Arab News Agency. The Egyptian authorities would uncover more details of the espionage ring as Swinburn confessed that they were planning a coup against ʿAbd al-Nasir.[230] No evidence exists to link the separate British attempts with those of members of the Society to assassinate ʿAbd al-Nasir, even though both parties clearly considered him their main enemy.

224. Ibid., 32. See also Joel Beinin and Zachary Lockman, *Workers on the Nile: Nationalism, Communism, Islam and the Egyptian Working Class, 1882–1954* (Princeton, NJ: Princeton University Press, 1987), 372.

225. Mitchell, *The Society of the Muslim Brothers* 112–13.

226. On Hudaybi's views on ʿAbd al-Nasir's land reforms, see ibid., 107.

227. Ibid., 182.

228. Dreyfus, *Devil's Game*, 101–2. For the history of US dominance of Saudi Arabia, see Robert Vitalis, *America's Kingdom: Mythmaking on the Saudi Oil Frontier* (Stanford, CA: Stanford University Press, 2007).

229. Stephen Dorill, *MI6* (London: Simon & Schuster, 2002), 632.

230. Ibid., 632, 636.

In January 1957, President Eisenhower announced the Eisenhower Doctrine in a much-touted speech. He declared that the US would come to the aid of any country in the Middle East threatened by Communism. In his speech Eisenhower insisted:

> The Middle East is the birthplace of three great religions—Moslem, Christian and Hebrew. Mecca and Jerusalem are more than places on the map. They symbolize religions which teach that the spirit has supremacy over matter and that the individual has a dignity and rights of which no despotic government can rightfully deprive him. It would be intolerable if the holy places of the Middle East should be subjected to a rule that glorifies atheistic materialism.[231]

In private meetings with the CIA's Frank Wisner and the Joint Chiefs of Staff, Eisenhower insisted that the Arabs should obtain inspiration from their religion to fight communism and that "we should do everything possible to stress the 'holy war' aspect."[232] The plan was for the US to support new "reformist" groups like the Society of the Muslim Brothers and shun traditional clerics. Later in the year and during an American embassy-sponsored palace coup by King Husayn against the democratically elected parliament, the anti-imperialist cabinet, and the nationalist army officers, members of the Jordanian branch of the Society would join British-trained Bedouin army units in fighting the anti-imperialist nationalist and pro-democratization forces in the country whom they dubbed "communists."[233] As we will see, this would not be the last time that American-sponsored Islamists would declare jihad on America's communist enemies in the Muslim world.

In the meantime, as the Saudis, who had been traditional enemies of the Hashemites, had sided with ʿAbd al-Nasir against the Western-created anti-Soviet Baghdad Pact, the American State Department decided "to detach Saudi Arabia from Egyptian influence."[234] Eisenhower was keen on propping up the Saudis as a counterweight to ʿAbd al-Nasir, especially as the Americans recognized the importance of Saudi control of Muslim holy places. Eisenhower's plan was that the Saudi "King could be built up, possibly, as a spiritual leader. Once this were accomplished

231. Speech by President Dwight Eisenhower, 5 January 1957, available on http://millercenter.org/scripps/archive/speeches/detail/3360 (accessed 19 February 2014).

232. Cited in Johnson, 127.

233. See Joseph Massad, *Colonial Effects: The Making of National Identity in Jordan* (New York: Columbia University Press, 2001), 194.

234. Quoted in Salim Yaqub, *Containing Arab Nationalism: The Eisenhower Doctrine and the Middle East* (Chapel Hill: University of North Carolina Press, 2006), 44.

we might begin to urge his right to political leadership."[235] As King Sa'ud seemed less responsive and not fit for the role, in 1962, Prince Faysal (Crown Prince of Saudi Arabia, who, with the support of the Americans, would force his brother King Sa'ud to abdicate in 1964 and would replace him on the throne) organized an international Islamic conference in Mecca to combat the popularity of Arab nationalism, socialism, and "secularism," and launched the Muslim World League. This was part of the new role that the US subcontracted to the Saudis against 'Abd al-Nasir during the Arab Cold War. Sa'id Ramadan attended the conference (indeed he was one of the founding members of the League)[236] while working with American intelligence and was instrumental in drawing up the bylaws of the League and pushing its anticommunist agenda.[237] The conference declared: "Those who disavow Islam and distort its call under the guise of nationalism are actually the most bitter enemies of the Arabs, whose glories are entwined with the glories of Islam."[238] In response to Faysal's attempt to replace Arab unity with Islamic unity, 'Abd al-Nasir accused the new Islamic alliance of being an "American-British conspiracy aimed at dividing the Arab world and undermining Arab hopes for unity."[239] He was not far off the mark. While the Americans were not closely involved in the formation of the League, they gave it their blessing and support as one more organ of their international networks to fight communism and anti-imperialist Arab nationalism simultaneously.

Using Muslim groups and Islamism more generally against communism was standard fare throughout the Cold War. The participation of right-wing Indonesian Muslim groups in the massacre of half a million to a million communists and alleged communists in 1965 Indonesia after a US-sponsored and financed coup was celebrated by an editorial in the *Chicago Tribune*: "We must say it's refreshing to read of young Muslims burning down Communist Party headquarters, for a change, and shout 'Long Live America.'"[240] Muslim leaders in Indonesia met regularly with the US embassy and the CIA, which provided the names and addresses

235. Quoted in ibid., 44.

236. A list of the founders of the league is provided by Reinhard Schulze, *A Modern History of the Islamic World* (New York: New York University Press, 2002), 172.

237. Johnson, 162–63.

238. "Islam against Nationalism," *Economist*, 2 June 1962, 903, cited in Abdullah M. Sindi, "King Faisal and Pan-Islamism," in *King Faisal and the Modernisation of Saudi Arabia*, ed. Willard A. Beling (London: Croom Helm, 1980), 186.

239. Sindi, ibid., 188.

240. "1 1/2 Cheers for Indonesia," editorial, *Chicago Tribune*, 12 October 1965.

of Indonesian communists, as well as weapons, for the massacre to continue unhindered. The support of the Indonesian Islamists went back to the 1950s, when the US and Britain provided arms for the anti-Sukarno rebellion which would be crushed in 1961 and of which the Islamist groups formed a major part, declaring Islamic republics in various parts of Indonesia that challenged Sukarno's rule.[241] Once Suharto consolidated his rule, he would rein in the Islamist groups, though some of the more extreme among them would be maintained as an anticommunist force. These same groups would join in the anti-Soviet effort in Afghanistan in the 1980s.[242]

The interest in Muslims fighting the Soviet Union, not only in Afghanistan but even inside the Soviet Union itself, remained part of US strategy, so much so that the US Defense Department commissioned a report from the Rand Corporation in 1982 on Nazi policy of co-opting Soviet non-Russian nationalities during World War II in preparation for its strategy to bring down the Soviet regime. The report would examine the policies that led many among Soviet Muslims to collaborate with the Nazis for possible use by the Americans.[243] In the 1960s and as part of the cultural Cold War, the CIA had set up an Arabic magazine in Beirut, *Al-Hiwar*, with generous CIA funding for its prospective editor with one stipulation, that it publish articles on the situation of Soviet Muslims.[244] By the late 1970s, the United States was already involved, in partnership with the Saudis and Egyptian president Anwar Sadat and later Husni Mubarak, in recruiting, financing, and training Islamists from Afghanistan to Pakistan, the Arab World, Europe, and the United States, readying them for the final battle against the Soviets. It was this US policy abetted by its subcontracted allies, Saudi Arabia and Pakistan, which led to the creation of the Taliban and al-Qaʿidah from the ranks of the US-created and trained Islamists who would come to rule Afghanistan and later fight the United States once it turned on them after the fall of the Soviets.[245]

It was in the light of the hegemony of these right-wing and anticommunist Islamist groups and their Saudi benefactor that the US began

241. See Mark Curtis, *Secret Affairs, Britain's Collusion with Radical Islam*, 77–82, 95–98.
242. Ibid., 98.
243. Alex Alexiev, *Soviet Nationalities in Nazi Wartime Strategy, 1941–1945: Report Prepared for the Net Assessment, Office of the Secretary of Defense*, Rand Foundation, Rand Publication Series (Santa Monica, CA: Rand, August 1982).
244. Mitchell, "The Middle East in the Past and Future of Social Science," 12.
245. On the history of US arming and conscripting Islamists in the 1970s through the 1990s, see John Cooley, *Unholy Wars: Afghanistan, America, and International Terrorism*, 3rd ed. (London: Pluto Press, 2002).

to seek a certain change in its tactics. As it once pushed for the issuance of religious fatwas to support jihad against local and international communism and the Soviets and support local dictatorships in Muslim-majority countries against local agitation for Western-style liberal "democracy" across "the Muslim world," it would soon turn to create and abet another variant of Islam for the era of the "War on Terror." Thus it appears that Western and American cultural and political commitments to democracy are as malleable as the "Islam" they seek to mobilize for different strategic ends. This change of tactics reflects what Foucault described as the "tactical polyvalence of discourse," which includes "a multiplicity of discursive elements that can come into play in various strategies."[246]

Mobilizing Islam for Democracy

The current US campaign to produce and support a "moderate" Islam is a continuation of these theological interventions, if a less robust effort. But this is hardly a new Western tactic; it rather harks back to the primal scene of the Napoleonic invasion of Egypt. It was on that occasion that Napoleon proclaimed in July 1798 to the Egyptians upon landing in Alexandria: "The Lord of the Universe, the Omnipotent, has commanded the annihilation of the [Mamluk] dynasty."[247] He proceeded: "It is the duty of the Shaykhs, the *ulama*, the judges, and the *imams* to keep to their functions. . . . Formal prayer will be held in the mosques as usual. All Egyptians must be grateful to God, glory be to Him and exalted is He for the termination of the dynasty of the Mamluks, saying loudly 'May God perpetuate the paying of honour to the Ottoman sultan, may God perpetuate the paying of honor to the French army, may God curse the Mamluks, and may He ameliorate the condition of the Egyptian nation.' "[248]

Napoleon's inaugural appeal to Islamic theological legitimacy for his colonial campaign would be picked up by the British later in the nineteenth century for their own. In 1857 and before Abdülhamid II would deploy his title as caliph against European encroachment, the British obtained a proclamation from the Ottoman sultan and caliph

---

246. Foucault, *The History of Sexuality*, vol. 1: *An Introduction*, 100.
247. "Proclamation of Bonaparte to the Egyptians. Muharram 1213 A.H.," in Saladin Boustany, ed., *The Journals of Bonaparte in Egypt, 1798–1801* (Cairo: Dar al-Maaref, 1971), 5.
248. Ibid., Article 5 of Napoleon's proclamation, 9.

ʿAbd al-Majid I addressed to Indian Muslims not to join the anti-British Mutiny in India and to remain loyal to the sultan's British allies.[249] This was not the first time the British had asked the Ottomans to invoke their caliphal authority. In the context of Napoleon's threat to British rule in India half a century earlier, British diplomats, who took the threat seriously, had interceded with the Ottoman caliph to address Indian Muslims and warn them of the "false promises of the French." Henry Laurens affirms that in doing so "the sultan would thereby engage unawares in pan-Islamism."[250] It was following the Mutiny and the removal of the Mughals from power that the British began in earnest to displace the "Anglo-Muhammadan" law in India, itself a "middle stage" British imposition towards the final Anglicization of Indian laws. The 1860s and the 1870s would witness this accelerated process so much so that "by the end of the century, and with the exception of family law and certain elements of property transactions, all indigenous laws were supplanted by British law."[251]

After the British occupied Egypt in 1882, they began to push for new Islamic theological understandings of governance, not to mention sociality. Lord Cromer, British Consul General of Egypt, an ardent anti-feminist in Britain who opposed women's suffrage and who obstructed women's education and the training of women doctors in Egypt, would champion unveiling as the way to modernize Muslim societies. His racist views of Islam were culled from a variety of Orientalist sources. Egyptian intellectual Qasim Amin's 1899 book *The Liberation of Women*, which borrows much of Cromer's Orientalism and lavishes praise on the British while condemning anti-imperialist Egyptians, among others, was not only a work about modernization but also a theological exegesis on the question of the hijab for women, where he delves into theological interpretations (more about his views in chapter 2).[252] According to rumors at the time, the book was said to have been written at Cromer's urgings and in conversation with him.[253] Moreover, the rise of one of

249. On the context of the proclamation, see Aziz Ahmad, *Islamic Modernism in India and Pakistan, 1857–1964* (Oxford: Oxford University Press, 1967), 123–24. See also Hamid Enayat, *Modern Islamic Political Thought* (Austin: University of Texas Press, 1982), 58, and Jacob M. Landau, *The Politics of Pan-Islam*, 185.

250. Henry Laurens in Tolan, Veinstein, and Laurens, *Europe and the Islamic World*, 272.

251. Hallaq, *Sharia*, 383.

252. See Qasim Amin, *Tahrir al-Marʾah*, in *Qasim Amin: Al-ʿAʿmal al-Kamilah*, ed. Muhammad ʿImarah (Cairo: Dar al-Shuruq, 1989), 352–59.

253. See Leila Ahmed, *Women and Gender in Islam: Historical Roots of a Modern Debate* (New Haven, CT: Yale University Press, 1992), 153, 159.

the most principal reformers of Islam in the late nineteenth century, Muhammad ʿAbduh, was not independent of British colonial power (it is also rumored without concrete evidence that ʿAbduh wrote one of the chapters of Qasim Amin's book). ʿAbduh would be appointed by the British occupation authorities as the Chief Mufti of Egypt in 1899. Whereas he was on bad terms with the ruling monarch of Egypt, the khedive Abbas Hilmi, ʿAbduh was on very good terms with Cromer. The latter would lavish praise on ʿAbduh's reforms in his Annual Report in 1905, the year of ʿAbduh's death, though he would criticize him in later years.[254]

In the same period, in 1899, the important Syrian intellectual ʿAbd al-Rahman al-Kawakibi moved from Aleppo to Cairo to escape Ottoman harassment and to express his anti-Ottomanism more freely. He was influenced in his ideas by Jamal al-Din al-Afghani and Muhammad ʿAbduh, though unlike the latter he was a friend of the khedive ʿAbbas Hilmi and on his payroll.[255] Al-Kawakibi first published his magnum opus The Characteristics of Despotism and the Demise of Subjugation (Tabaʾiʿ al-Istibdad wa Masariʿ al-Istiʿbad) against Ottoman despotism (which he does not name in the book) as a series of articles in the Cairo newspaper Al-Muʾayyad, between 1900 and 1902, which were later collected in book form. The book was highly influenced by the views of translated European works (al-Kawakibi knew Arabic, Turkish, and Persian but did not know European languages) on the question of Oriental and Ottoman despotism and was full of praise for French and British democracy (and other European governments and even the United States) while critical of colonialism (and this while Egypt was languishing under draconian British colonial rule locally presided over by Lord Cromer).[256] Al-Kawakibi, following Enlightenment thinkers, linked despotism to religion but insisted (like some of them) that Islam was not despotic though later Muslim rulers were. His major influence was the work of Italian thinker and playwright Vittorio Alfieri, who wrote Della Tirannide in 1777, which al-Kawakibi might have been acquainted with through an obscure Turkish translation.[257]

254. See Roger Owen, Lord Cromer: Victorian Imperialist, Edwardian Proconsul (Oxford: Oxford University Press, 2005), 361.
255. See Muhammad ʿImarah, ʿAbd al-Rahman al-Kawakibi: Shahid al-Hurriyyah wa Mujaddid al-Islam (Beirut: Dar al-Wihdah, 1984), 38.
256. ʿAbd al-Rahman al-Kawakibi, Tabaʾiʿ al-Istibdad wa Masariʿ al-Istiʿbad, in ʿAbd al-Rahman al-Kawakibi, Al-Aʿmal al-Kamilah lil-Kawakibi, ed. Muhammad Jamal Tahhan (Beirut: Markaz Dirasat al-Wihdah al-ʿArabiyyah), 516–18.
257. On the Turkish translation, see Ettore Rossi, "Una traduzione Turca dell'opera 'Della Tirannide' di V. Alfieri probabilmente conosciuta da al-Kawakibi," Oriente Moderno 34, no. 7 (July

In his book, al-Kawakibi distinguishes between Occidental and Oriental despotisms in several areas. Examples include that Occidental despotism "is wiser, more entrenched, and has a heavier impact though with some flexibility whereas Oriental [despotism] is unstable, has a short life, yet is unpleasant." There are other differences between them such as "when Occidental despotism is removed, it is replaced by a just government that lasts as long as circumstances allow, whereas the Oriental one when removed is replaced by a worse despotism, as it is the habit of Orientals not to think of the immediate future, as if their major concern were diverted to the afterlife only, or that they are afflicted with short sightedness."[258] Note al-Kawakibi's concern for the "future," which he borrows from imperial commentators. After another series of comparisons that privilege Occidentals over Orientals, al-Kawakibi concludes that "the Oriental is a creature of the past and of phantasy, while the Occidental is a creature of the future and of glory."[259]

In his earlier book, *Umm al-Qura* (first published in 1898), one of the names by which the city of Mecca is known, al-Kawakibi would support the replacement of the Ottoman caliph with an Arab one, as well as the limiting of his powers to the spiritual realm.[260] In *Umm al-Qura*, al-Kawakibi sets up a fictional assembly in Mecca among Muslims from across the Muslim world, including England, Iran, India, China, inter alia, as well as from Arab lands in order to set up a Muslim Society with its own bylaws. The fictional secret Society he convokes seeks to understand the "illness" and "degradation" (*futur*) that has afflicted Islam, in terms of "decadence" and "retrogression," as well as "moral degeneration,"[261] and Islamic politics which was transformed from a "fully socialist parliamentary, i.e. democratic" politics in the times of the rightly guided caliphs into a "kingly" politics "restricted by the basic legislative

---

1954): 335. See also Ahmad Amin, *Zuʿamaʾ al-Islah fi al-ʿAhd al-Hadith* (Cairo: Maktabat al-Nahdah al-Misriyyah, 1948), 254. For al-Kawakibi's citation of Alfieri, see al-Kawakibi, *Tabaʾiʿ al-Istibdad*, 529. On the controversy about how al-Kawakibi might have accessed Alfieri, see ʿAbbas Mahmud al-ʿAqqad, *ʿAbd al-Rahman al-Kawakibi, al-Rahhalah Kaf* (Beirut: Dar al-Kitab al-Arabi, 1969), 132–35. Al-ʿAqqad postulates that al-Kawakibi learned of Alfieri through the many Italians resident in Aleppo in his lifetime. Also see Sylvia Haim, "Alfieri and al-Kawakibi," *Oriente Moderno* 34, no. 7 (July 1954): 321–34. Haim suggests that the book could have been read out loud to him by interpreters, ibid., 333.

258. Al-Kawakibi, *Tabaʾiʿ al-Istibdad*, 483. For other comparisons see 461–62.

259. Ibid., 492.

260. ʿAbd al-Rahman al-Kawakibi, *Umm al-Qura*, in ʿAbd al-Rahman al-Kawakibi, *Al-Aʿmal al-Kamilah lil-Kawakibi*, ed. Muhammad Jamal Tahhan (Beirut: Markaz Dirasat al-Wihdah al-ʿArabiyyah).

261. See for example ibid., 299, 370.

rules which would become later absolutist."[262] This has lost "us" our "freedom" and "justice."[263] In the second half of the book and after detailing how Islamic practices have been adulterated over the centuries as a result of "decadence," the book begins to delve explicitly into Ottoman rule (in contrast to his book on despotism, where the Ottomans are not criticized by name), its discrimination against non-Turkish nationalities, specifically the Arabs, and begins to articulate the measures to be taken to address this illness, which would include the important "medication" of "the enlightenment of thought through education and the instilling of yearning for ascent/elevation [*taraqqi*] among the youth."[264] The meeting resolves on the importance of the Arabian Peninsula and the Arabs to bring about an "Islamic" or a "religious renaissance."[265]

The arguments put forth in this section resemble to a great deal the arguments put forth by Blunt two decades earlier as to the uniqueness of Arabia and the Arabs with regards to the question of the caliphate. Sure enough, at the conclusion of the meeting and the book, al-Kawakibi begins to explain the difference between "religion" and the "State," and that the purpose of the secret meeting is to create a renaissance of Islam, and not the worldly matters of statecraft; indeed that "religion is not governance."[266] His proposal was not only the separation of religion and the caliphate from the Ottoman sultan, but that the latter would be needed to support the former. He even provides a summary history of how the state and religion were separated in Islamic history except for the case of the rightly guided caliphs and a few others.[267] Al-Kawakibi would insist on the separation of the theological and the political and that Islam had authority only on matters of worship but not on matters of governance: "As is known, there is no religious authority whatsoever in Islamism except over matters of religious rituals."[268] In *Umm al-Qura*, al-Kawakibi, in a manner almost identical to Blunt's, would explicitly call for the "establishment of an Arab Qurayshi caliph," whose political rule

262. Ibid., 289.
263. Ibid., 290.
264. Ibid., 376.
265. Ibid., 384, 390, 393.
266. Al-Sayyid al-Furati (pseudonym for ʿAbd al-Rahman al-Kawakibi), *Umm al-Qura* (Cairo: published by Al-Maktabah al-Tijariyya and printed at Al-Matbaʿah al-Misriyyah bil-Azhar, 1931), 202. It is significant that this part of the conversation is missing without explanation from the version reproduced in the collected works of al-Kawakibi edited by Tahhan. See ibid., 394.
267. ʿAbd al-Rahman al-Kawakibi, *Umm al-Qura*, in ʿAbd al-Rahman al-Kawakibi, *Al-Aʿmal al-Kamilah lil-Kawakibi*, ed. Muhammad Jamal Tahhan (Beirut: Markaz Dirasat al-Wihdah al-ʿArabiyyah), 395.
268. Al-Kawakibi, *Tabaʾiʿ al-Istibdad*, 450. On his views of the caliphate and the state, see al-ʿAqqad, *ʿAbd al-Rahman al-Kawakibi*, 188–96.

would only encompass Hijaz, overseen by an elected assembly of two hundred people from around Muslim lands whose authority would be solely over "matters of religious public policy" and who would elect the caliph who would not "intervene at all in any political or administrative matter in the sultanates and principalities."[269] It would be "thus that the problem of the Caliphate would be resolved, and a cooperative Islamic union of solidarity can be facilitated in adopting its structure from the rules of German unity and American unity with certain changes."[270] These ideas are presented as a dialogue between the Indian delegate and a great Muslim commander and statesman with whom the discussion of the caliphate occurs two months after the conclusion of the secret meeting.[271] The ideas about the caliphate would be articulated by the fictional Muslim statesman.

To make the Arab caliphate safe for Europeans to support, al-Kawakibi would even counter Orientalist arguments about jihad as a war against unbelievers, reminding them that, for the prior seven centuries, no such jihad had ever been declared by the Arabs.[272] The interests of European Christians in an Arab caliphate were explicitly explained by al-Kawakibi's fictional commander: "If [European] politicians learn about these facts [about the Arabs] and their ramifications, they will not fear an Arab caliphate but rather would find that it is in their private interests and in the interests of Christianity and the interests of humanity that they should support the establishment of an Arab Caliphate with limited authority linked to a consultative council like the one I read to you."[273] He would call for the khedive ʿAbbas Hilmi to assume the caliphate instead of the Ottoman sultan Abdülhamid, something British policy would openly support by the beginning of World War I.[274] It is clear that al-Kawakibi's proposals on the question of the caliphate, the inappropriateness of the Ottomans to assume it, and the importance of the Arabs assuming it are highly influenced if not copied from Blunt. Even though Blunt's book *The Future of Islam* was not translated to Arabic, it is likely that al-Kawakibi knew of the book from his Cairo associates and might have even met with Blunt himself, who kept a house in Cairo at the time.[275] The internalization of Arab and Muslim intellectuals of the duality of despotism

269. Al-Kawakibi, *Umm al-Qura*, 397–98.
270. Ibid., 399.
271. Ibid., 393.
272. Ibid., 401.
273. Ibid., 402.
274. Ibid., 388. See also Muhammad ʿImarah, *ʿAbd al-Rahman al-Kawakibi*, 38.
275. On the influence of Blunt's book on al-Kawakibi's, see Haim, "Blunt and al-Kawakibi."

and democracy was, as is clear from works like al-Kawakibi's, hardly external to liberal colonial and Orientalist epistemology or pedagogy. Many such intellectuals were in fact the product of the colonial pedagogical strategy as elaborated by Edmond Douttée and William Marçais above.

The British, like the French before them, had a special concern with the "Caliphate Question," and whether the caliphate was indeed essential to "Islam," in light of the new state of war between them and the Ottomans at the start of World War I. This was the year when the Young Turks declared the first modern "jihad" against the Entente on 14 November 1914, weeks after announcing their entry into the war, a declaration that is said to have been "made in Germany" with the good offices of Kaiser Wilhelm II, who had instructed his diplomats and intelligence agents to "set the East aflame."[276] The jihad declaration was issued as a fatwa by the Ottoman chief jurisconsult (Shaykh al-Islam) and was eagerly awaited by Germany's political and military leaders, who sought to have it immediately translated to "Arabic and Indian [*sic*]" for leaflet propaganda targeting "enemy Moslem soldiers in France."[277] The kaiser recalled Max Freiherr von Oppenheim, a retired rich diplomat and amateur orientalist archeologist, and a friend of the khedive ʿAbbas Hilmi, who was on an excavation trip in Syria. Oppenheim had served as chargé d'affaires of the German consulate general in Egypt. During his service, he had dispatched a report in 1908 to Chancellor von Bülow with regards to "England and Islam," in which he warned that the British were attempting to weaken the Ottoman Empire by detaching the caliphate from the sultan to protect their dominion in India and Egypt from the influence the Ottoman caliph had over Indian and Egyptian Muslims.[278] Oppenheim's assessment would prove accurate. British strategy at the beginning of the war, as established in a Foreign Office secret document, would include the "nullif[ication] by action both within the Turkish Empire and outside the Turkish efforts to set Muslim against Christian by their declaration of a Holy War," which could only be declared by the Ottoman caliph.[279] The British, in the form of a letter sent by Lord Kitchener, had, a month earlier in October, informed ʿAbdullah, the

---

276. Susanne E. Marchand, *German Orientalism in the Age of Empire: Religion, Race and Scholarship* (Washington, DC, and Cambridge: German Historical Institute and Cambridge University Press, 2009), 439. There is considerable debate in the literature on the German role in the Ottoman declaration of jihad. On this see Marchand, *German Orientalism*, 439–46.

277. Cited in Ulrich Trumpener, *Germany and the Ottoman Empire, 1914–1918* (Princeton, NJ: Princeton University Press, 1968), 117.

278. Caesar Farah, "Great Britain, Germany, and the Ottoman Caliphate," *Der Islam* 66 (1989): 268.

279. Quoted in ibid.

son of the Hijazi sharif Husayn, that "Germany has bought the Turkish Government with gold, notwithstanding that England, France and Russia guaranteed the integrity of the Ottoman Empire. . . . It may be that an Arab of true race will assume the Khalifate at Mecca or Medina. . . . Till now we have defended Islam in the person of the Turks; henceforward it shall be in that of the noble Arab."[280]

Oppenheim would now prepare a memorandum for the kaiser on how the German Reich could use Islam as "one of our most important weapons" and organize "Islam" against the English. The caliph's participation in these efforts, wrote Oppenheim, was "the best propaganda tool."[281] The idea, which never materialized, was that British, French, and Russian Muslim subjects from India, central Asia, and Africa would respond to the Ottoman call and fight against their rulers, who were the declared enemies of the caliph.[282] Dutch Orientalist Snouck Hurgronje who (as we saw) had argued two decades earlier that European powers should not recognize the caliphate lest their own Muslim subjects revolt against them, was so incensed at the German role in the jihad declaration and its potential impact on the Dutch colony of Indonesia, that, despite his erstwhile friendship with German Orientalists, published a long vituperative article in early 1915 in the liberal journal *De Gids* titled "Holy War 'Made in Germany'" condemning their role in the matter.[283] In contrast, German Orientalist Martin Hartmann, who two decades earlier had declared that Islam was on the eve of a new "evolution," wrote the foreword to the commentary "the Truth of Jihad" written by Tunisian mufti Shaykh Salih al-Sharif al-Tunisi, a confidante of the Ottoman minister of war Enver Pasha, and published in Germany at the beginning of 1915.[284]

This would lead the British from 1914 on to consider supporting an Arab caliph instead of a Turkish one, which would engender all kinds of discussions with Sharif Husayn of Mecca as the major candidate for the job, though King Fu'ad of Egypt would also be a contender. But this was not only a British concern; in 1915 the French (whose Commission interministérielle des affairs musulmanes collected notes on the subject

280. Cited in ibid., 278.
281. Marchand, *German Orientalism*, 438.
282. On the role of Oppenheim, see also Jacob M. Landau, *The Politics of Pan-Islam*, 96–98.
283. Cited in Marchand, *German Orientalism*, 443.
284. Cited in Wolfgang G. Schwanitz, "The German Middle Eastern Policy, 1871–1945," in *Germany and the Middle East, 1871–1945*, ed. Wolfgang G. Schwanitz (Princeton, NJ: Markus Wiener, 2004), 8. Schwanitz's propagandistic account (and condemnatory tone) of the German role judges it as decisive in the issuance of the declaration. He does not seem to acknowledge at all that there is a scholarly debate on the matter among historians.

of the caliphate) in turn proposed the constitution of a "Western caliphate," in the words of General Hubert Lyautey, the French colonial ruler of Morocco, with the sultan of Morocco as commander of the believers, whose caliphal authority would encompass the French colonial empire as a whole, what would be considered a "French Islam." The plan did not come through due to protests by other colonial officials in North Africa who did not want to submit to Moroccan authority. At European colonial instigation, fatwas would be issued to that effect by religious authorities across the colonial empires.[285] In the spring of 1915, the British, in a telegram to their high commissioner in Cairo, declared that "the seat of the Mahommedan Khalifate should be in Arabia, which comprises Hedjaz, Syria, El Irak (Mesopotamia), Yemen and other places. . . . Arabia is the best and most suitable place for the new Khalifate on account of its religious and political importance to the Mahommedans."[286]

After the war, the British would obtain theological opinions from Arab Muslim scholars from the Sudan to the Yemen in the process, including a professor from al-Azhar, Shaykh Muhammad Hilmi Tummara, as well as the opinions of the Agha Khan in India and of British (Sir Thomas Arnold) and Italian (Carlo Alfonso Nallino's report was written for the Italian Colonial Ministry) Orientalists. This would lead British imperial policy makers to discuss Islamic theology on the question of the caliphate, and to arrive at conclusions about the importance of maintaining it and that it should go to an Arab rather than an Ottoman Turk.

The fact that the British Empire had a large Indian Muslim population was clearly in the forefront of the policy makers' minds.[287] Indian Muslim support of Abdülhamid and the Ottoman Empire began to manifest in earnest after the 1877–78 Ottoman-Russian War and steadily increased as Britain began to annex and occupy Ottoman territory (Cyprus in 1878, and Egypt in 1882). Concerned about the increasing popularity of (what European powers and Orientalists referred to as) "pan-Islam" among Indian Muslims, the British seemed interested in ending any spiritual or secular authority that the office of the caliph could have on Muslims of other countries (in line with Snouck Hurgronje's suggestions in *Questions diplômatiques et coloniales*).

---

285. Henry Laurens in Tolan, Veinstein, and Laurens, *Europe and the Islamic World*, 361.
286. Farah, "Great Britain, Germany, and the Ottoman Caliphate," 278–79.
287. See Sean Oliver-Dee, *The Caliphate Question: The British Government and Islamic Governance* (Plymouth, England: Lexington Books, 2009), chapter 2.

They thus included in the Treaty of Sèvres, signed in August 1920, article 139, wherein "Turkey formally renounces any rights of sovereignty or jurisdiction of any kind over Muslims who are subject to the sovereignty or protectorate of any other state."[288] This would anger Indian Muslims, delegations from whose organizations, especially the Khilafat Movement (which was founded in support of the Ottoman caliphate by Indian Muslims at a conference in November 1919 and lasted until 1925 when it petered out and finally disappeared after 1933), would object to the British about it. In the years that followed, Thomas Arnold's expertise on the matter would continue to be sought by the British authorities— the Foreign Office, the India Office, the Colonial Office, as well as British officials in Cairo. Arnold's correspondence with British officials would become more intense in the preparation for the Lausanne Treaty and of the phrasing intended to transport Article 139 of the Treaty of Sèvres into it. Finally and after much debate about the differing meanings of the word "spiritual" for Christians and Muslims, and the need to remain as ambiguous as possible about these differences, the wording of Article 27 of the Lausanne Treaty signed in July 1923 by Turkey and the British Empire and its allies would be finalized:

No power or jurisdiction in political, legislative or administrative matters shall be exercised outside Turkish territory by the Turkish Government or authorities, for any reason whatsoever, over the nationals of a territory placed under the sovereignty or protectorate of the other Powers signatory of the present Treaty, or over the nationals of a territory detached from Turkey. It is understood that the spiritual attributions of the Moslem religious authorities are in no way infringed.[289]

British painstaking debates over the wording of the article would soon prove unnecessary as Atatürk would abolish the caliphate altogether in a few months (in March 1924), ending the 700-year history of the Ottoman Empire and its association with Islam.[290] But the British abiding interest in the caliphate would be misunderstood by the Soviets as an interest *only* in maintaining it as a tool to advance British imperial

---

288. Cited in ibid., 93.

289. Lausanne Treaty, signed on 24 July 1923, Article 27.

290. The French in turn were also preoccupied with the Caliphate Question in relation to their African colonial subjects, a concern that was tempered by the French racist belief in the "innate docility of Africans." Indeed, the French Colonial Minister was so confident that caliphal concerns were of no interest to African Muslims that he wrote in October 1923 to Governor-General Carde in Dakar that "the conservatism of our African subjects keeps them outside the neo-Muslim movement." See Christian Harrison, *France and Islam in West Africa, 1860–1960* (Cambridge: Cambridge University Press, 1988), 164, 165.

policies. The Soviets did not seem to appreciate that the British were interested in pursuing the maintenance *or* the removal of the caliphate, depending on which they saw as serving their imperial interests better. Leon Trotsky would declare in April 1924 that "Turkey abolished the Caliphate and [British Prime Minister] MacDonald resurrects it."[291] Soviet concern about ongoing British policy at the time in Afghanistan led Trotsky to add: "MacDonald's Britain is toppling the left national bourgeois wing which is striving to Europeanize independent Afghanistan and is attempting there to restore to power the darkest and most reactionary elements imbued with the worst prejudices of pan-Islamism, the Caliphate and so forth."[292]

Yet British policy remained open to all possibilities. The postwar situation no longer lent itself to the grand ideas of empire, annexation, and the white man's burden, which "have been expunged from the popular political vocabulary," as British colonial diplomat Mark Sykes clearly recognized in the context of the British conquest of Mesopotamia and Palestine. He would declare in 1918, in line with the new notion of the right of nations to self-determination, that "protectorates, spheres of interest or influence, annexations, bases, etc, have to be consigned to the Diplomatic lumber-room. . . . If Britishers are to run Mesopotamia we must find up to date reasons for their doing so and up to date formulae for them to work the country on. We shall have to convince our own Democracy that Britishers ought to do the work and the Democracies of the world as well."[293] That "democracy" would be the "up to date reasons" and "formulae" that colonialism sought in order to justify itself to the colonized natives was hardly obscure to the latter, but that the so-called British democracy and other democracies had to be "convinced" of the colonial project and deceived into believing it was one of democratization has been a successful deception for so many of the natives of Western democracies and would become the main umbrella under which American imperialism would proceed after World War II and through the present.

It was in light of active British involvement in the colonies and its plans to control the Muslim population of the British Empire that Sir Thomas Arnold would publish his book *The Caliphate* in 1924, in which

291. Leon Trotsky, "Perspectives and Tasks in the East," speech delivered on the third anniversary of the Communist University for Toilers in the East in the USSR on 21 April 1924, http://www.marxists.org/archive/trotsky/1924/04/perspectives.htm (accessed 22 February 2014).

292. Ibid.

293. Cited in Helmut Mejcher, *Imperial Quest for Oil: Iraq 1910–1928* (London: Ithaca Press, 1976), 53.

he asserted that the caliph "enjoyed no spiritual functions," indeed that the very concept and theory of the caliphate was not elaborated in the Qur'an but much later by Muslim elites.[294] A year after Arnold published his book, Egyptian judge ʿAli ʿAbd al-Raziq followed with his own book, *Islam and the Bases of Governance*,[295] essentially arguing similar points, namely that the caliphate has no basis in the Qur'an, and that in this sense Islam is compatible with secularism and democracy. ʿAbd al-Raziq's explicit reliance on the views of Arnold, which he extols in his book, hardly mitigated the response of his critics, who accused him of propagating borrowed views from Arnold, whom a major critic identified as "the fiercest antagonist" of the caliphs and the caliphate system.[296]

The British would revisit the Caliphate Question in view of Egypt's King Faruq's interest in assuming the office in the late 1930s. They ultimately recommended against it.[297] They would discuss it one more time in the context of Pakistan's interest in 1949 to form a "Muslim Bloc" without reviving the caliphate, which the British were enthusiastic about as key to oppose and encircle the Soviets.[298] This would be picked up by the Americans in their later support for the Saudi-sponsored Muslim World League.

Following in the footsteps of Britain and France, which controlled the various parts of "the Muslim world" from the late nineteenth century through World War II, the United States, since the end of the war but more diligently since the mid 1950s, followed two simultaneous strategies to exercise its control over Arabs and Muslim peoples. The first, and the one most relevant to Muslims, was based on the early US imperial recognition and realization (like Britain, France, and Italy before it) that having learned the language of Western liberalism through

---

294. See Sir Thomas Arnold, *The Caliphate* (Oxford: Clarendon Press, 1924), 14, 31, as well as his first chapter more generally.

295. Abd al-Raziq states that "if you want to explore this research more, see the book *The Caliphate* by the great scholar Sir Thomas Arnold, as it contains in its second and third chapters a persuasive clarification." ʿAli ʿAbd al-Raziq, *Al-Islam wa Usul al-Hukm: Bahth fi al-Khilafah wa al-Hukumah fil Islam*, ed. Mamduh Haqqi (Beirut: Dar Maktabat al-Nahar, 1966). The original edition was published in Cairo in 1925.

296. See Muhammad Bakhit al-Mutiʿi, *Haqiqat al-Islam wa Usul al-Hukm* (Cairo: n.p, 1926?), 43. Some have argued, however, that ʿAbd al-Raziq's book was essentially in opposition to King Fuʾad becoming caliph, an ambition, which Muhammad ʿImarah, for one, claims the British supported, hence their neutral stance on the attacks on ʿAbd al-Raziq. See Muhammad ʿImarah, *Al-Islam wa Usul al-Hukm li-ʿAli ʿAbd al-Raziq: Dirasah wa Wathaʾiq* (Beirut: Al-Muʾassassah al-ʿArabiyyah Lil-Dirasah wa al-Nashr, 2000), originally published in 1972.

297. See Oliver-Dee, *The Caliphate Question*, 145–49.

298. Ibid., 150–53.

colonial education, Muslims (Arabs amongst them), like all other colonized peoples worldwide, articulated their political projects against imperialism and local dictatorship in the language of the European liberal tradition as struggles for "democracy" and "freedom" (though the political content of these liberal terms would differ from their European origins to include freedom from colonial and imperial rule), hence the early and anti-Orientalist recognition by the Americans that Islam was not guaranteed as an anticommunist force. For the United States, this necessitated the simultaneous establishment of security and repressive apparatuses across Muslim-majority countries, which the US would train, fund, and direct, and the creation and/or rendering of support to conservative religious anticommunist Muslim groups in order to suppress these struggles in support of dictatorial regimes whose purpose had always been and continues to be the defense of US security and business interests in the region. These interests consist principally in securing and maintaining US control of the oil resources of the region and the price of oil, ensuring profits for American business, fighting communism and anti-imperialist nationalisms, whether liberal or socialist, whose ascent would threaten US control, and strengthening the Jewish settler-colony.

Much of this was of course propelled by the beginning of the Cold War and the US strategy to suppress all forms of real and imagined communist-leaning forces around the world, which included any and all demands for liberal democratic change in these countries. This strategy was formalized in the Eisenhower Doctrine and continues through the present. The Eisenhower Doctrine essentially declared not only the Soviet Union as the enemy of the Muslim peoples of the Middle East, but also all local struggles seeking to establish nationalist democratic orders as enemies as well, on account of their socialist leanings and anti-imperialism. In his speech, Eisenhower stressed that the "independence" of the countries of the Middle East meant an alliance with the United States against international communism:

Many, if not all, of the nations of the Middle East are aware of the danger that stems from International Communism and welcome closer cooperation with the United States to realize for themselves the United Nations goals of independence, economic well-being and spiritual growth. . . . If the Middle East is to continue its geographic role of uniting rather than separating East and West; if its vast economic resources are to serve the well-being of the peoples there, as well as that of others; and if its cultures and religions and their shrines are to be preserved for the uplifting of the spirits of the peoples, then the United States must make more evident its willingness to support the independence of the freedom-loving nations of the area.[299]

Eisenhower refers to the dictatorial royal regimes of Saudi Arabia, Iraq, and Iran as "free" governments. He also addresses the question of "indirect aggression" by international communism, which he sometimes refers to as "subversion." This he proposes to remedy by strengthening these regimes' "loyal security forces." Indeed, Eisenhower speaks of these dictatorial regimes as "patriots":

We shall have heartened the patriots who are dedicated to the independence of their nations. They will not feel that they stand alone, under the menace of great power. And I should add that patriotism is, throughout this area, a powerful sentiment. It is true that fear sometimes perverts true patriotism into fanaticism and to the acceptance of dangerous enticements from without. But if that fear can be allayed, then the climate will be more favorable to the attainment of worthy national ambitions.[300]

Here, we go back to Foucault's tactical polyvalence of discourses, wherein the Western liberal discourse of democracy and despotism and its claims of an impossibility of an Islamic, Arab, or Muslim democracy made possible the appearance of "a reverse discourse," one that posits Islamic, Arab, and Muslim democracy as the basis of material and discursive resistance to Western liberalism and its imperial strategies.[301] In this context, there emerges a Western imperial recognition of the political inclinations of Arab and Muslim nationalists who, like non-Muslims worldwide, had adopted the modern Euro-American and European liberal political vocabulary of "democracy" and "despotism" and launched political struggles in support of the former and against the latter as a basis for "independent" forms of self-governance, which the US was

299. Speech by US President Dwight Eisenhower, 5 January 1957, http://millercenter.org /scripps/archive/speeches/detail/3360 (accessed 22 February 2014).
300. Ibid.
301. Foucault, *The History of Sexuality*, 1:100–101. The history of the rise of the question of Islam and democracy among Muslim scholars will be discussed in my forthcoming book *Genealogies of Islam*, but for the purposes of this chapter, see for example ʿAbbas Mahmud al-ʿAqqad, *al-Dimuqratiyyah fi al-Islam* (Cairo: Dar al-Maʿarif bi-Misr, 1964). Al-ʿAqqad partakes of the liberal concept of democracy when he asserts that "Islamic democracy as such is based on four foundations that no extant democracy can be established without, namely, (1) individual responsibility, (2) universal equal rights, (3) the imperative on rulers to seek [the people's] counsel, (4) solidarity among subjects regardless of sects or classes," indeed, that Islamic democracy "deserves to be called human democracy [*al-dimuqratiyyah al-insaniyyah*] as it established freedom based on the right of humans who had no rights or power before [Islam]," in al-ʿAqqad, *al-Dimuqratiyyah fi al-Islam*, 43, 47.

imperially committed to suppress. Evidently, Orientalism and its culturalist assumptions did not obscure this for US imperial strategy at all.

In contrast with its actual policies and commitments that sought to suppress struggles for liberal or social democratic self-governance around the world, the US has always insisted on marketing itself as a force for global democracy, and as we saw earlier as the oldest democracy of the modern world. Indeed, the US markets what its opponents recognize as "despotic" imperial rule around the globe as a form of "democracy" and "freedom." In line with this public relations campaign, the second strategy the US used to advance its antidemocratic policies in Muslim-majority countries was the importation of European Orientalism, which, as we saw, acquired a central place in postwar US academia. State Department funding assisted by funding from private foundations would solidify Orientalist research that asserted, in contradistinction with the imperial realization to the contrary, that it was Arabs and Muslims (among other non-Christian civilizations and cultures), rather than American imperial policy, who were incompatible with democracy and Western liberal values and that more often than not they love and prefer despotic rule and that it would be considered a sort of "human rights imperialism," as Huntington was prone to argue,[302] for the US to impose democracy and liberal values on them, leading to the conclusion that it would be best to uphold their despotic rulers whose repressive policies, we are told, are inspired by Islam and Arab culture.

This is to be contrasted with the United States, whose population seemed suddenly to be intent on being involved in the country's politics. In the context of the civil rights and the antiwar movements of the late 1960s and early 1970s, Huntington had complained that the problems encountered in the US stemmed from "an excess of democracy," due to the then recent development wherein the previously "marginal" black American population, which wished not to be "active" in politics on account of its "apathy," had by the 1960s begun to "involve" itself in the country's politics, thus overloading the system. This situation, Huntington advised, should be responded to with "a greater degree of moderation in democracy" with all groups in US society exercising "self-restraint" in their political involvement.[303]

---

302. Huntington, "Clash of Civilizations," 20.
303. Samuel P. Huntington, "The United States," in *The Crisis of Democracy: Report on the Governability of Democracy to the Trilateral Commission*, ed. Michael Crozler, Samuel P. Huntington, and Joji Watanuki (New York: New York University Press, 1975), 113, 114.

Huntington's apparent concern for cultural imperialism in the case of Muslim states appeals to the principle of the right of nations to self-determination. Framing this situation as an outcome of the incompatibility, if not outright contradiction, between "Islam" and "democracy," British and later American academia and the Western and US media would mobilize culture and/as religion as a ruse and alibi for imperial responsibility for the suppression of local attempts to establish forms of rule that defined themselves as "democratic" across Muslim-majority countries.

These culturalist arguments expectedly correspond to the post–World War I European and American promotion of the right of nations to "self-determination," initially articulated by Jan Smuts to grant white colonial settlers, but not natives, self-rule, in South Africa, and as Timothy Mitchell has shown, a principle wrongly attributed to US president Woodrow Wilson.[304] As Mitchell explains, British prime minister David Lloyd George would argue that this new rule should be extended to populations who "lived under the rule of chiefs or councils who were 'competent to speak for them.' In other words, self-determination would be a process of recognizing (and in practice, of helping to constitute) forms of local despotism through which imperial control would continue to operate,"[305] an antidemocracy strategy Britain would use in the Middle East after World War I and the US would pursue assiduously after World War II across "the Muslim World."

Models of Islam and Democracy

Timothy Mitchell explains how the production and transportation of coal, which would lead to the large-scale industrialization of Europe and the United States, created the need for materials unavailable in Europe (cotton, sugar, gold, rubber) which encouraged both the expansion of mining and of European colonization across the non-European world. It also "created the possibility of more democratic politics. The attempt to expand democratic control along the production and transport routes of these other materials proved more difficult [than the situation was with coal-mining and its transportation]. Democracy was becoming an ideal, a lightweight claim, translated into doctrines of self-determination."[306]

---

304. Mitchell, *Carbon Democracy*, chapter 3, 66–85.
305. Ibid., 80.
306. Ibid., 85.

Between the billions spent on repressing the Muslim and Arab peoples and the millions spent to explain academically and in the Western media the *need* to repress them and that their repression is compatible with their cultural and religious imperatives and hence a form of self-determination, this two-pronged US strategy in the region since World War II began to be imperiled at an accelerated rate since January 2011 with the advent of what the American media dubbed "The Arab Spring."[307] It was then that concern about the rise of Islamists, who might "exploit" this democratic opening, and who might be antagonistic to US imperial interests, began to be expressed in the Western media and by Western governments, though the latter remained ambivalent in recognizing that many of the Islamist groups vying for electoral victory were essentially friendly to, if not allies of, Western capital and neoliberal imperial strategy in the region.[308]

In the meantime, the US has continued to be the hegemon over much of "the Muslim world," including Indonesia, not only under the murderous regime of Suharto which it helped bring to power in 1965, but also and especially during the post-Suharto "democratic" phase where neoliberal former army generals would be elected to the presidency in accord with US interests.[309] The current president, Susilo Bambana Yudhoyono (a retired army general trained in the United States and an accused war criminal for his military role during Indonesia's US-supported genocidal occupation of East Timor), and his vice president Boediono (former governor of the Bank of Indonesia and a Wharton School graduate), are the crowning efforts of US policy in the country.

As the "War on Terror" went on, Western leaders began to offer Indonesia (and much more recently Turkey) as the viable example of Islam and democracy that they wanted to see instituted elsewhere. Having sponsored the massacres of Indonesian communists in 1965–66 and subdued the country completely to US diktat, representatives of US power would lavish praise on the new regime, as did US secretary of

307. On the invention of "The Arab Spring" and imperial policies, see Joseph Massad, "Love, Fear, and the Arab Spring," *Public Culture* 26, no. 1 (2014): 129–54.

308. See for example the series of articles published in *The Economist*, including "Islam and Democracy: Uneasy Companions," "Islam and the Arab Spring: Bring the Islamists In," "Islam's Philosophical Divide: Dreaming of a Caliphate," "The Turkish Model: A Hard Act to Follow," 6 August 2011. On the US backing of the Muslim Brothers in post-Mubarak Egypt, see Joseph Massad, "Arab Instability and US Strategy," *Al-Jazeera English Web*, 17 July 2012: http://www.aljazeera.com /indepth/opinion/2012/07/201271511521721772.html (accessed 22 February 2014).

309. On the role of the US in Indonesia, see Bradley R. Simpson, *Economists with Guns: Authoritarian Development and US-Indonesian Relations, 1960–1968* (Stanford, CA: Stanford University Press, 2008).

state Hillary Clinton when she declared in 2009 while on a state visit to the country: "If you want to know if Islam, democracy, modernity and women's rights can coexist, go to Indonesia."[310] In line with Clinton's showcasing Indonesia, British prime minister David Cameron repeated her mantra when he visited in 2012 and in the context of the rise of Islamists in the Arab world amidst the "Arab Spring." He declared: "What Indonesia shows is that in the world's largest Muslim-majority country, it is possible to reject this extremist threat and prove that democracy and Islam can flourish alongside each other."[311] Cameron further declared that it was the Islamists (rather than Western liberals) who "believe that democracy and Islam are incompatible."[312]

With such Western-approved "democratic" models being bandied about for Muslim-majority countries to emulate, the erstwhile contradiction between Islam and democracy as far as Western liberalism is concerned seems to have been resolved finally. After all, the American understanding has it that if British colonialism could use Islamic authority to influence Indian Muslims to accept its colonial rule in the nineteenth century, and later to try to impose a secular understanding of governance in Islam in Egypt and elsewhere across the Arab world, why can the Americans not do the same today with their sponsorship of new projects to secularize "the Muslim world" and introduce neoliberal norms of citizenship? The task for Western liberals from now on then is to impose the Indonesian (or Turkish) model or something akin to it on the rest of the Muslim world.

More than a century ago, in March 1910, while on a visit to British-occupied Egypt, former US president Theodore Roosevelt, who had just left office, addressed Egyptians at the then recently established Egyptian University (later Cairo University) on the question of self-government. He would invoke both Arab culture (in the form of proverbs) and Qurʾanic quotations to drive his message home. In his speech, aptly titled "Law and Order in Egypt," Roosevelt declared, echoing Lord Cromer:

The training of a nation to fit it successfully to fulfill the duties of self-government is a matter, not of a decade or two, but of generations. There are foolish empiricists who believe that the granting of a paper constitution, prefaced by some high-sounding

310. Mark Landler, "Clinton Praises Indonesian Democracy," *New York Times*, 18 February 2009.

311. Nicholas Watt, "Cameron calls on Islam to Embrace Democracy and Reject Extremism," *Guardian*, 12 April 2012.

312. Ibid. For a contrary view of Indonesia as intolerant toward non-Sunni Muslim religions and sects, see the op-ed piece written by Human Rights Watch researcher Andreas Harsono, "No Model for Muslim Democracy," *New York Times*, 21 May 2012.

declaration, of itself confers the power of self-government upon a people. This is never so. Nobody can "give" a people "self-government." . . . You know that the Arab proverb runs, "God helps those who help themselves." . . . . With any people the essential quality to show is, not haste in grasping after a power which it is only too easy to misuse, but a slow, steady, resolute development of those substantial qualities, such as the love of justice, the love of fair play, the spirit of self-reliance, of moderation, which alone enable a people to govern themselves. . . . When I was recently in Sudan I heard a vernacular proverb based on a text in the Koran, which is so apt that, although not an Arabic scholar, I shall attempt to repeat it in Arabic: "*Allah ma el saberin, izza sabaru*"— God is with the patient *if they know how to wait* [All emphases in the original].[313]

The Egyptian press, university officials, and members of the audience were outraged, though Roosevelt's personal secretary during his trip, Lawrence F. Abbott, who introduced the published version of Roosevelt's speeches, begged to differ. He noted in the only footnote to the speech that "this bit of Arabic, admirably pronounced by Mr. Roosevelt, surprised and pleased the audience as much as his acquaintance with the life and works of Ibn Batutu [Ibn Battutah] surprised and pleased the sheiks at the Moslem [al-Azhar] University two days before. Both Mr. Roosevelt's use of the Arabic tongue and his application of the proverb were greeted with prolonged applause."[314] Roosevelt not only engaged in mobilizing a theological dictum to preserve British colonialism, but also an American example of tolerance that Muslim countries should follow as a model. Addressing the issue of Muslim-Christian relations in Egypt following the assassination of Prime Minister Butrus Ghali, a collaborator with the British occupation, who was assassinated by Egyptian nationalist Ibrahim Nasif al-Wardani (who was significantly a member of the anti-British Egyptian National Party, or al-Hizb al-Watani, which supported the caliphate and 'Abbas Hilmi enthusiastically) for patriotic nonsectarian reasons, Roosevelt, who wanted to portray the assassination as sectarian in motive, instructed his audience to follow the American example of tolerance:

In my own country we have in the Philippines Moslems as well as Christians. We do not tolerate for one moment any oppression by the one or the other, any discrimination

313. Theodore Roosevelt, "'Law and Order in Egypt,' An Address before the National University in Cairo, 28 March 1910, With an Introduction presenting a description of the conditions under which the addresses were given during Mr. Roosevelt's journey in 1910 from Khartum through Europe to New York by Lawrence F. Abbott," 24–26, available from the *Almanac of Theodore Roosevelt*, http://www.theodore-roosevelt.com/trspeechescomplete.html (accessed 22 February 2014).
314. Ibid., 26.

by the Government between them or failure to mete out the same justice to each, treating each man on his worth as a man, and behaving towards him as his conduct demands and deserves.[315]

Presumably, Roosevelt was referring to the ongoing massacre of hundreds of thousands of Filipinos at the hands of the American military at the time of his speech, which, in fact, did not discriminate between them on a religious basis. As both Christian and Muslim Filipinos resisted the American occupation, the American pacification campaign of the Philippines during Roosevelt's presidency (1901–9), which followed the Spanish American War of 1899–1902, proceeding from 1902 to 1913, would target them both without discrimination. The most infamous example of the violence inflicted on Filipino Muslims by American troops was the Moro Crater Massacre of March 1906, when hundreds of Muslims, including scores of women and children, were butchered. US army general Leonard Wood, who led the American troops in their campaign and had been appointed as governor of the Moro province from 1903 to 1906 (he would later become Governor General of the Philippines), urged the extermination of all Filipino Muslims as he considered them fanatical. After the massacre, Roosevelt sent him a letter: "I congratulate you, and the officers and men of your command upon the brave feat of arms wherein you and they so well upheld the honor of the flag."[316] Clearly, Roosevelt's teaching Egyptian Muslims a lesson in tolerance was not on account of some anxiety about the intolerance of American imperial or domestic policies in 1910 toward nonwhite Christians and non-Christians alike, but imperial hubris and doublespeak. He would later aver to an interviewer: "That speech of mine at Cairo was a crackery Jack. You should have seen the Fuzzy Wuzzies' faces as I told them off. They expected candy, but I gave them the big stick. And they squirmed, Sir; they squirmed."[317]

A century later, in June 2009, US president Barack Obama addressed not only a local Egyptian audience but also the entire "Muslim World" from the same Cairo University at which Roosevelt had spoken. Obama also quoted the Qur'an, not once but three times, and greeted his audience in Arabic: "assalaamu alaykum."[318] Like Roosevelt, Obama wanted

315. Ibid., 27.

316. Miguel J. Hernandez, "Kris vs. Krag," *Military History* 23, no. 4 (June 2006): 64.

317. "Egyptian University," *Egyptian Gazette*, 15 April 1910, 4, quoting Walter Moore's interview published in *John Bull*, cited by Donald Malcolm Reid, *Cairo University and the Making of Modern Egypt*, 43.

318. See Barack Obama, "Text: Obama's Speech in Cairo," *New York Times*, 4 June 2009.

to provide a theological justification for an American-sponsored policy, namely the imposition of a "peace" between Palestinians and Israelis that preserves Jewish settler-colonialism and occupation at the expense of Palestinian rights. To do so, he spoke of how the "Holy Land of three great faiths is the place of peace that God intended it to be; when Jerusalem is a secure and lasting home for Jews and Christians and Muslims, and a place for all of the children of Abraham to mingle peacefully together as in the [Qurʾanic] story of Isra [sic], when Moses, Jesus, and Mohammed (peace be upon him) joined in prayer."[319] In doing so, Obama was clearly stating, in Zionist fashion, that the Jewish colonizers of Palestine are resisted because they are Jewish and not on account of being colonists, hence his call for tolerance and ecumenical peace rather than for an end to Jewish colonialism.

Obama also announced several cooperative projects between the United States and Muslim-majority countries, one of which was "a new global effort with the Organization of the Islamic Conference to eradicate polio."[320] We do not know what Obama might have intimated to administration officials after his speech and whether he thought his audience were a bunch of "Fuzzy Wuzzies," but his subsequent actions spoke louder than his words and indeed made many Muslims "squirm." His polio campaign was the same program that the CIA would use two years later in May 2011 to stage a fake polio vaccination campaign to capture and kill Osama Bin Laden in Pakistan. That the fake campaign, which used a Pakistani doctor for the task, has imperiled the lives of hundreds of thousands of Muslim children in Afghanistan and Pakistan due to a subsequent ban on the vaccinations by the Taliban and the refusal of local leaders to allow doctors in for fear of being CIA agents, has hardly been seen by Muslims as a tolerant form of cooperation.

Like Roosevelt, Obama did speak about the importance of religious tolerance of Egyptian and Lebanese Christians by their Muslim compatriots while promising to end institutionalized discrimination against American Muslims which followed 9/11, and justifying the ongoing murderous American military campaigns in Afghanistan and Pakistan (he could have added Yemen but he did not), though not in Iraq, as necessary. These were countries where his administration was killing not only non-American Muslims but also targeting American Muslim (non-white) citizens for assassination. Obama would precede his secretary of state in announcing Indonesia as a model of tolerance for the

319. Ibid.
320. Ibid.

Muslim world: "I saw it firsthand as a child in Indonesia, where devout Christians worshiped freely in an overwhelmingly Muslim country." Obama had lived in Indonesia from 1967 to 1971, in the wake of the massive US-sponsored massacres, yet, while he remembers well Muslim "tolerance" towards Christians, he seems to remember little of the US-imposed terror and American sponsorship of right-wing Muslim groups to kill communists in the wake of the 1965 Suharto coup, an intolerance the US had engineered, and which would expand later to Afghanistan and spill over to right-wing Muslim intolerance of Christians in places like Egypt (many of whose right-wing sectarian Islamists were recruited by the US for its anti-Soviet war in Afghanistan) to which Obama was now counseling tolerance.

Offensive Democracy

It is in the contemporary context and timeframe that the "Western" understanding of "Islamic culture" would lose the essentialist character that Western Orientalism and policy makers imposed on it in Orientalist studies and during the Cold War years when they supported right-wing antidemocratic Islamisms against all leftist democratic forces (secularist and religious alike) in the Muslim world, and would acquire a malleable notion of culture that could be used to bring the Muslim world closer to Western understandings of an imperialism-friendly "democracy" and (neo)liberal notions of citizenship, something that the liberal pluralization of Islam has made possible. As Talal Asad puts it:

The de-essentialization of Islam is paradigmatic for all thinking about assimilation of non-European peoples to European civilization. The idea that people's historical experience is inessential to them, that it can be shed at will, makes it possible to argue more strongly for the Enlightenment's claim to universality: Muslims . . . can be assimilated or . . . "translated" into a global ("European") civilization once they have divested themselves of what many of them regard (mistakenly) as essential to themselves. The belief that human beings can be separated from their histories and traditions makes it possible to urge a Europeanization of the Islamic world.[321]

The definitional flexibility of the imperial realpolitik understanding that all methods should be used to preserve imperial influence in the Muslim

---

321. Asad, *Formations*, 169–70.

world remains the operative criterion, and *not necessarily* an Orientalist epistemology. In this sense, it becomes clear that much of the liberal controversy about Islam and democracy has really been about the West's *own* antidemocratic imperial and domestic commitments (which denied and, in many cases still deny, rights to Native Americans, to blacks, to Catholics, to Mormons, to Jews, to Muslims, to women, to communists, et al.), *its* "hatred of democracy," *its* very checkered history in relation to this much touted political system and its fantastical deployment as the very essence of Western culture which allegedly emerged from the very bosom of Christianity. This liberal project is in effect a missionary project to convert Islam to the "highest stage" of Christianity reigning in the West, even if this is carried out under the banner of a "reformed" Islam.

Slavoj Žižek, a scholar who generally holds offensive views of Islam (see chapter 4), notes that "already in the 16th century the French naturalist Pierre Belon could note that 'the Turks force no one to live like a Turk.' Small surprise, then, that so many Jews found asylum and religious freedom in Turkey and other Muslim countries after Ferdinand and Isabella had expelled them from Spain in 1492—with the result that, in a supreme twist of irony, Western travellers were disturbed by the public presence of Jews in big Turkish cities."[322] Žižek quotes a report from N. Bisani, an Italian who visited Istanbul in 1788:

A stranger, who has beheld the intolerance of London and Paris, must be much surprised to see a church here between a mosque and a synagogue, and a dervish by the side of a Capuchin friar. I know not how this government can have admitted into its bosom religions so opposite to its own. It must be from degeneracy of Mahommedanism, that this happy contrast can be produced. What is still more astonishing is to find that this spirit of toleration is generally prevalent among the people; for here you see Turks, Jews, Catholics, Armenians, Greeks and Protestants conversing together on subjects of business or pleasure with as much harmony and goodwill as if they were of the same country and religion.[323]

Žižek concludes that "the very feature that the West today celebrates as the sign of its cultural superiority—the spirit and practice of multicultural tolerance—is thus dismissed as an effect of Islamic 'degeneracy.'"[324] Whereas Žižek quotes Mladen Dolar on the relationship of Europe to the Balkans, the Bisani quote helps us to produce a more general diagnosis

322. Slavoj Žižek, "Against Human Rights," *New Left Review* 34 (July-August 2005): 115–16.
323. Quoted in ibid., 116.
324. Ibid., 116.

of Christian Europe's relationship to "Islam" itself (and to despotism and democracy) and provides a response to Derrida's designation of Islam as "the other of democracy" discussed earlier. The Bisani observation should also be be contrasted with the recent remarks of British prime minister David Cameron and German chancellor Angela Merkel about the alleged "failure" of "multiculturalism" in their countries. What they see as a failure of multiculturalism is not the failure of a hegemonic white Christian culture, which markets itself as democratic, tolerant, and multi-cultural, to tolerate people who are nonwhite and non-Christian and who resist assimiliationist policies democratically, but the "utter" fail-ure of nonwhite non-Christian and despotic Muslims to assimilate into secularized Christian and democratic whiteness. Cameron was explicit in the questions he posed about British Muslim groups: "Do they believe in universal human rights—including for women and people of other faiths? Do they believe in equality of all before the law? Do they believe in democracy and the right of people to elect their own government? Do they encourage integration or separatism?" Cameron added: "Frankly, we need a lot less of the passive tolerance of recent years and much more active, muscular liberalism."[325] It is in the light of this European Christian intolerance and commitment to antidemocracy and "mus-cular liberalism" that it can be concluded, following Žižek, that *in the guise of the "otherness" of Islam as despotism, Europe takes cognizance of the "stranger in itself," of its own repressed.* Wendy Brown adds in this regard:

The Third World, and especially the Islamic world today, is categorized in one of two categories of *lack* vis-à-vis democracy: either undemocratic or democratizing. Third World nations, leaders, and cultures are either the radical Other of democracy or in a temporal lag vis-à-vis democracy. Of course, this is the way the non-Euro-Atlantic world has been positioned in relation to civilization, development, modernity, and Europe throughout modernity, as either their Other or their primitive precursor. This construction in turn establishes First World countries as always already democratic, not democratizing, but fully Arrived.[326]

Within the liberal deployment of the discourse of democracy, which is always articulated in the register of the imperial, Western Christianity, in the form of Protestantism, is said to have produced a culture of

325. "Merkel Says German Multicultural Society Has Failed," *BBC*, 17 October 2010, http://www.bbc.co.uk/news/world-europe-11559451 (accessed 24 February 2014). For Cameron, see "State Multiculturalism Has Failed, Says Cameron," *BBC*, 5 February 2011, http://www.bbc.co.uk/news/uk-politics-12371994 (accessed 24 February 2014).

326. Wendy Brown, "Sovereign Hesitations," 130.

secularism and democracy in the West, and the notion of liberal citizenship as their natural outcome, and therefore, there is nothing to say that it cannot bring them about also to "Islam" (or at least a version of it bolstered by the West) and its adherents. "Islam" and the anti-Western culture it is said to have fostered, as we saw, could very well be "defenseless" against such formidable forces backing this democratic offensive, including those of liberal forms of Islam, thus averting the long-predicted "clash of civilizations." The democracy offensive against "Islam" is therefore inseparable from the imperial offensive, indeed, the discourse of democracy turns out to be nothing short of camouflage *for* this imperial offensive.

In addition to Bryan Turner, other scholars have discussed how the deployment by Orientalists of the European Enlightenment and the Romantic era of the notion of Oriental despotism was also a way of speaking about the European despotism of the period, which they opposed.[327] The ongoing Western liberal discussions about Islam and democracy seem to betray a similar concern, or at least to displace the West's own despotisms and the West's problematic relationship to democracy onto Islam. Thus, once Muslim countries approximate the model set for them by the West, they could be said to have become the perfect foil for the United States—having become the youngest of democracies and the oldest of countries compared to the claim of the United States that it is the youngest of countries and the oldest of democracies. This contrast consolidates the Christian and Western precedence in "democracy" over "Islam's" achievement of it and maintains the same structure and logic of the comparison, providing a further push for the imperial argument organizing the relationship that, Western liberalism insists, links and de-links "Islam" and "democracy" and more importantly "democracy" and the "West." It is within the regnant system of knowledge-power we call liberalism that this is anchored in the service of imperial governance.

---

327. See for example Mohammed Sharafuddin, *Islam and Romantic Orientalism: Literary Encounters with the Orient* (London: I. B. Tauris, 1994). This is not unlike medieval Christian condemnations of Islam, which Norman Daniel identifies as "an aspect of other condemnations, of the oriental churches, as well as of the great heresies which sprang up in, or invaded Europe, and even of each individual intellectual eccentricity. It is in the context of European thirst for orthodoxy that we must see the passion for identifying the heresies that Islam resembled (or might be supposed to derive from), and for specifying minutely each separate count on which Islam must be detested. . . . [The anti-Islam] arguments . . . were intended for internal consumption, and were the better for that if they could be presented as having successfully silenced Muslims in debates which can rarely have happened at all, and never profitably." Norman Daniel, *The Arabs and Medieval Europe* (London: Longman, 1975), 245–46.

British, French, and US (and, as we saw, even at times German) imperial policies included, in the case of the British and the French since the nineteenth century and of the Americans since World War II, the production of certain forms of Islam that could be put in the service of colonial and imperial policies. This involved intermittently the imperial production of "liberal" forms of Islam, "jihadist" forms of Islam, and then again a "liberal-democratic" Islam, wherein the very relationship of "Islam" to "democracy" from the view of American, British, and French imperialisms was being determined by these policies. Concomitant with these policies, British, French, and American liberal political doctrine would deploy explanations of both, the emergence of liberal "democracy" in the so-called West, and the persistence of "despotism" in the non-West, with particular attention to and focus on "Islam." Much of this is a continuation of the othering of Islam that European liberal doctrine, since its inception, relied on to articulate its key concepts of secularism, tolerance, the individual, citizenship, and democracy, which it always opposed to the alleged Oriental and specifically Arab and Islamic practices of religious authority, intolerance, the community, subjection, and despotism. This, as I have demonstrated, is not only a projection of Western liberal imperial commitments to despotism at home and abroad onto "Islam" and the "Orient," but also to showcase Western cultural and political superiority ushered in by the age of secularism through a suspect claim to democratic governance that is deployed in the service of securing imperial aims in what came to be known and religiously defined as the "Muslim world."

What has been unfolding since the emergence of this Western discourse on Islam and democracy then is liberalism's production of a political vocabulary that is central to its understanding of itself and the world around it, whereby subjection and citizenship are produced not as the compatible and complementary terms instituted by liberal European systems of governance but as cultural, geographic, and religious antonyms through appeal to an Orientalist ontology, which in turn enables the production of despotism and democracy as irreconcilable essences that serve as a justification and casus belli for European universalism, actualized through imperialism.

TWO

Women and/in "Islam": The Rescue Mission of Western Liberal Feminism

If European liberalism understood its commitment to what it called and calls democracy as a contrast to and a disavowal of "Oriental despotism," which it projected onto Islam and the Orient more generally, it would soon understand its and Western Christianity's treatment of women as a repudiation of Oriental religions, cultures, and traditions, which, it claims, subordinate women through exotic and barbaric practices. This contrast, as in the case of democracy and despotism, would promote a similar European and Euro-American missionary zeal of proselytizing, converting, saving, and rescuing, this time *not all* Muslims (which liberalism, hard as it tried and tries, has so far failed to rescue from "Islamic" despotism), but specifically Muslim women from the religions, cultures, and traditions under whose yoke they live and from their misogynistic Muslim male captors.

This would not be a novel *mission* for Western liberalism. The Ottoman capitulations to European countries from the sixteenth century onward were predicated on conceding to these countries the right to protect and even to represent different populations residing within the Ottoman Empire. In addition to European nationals, European countries were interested in extending their "protection" to Ottoman Christians (and later to Jews) of various denominations and ethnicities, a condition that would continue until the

Lausanne Treaty of 1923, which put an end to the capitulations (in Egypt, this would happen as late as 1949).

From the 1830s onward, European countries would also seek to intervene and defend European colonial settlers (sometimes called "immigrants" or "residents") in majority Arab and Muslim countries including Algeria, Palestine, Egypt, Indonesia, and Morocco, to name the most obvious, which would conclude after the independence of these countries, except in the case of Palestine. It is with these precedents that interest in defending and protecting Muslim women would advance since the nineteenth century, culminating in the arguments of the Bush administration and its neoconservative allies to invade Afghanistan to *save and rescue* Afghani women following the events of September 11, 2001.

As in the case of democracy, the link between European civilization, Protestant Christianity, and women is an important one that emerges since the eighteenth century, not only on the part of colonial officials who emphasized the oppressiveness of Oriental cultures toward women, most manifest in Chinese foot-binding, Indian widow-burning (or sati), and child marriage, and the gender segregation of Muslim societies, their oppressive yet enticing institution of the harem, and most prominently the so-called veil or hijab, but also one that was constitutive of eighteenth- and nineteenth-century consciousness and analysis of the emergent white women's and white feminist movements, whether in Christian Europe, or in the very Christian United States (in this regard, Protestant arguments about Catholic repressive treatment of women are also important to note).

In this chapter, I will review the process of universalizing US and West European liberal feminisms on a global scale and the methods and tools by which they came to dominate the discourse and policies of emancipating Muslim women from gender-based discrimination in their societies and countries and how Western liberalism links and delinks the latter to "Islam." I will focus on the linkage of such emancipation to liberal definitions of rights, and specifically of women's rights as human rights. I will also show how this is a direct outcome of the weakening of the Soviet Union during the last decade of the Cold War, leading to its final collapse in 1991, thus neutralizing socialist and anti-imperialist resistance to Western liberalism and its developmentalist and anticapitalist agenda, which would be replaced by the successful rise of a US-led neoliberal order and its corresponding political agendas of globalizing capital that have dominated the globe since.

Beginning in the 1970s, the most obvious transformation has been the governmentalization of gender issues of equality, discrimination, violence, and sexuality under the rubric of "rights." If, as we saw in the previous chapter, European powers insisted on transforming Islam and Shariʿa to accord with a new conception of governance they termed "democracy," the governmentalization of women's rights, as we will see in this chapter, through American legislation and international agreements and United Nations protocols and accords, would lead to a new attack on what Western and Westernized liberals identified as the last bastion of Shariʿa in Muslim-majority countries, namely "personal status" laws, which had to be transformed in accordance with the governmentalized international norms imposed by the US and Western Europe through the United Nations on the rest of the globe.

In addition to transforming "Muslim" or "Islamic" laws, I will examine Western liberalism's project of also transforming Muslim cultures into cultures that are in line with Western liberal variants, if not of transforming Islam itself into a variant of Protestant Christianity, and the role linguistic and cultural translations are designed to play in such transformations that are seen as central prerequisites to the success and domination of the new neoliberal order which the United States and its West European junior partners seek to impose globally.

The second half of the chapter will examine in detail the Arab Human Development Report of 2005, which takes on the question of Arab women, and which is a most illustrative and authoritative document with the aim of bringing about this juridical, cultural, and religious transformation and the ensuing establishment of a neoliberal order. The chapter will also note that the hegemony of Western interventionism, as a humanitarian mission and as a moral imperative of sorts, is shared even by those scholars who write well-informed correctives to the prevailing liberal feminist discourse on Muslim women yet remain committed to feminist "human rights internationalism."

White Feminism and (Protestant) Christianity

It is hardly coincidental that it would be Montesquieu himself who would elaborate on the situation of Oriental and Muslim women in his 1721 novel *Lettres Persanes* (*Persian Letters*), as a precursor to his production of Oriental despotism in *The Spirit of the Laws* (as we already discussed in the previous chapter), published twenty-seven years later in 1748. It is in the *Persian Letters* that Muslim women are represented as enslaved in harems, deprived of "liberty," compared to women in Christian Europe. Following Montesquieu's *feminist Orientalism*, the theme of enslaved Muslim women would become a common theme in French literature. As Pauline Kra explains, in eighteenth-century France and following Montesquieu, "the image of oriental despotism was used in political writings as a negative model for the denunciation of French absolutism. Similarly, in social satire polygamy provided the negative standard by which to measure the corruption of morals and the subordination of women."[1] Joyce Zonana adds that while "the condition of women is not Montesquieu's central concern," he uses "the harem [a]s his functional model of despotism."[2]

But this did not only predominate in French literature. In her foundational text for Western liberal feminism, Mary Wollstonecraft would deploy the image of the enslaved Muslim woman to scandalize Christian Europeans for their treatment of Christian women, thus inaugurating a Western *Orientalist feminism* that persists to the present.[3] She would declare "that the books of instruction [for women], written by men of genius, have had the same tendency as more frivolous productions; and that in the true style of Mahometanism, [women] are treated as a kind of subordinate beings, and not as a part of the human species."[4] As Zonana explains, Wollstonecraft "reserves her fullest scorn for the gendered despotism that she sees as a defining feature of Eastern life and a perverse corruption of Western values. . . . [Indeed] any aspect of the European treatment of women that Wollstonecraft finds objectionable she labels as Eastern."[5] Wollstonecraft perpetuated the European Christian myth that women according to Islam have no soul. In her *Vindication of the Rights of Woman*, she "reproduces and intensifies the spurious 'fact' about 'Mahometanism,' indeed, using it as a cornerstone of her argument for women's rights in the West."[6] Zonana asserts that "the feminism of Wollstonecraft's *Vindication of the Rights of Woman* ultimately reduces itself to what would have been in her time a relatively noncontroversial plea: that the West rid itself of its oriental ways, becoming as a consequence more Western—that is, more rational, enlightened,

---

1. Pauline Kra, "The Role of the Harem in Imitations of Montesquieu's *Lettres Persanes*," *Studies on Voltaire and the Eighteenth Century* 182 (1979): 273.
2. Joyce Zonana, "The Sultan and the Slave: Feminist Orientalism and the Structure of *Jane Eyre*," *Signs* 18, no. 3 (Spring 1993): 598.
3. Mary Wollstonecraft, *A Vindication of the Rights of Woman* (New York: Dover, 1996).
4. Ibid., 6–7.
5. Zonana, "The Sultan," 600.
6. Ibid., 600, also 600–602. On the views of Western feminists of Muslim women, see also the pioneering article of Leila Ahmed, "Western Ethnocentrism and Perceptions of the Harem," *Feminist Studies* 8, no. 3 (Fall 1982): 521–34.

reasonable."[7] In this vein, Wollstonecraft would often analogize English society and its discrimination against women to "Eastern despotism."[8]

Wollstonecraft was following in the tradition of the late-seventeenth-century (1696) English pamphlet *An Essay In Defence of the Female Sex . . . Written by a Lady*, which posited African slavery and Muslim women, depicted as slaves, as analogical to the status endured by Christian English women. Bernadette Andrea argues that "when applied to the Islamic as opposed to the transatlantic case [of slavery]," the slave analogy posited as an antislavery argument "encapsulate[s] the orientalism associated with emerging liberal feminism, which articulated its goal of expanded property rights for 'freeborn Englishwomen' through the negative foil of those women who 'are born slaves' in the 'Eastern parts of the World.' "[9] That unlike Christian European women, Muslim women had a right to own property since the seventh century seemed immaterial to these European Christian projections.

Such were the dominant views of Muslim women, which were first propagated by Orientalist European Christian male travelers of the eighteenth century. Andrea reviews this literature and how this "patriarchal" male travel literature was often deployed in order to limit the rights of European Christian women, who were depicted as living in a paradise of gender relations, threatening them with the imagined slavery of Muslim women were they to get out of line.[10] That the emergent Christian liberal feminists would capitalize on this fantasy to describe their oppression as "Oriental" in nature, by accusing their Christian Western society of "Oriental despotism" of which the latter needed to rid itself as part of its own Occidentalization, clarifies the early alliance between feminist Orientalists and Orientalist feminists.

Margaret Hunt asserts in this regard that early feminists like Wollstonecraft "assumed that Western European women were far better off than women living in Muslim lands."[11] Yet, and as Andrea asserts, this was being argued when European Christian married women had no right to property until the end of the nineteenth century when

---

7. Zonana, "The Sultan," 602. On Wollstonecraft's consolidation of Orientalist feminism, see Bernadette Andrea, "Islam, Women, and Western Responses: The Contemporary Relevance of Early Modern Investigations," *Women's Studies* 38 (2009): 273–92.

8. Margaret R. Hunt, "Women in Ottoman and Western European Law Courts: Were Western European Women Really the Luckiest Women in the World?" in *Structures and Subjectivities: Attending to Early Modern Women*, ed. Joan E. Hartman and Adele Seeff (Dover: University of Delaware Press, 2007), 176.

9. Bernadette Andrea, "Islam, Women, and Western Responses," 282.

10. Ibid., 276–80.

11. Hunt, "Women in Ottoman and Western European Law Courts," 176.

"The Married Women's Property Act" was passed; correspondingly, under Islamic law, Muslims cannot be enslaved (hence, the fallacy of the "Muslim wife as slave") and Muslim women always had an inalienable right to own property. However, despite challenges within the feminist camp to the alliance between the advocacy for English women's rights and their complicity with orientalism and other imperialist discourses, the view that Western women—and in the contemporary world, American women—are the "freest" women in the world as opposed to inherently oppressed Muslim women is still widespread.[12]

These dominant views were not all-encompassing at the dawn of the West European liberal era. Some voices of dissent were present, but they would remain marginal. The most prominent among them was perhaps Lady Mary Wortley Montagu, wife of the British ambassador to the Ottoman Empire in 1717–18. She was the earliest to question many of the European Christian fantasies about Muslim women. Montagu's impression of Ottoman Muslim women in Istanbul, which she recorded in her 1761 posthumously published book *Turkish Embassy Letters* (though the book was written around the same time as Montesquieu's *Persian Letters*), was so positive that she lamented the absence of the freedoms they enjoy among European Christian women.[13] She would go as far as to describe Ottoman Muslim women as "the only free people in the empire."[14]

Montagu's observations, however, have, as Andrea notes, often been dismissed by modern scholarship "as 'perverse' rather than based on historical realities. In [Katherine] Rogers's words, 'Of course [Montagu] must have realized that this was a frivolous proof of liberty and that Turkish women were even more restricted and less valued than English ones.' . . . But it is just this fallacy . . . that blinds Western women to their own disabilities, which continue to this day despite the dogma that Western women are 'the luckiest . . . in the world.'"[15] Montagu would not be alone. There emerges in the early twentieth century more "legitimations by reversal" in the African case. In 1913, John Weeks in *Among Congo Cannibals* writes of the case of female-initiated divorce amongst the Bakongo in the Congo at a time when English women had no such rights, thus unwittingly showing how "primitive" African

12. Andrea, "Islam, Women, and Western Responses," 274.
13. See Leila Ahmed's discussion of Montagu in Leila Ahmed's *Women and Gender in Islam* (New Haven, CT: Yale University Press, 1992), 121–22.
14. Quoted in Andrea, "Islam, Women, and Western Responses," 280.
15. Andrea, "Islam, Women, and Western Responses," 287.

women had greater freedom than their ostensibly liberated English counterparts.[16]

On the American scene, the alliance between white feminist American women and imperialism, as Louise Newman has demonstrated, follows directly from the linking of Protestant Christianity and Western civilization with the treatment of women, and partakes of evangelical imperial missions not only externally, as far as Africa, but also internally, to African Americans and most palpably in the late nineteenth century to Native Americans.[17] As Newman explains,

White middle-class women generally found missionary work appealing because it permitted them to exercise cultural authority over those they conceived as their evolutionary and racial inferiors. Espousing their superior capacities as reformers and civilizers, white women generated unprecedented visibility and status from their roles as special government agents (Alice Fletcher), as appointed state commissioners on various boards dealing with urban problems (Josephine Shaw Lowell), as leaders of the settlement house (Jane Addams) and temperance movements (Frances Willard), or as missionaries either at home or abroad (Helen Montgomery). The woman's foreign mission movement eventually became the largest movement of white women in the United States, attracting more than three million women as members by 1915.[18]

The belief that Protestant Christianity is a precondition to the liberation of women and the advancement of their rights would become a cornerstone of the women's movement, which set itself the double task of evangelizing both the Protestant religion as well as the new gospel of (white) women's rights. This was not only the case in the United States but also in Britain, whose feminists (especially Josephine Butler) had a high value placed on Christianity, especially when it came to evangelizing the Bible and the cause of women in British India.[19] The status of Oriental women would be the reference against which white women would and could measure their advanced status in Christian society, further entrenching the already existing understanding of the liberatory

16. John Weeks, *Among Congo Cannibals* (Philadelphia: J. B. Lippincott, 1913), 128.

17. See Louise Newman, *White Women's Rights: The Racial Origins of Feminism in the United States* (Oxford: Oxford University Press, 1999).

18. Ibid., 53.

19. See Antoinette Burton, *Burdens of History: British Feminists, Indian Women, and Imperial Culture, 1865–1915* (Chapel Hill: University of North Carolina Press, 1994), 42–43, 142–48. See also Barbara N. Ramusack, "Cultural Missionaries, Maternal Imperialists, Feminist Allies: British Women Activists in India, 1865–1945," in *Western Women and Imperialism: Complicity and Resistance*, ed. Nupur Chaudhuri and Margaret Strobel (Bloomington: Indiana University Press, 1992), 119–36.

basis of Western Christian society as opposed to the repressive basis of Oriental societies. Tracey Fessenden argues in this regard:

The evangelical Christianity of the emergent white middle class, with its gendered spheres of home and world, proved especially amenable to an alliance between women's rights and imperialism: the assumption that Protestant Christianity was the most advanced religion, one in relation to which others were primitive, allowed evangelical women to take part in the "civilizing" operations of empire, associated with men, without appearing to depart from their appointed sphere, associated with Christianity.[20]

It is noteworthy that the Christian reference would even be used by Muslim Arab modernizing and feminist men of the same era in their own conceptions of women's rights, especially within marriage. Thus, for example, in his 1901 book *The New Woman*, Qasim Amin imagines the best form of marriage among Muslims as one that emulates that of Western Christian precedents, including that of Louis and Marie Pasteur and John Stuart Mill (whom he quotes) and his late wife Harriet. He echoes Christian marriage vows when he declares: "What interest would a man have better than to live with a female companion beside him who accompanies him day and night, at home and during travel, in sickness and in health, in good and bad, a companion who is rational and cultivated, who knows all of life's concerns."[21]

Amin's Orientalist descriptions of Muslim women would be echoed by Euro-American and European Christian women missionaries in Muslim countries. In her 1907 book, decrying the conditions under which Muslim women live, Christian missionary Annie Van Sommer cited Amin (and the Agha Khan) as evidence of the unhappiness of Muslim women and the miserable conditions under which they live in their "lands of darkness." The notion of "sisterhood is global," so familiar after US second-wave feminism (especially following Robin Morgan's publication of her book by that title in 1984, which included many contributions on the status of women in Muslim-majority countries, and the Sisterhood Is Global Institute she founded the same year as the "first international feminist thinktank"),[22] had already been her motto. Van

---

20. Tracey Fessenden, "Disappearances: Race, Religion, and the Progress Narrative of US Feminism," in *Secularisms*, ed. Janet R. Jakobsen and Ann Pelligrini (Durham, NC: Duke University Press, 2008), 140.

21. Qasim Amin, *Al-Mar'ah al-Jadidah*, originally published in 1901, republished in *Qasim Amin: al-A'mal al-Kamilah*, ed. Dr. Muhammad 'Imarah (Cairo: Dar al-Shuruq, 1989), 478.

22. Robin Morgan, *Sisterhood is Global: The International Women's Movement Anthology* (New York: Anchor Press/Doubleday, 1984).

Sommer appealed on behalf of "our Moslem sisters" to "Christian womanhood to right these wrongs and enlighten this darkness by sacrifice and service." She includes in her edited book a 1906 appeal issued by Christian women missionaries in Cairo: "We, the women missionaries, assembled at the Cairo Conference, would send this appeal on behalf of the women of Moslem lands to all the women's missionary boards and committees of Great Britain, America, Canada, France, Germany, Switzerland, Denmark, Norway, Sweden, Holland, Australia, and New Zealand." The appeal, which bemoans the horrible conditions of Muslim women, affirms:

The same story has come from India, Persia, Arabia, Africa, and other Mohammedan lands, making evident that the condition of women under Islam is everywhere the same—and that there is no hope of effectually remedying the spiritual, moral, and physical ills which they suffer, except to take them the message of the Saviour, and that there is no chance of their hearing, unless we give ourselves to the work. No one else will do it. This lays a heavy responsibility on all Christian women.[23]

In colonial Egypt, it would be British strongman and ruler of the British-occupied country Lord Cromer who would champion the unveiling of Egyptian women, denigrating "Islam's" oppression of Muslim women and extolling both Christianity and "Western civilization" for their treatment of women. But if John Stuart Mill was a democrat at home and a despot abroad, Cromer was in fact a misogynist at home and a feminist abroad. As Egyptian Muslim feminist Leila Ahmed observes, "this champion of unveiling of Egyptian women was, in England, founding member and sometime president of the Men's League for Opposing Women's Suffrage. Feminism on the home front and feminism directed against white men was to be resisted and suppressed; but taken abroad and directed against the cultures of colonized peoples, it could be promoted in ways that admirably served and furthered the project of the dominance of the white man."[24] This is not unlike President Bush's interest in Afghani women in the more recent past, when his own country is one of the few worldwide who continuously refuses to ratify the

---

23. Annie Van Sommer, *Our Muslim Sisters: A Cry of Need from Lands of Darkness Interpreted by Those Who Heard It* (New York: F. H. Revell, 1907), introduction. I have consulted with an online unpaginated version of the book. http://archive.org/stream/ourmoslemsisters30178gut/30178-8 .txt (accessed 24 February 2014). On similar Christian missionary views of Islam, see Leila Ahmed, *Women and Gender in Islam*, 153–54.

24. Ahmed, *Women and Gender in Islam*, 153. On Cromer's position on women's suffrage in Britain, see also Roger Owen, *Lord Cromer* (Oxford: Oxford University Press, 2004), 374–76.

Convention on the Elimination of all Forms of Discrimination against Women (CEDAW) in any form. Zillah Eisenstein asserts that "Bush's policies [at home] undermine gender rights for women. Shortly after Bush took office he closed and downsized numerous government offices focused on women's interest and rights in the realm of work," in addition to numerous other measures weakening the position of American women and withdrawing existing state benefits to them.[25]

In addition to Christianity and religion more generally, racial debates and Social Darwinism would also be highly influential factors in the white American women's movement. Whereas second- and third-wave American feminisms in the second half of the twentieth century dissociated themselves from white feminism's earlier connections to Protestant Christianity, their secularism would depend on narratives of social evolution and progress that are not unconnected to the values ascribed to nineteenth-century Protestantism that would become central to their projects. Indeed, contemporary secular academic feminism in the United States, as Fessenden points out, continues to announce and obscure "its debt to an implicitly Protestant narrative of emancipation" in instructive ways.[26] The emergence of Muslim women as another pole of contrast to white Christian women since the nineteenth century is central to this Weltanschauung. That the so-called Muslim veil would become, as Jasbir Puar astutely observes, "one of the most self/othering mechanisms in the history of Western feminisms,"[27] is one of its more obvious manifestations. This would have its impact in Muslim societies. Leila Ahmed recognizes that "colonialism's use of feminism to promote the culture of the colonizers and undermine native culture has . . . imparted to feminism in non-Western societies the taint of having served as an instrument of colonial domination. . . . That taint has undoubtedly hindered the feminist struggle within Muslim societies."[28]

This understanding of the structural position of Muslim women and "Islam's" attitude towards them would also be adopted by the Westernizing Russian Bolsheviks during the Soviet state's expansion of its authority over Central Asia. Soviet Socialism's understanding of the

---

25. Zillah Eisenstein, *Sexual Decoys: Gender, Race and War in Imperial Democracy* (London: Zed Books, 2007), 171. On the diminution of the status of American women in US society after 9/11 in the context of their recruitment to save Afghani women, see also Susan Faludi, *The Terror Dream: Fear and Fantasy in Post-9/11 America* (New York: Metropolitan Books, 2007).

26. Fessenden, "Disappearances." 141.

27. Jasbir K. Puar, *Terrorist Assemblages: Homonationalism in Queer Times* (Durham, NC: Duke University Press, 2007), 181.

28. Leila Ahmed, *Women and Gender in Islam*, 167.

Woman Question, unlike its position on other liberal forms of justice, seemed to meet liberal feminism when it came to Muslim women. Leon Trotsky would express this clearly in a speech he delivered in 1924:

In the movement of the peoples of the East woman will play a greater role than in Europe and here. [*applause*] Why? Just precisely because Eastern woman is incomparably more fettered, crushed and befuddled by prejudices than is the Eastern man and because new economic relations and new historical currents will tear her out of the old motionless relations with even greater force and abruptness than they will man. Even today we can still observe in the East the rule of Islam, of the old prejudices, beliefs and customs but these will more and more turn to dust and ashes. . . . And so in the East the old beliefs which appear to be so deep are actually but a shadow of the past: in Turkey they abolished the caliphate and not a single hair fell out of the heads of those who violated the caliphate; this means that the old beliefs have rotted and that with the coming historical movement of the toiling masses the old beliefs will not present a serious obstacle. And this, moreover, means that the Eastern woman who is the most paralyzed in life, in her habits and in creativity, the slave of slaves, that she, having at the demand of the new economic relations taken off her cloak will at once feel herself lacking any sort of religious buttress; she will have a passionate thirst to gain new ideas, a new consciousness which will permit her to appreciate her new position in society.[29]

The policies of the Soviet authorities and their understanding of the "inferiority" of Muslim women as a "surrogate proletariat" would lead them to see in them a revolutionary potential that could overturn "traditional" authority in Muslim societies which lacked an industrial male, let alone a female, proletariat.[30] The Zhenotdel (the Soviet Department for Work among Women which was set up in 1919 and dissolved by Stalin in 1930) would be actively involved in this mission.[31] The leadership in charge of liberating Muslim Central Asian Women was "almost exclusively in the hands of outsiders. Characteristically, most of the latter were Russian, Armenian, or [European] Jewish. . . . They brought with

29. Leon Trotsky, "Perspectives and Tasks in the East," Speech delivered on the third anniversary of the Communist University for Toilers in the East in the USSR on 21 April 1924 (London: Index Books, 1973), available online on http://www.marxists.org/archive/trotsky/1924/04/perspectives .htm (accessed 24 February 2014).

30. For a history of the Soviet approach, see Gregory J. Massell, *The Surrogate Proletariat: Moslem Women and Revolutionary Strategies in Soviet Central Asia, 1919–1929* (Princeton, NJ: Princeton University Press, 1974).

31. For their work among Russian women and the differing approaches to their liberation, see Elizabeth A. Wood, *The Baba and the Comrade: Gender and Politics in Revolutionary Russia* (Bloomington: Indiana University Press, 1997).

them . . . a sense of moral outrage characteristic of European radicals exposed to feminist as well as socialist ideology."[32]

This is not to say that Westernized Muslim women did not partake of the effort. Several did. Prominent amongst them was the feminist Soviet ideologue Anna Nukhrat, "a talented Chuvash teacher and writer, raised first in a Moslem and then in a Russian milieu of Bashkiria, passionately committed to the causes of secular revolution in Russia's traditional societies, and devoting all of her energies to organizational and propaganda work among Central Asian women."[33] The Second International Conference of Communist Women in June 1921, attended by Alexandra Kollontai, Clara Zetkin, Nadezhda Krupskaya, and Inessa Armand, provided "the most impressive and memorable moment at the conference," namely the sight of Central Asian women, "most of them veiled, and some removed their veils briefly in order to address the assembly."[34] A number of Soviet European women were touched by the fact that they were being addressed by those who might have been "harem girls," living under "grim, barbarian slavery" before the revolution. Members of the audience were reportedly "deeply moved," "stunned," and "reduced to tears."[35] That the course the Soviets followed to "liberate" these women was a liberal and not a socialist one, and addressed their situation "primarily in individualistic and libertarian" terms, is significant.[36]

That Muslim Central Asian women who were veiled were urban (and sometime rural) elites, and not the urban poor, peasant or nomadic women, and were thus a minority population among the mostly non-urban Muslim women, did not deter Soviet feminists from staging public unveilings across cities in Central Asia as a sign of liberation (ironically, Soviet feminists seemed interested in liberating the rich "feudal" and "bourgeois" women who were veiled, rather than focus on the struggles of the majority of poor peasant and nomadic tribal women who were not).[37] The issue of unveiling, however, was not initially seen as the necessary condition for the liberation of women of the "East." Major voices in the Soviet leadership had opposed unveiling as not a priority and did not see veiling as an obstacle to liberation. Indeed, calls

32. Massell, *The Surrogate Proletariat*, 134.
33. Ibid., 133–34.
34. Ibid., 135.
35. Ibid.
36. Ibid., 141.
37. See Douglas Northrop, *Veiled Empire: Gender & Power in Stalinist Central Asia* (Ithaca, NY: Cornell University Press, 2004), 42–46.

for public unveilings would be labeled "Left deviation."[38] By the mid 1920s, the Zhenotdel, among other Soviet organs, would increasingly insist on and push for unveiling, which would finally become official Soviet policy in 1926–27, and would manifest spectacularly in the public unveilings in Uzbekistan on International Women's Day, 8 March 1927. That the mid 1920s efforts pushing for unveiling would coincide with the emergent liberal feminist attack on the veil, worn by elite and middle-class urban women, in Cairo (which followed British colonialism's condemnation of it) led by Huda Sha'rawi, an elite woman herself, who took off the veil in 1923 after she attended a woman's suffrage conference in Rome (upon her return from Rome, she founded the Egyptian Feminist Union), shows the shared liberal values between Western Christian missionary women and European colonial feminists more generally, liberal Muslim elite women, and Soviet socialist women, whether European or Central Asian, in this period. The Turkish example would also be ever present in Soviet strategy in light of Atatürk's Europeanization campaign introduced in 1924, leading to the Latinization of the Turkish alphabet and the legal ban on the fez for men and the veil for women.[39] If the bourgeois Turkish regime banned veiling, the argument went, would the Soviet communists be any less radical? The Soviet mission to liberate Muslim women in the 1920s, as we will see, would find many parallels in the "women's rights" movement led by Euro-American and West European liberal feminists half a century later, and by the US government itself to achieve similar goals.[40] It would not be until the dawn of African and Asian anticolonial revolts that the Soviet Union would shift its approach to women's issues, especially Third World women's issues, from the liberal individualism of its early years to a more developmentalist socialist approach.

In the context of the more recent battle represented by Western feminisms as one between a feminist West and a misogynist Islam(ism), Rosalind Morris astutely summarizes this feminist mission in the wake of 2001:

The Eastern Question was always also the Woman Question. . . . To understand the current moment as one in which the Woman Question dominates, constituting as it does the justificatory rationale for both Islamist and anti-Islamist policy, requires a

38. Ibid., 81.
39. Ibid., 79–82.
40. On the Soviet effort to end veiling through their 1927 policy of "hujum" in Uzbekistan, see Northrop, *Veiled Empire*, 69–101.

recognition that this question is not interior to Islamism, but that it is perhaps the most important site of complicity and mutual entailment in a war that encompasses us all. The Woman Question is, in fact, the hinge or point at which a politics of the nation become that of international relations. It is there that absolute freedom and absolute lack of freedom turn on each other. Which is to say, the Woman Question is also always the Eastern Question.[41]

We can add to Morris's formulation that *the Western Question is also the Woman Question*, and that the Woman Question has also become in turn the Western Question. It is the position of women in the West and inside Christianity that is fantasized and fictionalized as one of equality, and that, indeed, violations of such equality, "rare" as they are, are always already noncultural and nonreligious aberrations. Part of the ongoing self-making of the West today is its projection and championing of itself on account of the (fictional) equal position of its women with its men, which must always be contrasted primarily with the position of Muslim women of the East and especially in "Islam." If, as we observed in chapter 1, the Eastern Question was always the Western Question, and the Question of Oriental and Islamic despotism was always the question of the Western "hatred of democracy," then the Woman Question as the Eastern and Western Questions is just another instance (and there are more) in this series of Western projections.

A major example of this is the French government's ban on the headscarf in French public schools and the controversy this generated. In her important book about the subject, Joan Scott wonders "what is it about the status of women in Islam that invites special remedial attention [by Europeans]?"[42] Scott situates the French legal ban in Europe's own identity crisis in the context of the emergence of the European Union and the attendant threats to national sovereignty of member states:

Depending on particular [European] national histories, the idealization of the nation has taken various forms. In France it has taken the form of an insistence on the values and beliefs of the republic, said to be the realization of the principles of the Enlightenment in their highest, most enduring form. This image of France is mythical; its power and appeal rests, to a large degree, on its negative portrayal of Islam. The objectification of Muslims as a fixed "culture" has its counterpart in the mythologizing of France as

41. Rosalind C. Morris, "Theses on the Question of War: History, Media, Terror," *Social Text 72*, vol. 20, no. 3 (Fall 2002): 154.

42. Joan Wallach Scott, *The Politics of the Veil* (Princeton, NJ: Princeton University Press, 2007), 6.

an enduring "republic." Both are imagined to lie outside history—antagonists locked in an eternal combat.[43]

Objecting to the deployment of the cultural as the cause of differences between France and "Muslims," Scott insists that the idea of "culture" itself in these debates is "the *effect* of a very particular, historically specific political discourse" that essentializes France and its imagined antagonists and their difference.[44] Attempting to answer a similar question about the European obsession with Muslim women, Sarah Farris posits the politics of Muslim women's migrant labor and their domestic employment as nannies and maids in European households, as essential. It is in this context that what Farris calls European "femonationalism," in reference to the mobilization of feminist ideas by European (and US) nationalist parties and neoliberal governments rears its ugly head:

The image of the immigrant as male *Gastarbeiter* (guest worker) that was diffused in the 1950s and 1960s, when Europe received the first significant flows of foreigners from all over the world, has not been replaced by the figure of the migrant as female maid. Rather, when women migrants are mentioned at all, they are portrayed as veiled and oppressed Orientalist objects. The public debate on the role of migrations and contemporary Europe's status as a multicultural laboratory has indeed been dominated by an insidious discursive strategy that tends to obscure the importance of those women as care and domestic workers and instead represents them as victims of their own culture.[45]

These discursive strategies are embedded in European anxieties about identity and economics. Farris explains:

Recent discourses about multiculturalism and migrants' integration, particularly in the case of Muslims, have been strongly marked by demands for migrants to adapt to Western culture and values. We should note that one of the essential items in such a list of values is gender equality. The mobilization, or rather instrumentalization, of the notion of women's equality both by nationalist and xenophobic parties and by neoliberal governments constitutes one of the most important characteristics of the current political conjuncture, particularly in Europe.[46]

43. Ibid., 7.

44. Ibid., 7. For another important analysis of the ban in some European countries of the "burqa" or "niqab," see Wendy Brown, "Civilizational Delusions: Secularism, Tolerance, Equality," *Theory and Event* 15, no. 2 (2012).

45. Sarah R. Farris, "Femonationalism and the 'Regular' Army of Labor called Migrant Women," *History of the Present* 2, no. 2 (Fall 2012): 184.

46. Ibid., 185.

That many European feminists have joined in these campaigns is symptomatic of this new European anti-Islam and femonationalist alliance.

The consensus among European liberal and socialist colonial feminists over the centrality of Islam and the cultures and traditions from which it emerged and those it itself generated to the condition of women would be seriously questioned and resisted by many Muslim women, feminists and non-feminists alike, since the 1970s. Their challenge, however, would retreat significantly in the wake of the institutionalization of liberal American women's feminism and its Protestant biases in US government policies that would, since the mid 1980s, be universalized through the United Nations and US imperial organs worldwide, and which would produce a new class of Muslim liberal feminists who would abet and endorse many of Western liberal feminism's positions on women and Islam.[47]

Western Liberal Feminism on a Global Scale

In the 1970s, as a certain white American liberal feminism begins to entrench itself in the United States political sphere at the official level and more principally in US law (though this would involve some important defeats, notably of the Equal Rights Amendment guaranteeing legal equal rights between men and women, which had passed both houses

---

47. It is important to note here that US (and West European) liberal feminisms had many American and European feminist detractors in the 1970s and especially in 1980s, let alone detractors from "Third World" women, including varieties of socialist feminisms, psychoanalytic feminisms, as well as antiracist feminisms. While the bibliographic references to this literature are enormous, some of the following are important to note: Angela Davis, *Women, Race, & Class* (New York: Vintage, 1983), and *Women, Culture, and Politics* (New York: Random House, 1984), bell hooks, *Ain't I A Woman: Black Women and Feminism* (Boston: South End Press, 1981), and *Feminist Theory: From Margin to Center* (Boston: South End Press, 1984). See also Kumari Jayawardena, *Feminism and Nationalism in the Third World* (London: Zed Books, 1986), and Chandra Talpade Mohanty, Ann Russo, and Lourdes Torres, eds., *Third World Women and the Politics of Feminism* (Bloomington: Indiana University Press, 1991). See also Lydia Sargent, ed., *Women and Revolution: A Discussion of the Unhappy Marriage of Marxism and Feminism* (Boston: South End Press, 1981), Annette Kuhn and AnnMarie Wolpe, eds., *Feminism and Materialism: Women and Modes of Production* (London: Routledge and Kegan Paul, 1978). See also Juliet Mitchell, *Psychoanalysis and Feminism* (New York: Pantheon Books, 1974). Since the 1990s, such US and West European critiques of liberal feminisms have become legion, including in the form of poststructuralist and deconstructive feminisms and the epistemological break instantiated by Judith Butler's *Gender Trouble: Feminism and the Subversion of Identity* (London: Routledge, 1990). It is, however, the liberal (and often racialized) variety of feminism that would be taken up by US state institutions. As for the many Third World feminist criticisms (including by Muslim women), some of them are cited in the text above and are discussed later in the chapter, given their direct relevance to the arguments of this chapter regarding the imposition of First World liberal feminisms on the rest of the world.

of Congress in 1972 but failed to be ratified by state legislatures, which led to its final defeat in June 1982), it also launched itself internationally by exporting its agenda to the United Nations and the rest of the non-Euro-American world.[48] Part of its effort was dependent yet again on non-Protestant and non-European religious and cultural contrasts that were presented as impediments to women's rights and emancipation. Whereas this effort would be channeled through the increasingly powerful discourse of human rights and the emergent human rights industry developing around it, it would yet again appeal to secular, read Protestant, cultural values as those that should be imposed as the norm on an international scale. Samuel Moyn put it thus: while the notion of "human rights" which emerged in the 1940s "implied a politics of citizenship at home, the [notion of "human rights" that emerged in the 1970s implied] a politics of suffering abroad."[49]

The ascendance of "rights" discourse took place at the dawn of the neoliberal global order and would coincide with the weakening of the USSR and its ultimate collapse. The institutionalization of neoliberalism through US-dictated local economic legislation inside the United States was and is imposed by the International Monetary Fund and the World Bank on Third World countries, and more recently on some European countries as well. This is coupled with the proliferation of Western-funded nongovernmental organizations propounding neoliberal arrangements of economic and social opportunities that protect and enshrine "human" and property rights and often ignore or downplay economic and social rights, all the while presenting themselves as, while supplanting, local "civil society" and the state's social welfare function.

A major area where this becomes operative is the international human rights movement to end violence against women, which produced new categories of meaning that it applied to social practices internationally that are quickly adopted by local actors in order to criticize everyday practices of violence. In her examination of how the Euro-American and European discourse of human rights and international law are translated into "local justice," Sally Engle Merry addresses the embeddedness of international human rights activism in a "transnational legal culture [that is] remote from the myriad local social situations in which human rights are violated," rendering translating human rights into the vernacular of

48. On these developments, see Ratna Kapur, "Resurrecting the Native Subject in International/PostColonial Feminist Legal Politics," *Harvard Human Rights Journal* 15, no. 1 (2002): 1–38.

49. Samuel Moyn, *The Last Utopia: Human Rights in History* (Cambridge, MA: Belknap Press of Harvard University Press, 2010), 12.

126

the local "difficult."[50] Nonetheless, it is as translators that human rights "activists," both Euro-American, Europeans and local, "serve as intermediaries between different sets of cultural understandings of gender, violence, and justice."[51] In the age of the proliferation of Western private and governmental financing of international and local nongovernmental organizations defending human rights, it is exceedingly inaccurate to describe those who work in international campaigns of human rights simply as "activists" when they are largely paid employees of NGOs and not voluntary activists in any traditional sense. Their institutional interests, while possibly, though not necessarily, intersecting with their ideological commitments, complicate matters, rendering a disaggregation of these interests a difficult if not an impossible task. Nonetheless, their mediation of the Euro-American and the European to the local is their paramount function: "Intermediaries such as NGO and social movement activists play a critical role in interpreting the cultural world of transnational modernity for local claimants."[52]

But their role is in fact a double one; as Merry recognizes, these actors transmit Euro-American and European (coded as "transnational" or "international") knowledge to local settings and local knowledge to transnational settings.[53] They act internationally as spokespersons for and against local culture and locally as translators of "international" human rights norms. This becomes especially important as gender violence, which is a relative newcomer to the category of human rights violations, has become, since the 1990s, "the centerpiece of women's human rights," with specialized, highly funded NGOs and world conferences convening in the 1980s and 1990s stressing that violence against women is a "human rights" violation.[54] It is within this context that Euro-American and West European human rights enforcers and many, though not all, of their local affiliates "must adhere to a set of standards that apply to all societies if they are to gain legitimacy. Moreover, they have neither the time nor the desire to tailor these standards to the particularities of each individual country, ethnic group, or regional situation."[55] What they ignore, of course, is both the general white Euro-American middle class and Protestant culture from which they and their

50. Sally Engle Merry, *Human Rights and Gender Violence: Translating International Law into Local Justice* (Chicago: University of Chicago Press, 2006), 1.
51. Ibid., 2.
52. Ibid., 3.
53. Ibid., 20.
54. Ibid., 2.
55. Ibid., 3.

norms issue, and the "international" culture of modernity ("one that specifies procedures for collaborative decision-making, conceptions of global social justice, and definitions of gender roles") that is nothing less than the institutionalization of these cultural norms. They remain oblivious to the fact that human rights law itself is "primarily" a Euro-American "cultural system."[56]

The campaign to end violence against women internationally becomes the main theater of events. While the issue of violence against women as a human rights violation was not a major issue at the international women's conferences of 1975 and 1980 (though the Copenhagen document of the 1980 conference does mention it), it begins to be broached at the 1985 Nairobi conference as a "basic strategy to address the issue of peace" but not as a human rights violation. It would be in 1992 that the monitoring committee of CEDAW (which was established in 1979 and whose founding documents did not refer to violence against women) would define gender-based violence as a form of discrimination and placed it within the rubric of human rights. In 1993, the General Assembly unanimously adopted the Declaration on the Elimination of Violence Against Women issued by the Commission on the Status of Women, and in 1994, the UN appointed a special rapporteur on violence against women. The Declaration cautions against and prohibits the use of "customs" or "traditions" to avoid compliance with its obligations. The Beijing fourth world conference on women in 1995 reasserted more strongly its rejection of "the culture defense." The 1990s expanded institutional organizing so much that by 2003 Amnesty International USA would launch an international campaign against violence toward women as a human rights violation.[57]

The general approach then, as now, remains for states to reconcile "conflicts" between rights and "culture," eliding the fact that the "conflict" was principally one between a new Euro-American and European "culture" that insists that the state must bestow rights domestically and the role it demanded of the United Nations that it impose this recently invented US "culture" internationally. The conflict was therefore

56. Ibid., 16.

57. Ibid., 22–23. The more recent United Nations General Assembly Human Rights Council resolution of September 2012, calling for "Promoting human rights and fundamental freedoms through a better understanding of traditional values of humankind," sponsored by the Russian Federation and supported, inter alia, by Pakistan, on behalf of the Organization of Islamic Cooperation, can be seen as an attempt to contest this move. For the text of the resolution, see http://www.wunrn .com/news/2012/09_12/09_24/092412_traditional_files/Traditional%20Values%20HRC%2021%20 Resolution.pdf (accessed 25 February 2012).

between Euro-American and West European imperial and liberal culture that redefined itself in relation to women in the 1970s and 1980s and non-European cultures that had not done so, or at least had not done so in the same way. That Euro-American and European culture is dissimulated under the heading of "rights" and not as "culture" was hardly unnoticed by those fighting imperialism, male privilege, or both.[58] This is not unlike how a Protestant-inspired secularism defines its opponents as "religious" while inventing the very division by which it defines itself as non-religion.

In so doing, however, and as Ratna Kapur has explained, "the VAW [Violence Against Women] agenda has taken up issues of culture and religion in ways that have not only reinforced gender essentialism but have also essentialized certain features of culture and reinforced racial and cultural stereotypes."[59] Kapur provides the example of "dowry deaths" in India and how white Euro-American and West European feminisms are invested in saving Indian women and how some Indians perpetuate these Orientalist views of "death by culture." The white liberal women's campaign to end "dowry deaths" is not unlike the campaign against "honor crimes" in Arab countries. A whole slew of Western-funded nongovernmental organizations, based in the United States and Europe as well as locally, where, in the latter, they are largely staffed by Indian and Arab women, would undertake these tasks.[60] Kapur insists:

In the international arena, the victim subject, in the context of the primary focus on violence against women, creates an exclusionary category built on racist perceptions and stereotypes of Third World women. This category is disempowering and does not translate into an emancipatory politics. It produces the fiction of a universal sisterhood, bonded in its experience of victimization and violence. There is no space in this construction for difference or for the articulation of a subject that is empowered. Indeed, the victim subject collapses easily into Victorian/colonial assumptions of women as weak, vulnerable, and helpless. It also feeds into conservative, right-wing agendas for women, which are protectionist rather than liberating.[61]

---

58. For the US context in which "bad" behavior is identified as "cultural" and collective when the matter involves racial and ethnic minorities, and as an individual aberration when the matter involves white people, see Leti Volpp, "Blaming Culture for Bad Behavior," *Yale Journal of Law and Humanities* 12 (2000): 89–117. On how "culture" is deployed in the US court system in the case of criminal cases, see also Leti Volpp, "(Mis)Identifying Culture: Asian Women and the 'Cultural Defenses,'" *Harvard Women's Law Journal* 57 (1994): 91–93.

59. Kapur, "Resurrecting the Native Subject," 11.

60. Ibid., 13–17.

61. Ibid., 36.

The development of this campaign has much to do with the history of the Cold War, and especially with the US victory over the Soviets, which ended it, and the rise of neoliberalism as the New World Order. In writing the history of this campaign, Margaret Keck and Kathryn Sikkinik, significantly, do not place it within this Cold War and post-Cold War history.[62] While the UN-sponsored conferences on women that began in Mexico City in 1975 and resumed in Copenhagen in 1980 and in Nairobi in 1985 encouraged the creation of international networks of women's organizations, establishing links and mailing lists amongst them, the issues they championed were at odds with one another, and split neatly along the North–South divide. European and US organizations, alongside the UN, pushed discrimination and equality as "the master frames" of the women's movement, though "the discrimination frame did not always include the concerns of Third World women's organizations, as revealed in many of the debates at the International Women's Year Conference in Mexico City in 1975."[63] Soviet, East European, and Third World women's organizations stressed development issues and social justice as key to both women and men, rather than the West European and US insistence on the discrimination frame. The acrimony would be exacerbated in Copenhagen, especially as relates to Zionism and the Jewish settler-colony. These were not only North–South divides, but to some extent would also emerge as differences inside Northern and Southern NGOs.

The Soviet/US struggle over defining human rights is now the stuff of Cold War history given the US victory in the Cold War, but a brief review is necessary. While the US insisted that having the right to work, to free or universally affordable health care, free education, daycare, and housing (which the Soviet system granted in the USSR and across Eastern Europe as substantive and not merely as formal rights) are not human rights at all, the Soviets, in the tradition of socialism, insisted they were essential for human life and dignity and that the Western enumerating of the rights to free speech, free association, free movement, freedom to form political parties, etc., were "political" and "civil" and not "human" rights, and that in reality in the West, they were at any rate only formal and not substantive rights except for the upper echelons of society and those who owned the media and could access it and who could fund election campaigns, etc.

---

62. See Margaret E. Keck and Kathryn Sikkinik, *Activists Beyond Borders: Advocacy Networks in International Politics* (Ithaca, NY: Cornell University Press, 1998), 165–98.
63. Ibid., 168.

Moreover the Soviets argued that it was essential for humans to have human rights in order to be able to access civil and political rights in a substantive manner and that granting formal civil and human rights while denying substantive human rights amounted to granting no rights at all.[64] Perhaps most important in this regard is that the post–World War II US definition of human rights did not encompass in the 1950s and 60s the rights of African Americans to vote, to receive the same social services as whites, and not to face officially institutionalized racial discrimination—all of which were referred to in the US lingo as mere "civil rights." Malcolm X's insistence that US violations of the human rights of African American citizens should be taken up by the United Nations, which had the power to impose sanctions on the United States as a racist state, earned him much opprobrium and a much lesser status in later official commemorations than Martin Luther King, who was satisfied principally with limiting the Black struggle in the US to the arena of "civil rights."[65]

While the Soviet form of a "popular democracy" was anchored in the hegemony of this system of rights and its resultant substantive and massive benefits and massive restrictions applied universally to all Soviet citizens, the US system of liberal "democracy" was anchored in its own system of rights that granted substantive and massive benefits to smaller portions of the citizenry while applying massive restrictions to the larger portions. The post–World War II Soviet system did not need to resort to major coercive means when its hegemonic system did not seem all-encompassing; indeed in a country of some 260 million people, at the height of the 1960s and 1970s Brezhnevite repression, there were no more than 500 political prisoners in the country. Amnesty International's count in 1980 was that the Soviets had no more than 400 people imprisoned for political dissidence between 1976 and 1980.[66] The postwar United States, in contrast, had to rely, especially since the late 1940s, on more massive coercive means when the hegemony of its system was weakened, as evidenced by McCarthyist repression and by the repression of the antiwar and civil rights protests of the 1950s–1975, and had hundreds of political prisoners (under varying legal pretexts

64. See Albert Szymanski, *Human Rights in the Soviet Union: Including Comparisons with the USA* (London: Zed Books, 1984).

65. Malcolm X, "Malcolm X: Human Rights and the United Nations," in *Malcolm X: A Historical Reader*, ed. James L. Conyers Jr. and Andre P. Smallwood (Durham, NC: Carolina Academic Press, 2008), 125–30.

66. "Amnesty International Says Soviet has detained 400 Dissidents; Abuse of Psychiatry Reported," *New York Times*, 30 April 1980.

used to prosecute activists), who are harder to count due to the use of criminal charges to imprison them.[67] The reassertion of the US coercive system would be strengthened through its new racialized and repressive criminal justice system since the 1980s and more so after September 2011 with the legislation of the Patriot Act and related repressive measures.[68]

While in the late 1980s and early 1990s, as the hegemony of Soviet-style "popular democracy" eroded under the increasing US Cold War assaults on the USSR, most Soviet and East European citizens hoped to end the "popular democratic" systems of their ruling Communist Parties and gain Western-style political and civil rights. They wanted the latter not instead of but in addition to retaining those human rights that the Soviet system guaranteed them. In the end, they lost all their existing human rights and gained very little Western political and civil rights, and even the modicum of rights they did gain were more formal than substantive and subjected to the vagaries of financial and class power.[69] It was in this context of an all-pervasive imposition of neoliberalism on a global scale that the US discourse of human rights and the meanings the US gives to "human rights" reigned supreme.[70]

The debates on women and issues of development versus liberal definitions of human rights would begin to recede at the Nairobi conference in 1985, which was held a few months after Gorbachev had taken over as the leader of a weakened USSR. This was hardly coincidental. With the ascendance of the US since the late 1970s and the retreat of the USSR and its increasing economic weakness, development policies which had been advocated at earlier conferences did not seem to bear much fruit in improving the lives of women, most notably as they could not address the world economic system and the structural position of Third World countries, where development was needed, in the international capitalist economy. It is with this notable failure, the increase of the debt crisis, and the retreat of the USSR, that the development and social justice agenda would retreat in Nairobi, allowing the ascendance of the human rights agenda. In contrast, "the issue of violence . . . appeared to offer

67. For comparisons, see Szymanski, *Human Rights in the Soviet Union*, 152–203.

68. Michelle Alexander, *The New Jim Crow: Mass Incarceration in the Age of Colorblindness* (New York: New Press, 2012). Alexander discusses in detail the racialization of the US criminal justice system since the 1970s.

69. Naomi Klein, *The Shock Doctrine: The Rise of Disaster Capitalism* (New York: Picador, 2008).

70. In the above review of US and Soviet definitions of human rights, I am reproducing my arguments in my article "Love, Fear, and the Arab Spring," *Public Culture* 26, no. 1 (Winter 2014): 127–52.

clearer avenues for activism. . . . Violence and development could also be linked, since in many cases violence against women limited the role they could play in development."[71]

It should be noted here that whereas the special organs of the UN have a relationship with the IMF and the World Bank, they are not coterminous with them. They both lack mechanisms of democratic accountability, but something like the World Bank is constituted very differently from something like United Nations Human Rights Commission or the gender and development initiatives. Its imperial mission aside, the discourse (and organized campaigns) of human rights has more of a symptomatic relationship to neoliberal global capitalism: it broaches moments of critique; it attempts to inoculate against neoliberalism's worst excesses; sometimes it pretends to offer something almost like a counter-public, yet it continues to operate insistently outside the economic sphere, the most important of neoliberalism's theaters of operations.

Following the collapse of the USSR, preparations for the Cairo conference of 1994 and the Beijing conference of 1995 "further extended and solidified this network" of international NGOs and the new human rights frame.[72] The situation of Muslim women would become paramount. It was in light of the success of the Beijing conference that Mahnaz Afkhami and Erica Friedl observe that "Islamists" seek to "couple" law and culture and that "Islamic fundamentalism must logically debilitate Islam as religion":

Because Muslims, however, including, Muslim women, need to believe as Muslims, it follows that Islam will have to be reclaimed against, or reimagined independently of, fundamentalism. . . . Muslim women have begun to take an active interest in theological arguments regarding women. They claim the right to interpret laws and religious texts themselves and to learn the skills necessary for such interpretation; they challenge the androcentric and misogynist interpretations of texts; and they are determined to find in Islam justifications for demanding individual freedom and women's rights. . . . Nowhere is this more difficult than in Muslim countries where religious authorities, anti-Western and anti-modernist sentiments, Islamist agendas, and weak economies form very strong barriers to women's realization of their rights.[73]

71. Keck and Sikkinik, *Activists beyond Borders*, 171.
72. Ibid., 169.
73. Mahnaz Afkhami and Erika Friedl, eds., *Muslim Women and the Politics of Participation: Implementing the Beijing Platform* (Syracuse, NY: Syracuse University Press, 1997), xii, xiii.

133

Regarding the "coupling" of Islamic "law" and culture, Afhkami and Friedl understand that there exists an essentialist use of terms like "Muslim" and "Islam," and even "Muslim women," despite the many differences among those identified as such, including "local cultural traditions that historically cannot be justified with reference to Islam. Yet, they frequently are used to deny women rights in the name of Islam."[74] They add that "for activists working for the advancement of women's rights in these various Muslim societies skills in separating cultural conditions that impede women's rights from 'Islam' often are crucial to success."[75]

Here it seems that the task is a double one, namely, separating Islam from "local cultural traditions" and reclaiming it from "misogynistic" religious authorities. Note that Afkhami and Friedl understand Muslim women's "reclaiming" of Islam along liberal feminist lines of "individual freedom and women's rights." In the world of the Western-funded women's NGO activism, Afkhami and Friedl may not be off the mark, but they do seem to leave out those Muslim women who are invested in theological and nontheological interpretations that favor women outside of Western feminist liberalism, like the many Iranian Muslim women who would reverse policies that discriminated against women after the Iranian Revolution and enlisted the support of Iran's mullahs to their cause, with the latter using the mosque itself to spread the message of women's right to work and the importance of contraception, among other issues.[76] They also seem to leave out pious Muslim women who are part of new social movements in Egypt for example, and Muslim women activists and academics like Heba Raouf Ezzat (more on her views later), who do not speak the Western liberal language of rights or an Islamized version of it, none of whom is among the contributors to Afkhami's and Friedl's edited volume.

This is perhaps because these women were not invited (or if they were invited did not attend) to participate in the May 1996 conference organized and hosted by the Sisterhood Is Global Institute in Washington, D.C., whose executive director at the time was Afkhami herself, under the banner "Beijing and Beyond: Implementing the Platform for Action in Muslim Societies," and whose papers (or "some" of them) were included

74. Ibid., xiii.
75. Ibid., xiv.
76. See Parvin Paidar, *Women and the Political Process in Twentieth-Century Iran* (Cambridge: Cambridge University Press, 1995), 286–89, 322–35. On the lively debate on women and feminism in the Islamic Republic of Iran, see Ziba Mir-Hosseini, *The Religious Debate in Contemporary Iran* (Princeton, NJ: Princeton University Press, 1999).

in Afkhami's and Friedl's book.[77] Of the seventeen contributors to the book whose mission is to implement the Beijing platform in "Muslim Societies," only two are Muslim women who live in Muslim communities in India and Malaysia.[78] As for the task of "reclaiming Islam" that the editors set for the implementation of the Platform, "most [participants] dismissed the project as too intellectually, emotionally, and politically taxing . . . or thought it better left to religious scholars."[79]

Violence against Women on an International Scale

The term "violence against women" would receive its first definition in 1994, by the Organization of American States, which adopted the Inter-American Convention on the Prevention, Punishment, and Eradication of Violence Against Women. "Violence against women" had emerged a few years earlier as a term that grouped together specific practices, including domestic abuse and rape in the United States and Europe, female circumcision/clitorodectomy/infibulation in African countries,[80] dowry death in India, torture and rape of political prisoners in Latin America, and female sexual slavery in Asia and Europe. The category "had to be created and popularized before people could think of these practices as 'the same' in some basic way."[81] Keck and Sikkinik add that the category would also serve

key strategic purposes for activists trying to build a transnational campaign because it allowed them to attract allies and bridge cultural differences. The strategy forced transnational activists to search for a basic common denominator—the belief in the importance of the protection of the bodily integrity of women and girls—which was central to liberalism, and at the same time at the core of understandings of human dignity in many other cultures.[82]

77. Afkhami and Friedl, *Muslim Women and the Politics of Participation*, xvi.

78. Ibid., xxi–xxiii. For a critique of the conference and its liberal rights agenda, see Mervat Hatem, "Islamic Societies and Muslim Women in Globalization Discourses," *Comparative Studies of South Asia, Africa, and the Middle East* 26, no. 1 (2006): 26–27.

79. Hatem, "Islamic Societies," 26.

80. On the question of naming the practice and the investment of American white and African American feminists in rescuing African "victims" of the practice, see Hope Lewis, "Between Irua and 'Female Genital Mutilation': Feminist Human Rights Discourse and the Cultural Divide," *Harvard Human Rights Journal* 8 (1995): 1–55. See also Hope Lewis and Isabel Gunning, "Cleaning Our Own House: 'Exotic' and Familial Human Rights Violations," *Buffalo Human Rights Law Review* 4 (1998): 123–40.

81. Keck and Sikkinik, *Activists beyond Borders*, 171–72.

82. Ibid., 173.

That the championing of the campaign to end violence against women would begin to gain traction at the United Nations by 1987 is hardly surprising. In fact, an "explosion of organizing" in NGOs would ensue from that moment on.[83] That the Euro-American liberal discourse of women's rights won out by the time of the Cairo and Beijing conferences, half a decade after the US Cold War victory and the collapse of the Soviet regime, is hardly a surprise occurrence. Whereas groups from the North would initiate the campaign with "counterpart" organizations in the developing world, it would be the Latin Americans who would become the most active members.[84]

From the late 1980s on, it was the US-based Ford Foundation that would become the major funder of the campaign, accounting for half the contributions of all US foundations put together (it should be noted here that the Ford Foundation was also one of the main contributors to the creation of Helsinki Watch in 1977, which would later become Human Rights Watch).[85] European funding would also increase substantially in this period. That a major increase in funding would occur in 1990, the year the Soviet Union was collapsing, is instructive. American and West European "foundations would be key supporters of the organizing efforts that made women's groups a powerful presence at the Vienna World Conference on Human Rights [in 1993], as well as the Cairo Population Conference and the Beijing Women's Conference."[86] The money would expectedly go to Northern NGOs and not to ones in the Third World, which led to tensions and claims that the Northern NGOs did not represent Southern NGOS as they claimed to.[87] Keck and Sikkinik do not see a role in the collapse of the Soviet Union and the imposition of the US neoliberal order globally in its wake in any of this. On the contrary, their analysis of why American foundations suddenly took on the mantle of women's rights is due to "staff changes within foundations" and how some of the new women employed in these foundations felt "passionately" about the issue of violence against women and supported women's rights. The reasons why the foundations

83. Ibid., 179.
84. Ibid.
85. William Korey, *Taking on the World's Repressive Regimes: The Ford Foundation's International Human Rights Policies and Practices* (New York: Palgrave Macmillan, 2007), 93. Korey's book is a hagiographic account of the Ford Foundation. For a critical assessment of the role of the Ford Foundation in abetting right-wing dictatorships around the world, see Naomi Klein, *The Shock Doctrine*, 73–75, 152–53.
86. Keck and Sikkinik, *Activists beyond Borders*, 182.
87. Ibid., 183.

employed these women in the first place remained unexplored by the authors.[88]

It was in Vienna where "women's issues were incorporated into a 'rights' frame, or master frame, supplementing the 'discrimination' frame of the 1979 women's convention and the 'development' frame in the women in development debate."[89] But some American activists did not think the human rights frame was adequate. Marsha Freeman, for example, argued that "women are rarely prisoners of conscience but they are always prisoners of culture," except, presumably, among white women in Europe and the United States where culture only makes an appearance in the case of nonwhite ethnic and racial minorities.[90]

Keck and Sikkinik criticize "critics who sometimes argue that trans-national networks are vehicles for imposing concerns of Western states, foundations, or NGOs, upon social movements in the third world," by insisting that "the violence frame helped women overcome this often sterile north-south debate by creating a new category: when wife batter-ing or rape in the United States, or female genital mutilation in Africa, or dowry death in India were all classified as forms of violence against women, women could interpret these as common situations and seek similar root causes."[91] But this, in fact, did not happen, as rape and wife battery in the United States or Western Europe, as many have noted, are not considered human rights violations.

Indian-American feminist scholar Inderpal Grewal put it bluntly and without equivocation: "In countries like the United States, with patri-archal and often anti-feminist legal cultures, feminist groups did not resort to claims of human rights; it was taken for granted, however er-roneously, that the American legal system and others like it were ad-equate to the task of ensuring the rights of women without resorting to international instruments or the UN."[92] The general consensus that accompanied the new human rights NGO regime was one that claimed that "the North has human rights (with certain aberrations) and the South needs to achieve them."[93] Clearly in these cases, American (and European) liberal feminists followed the Martin Luther King approach domestically and the Malcolm X approach in the Third World.

88. Ibid., 182.
89. Ibid., 184.
90. Quoted in Ibid., 184. On this, see Leti Volpp, "Blaming Culture for Bad Behavior," 89–90.
91. Keck and Sikkinik, *Activists beyond Borders*, 197.
92. Inderpal Grewal, *Transnational America* (Durham, NC: Duke University Press, 2005), 129.
93. Ibid., 133.

In his analysis of the emergence of "military humanitarianism," David Chandler notes that the development of the NGO regime prevalent in the 1980s focused on "capacity building," "empowerment," and "civil society" (and this is of course in line with the democratization ideas we discussed in chapter 1, namely, that Muslims lack civil society and one has to be created for them to advance democracy), "as they argued the need for a long-term involvement in society and a sphere of influence independent from the Third World state."[94] In their stead, the human rights NGOs created a Third World "hapless victim in distress" that needed to be rescued by the NGOs of the First World who play the role of their "saviour" from "the villain, the non-Western government or state authorities that caused famine and poverty through personal corruption or wrong spending policies or that consciously embarked on a policy of genocide or mass repression."[95] For those deploying it, the narrative of salvation and rescue, remains, consciously or unconsciously, within the Christian tradition and mission underlining it, and a continuation of the history of the capitulations Christian Europe imposed on the Ottomans.

The question of women and development would be a crucial part of the human rights NGO agenda, but it was not the same question posed by East European socialist and Third World anti-imperialist activists in the 1970s and 1980s. Now it involved individualistic solutions, including micro-financing provided by private banks, NGOS, and other development funds. This schema not only delegitimizes non-Western states but it also legitimizes Western NGO activism in one fell swoop. It is this, argues Chandler, which led, with the support of these NGOs, to "humanitarian" military interventionism on an "ethical" basis, an interventionism which was inaugurated in Kosovo in the late 1990s and has not abated since.

The role of US imperialism in this would be paramount, so much so that some of its critics would argue that *it should be*. After explaining the racist depiction of exotic gender crimes outside and inside the United States, and after explaining the racialized basis of human rights imperialism, whether of the feminist or nonfeminist varieties, African-American feminist scholars Hope Lewis and Isabelle Gunning, for example, still insist that the US must play its traditional imperialist role, but this time to produce good results, which somehow mitigate its imperialism:

94. David Chandler, "The Road to Military Humanitarianism: How the Human Rights NGOs Shaped a New Humanitarian Agenda," *Human Rights Quarterly*, no. 23 (2001): 687.
95. Ibid., 690.

Rather than function solely as voyeurs of exotic foreign practices such as FGS [Female Genital Surgery], American activists could stop to examine whether and how US policies contribute to the violations we seek to end. For example, American activists could urge the United States government to facilitate the provision of material support for indigenous groups that work against FGS. Such grassroots organizations are often small and underfunded. Their leaders may be castigated as traitors to indigenous cultural tradition and as apologists for Western imperialism. Despite the controversial ways in which aid conditionality can operate, the US could use its influence to promote respect for human rights of women among national governments with which it has aid and trade relationships.[96]

Lewis and Gunning are not alone in their call. In the context of the US war on Afghanistan and American championing of the "rights" of Afghani women and its commitment to their "liberation," anthropologist Lila Abu-Lughod (an American scholar born in the United States to an American Ashkenazi Jewish mother and a Palestinian Arab Muslim father) issues a similar call to liberal American feminists. She does so after cogently reproducing the arguments of anticolonial feminist critics of the last several decades against the racism, stereotyping, and Western-centric views characterizing Western feminism since the nineteenth century and the role the latter assigned to liberal American feminists to rescue and save Muslim women from their male captors:

My point is to remind us to be aware of differences, respectful of other paths toward social change that might give women better lives. Can there be a liberation that is Islamic? And, beyond this, is liberation even a goal for which all women or people strive? Are emancipation, equality, and rights part of a universal language we must use? . . . In other words, might other desires be more meaningful for different groups of people? Living in close families? Living in a godly way? Living without war?[97]

Abu-Lughod volunteers her Egyptian native informants to authorize her plea to Western feminists: "I have done fieldwork in Egypt over more than 20 years and I cannot think of a single woman I know, from the poorest rural to the most educated cosmopolitan, who has ever expressed envy of US women, women they tend to perceive as bereft of community, vulnerable to sexual violence and social anomie, driven by individual success rather than morality, or strangely disrespectful

96. Lewis and Gunning, "Cleaning Our Own House," 133.
97. Lila Abu-Lughod, "Do Muslim Women Really Need Saving? Anthropological Reflections on Cultural Relativism and Its Others," *American Anthropologist*, n.s., 104, no. 3 (2002): 788.

of God."[98] Abu-Lughod's plea is contextualized in the American feminist endorsement of the US attack on Afghanistan. It is these feminists whom she addresses as her primary audience:

Could we not leave veils and vocations of saving others behind and instead train our sights on ways to make the world a more just place? The reason respect for difference should not be confused with cultural relativism is that it does not preclude asking how we, living in this privileged and powerful part of the world, might examine our own responsibilities for the situations in which others in distant places have found themselves. . . . A more productive approach . . . is to ask how we might contribute to making the world a more just place. A world not organized around strategic military and economic demands.[99]

While noting the differential of political power between North and South, Abu-Lughod strangely manages to deploy the language of equality in North–South relations when it comes to women's activism. Her concern (which, like that of Lewis and Gunning, opposes harmful US interventionism), is not necessarily the ongoing involvement of American women in the lives of women in distant places, but the "salvation" form this has taken (and here she differs from Lewis and Gunning who continue to be invested in salvation): "Were we to seek to be active in the affairs of distant places, can we do so in the spirit of support for those within those communities whose goals are to make women's (and men's) lives better . . . ? Can we use a more egalitarian language of alliances, coalitions, and solidarity, instead of salvation?"[100] She concludes by affirming that "missionary work and colonial feminism belong in the past. Our task is to critically explore what we might do to help create a world in which those poor Afghan women, for whom 'the hearts of those in the civilized world break,' can have safety and decent lives."[101]

It remains unclear though how this "help" can take nonsalvational forms, especially as the American feminist movement was in fact revitalized after suffering a backlash in the late 1970s and early 1980s precisely through taking on the mantle of "international" work. Also, as significant (though by no means comprehensive) legislation protecting (some American) women from sexist discrimination and abuse began to be enshrined in American law and practice, the dominant branch of the

98. Ibid.
99. Ibid., 789.
100. Ibid.
101. Ibid., 790.

American women's movement saw these as gains that have remedied the domestic situation in the US and which it should use to revitalize itself though universalization. As Amy Farrell and Patrice McDermott have argued, "'international feminism' and the plight of African, Bosnian, and Middle Eastern women were key to keeping the US [feminist] movement alive" and "this activism and the emphasis on the victim status of Third World women were central to the very construction of American feminism in the late twentieth century. Protecting Third World women formed these understandings of American womanhood and feminist struggle."[102]

In contrast to Abu-Lughod's call for peace and cultural understanding, Inderpal Grewal takes on the difficult task of explaining that the universalization of women's rights as human rights, which presumes women to be "subject to what is called 'domestic violence' across national, cultural, social, and economic divides," has led to the essentialization of the female subject.[103] While Abu-Lughod understands the history of colonial and Christian feminism as something that should not be replicated by contemporary American liberal feminists in their globalizing efforts, Grewal proceeds from an understanding that American feminist imperialism is not just an outcome of certain historical processes but also one that is constitutive of the movement ontologically and epistemologically. She concludes that the "women's rights as human rights project universalized and stabilized the category of 'women' at the same time as it addressed their situations in terms of a discourse of rights and civil society. In forming an 'international' struggle, in which all women from all nations could speak or to understand each other or work together for a 'common' goal, gender was stabilized through practices articulated as human rights violations essentially linked to gender."[104]

In this regard, Anne Norton explains how the enlistment of Western women in "the project of liberating—or simply defeating—the Muslim world"[105] has implications for women at home:

In participating in this campaign, [these Western women] learn to look upon Western models of sex and sexuality as liberating, universally valid, and exempt from criticism.

102. Amy Farrell and Patrice McDermott, "The Challenge of Human Rights Discourse for Transnational Feminism," in *Just Advocacy: Women's Human Rights, Transnational Feminisms, and the Politics of Representation*, ed. Wendy S. Hesford and Wendy Kozol (New Brunswick, NJ: Rutgers University Press, 2005), 47.

103. Grewal, *Transnational America*, 136.

104. Ibid., 137.

105. Anne Norton, *On the Muslim Question* (Princeton, NJ: Princeton University Press, 2013), 72.

They are turned away from the advancement of women's position at home and enlisted in projects of imperial domination.[106]

The Western cultural and political basis of these definitions continues to reign supreme. American and European women who were active in these NGOs are suffused with American and European nationalisms which make them see themselves as "'free' in comparison to their 'sisters' in the developing world" amounting to a "hegemony of first world women's groups to affect women's lives and women's groups worldwide by creating a 'common agenda' that produced women as their subjects and as a target population."[107] Human rights internationalism, as Grewal calls it, "represented the use of [human rights] instruments by 'nonwestern' subjects as a mark of their undisputed applicability rather than as a discourse of power created by cosmopolitan knowledges."[108]

That "rights discourse" was/is associated with "leftist" American and European forces before and even after their institutionalization in imperial state policies, however, obscures how they had always been put to good use by conservative right-wing capitalists in the United States. Indeed, right-wing Americans had invoked the "rights of man" and "natural rights" during the economic crisis of the interwar period to support freedom of contract and safeguard private property from social regulation. As Samuel Moyn demonstrates, this chapter of the history of the use of "rights" is "always omitted from attempts to reconstruct their history as one of uplift because it is an episode that does not fit" in the ideological invocation of rights by its Euro-American and West European proponents as a leftist non-imperial cause.[109] If in the build up to World War II, Pope Pius XI would invoke human rights as a Christian idea, as would many European Catholics, not to mention American Catholic and Protestant groups, in the postwar period it would be conservative West Europeans who would invoke the language of "human rights," as their Americans counterparts had already done, as one that was "most often, linked so inseparably to Christian, Cold War identity."[110] Even in the case of the three framers of the Universal Declaration of Human Rights, it would be "Christianity that defined the[ir] worldviews."[111] That one of the three (the other two were Eleanor Roosevelt and John Humphrey)

---

106. Ibid., 67.
107. Grewal, *Transnational America*, 142, 143.
108. Ibid., 143.
109. Samuel Moyn, *The Last Utopia*, 35–36.
110. Ibid., 50, 53, 55, and 47.
111. Ibid, 64.

was the Lebanese sectarian, anti-Muslim, and anticommunist conservative Christian Charles Malik is symptomatic.[112] Malik would reiterate his understanding of the Christian origins of human rights in 1968 when he avowed that "nothing" in the Universal Declaration "cannot be traced to the great Christian religious matrix." He added that the present forms that Islam took had made it unable to contribute to human rights in contrast with its erstwhile "remarkable humane tradition which should be revived for our times independently from the transience of politics."[113] While the Americans would inaugurate the use of human rights in Cold War attacks on the Soviets in the late 1940s, the campaign would move slowly in the 1960s until it was revived in full force during the Carter Years, in the second half of the 1970s, when the human rights industry itself was born as part and parcel of the adoption of its agenda as official US imperial policy.

Amnesty International, which was born in 1961 in Britain as part of the ongoing anti-Soviet campaigns, would also arm itself with Christian ideals. Its founder Peter Berenson was a Jewish convert to Christianity (and would develop ties to British intelligence), whose conversion partakes of this very same history of the centrality of Christianity to liberal conceptions of human rights.[114] If democracy, as shown in the previous chapter, was being advanced as *the highest stage of Christianity*, human rights would be tagged as the core Christian (and "Western") principle from which the quest for democracy issues, and one of the instruments through which democracy can be promoted. The internationalist dimension of this campaign is crucial. Though communism was the ideology that called for internationalism as a way of combating the world capitalist class that had always organized itself on an international scale, bourgeois liberalism would find its calling in human rights internationalism since the 1970s, an internationalism deployed *not to facilitate resistance* to an oppressive force that is organized internationally, but one that imposes a Euro-American and West European imperial will on the globe engineered precisely to quash any *local* resistance (cultural, social, or economic) to imperialism in its myriad forms.

Reaction in the Third World to the transnational agenda of "women's rights as human rights" seems to vary depending on geographical

---

112. Ibid., 65. Malik would become one of the founders and leaders of Jabhat al-Hurriyyah wa al-Insan (The Front of Liberty and Man), which led the sectarian Christian right-wing militias in Lebanon during the Civil War to defend the "Christian" cause.

113. Ibid., 127.

114. Ibid., 130–31.

location.[115] Amrita Basu argues that "women's groups most enthusiastically have supported campaigns against sexual violence in countries where the state is repressive or indifferent and women's movements are weak. Conversely, transnationalism has provoked more distrust where women's movements have emerged, grown, and defined themselves independently of Western feminism."[116] Basu provides two reactions as examples to illustrate her point, one by the Iranian-American feminist scholar Valentine Moghadam and the other by the Cuban-American feminist scholar Sonia Alvarez. To explain the difference between Moghadam's enthusiasm for human rights internationalism and Alvarez's reservations, Basu states that "Moghadam's optimism about the role of transnational networks may be born of the pessimism she feels about the potential of the women's movements in face of the growth of Islamic fundamentalism in the Middle East. By contrast, Alvarez expresses concern about cooptation because historically women's movements in Latin America have been strong and closely tied to left-wing parties and human rights movements."[117] Rather than look for the Eurocentric and Protestant/secular horror at Islam and religion that sees Muslim women as lacking movements and resistance to oppression, which are abundant across the "Muslim world," or discerning the state feminism of the Iranian Islamic Republic and Iranian societal activism, which would take shape several years after the Iranian Revolution and which forced the government to reverse key discriminatory policies it had enacted against women and to adopt a feminist activist stance on several of them, Basu seems to share Moghadam's pessimism rather than question it. That Latin America continues to be dominated by a class of descendants of white colonial settlers who view themselves as part and parcel of "Western culture" is also not investigated when examining how Latin America, while part of the Third World, does not fit neatly with Asia and Africa in the category of "non-Western" countries.

115. Indeed, this would be the case in an earlier historical period, when the Universal Declaration of Human Rights was issued in 1948. For the varying reactions of Muslim-majority countries to a number of articles, including gender equality in marriage, see Susan Eileen Waltz, "Universal Human Rights: The Contribution of Muslim States," *Human Rights Quarterly* 26, no. 4 (November 2004): 799–844.

116. Amrita Basu, "Globalization of the Local/Localization of the Global: Mapping Transnational Women's Movements," *Meridians: Feminism, Race, Transnationalism* 1 (2000): 76.

117. Ibid., 76. For Moghadam's work, see her "Feminist Networks North and South: DAWN, WIDE and WLUML," *Journal of International Communication* 3, no. 1 (1996): 111–25. For Alvarez, see her "Latin American Feminisms 'Go Global': Trends of the 1990s and Challenges for the New Millennium," in *Cultures of Politics/Politics of Cultures: Revisioning Latin American Social Movements*, ed. Sonia E. Alvarez, Evelina Dagnino, and Arturo Escobar (Boulder, CO: Westview Press, 1998), 62–85.

Grewal importantly views the globalization of these campaigns as internal to a "technology of transnational governmentality." She asserts that "in the 'global' struggle against 'domestic violence,' we see a link between those who recognized this as one of the main 'problems' standing in the way of a better world constituted without gendered inequalities and those who, through this sort of recognition, constituted themselves as ethical subjects and thus as 'global citizens' of an interconnected world." The creation of statistical data, the innovation of new and effective strategies to eradicate violence against women, global networking aiming to produce domestic violence as a global human rights problem "become the tactics through which the question of violence posed by feminist movements become governmentalized."[118] She concludes that this is constitutive of "the power of the West and in particular the United States to institute these new forms of governmentality that reshape the relations between West and non-West, and between populations and states." Instruments of liberal citizenship, Grewal concludes, "produce liberal subjects as objects and subjects of rescue. . . . Feminist NGOs were constituted as key to this goal, and they worked to manage the 'global' population of women whose welfare became increasingly their concern."[119]

This rescue operation continues the coupling of the liberal and the Christian missions of salvation as one and the same. Moreover, the governmentalization of saving and rescuing women renders both the Euro-American and European states and Western and local NGOs the main imperial agents of rescue at the same time as it enjoins the local state to limit its role to the issuance and enforcement of legislation in line with Western norms while forcing it, in line with the neoliberal order, to withdraw from the provision of economic and social services to the population.

Defining the Struggle for/of Muslim Women

Recruiting local actors in the Arab and Muslim worlds would be a paramount task of this effort. The Beirut-based *Al-Raida* magazine, for example, would live up to its name (al-Raʾidah means "Female Pioneer" in Arabic) by pioneering the campaign. *Al-Raida* began publication in 1976

---

118. Grewal, *Transnational America*, 157.
119. Ibid. On the views of the state and secular and Islamist women on this globalization agenda and the way they are represented in it, see Mervat Hatem, "Islamic Societies," 22–35.

and is published by the Institute for Women's Studies in the Arab World, which was established with Ford Foundation money in 1973 at the all-women Beirut University College (later the co-ed Lebanese American University). The magazine released a special double issue in the summer and fall of 1996 partaking of these global changes under the title "Women's Rights are Human Rights: Perspectives from the Arab World." As the Beirut University College had been established by American Christian missionaries, its commitment to the English language is unwavering. The magazine's language is accordingly exclusively English with Arabic never making an appearance except in its title (significantly, the magazine would only begin to issue an Arabic edition beginning in the fall/winter 2001–2002).[120] That the language of publication of the magazine explicitly and primarily addressed itself to an international audience, which includes English-literate elite Arabs, is clear enough. It is also noteworthy that the editor-in-chief of the magazine at the time was Laurie King-Irani, a white American Protestant woman married then to a Lebanese Christian.[121] King-Irani made not less than five contributions (in addition to the opening editorial which she also wrote, she contributed articles and interviews that she conducted with non-Arab feminist heads of US-based women's rights NGOs and with a Lebanese activist) to the issue out of the total of thirteen short contributions.[122]

King-Irani expressed her gratitude to the United States Aid for International Development (USAID) "for providing us with a grant to enable wider dissemination of *Al-Raida* throughout the world."[123] The opening editorial for the issue reports with much excitement about "The Arab Women's Tribunal" held in Beirut in 1995, which, according to King-Irani, who emphasized the question of domestic abuse, allowed Arab women "to join together and form networks to confront . . . violence against women in all its permutations." The Tribunal was organized by El-Taller, "an international non-governmental organization, in co-operation with Secours Populaires Libanais, and was conducted under the patronage of Lebanese First Lady Muna al-Hrawi."[124] King-Irani's opening essay situates Arab women's struggles in a global context as exceptional: "Although the topic of human rights has been high on the

---

120. See *Al-Raida* 19, nos. 95–96 (Fall/Winter 2001–2002).

121. For the history of the institute, see Laurie King-Irani, "Imperiled Pioneer: An Assessment of the Institute for Women's Studies in the Arab World," in *Muslim Women and the Politics of Participation*, ed. Afkhami and Friedl, 101–8.

122. Her Palestinian assistant editor, Ghena Ismail, contributed three of the articles.

123. *Al-Raida* 13, nos. 74–75 (Summer/Fall 1996): 2.

124. Ibid.

world's political agenda since the end of the Second World War, only recently have the human rights of Arab women received the attention and concern they deserve in local, regional, and international fora of discussion and debate." She stresses, however, that these debates "have neither altered traditional mentalities nor broadened narrow visions of Arab women's role in society." King-Irani echoes the concerns of white liberal feminists and Arab liberal feminists when she declares:

The topic of women's human rights in the Arab world evokes controversy and debate because it sits uncomfortably atop several cultural 'fault-lines.' Discussing Arab women's rights . . . forces us [sic] to confront a number of contentious issues: What is the dividing line between private, familial matters, and public policy concerns? What is the difference between legality and morality? What is the role of 'culture' in shaping conceptions of women's human rights, and to what extent is culture immutable? Which should prevail: the needs of the individual or the demands of the group? To what extent is the human rights debate in the Arab world constricted and confused by the ongoing and politically charged confrontations between East and West, liberalism and communitarianism, the developing world and the advanced industrial nations?[125]

King-Irani then "presents" without irony this special issue of *Al-Raida*, which again is entirely written in English, "in the hope that it will be discussed actively, not just read passively, by individuals and groups in *all sectors* of contemporary Arab society [emphasis added]."[126]

In King-Irani's interview with Jessica Neuwirth and Surita Sandosham, "founders of the international women's rights monitoring organization, Equality Now," the American Neuwirth and Singaporean Sandosham inform King-Irani that one of the "first" stories that impelled them to begin the organization was of an Indian Muslim girl who "had been sold in marriage" to a Saudi businessman. Other stories they cite include the case of a Togolese woman who sought asylum in the US to avoid clitorodectomy, a Filipina woman entertainer who was killed in Japan, an American woman killed by her husband who had a sympathetic trial judge, the Egyptian government's attempt to medicalize "FGM" before it finally banned it, a Filipina woman sentenced to death in the United Arab Emirates for stabbing her employer who tried to rape her, the right of Afghan women to work against the Taliban, and a Saudi woman seeking asylum in Canada on account of being mistreated by

125. Laurie King-Irani, "Women's Rights are Human Rights," *Al-Raida* 13, nos. 74–75, (Summer/Fall 1996): 11.
126. Ibid., 12.

her parents in Saudi Arabia. That all the cases, except for the one US case, issue from Africa, India, the Philippines, and the Arab world and not from Latin America or Europe seems to testify to the specifically dire situation of Muslim and non-Muslim women living in Muslim majority countries compared to others.[127] It is in this context of a proliferation of atrocity exhibitions of Muslim and other Third World women that the 1995 Beijing conference would establish the universality of liberal conceptions of rights, of the political, of gender and sexuality, and of citizenship.

The inclusion of women from the formerly colonized world is often asserted as the mark of universalization of white middle class women's liberal feminism as "global" feminism. Class here is sacrificed as a diagnostic at the altar of race, gender, and a homogenized culture. Gayatri Chakravorty Spivak has always cautioned against postcolonial middle-class women's claims of representativity of women in their societies, let alone of what is deemed their "culture." These "experts probably know the local languages," Spivak tells us, "but here class, and yes, cultural difference kick in—feudality without feudalism operates as impatient stakeholding benevolence." She elaborates:

This is not to say that the people from the culture who have remained in the nation of origin in social strata separated from the general academic culture are more authentic representatives of the culture in question. It is to say that there is an internal line of cultural difference within 'the same culture.' This holds not only for the nation of origin but also for the state to which the cultural minority has immigrated. The academy is a place of upward class-mobility, and this internal cultural difference is related to the dynamics of class difference. . . . It also marks the new culture of international non-governmental organizations, involved in development and human rights, as they work upon the lowest social strata in the developing world.[128]

Indeed, what has come to legitimate much of the discussion of "women's rights as human rights" and the relationship they should have to "culture," and in the case of Muslim-majority countries to "Islam," is "the alliances of the international civil society with the benevolent feudal feminism of the global South."[129] Algerian sociologist and feminist scholar Marnia Lazreg has astutely analyzed this structure:

127. See "Equality Now," interview conducted by Laurie King-Irani, *Al-Raida* 13, nos. 74–75 (Summer/Fall 1996): 26–31.

128. Gayatri Chakravorty Spivak, *An Aesthetic Education in the Era of Globalization* (Cambridge, MA: Harvard University Press, 2012), 127.

129. Ibid., 131.

The search for the disreputable which reinforces the notion of difference as objectified otherness is often carried out with the help of Third World women themselves. [American] Academic feminism has provided a forum for Third World women to express themselves and vent their anger at their societies. But the Western mode of feminist practice is no free gift, any more than anger is conducive to lucid inquiry. Individual Third World women are made to appear on the feminist stage as representatives of the millions of women in their own societies.[130]

One could observe this trend since the mid 1980s. But Arab and Muslim women do not only need to deal with the Westernized amongst them who assume the mantle of speaking for them, but also with white European and American Christian women who pretend to do the same. Lazreg explains that "two extreme interpretations of women have ensued. Women are either seen as embodiments of Islam, or as helpless victims forced to live by its tenets."[131] It was in the mid 1980s that Marie-Aimée Hélie-Lucas, a descendent of French colonial settlers in Algeria, and "illustrating this second interpretation," started an "international solidarity network" she called "Women Living Under Muslim Laws."[132]

In a 1984 interview with a British feminist magazine in which she used a pseudonym, Hélie-Lucas (who had been formerly married to an Algerian Muslim man) presented herself as a repentant Algerian nationalist who decided to replace her erstwhile nationalism with feminist internationalism. Speaking to her white British interviewer, Sophie Laws, she declares: "I personally believe in internationalism, also among women's groups, but I am not representative of the opinion of Algerian women and Third World women in general, because you will usually find a lot of racism amongst us, towards you people."[133] The interview seems cathartic for Hélie-Lucas. She explains that "it took me ten years to decide [to talk to you], because I was nationalist enough to think that I should not speak outside." The information Hélie-Lucas wanted to relay to British feminists was not "a one-way process," wherein only Algerian women benefit, "I'm sure we can also give information that would be useful to you."[134] In a postscript she added to the interview in 1987, her concerns moved quickly beyond the situation of women

---

130. Marnia Lazreg, *The Eloquence of Silence: Algerian Women in Question* (New York: Routledge, 1994), 10.

131. Ibid., 14.

132. Ibid.

133. Her interview with a postscript is reproduced as "Bound and Gagged by the Family Code," in Miranda Davis, *Third World, Second Sex* (London: Zed Books, 1987), 2:11.

134. Ibid.

in Algeria to the entire Muslim world. Concerned about personal status laws and the way they affect women, she declared that "one has to face the fact that justice for women is threatened all over the Muslim world."[135] Even though Hélie-Lucas unapologetically generalizes about the entire "Muslim world," she is aware of differences inside it and that certain practices that are injurious to women, like infibulation, that are practiced in "Africa" are not practiced in "Asia," or like the veil "worn in Arab countries is not there in Africa," and that "none of these practices rely on religious principles, but that religion everywhere backs such practices wherever they allow more control over women."[136] Hélie-Lucas is conscious that her repentant nationalism is just like the repentant communism of East European dissident Cold Warriors of the period. Though "I have been blindly nationalist in the past," she confesses, "we have everything to gain in being truly internationalist: in exchanging all useful information, and in solidarity and support. . . . This is the dream which lies behind the network 'Women Living Under Muslim Laws.'"[137]

Hélie-Lucas's focus on information exchange is key to her internationalist networking, both as strategy and as goal. This is hardly incidental to her cause. Spivak recognizes that "powerful international NGOs . . . now control . . . extra state circuits globally. Indigenous NGOs typically have large components of foreign aid. This self-styled international civil society (since it is extra-state) has a large cultural component, especially directed toward gender issues. It is here that the demand for translation—especially literary translation, a quick way to 'know a culture'—has been on the rise."[138]

Hélie-Lucas acknowledges on behalf of Muslim women that "we are in debt to the early Western internationalist feminists, who, 20 years ago, started inviting women from the so-called Third World to international feminist gatherings, granting some of us the privilege to not only be in contact with feminists from all over the Western world, but also meet other Third World women. It is through international meetings that we came to know each other and later found associations at regional or continental level."[139] It was at such a gathering that "Women Living Under Muslim Laws was founded, that women from Muslim countries came to know each other."[140] Insistent that the relationship

135. Ibid., 12.
136. Ibid., 13.
137. Ibid., 14.
138. Ibid., 258.
139. Ibid., 14–15.
140. Ibid., 15.

between Muslim women and Western feminists is a two-way street, where Muslim women can help their Western counterparts, just like Western women have helped Muslim women, Hélie-Lucas gives the example of how her network is supporting five French women "whose children were taken away from them after their Algerian husbands had divorced them. We have much experience of such situations, which are common in all Muslim countries."[141] Recognizing that Western women and Muslim women have a common enemy in Muslim men, Hélie-Lucas, who recently began to use the Arabic-sounding "Marieme" for her first name (instead of Marie-Aimée), declares "for the first time, European women are supported in their struggle against unjust laws by women from Muslim countries who suffer under the same laws and traditions. Their fight is ours."[142]

This internationalist commonality of the struggle of "Western" and "Muslim" women was interrogated by Spivak, who recognizes, in contrast with Hélie-Lucas's claims, that "the Family Code occupies a space within a diversified womanspace. The possibility of the exercise of the Law as right is class-stratified."[143] Despite her generous reading of Hélie-Lucas, with whose views she takes some issue, Spivak insightfully speaks of "a section of the generation of emancipated colonial bourgeois women whose daughters can be and are the agents of negotiation in decolonized feminist space, represented by Hélie-Lucas."[144]

The move to transform what is named as "Muslim" and "Islamic" laws is a strategy that is complementary to that of religious and cultural transformation. Hélie-Lucas is a pioneer in this regard, as her campaign

141. Ibid.
142. Ibid.
143. Gayatri Chakravorty Spivak, *Outside in the Teaching Machine* (New York: Routledge, 1993), 141.
144. Ibid., 146. Hélie-Lucas was not the only one launching such advocacy in the 1980s. The London-based Lebanese Christian activist May Ghoussoub, a former Trotskyist who converted to Western liberalism in the 1980s, would adopt a wholesale Orientalist perspective on Arab and Muslim women and call upon them to abandon Arab "culture" and "Islam." She would be able to air out her liberal views on the pages of the English Marxist journal *New Left Review*, which prominently featured her article. See May Ghoussoub, "Feminism—or the Eternal Masculine-in the Arab World," *New Left Review* 161 (1987): 1–18. Ghoussoub concludes her Orientalist attack on Arab and Muslim feminists who rejected Western liberal feminist Orientalism by asserting that "the double knot tied by the fatal connexions in Arab culture and politics between definitions of femininity and religion, and religion and nationality, have all but throttled any major women's revolt so far," and that "as long as women's organizations or currents in the Arab world seek to conjugate together—either from tactical desire to win toleration or fervent identification with existing society—Islamic tradition and female emancipation, they are bound to end by putting up with women's oppression itself, or many of its dimensions" (17, 18). See also the strong response to Ghoussoub's Orientalism by Rema Hamami and Martina Reiker, "Feminist Orientalism and Orientalist Marxism," *New Left Review* 170, (July–August 1988), and the reply of Ghoussoub to them in the same issue, 91–109.

began during the height of the second Cold War when the Soviet Union was in serious retreat. Her call to transform/reform "Muslim laws" would become much more protracted and generalized, as we will see, and a key item on the agenda of contemporary feminist reform. But what are the limitations of these reforms, be they external or internal to "Islam," for which Western and Western-identified feminisms are calling? Talal Asad questions the intention and the effects of these types of reforms that are often demanded by Western and Westernized feminists. He asks:

Are the Western-inspired reforms in the domain of 'family law' a consequence of moral weaknesses? Or a consequence of the superior power of Western or Westernized re-formers? Before we attempt to answer these questions, it is worth noting that reform in these matters takes the line of restricting the traditional rights of Muslim men and not of enlarging the traditional rights of Muslim women. Thus, modern reform in the Muslim world has never empowered . . . women to contract polyandrous marriages. More significantly, it has never empowered a wife to effect a dissolution of her own marriage unilaterally and without judicial intervention. The reason such forms of in-equality have not been inscribed by the law has to do with the dominant practices of state, selfhood, and sexuality in modern Western societies; it has nothing to do with moral principle as such. Or rather, if it has anything to do with the latter, it is precisely because morality is constructed by the former.[145]

This indeed also applies to the question of child marriage and the attempt to introduce age of consent legislation by colonial and contemporary Western feminist activists in the name of emancipation and gender equality. Asad shows how age of consent legislation in England, for example, introduced in the late nineteenth century, had much to do with concern over prostitution and the increasing criminalization of sexual acts of all sorts. While Euro-American and European feminist crusades to criminalize "child-marriage" in the non-European world have been launched to protect against the sexual exploitation of young girls by more powerful older men, this is not what the reforms achieve, as they

do not forbid marriage in all cases where the parties differ greatly in age—a middle-aged man of forty-eight, say, can marry a very young woman of sixteen; they do forbid it in certain cases where the parties are equivalent in age—a boy and a girl both of twelve, for example. The dominant concern seems to be to prevent sexual intercourse

145. Talal Asad, "Conscripts of Western Civilization," in *Dialectical Anthropology: Essays in Honor of Stanley Diamond*, vol. 1, *Civilization in Crisis: Anthropological Perspectives*, ed. Christine Ward Gailey (Tallahassee: University Press of Florida, 1992), 341–42.

where either party is a child. Indeed, the normative conception of 'childhood' here is that sexual excitation is dangerous to it; that sexuality is proper only to 'adults,' individuals 'mature' enough to handle its conditions. These ideas have a particular—and often bizarre—history in the modern West and have often formed the basis of modernizing reform in the non-European world.[146]

Thus, for Asad, "Western-inspired legislation outlawing child-marriage is therefore part of a complex, ambiguous movement that is not fully described as the self-evident elimination of inequality and exploitation. Such legislation works toward the forcible construction of new, and contradictory, social relations that define the autonomous (and suspicious) modern self."[147]

While, as we saw earlier, the relationship of Western feminism to Christianity was a formative one, despite second-wave feminism's attempt to conceal its debt to it, the relationship of feminism to religion more generally, as Saba Mahmood has affirmed, "is most manifest in discussions of Islam."[148] As Islam and Islamists are seen widely in Western feminist accounts (from nineteenth-century colonial feminism to the present), activist and academic alike, as injurious to women and as taking away women's freedom (something that Hélie-Lucas reproduces in her work), the Western liberal and feminist mission has been to *save and rescue* them from their male captors. To do so, whatever self-reflection is exercised by advocates of women's human rights outside Europe and Euro-America always leads back to the necessity of accomplishing their task. As Mahmood asserts, "freedom is normative to feminism, as it is to liberalism, and critical scrutiny is applied to those who want to limit women's freedom rather than those who want to extend it."[149]

The Question of "Islamic Law"

A case in point is the debate that an article on women and multiculturalism by US philosopher Susan Okin generated in the late 1990s. Rather than ask the question, *Is Christianity, or imperialism, or racism, or secularism, or liberalism bad for women?*, the question for Euro-American liberalism in the last quarter century, as summarized by Susan Okin, has

146. Ibid., 343.
147. Ibid., 344.
148. Saba Mahmood, *Politics of Piety: The Islamic Revival and the Feminist Subject* (Princeton, NJ: Princeton University Press, 2005), 1.
149. Ibid., 10.

been "Is multiculturalism bad for women?"[150] Okin's concern is how "multiculturalism" affects "women" who live in white-majority societies with a "Western liberal culture" like the United States and Western Europe from which her examples are drawn. Okin, true to Western anthropological approaches, sees nonwhite cultures through the binary of developmentalism and radical alterity, and deals with them the way the US military approaches them—namely that in the case of radical alterity, the culture in question should be eliminated altogether:

In the case of a more patriarchal minority culture in the context of a less patriarchal majority culture, no argument can be made on the basis of self-respect or freedom that the female members of the culture have a clear interest in its preservation. Indeed, they *might* be much better off if the culture into which they were born were either to become extinct (so that its members would become integrated into the less sexist surrounding culture) or, preferably, to be encouraged to alter itself so as to reinforce the equality of women—at least to the degree to which this value is upheld by the majority culture.[151]

Leila Ahmed had already exposed this feminist racist fallacy in her 1991 classic book, *Women and Gender in Islam*. Ahmed argued against the Western liberal feminist (or what she accurately describes as "colonial feminism") connection established between "culture" and the status of women. Ahmed notes that it was never

argued, for instance, even by the most ardent nineteenth century feminists, that European women could liberate themselves from the oppressiveness of Victorian dress (designed to compel the female figure to the ideal of frailty and helplessness by means of suffocating, rib-cracking stays, it must surely rank among the most constrictive fashions of relatively recent times) only by adopting the dress of some other culture. Nor has it even been argued, whether in Mary Wollstonecraft's day, when European women had no rights, or in our own day and even by the most radical feminists, that because male domination and injustice to women have existed throughout the West's recorded history, the only recourse for Western women is to abandon Western cultures and find themselves some other culture. The idea seems absurd, and yet this is routinely how the matter of improving the status of women is posed with respect to women in Arab and other non-Western societies.[152]

---

150. See Susan Moller Okin et al., *Is Multiculturalism Bad for Women?* (Princeton, NJ: Princeton University Press, 1999).

151. Ibid, 22–23.

152. Ahmed, *Women and Gender in Islam*, 244.

Okin also seems to think that in addition to all men, the older women from nonwhite cultures are also beyond the pale, "since older women often are coopted into reinforcing gender inequality," thus rendering young women from nonwhite cultures the target of white feminist concerns,[153] something that even a scholar like Homi Bhabha, not a friend of Islam or Islamisms, identifies as the erstwhile colonial policy of "divide and rule."[154] Okin also considers Islam and Islamic laws as central culprits in this regard. In response to what she identified as Okin's "condescending, even patriarchal" judgment, the Lebanese Muslim feminist scholar Aziza al-Hibri posed the question of whether "Western Patriarchal Feminism is Good for Third World/Minority Women?"[155]

But the problem with the question of "Muslim laws" or "Islamic law" or Shari'a, as presented and analyzed in such texts, is not only the ahistoricity with which they are presented, let alone their classed application (as Spivak recognizes), and their universality and uniformity in the "Muslim world," which is often posited by their detractors, but also how they are related in these discussions to "Islam" itself as a place of origin, or one that is claimed as such. This of course neglects the history of the imposition of European laws since the eighteenth century on the Ottoman Empire through the mechanism of the capitulations and on India through direct colonization.[156] While the larger part of Ottoman legal transformation would take place in the nineteenth century, it would initially set what the Europeans called "family law" aside by maintaining its Shari'a form "at least nominally; although by casting it in a codified form it ceased to be part of the Shari'a as a 'process.' . . . It also changed masters, the state taking over in this role [from the independent judges]."[157] The emergence of "family law" in the European world in the nineteenth century was part and parcel of the new liberal and capitalist order, wherein "family" would be separated from the market as the domain of persons (wife, children, not to mention the insane) incapable of entering into contracts versus the individual and

153. Okin, *Is Multiculturalism Bad for Women?* 24.

154. Homi Bhabha, "Liberalism's Sacred Cow," in *Is Multiculturalism Bad for Women?* 83. For Bhabha's anti-Islamist (and anti-Palestinian) views, see Joseph Massad, "Affiliating with Edward Said," in *Emancipation and Representation: On the Intellectual Meditations of Edward Said*, ed. Hakem Rustom and Adel Iskander (Berkeley: University of California Press, 2010), 40–42.

155. Aziza al-Hibri, "Is Western Patriarchal Feminism Good for Third World/Minority Women?," in *Is Multiculturalism Bad for Women?* 41–46.

156. See Wael B. Hallaq, *Shari'a: Theory, Practice, Transformations* (Cambridge: Cambridge University Press, 2009), 371–442. For an erudite study of how "Shari'a" functioned in relation to women before the colonial encounter, see Judith Tucker, *In the House of the Law: Gender and Islamic Law in Ottoman Syria and Palestine* (Berkeley: University of Californian Press, 1998).

157. Hallaq, *Shari'a*, 428.

male citizen able to enter into contracts in the realm of the market.[158] This is a division unknown in Shariʿa, as Muslim men and women were always equal in their rights to own property and to enter into contracts.

When the French arrived in Morocco, "Family Law" was not of interest to them, and "they left it alone, at least initially. As happened in Algeria, the French government deployed the skills of French Orientalists, who, drawing on their predecessors' achievement in Algeria, started their Moroccan 'project' in earnest in 1930." The very name by which the family code would become known across Arab countries, would be *al-ahwal al-shakhsiyyah*, which was a neologism introduced into Arabic from the European "personal status" or more accurately from the French "statut personnel."[159] It was the colonial efforts to shape native knowledge of the natives' own history which would mark the history of "Islamic law" in accordance with colonial interests. That the modernization of Shariʿa and the importation of European laws focused on matters of economic interest to the colonizing Europeans is exhaustively documented by Wael Hallaq's magisterial work, but therein lies the particularity of family law, now rendered "personal status" law:

When European colonists did not accord Islamic laws of personal status any strategic importance (since these laws did not interfere with the processes of systemic (re)orderings for the purposes, inter alia, of material exploitation), their scholars promoted the idea that these governments had refrained from instigating 'reform' out of respect for the sanctified regard in which Muslims held their laws of personal status. . . . The sacredness and sensitivity of the laws of personal status, once marked as such, were taken as the point of reference for the modern politics of identity.[160]

Responding to the claims put forth by Hélie-Lucas that family law has emerged as "the preferential symbol of Islamic identity," Hallaq replies that "it did so not only because it was built into Muslim knowledge as an area about which they should display sensitivity, but also because it represented what was taken to be the last fortress of the Shariʿa to survive the ravages of [colonial] modernization."[161] But even this proves to be an inaccurate assessment by those who uphold personal status laws as "Islamic." Hallaq explains that "even this sphere of law underwent structural and foundational changes that ultimately resulted in its

158. On the genealogy of family law, see Janet Halley, "What is Family Law? A Genealogy, Part I," *Yale Journal of Law and the Humanities* 23, no. 1 (2011): 1–109.
159. Hallaq, *Shariʿa*, 441.
160. Ibid., 445–46.
161. Ibid., 446.

being severed from both the substance of classical *fiqh* and the methodology by which *fiqh* had operated. . . . Thus, it was both essential to and an inevitable consequence of the ways of the nation-state that personal status had to be severed from its own indigenous jural *system*."[162] Indeed, the call for a reform of personal status laws continues the colonial tradition of transforming what it considers to be forms of "Muslim" or "Islamic" governance into what it identifies as "Western" forms of governmentality.

Translating Euro-America to Islam and Arabic

But translating European conceptions of law into forms of "Shari'a" and translating Shari'a itself into European codes, like personal status, would be part of a larger process of translation that colonial modernity ushered into Muslim-majority countries, from Morocco to Indonesia and from Central Asia to Central Africa. These translations were always anchored in European colonial claims to universality. But even in the postcolonial period, there has been "no cultural consensus on an international level about what ought and ought not to be a claim to universality, who may make it, and what form it ought to take."[163] Judith Butler argues that for the claim to universality to compel international consensus "it must undergo a set of translations into the various rhetorical and cultural contexts in which the meaning and force of universal claims are made."[164] Thus "no assertion" of universality "can be made without at once requiring a cultural translation."[165] Consequently, Butler asserts:

Without translation, the very concept of universality cannot cross the linguistic borders it claims, *in principle, to be able to* cross. Or we might put it another way: without translation, the only way the assertion of universality can cross a border is through a colonial and expansionist logic.[166]

162. Ibid., 446–47. For some of the examples where the new personal status laws differ markedly from the premodern understanding of, say marital relations, see Hallaq, 456. For the creation of "personal status" laws in the case of Jordan, for example, see Joseph Massad, *Colonial Effects: The Making of National Identity in Jordan* (New York: Columbia University Press, 2001), 51, 79–84. On French intervention in "family law" in Algeria, see Marnia Lazreg, *The Eloquence of Silence*, 88–92.
163. Judith Butler, "Restaging the Universal: Hegemony and the Limits of Formalism," in Judith Butler, Ernesto Laclau, and Slavoj Žižek, *Contingency, Hegemony, Universality: Contemporary Dialogues on the Left* (London: Verso, 2000), 35.
164. Ibid.
165. Ibid.
166. Ibid., 35.

For Butler, this is the situation in which Anglo-feminism in the academy has proceeded (she cites Okin and Martha Nussbaum as examples) "without regard to prevailing norms in local cultures, and without taking up the task of cultural translation." In attempting to overcome the issue of local cultures "international feminism does not understand the parochial character of its own norms, and does not consider the way in which feminism works in full complicity with US colonial aims in imposing its norms of civility through an effacement and a decimation of local Second and Third World cultures." Butler is aware that

translation by itself can also work in full complicity with the logic of colonial expansion, when translation becomes the instrument through which dominant values are transposed into the language of the subordinated, and the subordinated run the risk of coming to know and understand them as tokens of their 'liberation.'[167]

She invokes Spivak's important caveat with regards to the colonized emerging as a subject for Europe only in terms that European liberalism can recognize. Thus, it is not that the subaltern cannot speak, it is that she cannot speak in terms that are intelligible and recognizable to Eurocentrism, terms that do not lend themselves to the European homogenization of peoples that occupy the position of the subaltern except through European epistemic violence. Euro-American and European attempts to speak for the subaltern, to represent her, will always require a translation which "always runs the risk of appropriation."[168]

While translation could have a "counter-colonialist possibility," to do so it would have to expose "the limits of what the dominant language can handle" by altering its meaning as it is being repeated, iterated, and mimed.[169] Alas, this is not a common occurrence in feminist (or non-feminist) translations, let alone in sexual libertarian translations, as we will see in the next chapter. In the case of feminist terms, translation seems often as either lacking or in excess. What to do about the English term "gender" that was being forcefully universalized, through the United Nations and human rights instruments and NGOs around the world, became a central question. While one of the more accepted translations of the term in the early days of its entry into Arabic is *al-naw'al-ijtima'i*, meaning "social type," the term was not immediately

167. Ibid., 35.
168. Ibid., 36.
169. Ibid., 37.

intelligible, anymore than "gender" itself would have been intelligible to the English reading public before its proliferation through the mass media since the 1970s in its new idiomatic use. In a special issue in the bilingual American University in Cairo journal *Alif* on "gender and knowledge," Iraqi literary scholar Ferial Ghazoul proposed a solution:

Gender does not have a ready-made unequivocal signifier in Arabic, nor for that matter in many European languages, thus *Alif*, after lengthy discussions with linguists, critics and poets, decided not to Arabize the term "gender" by giving it an Arabic pronunciation and script, but to derive a term from the Arabic root which corresponds to the etymological significance of "gender." The tri-literal root j-n-s has mothered so many specifically defined terms such as *jins* (sex), *jinsaniyya* (sexuality), *ajnas* (races), *jinas* (alliteration), *tajnis* (naturalization and homogenization), among others. To use any of these terms would add confusion to an already misunderstood concept. While the biological factor is present in gender, the term is not biological in the first place, but cultural. Thus, we rendered gender (the collective formalization of the image, status, tasks, potential rights and responsibilities of males and females in a given culture at a certain historical moment) in Arabic in the neologism *j[u]nusa* which corresponds morphologically to *unutha* (femininity) and *dh[u]kura* (masculinity). *J[u]nusa* (gender) incorporates notions of the masculine and the feminine as they are perceived in a given time and place, with all the ideological twists and politics that such a construction and a vision imply.[170]

Indeed, here we should be reminded the Arabic *jins*, meaning sex, which has been part of Arabic for two millennia, has Greek etymological origins, namely "genos," from which the English world "gender" also issues.[171] Egyptian literary scholar Samia Mehrez notes that despite the editor's introducing of *junusa*, the contributors to the special issue used a variety of other terms like *jins* and *naw* (meaning "kind"), including the transliterated term "gender," borrowed from English, as "jindar"

170. Ferial Ghazoul, "Gender and Knowledge: Contribution of Gender Perspectives to Intellectual Formations," *Alif*, no. 19 (1999): 6 of the English pagination. It is most ironic that the term chosen by the editor is misspelled in its English rendering as "jinusa" instead of "junusa." For Ghazoul's more elaborate linguistic discussion, see her Arabic editorial in the same issue titled "Al-Junusah wa al-Ma'rifah: Siyaghat al-ma'arif bayn al-ta'nith wa al-tadhkir," 6 of the Arabic pagination (as a bilingual issue, the journal has two sets of pagination, Arabic and English). In opposing the transliteration of "gender" as is in Arabic, Ghazoul mentions in the Arabic editorial that indeed the word "jandara" in Arabic, which NGOs often use as the Arabized form of "gender," means "a wooden device used to dye and flatten [worn out] clothes."

171. On *jins*, *genos*, and *genus*, see Joseph Massad, *Desiring Arabs* (Chicago: University of Chicago Press, 2007), 171–72.

in Arabic ("which alienates rather than communicates anything to an Arabic speaker and, given the hypersensitivity to 'Western' hegemonic discourses today, can result in combative nationalistic responses"), and resisted adopting the recently minted Arabic term "junusa."[172] I am not certain though that "the hypersensitivity to 'Western' hegemonic discourses today" has to be necessarily nationalistic, though it is indeed always anti-imperialist.

Mehrez, however, is frustrated, because she wishes to link the notion of translation as "the process of meaning construction" to "the urgency of translation politics for gender studies [in the Arab world] in particular." Yet, the contributors to *Alif* refused to heed the editor's term, and used instead "essentializing terms," thus squandering the creative potential of Arabic and the necessity of its "modernization."[173]

Spivak had already alerted us to the politics of the translation of "gender" more than two decades ago:

Farida Akhter has argued that, in Bangladesh, the real work of the women's movement and of feminism is being undermined by talk of "gendering," mostly deployed by the women's development wings of transnational nongovernment organizations, in conjunction with some local academic feminist theorists. One of her intuitions was that "gendering" could not be translated into Bengali. "Gendering" is an awkward new word in English as well. Akhter is profoundly involved in international feminism. And her base is third world. I could not translate "gender" into the U.S. feminist context for her. This misfiring of translation, between a superlative reader of the social text such as Akhter, and a careful translator like myself, speaking as friends, has added to my sense of the task of the translator.[174]

But not only gender, even the term "feminism," which remains contested in major ways in academic and vernacular cultures in the United States and Western Europe, is at issue when it comes to Muslim women. Heba Raouf Ezzat, for one, objects to the scholarly use of the term "feminist" to describe Muslim women who "demand respect . . . [and that] they participate in economic and political processes" within the rubric of "religious traditions," although "they themselves choose not to identify themselves as such." Such appellation, Raouf Ezzat contends,

---

172. Samia Mehrez, *Egypt's Culture Wars: Politics and Practice* (London: Routledge, 2008), 111.
173. Ibid.
174. Gayatri Chakravorty Spivak, "The Politics of Translation," in *Outside in the Teaching Machine*, 188.

"obscures the deep differences between Islamic trends and the feminist epistemology/discourse regarding the [contested] issues of family, morality, the scope and role of religion and many other questions."[175]

But the question of translation of terms having to do with women, gender, feminism, and human rights is a more protracted one. The United Nations Development Program (UNDP), which began to issue "Arab Human Development Reports" (AHDR) in 2002, focused on the question of translation in its 2003 report on "Building a Knowledge Society."[176] To achieve its vision of how the Arab world can achieve this "knowledge society," the report lists the item "Opening up to other cultures" as part of its strategy: "Such interaction would be strengthened by translation into other languages; promoting an intelligent and generous exchange with non-Arab cultures and civilisations; maximising benefits from regional and international organisations and initiating reform in the world order through stronger inter-Arab cooperation."[177] Understanding translation as a way to transform Arab societies, the report acknowledges that "the question facing Arab countries is: how can translation become an asset in building knowledge? How can it be mobilised to enhance the frame of mind of individuals and increase the intellectual and cultural reference of society? How can it contribute new values, new ways of thinking and new forms of empowerment?"[178]

The problem that the AHDR writers found was in the current state of translation in Arab countries:

Most Arab countries have not learned from the lessons of the past and the field of translation remains chaotic. In terms of quantity, and notwithstanding the increase in the number of translated books from 175 per year during 1970–1975 to 330, the number of books translated in the Arab world is one fifth of the number translated in Greece.

The aggregate total of translated books from the Al-Ma'moon era to the present day amounts to 10,000 books—equivalent to what Spain translates in a single year (Shawki Galal, in Arabic, 1999, 87). . . . This disparity was revealed in the first half of the 1980s when the average number of books translated per 1 million people in the Arab world

175. Heba Raouf Ezzat, "Secularism, the State, and the Social Bond: The Withering Away of the Family," in *Islam and Secularism in the Middle East*, ed. Azzam Tamimi and John Esposito (London: Hurst, 2000), 137.

176. United Nations Development Program, *Arab Human Development Report 2003: Building a Knowledge Society* (New York: UNDP, 2003).

177. Ibid., 13.

178. Ibid., 66.

during the 5-year period was 4.4 (less than one book for every million Arabs), while in Hungary it was 519, and in Spain 920.[179]

Literary scholar Richard Jacquemond begs to differ. He explains that "these striking figures have been widely publicized, to the extent that the weakness of the translation movement is commonly quoted now as one of the indicators of the crisis of contemporary Arab culture. However, they are highly questionable."[180] Jacquemond demonstrates that all the sources on which AHDR report depended had faulty and grossly inaccurate data. Jacquemond in turn provides his own well-documented findings, which deserve to be cited at length:

On the whole, according to my own research, the total number of translations published in the Arab World during the current decade amounts to around 2000 titles a year, compared to 330 according to the AHDR. . . . Franck Mermier, in one of the finest and most recent analyses of the Arab book market, goes even further and suggests an estimate of "between 2,000 and 3,000 titles" translated every year. . . . We cannot but notice that while the AHDR usually resorts to emergent Asiatic countries such as Taiwan, China, or Indonesia as 'comparators' in other fields, when it comes to translation, it turns to European countries (Greece, Spain, Hungary), thus producing a false comparison because the latter have a much more developed publishing industry than those of the Arab World. For instance, let us take the striking figure, "less than one book translated every year for every million Arabs." If we divide the total Arab population (let's say, 250 million) by the number of translations recorded by the Index translationum over the last 25 years (around 8500 titles), the result is less than 30 books per million, that is, roughly one book per year and per million inhabitants. But the same calculation gives roughly the same results for countries like Indonesia (17 books per million over the last 25 years), Thailand (19) or Malaysia (50); and in the developed countries, the results are extremely variable, from 132 books per million in the United States and around 700 in Japan to more than 2000 for France and Germany—and 10,000 for Denmark, which seems to be the world champion of translation! In other words, this kind of indicator does not tell us much and is quite misleading. It is the typical kind of number made up to provoke public opinion—which it did, probably even to a greater extent than expected by the authors of the report themselves.[181]

179. Ibid., 67.
180. Richard Jacquemond, "Translation Policies in the Arab World: Representations, Discourse, and Realities," *Translator* 15, no. 1 (2009): 5.
181. Ibid., 5–6.

In fact, Jacquemond's research shows that the number of translations into Arabic since World War II hovers somewhere between 29,000 and 39,000 books, which include "despite some gaps here and there, the major works of world literature and thought."[182] The questionable methodology of the AHDR researchers notwithstanding, we need to take account also of US translation efforts in the Arab world since the dawn of the Cold War. It was in 1953 that the US opened the Cairo office of Franklin Publications, a private nonprofit organization whose creation was "encouraged" by the State Department and which was "entrusted" with the promotion of the translation of American works in multiple languages and in various countries.[183] The US imperial propaganda arm at the time, namely the International Information Administration (later the US Information Agency) of the State Department, worried in an internal top-secret letter that the Arabs do not view Soviet Communism as an immediate threat to them and "dismiss" it as "remote and unfamiliar" compared with the threat of Western control, including Western and US support for the establishment of Israel.[184] As a result, the letter asserts, in anticipation of the Eisenhower Doctrine, that "it is desirable that Arabs have a healthy awareness of Soviet Communism as the implacable enemy of all of their aspirations in order to provide a stimulus toward prompter association with the West in measures of common defense."[185] The letter then moved to explain the objectives of the translation project in the Arab world as:

Minimizing the difficulty of Arab-American negotiations by reducing Arab ignorance, suspicion and resentment of the West and particularly the United States . . . , creating a realistic and comprehensive world view in which Arabs can see a secure and respected role for themselves . . . , aiding in the acquisition by Arab literate groups of insights into the character of responsible government, of sound social and economic policy, and of effective economic organization . . . establishing an understanding of and a sense of communion with the central themes of Western thought, with especial emphasis on those most eloquently stating Western ideals of dignity and freedom of individual men.[186]

182. Ibid., 18.
183. Ibid., 7.
184. The letter written by Dan Lacy, Director of Information Center Service, to Mr. Datus C. Smith of Franklin Publications, is dated on 27 October 1952 and is available on http://www.gwu.edu/%7Ensarchiv/NSAEBB/NSAEBB78/propaganda%20078.pdf (accessed 26 February 2014).
185. Ibid., 4.
186. Ibid., 5.

While this preceded the heyday of the American state-supported feminism of the 1970s and beyond, one could imagine the current top-secret letters, just like the public ones, emphasizing the "freedom of individual women."[187] This would change with the new American translation programs, which started in Cairo and Amman in the 1980s. Their titles would include *Islam, Gender, and Social Change, Individualism and Democratic Culture, Women's Rights* by Christine Lunardini, and *Activists beyond Borders* by Margaret E. Keck and Kathryn Sikkinik.[188] Jacquemond, however, shows that Arab translation projects championed by national liberation regimes in Egypt and Syria have been more than open about Euro-American titles:

What strikes the researcher who goes through the titles published as part of these two programmes is the presence of numerous translations of classic works of (mainly) Western literature and thought, without distinction of period, original language or ideological trend, manuals and essays pertaining to the social sciences in a broad sense, chosen in a very eclectic way and covering the whole spectrum (from 'left' to 'right,' so to speak), alongside a militant, Marxist and third-worldist literature characteristic of the 1960s and 1970s. This eclecticism is an eloquent demonstration of how intellectuals trained in the liberal, colonial age (between the two World Wars) rallied to the cultural project of the new states, whether Nasserist or Baathist. It also demonstrates the eclectic nature of these states' cultural projects themselves and their genuine openness towards world culture.[189]

While these translations would Arabize foreign specialized vocabulary into a contemporary Arabic idiom, increasingly and since the 1980s, aside from terms referring to some recent technological devices, one witnesses attempts to import key ideological English terms wholesale into the language as part of multiple Western campaigns to transform Arabs and Muslims into Westernized mimic women and mimic men: these include "democratization" (which elicited debates as to the verbal derivation of the Anglicized Greek term, which was rendered "daqrata" and "damaqrata," though the former was selected as being in line with correct Arabic forms), "holocaust" (the latter has the Arabic equivalent of "mihraqah" and yet the transliterated Greek-based English term "hulukust" has increasingly dominated in the press and televised media

187. For the details of how Franklin publications would choose its titles, see Jacquemond, "Translation Policies in the Arab World," 8.
188. List is provided on http://egypt.usembassy.gov/pa/rbo_.html.
189. Jacquemond, "Translation Policies in the Arab World," 11.

given its ideological resonance in the West), and "gender" (not to mention "gay" and "queer," which will be discussed in chapter 3). The Arab Human Development Reports would not restrict themselves to the general question of knowledge and translation but would also take up the issue of women head-on two years later.

Women, Culture, and Islam

The UNDP, which identified "freedom" as a "deficit" it wanted to critically assess and remedy in the Arab World in its 2004 report, moved in the following year to the question "women's rights," which it had identified in 2002 as one of the three areas of "critical development 'deficits'" that have held back "human development" in the Arab world. In 2005, the UNDP dedicated its Arab Human Development Report (AHDR) to this matter, explaining that "given the contentious nature of the issues covered in the AHDRs, it should come as no surprise that their preparation has tended to fall into this latter category, with this year's report being no exception."[190] In the following sections, taking the AHDR 2005 as a case study, I will analyze in detail how Arab feminist intellectuals, the United Nations, international NGOs, human rights discourse, and the hegemony of neoliberalism interact to produce and articulate policy recommendations for Arab and Muslim women that are fully in line with Western liberal feminism's rescue mission. While a number of important criticisms have been leveled against the AHDR 2005, my critique and analysis for the remainder of this chapter will focus on tracking how religion (specifically Islam) and culture (specifically Islamic, but also Arabness) are deployed in the AHDR's strategic recommendations.

Shedding any responsibility that the reports it issues represent the UN or the UNDP or indeed any organization except for the authors themselves (which the UNDP management selects and whose views it promotes in these reports to the exclusion of others), the Turkish UNDP administrator Kemal Dervis affirms: "The AHDRs—this year's included— articulate some views that UNDP does not share, and at times uses language that is unnecessarily divisive. Since 2002, UNDP has helped provide a platform for debate in the region and beyond. Unfortunately,

190. United Nations Development Programme, *The Arab Human Development Report 2005: Towards the Rise of Women in the Arab World*, i. Henceforward, I will refer to the report in the forthcoming footnotes as *AHDR*.

the language used in part of this debate has not always been compatible with the cause of reform and understanding based on reasoned arguments."[191] As for the views of the UNDP itself, the administrator articulates them thus:

UNDP management believes the building of freedom and good governance, which is the stated aim of the AHDRs, requires moderation and arguments based on reason and respect for the views of the "other," all hallmarks of the golden age of Arab greatness, a time when the Arab and Muslim worlds were prosperous, strong and standard-setters for others. Progress in the Arab world in this age of global economic forces will also require much closer cooperation and economic integration, a process which can only take place if Arab countries, governments and civil societies can move closer together, despite their diversity.[192]

Due to huge internal differences among its cohort of authors, the release of the AHDR 2005 was delayed until the end of 2006. One of the authors, Islah Jad, an Egyptian women's studies professor at the West Bank-based Birzeit University, who would later serve as the director of its women's studies program, averred that the report was the first among the AHDRs to

be criticized and even attacked by its own authors. Some contested not being "fully" the "owner" of the report because they were forced to share it with some "disappointing" partners; some attacked it for not fully representing their fundamentalist secular beliefs. Others showed their discontent with its theoretical incoherence and its clear neoliberal approach. These differing stands reflect the spectrum of conflicting views and approaches in the Arab world about women's issues; they also reflect the lack of a spirit of teamwork. . . . The neoliberal line and the contradictory stand over postcolonial authoritarian regimes vis-à-vis women's issues resulted purely from the lack of consensus among the authors and the advisory board over almost every single statement in the report. Hours of discussion focused on what to call what is happening in Iraq (occupation or liberation?), whether Islamist movements are empowering or disempowering women, the envisioned role of the state, whether women's movements and activists work from within or outside the state, and so forth. Thus, the report is full of compromises to accommodate all "real" emerging differences in the region.[193]

191. Ibid., i–ii.
192. Ibid., ii.
193. Islah Jad, "Comments from an Author: Engaging the *Arab Human Development Report 2005* on Women," *International Journal of Middle East Studies* 41 (February 2009): 61.

It is not clear what the nature of the debates on the question of religion and Islam were, as Jad does not elaborate beyond the truncated list she provides, though her reference to many of the authors as avowing "fundamentalist secular beliefs" provides some evidence of the acrimonious nature of the debates. Jad attributes the neglect of the impact of globalization on women in the report to the fact that some of the authors "were strongly driven by a neoliberal and women's liberal rights approach and 'confident' in their beliefs about what is 'good' for women."[194]

The commitment to neoliberalism is not only linked to women's emancipation but to the alleged inclusion of Arabs and Muslims in the global market and the post-Cold War international community. While this would begin in the 1980s with the International Monetary Fund's push to dismantle the welfare state in the Third World more generally, it would get another strong push following the events of September 11 and the US invasion of Iraq in 2003. It was in that context that large public relations campaigns were launched in Egypt, Jordan, Lebanon, and the Gulf states, among others, to transform Arab and Muslim cultures into cultures that can advance the neoliberal agenda.

In 2005 Queen Rania of Jordan with the help of USAID and public relations firm Saatchi and Saatchi launched the "Culture of Hope" campaign to accompany the final dismantlement of the Jordanian welfare state and the massive privatization and corruption and impoverishment of the population that accompanied it. In Lebanon in 2006, the neoliberal Hariri financial empire sponsored the "I Love Life" campaign, while in Egypt, internationally sponsored conferences launched the pan-Arab "Culture of Optimism" campaign. All three campaigns stressed the liberal value system of individualism, free enterprise, markets, personal responsibility, privatization, human rights, etc., and aimed at transforming "Arab culture," which was posited as responsible for Arab "failures" in development, into one that could advance neoliberal success. These campaigns became "the most visible manifestations of a broader set of reform programs that have been launched throughout the Arab world after 9/11."[195] We will see how the AHDRs generally, and the AHDR 2005 specifically, are part and parcel of this neoliberal effort at cultural, religious, and juridical transformation, in short, at instituting a new form of governmentality that extends the reach of US and West European imperialism across the globe.

194. Ibid.
195. See Mayssoun Sukarieh, "The Hope Crusades: Culturalism and Reform in the Arab World," *Political and Legal Anthropology Review* 35, no. 1 (May 2012): 115.

In her forward to the report, Amat Al Alim Alsoswa (an Arab Muslim woman from Yemen), UNDP Regional Director of the Bureau for Arab States, explains that the authors of the report have "a firm stake in the issues at hand and accept the risks entailed in tackling a subject loaded with cultural, religious and social sensitivities."[196] Concerned over the angry tone of parts of the report, the regional director explains:

An Arab intellectual who today brings "Western" ideas of gender equality into such polarised arenas faces outright dismissal. In this environment, one who advocates for homegrown democratic change to speed women's empowerment while Israel's occupation of Palestinian territory, its aggression against neighbouring countries and the military interventions of foreign powers continue, is seen as the pawn of a discredited model. With their arguments derailed by intervention from abroad, and stifled by reactionary forces at home, Arab moderates are increasingly embattled, frustrated and angry.[197]

The AHDR, we are told by the regional director, "stresses the need to eliminate the seeds of discrimination against women in Arab tradition and to promote ijtihad (interpretative scholarship) in religious matters to overcome cultural obstacles."[198] As we will see, the report was less interested in the economic and social conditions that lead to discrimination against Arab women and diagnoses their situation mainly as "cultural," which may very well be the mark of "moderation," read liberalism, of which the director speaks. But these "moderates" understand that a liberal commitment to democracy is not always good for women. The authors do seem to see advantages to despotism over democracy in Arab society as relates to women's rights:

On the one hand, repressive regimes have contributed to important achievements in favour of women's rights that might not been [sic] achieved if matters had been left to the natural progress of society, given its imposed constraints. At the head of such achievements is the exponential expansion in girls' education within a conservative environment; here it is possible to say that the various authorities, despotic as they may be, have been ahead of society. However, this sort of progress is not limited to this one achievement, which is common to nearly all Arab regimes. Important achievements, pioneering by any standard, have been realised in Arab

196. *AHDR*, iii.
197. Ibid.
198. Ibid., iv.

countries under regimes that lack components of the society of freedom and good governance.[199]

Decoupling women's rights from democracy is important in this regard, though given the overall commitment to liberalism and neoliberalism by many of the report's authors, it is not a recommended course. The problem seems to center less on despotism and democracy and more on religion and secularism, on "traditional" culture and "Western" modern culture.

In his foreword to the report, Talal Bin Abdul Azim, president of the Arab Gulf Programme for United Nations Development Organizations (AGFUND), identifies "the continuance of outmoded attitudes towards women, their status and role" as

regrettably, linked to certain interpretations of religion, even though a careful study based on the facts will reveal that they have their origins in custom and tradition. Religion has no connection with any of the mistaken practices that are carried out against women. Our societies, however, give precedence to custom over true worship and provide foundations for assumptions that have no grounding either in the Holy Qurʾan or in the authenticated practices and sayings of the Prophet (the Hadith). . . . *Most of the sufferings of Arab women is attributable to the accumulation of such customs and traditions* [emphasis added]. It follows that the correction of outmoded assumptions and attitudes is a leading priority, one that demands, in the first place, cultural and societal measures to instil in coming generations a balanced vision of women and their role. . . . *Indeed, no change can be expected if we do not begin by developing the inner workings of our culture, which determines our rules and how we see ourselves* [emphasis added].[200]

Here, we see an attempt to decouple culture and traditions from Islam and its theology, focusing on *culture* as that which is responsible for the inferiority of women in Muslim societies, indeed even for the alleged misinterpretations of Islam and its scriptures. Furthermore, the report wants also to decouple culture itself, as a reified notion, from the *local* and juxtapose it to the "international." *It is this series of decouplings of women's rights from democracy, of Islam from local culture, and of culture itself from its local setting, that, the writers believe, will bring Arab (and Muslim) societies closer to achieving Western norms of gender equality.*

199. Ibid., 64.
200. Ibid., vii–viii.

As my engagement with the AHDR 2005 will focus on its relationship to culture and religion (and laws associated with the latter) and the latter's role in producing gender inequality primarily, I will not reiterate the other limitations of the report which many have already criticized—its deployment of certain kinds of statistical instruments by which it homogenizes all women internationally and reifies "Arab" women as an intelligible statistical category, its use of "the Arab world" as a unit of analysis, the homogenization of Arabs who live in various states with highly differing GNPs and GDPs, literacy rates, employment rates, health standards, legal instruments, economic structures, security structures, etc., and the reification of the "Arab family" and kinship relations that are rendered uniform and ahistorical, and its commitment to a US imperial and liberal approach and definitions of what constitutes "human development" and gender equality which have led and lead to "humanitarian" military invasions by the US to "rescue" the population, especially women and so forth.[201]

Culture, Bounded and Unbounded

The report's deployment of key terms like "culture," "religion," "Islam," "traditions," and "the tribe," in reified forms, as bounded categories endowed with the power of immediate causality when it comes to the condition of Muslim and Arab women is its central methodological approach. Yet, the authors seem clear that the boundedness of these categories is breakable through international and local interventions, which will render them unbounded, and therefore open to change in a westward direction.

Bounded or not, the authors' intervention is at the level of causality of which they seem certain. If indeed culture, Islam, religion, tribes, and traditions (including legal traditions) are responsible for the situation of Arab and Muslim women, then they will always continue to be so in the future. Hence, any project that seeks to change the condition of

201. See the important critiques of Frances Hasso, "Empowering Governmentalities rather than Women: *The Arab Human Development Report 2005* and Western Development Logics," *International Journal of Middle East Studies* 41 (February 2009): 63–82, and Fida Adely, "Educating Women for Development: *The Arab Human Development Report 2005* and the Problem with Women's Choices," *International Journal of Middle East Studies* 41 (2009): 105–22. For critiques of similar UN methods in its reports, see Gina Naheed Aaftaab, "(Re)Defining Public Spaces through Developmental Education for Afghan Women," in *Geographies of Muslim Women: Gender, Religion, and Space*, ed. Ghazi-Walid Falah and Caroline Nagel (New York: Guilford Press, 2005), 44–67.

women in Muslim societies must perforce target these causes for change and transformation in a direction that can ensure the elimination of discrimination and injustice. As the authors recognize Western liberal feminist approaches as *the cause* of the emancipation of women in the West, and that their internationalization and governmentalization will lead to the emancipation of Arab and Muslim women, their task would be clear and elementary—namely the employment of Western liberal feminism and its governmentalization of women's issues in the United States and Western Europe as the guide and the blueprint for transforming Islam, Muslim culture(s), "Islamic" law, social structures (including the elimination of "tribalism"), and tradition(s).[202]

Let us begin with the modular case of "honor crimes," which seems to straddle, as far as liberal feminists are concerned, the issue of culture, law, and religion. The identification of "honor" crimes as Arab and Muslim crimes in Western liberal accounts, which the report fully espouses, and wherein such crimes are discussed without any comparison to the Western category of "crimes of passion" let alone "domestic abuse," and Arab laws related to them are discussed without any discussion of the Napoleonic legal legacy from which they derive. Indeed, "honor" killings or crimes are identified as an "old tribal custom" in origins without any evidence being provided.[203] In fact, the very category "honor" killings is an Orientalist category that has been translated to Arabic as "jaraʾim al-sharaf," and still lacks a translation in Hindi, where the Hindi language press in India still uses the English term to designate such crimes.[204] The very category relies on what Inderpal Grewal has termed the "outsourcing" of the Western notion of patriarchy to non-European, especially Muslim, societies, including Muslim immigrant communities residing in Europe and the United States. She states that

'honour killings' refer not simply to a cause of death, but also to the cause as the work of a patriarchy. The term 'honour killing' enables the articulation of this patriarchy in some sites, locations and communities but not in others—the term sticks to a crime by certain bodies against other bodies. It seems to have little explanatory value for societies seen as 'Western' but a great deal of meaning is produced if the concept is yoked to Middle East or South Asian bodies and groups.

202. For an excellent critique of these Orientalist methods and solutions in the context of Saudi Arabia, see Madawi Al-Rasheed, *A Most Masculine State: Gender, Politics, and Religion in Saudi Arabia* (Cambridge: Cambridge University Press, 2013).

203. *AHDR*, 116.

204. Inderpal Grewal, "Outsourcing Patriarchy: Feminist Encounters, Transnational Mediations and the Crime of 'Honor Killings,'" *International Feminist Journal of Politics* 15, no. 1 (2013): 11.

As "honor" killings have been part of the atrocity exhibition of Western feminisms and Western media as exclusively Arab and Muslim crimes,[205] the report does nothing to disabuse its Western or Arab readers of such an understanding:

In a questionnaire put to a number of [Arab] girls who took refuge in shelters in Switzerland, the sentence repeated by most of them was, "Murdering me costs the murderer nothing." The sentiments expressed in the statement "Stop Killing Women," signed by tens of thousands of people inside and outside Syria, give an idea of the size and significance of this social and legal cancer.[206]

The situation of Arab and Muslim women in the Arab world is presented by the authors in the context of a world which has been provoked to action by Western liberal feminisms and their influence on Western governments. The establishment of Western feminist solidarity with oppressed women outside the West is noted with much celebration. This includes the report's excitement about the rise of Western-funded NGOs and the supremacy of "international" legal norms and standards.

Starting with the 1975 First United Nations World Conference on Women in Mexico City and under the influence of international mechanisms working for the rise of women, new instances of the so-called feminisation of the State began to emerge. Countries committed themselves to develop their legislation in accordance with international conventions calling for the abolition of all forms of discrimination against women. A host of centers, foundations, and organizations concerned with women's affairs grew up in the region.[207]

The authors are clear on the importance of theological interventions based on these legal norms, as they rush to tell us that the new NGOs "demanded that the door to independent religious thinking (ijtihad) be opened on questions connected with women in the belief that *enlightened* [emphasis added] readings of the regulatory Qurʾanic verses would

205. See Joseph Massad, *Desiring Arabs*, 37, 319–20.
206. *AHDR*, 173. It should be noted that many liberal Arab and Muslim scholars rely on such Orientalist representations and methods in culturalizing crimes against women. Lama Abu-Odeh, for one, and in line with such Orientalist traditions, terms Arab societies "honor-shame social-system[s]," "honor-based societ[ies]," and "honor societ[ies]." See Lama Abu-Odeh, "Crimes of Honor and Constructions of Gender in Arab Societies," *Comparative Law Review* 2, no. 1 (Spring 2011): 10, 11, 15, 22. In her earlier rendition of the same article, Abu-Odeh did not use these terms but referred to Arab society as a "traditional society." See her "Crimes of Honour and Constructions of Gender in Arab Societies," in *Feminism and Islam: Legal and Literary Perspectives*, ed. May Yamani (Beirut: Ithaca Press, 1996), 141–94.
207. *AHDR*, 128.

establish a new discourse on women nourished by the heritage."[208] Lacking any class analysis of the relation of local women who run the NGOs and the majority of women in their own countries for whom they purport to speak, the report collapses the two as one and the same:

The new generation of women's associations is distinguished by its qualitative closeness to women's issues. In spite of their affiliation with democratic parties, these associations clearly emphasise that women's issues are no longer a minor detail among party preoccupations and concerns. On the contrary, the constitutions of these new associations, the resolutions passed at their conferences and their writings in the press all underline that these issues have become, perforce, no less central than those of democracy, development or human rights.[209]

The report correctly claims that "the global discourse on women has been a significant influence on the Arab women's movement and a driving force in the latter's reformulation of its goals and perseverance in its struggle. It has helped in Arab women's efforts to bring laws and national legislative initiatives into line with universal objectives."[210] No mention, however, is made in this context of foreign funding, imperial interests, cooptation of activists for the NGO industry, etc. Under the heading culture, the report adds that "religious heritage, above all, is a key determinant of the cultural norms underpinning the position of women in the Arab world."[211]

In their rush to deploy Western liberal feminisms as the cure to the disease of Muslim and Arab misogyny, the authors' views of the situation of women in Europe suffer from similar blind spots and misapprehensions as their views of Arab and Muslim women do. They assert, in an implicit comparison with Arabs and Muslims, that with the "dawn of modern civilization" Europeans "advanced the woman, taught her and raised her status. She then started demanding her rights. There was disagreement among writers over the extent of those rights but they agreed in [sic] respecting the woman and holding her in high esteem."[212] It seems this was a direct result of Europe's commitment to liberalism which Muslim societies lack:

208. Ibid., 129.
209. Ibid., 131.
210. Ibid.
211. Ibid., 143.
212. Ibid., 150.

Unlike the situation in developed countries, wage labour in the poor socio-economic sectors does not allow for the individualisation of women or vulnerable groups. This is owing to the weakness of individualisation in general and its complete absence when it comes to the weakest element of society, meaning women, who do not enjoy rights as individuals per se. Indeed, only in the dominant value system can a woman enjoy any rights—through her role in the group and/or the home.[213]

Recognizing the irrelevance of the local and the supremacy of the West, the authors assert that "Western culture and the Western lifestyle represented the main source of inspiration for most advocates of woman's liberation and equality between the sexes for over a century. In most cases, the 'Western exemplar' was seen as a new Mecca. In other words, it was approached in a spirit of imitation and discipleship."[214] Here, Grewal's important understanding of how in the self-making of the modern West patriarchy seems to have disappeared and sticks only to non-Europeans is absent from the AHDR authors' West-worship. Grewal insists:

Patriarchies are now consolidated and exist in the USA in many localized social and political formations. Religious groups, right-wing conservatism, homophobic and racist projects and corporate capital—all of these may nurture patriarchy as a networked form of power. Fraternities—male identified collectives or networks—may not depend on the control of women to gain legitimacy, but still create networks of power and support that are racial, sexual, financial, social and political. Societies that see themselves as liberal may retain male power as hegemonic while enabling some groups of women to gain power. Yet in order to consolidate the West as modern, patriarchy is both disavowed and also outsourced by liberal Western cultures. Violence against women is blamed on individual criminality rather than cultural factors in the case of white males; for minority groups, it is linked to pathological cultures.[215]

Whereas Grewal's understanding of the ontological implications of Western feminist internationalism for the self-making of the West and of Western feminism and feminists themselves is paramount, the pervasiveness of Western human rights internationalism is such that a scholar like Lila Abu-Lughod, who agrees with the important critiques made by anti-imperialist feminists of such activism and of its racism and imperial pedigree, cannot help but persist in her determination to *save and rescue* liberal Western feminist activism from these very implications, believing

213. Ibid., 168.
214. Ibid., 176.
215. Grewal, "Outsourcing Patriarchy," 7.

in the necessity and inevitability of such activism as a form of solidarity with Muslim women. Addressing Western feminists, she declares:

Categories like the honor crime trap feminist scholars and activists in difficult binds: how are we to publicize and work against violence against women in the Middle East, South Asia, and Muslim Europe without being complicit in other serious forms and institutions of harm? The political and historical context in which the culturo-legal category was constructed and the campaigns in its name have gained momentum has opened feminists to the charge of inadvertent collusion with many of the processes they deplore. Representations of Muslim women are particularly fraught in this era. *This imposes on those who work on anything to do with them a responsibility to think critically and to be vigilant against having our analyses hijacked by others or unconsciously infiltrated by divisive values or fantasies* [emphases added].[216]

Abu-Lughod's approach, consisting largely of pleas to liberal American feminists and women's rights activists (as we saw earlier), is a consistent mark of her scholarship. In a later article, her "plea" is made most explicit in her title: "A Plea for Ethnography."[217] Understanding that American feminists, who constitute the group with which she identifies, as having "well-meaning concerns" about Muslim women (indeed, despite her disagreement with his policies, Abu-Lughod

---

216. Lila Abu-Lughod, "Seductions of the 'Honor Crime,'" *Differences: A Journal of Feminist Cultural Studies* 22, no. 1 (2011): 53. I should note that Abu-Lughod often uses the subject and object pronouns "we" and "us" when addressing the question of US liberal feminism's discourse and politics regarding Muslim women. Her identification seems at times to be with "people in the West," with feminists more generally, anthropologists more particularly, but also with those in the West who are concerned with the lives of Muslim women. See her multiple invocations of these pronouns in Lila Abu-Lughod, *Do Muslim Women Need Saving?* (Cambridge, MA: Harvard University Press, 2013).

217. In this article, Abu-Lughod posits ethnography as the best method to understand how Muslim women's "rights" operate: "Only ethnography can reveal the different place of 'rights' in these lives, and the multiple registers and tracks they follow in specific locations. When we treat 'Muslim women's rights' as a social fact rather than a rallying cry, we can begin to use them to better understand the complex dynamics of gendered power, global, national, and local." Lila Abu-Lughod, "The Active Social Life of 'Muslim Women's Rights': A Plea for Ethnography, Not Polemic, With Cases from Egypt and Palestine," *Journal of Middle East Women's Studies* 6, no. 1 (Winter 2010): 34. This is not a new plea by Abu-Lughod, who seems to have also believed earlier in her career that "anthropological theorizing about Islam . . . [is] more promising than other sorts of theorizing about Islam." To that end, her constant attempts to rescue white liberal feminists from their Orientalist pitfalls by issuing friendly *pleas* to them should be contrasted with her much earlier attempt to rescue a British anthropologist of Islam from the clutches of Talal Asad's criticisms. Rather than issue a plea to Asad, she *chastises* him for criticizing and neglecting some British and American anthropologists of Islam (whose works she defends), his alleged refusal to "appreciate" them, and his alleged "undervalu[ing]" of their contributions. See Lila Abu-Lughod, "Anthropology's Orient: The Boundaries of Theory on the Arab World," in *Theory, Politics, and the Arab World: Critical Responses*, ed. Hisham Sharabi (London: Routledge, 1990), 109, 111.

believes that George W. Bush's "desire to understand our sister 'women of cover' . . . is laudable"),[218] her goal is that the kind of ethnography in which she engages would "teach us" and "help us" reflect more critically about the question of transnational solidarity, which would make "us" more vigilant and avert the rescue mission of Western liberal feminists.[219]

The problem with this approach, however, is that it never bothers to think why international solidarity is always already unidirectional, white women having "well-meaning concerns" about brown and black women, or Christian and Jewish American and European women (secular and religious alike) having "well-meaning concerns" about Muslim women of all nationalities. Why is it that there is no international solidarity projects and transnational feminism among Asian and African women, Muslim or otherwise, that express "well-meaning concerns" about their white and non-white American and European sisters who continue to suffer under legal, political, social, and economic regimes of discrimination is a question that is not asked. Is it that the former are more narcissistic, more nationalistic, parochial, devoid of altruism, and more localist than European and American women or is it that transnational forms of feminist solidarity can only issue from imperialist countries toward the Third World as part of imperial networks that these types of feminist solidarity support and/or resist? If the latter, then questions of "well-meaning concerns" and pleas for anti-culturalist vigilance turn out to be nothing short of misnomers at best and liberal imperialist dissimulations at worst. It is not a simple matter of Westerners having to heed Abu-Lughod's advice (which is intended to save them from their culturalist pitfalls) before launching their interventions, namely that they should "look and listen carefully, think hard about the big picture, and take responsibility," but rather that given the very international imperial power structures (which are not reducible to the human subjects formed by them taking "responsibility") within whose circuits such interventions are always launched, they can never escape their "save and rescue" mission at all.[220]

Many of the authors of the AHDR insistently reject even this mild responsibility of vigilance about culturalist explanations, which Abu-Lughod advocates, as they proceed with their project of imagined cultural transformation. Indeed, the importance of education for the AHDR

218. Lila Abu-Lughod, *Do Muslim Women Need Saving?* 29.
219. Ibid., 26.
220. Ibid., 224.

project of cultural transformation, including religious education, is identified as one of the major areas where secular, liberal, and feminist intervention should be made. The authors explain:

It was only the latter stage that saw a transition from conformity (to history and to the West) to creativity in the field of socialisation and education. This transition, however, requires what Munir Bashshur calls "a spiritual and cultural maturity in the family that no longer distinguishes between female and male in education or anything else, just as it requires that the other various institutions of the society, including the school, be in tune with, strengthen and support this maturity. But from where will this maturity come, if not from the educational institutions, including the school, which thus become both the means to, and the object of reform?[221]

The report proceeds to discuss the representation of women and men in school textbooks, pointing out the inferior position of women in these depictions; but these are not contrasted, for example, with the high level of female education in places like Palestine, Jordan, Syria, Tunisia, or Lebanon, which the report recognizes. Yet no explanation is provided as to how these representations, which are credited with producing women's inferior status in society, fail to affect the rate of women's education, which, instead of being lowered, has increased measurably. Another question would be how society has been able to overcome these persistent representations by educating women at the same rate as men in several Arab and Muslim countries. Indeed, given the comparative grid with the United States and Western Europe with which the Arab world is always placed, it is significant that in several fields of higher education, Arab women, as Fida Adely has shown, "are actually doing better than women in the United States."[222] Yet neither are such conclusions drawn nor are they explained. Such analytical questions seem immaterial to the report writers.[223]

The report is rather confused and contradictory on its deployment of Western versus "authentic" values. In the context of addressing the resistance of certain social forces in the Arab world to the gender agenda of NGOs and governments, the report affirms:

An enforced anatomic separation between what is deemed local and what is deemed foreign is no longer possible in this age. What we call "foreign" culture actually thrives

221. *AHDR*, 176.
222. Fida Adely, "Educating Women for Development," 112.
223. For an important critique of the *AHDR 2005* on the question of education, see ibid., 105–22.

within Arab societies—particularly in terms of values and modes of behaviour—owing to the increasing globalisation of Arab societies. Nor is such a separation beneficial for the aspiration for progress in the Arab world—which is an *authentic* [emphasis added] aspiration—and which has continued, since the beginning of the Arab Renaissance, to be positively influenced by the best human accomplishments of the prevailing Western civilisation.[224]

The link made between the local and the international is used by the report writers as the mechanism by which they argue in favor of international NGO interventions, although the report claims opposition only to the "crassness of the call from outside for reform."[225] Thus after decoupling culture from the local (bounded) and linking it to the international (unbounded), the work of solidarity will no longer be seen as external to "culture" at all:

To be more precise, there is a largely beneficial collaboration between the struggle for women's emancipation in Arab countries as a liberating dynamic in society, and women's movements around the world, including those in the West. The efforts of international organisations are particularly important here, especially the agreements, resolutions, mechanisms and international activities aimed at protecting women's rights and equal treatment.[226]

As for the socioeconomic effects that produce discrimination against women, they seem to have very little to do with globalized business ventures; rather, the opposite seems to be true. In addition to globalization being an instrument of the spread of a culture that seems conducive to gender equality as identified above, the report argues that market economics has continued the work of "Islam" itself with regards to women's equality in business ventures:

Even before the advent of Islam, women played a role in business in Arab countries that did not go unrecognised. One of the legacies of Islam for women's rights is that it conferred upon women autonomous financial rights, which helped to sustain the presence of women in commercial affairs, whether directly or as partners of male relatives or other men. Today, the move towards free market economies, together with growing advocacy for the empowerment of women in Arab countries, has worked to increase the contributions of women entrepreneurs in Arab economies. It has augmented their

224. Executive Summary, *AHDR 2005*, 6. See also elaboration of this point at 61.
225. Ibid., 6.
226. Ibid., also part of the report on page 61.

influence in private-sector business organisations and, indeed, has given rise to their own organisations, even in those Arab countries that are the most conservative with respect to women's issues.[227]

The latter segment of the above quote is so important, that it is reproduced in its entirety in the report's executive summary.[228]

This neoliberal agenda and the attempt to invoke the history of "Islam" to legitimize it aside, the report employs the language of "balanced" journalism to assess the impact of structural adjustment and neoliberal economics on women:

Throughout the eighties and nineties a number of Arab States adopted structural reform programmes to liberalise trade, privatise, strengthen the private sector and increase production efficiency in order to establish internal and external equilibrium and promote economic development. Views differ over the effect that these policies have had on women, their employment and their participation in economic activity. While contraction of the public sector has led to a reduction in formal job opportunities for women, some see these policies as affording women wider job and economic opportunities in the informal sector. Although this sector has grown, it does not, by its nature, provide women with any legal protections or guarantees of work.[229]

Some criticisms of neoliberalism, most likely on account of the resistance of some of the authors of the report to the overall neoliberal language, are, however, mentioned:

Women, however, pay a high price under the rules of the new market, which provide them with insecure temporary work contracts and humiliating work conditions in free economic zones. Such conditions often represent no real gain for women despite the fact that these very changes (flexible working hours; opportunities to work from home) could, in principle, facilitate a reconciliation of wage labour with family-building. The absence of social policies that protect women and the limited services that the government provides play a role in making women victims rather than beneficiaries of flexible work opportunities.[230]

No matter the criticism, it seems that the linkage the report establishes between the local and the international is not only good for Western

227. Ibid., 110.
228. Ibid., 9.
229. Ibid., 92.
230. Ibid., 171.

solidarity work with Muslim women but is also good for business ventures which also are said to benefit Muslim women's rights.

While discussing the rise of Islamism, which is identified as the conservative right-wing Islamism that opposes women's rights, the Executive Summary suddenly inserts the following paragraph regarding the links between the local and the international: "Starting with the 1975 UN Conference in Mexico and under the influence of international organisations working for the rise of women, new instances of the so-called 'feminisation of the state' began to emerge."[231] Note the report's use of "international" as opposed to Euro-American and European organizations. To explain the influence of these international organizations on the rise of Arab women's organizations in the 1970s and the 1980s, the authors assert:

The international discourse on women has been a significant influence on the Arab women's movement and a driving force in the latter's perseverance and reformulation of its goals. The new consciousness was reinforced at international conferences, chiefly those convened under the auspices of the United Nations. The new approach aimed to dislodge traditional views still clinging to the women's question. Thus, personal status laws were the most important priority among these goals, followed by the enactment of legislation guaranteeing the equality of women and men in political and economic life. Women's associations were also active in urging Arab governments to implement the international agreements that they had approved, especially the Convention on the Elimination of All Forms of Discrimination against Women (CEDAW).[232]

As is clear, the report authors do not engage the critical work done on CEDAW's normalizing and universalizing notions and its hostility to local "traditions," cultures, and religions, which it deems responsible for women's inequality, as they themselves seem to share these biases. Shaheen Sardar Ali, for example, has shown in a UN-sponsored study how CEDAW's articles rely on Western liberal feminist discourse that insists on individual rights and excludes women's multiple identities, and that such an approach and the language of equal rights fail to apply to Asian and African contexts where "most women rely on entitlements embodied in family and community relationships that do not relate to the 'equal rights' language."[233] Sardar Ali adds that, given the

231. Ibid., 11.
232. Ibid., 11–12.
233. Shaheen Sardar Ali, *Conceptualizing Islamic Law, CEDAW and Women's Human Rights in Plural Legal Settings: A Comparative Analysis of Application of CEDAW in Bangladesh, India and Pakistan,*

importance of religion in the identity of many of these women, "they are not comfortable with being asked to frame their identities within a discourse that is avowedly secular."[234] She points out that critiques of CEDAW have noted the contradiction in the document between the simultaneous commitment to gender equality and the right to freedom of religion, culture, and custom. As such:

It was argued that the Religious Tolerance Declaration of 1981, in conjunction with Article 18 of the Universal Declaration of Human Rights and Articles 18, 26 and 27 of the International Convention of Civil and Political Rights (ICCPR), creates an invisible hierarchy of human rights by placing freedom of religion at a higher level than right to equality irrespective of sex and gender. It follows, therefore, that if the freedom to manifest and practice one's religion or belief led to discrimination against women, such discrimination could be upheld on the basis of the right to practice one's religion or belief.[235]

The AHDR authors are unencumbered by such concerns and critiques for the most part, and proceed as if they could be resolved through appeal to international norms with certain caveats that function more as alibis than vigilance in resisting Western-imposed norms. Frances Hasso adds in this regard that the AHDR's commitment to the application of CEDAW is registered by the authors "despite the fact that many, even the vast majority, of poorer Muslim women will reject the CEDAW premise of total gender equality with regard to housing provision, economic maintenance of the marital home and children, and child support in case of divorce, given that Islamic jurisprudence has historically placed great emphasis on male responsibility in these arenas. Indeed, this 'traditional' logic may explain why poverty and economic wellbeing in Arab countries are not necessarily feminized and masculinized."[236]

As part of their consideration of the axis of culture in relation to women, the AHDR wants to study "social patterns that contribute to shaping the position of women in Arab societies today." To do so, it "focuses on three central sources of influence: religious heritage, popular culture and Arab intellectual, artistic and media production."[237] In addition to legitimizing neoliberal economics in Islamic terms as beneficial for women, as we saw above, the report's other task is to intervene in

---

in *Islamic Law through the CEDAW Lens*, a publication of UN Women, South Asia, United Nations Entity for Gender Equality and the Empowerment of Women, 2006, 87–88.

234. Ibid., 88.

235. Ibid.

236. Hasso, "Empowering Governmentalities rather than Women," 67.

237. *AHDR*, 13.

theological and especially jurisprudential matters in preparation for the
neoliberal order:

Because the dynamics of transformation in contemporary Arab societies are different
from those in Arab societies at the time when the schools of jurisprudence were established, earlier endeavours are no longer appropriate to either the nature or pace of
current social transformations. Rather, it is a right to try to open the gates of interpretation anew and to seek further understanding of the spirit of the Qurʾanic text in order
to produce jurisprudential texts based on values of equality. Such texts will seek to
embody a jurisprudence of women that goes beyond the linguistic and historical equation of what is feminine with what is natural (pregnancy, childbirth, breast feeding,
upbringing and cooking). They will contribute to the promotion of feminine cultural
values and transform them into a general attitude.[238]

While accusing "Islamists" of seeking to return Muslims to the time of
the Prophet, ironically, it is the report's writers who insist on linking
contemporary Arab society to the time of the Prophet, bypassing the
fourteen centuries that had elapsed in the interim. Whereas much has
been said in scholarship about post-Qurʾanic Muslim condemnation of
the pre-Islam period as a society of "jahiliyya" or "ignorance," alleging
that it was a society that uniformly practiced female infanticide which
Islam banned (we have no other evidence that this was in fact the case),
the report writers tell us that contemporary Arab society still practices
infanticide by other means: "Hundreds of popular proverbs project an
attitude akin to that which led to the burying of girls alive."[239]

Whereas the report is sometimes critical of Western intervention promoting "women's rights," it registers such criticism not on account of
this interventionism being foreign or imperialist, but rather, and here it
is not dissimilar (mutatis mutandis) to Abu-Lughod's advice to Western
feminists discussed above, that the intervention occurs in the wrong
places and without adequate studies:

The new wave of Western interest in advancing the position of women has led donors
to support projects solely because a visible women's or feminist institution puts them
forward; or to support any projects to strengthen the status of women that seem topical. Seldom are proper studies carried out to measure the effect of these projects on
the status of Arab women in their society, in the family or in relation to the state.[240]

238. Ibid., 13, and the paragraph is repeated on page 147.
239. Ibid.
240. Ibid., 22.

Finally, the report concludes by appealing to the application of Euro-American instruments (CEDAW) on the Arab world as the only way to achieve women's equality:

In line with the calls in previous Reports for comprehensive, rights-based societal re-forms, the rise of Arab women entails: • Total respect for the rights of citizenship of all Arab women. • The protection of women's rights in the area of personal affairs and family relations. • Guarantees of total respect for women's personal rights and freedoms and in particular their lifelong protection from physical and mental abuse. The achievement of these rights requires extensive legal and institutional changes aimed at bringing national legislation in line with CEDAW.[241]

The report also supports American liberal instruments for race and gen-der, such as affirmative action, and commits itself to an antihistorical es-sentialist view of contemporary gender discrimination: "This will allow the dismantling of the centuries-old structures of discrimination against women."[242]

In addition to the matter of culture and traditions, the question of Islam and theological transformation is central to the report, which seeks to intervene actively in the religious field. Unlike Western secular-ism more generally, which claims to want to separate religion from gov-ernance and not to intervene in theological questions as such (which, as critical research on secularism has shown, it invariably does), the re-port, in the name of secularism but in a nonsecularist fashion, explicitly calls for theological reformulations and interventions. It calls for what it terms "Societal Reform for the Rise of Women" which aims to

address attitudinal shifts and the reform of cultural frameworks. In particular, it will modernise religious interpretation and jurisprudence through the widespread adop-tion of the enlightened readings of ijtihad. The latter must escape the thrall of existing religious institutions and personages to become the right and duty of every Muslim of learning, woman or man, who has the capacity to engage in the study of her or his religion.[243]

Caricaturing "defensive" responses to the women's movements, espe-cially in relation to the question of religion, the report explains:

241. Ibid.
242. Ibid.
243. Ibid., 23.

Sadly, even today whenever the situation of Arab women is raised as an issue, the ensuing debate tends to be heated, defensive and attended by a volley of questions. Is the Arab women's liberation movement at odds with the demands and needs of society as a whole? Is it anti-male? Do Arab women activists have an authentic agenda drawn from the reality of Arab societies? Are Arab feminists merely imitating women's liberation movements in the West? How is one to interpret Western interest in the situation of women in the East? Do women's liberation movements work against the interests of the Arab family? Is there a hidden agenda to destroy the Arab family? Do demands for women's rights seek to undermine religion?[244]

The report clearly believes that its intended reform of "Islam" will undermine extant understandings of religion and strengthen new ones. To do so, the report engages in its own Qur'anic interpretation. It discusses and summarizes Qur'anic verses on the question of gender equality[245] and concludes:

The general principles embodied in these verses, as well as others, enable one to infer the broad outlines of a social system that responds to the objectives accepted by the Islamic community in order to live a life of interdependence and consensus, while recognising the equality of all human beings, males and females. Nevertheless, several jurists set the examples given in these Qur'anic verses on a lower level than other suras devoted to the legislation of minute details concerning the relationship between men and women. Instead of bringing the subsidiary verses closer to the spirit of those dealing with the fundamental and general, the suras indicating equality were used to justify its opposite, i.e., to justify and legitimise the existing hierarchy.[246]

The report goes as far as rendering religious judgment, going beyond mere observation and analysis: "It may be said here that the male viewpoint in the history of Islamic societies has violated the divine principle of equality bestowed upon human beings as a whole."[247]

Thus, the report's call for reform does not aim to produce new juridical readings of the Qur'an by Muslims, but rather to make new juridical readings congruent with "international" liberal legislation:

244. Ibid.
245. Ibid., 143–45.
246. Ibid., 145.
247. Ibid.

The Qur²an has granted human beings (women and men) an elevated position on earth. If Islamic jurists of old were loyal to the needs of their customs and the requirements of their society, those customs and requirements no longer satisfy the needs of our age and society. Thus, turning to international laws that eliminate all forms of discrimination between men and women in no way contradicts religious belief, since these laws are closer to the spirit of the religious texts while also being closer to the changes taking place in contemporary Arab societies.[248]

The report is clear that it wants to support one side of existing theological debates on the question of women:

Many interpreters of legislation echo this discriminatory tendency when faced with the principle of equality before the law. The Report team will not emphasise here the commentaries of some modern scholars of Shari²a, who still recite the views of classical Islamic jurists regarding men's custodianship over women. In sharp contrast to such views, there exists a body of enlightened Islamic jurisprudence that interprets such texts in their context and inclines, to a considerable extent, to the espousal of the principle of gender equality.[249]

As culture and religion seem to be conflated, even if at times they are presented in variegated forms, the report seeks to excise their objectionable parts (or is it the whole of Arab "culture"?) from Arab society. In an Orientalist fashion, the report wants to intervene even in the matter of existing Arab proverbs (which, as we saw above, it depicts as a form of female infanticide) that are seen as discriminatory towards women (a project no one has ever approached in Euro-American and West European cultures despite the preponderance of popular maxims hostile to women and femininity in these cultures):[250]

Hundreds of popular proverbs imply that women should be segregated. These are common in more than one Arab country (Arab Mashreq countries, Egypt and the Arab Maghreb). They project an attitude akin to that which led to the burying of girls alive. In order to justify their retrograde spirit, these proverbs use moral and other arguments expressed in the language of tales and myths. Some also rely on psychology. In their various forms, these proverbs serve to underline the inferior social and moral position of women in society.[251]

248. Ibid.
249. Ibid., 198.
250. Ibid.
251. Ibid., 148.

The report cites two proverbs that seem to be only known to the re-port writers (along with many other unknown proverbs—there is no selection criteria presented for identifying the proverbs, where they are used, when they are used, who uses them, and the evidence that they are widely used at all) without any source for the citation except for the work of Fatima Mernissi, who, at any rate, writes on "Moroccan" proverbs which are suddenly generalized as "Arab" proverbs across the Arab world.[252]

In the realm of contemporary cultural production, the report, rather than seeing cinema as producing and creating an "Arab" or "Islamic" tradition that the report writers want to oppose, it takes cinema as a faithful representative of such traditions. The authors assert that "the most important contribution of Arab cinema to challenging society's sexual hierarchy is its graphic exposure of the broken spirit of submissive women. Such films openly confront inherited values of submission legitimised by obsolete traditions."[253]

The authors also discuss the tribe in a classic anthropological and anachronistic way, insisting on going back in time to tell us how "Islam" dealt with tribes. In some ways, it seems that tribes and tribalism have no history, and surely no colonial history to speak of.[254] Whereas the report speaks of "two" shocks to the tribal system (during the Ummayad pe-riod and again at the dawn of colonial capitalism), it seems the modern state has brought it back unscathed. Then comes the authors' attempt to claim that if Islam is not the culprit, then surely it is Arab culture, which persists despite Islam's new system of equality: "Although Islam established the notion of individual responsibility for both men and women, as well as emphasising respect for both sexes and their rights, the socio-cultural and economic-political formation of the conquests imposed limits on these broad vistas that the new religion had opened for women."[255]

Like classic Orientalism, the faults of Arab society today, according the authors, are its inheritance from Arab society of yesteryear. Such methods would surely never be used by analysts of the European, or say the English, present. Imagine if researchers of the situation of women today in England would go back to the history of the founding of Londinium by the Romans to explain what befell women's "rights"

252. Ibid.
253. Ibid., 158.
254. Ibid., 164–65.
255. Ibid., 165.

today, or that such researchers would explore the history of the entry of Christianity to the British isles and the impact of the gender system it introduced on the present, being mindful that Anglican Protestantism (and its guardian the Church of England) is the official religion of England to this day.

Here it is the alleged tribal culture of Arab countries that is the culprit,[256] and not Islam, the report proceeds to tell us:

The very strength of social structures based on traditional tribal values should not conceal the strong and violent reactions expressing rebellion and revolution. Rebellion against restrictive and undemocratic family relations does not, however, lay the foundations of a culture based on equal rights and obligations. Individual revolt does not produce a culture with a human rights structure that considers woman's rights an indivisible part of its identity and content. . . . It is important to note that submission to, or rebellion against, kinship bonds does not necessarily flow from religious considerations, given that, on both sides, one can find veiled women or women who participate in public work through educational or charitable religious institutions.[257]

The decoupling of Islam and its theology from local culture and blaming the latter for misapprehending Islamic scriptures is a central "discovery" made by the authors (which they borrow from the work of a good number of modernizing and Westernized Arab intellectuals over the last century and a half) who then move to address how this misinterpretation has taken the form of law itself, and specifically of laws identified with Shariʿa. This move will be key to their recommendations for legal reform.

Islam, the Law, and Women's Rights

While in the modern West, in many contexts, it is law rather than religion that specifies the identity of people, Winifred Fallers Sullivan argues that even though "modern law itself looks deeply self-contained, all-powerful and secular, we know that it was profoundly shaped by religion in its origins and continues to depend in fundamental ways on religious understandings of the nature of the human person and of

256. For a debunking of the "tribe" as cause of oppression of Saudi women, see Al-Rasheed, *A Most Masculine State*.
257. *AHDR*, 171.

society."[258] The situation is not that different in most Muslim-majority countries, which are also run in accordance with European secular law and with a very modern decontextualized and excised form of Shari'a, as Hallaq has demonstrated. Whereas law came to be separated from religion in the early modern West, in the Muslim world, this separation would come about with the onset of European direct and indirect colonialism. Even as religion became the object of the law in the West, a similar process came to stand in Muslim-majority countries despite the persistence of those parts of the Shari'a that were reformulated by European colonialism as "personal status laws." Inattentive, if not ignorant, of this significant historical transformation, the report finds that Shari'a and personal status laws (as a subset of Shari'a but not remnants of colonial secular laws), which are seen ahistorically and outside the colonial context, are central to the status of Arab and Muslim women:

To the present day, personal status laws constitute the most symbolic and profound embodiment of this problem. Matrimony is the first and foremost form of the relationship between women and men whether in the conscious or unconscious mind, in religion or society, in terms of the permissible or prohibited and the sacred or the desecrated. These laws may well represent the most pronounced embodiment of the relationship between Arab patriarchy and the forbidden and the taboo. The most important laws that relate to gender discrimination find refuge in it, allowing family laws to become the lair protecting culture, traditions, and customs, whether religious or popular.[259]

It is unclear why discrimination in the civil code, nationality laws, labor laws, passport laws (all of which are borrowed directly from European laws in most Muslim countries), which affect women's lives on a daily basis, find refuge outside the personal status laws. Still the report is concerned with a new category of sexual crimes that has emerged in 1970s and 1980s US feminism and US legislation, including sexual harassment:

In general, Arab penal codes contain no concrete definition of the crime of sexual harassment. There are laws punishing sex crimes such as rape, sexual assault, sexual

---

258. Winifred Fallers Sullivan, "Comparing Religions, Legally," *Washington and Lee Law Review* 63, no. 1 (2006): 913.
259. *AHDR*, 173.

abuse, and extorting sexual favours. However, while these laws provide for harsher penalties against offenders in a position of power over their victims, the crime of sexual harassment, as defined internationally, is not punishable by law unless it overlaps in some manner with the sex crimes designated in Arab penal codes. Arab legislators should, therefore, take steps to define sexual harassment as a crime in its own right even if it is not as grave as the crimes of rape, sexual assault, and sexual abuse that are already addressed in existing legislation.[260]

Notice that the test is always to accede to "international," read Western, standards, and not locally relevant legislation that springs from the kinds of sexual harassment to which women may be subjected. Here also, the report writers do not see "international" norms that follow Western law as having anything to do with Protestant Christianity, the religion of the majority in the modular cases of Britain and the United States.[261]

In elaborating on discrimination in "Arab" laws as relates to adulterous men and women and to crimes of passion, the report writers conclude by suggesting more changes in theological interpretations, and therefore in religion:

Arab personal status laws, with regard to Muslims and non-Muslims alike, are witness to legally sanctioned gender bias. This stems from the fact that personal status statutes are primarily derived from theological interpretations and judgments. The latter originate in the remote past when gender discrimination permeated society and they have acquired a sanctity and absoluteness in that confused area where the immutable tenets of religious creed interact with social history. Fortunately, evidence from the Report's public opinion survey indicates that the Arab public is moving towards a more liberal perspective on personal status issues.[262]

But how is discrimination in cases of adultery, nationality, right to work, etc. "derived" from theological interpretations? The writers provide no such genealogy. This is so because these laws are derived from colonial liberal and secular laws that survived after independence. Yet, these laws continue to be invoked as if they are part of Shariʿa rather than liberal colonial law. In this regard the report mentions the following:

260. Ibid., 187.
261. Sullivan, "Comparing Religions, Legally," 915.
262. *AHDR*, 189.

For example, Egypt recently passed Law 154/2004, which grants children of an Egyptian mother and a foreign father the right to nationality. This law consequently addresses the problems of thousands of people with an Egyptian mother and a foreign father who had previously been unable to obtain the Egyptian nationality. From the Report's public opinion survey, it is clear that Arab society is prepared to accept a woman's equal right to pass on her citizenship to her children.[263]

Notice that when a law is recognized as not part of Shariʿa (though its derivation from European colonial liberal law is still not explicitly stated or recognized), the authors make no mention of its genealogy, though the implication is that Arab culture is responsible. A unique divorce case is presented, however, as emblematic of the hegemony of Shariʿa:

Deferring to classical Islamic jurisprudence can produce rulings repulsive to the spirit of the age and to a human rights culture. A notable instance is to be found in the ruling, upheld by the Court of Cassation, ordering the divorce of an Egyptian intellectual from his wife on the grounds of his alleged apostasy in certain books that he had published. The ruling was founded upon the Hanafi opinion that an apostate must be divorced from his spouse. Clearly, then, it is essential to have clear, precise codification of personal status regulations; the legislative clarity to which this will contribute is a precondition for combating discrimination.[264]

But how is this example "discriminatory" against women or the wife? It is one thing to consider it coercive of citizens' (of either gender) choice of spouse, and another to consider it "discriminatory." The cited Hanafi jurisprudential opinion is not gender-specific at all. Also, why is it "repulsive to the spirit of the age and to a human rights culture"? What does this legislation have to do with human rights? The suggestion is that the right to marry has also become a "human right"? The confusion of the report writers, who find anything that offends their (mis)understanding of "liberal" values as a form of "gender discrimination" or a "human rights" violation, is often nonsensical and borders on the propagandistic. Indeed, this divorce case and the importance of religious views with regards to it could be compared, say, to the case of England, where people can still be prosecuted for blasphemy in accordance with current English law.[265] Yet, the authors insist:

263. Ibid., 196.
264. Ibid., 189.
265. Sullivan, "Comparing Religions, Legally," 921–23.

Over twenty years ago, the secretariat of the Council of Arab Ministers of Justice drafted a model Unified Personal Status Code. The project adopted the personal status regulations that prevailed in Arab States at the time and that continue today in many of them, bearing the stamp of classical Islamic jurisprudence. It featured no notable attempts to weed out gender bias in Arab personal status laws.[266]

Note here that while much of contemporary law in the Arab (and Muslim) world is a carryover from colonial liberal law, the authors only assume that laws derived from Islamic jurisprudence are discriminatory and that liberal colonial laws do not discriminate at all.

The report recommends in this regard that "the Arab League should take upon itself two tasks. The first is to revise the draft code so as to bring it into conformity with the demands and spirit of the times and with the international obligations of Arab States."[267] Note again the use of "spirit of the times," which seems to be nothing less than Western liberal times, whereas the Arab world is backwards and lives in a preliberal, premodern time. This does not apply only to Muslim Arabs, but also to Christian Arabs:

Personal status regulations for non-Muslims are derived from the canons of their respective religious sects or denominations. For the most part, these regulations sharply curtail the right of both spouses to divorce and, in some cases, prohibit it altogether. Adherents of Orthodox Christian denominations may, on various grounds, appeal for a judicial ruling granting a divorce, whereas Catholics may only sue for physical separation, in spite of allowing for the possibility of annulment of the marriage contract or declaring it invalid owing to flaws inherent from its initiation. On the whole, the notion of male superiority appears to have governed the formulation of such provisions pertaining to matrimonial relations.[268]

It remains unclear why curtailment of divorce for non-Protestant Christian denominations in Arab countries is seen as an exercise in "male superiority" rather than the insistence of the various Christian churches on a lifetime commitment of monogamous heterosexual marriages for both men *and* women.

In line with such an approach, the AHDR theorizes the political situation today through an assessment of the political-economic-sociocultural past of "Islam" which resists the modern order:

266. *AHDR*, 190.
267. Ibid., 191.
268. Ibid., 192–93.

The emergence of the modern authoritarian system played a large role in curtailing the growth of civil institutions. Though European capitalism brought with it new values relating to the state, politics and society, these did not originate in local conditions. Hence the cycle through which the foundations of a law-based state and an independent civil society resistant to oppression might have been established was never completed.[269]

The report's commitment to Western liberal instruments of imposing a Western vision of gender equality is unwavering and never subject to questioning. It objects to the reservations registered by Arab states that ratified CEDAW (which non-Arab and non-Muslim states also registered, barring the fact that the US refused to ratify it in any form),[270] and calls for a quota system for women in electoral systems.[271] The sense one gets is that all objections to and limitations on women's equality in Arab countries are due to Shariʿa or theological interpretations more generally, rather than discriminatory state policies based on other legal and administrative traditions. As already stated, the report never historicizes many existing laws that remain operative in Arab states as European colonial laws, but presents them as local and native laws reflecting local and often Islamic biases. Under the heading "Nationality," the Executive Summary of the report states:

In general, in Arab legislation, native nationality is determined by paternal descent. If a father is a citizen of a particular Arab country, his children acquire his nationality automatically. The children of a female national only acquire their mother's nationality if the father's identity is unknown or if he is stateless. Recently, Arab lawmakers have been working to counter the inhumane consequences of Arab states' long-held refusal to grant nationality to the children of female citizens married to foreigners (Egypt, Algeria, Lebanon).[272]

But these nationality laws are borrowed wholesale from English and French laws during the colonial period and do not issue from anything connected to Shariʿa, "Arab culture," or Islam.[273] Given the antireligion tenor of the report, it would have behooved the authors to distinguish

269. Ibid., 16.
270. Ibid., 17. Clearly the refusal of the US to ratify CEDAW does indicate fissures between US State feminism and extra-state US actors who work for its ratification internationally.
271. Ibid., 18.
272. Ibid., 19.
273. On how these laws were derived, especially in the case of Jordan, see Massad, *Colonial Effects*.

between those legislations that are claimed as "Islamic" and those that are not, a task they do not attend to or even consider.

In contrast with Muslim and non-Muslim personal status laws in Arab countries, the sexism of European liberal laws that pervades European societies and their former Muslim colonies does not seem to indict European cultures with misogyny, patriarchy, sexism, and related liberal failures. Arab culture, however, is immediately condemned for these very same liberal failures:

It requires little scrutiny of history to realise that Arab tribal culture, which sanctions discrimination against women, has strongly influenced the discriminatory juristic interpretations that establish the inferiority of women to men. Otherwise put, the male-dominated culture has been a crucial factor in shaping juristic judgments and endowing them with religious sanctity.[274]

After railing against Shariʿa's gender discrimination, conflated with a phantasmatic entity called "Arab tribal culture," the authors conclude with a self-contradictory statement: "Gender inequality in Arab legal systems is more the product of history, customs and conventions than of authentic religious precepts. Such considerations make it all the more imperative to revise Arab family law in order to end discrimination against women."[275]

Which is it then, Islam, or Arab society, or Arab culture? Perhaps it is all three. The confusion of the authors on this question is illustrated in their overall recommendations. On the one hand, "change has come from the direction of Arab ruling elites, which may have acted in part under overt or covert foreign pressures. However, sustainable and wide reforms in the law will require the creation and development of a domestic movement for change centred on civil society. It will also require changes in public awareness so as to generate a grass-roots culture favourable to gender equality."[276] On the other hand, the report recommends that

A review of the legal system relating to personal status in Arab countries should be undertaken to eliminate discrimination against women. In this regard, it is essential that Arab countries lacking unified personal status legislation adopt such legislation. Moreover, Arab legislators must act to adopt the most enlightened efforts in Shariʿa

274. Ibid., 197.
275. Ibid., 195.
276. Ibid., 200.

and other religious laws for achieving conformity with the principle of equal treatment for men and women, one that accords with the overall intentions of Islamic and non-Muslim religious law.[277]

Thus in one fell swoop, the report calls for eliminating religious freedom in matters of personal status and then calls for transforming religion to bring it in conformity with Western liberalism.

The report also pretends to know the difference between locally generated change and international reform initiatives that are imposed on Arabs, and does not recognize that this is in fact what it itself does. In specifying the best form of international solidarity with Arab women, it states:

Such solidarity will have the greatest impact if it takes the form of effective cooperation through equal partnerships between like-minded international civil society organisations, international agencies and Arab women's groups without the political and cultural biases that often vitiate external reform initiatives.[278]

The authors are clear that the conflict between women's rights and opposition to gender discrimination is not internal to Arab and Muslim societies but rather signifies a conflict between local culture and international, read contemporary Western, norms:

At the level of culture, the fundamental obstacle to the rise of women remains how to deal with certain conflicts between international standards on the one hand and religious and cultural beliefs on the other. The issue is sometimes referred to as "the conflict of authorities." "Religious beliefs" here does not refer to the Islamic religion alone, though that is always the focus, but also includes Christian beliefs since the stance of both divinely revealed religions towards issues such as abortion and a number of reproductive health issues is similar.[279]

This understanding, however, is fundamentally mistaken due to its historical ignorance of laws that limited abortion, as, in fact, it has been again liberal laws, inspired by Protestant and Catholic Christianity, imposed on Muslim countries that made abortion illegal, and not the different schools of Shariʿa which have historically permitted abortion, some without the father's consent and up to three months into the pregnancy

277. Ibid., 225.
278. Ibid., 227.
279. Ibid., 222.

(as for American "secular" laws that prohibited abortion in accordance with Protestant Christianity until 1973, and currently threatens to re-criminalize many of its forms, the report remains silent).[280] Selectivity of comparison within this almost mythic term "international standards" means that an accusation of hypocrisy can be fairly leveled at the report. The authors are explicit in their understanding of the nature of the con-flict in which they themselves are part:

Responses to this conflict take one of two forms. One approach, prominent in inter-national efforts and adopted by many supporters of women's rights in the region, is inclined to favour international standards. The other seeks to bridge the gulf be-tween international standards and religious principles through initiatives in interpre-tation. Undoubtedly, forcing the public to choose between international standards and their own religious beliefs and cultural traditions will create an insurmountable obstacle to the rise of women. Thus, in the view of the Report team, there is no alter-native to supporting the second approach, which tries to use independent interpreta-tion to establish congruence between international standards and religious cultural principles evolving, in the case of Islam, from a holistic understanding of the Islamic shari'a. Since "there is no priesthood in Islam," it follows that such initiatives in ju-risprudence must be released from the grip of religious institutions and personages. Rather, independent interpretation must become the right and duty of every qualified Muslim, woman or man, who has the capacity to engage in the study of her or his religion.[281]

As is evident, the report essentially calls for overthrowing existing reli-gious authorities as the custodians of theological interpretation and for the creation of new ones that support international, read Western lib-eral, norms. But all of this is done in the name of secularism and of lib-eral tolerance of religion. In her critique of the AHDR, Lila Abu-Lughod, echoing Saba Mahmood's arguments about Western liberal feminism and religion, recognizes this:

In general, the alternative language of Islamic piety that has a great deal of currency among ordinary women across the Arab world is dismissed because the intelligentsia involved in the *AHDR 2005* are so staunchly secular. The fact that for a majority of nonelite Muslim women across the Arab world being a good Muslim is a moral ideal or that their dignity as humans and women has a good deal to do with their sense

---

280. On this, see Basim Musallam, *Sex and Society in Islam: Birth Control before the Nineteenth Century* (Cambridge: Cambridge University Press, 1983).
281. Ibid., 222–23.

of themselves as good Muslims—whatever they think of formal groups or political Islam—is given no weight at all.[282]

The report's exclusive and insistent demand for a reform of "Islam" and of the laws derived from Shariʿa is so pervasive that it sacrifices any and all methodological rigor in its approach.[283] As Marnia Lazreg has remarked about such approaches:

The point is neither to dismiss the role that Islam plays in women's and men's lives, nor to inflate it. More importantly, it is to study the historical conditions under which religion *becomes significant* in the production and reproduction of gender difference and inequality. The historicization of the relationship between gender and religion permits an appreciation of the complexity of the lives of women hitherto subsumed under the homogenizing and unitary concept of 'Muslim.'[284]

In some ways, the debate on law and the insistence of the report that therein lies the imperative for change betrays a particular missionary and imperial legal regime (abetted by lawyers and international legal institutions) proselytizing for liberalism.

The report on occasion shows schizophrenic tendencies on the question of Western and international pressure and norms. This could very well be due to the differing agendas of the various authors. Thus, in contrast with the celebration of Western norms and NGO interventions and Western feminist solidarity, the following assessment is included more in the form of alibi than as part of an integrated analysis:

If Western criticism of the condition of the Arab woman from the academic, feminist and even political standpoints is sometimes based on fact, it does not occur in a pure form but is often mixed with concepts and ideas circulating in the West about women's liberation. These in turn are linked to developed market economies and the fragmentation of society. They can also include Orientalist concepts characterised by

282. Lila Abu-Lughod, "Dialects of Women's Empowerment: The International Circuitry of the Arab Human Development Report 2005," *International Journal of Middle East Studies* 41, no. 1 (February 2009): 97.

283. The lack of methodological rigor is pervasive throughout the report. This is most pronounced in the example of the report's citing of findings of Arab public opinion. A box is included about "young" Arabs' opinions on women, which turns out to be the summation of the opinions of eleven people invited to a session sponsored by the *AHDR*. No criterion is provided as to the selection process or how these eleven people represent anyone but themselves, nor is the method of obtaining these opinions discussed. The key question of whether the participants have been *prompted* by AHDR staff to express the opinions listed in the box is never contemplated. See page 93, Box 3–3, and Annex V.

284. Lazreg, *The Eloquence of Silence*, 14–15.

the demonisation of Arab men and an almost theatrical crusade to free women, in body and spirit, from their domination. The new wave of Western interest in advancing the position of women has led donors to support projects solely because a visible women's or feminist institution puts them forward or to support any projects to strengthen the status of women that seem topical. No proper studies [have been] carried out to measure the effect of these projects on the status of Arab women in their society, in the family or in relation to the State. Nonetheless, the Western trend in general is to provide support to women in the public arena who speak on behalf of women's issues demanding appointments in the administration and membership in parliament.[285]

This alibi aside, the transformation of Islam and this ahistorical self-consolidating fantasy of Arab culture remained the operative criterion to bring about women's emancipation. If at the turn of the twentieth century, European and Euro-American Christian and feminist missionaries would legitimize their views by quoting Qasim Amin, at the turn of the twenty-first century, they would cite the UN and AHDR Arab researchers. The indictment of Arab culture is so pronounced in the AHDR that, as Mayssoun Sukarieh concludes:

Western commentators have been given greater license to blame contemporary problems in Arab countries on Arabs themselves, while Western leaders have found a way to legitimize their reform programs for the region. Arabs, according to *The Economist* (2002), are "self doomed to failure." "Cultural values . . . are [the] chief obstacle to Arab progress," claims the Hoover Institute's William Ratliff, invoking the AHDR as the grounds for his argument. . . . Colin Powell, in his speech to launch the U.S. State Department's Middle East Partnership Initiative program, quoted from the report saying, "[T]hese are not my words. They have come from the Arab experts who have looked deeply into these issues."[286]

The circulation of the report through the international system of NGOs, as policy recommendations for US and European imperial policies, and through the international channels of Western liberal feminisms has served to confirm "Islam" and Arab "culture's" oppression of women and the need for Western and Muslim liberal feminists to rescue and save them.

The report's lead author, the Egyptian Nader Fergani, would insist on disowning the neoliberal parts of the report by blaming Rima Khalaf, the Palestinian-Jordanian Assistant Secretary-General and Director of

285. *AHDR*, 212.
286. Sukarieh, "The Hope Crusades," 126.

the Regional Bureau for Arab States at the United Nations Development Programme (UNDP) from 2000 to 2006, for the neoliberal bias. Khalaf, a neoliberal economist who served as a pro-privatization minister of planning and of industry and later as deputy prime minister in Jordan before acceding to her new position at the UN, is the official who founded and started the AHDRs. According to Fergani, who wants to blame her for whatever failings the reports had, Khalaf "did not have major intellectual qualifications, in the sense of not having any known scholarly or intellectual achievement."[287] Clearly, Fergani's feminist commitments seem to fail him when assessing Khalaf's curriculum vitae.

Fergani mentions the wide criticism of the report in the Arab world, which targeted the report's attack on Islam and religion more generally, by revealing the amount of discord among the more than one hundred researchers involved in writing it. However he would insist on the report's positive attitude towards Islam and religion more generally:

The report team included, especially its committee of consultants, a number of enlightened Islamist thinkers, as it included sometimes some of the ultra-secularists who felt that academic and scholarly standards demand that we not get into religious matters even if they related to the report's topics. This is why, in order for the report's [positive] position on religion, especially Islam, to be maintained, a heated battle was fought during the work on every publication [of the four AHDRs].[288]

Fergani explains the report's position on Islam by reiterating the report's call on new interpretations of religious dogma and jurisprudential opinions:

To establish . . . a renaissance in the Arab homeland demands opening the way to [new] jurisprudential opinions [al-ijtihad al-fiqhi] in order to establish the bases for coherence between . . . [a contemporary] human development in its comprehensive sense and the overall goals of Islamic shari'a, bypassing much of the jurisprudential opinions that prevailed during the age of decadence [in reference to the period of Ottoman rule], and which maintained oppression and despotism, left behind retardation and delay [takhalluf], and left the nation undefended before its enemies.[289]

287. Nadir Firjani, "Sirat Taqrir al-Tanmiyyah al-Insaniyyah al-'Arabiyyah: al-nashʾah, al-risalah, al-manhajiyyah, wa rudud al-fiʿl," *Majallat Idafat*, no. 1 (Winter 2008): 83–85.

288. Ibid., 84.

289. Ibid., 106.

Fergani also defends the report's findings and in a classic Orientalist move blames the "Arab mentality" (*al-ʿaqliyyah al-ʿarabiyyah*), Arab intellectuals, "the cultured/intellectual Arab self" (*al-dhat al-ʿarabiyyah al-muthaqqafah*), and Arab culture for not learning, or being open to, self-criticism. Indeed, it is not the report's failings that prompted Arab intellectuals to level criticisms against it, but rather their alleged inability to engage in self-criticism of their societies and culture.[290] The fact that Arab intellectual production since the nineteenth century has in its overwhelming majority expressed the most radical forms of "self-criticism" and "auto-critique" across the board (indeed one would be at a loss to find any serious Arab intellectual writing anything in celebration of modern Arab culture or anything related to it at all), and especially on the question of women's social position, often bordering on outright self-hatred, seems immaterial to Fergani, the liberal feminist.[291]

Expectedly and in the context of the international scope of liberal feminism, rather than setting a good standard of scholarship, the AHDR's approach to the study of the question of women in the Arab world is perhaps an excellent example of how one should *not* study gender and women in the Arab and Muslim worlds.

The Culture of Islam, or, How Not to Study Gender in the Muslim World[292]

One of the major developments in the last four decades on the academic scene of English-language (and some French) Middle East Studies is the emergence of many serious attempts to study "the woman question" in the Arab and Muslim worlds, provide histories of the different women's movements across this vast geographic and cultural area, historicize the emergence of women's education, political and cultural groupings, the women's press, women and religion, women's standing under the law (both positive and what is misnamed as "Islamic" law), and to a lesser extent, women and health, women and labor, women and capital, and much more.

While the focus on "the woman question" in the Arab and Muslim worlds specifically has had, as we saw, important Orientalist and colonial

---

290. Ibid., 98.

291. See Massad, *Desiring Arabs*, which documents how pervasive such self-criticisms are and have been across the Arab world since the nineteenth century to the present.

292. An earlier version of this section of the chapter was published in Arabic as "Kayfa ʿalayna alla nadrus al-nawʿ al-ijtimaʿi (al-jindar) fi al-ʿalam al-ʿarabi" (How Not to Study Gender in the Arab World), *Majallat al-Adab*, Beirut, June 2009.

precursors as well as local nationalist and liberal intellectual precedents from the early nineteenth century onwards, if not since the European Enlightenment, something different was emerging since the early 1970s that mainly attempted to critique as well as engage Orientalist colonial representations of Arab and Muslim women as well as anticolonial nationalist or liberal representations.[293] The decade of the 1970s saw the pioneering efforts of the Egyptian Nawal al-Saʿdawi in this regard, who engaged both with the Western women's movements and feminist critiques, colonial and nationalist histories, as well as apologist local representations of women.[294] Concomitant with the writings of al-Saʿdawi were the writings of the Moroccan professor Fatima Mernissi, who employed a Western academic idiom in her focus on women in the Arab or Muslim worlds and addressed mainly a Western audience with books and articles that on occasion critiqued Western understandings while reproducing Orientalist generalizations and Eurocentric epistemologies in analyzing Arab and Muslim societies, which she often conflated as one and the same.[295]

All this, however, would change with the advent of the 1980s and especially in the 1990s with the institutionalization of the category "gender" in academic discourse in Western universities, and also its proliferation to state decision makers and state policies in a number of Western countries, foremost among them the United States, and later, and as we saw, the imposition of this particular interpretation of human relations along an axis identified as "gender" through the United Nations and its many arms and branches across the globe as well as private US and European foundations, especially in the field identified as "development." As discussed in the early part of this chapter, Western development agencies and their local branches as well as Western human rights organizations and their local branches are beholden not only to these Western liberal definitions of rights and social structures but more importantly to universalizing them across the globe and reproducing the globe in the image of Europe as the only possible and viable model for ending different forms of injustice that are based on this thing called "gender."

293. For a review of Western academic scholarship on Muslim women inspired by Edward Said's *Orientalism*, see Lila Abu-Lughod, "*Orientalism* and Middle East Feminist Studies," *Feminist Studies* 27, no. 1 (Spring 2001): 101–13.

294. For her collected theoretical and historical works, see Nawal al-Saʿdawi, *Dirasat ʿan al-Marʾah wa al-Rajul fi al-Mujtamaʿ al-ʿArabi* (Studies about Women and Men in Arab Society) (Beirut: al-Muʾassassah al-ʿArabiyyah lil Dirasat wa al-Nashr, 1986).

295. See Fatima Mernissi, *Beyond the Veil: Male-Female Dynamics in Modern Muslim Society* (Cambridge: Schenkman, 1975). For a discussion of al-Saʿdawi and Mernissi's contributions in relation to women, culture, Islam, and sexuality, see Massad, *Desiring Arabs*, 152–57.

More recently, academic work on the gender question in Arab and Muslim societies began to involve masculinities and not only femininities and men and not only women. This is an important change that avoids the earlier collapse of women into gender. Moreover, while academic studies of the Muslim world produced in Western Europe and the United States have changed considerably since the 1970s, especially in the humanities, through taking more care in abandoning Orientalist methods, and have become more sophisticated in providing nuanced social and institutional histories, there remain important blind spots, especially in the social sciences by virtue of the insistence on universalizing Western taxonomies across the globe. While this major change in academe has been welcomed by many in the field, Western media representations of issues of gender in the Arab and Muslim world have not only remained within the confines of Orientalist and culturalist methods but have become more entrenched in their assumption of these positions. In this vein, predominant media representations, Western-funded NGO policies and activism, and some of the academic work on gender in the Arab world, often focus, as we saw, on certain kinds of gender-based crimes as exemplary of gender relations and on essentializing what are referred to often as "Arab masculinity" and "Arab femininity."

As already noted, some of the more important and particular crimes that seem to be the specialty of Arabs and Muslims in this discourse of "gender" injustice, whether in the Western media, some academic circles, European governments, and NGO discourse, is the hijab or certain and specific forms of it, "honor crimes," which we discussed above, and female circumcision or Female Genital Mutilation or Surgery (FGM or FGS). The hidden normativities of an ostensibly more neutral category like "health," or particularly "women's health," is surely also an important player on this terrain. These have been supplemented on occasion with notions like Arab or Muslim "patriarchy," the so-called special character of discrimination against women living under what is called "Islamic" or "Muslim law," and much more.[296] The UN and an entire industry of subsidiary organizations from the UNDP to ESCWA (Economic and Social Commission for Western Asia), including the AHDRs and other Western and Western-funded do-gooder NGOs, have flooded the region with offices and "development" policies that require the generation

---

296. On the question of patriarchy, see Mervat Hatem, "Class and Patriarchy as Competing Paradigms for the Study of Middle Eastern Women," *Comparative Studies in Society and History* 29, no. 4 (1987): 811–18, and Deniz Kandiyoti, "Islam and Patriarchy: A Comparative Perspective," in *Women in Middle Eastern History*, ed. Nikki R. Keddie and Beth Baron (New Haven, CT: Yale University Press, 1991), 23–42.

of unprecedented amounts of data for the purpose of fashioning policies based mainly on one of the major European and Euro-American epistemological approaches to non-European peoples, namely developmentalism, i.e., the Social Darwinist approach that stresses that non-Europeans live at the childhood stage of development and that mature adult Europeans and Euro-Americans, represented by these NGOs, will help to bring them to maturity through "development," which often includes Malthusian principles of population control usually enforced at the expense of women "for their own good."

The other major Western approach, namely radical alterity, is only adopted by Western militaries. Radical alterity is the approach that views non-Europeans as essentially so different from Christian Europeans and Euro-Americans that only destroying the infrastructures that maintain their "backward" and "oppressive" societies can usher them into Western modernity that is said to be characterized by equality and justice and prepare them for the badly needed developmentalist work of the NGOs—here the violent and quasi-genocidal destruction of Iraq and Afghanistan through massive US and allied invasions hoped to bring about the same sought-after "development" results that Western NGOs seek in other Third World countries by more "peaceful" means. Thus while developmentalism ushers in social and economic strategies whose effects can be violent by destroying local civil society activism in favor of one supported, created, funded, and inspired by Western strategies, and by reconfiguring social relations as replicas of a Western, mainly US-based model, seen as free from oppression, it differs from the radical alterity approach in the degree of violence it visits on "developing" societies, which in the case of radical alterity is a two-stage process that begins with military invasion and destruction of a society before the NGOs can enter to develop it along the right Western liberal path. Both developmentalism and radical alterity are deployed as internal to and supplemental aspects of imperial policy—including the central imperial interest in oil, stabilizing and/or producing Third World dictatorships, imposing a neoliberal economic order, and the backfiring of a Bismarckian short victorious war in relation to internal US electoral politics in the case of both US invasions of Iraq and the Gulf in 1991 and 2003 and of Afghanistan in 2001.

The proliferation of all these NGOs and of Western development discourse has had a drastic effect on local, national, and regional civil society activism, which NGOs not only help to demobilize by design but also replace with highly paid Western-funded Western and local experts, whereby many of the local experts were transformed from civil society activists into enforcers of Western developmentalism or simply replaced by new personnel conversant with Western methods of development (and here those chosen to contribute to all the AHDRs fit the role assigned them perfectly).[297] NGOs also produce local experts who can articulate the developmentalist issues in society in a Western academic and rights idiom that is fully in line with the reigning discourse. Commenting on this phenomenon in relation to women, Lazreg put it thus: "to what extent [these Arab women] do violence to the women they claim authority to write and speak about is a question that is seldom realized."[298]

Data generation is an essential part of the new NGOs masquerading as civil society. This is in line with neoliberalism as the ideology of experts from the International Monetary Fund and the World Bank down to local development NGOs, which amounts to no community accountability. The deployment of the discourse of expertise is a principal way for bypassing both local "cultural" norms and whatever structures of democratic representation and accountability may be extant on the ground. The production of data that is tabulable requires that new categories of thought and society be in place not only to make the data intelligible but also to produce it in the first place, and then to translate it and interpret it. Here the acts of production, translation, and interpretation are not necessarily consecutive steps but are in fact simultaneous because all three presuppose one another under the banner of assimilation. Thus if one begins with the premise that covering women's hair with a hijab is a sign of the restriction, say, rather than the expansion of women's sartorial choices, then the data collected on the numbers of women wearing the hijab in an Arab or Muslim society is already produced, translated, and interpreted by the initial epistemological consideration of hijab as restrictive and the political judgment attendant to it as discriminatory.

How can one, for example, collect data on whether people's sexuality is "repressed" if the notion of sexuality itself is not first imposed on people as an epistemological and ontological category that is said to constitute identity? How is one to analyze clitorodectomy in a society, like that of Egypt, where male and female "circumcision" are equalized as rites of passage and rituals and are called by the same name for boys and girls, *khitan* and/or *tuhur*? A related and more revealing question is why female circumcision is found to be violent and inhuman in developmentalist gender discourse but not so male circumcision? Indeed, the

297. On how this was done in the Palestinian case, see Islah Jad, "The Demobilization of the Palestinian Women's Movement," in *Women's Movements in the Global Era*, ed. Amrita Basu, 329–58.
298. Marnia Lazreg, "Feminism and Difference: The Perils of Writing as a Woman on Women in Algeria," *Feminist Studies* 14, no. 1 (Spring 1988): 89.

fact that male circumcision has been hegemonic in the United States since before World War II, as a result of a dominant Protestantism, and therefore considered normative and civilized, is the reason why it does not enter the developmentalist discourse either of the US government and its agencies, or of the United Nations and its subsidiary agencies as a "horrific cultural practice," which is reserved only for female circumcision. The practices held under the label "female circumcision" or more polemically "FGM," as has been asserted *ad nauseum* in the literature, vary radically from the nicking of the clitoris to infibulation. While the arguments usually explain the evidently different physiological effects of circumcision or genital mutilation on males and females to explain the horror at the latter, what it insists on sidestepping is the issue of genital mutilation *without consent* (for both boys and girls), which is a central basis of the FGM argumentation.

My point here is not to call on NGOs to launch more interventionist campaigns in Muslim countries to prohibit male circumcision (though racist and anti-Semitic European countries are already campaigning on this front)[299] but rather to demonstrate that their normative agendas of intervention are invariably based on what is considered normative and civilized in white Protestant middle-class society in the United States, and which they adopt and insist on disseminating across the globe. Indeed, were white Protestant American society to ever decide to stop circumcising boys and to launch an international campaign against male circumcision, imposing it globally through the United Nations, it would be yet again fully implicated in Islamophobia and anti-Semitism, let alone other forms of racism, in its quest to force Muslims and Jews to adopt Western Protestant norms (something that Europeans, most of whom do not circumcise their sons, are not reticent to do). The reaction to the 2012 ban by the Cologne regional appellate court in Germany on "religious" male circumcision is a case in point, especially as it was instigated by German Islamophobia that targeted German citizens of Turkish Muslim background whose circumcision of their male children

299. See the recent "Resolution 1952" passed by the European Assembly of the Council of Europe (an intergovernmental body that includes forty-seven European countries, including Turkey, twenty-eight of which are members of the European Union) in October 2013 on "Children's Right to Physical Integrity," which it considers violated by the following: "female genital mutilation, the circumcision of young boys for religious reasons, early childhood medical interventions in the case of intersex children, and the submission to, or coercion of, children into piercings, tattoos or plastic surgery," http://www.assembly.coe.int/nw/xml/XRef/Xref-XML2HTML-en.asp?fileid=20174&lang=en. Both Turkey and Israel (the latter has observer status in the Council) condemned the resolution. See Elcin Poyrazlar, "Turkey's Foreskin Wars," 5 February 2014, http://www.vocativ.com/world/turkey-world/turkeys-foreskin-wars/.

was represented as causing them bodily harm. German Muslims and Jews strongly opposed and condemned the measure.[300] The German Medical Association "condemned the ruling for potentially putting children at risk by taking the procedure out of the hands of doctors, but it also warned surgeons not to perform circumcisions for religious reasons until legal clarity was established." The ruling was, however, supported by *Deutsche Kinderhilfe*, a German child rights organization, which, invoking the discourse of rights, pointed out that religious circumcision may contravene the Convention on the Rights of the Child.[301]

When it comes to studying and representing gender in the Muslim world, we can summarize the major pitfalls of this type of research into three widespread approaches: culturalism, comparatism, and assimilationism. Let me turn to each separately:

Culturalism is the general approach of the Western media NGO discourse, and a good number of Western and Muslim academic and policy analyses, wherein any aspect of gender inequality in Arab or Muslim societies is reducible to cultural factors and explanations. The AHDR report discussed extensively above is a major case in point. This includes the major crimes and restrictions alleged to be practiced against women, including hijab, FGM, and "honor crimes," as well as notions like Arab or Muslim patriarchy exemplified by a special kind of machismo manifested in "Arab" or "Muslim masculinity," seen in the singular, and the oppressive nature of so-called Islamic law. Another aspect of culturalism is the transhistoricism of Western values—wherein the Qurʾan and medieval Muslim and Arab societies must correspond to modern Western and Christian values of judgment and must be evaluated accordingly. Their failures to accord with a fantastic version of modern Western societies will be subject to harsh judgment. Thus, the Prophet's marriage to the young Aisha has been condemned by Orientalist studies, which never bother to note that until the 16th century (a thousand years after the era of the Prophet), girls in Europe were married off at a similar young age.

Take another example of the attacks on Islamists as sexist, which many of them, though not all, are, not unlike most upholders of other political trends, and that Islamist political parties should be opposed

300. Melissa Eddy, "In Germany, Ruling Over Circumcision Sows Anxiety and Confusion," *New York Times*, 13 July 2012.

301. See "Anlässlich des Weltkindertages fordert die Deutsche Kinderhilfe ein klares Bekenntnis zu Kinderrechten statt Festtagsreden: Keine nicht-medizinische Beschneidung für einwilligungsunfähige Kinder," https://www.kinderhilfe.de/blog/artikel/anlaesslich-des-weltkindertages-fordert -die-deutsche-kinderhilfe-ein-klares-bekenntnis-zu-kinderrechten-statt-festtagsreden-keine-nicht -medizinische-beschneidung-fuer-einwilligungsunfaehige-kinder/.

on the basis that they would discriminate against women were they to come to power. This would be a credible claim if those making it would also condemn secularism and liberalism, whose laws and methods of governance ushered in what we identify today as legally based sexism and gender discrimination, or what Joan Scott calls "sexularism," since the French Revolution in Europe and, through colonialism, in the post-colonial Muslim-majority states.[302] This seems to be based on the false assumption, which Wendy Brown interrogates, that "Western secularism generates gender freedom and equality."[303]

Most laws on the books today that discriminate against women in formerly colonized Muslim-majority countries, including nationality laws, as we saw, are derived from Western liberal and secular colonial and national laws, yet no slogans that oppose secularism and liberalism, seen as European par excellence, have identified these ideologies as essentially sexist and gender-discriminatory; yet somehow all Islamists are often condemned for allegedly being *essentially* sexist and that this is the main characteristic of their social programs. The point here is that if the concern with Islamists taking power is because of some Islamists' gender policy or views (and many Islamist parties in fact have a far better record on gender equality and women's representation than secular parties across the region),[304] then why is opposition not articulated as strongly against non-Islamist parties whose record on women is often worse?[305] I do not mean to say that much of the academic and NGO research that is carried out in the Arab world ignores the local, which

302. On the problematic and undefended contention that secularism leads to nullification of sexism or to the end of gender discrimination, see Joan Wallach Scott, *The Fantasy of Feminist History* (Durham, NC: Duke University Press, 2011), chap. 4, on "sexularism," 91–116.

303. Wendy Brown, "Civilizational Delusions."

304. On Hamas's record on inclusion of women throughout the different levels of decision-making in the organization compared to leftist and secularist Palestinian groups, see Islah Jad, "Islamist Women of Hamas: A New Women's Movement," in *On Shifting Ground: Muslim Women in a Global Era*, ed. Nouraine-Simone (New York: Feminist Press at CUNY, 2005), 172–202. On the sexism of the secular Palestinian national movement, see Joseph Massad, "Conceiving the Masculine: Gender and Palestinian Nationalism," *Middle East Journal* 49, no. 3 (Summer 1995): 467–83.

305. In a similar vein, Saba Mahmood states that "I have seldom presented my work publicly without being asked if my analysis implicitly endorses a toleration for the injustices meted out to women in Iran, Pakistan, or by the Taliban government of Afghanistan. . . . Far more problematic is the assumption undergirding this concern that a critical attitude toward secular politics and its humanist assumptions, especially one that does not engage in repeated denunciations of all the harm done by Islamic movements around the world, is necessarily complicitous with their authoritarian practices. That an analysis of secular-humanist projects does not elicit a parallel demand for a denunciation of the crimes committed in their name, the unprecedented violence of the last century notwithstanding, is evidence of the faith that secular humanism continues to command among intellectuals." Saba Mahmood, "Feminist Theory, Embodiment, and the Docile Agent: Some Reflections on the Egyptian Islamic Revival," *Cultural Anthropology* 16, no. 2 (2001): 224–25.

is essential to understand the circumstances at hand, but rather that in many cases, and as we saw in the case of the AHDR, the attention to the local collapses into attention to the cultural and the religious.

Comparatism: This mainly means the transgeographism of Western values. It is a process by which the West, or a fantastic version of it, is taken as a comparative reference point and the rest of the world is studied to identify how it converges with or diverges from it. The comparison is often with a fantastical vision of Europe and the United States, which societies are not subjected to an analysis characterized by culturalist reductionism, and in which gender crimes are not exoticized or universalized. Let us take this example: if a man kills a woman in the United States or a European country (and according to statistics, over 30 percent of women killed in the US are killed by their husbands and boyfriends whereas more recent statistics from Italy reveal that 75 percent of women who are killed in the country are murdered by their current or former husbands or boyfriends),[306] the killing is not seen as part of a highly sexist Christian American or European culture in need of culturalist analysis, or even as part of a universal phenomenon (cultural or otherwise) of violence against women, and it is not subjected to special television programs and media campaigns that emphasize a culturalist schema, nor is it referred to in a category called "crimes of passion" or "honor crimes"; there are no UN campaigns, and no international NGO interventions to stop such killings (though local US women's groups attend to them as a local or national problem without using culturalist

---

306. See "Violence against Women: A National Crime Victimization Survey Report," US Department of Justice, Washington, D.C., January 1994, and Lawrence Greenfeld et al., eds., *Violence by Intimates: Analysis of Data on Crimes by Current or Former Spouses, Boyfriends, and Girlfriends* (Publication NCJ167237), (Washington, DC: US Department of Justice, Office of Justice Programs, Bureau of Justice Statistics, 1988), and available at http://www.ojp.usdoj.gov/bjs. See also the US-based Domestic Violence Resource Center, which provides more detailed statistics on these murders: http://dvrc-or.org/domestic/violence/resources/C61/#hom.

On Italy, see Elisabetta Povoledo, "A Call for Aid, not Laws, to help women in Italy," *New York Times*, 18 August 2013. In the case of Italy, there persist all kinds of Northern European and Protestant stereotyping (let alone northern Italian racial and cultural patronization toward southern Italians) which is also adopted by Italian feminists who invoke Italian "culture" as a problem for women. According to Povoledo, "victims' advocates also say that cultural factors contribute to violence against women. So-called honor killings of women said to have disgraced their family were legal until 1981, said Luisa Pronzato, who runs a blog about women for the Milan newspaper *Corriere della Sera*. Paternalism 'is part of our culture,' and it continues to permeate Italian society, she added." Despite the use of these cultural arguments, they are not the central arguments that are invoked, nor are women's murders presented as human rights violations. For how Italy is conceived in the making of Europe, see Roberto M. Dainotto, *Europe (In Theory)*, (Durham, NC: Duke University Press, 2007).

language and often insist that these crimes are at odds with a US "culture" that is allegedly based on equality).

Such statistics and practices are not compared to murder of women under the heading of "honor crimes" in a place like Jordan, where 25 percent of women who are killed every year are killed by male members of their families, and which is the highest rate of the crime in Arab and Muslim countries, even though it is lower than the rate of the murder of women in the US by their husbands and boyfriends. Yet Western media coverage and NGO attention and research have been extensively done on the case of Jordan, especially in the US, without comparisons to crimes against women in Europe and the United States but rather with comparisons to how in the West women are protected from these barbaric crimes. Some would say that in the US and West European countries, at least since the mid 1980s, laws that protected men who commit crimes against women have been removed but in Jordan they remain on the books. But if this is so, research has not turned to a condemnation of the Jordanian government and regime which uphold this law, and which is derived from the Napoleonic code, but Arab culture and "Islam" *tout court*, when as already stated above, all Islamic jurisprudential schools are condemnatory of "honor crimes" as murder and refuse to offer mitigating circumstances to men who commit them. Grewal explains how central the role of the media is in this campaign:

There is little doubt that 'honour' is now an overdetermined concept—the preferred term, in many regions, for practices linked to reputation, pride, masculinity or respectability. Honour enables sexual, economic and political control, through gendered violence and governmentality, and through the protection of women. It has thus become 'real,' incorporated within lived experience among those who claim to practise it and those who claim to eradicate it. Media circulation is an important aspect of how honour remains overdetermined in the contemporary moment, especially given the speed and reach of transnational media. A long colonial and newly racial history of anti-Muslim and anti-immigrant practices and beliefs ensures such media circulations.[307]

When culture is invoked in the West, it is mostly class-based or profession-based and not civilizational. Thus the working class or rich old white businessmen might be said to hold sexist attitudes or to have a sexist culture. Studies could also invoke the culture of the corporation, or of the law profession, or of surgeons, as sexist, but not of Western

---

307. Grewal, "Outsourcing Patriarchy," 15.

civilization as such. Yet in the Muslim world, every class and every profession seems to carry the burden of civilizational representation. Thus comparatism most often means that so-called Muslim failures should always be compared to Western achievement and successes. Those rare comparative studies of failures in both the West and the Muslim world, or the Third World more generally, on gender equality have failed to establish methodological hegemony and continue to languish outside it.

This sort of comparatism is also very much connected to media representations. While American television networks and the press often highlight the so-called Muslim failures on gender equality, let us imagine these kinds of representation if Al-Jazeera television were to undertake periodic reports on women in the United States highlighting the high rate of violence against them, through murder, rape, and domestic abuse. This is aside from labor discrimination, low rates of political representation, sexual harassment on the job front. Imagine that Al-Jazeera would undertake to explain the rate of American women who suffer from eating disorders, including Bulimia and anorexia, as examples of the barbarism of Euro-American culture, or that adult women not only choose to mutilate their bodies in the US and Europe at a staggering rate, but also that this mutilation is neither illegal nor condemned by civil society and that the media has flooded the airwaves with television programs glorifying and pushing for more such physical mutilation under the banner of plastic surgery and beauty. I should note here that FGM activism's main point is that girls who undergo circumcision or other forms of FGM have no choice in their mutilation. Yet, no activist horror is shown in NGO work or media representations about how large numbers of women and teenage girls in the US *choose* to mutilate their bodies. My point is to affirm that if Al-Jazeera were to undertake these reports on a culturalist and comparatist basis, it would be rightly accused of reductionism.

Another aspect would be if those who have flooded the academic market with studies of the hijab would ever turn their attention to gendered sartorial codes in the West and whether they exemplify gender inequality, oppression, etc. This is not to say that there are no commentaries or studies of these sartorial changes in Western countries, and about the radical sartorial revolution that the 1960s have ushered in, but that they are never highlighted as the most important sociological or cultural factor in gender inequality or women's oppression. In noting a feature in the *New York Times* about "real" New York women on the streets wearing high heels and platform shoes, Wendy Brown wonders:

Decades after Euro-Atlantic women rose up against the sexual codes that bound them to roles of subservience, unpaid and unrecognized labor, sexual availability and decorative objectification, what is to be made of these New York women teetering on the balls of their feet on stilts? Imagine walking for an hour in such shoes, let alone running for a bus, chasing after children, navigating inclement weather, standing all day at work or even for just two hours at a cocktail party in them. In Islamic female religious dress, one would surely be more comfortable, far less likely to sprain an ankle, slip on ice, trip on an uneven sidewalk, permanently damage one's feet, or succumb to chronic sciatica or other back injuries. One might also have better concentration, a wider subjective imaginary, and more versatility in greeting the various episodes and possibilities of a day. In short, if shoes nearly impossible to stand let alone walk in are freely chosen, that does not make them shoes of freedom, something of course that can be said of hijab or niqab as well. Yet to my knowledge, no one, anywhere in the Western world, has ever seriously considered passing legislation to outlaw such shoes, their making or their wearing, including in schools or state offices.[308]

While societal attitudes towards women's clothes in the Arab world are often invoked to connect them to a fantasized Arab patriarchy or so-called Muslim conservatism, they are never compared to similar Western societal attitudes and trends. The results of a poll conducted for the Home Office in Britain a few years ago revealed that one in seven people in the UK believe that women wearing revealing and sexy clothes deserve to be beaten up by their husbands, and that women who nag and moan at their husbands deserve to be slapped by them. The findings of the poll also disclosed that "about a quarter of people believe that wearing sexy or revealing clothing should lead to a woman being held partly responsible for being raped or sexually assaulted."[309] Cultural condemnation of Britain does not usually follow such polls, neither from the Western media nor from NGOs. Indeed, such sentiments about women are usually attributed in the gender discourse to "Muslim" attitudes on women's clothing. Irrespective of whether the measurement of these alleged Muslim attitudes are methodologically sound, what I want to stress is that comparisons of failures in Muslim-majority countries and the West are not evident in most research on gender. This is not to say that this is not invoked on occasion; it is to say that the

308. Wendy Brown, "Civilizational Delusions."
309. Richard Ford, "Women should be hit for wearing sexy clothing in public, one in seven believe," *Times*, London, online edition, 9 March 2009.

predominant approach remains culturalist and comparatist only in relation to Western success and Muslim failure.

Let me turn to the third approach: Assimilationism, or universalism as a cover for the supremacy of European and Euro-American social and cultural values. This factor is clearly related to comparatism and culturalism, since it presupposes both. If Arab and Muslim culture, seen as singular, unlike European and Euro-American culture, also seen as singular, is blamed for gender inequality, then this Arab and Muslim culture must be brought in line with European and Euro-American cultural achievement to be tolerable; it must be assimilated into a Western modern paradigm of gender rights and equality, otherwise it will continue to produce failures which will necessitate comparatism as the only way to analyze this failure. Assimilationism then is offered as the antidote not only to the problems of gender inequality but also to those who complain that Muslims are viewed through a culturalist or comparatist lens. If Muslims assimilate their values to European values, then they will cease to be studied in a culturalist or comparatist way, as they will have become the same as Europeans, which is the stated goal of developmentalism and modernization theory as carried through by the NGOs.

Thus to follow one or more of these three strategies—and they are invariably connected to one another so much so that if one follows one of them, then one perforce follows all three—is how analysts should not study gender in the Muslim world. Ultimately, the culturalist, comparatist, and assimilationist questions analysts pose prompt the very answers that this research assumes exists independently of the question. The only answers that such approaches produce are the ones wherein if scholars or NGO personnel use these approaches, they will produce these specific answers, which do not exist independently of their epistemological framework (the focus on outcomes for funding proposals reproduces this framework with a vengeance). In doing so, they would not be studying gender in the Muslim world but would be producing readymade answers that are prescribed by the very methods that are said to be discovering them.

Ultimately then, there are no tricks as to how to study "gender" in the Muslim world. If analysts attend to the social and economic factors, to the geographic and historical factors and *actors*, to culture as a dynamic entity that produces and is produced by social, economic, historic, and geographic factors and actors, analysts, whether Asian or African or European or American, will be able to begin to understand and analyze social phenomena based on terms and methods that the local situation on hand itself determines, rather than script them *a priori* with research agendas that are connected to imperial policies, namely developmentalism, and Orientalist methodologies of culturalism, comparatism, and assimilationism. Otherwise it would not be gender in the Muslim world that analysts are studying, but rather, and as we saw in much of this chapter, different strategies to transform Muslims into "liberal" Christian Europeans and to recreate the Muslim world in the image of an imagined liberal Christian Europe.

Recreating Muslims and Islam in the image of Christian and liberal Europe is therefore more about the relationship of Western liberal feminism to Christianity, liberalism, and Europe that can be consolidated in the act of repudiating Islam, conservatism, and the Orient as their opposites. The problems, identified in feminist scholarship, that American and European women had encountered with European religious, cultural, economic, social, and political practices over the last two centuries fall by the wayside in the production of Europe and its American extension as spaces of women's equality, of (Protestant) Christianity as a religion that accords women respect, and of liberalism as the secular variant of Protestantism that ensures these allegedly prevailing conditions in the form of "rights," which American and European feminists, in an act of Christian generosity to their kin, want to extend to their "Muslim sisters" through proselytization and conversion.

THREE

Pre-Positional Conjunctions: Sexuality and/in "Islam"

One could perhaps describe recent attempts in the Western academy as well as in the Western media, in NGO policies, and in human and sexual rights activism to create a conjunction between something called "sexuality" and another called "Islam" as a linking of objects of translations that purportedly have an immediate European and Euro-American liberal intelligibility that parades itself as universal. Thus this object called "Islam" is assumed to be translatable into the liberal European and Euro-American epistemology of religion, culture, civilization, system of thought, ethics, and more, just as corporeal practices of pleasure across the globe, among humans and animals alike, are said to be translatable into the modern European category of sexuality. As these acts of translation are assumed to be unproblematic or, if problematic are surmountable *a priori*, the conjunction which links them follows neatly in the footsteps of apprehending their translated significations, preparing them for the myriad intellectual and political projects the conjunction aims to generate.

To speak of "sexuality and Islam" already presumes that the speakers and the listeners already know what sexuality is and what Islam is and that all that is left to know and understand is the conjunction between the two, which is immediately transformed into a unidirectional pre-position, something along the lines of "sexuality *in* Islam" and almost never "Islam *in* sexuality." I will try to address what this means in the context of ongoing efforts by some to create and formulate, or even to assume a prior existence of a field of scholarship that is named, or, certainly, according to a number of scholars, should be named and constituted as "Queer Middle East Studies" under which rubric the question of sexuality and/in Islam can be posed.

Some thinkers have attended to the complications of the multiple referents Islam acquired since the eighteenth century. For example, Marshall Hodgson attempts to extricate Islam from its many meanings and confine its meaning to "the religion of the Muslims," suggesting that new terms that he coined such as "Islamdom" will clarify the general confusion created by the multiple referents Islam has. For Hodgson, "Islamdom" refers to "the society in which the Muslims and their faith are recognized as prevalent and socially dominant, in one sense or another . . . it does not refer to an area as such, but to *a complex of social relations*, which to be sure, is territorially more or less well-defined."[1] Similarly, Hodgson wants to deploy the term "Islamicate" to refer to "a *culture*, centered on a lettered tradition, which has been historically distinctive of Islamdom the *society*, and which has been naturally shared by Muslims and non-Muslims who participate at all fully in the society of Islamdom."[2] Yet, despite Hodgson's clarifying, because specifying, efforts which are informed more by a taxonomic need rather than concern about the historicity of the uses of "Islam," and leaving aside the problematic aspect of considering Islam as "religion," Hodgson himself titles his massive magnum opus about all aspects of "Islam," "Islamdom," and "Islamicate" *The Venture of Islam*.[3]

This has not dispelled the hope of some scholars that the term "Islamicate" is not essentializing in the way the terms "Islamic" or "Middle Eastern" can be, without clarifying how this is so, and that the term, for them, seems to be able to translate whatever they think must be translated into a European and Euro-American idiom more accurately than other terms. Thus Afsaneh Najmabadi and Kathryn Babayan insist on titling a recent book they edited *Islamicate Sexualities*, because they "wanted to move away from [the] geopolitical category [of Middle East] and its attendant Western ethnocentrism, which carries the additional burden today of disciplinary politics of area studies. Instead, we chose . . . Hodgson's coinage, Islamicate . . . [which] was intended to highlight a complex of attitudes and practices that pertain to cultures

---

1. Marshall G. S. Hodgson, *The Venture of Islam: Conscience of History in a World Civilization*, vol. 1, *The Classical Age of Islam* (Chicago: University of Chicago Press, 1974), 58.

2. Ibid.

3. See his discussion of the matter in ibid., 56–60.

and societies that live by various versions of the religion Islam." The editors recognize that "although the designation *Islamicate* carries its own limitations for our project, as it tends to reproduce a tradition of equating the Islamic world with its initial Arabo-Persian center, we use it here because of its conceptual movement away from the nineteenth century universalizing European idea that distinguishes between the world's cultures in part on the basis of religious denomination and that had dominated Islamic studies until Hodgson's proposition."[4] Admirable as their efforts are, however, it remains unclear how "Islamicate" escapes the distinction of religious denominationalism when it still names the "cultures" it seeks to know via the "religion" of which they are presented as the expression. Even though the authors, following Hodgson, compare "Islamicate" to "Italianate," they fail to see how "religions" and national adjectival affiliations have different genealogical trajectories and are not as assimilable into one another as they or Hodgson suggest.

Najmabadi and Babayan, and other contributors to their volume, do not clarify how Islamicate is different from Islamic or Muslim, especially as these three terms and even the term "Middle East" continue to be used interchangeably in their texts (notably in the introductory text by Valerie Traub), and often the word Islamicate seems to be used the very same way the word "Islamic" is used.[5] These problems notwithstanding, this thoughtful move on the part of the editors from an imperial nomenclature of "Middle East" to one that is presumably not imperial, albeit an archaic one, is not as successful as they intend, as the authors simply move from one post–World War I imperial nomenclature to another one, namely Islam and its derivatives, that emerged hegemonically after the United States won the Cold War and brought about the collapse of the Soviet Union.

Indeed, less careful scholars and activists continue to insist on this problematic deployment of "Islam," as do Samar Habib and Scott Kugle in recent books they unapologetically title *Islam and Homosexuality* and *Homosexuality in Islam* respectively.[6] In this chapter, I will address this

4. Kathryn Babayan and Afsaneh Najmabadi, *Islamicate Sexualities: Translations across Temporal Geographies of Desire* (Cambridge, MA: Harvard Center for Middle East Studies, 2008), ix.

5. Indeed, it often seems that the authors and editors employed the search function of their word processor and substituted the word "Islamic" with "Islamicate" across their texts with some exceptions. Najmabadi herself, in her book *Women with Mustaches and Men without Beards* (Berkeley: University of California Press, 2005), speaks of "Islamic societies of the Middle East" as a meaningful category, 8.

6. Samar Habib, *Islam and Homosexuality*, 2 vols. (Santa Barbara, CA: Praeger, 2010). The book, uninterested in theoretical questions, is a collection of twenty papers written by graduate students, journalists, sex tourists, activists, businessmen, and a few professors, only one of whom is

more recent Western liberal linkage of sexuality and/in Islam and review the most recent scholarly literature about it and the mission it sets itself to rescue and save Muslim "homosexuals" and "queers" from "Islam's homophobic grip." I will build on the arguments I made in my previous work on desire and sexuality and will elaborate on them in relation to the question of Islam in liberalism.[7]

The main arguments I base my analysis on and which much of the literature under review misses, neglects, misunderstands, or sidesteps include:

1. The important understanding that sexuality is a historically and culturally specific epistemological and ontological category and is not universal or necessarily universalizable—this includes sexuality's derivatives, homosexuality and heterosexuality (and bisexuality), whose consolidation as medical, juridical, and later social categories in late nineteenth- and early twentieth-century Western Europe and the United States is their hallmark, and heterocentrism, heterosexism, and homophobia as socially and culturally specific companions to these developments at the level of "Western" ontology.

2. The specific history of the US gay movement as part of American social and cultural history (and the correlate development of "straightness" as its normative counterpart), its export to Britain and non-English-speaking Western Europe and the attempt to export it to the rest of the world as an Anglo-American-centric identity category whose proponents insist on its universality and universalizability while maintaining its specific English name across languages and cultures.

3. The scholarly and activist commitment to the Euro-centric and imperial insistence that these culturally and historically specific categories be made universal and that the world be assimilated into European and Euro-American normativity as the only path to civilized modernity that merits "Western" tolerance and recognition.

---

specialized in anything connected to "Islam" (namely, the history of the Muslim Brotherhood). See their biographies in 2:489–93. See also Scott Kugle, *Homosexuality in Islam: Critical Reflection on Gay, Lesbian, and Transgender Muslims* (Oxford: Oneworld Publications, 2010). This trend continues unabated. More recently, the *Journal of Lesbian Studies* published a special issue on "Lesbians, Sexuality, and Islam," edited by Huma Ahmed-Ghosh, who speaks in her introduction of "lesbians in Islam"; see *Journal of Lesbian Studies* 16, no. 4 (2012): 378.

7. See Joseph Massad, *Desiring Arabs* (Chicago: University of Chicago Press, 2007). Much of the work under discussion in this chapter had not yet been published when my book *Desiring Arabs* went to press in 2006–7. In the rest of this chapter, I will recapitulate the arguments made in *Desiring Arabs* as well as address some of the responses that the book garnered since its publication. While *Desiring Arabs* elicited a great number of responses and comments, most of it positive, it has also elicited hostile and sometimes (expectedly) abusive responses by some scholars and activists, often intent on misrepresenting the arguments the book makes. I shall attend to some of these in an effort to explain what is at stake in these scholarly and political disagreements.

4. That these assimilationist activities, effected through the process of translation, result in the production of precisely what liberal Western-based scholars and sexual rights activists claim to be resisting in Europe and Euro-America and outside them, namely that by universalizing the hetero-homo binary, they end up heterosexualizing the world, not "queering" it.

5. A scholarly and activist commitment to what Foucault calls "the repressive hypothesis" in looking at sex and desire outside Europe and Euro-America, especially among Muslims, as "repressed," "confined," "restricted," and that their intervention will set it "free" and rescue and save their Muslim practitioners from their Muslim oppressors.

I will argue in conclusion, as in the cases of despotism and women's oppression discussed above, that much of this has less to do with something called "Islam" and everything to do with "sexuality" as a field of research and theater of rights activism in Western Europe and Euro-America and outside them. Deploying sexuality and sexual rights in the global arena will be shown to be essential to the consolidation of European and Euro-American identity and the continuing presentation of European "culture" and "civilization" as liberal, hence tolerant, just, liberatory, progressive, and enlightened, in contrast to a dark unjust, intolerant, regressive world to which Europe and Euro-America are constitutionally opposed and which they are committed to enlighten.

Universalizing Sexuality

As we have already reviewed in the first two chapters, Islam and its attendant adjectives are today what constitute the main targets of imperial policies. The name Islam is also generally and specifically the translation of everything that Euro-America and "Europe" wants to project onto its other. Islam has become indeed not only the principal name of the other, but the principal name through which Europe and Euro-America other all that they want to disavow to constitute and consolidate their modern civilized self—what psychoanalysis calls reaction-formation. The archives of evidence for this development abound, including official political discourse, media representations, academic analysis, human rights activism, and much more. Based on the uses and naming strategies to which Islam has been subjected in recent years, the question that needs to be addressed is not just an imperial political one but rather, and more centrally, an imperial *epistemological* one.

The problem with terms is not only a question of epistemology but expectedly has a number of ontological implications. This does not only apply to the term "Islam" but also to the term "sexuality" and subsidiary terms like "queer," "gay," "MSM," among others. Perhaps Michel Foucault's definition of sexuality can be our starting point:

The term itself did not appear [in Europe] until the beginning of the nineteenth century, a fact that should be neither underestimated nor overinterpreted. It does point to something other than a simple recasting of vocabulary, but obviously it does not mark the sudden emergence of that to which "sexuality" refers. The use of the word was established in connection with other phenomena: the development of diverse fields of knowledge . . . the establishment of a set of rules and norms—in part traditional, in part modern—which found support in religious, judicial, pedagogical and medical institutions; and changes in the way individuals were led to assign meaning and value to their conduct, their duties, their pleasures, their feelings and sensations, their dreams. In short, it was a matter of seeing how an "experience" came to be constituted in modern Western societies, an experience that caused individuals to recognize themselves as subjects of "sexuality," which was accessible to very diverse fields of knowledge and linked to a system of rules and constraints. What I planned [to write], therefore, was a history of the experience of sexuality, where experience is understood as the correlation between fields of knowledge, types of normativity, and forms of subjectivity in a particular culture.[8]

But if sexuality has a specific European history, even though, as Kobena Mercer and Ann Laura Stoler have demonstrated, this history is an effect and a product of European colonial encounters and is imbricated with the category and epistemology of race, the epistemological and ontological implications of the term are not easily transportable much less translatable to non-European contexts.[9] Also, Foucault's caveat that the appearance of the term "does not mark the sudden emergence of that to which 'sexuality' refers," undermines a good part of his project, as "sexuality" here, or its history, seems to signal not a new regime of subjectivity *tout court* but also, as Greg Thomas put it, "a more comprehensive genealogy of desire of which the contemporary sexual formation is

8. Michel Foucault, *The History of Sexuality*, vol. 2, *The Uses of Pleasure* (New York: Vintage, 1984), 3–4.

9. See Kobena Mercer and Isaac Julien, "Race, Sexual Politics and Black Masculinity: A Dossier," in *Male Order: Unwrapping Masculinity*, ed. Rowena Chapman and Jonathan Rutherford (London: Lawrence and Wishart, 1988), and Ann Laura Stoler, *Race and the Education of Desire: Foucault's History of Sexuality and the Colonial Order of Things* (Durham, NC: Duke University Press, 1995).

simply one part."[10] Thus becoming a "subject of sexuality," according to Foucault, is simply the most recent mode of how "Western man" had conceived of himself as a "subject of desire,"[11] rather than signaling the emergence of a classed and racialized *and* racially supremacist Western subjectivity more generally.

Foucault's problematic caveat aside, my point here is not to say that "sexuality" is experienced differently in different historical or geographical contexts and that it has distinct "cultural" interpretations that shape it, but rather, that "sexuality" itself, as an epistemological (that the world can only be apprehended and conceived through the regime of sexuality) and ontological (that sexuality tells/is the truth of the subject) category, is a product of specific Euro-American and European histories and social formations, that it is a Euro-American and European "cultural" (and institutional) category that is not universal *or necessarily universalizable*. Indeed, even when the category "sexuality" has traveled with European colonialism to non-European locales, its institutional, let alone "cultural," adoption in those contexts where it occurred was neither identical nor even necessarily symmetrical with its deployment in Europe and Euro-America.[12]

The category of sexuality continues to travel with imperial capital to the periphery, but its impact again is neither an assured one nor necessarily productive of the same effects it has at home. John D'Emilio has argued: "Gay men and lesbians have *not* always existed. Instead, they are a product of history, and have come into existence in a specific historical era . . . associated with the relations of capitalism."[13] I will add that this also applies to heterosexual and *straight* men and women who also are a product of a specific historical era and that, like gays and lesbians, their historical emergence and production was also specific to those geographic regions of the world and those classes within them where a specific type of capital accumulation had occurred and where certain types of capitalist relations of production prevailed.

10. Greg Thomas, *The Sexual Demon of Colonial Power: Pan-African Embodiment and Erotic Schemes of Empire* (Bloomington: Indiana University Press, 2007), 3.

11. Foucault, *The History of Sexuality*, 2:5–6.

12. This of course also means that sexual "orientation" (would it not be more appropriate to call it "occidentation"?) is also a culturally and historically specific concept. On this see Sonya Katyal, "Exporting Identity," *Yale Journal of Law and Feminism* 14, no. 1 (2002): 99.

13. John D'Emilio, "Capitalism and Gay Identity," in *The Lesbian and Gay Studies Reader*, ed. Henry Abelove, Michèle Aina Barale, and David M. Halperin (New York: Routledge, 1993), 468. For a recent discussion of the literature on globalization, see Jon Binnie, *The Globalization of Sexuality* (London: Sage Publications, 2004).

But if capitalism is the universalizing means of production and it has its own intimate forms and modes of framing them, these forms and modes have not been institutionalized across national laws and economies and in the quotidian and intimate practices of various peoples in the same way and have not produced similar effects as they have in the US and Western Europe (which is not to say that the hetero/homo binary was fully successful in normalizing Euro-American societies either, but, rather, that it set itself as the hegemonic form of organizing identities and continues to normalize populations in the West who resist it). The inability of the hetero/homo binary and its commensurate socio-sexual identities to institute themselves in the same way everywhere is also not unlike many other categories and products that travel with imperial capital from the metropole to the unevenly developed periphery and are not always used or consumed in the same metropolitan way. As Greg Thomas argues, "the possibilities of erotic identity or embodiment are by no means exhausted by what Europe would call heterosexuality and homosexuality. This narrow opposition is neither natural nor universal; it is modern, Western, and bourgeois or ruling-class. It is conventionally white and white supremacist as it upholds a much larger sexual opposition between the 'civilized' and the 'uncivilized,' the colonized and the colonizer."[14] Even in early twentieth-century New York, as George Chauncey has shown, sexuality had not yet been established as the dominant regime of truth for everyone: "The most striking difference between the dominant sexual culture of the early twentieth century and that of our own era is the degree to which the earlier culture permitted men to engage in sexual relations with other men, often on a regular basis, without requiring them to regard themselves—or be regarded by others—as gay. . . . Many men . . . neither understood nor organized their sexual practices along a hetero-homosexual axis."[15]

Indeed the sexual order of the postcolonial context in which contemporary Western sexual identities are introduced is already the effect of a colonial epistemology that has been translated and iterated earlier. As I chronicled in *Desiring Arabs*, the European shaming of non-Europeans on the basis of sexual desires and practices begins at the dawn of the colonial encounter, inciting a reactive discourse of assimilation into

14. Thomas, *The Sexual Demon of Colonial Power*, 22. Thomas adds: "Like heterosexuality, and all sexual neurosis in the West, homosexuality is a culturally specific rather than natural, universal phenomenon. And, like heterosexuality and neurosis, it can only be universalized through imperialism" (87).

15. George Chauncey, *Gay New York: Gender, Urban Culture, and the Making of the Gay Male World, 1890–1940* (New York: Basic Books, 1994), 65.

(and, at times, difference from) the then prevailing European Victorian norms. Thus the more recent imperial export of the homo-hetero binary and specifically of gay (and much less so lesbian) identity takes place in a context that has already suffered a prior process of translation that produced particular "peripheral" understandings of normative and natural desires inflected with Western medical and scientific arguments and taxonomies, but which mostly failed to institute a Western regime of sexuality.

My argument is not that these sexual identities always fail to institute themselves inside or outside the West and that this failure is total, but rather that they succeed and fail differentially across classes and countries depending on the effect of capitalist structures and their production of certain lifestyles and forms and modes of intimate life on different classes, which are in turn the outcome of uneven capitalist development. Moreover, while imperial capital is often productive of new identities, including sexual identities commensurate with its dissemination of the heterosexual bourgeois nuclear family form globally, whatever new sexual identities it creates and generates in the periphery are not always or often mappable onto the homo-hetero binary. That international sexual identitarians and some among peripheral elites seek to assimilate these identities into the homo-hetero binary in a procrustean fashion is itself, as Dennis Altman famously argued, a (culturally imperialist) symptom of imperial capital's penetration and not its effect.[16] Here

16. See Dennis Altman, "On Global Queering," *Australian Humanities Review*, electronic journal: http://www.australianhumanitiesreview.org/archive/Issue-July-1996/altman.html#2 (accessed 1 April 2014) and the responses the essay garnered in the same journal issue. While often critical of the universalizing projects of gayness and queerness, Altman's work unfortunately invokes some universal "shared [homo]sexuality," failing to question the universalization of the category "sexuality" itself. See his "Global Gaze/Global Gays," *GLQ* 3, no. 4 (1997): 433. In contrast with Altman, Tom Boellstorff is so committed to a conflation of same-sex practitioners and homosexual *and* gay identities, that he misreads my assertion in my article "Re-Orienting Desire: The Gay International and the Arab World" (published in *Public Culture*, Spring 2002) that the adoption of gay identity in the Arab World is restricted to those in the upper and upper middle classes, on account of their economic transformation and access to Westernization and Western cultural and consumer products, as evidence of my "participation in the [Western] stereotype that homosexuals are upper class"! Reading my neologism "Gay International" (not as the intended irony that unlike the Communist International, which sought to include all communists and wage laborers under capitalism globally into its revolutionary goals—the cultural and economic limitations of which notwithstanding—the Gay International produces the very subjects it claims to defend) through an anticommunist ideological framework which he does not question and which he unfortunately projects onto me, Boellstorff believes the neologism "could be seen to suggest a global gay menace by participating in the McCarthyist stereotype that homosexuals recruit." Note how in his use, gay and homosexual are mere synonyms. See Boellstorff, *The Gay Archipelago: Sexuality and Nation in Indonesia* (Princeton, NJ: Princeton University Press, 2005), 233n. Boellstorff also criticizes Neville Hoad's seminal book *African Intimacies: Race, Homosexuality, and Globalization* (Minneapolis: University of Minnesota Press, 2007) in relation to his arguments about the imperial character of much gay internationalism

we must bear in mind that, as Edward Said reminds us, "imperialism is the export of identity."[17] It operates in the register of producing non-Europe as other, and sometimes as almost the same as (or potentially the same as) Europe.

D'Emilio sought to demonstrate that the effect of capitalism on the emergence of gay and lesbian identities in the West was both an outcome of the objective *and* subjective effects of capital, in that it was following the *objective* development of labor relations that required new residential and migratory activities and the dissolution or weakening of kinship and family ties and the development of a consumer society *and* the *subjective* emergence of social networks that produce, shape, and articulate sexual desires that are commensurate with these changes, which led to the development of sexual identities. The extent to which crusading sexual identitarians have insisted on the presence of such identities in a number of countries in the periphery as proof of a parallel development of what happened in Europe and the United States, however, appeals to the subjective identifications of few elite members of these societies, and neglects the absence of economic and social structures that led to their emergence in the West.

American and West European sexual identitarians never question the teleological schema that there is one possible outcome that the global-

---

by insisting that such arguments are polemical and devoid of facts: "These kinds of accusations, found also in the work of scholars such as Joseph Massad, are typically made at a polemical level, with little supporting evidence and significant mischaracterisations as to the size, power, composition, and intentions of transnational queer activist networks," in Boellstorff, "Queer Trajectories of the Postcolonial," *Postcolonial Studies* 11, no. 1 (2008): 116. In a review of the literature of queer studies, Boellstorff continued to propose similar unsubstantiated claims and misreadings of the scholarship of Jasbir Puar (he cites her "Circuits of Queer Mobility: Tourism, Travel, and Globalization," *GLQ* 8, nos. 1–2 [2002]: 101–37) and my own, charging that "in comparison with more ethnographically informed research, such work often presumes that persons outside the West terming themselves lesbian or gay are inauthentic: wealthy, connected to nongovernmental organizations, mobile, and ultimately estranged from their own cultures." See Tom Boellstorff, "Queer Studies in the House of Anthropology," *Annual Review of Anthropology* 36 (September 2007): 23. This strikes me as a gross misunderstanding, as neither my scholarship nor Puar's has any investment in anything resembling "authentic" or "inauthentic" identities. Boellstorff's frustration with my scholarship on this issue may very well be on account of my insistent refusal to function as a native informant for "Arab," "Muslim," or "Islamic" sexuality by producing such data in the form of ethnography, and my refusal to accept the notion of "sexuality" itself as a transhistorical and transgeographic descriptive and analytic concept with universal applicability. In his review of the literature Boellstorff admirably questions the historicity and possible universalization of identities that come together under the rubric of LGBTIQ, but not the notion of "sexuality" itself, which he holds as both objective and universal. He concludes by announcing that his survey "has provided insights on the place of sexuality in the human journey," where "human" is presumably the universalizing code for European and Euro-American (ibid., 27).

17. Edward W. Said, *On Late Style: Music and Literature against the Grain* (New York: Pantheon, 2006), 85.

ization of capital will bring about in modes and forms of sexual intimacies and identities around the world, namely the same outcome that capital produced in their parts of the world. Indeed, if like Leninists in a different register, they believe that capital will only create the *objective* conditions for the institution of the homo-hetero binary, they hope to play the role of the vanguard party in bringing about the subjective conditions and lead the masses to the achievement of homo- and heterosexuality, which on their own the masses would not be able to bring about. Even though neither the subjective nor the objective conditions that capital produced in the West are in evidence elsewhere, sexual identitarians churn out a lone example to support their position on the Arab world, namely Lebanon's Helem organization, which was founded at the end of 2004 and is currently made up of some thirty "homosexual" members in a country of four million people in a region of 350 million Arabs.[18] But Helem is hardly original in its endeavors. Dennis Altman argued in 1996 that

many non-Western homosexuals are nonetheless attracted to a Western model, which they seek, consciously or not, to impose on their own movements. They are aided by discourses of human rights and the more specific language of AIDS/HIV (thus recognition of a gay community becomes a frequent demand at most international AIDS conferences). When such demands are voiced in the name of representing Asians or South Americans, is it to be understood as the oppressed demanding to be heard or as a new stage of internalized imperialism?[19]

It is my estimation that the record of the last fifteen years suggests the latter more emphatically than the former, and not only in the case of "non-Western homosexuals" but also and equally of non-Western homophobes.

In the case of Helem, the organization has been financed since 2005 by the Ford Foundation and the Astraea Lesbian Foundation for Justice, a New York-based Gay-Internationalist organization that funds gay organizations separated from the US by "continents, language, and culture," and which itself receives large funds from the Ford Foundation.[20] Helem

18. On the Lebanese Helem (the acronym for Al-Himayah al-Lubnaniyyah lil-Mithliyyin, or "Lebanese Protection for Homosexuals"), the number is given by the organization's "social counselor" Sharbil Maydaʿ as forty members "twenty percent of whom are not homosexual but support our rights." See "Hulm Taʿtasim Didd al-ʿUnf" (Helem stages a sit-in against violence), *Al-Safir*, 23 February 2009.

19. Dennis Altman, "Rupture or Continuity? The Internationalization of Gay Identities," *Social Text*, no. 48 (Autumn 1996): 85.

20. See Astraea's website, http://www.astraeafoundation.org/about/. On Astraea's financial backers, see Astraea's 2008 Annual Report available on its website, 36.

is also financed by grants from the Dutch Embassy, the Heinrich Böll Foundation, the Chicago-based Heartland Alliance (which funds gay organizations only in the Third World—Nigeria, Sri Lanka, Guatemala, and Lebanon),[21] UNAIDS, and the World Bank.[22] It is important to stress here that Helem was not founded by an existing gay community in Lebanon; rather, Helem's purpose is to *create* such a community.[23]

How then can one study a category of knowledge, an object of socio-logical research, an epistemology of experience, and an institutionalized notion deployed to effect social normativity, let alone one that is crucial to subject formation, which is principally what sexuality is as a modern European usage, in societies that do not deploy it as a means of subjec-tive identification or apprehension of human conduct or human sexual desires? Perhaps a remark by Foucault here is in order with regards to the specific class basis of European sexuality:

If it is true that sexuality is the set of effects produced in bodies, behaviors, and social relations by a certain deployment deriving from a complex political technology, one has to admit that this deployment does not operate in symmetrical fashion with re-spect to social classes, and consequently, that it does not produce the same effects in them. . . . [W]e must say that there is a bourgeois sexuality, and that there are class sexualities. Or rather, that sexuality is originally bourgeois, and that, in its successive shifts and transpositions, it induces specific class effects.[24]

21. See their website at http://www.heartlandalliance.org/international/partners/global-equality-network.html.

22. See *HELEM: A Case Study of the First Legal, Above-Ground LGBT Organization in the MENA Region*, report published 21 October 2008, 11–12. The organization's website is entirely in English, even though it posts Arabic-language newspaper articles in Arabic. For a recent exchange between Helem's executive director Ghassan Makarem and me over my comments about Helem in an in-terview, see the following: "The West and the Orientalism of Sexuality: Joseph Massad (Columbia University) talks to Ernesto Pagano," *Reset DOC*, 1 December 2009, http://www.resetdoc.org/EN/Massad-interview-gay.php (accessed 1 April 2014). See also the letter to the editor written by Ghassan Makarem, "We are not Agents of the West," *Reset DOC*, 10 December 2009, http://www.resetdoc.org/EN/Helem-replies-Massad.php. My reply to him was published on 14 December 2009, http://www.resetdoc.org/EN/Massad-counter-replies.php.

23. In a recent article purporting to present the "story" of Helem's founding, its current director Ghassan Makarem does not even list the names of the founders of the organization or the internal disputes that led to the exit of many among them and among many Helem members over the past few years, much less the disputes that led to his takeover of the organization. Indeed, the history he provides is so general that one learns very little about the organization beyond rhetorical flour-ishes about its alleged anti-imperialism while being on the payroll of imperial organizations whose agenda Helem pursues with much zeal. See Ghassan Makarem, "The Story of Helem," *Journal of Middle East Women's Studies* 7, no. 3 (2011): 98–113.

24. Michel Foucault, *The History of Sexuality*, vol. 1, *Introduction* (New York: Vintage, 1980), 127. Foucault is surely not the first theorist to speak of the class basis of sexuality. In a different register V. N. Voloshinov asserts in his 1920s critique of psychoanalysis that "the homosexual inclinations of an ancient Hellene of the ruling class produced absolutely no conflicts in his behavioral ideology;

This asymmetry in the deployment of European bourgeois sexuality in the colonies is compounded by the sexual identities generated by nineteenth- and early twentieth-century European discourses on identity in general and the invention of categories, experiences, and objects of knowledge named heterosexuality (whose normative sense did not emerge till the twentieth century),[25] bisexuality, and homosexuality, let alone later social identities that developed in specific contexts in the United States under the banner of gay and lesbian identities and their straight other.

Moreover, if the history of gay and lesbian activism in the United States proceeded from a cultural oppositional movement demanding the right to be *different* from heterosexuals but have the same rights, its second phase was its very demobilization as a movement and its institutionalization in committees, academic programs, government and civil society policy-making bodies, and local and international nongovernmental organizations that work to bring about the recognition of the right of gays and lesbians to be the *same* as heterosexuals. As Lisa Duggan puts it:

No longer representative of a broad-based progressive movement, many of the dominant national lesbian and gay civil rights organizations have become the lobbying, legal, and public relations firms for an increasingly narrow gay, moneyed elite. Consequently, the push for gay marriage and military service has replaced the array of political, cultural, and economic issues that galvanized the national groups as they first emerged from a progressive social movement context several decades earlier.[26]

That no similar social movements exist anywhere in what is misnamed as the "Islamic world" has not stopped European and Euro-American efforts to institutionalize gay and lesbian (though the latter is rarely emphasized beyond the rhetorical) identities via Western and Western-funded NGOs crowding civil society in this "Islamic world" and via academic projects located in US and some European universities. It is hardly incidental that the historical moment when the Gay International emerges is the globalizing neoliberal moment that proliferated in the United States and Western Europe and coincided with the

---

they freely emerged into outward speech and even found formulated ideological expressions (e.g. Plato's *Symposium*)." V. N. Voloshinov, *Freudianism: A Marxist Critique* (London: Verso, 2012), 145. Here Voloshinov is of course speaking of same-sex desires and practices, not of identities.

25. See Jonathan Ned Katz, *The Invention of Heterosexuality* (New York: Dutton, 1995).

26. Lisa Duggan, *The Twilight of Equality? Neoliberalism, Cultural Politics, and the Attack on Democracy* (Boston: Beacon Press, 2003), 45.

increasing weakness and ultimate collapse of the Soviet Union. Indeed, it was in the era of Reaganism and Thatcherism that a major incitement to tether gay rights to anticommunism would be made, namely in 1984 with the launch of the French-produced anti-Cuban regime propaganda film *Improper Conduct* (*Mauvaise Conduite*, directed by Cuban dissidents Néstor Almendros and Orlando Jiménez Leal), which targeted the Cuban regime as a tyrannical violater of the rights of homosexuals. The film won several human rights prizes in Western Europe in addition to the Best Documentary Audience Award at the 1984 San Francisco International Lesbian and Gay Film Festival.[27]

The case of Helem is emblematic of what happened to the women's movements in the Arab world after the proliferation of US- and European-funded nongovernmental organizations beholden to Western neoliberal agendas. What is noteworthy here is the institutionalization in US governmental policies and law of a major strand of 1970s American feminism, which was then forced upon the world by the US government through the mechanism of the United Nations and Western private foundations.[28] If 1970s-style feminism lost much steam in the US academy by the end of the 1980s in favor of more sophisticated feminist methods that critiqued liberal and moralist approaches, what was internationalized and became institutionalized in the emerging Western-funded nongovernmental organizations that invaded the Third World as part of the neoliberal era was, as we saw in chapter 2, this earlier white middle-class Protestant feminism as *the* universal model. It is the emergence of such NGOs, as a substitute for local civil society, with their cooptation of many activist women who were transformed into salaried managers of organizations, that shifted existing strategies and goals of local activism to 1970s American-style feminism. Indeed, not only local activists but also local intellectuals, many of whom are Western-educated, who staff these NGOs, are utterly ignorant of later trends in US feminism, except for the multiculturalist turn that solidified 1970s feminism in new guise, and boast of their recent adoption of such feminism as contemporary academic theory and show little awareness of the massive critiques leveled against it since the 1980s in the US academy

27. On the question of Cuban communism and homosexuals, see Lourdes Arguelles and B. Ruby Rich, "Homosexuality, Homophobia, and Revolution: Notes toward an Understanding of the Cuban Lesbian and Gay Male Experience," part 1 in Signs 9, no. 4 (Summer 1984): 683–99, and part 2, Signs 11, no. 1 (Fall 1985): 120–35.

28. On the institutionalization of 1970s American feminism in the United States, see Janet Halley, *Split Decisions: How and Why to Take a Break from Feminism* (Princeton, NJ: Princeton University Press, 2008).

by white and nonwhite US feminist scholars as well as by Third World (including Arab and Muslim) feminist scholars (which we discussed in the previous chapter). It is also the discourse of activist gay internationalism that follows 1970s feminism that the US government and American funders push on the rest of the world and that organizations like Helem adopt, completely oblivious to the critiques leveled by queer theory since the 1990s about the sexual theories and politics pushed by the earlier phase of gay activism and scholarship.

The US governmental adoption of gay internationalism has become so institutionalized and so focused on what it terms the "Islamic" world that the US embassy in Islamabad and its "Chargé d'Affaires Ambassador Richard Hoagland and members of Gays and Lesbians in Foreign Affairs Agencies (GLIFFA)" hosted the embassy's "first ever gay, lesbian, bisexual, and transgender (GLBT) Pride Celebration" on 26 June 2011. The US embassy in Pakistan's press release explained: "This gathering demonstrated continued U.S. Embassy support for human rights, including LGBT rights, in Pakistan at a time when those rights are increasingly under attack from extremist elements throughout Pakistani society." The press release informs us that "Addressing the Pakistani LGBT activists, the Chargé, while acknowledging that the struggle for GLBT rights in Pakistan is still beginning, said 'I want to be clear: the U.S. Embassy is here to support you and stand by your side every step of the way.'"[29] This US imperial neoliberal model of universalizing sexual and gender conceptions, especially in the "Islamic" world, informs much of the contemporary politics and polemics about "sexuality" and "Islam." The announcement by the Obama White House in December 2011 that the US government would link its foreign aid program to the adherence of other countries to its vision of sexual rights and the "protection" of sexual identities, which was also articulated in a speech by Secretary of State Hillary Clinton, is the most recent and grandiose of these imperial policy gestures.[30] It should be mentioned that Obama is actually following British prime minister David Cameron, who threatened suspension of aid to Nigeria in October 2011 over the issue of gay rights.[31]

29. From the US embassy website: http://islamabad.usembassy.gov/pr_062611.html (accessed 1 April 2014).

30. See "Memorandum for the Heads of Executive Departments and Agencies: International Initiatives to Advance the Human Rights of Lesbian, Gay, Bisexual, and Transgender Persons," issued by The White House Office of the Press Secretary, 6 December 2011.

31. Dotun Ibiwoye, "Gay Right Controversy: A Gathering Storm over Cameron's Comments," *Vanguard*, 23 November 2011.

This is not necessarily separate from the fact that while earlier scholars who wrote on sexuality "in Islam" were Arab liberals,[32] some of
those writing on the question of "sexuality and Islam" since the late
1980s belong to right-wing neoliberal imperial political currents. For example, Stephen O. Murray, co-editor of one of the earlier volumes on
"Islamic homosexualities,"[33] is a member of the right-wing and neoliberal Independent Gay Forum to which he contributed an article titled
"Why I Don't Take Queer Theory Seriously."[34] Afsaneh Najmabadi herself, a former leftist, had turned right-wing and pro-imperialist a decade
before 9/11 and attacked Edward Said for daring to criticize the 1990/91
pro-war stances of Thomas Friedman, Bernard Lewis, Fouad Ajami, and
her ex-husband Kanan Makiyyah, all of whom she zealously defended
against Said, whose criticisms, she insisted, amounted to the "rhetorical
equivalent of political murder." In her diatribe against Said, Najmabadi
volunteered the example of her half-Iraqi daughter, who was allegedly
embraced by her (white) American teachers at school during the Gulf
War of 1990/91 as proof of the absence of anti-Arab racism in the US
and as a solid refutation of Said's contention that such racism exists.[35]

The more contemporary move to queerness in the United States as a
resistance to identitarian essentialism, however successful or unsuccessful it is, also retains its localist coloring and is not so easily transmutable
or translatable as many authors and activists in the field of sexuality in
the United States and Western Europe imagine. This does not mean that

32. Examples include Fatima Mernissi, *Beyond the Veil: Male-Female Dynamics in Modern Muslim Society* (Cambridge: Schenkman, 1975) and Abdelwahab Bouhdiba, *La sexualité en Islam* (Paris: Presses universitaires de France, 1975). For a discussion of their books, see my *Desiring Arabs*, 144–57 and 152–57 respectively. See also B. F. Musallam, *Sex and Society in Islam: Birth Control before the Nine-teenth Century* (Cambridge: Cambridge University Press, 1983).

33. Stephen O. Murray and Will Roscoe, eds., *Islamic Homosexualities: Culture, History, and Liter-ature* (New York: New York University Press, 1997). For a discussion of the book, see *Desiring Arabs*, 170–71.

34. Cited in Duggan, *The Twilight of Equality*, 49.

35. Afsaneh Najmabadi, "Said's War on the Intellectuals," letter to the editor, *Middle East Report* 2 (November-December 1991): 42–43. Najmabadi's right-wing politics manifested strongly after 9/11 when she was overcome with a sense of "shame" and "responsibility" for what happened. She insisted that any Arab or Iranian who condemns these acts but tries in any way to explain the history behind the bitterness felt by Arabs and Iranians against the US for the harm it had caused and continued to cause them would be complicit in terrorism: "every time that we say 'but', every time we choose to 'explain', we become implicated in regenerating a political culture and an ethical outlook that becomes part of the state of being in the world that allows hostage-taking and suicide bombing. It allows the September 11th tragedy." She insisted that Palestinians and Iranians should always apologize to white Americans and Jewish Israelis for any act of violence against them com-mitted by any Palestinian or Iranian, short of which all Palestinians and Iranians (indeed all "Middle Easterners") would be "implicated in that tragedy." Afsaneh Najmabadi, "Wrong Regardless," let-ter to the editor, *Iranian*, 18 September 2001, http://iranian.com/Opinion/2001/September/Wrong /index.html.

European colonial powers have not deployed or tried to deploy the category and object sexuality and its attendant identities as a mode of subject formation in ruling colonially subjected non-European populations. It is to say that this deployment was commonly internalized (and sometimes resisted) at the level of intellectual (and rarely, juridical) discourse, but seldom internalized and often resisted at the level of practices and failing to become a hegemonic epistemology or ontology—something that European and Euro-American anthropology of non-European cultures assiduously studies and observes with much curiosity.

On an academic level, the most salient problem of research on sexuality and culture is perhaps the inclination toward assimilating others into the European self under the sign of universalization as identity, or representing the other as exemplifying an unbridgeable radical alterity, under the sign of localism as difference. The outcome of such approaches leads not only to the commission of scholarly mistakes by reading signs through a Western grid of interpretation, but also of methodological ones, by risking the reification of the recently hegemonic hetero-homo binary prevailing in the West as either a transhistorical, transgeographical, and transcultural phenomenon, or as a feature characterizing the superior notion of the human as defined by the European experience and its interpreters, or even as the intimate consequence of capitalist penetration.[36]

Since the institutionalization of the hetero-homo binary in Western medicine and law in the nineteenth and early twentieth centuries and its proliferation across the surface and interstices of cultural products, cultural historians and literary critics in the US and West European academy have espoused the binary as a transhistorical and transcultural truism that the hand of scholarship need only reach to interpret accordingly. Eve Kosofky Sedgwick had put it thus: "An understanding of virtually any aspect of modern Western culture must be, not merely incomplete, but damaged in its central substance to the degree that it does not incorporate a critical analysis of modern homo/heterosexual definition."[37] While Sedgwick has been careful to limit her claim to the "modern West," others have been less so. Not only were figures from the constructed past of Europe and the rest of the globe (from Plato, Sappho, Catullus, Ovid, and Abu Nuwas, to Oscar Wilde and

36. I have adapted this from my essay "Sexuality, Literature, and Human Rights in Translation," in *Teaching World Literature*, ed. David Damrosch (New York: Modern Language Association, 2009).

37. Eve Kosofsky Sedgwick, *Epistemology of the Closet* (Berkeley: University of California Press, 1990), 1.

Marcel Proust) brought to the present and endowed with sexual identities commensurate with the recently invented binary as definitional of their sexual desires, experiences, and identities, but so were figures from the contemporary world that lie outside Western definitions brought into this new sexual binary as the only possible interpretative grid of their desires, experiences, and identities.

Kath Weston argued in a 1993 survey that "lesbian/gay studies in anthropology reached a turning point when researchers moved beyond fact-finding missions, typologies, and correlational studies to formulate questions about historical change, material relations, and how 'the natives' conceptualized behaviors that observers glossed as transgendering and homosexuality."[38] Carole Vance in turn offered a forceful evaluation of such research prior to 1990:

The cultural influence model assumes that sexual acts carry stable and universal significance in terms of identity and subjective meaning. The literature routinely regards opposite gender sexual contact as 'heterosexuality' and same gender contact as 'homosexuality,' as if the same phenomena were being observed in all societies in which these acts occurred. With hindsight, these assumptions are curiously ethnocentric, since the meanings attached to these sexual behaviors are those of the observers and 20th century complex, industrial society. Crosscultural surveys could fairly chart the distribution of same or opposite gender sexual contact or the frequency of sexual contact before marriage. But when investigators report instead on the presence or absence of "homosexuality" or "sexual permissiveness," they engage in a spurious translation from sexual act or behavior to sexual meaning and identity, something later theoretical developments would come to reject. . . . To summarize, the cultural influence model recognizes variations in the occurrence of sexual behavior and in cultural attitudes which encourage or restrict behavior, but not in the meaning of the behavior itself. In addition, anthropologists working within this framework accept without question the existence of universal categories like heterosexual and homosexual, male and female sexuality, and sex drive.[39]

This trend unfortunately persists in academic works that purport to link "sexuality" and "Islam." David Valentine identifies the Social Darwinist implications of this scholarship as follows: "The concern of gay male an-

38. Kath Weston, "Lesbian/Gay Studies in the House of Anthropology," *Annual Review of Anthropology* 22 (1993): 359. For a critical and comprehensive review of the literature of Performance Theory on sex and gender, see Rosalind Morris, "All Made Up: Performance Theory and the Anthropology of Sex and Gender," *Annual Review of Anthropology* 24 (1995): 567–92.

39. Carole Vance, "Anthropology Rediscovers Sexuality: A Theoretical Comment," *Social Science and Medicine* 33, no. 8 (1991): 879.

thropologists to describe and valorize non-Western (male) homosexualities can be interpreted (if not by anthropologists themselves, at least by
others) as forerunners of modern ('sexual') homosexuals."[40]

Najmabadi herself seems so taken with metropolitan theories about
Western history that she rewrites her own research project on Iran
in light of them. She tells us that after her reading of the seminal work
of Eve Sedgwick and the latter's proposition about reading Western cultural history through incorporating a critical analysis of the modern
homo/heterosexual definition, she (Najmabadi) "ended up reconceptu-
alizing and rewriting [my] entire manuscript. Indeed, I had to reread my
sources."[41] In doing so, Najmabadi does not document or demonstrate
the process through which the hetero-homo binary emerged, was produced, imposed, or institutionalized in Iran (assuming this transformation had even taken place at all), but rather she imposes the hetero-homo
binary on Iranian history as an interpretative grid of some of its documents, as an epistemology through which she arrives at certain preset
conclusions. Thus, even though Sedgwick took great care to specify her
claim about Western modern culture, the temptation to emulate, apply,
universalize, and identify with this modern Western history as paradigm
produces research projects with potential assimilationist ambitions.

Translating Queerness

In commenting on Michael Warner's book *Fear of a Queer Planet*, Neville
Hoad, while aware of the metaphoric use of the term "planet," registers
an important concern:

I cannot see the metaphor of a queer planet as only a metaphor, unrelated to the site of
queer subjectivity in the US and innocent of its own colonizing fantasies. In as much as
queer theory points to the underlying historical script of sexuality in the constitution of

---

40. See David Valentine, *Imagining Transgender: An Ethnography of a Category* (Durham, NC: Duke
University Press, 2007), 171. Even those who recognize that Western sexual identities are not universalizable continue to believe that the Western gay movement should intervene to liberate sexual
minorities around the world. For example Sonya Katyal, in an otherwise thorough and insightful article of legal and discursive analysis, affirms that "[i]nstead of liberating sexual minorities, the use of
identity-based frameworks may paradoxically exclude them from protection. I contend, therefore,
that a global gay rights movement must take into account sexualities and behaviors that fall outside
of traditional categories of sexual orientation. If a constitutional framework for protection of sexual
minorities is to be globally effective, it must recognize that many individuals who fall outside of
neatly circumscribed categories of sexual identity are just as deserving of a model of liberation that
includes them" (Katyal, "Exporting Identity," 100).
41. Najmabadi, *Women with Mustaches*, 3.

the terms of class and gender analysis, it needs to be equally sensitive to the historical conditions of the production of the category sexuality and to its contemporary global deployments and continual resignifications.[42]

The normalizing, because assimilationist, move by a number of scholars has therefore foreclosed any possible reading of the past of Europe and the rest of the globe and the present of Europe and non-Europe outside its epistemological limitations. The error here is not merely political, where sexual liberation and a commitment to the affirmation of the identities of sexual minorities are at stake, but, more egregiously, epistemological, where sexual desires, identities, and practices can only be viewed through a post-binarized world, a view that can only perform epistemic violence on those coerced and conscripted into assimilation. This is part of the same process begun by Western imperialism since the nineteenth century. As Talal Asad affirms, "the image of 'conscripts' as opposed to 'volunteers' does not suggest merely the recruits' initial attitude, but also the nature of the army and the war it has been fighting. To instill the desire for progress in the non-European world, it was necessary to inscribe modern Western categories into the administrative and legal discourses of that world. It was through such discursive powers that people undergoing 'modernization' were compelled to abandon old practices and turn to new ones."[43]

This type of research is further complicated by the attempt to disseminate the nascent field of queer theory universally across cultures (presumably on account of the anti-identitarian approach of the field) and of the notion of sexuality trans-geographically and transhistorically. But queer anti-identitarianism, which is dependent in its historical emergence on its constitutive opposition to hetero-homo identitarianism, is also not easily universalizable outside West European and Euro-American societies (and arguably even inside them), and "sexuality" as biopolitics cannot travel across time and space peremptorily no matter what caveats scholars or activists deploy as alibis.[44] Attuned to its racializing implications, "universal 'queer,'" as Greg Thomas argues, is "the latest, though not the last,

42. Neville Hoad, "Arrested Development or The Queerness of Savages: Resisting Evolutionary Narratives of Difference," *Postcolonial Studies* 3, no. 2 (2000): 150.

43. Talal Asad, "Conscripts of Western Civilization," in *Dialectical Anthropology: Essays in Honor of Stanley Diamond*, vol. 1: *Civilization in Crisis: Anthropological Perspectives*, ed. Christine Ward Gailey (Tallahassee: University Press of Florida, 1992), 340.

44. See Lara Deeb and Dina Al-Kassim, "Introduction," *Journal of Middle East Women's Studies* 7, no. 3 (Fall 2011).

embodiment of the humanist imperialism of Europe."[45] The condition of a term like queer, which has on occasion been abducted by liberal strategies as a form of pluralism, is precisely about resistance to assimilation and normativization. Queer, following Lee Edelman, occupies the place of the negative. To universalize it runs counter to its very constitution. It "finds its value not in a good susceptible to generalization, but only in the stubborn particularity that voids every notion of the general good."[46] This is not to say that queer politics does not partake of much liberal understanding of sociality. As Michael Warner argues:

Queer politics continues regularly to invoke norms of liberal modernity such as self-determination and self-representation; it continues to invoke a civil-society politics against the state; and most significant to my mind, it continues to value sexuality by linking it to the expressive capacities of individuals. . . . Although queer theory expresses skepticism about other elements of the modern sexual ideology, it relies absolutely on norms of expressive individualism and an understanding of sexuality in terms of those norms.[47]

It is this liberal epistemology that informs much of this effort at producing and assimilating the entire world into the image of Europe, an effort that hinges on two strategies—*universalization of the West as humanity, and translation of the non-West into modes of subjectivity that the West can recognize and tolerate.*[48] Western sexual epistemology and ontology are universalized *a priori* as human and not as products of particular histories; although when different sexual notions arise, translation into Europe can render them intelligible and in accordance with Western judgment of analogical notions—hence what is presented and translated as "sexual violence against women," "homosexuals," and "children" outside the West must be held accountable to Western norms of moral and juridical

45. Thomas, *The Sexual Demon of Colonial Power*, 108.
46. Lee Edelman, *No Future: Queer Theory and the Death Drive* (Durham, NC: Duke University Press, 2004), 6.
47. Michael Warner, "Something Queer about the Nation-State," in *After Political Correctness: The Humanities in the 1990s*, ed. Christopher Newfield and Ronald Strickland (Boulder, CO: Westview Press, 1995), 367.
48. Timothy Mitchell argues that Western scholarship on "political Islam" is carried out precisely through a process of translating: "The languages of political Islam, for example, can appear in Western scholarship only through a process of translation that enables them to speak in terms of the modernizing discourse of the West. There is no way around this problem of translation. But those anxious to contribute to the universal knowledge of the social sciences seldom seem to recognize it as a problem." See Timothy Mitchell, "The Middle East in the Past and Future of Social Science," in *The Politics of Knowledge: Area Studies and the Disciplines*, ed. David Szanton (Berkeley: University of California Press, 2002), 22–23.

judgment. Therefore, translation here seems superfluous, except at the linguistic level, as all it is doing is identifying the approximate correspondence between words and notions in non-European and even in other European languages and the contested English idiom. Translating the world into English becomes then an easy task of presenting the world as an extreme or more primitive form of this imaginary Europe (of which the United States is the constitutive part), *before* it was transformed by sexual liberation, sexual rights, and sexuality studies or even by queer theory. The world therefore must be brought closer to this imagined liberated Europe. When I speak of translation as assimilation, I am referring not only to the translation of European and non-European texts into English, but also of European and non-European corporeal practices, ontological structures, epistemologies, identities, and much more.

This also applies to the active work of translating Europe into non-European languages to effect epistemological shifts, something often preceded by the adoption of English terms and coinages (gay, queer) by other European languages. Oblivious to queer anti-identitarianism and determined to find an equivalent for it in Arabic, Hala Kamal, while working on the translation of *The Encyclopedia of Women and Islamic Cultures* from English to Arabic, discusses the practical problems of translation. She states:

Unlike the term "gender," which does not seem to require explanation in specialized writings, we faced a term for which we could not but use an explanatory translation.[49] Seham Abdel-Salam and Aida Seif el-Dawla, in two of the articles they were translating, faced the term "queer" in relation to specific sexual individual and group identities. Although the word "queer" (*kwir*) has started appearing in Arabic on certain Web sites, it remains unknown to the vast majority of the public; hence the demand for an explanatory translation of the concept, which had not developed with its sexual and cultural connotations up to the 1990s.[50]

Kamal adds:

Aida and Seham involved me in the problem facing them in the translation of this term, for which there does not yet exist in Arabic an accurate equivalent that is reflective of

49. As already noted in chapter 2, the recent rendering of "gender" in Arabic as *jindar*, which was not the pre-Western NGOs' translation of the term, contrary to Kamal's assertion, requires much explanation, and not only in Arabic.

50. Hala Kamal, "Translating Women and Gender: The Experience of Translating *The Encyclopedia of Women and Islamic Cultures* into Arabic," *Women Studies Quarterly* 36, nos. 3–4 (Fall/Winter 2008): 264.

its gender and political dimensions. So far, when not using a transliteration of 'queer,' the word is usually mistranslated [to Arabic] in terms of either the judgmental notion of 'deviance' (*shudhudh*) or through the misguided oversimplification in 'gays and lesbians' (*mithliyyun wa mithliyyat*). Aida, Seham, and I worked on a translation of 'queer'; during our discussions and our endeavors to come up with the closest possible translation, Aida suggested the use of the phrase *al-hawiyat* [*sic*] *al-jinsiya al-la namatiya*, more or less equivalent to 'atypical sexual identities.'[51]

Still unperturbed by the rendering of queerness as an identity category and emphasizing that this is precisely what queerness is, Kamal concludes:

The significance of this formulation, at this stage of translation, lies in translating the term into a value-free explanatory equivalent; and the focus was therefore placed on a sexual identity and its reference particularly to a specific atypical identity. As we put forward this explanatory translation of "queer," we are well aware of its shortcoming in highlighting a gender identity ("gender" being already a problematic term in its translation into Arabic). Nevertheless, with the current absence of an equivalent of "queer" in Arabic, we hope that perhaps with an increasing interest in tackling and writing about this issue in Arabic in the years to come, translation alternatives will appear, either turning the word "queer" into a familiar term in Arabic, or using shorter derivative forms (such as "*al-la namatiya*" and so on).[52]

This presentation of "queer" by Kamal as not "judgmental" misses completely the Anglo-American history of the term which was never "value free," and that its more recent use is a reappropriation of an insult, and that it is a term that tries to transvalue itself from a designation of abjection to an imagining of political agency, which also wishes to reconfigure the terrain of political agency.[53]

51. Ibid., 265.
52. Ibid.
53. Kamal expresses concern that in *Desiring Arabs* I do "not tackle the 'queer' identity [*sic*], nor . . . address the forms of existence (or absence) of its cultural equivalent in the Arab world or the Arabic language" (ibid., 267n5). An Ashkenazi Israeli scholar, Gil Hochberg, who is also the vice chair of the program in LGBT studies at UCLA, finds solace in Kamal's concern, as it authorizes her to add: "This avoidance on Massad's part, I believe, is significant, as it reflects his failure to confront the political challenges presented by the term queer in its rejection of naturalized (sexual) identity categorizations, a political potential perhaps stored also in the reclaiming of the Arabic term Shaz (irregular, deviant, pervert, abnormal)." Hochberg's poor command of Arabic notwithstanding (the term she references is "shadh" not "shaz"), her universalizing mission, as is made clear in her assertion, encompasses not only the need to globalize queerness but also the assumption that "naturalized (sexual) identity categorizations" are also always already universal! See Gil Hochberg, "Introduction—Israelis, Palestinians, Queers: Points of Departure," *GLQ* 16, no. 4 (2010): 512n. For

This "demand" for a linguistic equivalent to "queer" is clearly registered by Kamal and her associates as one that requires patience and hope that Arabic and Arabs will be transformed epistemologically and ontologically soon enough into cultural and linguistic versions of Europe and Anglo-America which would bring forth an "accurate" translation of "queer" in Arabic. As Gayatri Chakravorty Spivak put it: "If you are making anything else accessible [when translating], through a language quickly learned with an idea that you transfer content, then you are betraying the text and showing rather dubious politics."[54]

Hochberg's absurd invocations and invention of Arabic words like "luwatat" and her providing fantastical etymologies and meanings of "sahaqa" and "suhaq," which she renders wrongly as "sahq" and "sihaqa," see ibid., 498. It is notable that as a Euro-Israeli, Hochberg, without any self-reflection on her racial/colonial authority, embarked on editing a special issue of GLQ on "Queer Politics and the Question of Palestine/Israel," with no essay contributions by Palestinian scholars save an "afterword" by a token Palestinian. This of course also attests to the political limitations and racial biases of the editors of GLQ, who presumably invited her or accepted her proposal to edit such an issue even though her previous scholarly work had little to do with sexuality studies. Hochberg indeed dominates the journal's special issue in contributing not only an introductory essay but also a research essay as well as an interview she conducted with Palestinian activists who are citizens of Israel. Perhaps this was on account of the refusal of Palestinian scholars to contribute to her issue, even though she invited many of them. When Hochberg invited me to contribute an essay, she listed a number of Palestinian scholars to whom she had issued invitations, none of whom appears in the published issue. Perhaps reacting to my polite refusal to contribute, in her introduction to the special issue, Hochberg launches into a diatribe against *Desiring Arabs*, manufacturing and fabricating quotes and arguments nowhere to be found in my writings, including my alleged concern about and defense of "authentic" Arab desires (a term and a notion which she claims to quote from my work without providing any documentation), my alleged denial "that there are Arab homosexuals," and my alleged labeling those who identify as gay as "sellouts" (ibid., 506–7). The "authentic" charge is also deployed by other contributors to her issue as it has been by other Gay Internationalists. In advancing these charges, Hochberg, unfortunately, imitates the methods of traditional Zionist propaganda, which is predicated on the distortion of the claims made by those whom Zionism and Hochberg target and see as a threat to their/her ideological interests. I was quite surprised and taken aback by this unwarranted attack on *Desiring Arabs* given the previous communications I had received from Hochberg, whom I have never met. Before my refusal to contribute to her special issue, Hochberg had thanked me and a number of other scholars in her book *In Spite of Partition: Jews, Arabs, and the Limits of Separatist Imagination* (Princeton, NJ: Princeton University Press, 2007), asserting that our writings "on the question of Palestine have accompanied me throughout the process of writing this book and have provided me with much inspiration and hope" (xii). She e-mailed me several times to express admiration of my work and identified herself as an "old fan" and informed me that she was "very excited about your new book [*Desiring Arabs*], which I have just started to read." She added in a later e-mail to a colleague at Columbia University, which my colleague forwarded to me at the time, that she found the book "quite an achievement" and asked my colleague to "pass on my compliments on the book." In her letter of invitation to me to contribute an essay, Hochberg emphasized that "I would love to have you contribute a paper. . . . It could be anything you'd like it to be as long as [it] touches on issues of gay/queer politics (academic, activism, art etc.) and the question of Palestine. Truthfully, [I] cannot think of a better candidate to write such [a] paper than you, and I do very much hope you would be interested in participating in this project." Needless to say, I was as surprised to receive her praise as I was to be a target of her attacks and careless misreading.

54. Gayatri Chakravorty Spivak, "The Politics of Translation," 191. Talal Asad and John Dixon note the inequality of languages in the process of translation, pointing out the unequal power of

Kamal seems to want to follow Clifford Geertz's view that all one need do when "translating across cultures is to make strange concepts familiar," as Talal Asad paraphrases him. But Asad argues that this is too "comforting" and that "in translation we ought to be bringing things into our language even though they cause a scandal. Now, one can respond to scandal in two ways; one can throw out the offending idea or one can think of what it is that produces the horror. I would like to think that that kind of translation forces one to rethink some of our own traditional categories and concepts. If you just say, 'Well, I am going to find an equivalent word that is nice and familiar in our own language,' you are simply domesticating the original."[55] Kamal's horror, however, is not the effect of the "strangeness" of a term like "queer" to Arabic, but at the resistance of Arabic to grant the word admission, much less to provide any equivalency for it—a resistance that Kamal is determined to quash. Kamal's commitment to European and Euro-American normativity registers horror and the sense of the scandalous not at the realization that Euro-American and European epistemologies and the English language have produced something like queerness, but that Arabs have not, which is an indication of their failure, and that they must and should create an equivalence for queerness as part of the recipe for success. As Asad put it, "incomplete or unsuccessful translations have come to be seen as evidence of *failure* on the part of entire societies and not as indications of other kinds of history."[56] The translational predilection in Kamal's (and others') accounts is precisely that translation must operate in the economy of the production of sameness, which will always register horror at encountering difference *from Europe*.[57]

---

dominating and dominated languages: "A readiness to expand and deepen the translator's own language is not, we think, encouraged equally by the wider conditions that define relations between dominating and dominated cultures. . . . Arabic speakers are in general readier to acquire new concepts, metaphors, and images for their language . . . in their engagement with English, than English-speakers are when they encounter . . . Arabic." Asad and Dixon, "Translating Europe's Others," in *Europe and Its Others*, ed. Francis Barker, Peter Hulme, Margaret Iversen, and Diana Loxley (Colchester: University of Essex Press, 1985), 1:174.

55. "The Trouble of Thinking: An Interview with Talal Asad," in *Powers of the Secular Modern: Talal Asad and his Interlocutors*, ed. David Scott and Charles Hirschkind (Stanford, CA: Stanford University Press, 2006), 275. Asad makes similar points in his "Cultural Translation in British Social Anthropology," in Talal Asad, *Genealogies of Religion: Discipline and Reasons for Power in Christianity and Islam* (Baltimore: Johns Hopkins University Press, 1993), 171–99.

56. Talal Asad, "A Comment on Aijaz Ahmad's *In Theory*," *Public Culture* 6, no. 1 (Fall 1993): 38.

57. Talal Asad and John Dixon explain how Arabic has been substantially influenced by European languages in the modern period on many levels (literary style, lexical, syntactic, etc), but that "such changes tend to take place in a determinate direction, and that this clearly has to do with the political and economic inequalities between societies. There is, for example, no list of modifications in English or in French deriving from their reception of translations from the Arabic, comparable

But Kamal is not alone in her quest. Samar Habib, a Palestinian-Australian scholar, goes further by arguing that the sexuality that exists in the Arab World is always already "queer." While claiming that resisting the universalizing reach of the Gay International "oppresses those who, against all odds . . . initiated local grassroots campaigns for LGBTIQ rights in the Arab world by reducing these initiatives, in an academic discourse, to nothing more than agents of Western/imperialist sabotage of Arab nations," Habib, in a sensationalist account, asserts unequivocally that the "irony is that the Western term 'queer' has a way of capturing the sexual flux with which the Arab world is often characterized."[58] Habib proceeds to issue a call for "queer-friendly Islamic hermeneutics," and speaks of "queer citizens in the Muslim world" as actual legal subjects.[59]

Thus, not only is "queer" universalizable, as the sexual relations it names are posited already as the hegemonic form extant in Arab or Muslim-majority countries and wherein its practitioners are already constituted as such before the very act that names and interpellates them as "queer," this American term itself is taken out of its contemporary American context where its value lies in contesting the hegemony of reproductive heteronormative sexual relations and identities to an Arab and Muslim context where queerness is allegedly already hegemonic as the norm. But if the value of queer is in its opposing and resisting heteronormative hegemony, will it not lose its ideological and sociopolitical function (a function that is its very *raison d'être* in its American setting) if it is the sexually hegemonic form? What emerges here then is not only Habib's insistence on translating and "capturing" Muslim sexual desires, practices, and identities by an American term, but also her misapprehension

---

to the one we have mentioned for the latter language," in Asad and Dixon, "Translating Europe's Others," 1:172. One of the most comical episodes of the deployment of the term "queer" in Arabic was its recent use by a Palestinian panelist representing a new Palestinian group calling itself "Queer Palestinians for Boycott, Divestment, and Sanctions" (PQBDS), rendered in Arabic "Kwiriyyun Filastiniyyun min ajl Muqata'at Isra'il," at a BDS conference that took place in Istanbul in mid April 2012. Most of the conference attendees were at a loss during his presentation, whispering to each other and wondering about what they understood to be his topic, namely "Palestinian Koreans for BDS," as the word he used "kwiriyyun" (his Arabic rendering of "queers" in the plural) sounded to their ears as "Kuriyyun" meaning "Koreans," especially as many of them did not believe there was such a community as Palestinian Koreans! One woman attendee shouted out that he must have said "Suriyyun," meaning Palestinian Syrians for BDS, but she was promptly corrected that this was not what he said or meant. I thank Ali Abunimah and Shakir Jarrar, who participated in the conference, for sharing this episode with me.
58. Habib, *Islam and Homosexuality*, 1:xix.
59. Ibid., 1:lviii.

and mistranslation of that term itself in the interest of universalism and universalization.[60]

In his recent book *Homosexuality in Islam* that examines Islamic theology and the history of jurisprudential opinions on "homosexuality," Scott Kugle, a white American convert to Islam, "hopes to provide a bridge between Islam as a tradition and Muslims as a living people."[61] While he seems interested especially in Muslim immigrants and converts in Europe or European settler colonies, especially the US, Canada, and South Africa (the last is the only one with an indigenized Muslim community), with whom he conducted interviews exclusively, he often speaks of Muslims in Muslim-majority countries in Asia and Africa as well.[62] Indeed he refers to "straight" and "gay" Muslims as self-evident identities espoused by Muslims everywhere.[63] While Kugle speaks often in the name of gay and lesbian Muslims and uses the pronoun "we" in representing them, he does not quote them, except in rare cases, when he quotes an African-American gay convert to Islam named Daayiee Abdullah.

Kugle holds fast and unapologetically to essentialist notions of homosexuality and heterosexuality, because "'essentialist' approaches are more useful to mount a political campaign to actually change social relations rather than just comment on them."[64] He uses the two terms transhistorically to claim that the Qur'an refers to these groups, as does the Islamic legal tradition.[65] In doing so, he avoids the whole conundrum of translation altogether by bringing his strange ahistoric imputations of modern notions to bear on a seventh-century text. Kugle heavily relies on an academically discredited notion of "patriarchy" as a buzzword to explain "Islamic" societies and refers to "the patriarchal culture of most Muslims."[66] It is never made clear if most non-Muslims have a matriarchal culture or at least a nonpatriarchal one, although this is often implied when Kugle discusses Europe and its settler colonies. Kugle also is not interested in speaking or addressing bisexuality in "Islam,"

60. Habib's misunderstanding, false attributions, and distortions of the argument I make in my 2002 article on the Gay International (she never cites *Desiring Arabs* and appears either not to have read it or not interested in the larger arguments it makes), has me positing Arab men as "culturally bisexual." Of course, nowhere in my account have I posited or represented the desires of Arab men or women. My book is in essence an examination of such representations that are made in a wide and various body of literature. See Habib, *Islam and Homosexuality*, 1:xlvi.

61. Kugle, *Homosexuality in Islam*, 14.

62. Ibid., 7.

63. Ibid., 8.

64. Ibid., 9.

65. See ibid., 2, 10, where he first makes these claims.

66. Ibid., 3.

as he seems to believe that in contrast to the natural "dispositional" homo- and hetero-sexuality, bisexuality is "behavioral" and results from sexually "segregated" societies and therefore to speak of this "behavioral bisexuality . . . obscures 'dispositional homosexuality.'"[67] While most scholars who deal with these topics address the question of translation and the difficulty it presents, Kugle proceeds unencumbered by such imagined irrelevancies.

Valerie Traub in turn thinks the editors of *Islamicate Sexualities* avoid the trap of translation as assimilation by opposing the two terms. She states: "Resisting the imperative of assimilation, the editors have chosen to put an additional metaphor in play—translation."[68] Traub and Hala Kamal would do well complicating their accounts by incorporating Gayatri Chakravorty Spivak's notion of translation as "violation," which is most applicable when we understand translation *as* assimilation.[69]

Thus Najmabadi and Babayan speak of "the need for materially localized readings of past sexualities represented within Islamicate textual milieus," inattentive to the temporal travel their use of "sexuality" is undertaking in their research.[70] Moreover, their desire to "queer" "Islamic historiography" or "Islamicate history and culture" is complicated for them, as they note, not by the imposition of these terms on non-European contexts, but more so because of the "problematic" aspect of "'translating' sex and relevant cultural, linguistic, and epistemological practices from Islamicate contexts into European and Anglo-American 'counterparts.'"[71] Even though Najmabadi and Babayan are mindful of the need to be vigilant about questions of translatability, they naturalize their use of these problematic, even untranslatable, terms as useful for analysis—especially as they pose to themselves the question of "how do we go about 'translating' Islamicate sexualities, based on their own historically determined notions, to English-speaking and -reading audiences?"[72]—failing to realize that christening whatever they seek to translate into English as "Islamicate sexualities" is already an act of (mis)translation that forecloses whatever specificity or historical determination they hope to clarify in their translational practices. This is mostly so because both "Islamicate" and "sexuality" are *only* intelligible

67. Ibid., 11.
68. Valerie Traub, "The Past Is a Foreign Country?" 30.
69. Gayatri Chakravorty Spivak, *A Critique of Postcolonial Reason: Toward a History of the Vanishing Present* (Cambridge, MA: Harvard University Press, 1999), 163.
70. Babayan and Najmabadi, *Islamicate Sexualities*, viii.
71. Ibid., ix, x.
72. Ibid., x.

to "English-speaking and -reading audiences" and therefore what the authors seem to be doing is "translate" English concepts that are projected onto non-English societies back to "English-speaking and -reading audiences." This act of (re)translation therefore turns out not to be a translation at all, but rather a universalizing application of English concepts, an *assimilation* of the world in the image of "English-speaking and -reading audiences" that mistakes itself for an act of translation from other cultures in the literal and metaphorical senses. Saba Mahmood described some Western feminisms' translation of the lives of Muslim women as "a mode of encountering the Other which does not assume that in the process of culturally translating other lifeworlds one's own certainty about how the world should proceed can remain stable."[73] It is precisely the stability of this certainty to which Najmabadi and Babayan's project remains committed. I am not claiming here that other reified categories like class, race (or gender, as we saw in the last chapter) do not face problems of translatability, but that the specific political valences in the case of translating sexuality go mostly unrecognized in these accounts.

Valerie Traub and Dina Al-Kassim, one a Europeanist, the other an Americanist, who were invited by Najmabadi and Babayan to effect the "queering" of Middle East Studies and to "frame" a book whose other contributors are from within Middle East Studies, as the editors tell us,[74] and who subscribe to and ferociously defend this assimilationist project, insist on the need to create this new field of study. Traub declares that Najmabadi's and Babayan's project "aims to create, through tenacious acts of dialogue, translation, and comparativism, a new field of historical knowledge and site of knowledge production—that of Islamicate sexuality studies."[75] She adds that the unique contribution of *Islamicate Sexualities* is reproductive, wherein "no other group of scholars has taken on the responsibility to think capaciously about what it would mean to facilitate the birth of a new field of knowledge."[76] Al-Kassim, in turn, speaks of this project as one of "queering Middle East Studies" and indeed proceeds to assume the *a priori* existence of "a field as fragile as queer Middle East studies" as a *fait accompli*.[77] George Chauncey was

73. Saba Mahmood, *Politics of Piety: Islamic Revival and the Feminist Subject* (Princeton, NJ: Princeton University Press, 2005), 199.

74. Babayan and Najmabadi, *Islamicate Sexualities*, vii, viii.

75. Traub, "The Past Is a Foreign Country?" 3.

76. Ibid.

77. Dina Al-Kassim, "Epilogue," *Islamicate Sexualities*, 299. For a survey of English-language academic histories of "sexuality" in the Middle East, see Leslie Pierce, "Writing Histories of Sexuality in the Middle East," *American Historical Review* 114, no. 5 (December 2009): 1325–39.

cautious about constituting and institutionalizing intellectual inquiry about sexuality and queerness, *inter alia*, in academic programs, as such institutionalization threatens to "reify and naturalize the very categories it was initially designed to critique."[78] In contrast, the editors and some of the contributors of *Islamicate Sexualities* do not seem burdened by such caution. What is exceptionally refreshing about their volume, however, is that many of the important questions about Eurocentrism, assimilationism, universalism, and translation are posed, but what is stale in it, unfortunately, is that the editors and the discussants fall back on and repeat familiar modes of thinking by redeploying the very same notions they questioned through what they deem a resolution to the theoretical conundrums they identify.

It was left to one of the contributors, Leyla Rouhi, to point out the imperialist deployment of the term "queer" in non-Anglo American contexts.[79] Rouhi cites Gregory Hutcheson, who reevaluates the title of the book he and Josiah Blackmore had published in 1999 under the title *Queer Iberia* to make her point. In that volume, both Hutcheson and Blackmore aver that "the celebration of queerness is certainly implicit in our project, both in our choice of title and in the sheer delight we take both individually and collectively in the telling of stories of heterodoxy and transgression."[80] This assertion of an (anti)normative bias is made more explicit in the authors' citation of Michael Warner in *Fear of a Queer Planet*, namely his call "not only [for] the recovery of queer histories and identities as a means to fostering tolerance, but the active imagining of a 'necessarily and desirably queer world.'"[81] When reviews in Spanish periodicals accused the authors of Anglo-American centrism and imposing Anglo-American gay agendas on Iberian Studies, Hutcheson reflected on the reaction: "If truth be told, however, the 'queer' of *Queer Iberia* is the extent of our gay Anglo-Saxon posturing. Joe Blackmore and I had certainly intended the title as an activist act, one we aimed at the American academy in hopes of destabilizing the rigid academic discourse inherent in medieval studies."[82] Hutcheson, unlike Hala Kamal,

78. George Chauncey, "The Queer History and Politics of Lesbian and Gay Studies," in *Queer Frontiers: Millennial Geographies, Genders, and Generations*, ed. Joseph A. Boone et al. (Madison: University of Wisconsin Press, 2000), 305.

79. Leyla Rouhi, "A Handsome Boy among Those Barbarous Turks: Cervantes's Muslims and the Art of Science and Desire," in *Islamicate Sexualities*, 45.

80. Gregory Hutcheson and Josiah Blackmore, *Queer Iberia: Sexualities, Cultures, and Crossings from the Middle Ages to the Renaissance* (Durham, NC: Duke University Press, 1999), 21.

81. Ibid.

82. Hutcheson, "Return to Queer Iberia," *La Corónica*, Fall 2001, accessed 1 April 2014 at http://college.holycross.edu/lacoronica/qi/2-Hutcheson.htm.

came to understand well the imperialist implications of the book title. He adds:

> While attending "The Future of the Queer Past" conference at the University of Chicago in Fall of 2000, I was struck by Argentinean activist Alejandra Sardá's intervention in the closing plenary session. She warned against what she called "American gay cultural imperialism," that is, the deliberate forging of a global gay culture and the presumption of a common sociopolitical agenda. The Stonewall model, she pointed out in what came surely as a shock to many of the American activists in attendance, is not necessarily consonant with the social, cultural, and political realities of other countries, and indeed, it might very well be the exception rather than the rule. Latin America in particular, while certainly embracing American models, has also begun resisting these same models. I suppose we shouldn't underestimate the extent to which our selection of the title *"Queer" Iberia* smacks precisely of this sort of imperialism, the extent to which the term "queer" is shorthand in some circles for Anglo-American gay activism at its most self-serving and myopic. What we didn't bank on when devising the title was its absolute resistance to translation. . . . Ultimately, "queer" is a term so entrenched in both its etymology and the history of its deliberate appropriation by the Anglo-American gay community that it cannot be rendered by any single term in the Spanish. By using "queer" in our title, we unwittingly created an entity that resists *a priori* a quick-and-easy translation of the whole, that appears to impose English as the default when speaking about the Iberian subjects we study, that perpetuates Anglo-American models of writing queer history.[83]

Warner himself had asserted that "both the word 'queer' and the concept of queerness turn out to be thoroughly embedded in modern Anglo-American culture." He added:

> The term does not translate very far with any ease, and its potential for transformation seems mostly specific to a cultural context that has not been brought into focus in the theory of queerness. Even in cultures with well-organized gay movements and a taste for Americanisms there has been little attempt to import the politics with which the label has been associated here. In the New World Order, we should be more than usually cautious about global utopianisms that require American slang.[84]

This sober recognition of the limitation of the term queer, its imperialist function and specificity is strangely evaluated by Al-Kassim as a *resolution*. She concludes: "The problem is eventually resolved by allowing the

---

83. Ibid.
84. Michael Warner, "Something Queer about the Nation-State," 361.

English word to linger as a failed translation that is accused of cultural imperialism."[85] But simple acknowledgment will resolve very little if one proceeds with the same assimilationist project whose pitfalls one recognizes. Gayatri Spivak has cautioned against such carelessness:

> The word 'culture' belongs to the history of Western European languages. If we want to move into the elusive phenomenon in other places, below the shifting internal line of cultural difference, we will not look for translations and approximations of the word. Such synonyms carry on their back the impulse to translate from the European, which is a characteristic of the colonized intelligentsia under imperialism, and this is the condition as well as the effect of that differentiating internal line. They will not let us go below it. We must rather learn a non-European language well enough to be able to enter it without ready reference to a European one. We may encounter creole versions of the word 'culture' which will complicate our argument. But they are neither the same word nor its translation.[86]

The attempt to impose these English words in a social engineering project, like the one Al-Kassim is resolving to do, on non-English languages, however, has not resulted in a creolization that marks itself as a *different* word and as *not translation*, but rather precisely as part of an imperial pedagogy that is assertive and proud of its lineage.

In the context of discussing "marginal sexualities in the Maghreb," Jarrod Hayes worried that Warner's assertion "in spite of its anticolonial intentions, might lead to an Anglo-American monopoly on queerness that repeats the exclusionary gestures many constructionists have used to define Western homosexuality."[87] Warner's point, however, is not an argument that pits constructionism against essentialism, rather a point about the specificity of certain forms of cultural, social, and political histories and identities that are only universalizable *through* imperial gestures. Hayes, however, is unpersuaded, though he remains more careful than Al-Kassim. He asserts that "in spite of the potential applicability of the term 'queer' to the Maghreb, I shall use it here less as an adjective to describe sexual acts than a verb to signify a critical practice in which nonnormative sexualities infiltrate dominant discourses to loosen their

---

85. Al-Kassim, "Epilogue," *Islamicate Sexualities*, 320.

86. Gayatri Chakravorty Spivak, *An Aesthetic Education in the Era of Globalization* (Cambridge, MA: Harvard University Press, 2012) 121.

87. Jarrod Hayes, *Queer Nations: Marginal Sexualities in the Maghreb* (Chicago: University of Chicago Press, 2000), 6.

political stronghold."[88] Unfortunately, his adjectival use of the term is what dominates his book, whose very title *Queer Nations* insists on that grammatical identitarian form.

The Price of Sexual Agency

In large measure, the approach of the editors and discussants of *Islamicate Sexualities* is encapsulated and summarized in this telling dilemma that Al-Kassim articulates uncritically. Indeed, Al-Kassim seems resistant to concerns about Anglo-American taxonomical and identitarian hegemony, if not imperialism. She concludes that "this scandal of translation is another version of the injunction against mixed productions that seems to shadow studies of gay and lesbian figuration in the form of a warning to avoid such anachronistic projection and that, at least in the case of this title [*Queer Iberia*], may reveal more about fears of gay dissemination than any actual threat of gay hegemony."[89] Here, I am more interested in the fear expressed and felt by Al-Kassim herself of any resistance to Anglo-American universalization of identities whether within Euro-America or outside it. Her fear is also shared by Najmabadi, who remarks that she

generally share[s] this reluctance to map later formations of desire onto those of earlier sociohistorical periods. Yet one needs to be aware of the current effects of pushing this argument to the limit of drawing lines of alterity. First, by locating same-sex identification in modern Euro-America, one renders homosexuality external to other places, an alien concept for formation of desires in these other cultures, an argument fully used by homophobic cultural nativists who are happy to (al)locate homosexuality in 'the West.' Second, it introduces radical alterity with the past, producing the premodern as a radically different time.[90]

Najmabadi's argument is not only a politically motivated move against a real or imagined nativist enemy but also elides the epistemological complicity of certain "Islamicate" nativists and Western gay activists who both call for the identification (and subjectification) of people based on sexual practices and desires and insist that the state should arbitrate their

88. Ibid., 7. Hayes however remains ambivalent in the remainder of his text, as he continues to use the term "queer" in both its adjectival and verbal forms.
89. Al-Kassim, "Epilogue," *Islamicate Sexualities*, 320.
90. Najmabadi, *Women with Mustaches*, 19.

subjective rights.[91] It is unclear why Najmabadi is only concerned with non-European "homophobic cultural nativists" who reject homosexuality as alien, but not with Islamophobic European universalists and cultural nativists who want to impose it on a world they seek to assimilate in the image of modern Europe. She does not seem to realize that it is essentialist claims about homosexuality that rewrite the history of Europe and the rest of the globe in Social Darwinist terms of developmentalism toward the telos of gay liberation while at the same time claiming the post-Enlightenment European world as alien to its prehistory of oppression and to the present and past of non-European geographies. It is this projection of recent normative identities and invented histories that renders the premodern and the non-European *other* in terms of both developmentalism and radical alterity, and not the scholarly or political resistance to them.

Not letting go of her commitment to the explanatory powers of metropolitan theories, Najmabadi deploys one last strategy to fight off those who resist them, namely the production of anthropological evidence from the local through her insistence on the facticity of the adoption of "gay" identity in Iran (to use her only empirical example), even if with a twist. She declares: "How do these enunciations mean differently, and do a different cultural work, in Tehran compared with New York? Perhaps one of the problems with the current heated debates between proponents of 'global gay' and opponents of 'gay international' resides in the presumption, common to both groups, that 'I am gay,' or 'I am transsexual' means the same thing anywhere it is pronounced."[92] But no scholar who critiques gay internationalism has ever made such a naïve argument, and Najmabadi cites no one who does. However, if as Najamabadi claims, men in Tehran use the term "gay" for men who assume the "passive" role during coitus with other men but not those who assume "active" roles, on what basis could this local configuration of "gay" then become the basis of international gay solidarity, to which Najamabadi seems committed despite her investment in a suspect neutrality that always fails to register as neutral (assuming such a position is even possible outside the liberal imaginary)?

Najmabadi clearly shares the facile defensive position taken up by Gay Internationalists against their critics, namely the undefended allegation that their critics are nativist apologists for the local and the

91. On this complicity, see Massad, *Desiring Arabs*, 195.
92. Afsaneh Najmabadi, "Transing and Transpassing across Sex-Gender Walls in Iran," *Women's Studies Quarterly* 36, nos. 3–4 (Fall–Winter 2008): 37.

authentic. The contradictions in Najmabadi's position on this point are troubling. On the one hand, she wants to paint critics of the Gay International as cultural nativists who view the Gay International as part of an imperialist plot, while on the other hand, she herself makes a nativist argument by insisting that the use of "gay" in Iran is indeed a local authentic native development and not an outcome of imperial politics or dynamics (and therefore it should not be opposed):

The entry into Persian and wide circulation of the words "gay" (pronounced as in English) and, less frequently, "lezbish" (lesbian butch) may indicate (contrary to the presumption of imitation of or imposition by the "gay international" on unsuspecting naive Iranians) in part an attempt to move away from the burden of the stigma that the term *kuni* (and, to a lesser extent, *baruni*, used for the "active" partner in a lesbian relationship) carries with it. In other words, to the extent that the adoption of the terms gay and lesbian into Persian nomenclature can be viewed as some sort of mimicry, it is a strategic move to shed the cultural stigma of *kuni* (and *baruni*). . . . Whether these language moves work or fail is not determined because of the presumed shortcoming of "mimicry," or because of the cultural power of domination by a presumed "gay international" that is exporting its identity categories in imperial fashion. Its potential source of trouble is the tight gender grid within which same-sex relationships in contemporary Iran are configured. This configuration is in turn an effect of the marriage imperative . . . that shapes particular notions of masculine and feminine performance (within heterosexual relationships as well).[93]

Najmabadi seems to miss that the point of the use of the term "queer" in the United States is precisely in having the term *linger in cultural stigma* rather than to "shed" it. Moreover, she seems to want to deploy a variant argument for universalism. If Gay Internationalists seek actively and consciously to universalize sexual identities from its US location to the world at large, Najmabadi's universalism insists that sexual identities are in fact already existing universal phenomena that sprang up on their own and that her endorsement of them is not an endorsement of universalizing US forms but of existing universal phenomena independent of US influence (in this, she is not dissimilar to Samar Habib in the latter's claim of Arab "sexuality" as always already "queer" noted above, or to al-Kassim who thinks sexuality developed in the East and West "coevally").[94] That some Iranians use the term "gay" to define

---

93. Ibid., text of endnote 10, 39–40.
94. In Lara Deeb and Dina Al-Kassim, "Introduction," *Journal of Middle East Women's Studies* 7, no. 3 (Fall 2011): 2.

themselves differently from its use in the West, according to Najmabadi, is not on account of the influence of Gay Internationalism at all, but rather the proof of local and independent agency! This is not unlike the scholarly trend that David Valentine astutely observes in much of the academic literature about "sexuality" in the non-Western world, wherein "transnational appropriations of Western identities such as 'gay' or 'lesbian' are seen as evidence of contemporary 'traditional' people adopting 'modern' homosexuality."[95]

Najmabadi's metropolitan anthropological foray (or is it a native informant account?) into explaining the *intent* of those who use the term "gay" in Iran is presented by her as nothing short of a legitimizing defense of the "local" for not mimicking the "imperial," which fancies itself as an argument against critics of the epistemic and physical violence brought about by Gay Internationalism, who are trivialized and neutralized as apologists for the local and are simultaneously presented as denying the agency of those locals who insist on gay identification.

The question of refusing to recognize local gay agency is important here, as it is often leveled by those who criticize opponents of Gay Internationalism.[96] It is noteworthy, however, that none of the critics of the arguments against Gay Internationalism had objected to the Orientalist representations of Arab (and "Islamic") "sexuality" before the publication of my essay on the subject in 2002; their subsequent intervention, while feigning agreement with some of the criticisms of Orientalist representations the essay makes, moves swiftly to tackle the question of Arab and Muslim sexual "agency," which, they believe, the argument about the Gay International eliminates. But the question of agency, which was often used in leftist political activism in the 1970s and 1980s to criticize metropolitan racisms, sexisms, heterosexisms, and classisms, was appropriated in the 1990s and in the new century by right-wing conservatives and imperial liberals in defense of those African Americans, women (both in Euro-America and outside it), homosexuals (also, both in Euro-America and outside it), and Third World nationals who uphold liberal and conservative metropolitan notions of universalism as expressing their own agency, and how opposing them from the left would be a denial of such agency, one which is itself implicated in imperialism and orientalism! Indeed, immigrant and first

95. Valentine, *Imagining Transgender*, 158.
96. In addition to Najmabadi, see Ghassan Makarem, "We are not Agents of the West," *Reset DOC*, 10 December 2009, http://www.resetdoc.org/EN/Helem-replies-Massad.php (accessed 1 April 2014).

generation Muslim women and gays in the United States and Europe (as well as those who uphold similar views and staff the local NGOs in Muslim-majority countries) have figured prominently in this (neo) liberal discourse of agency. In the case of such Muslim women in Europe and the United States, Yasemin Yildiz states that they

> speak publicly as potential objects of tolerance or guilt, even if they reject those terms for themselves. They thus have a legitimating function in the discourse. Moreover, their participation seemingly disables the kind of critique that Gayatri Spivak formulated when she spoke of "white men . . . saving brown women from brown men." . . . Now the formula seems to read: "brown women saving brown women from brown men." What makes this new version so effective is the seeming identity between those "brown women" who need to be saved and those "brown women" who act to save them. Rather than being identical, however, "brown women" come in two distinct guises in the current discourse, namely, as subjects with agency and as victims without agency. Those public figures, who position themselves as agents, in fact rely on the constant reproduction of others as voiceless victims.[97]

Indeed, Spivak's formula has become much more complicated in the age of right-wing investment in "agency," so much so that it should now be read as: brown women (gay and straight) and brown gay men (located in the western and northern European and the US metropole and those who work for NGOs with west and north European and US funding in their home countries), and their white allies of all genders and sexualities, are engaged in saving brown women ("straight" and "gay") and brown "gay" men (in the Third World and in western and northern Europe and the Unites States) from brown "straight" men. As we have already seen in this chapter and the last, this has become a huge industry.

I have argued in *Colonial Effects* that much of what passed as anticolonial nationalism in the former Asian and African colonies expressed very little that was anticolonial, and that except for the questioning of colonial racial hierarchies, the agency of Third World nationalists was often one of replicating, not opposing, colonial forms of subjectivity under the banner of anticolonial nationalism, and that "the irony of this

---

97. Yasemin Yildiz, "Governing European Subjects: Tolerance and Guilt in the Discourse of 'Muslim Women,'" *Cultural Critique* 77 (Winter 2011): 86. For the US context, see Saba Mahmood, "Feminism, Democracy, and Empire: Islam and the War on Terror," in *Women's Studies on the Edge*, ed. Joan Wallach Scott (Durham, NC: Duke University Press, 2008), 81–114.

is in having us believe that this colonial subjection and subjectivation *is* anticolonial agency."[98]

Thus explaining the process through which a small number of people outside Europe and its settler colonies come to adopt the term "gay" is not a refusal to recognize the agency of these individuals but rather a *recognition* of the complicity of such agency with gay universalism and, as I argued in my response to Helem director Ghassan Makarem, an insistence "that everyone must [also] recognize the agency of all of those who practice same sex and different sex contact *not to assimilate* into gayness and straightness."[99] Furthermore, it is a recognition that Euro-American and West European gayness as a quest for the social is predicated upon a reproductive model that can only be actuated by rendering itself normative and by coercing all those who have same-sex desire into its identity structure as the "gay social"—thus gayness does interpellate other men and women by coercing them into joining its social identitarian collective through a variety of instruments (state-sanctioned social services, access to community and kinship structures, law, media, political organizations, human rights work, etc.) as its homophobic detractors often claim, though contrary to the homophobes' contention, it does not do so by creating same-sex desires or by urging those who have them to pursue same-sex practice, but by its simple insistence, as does compulsory straightness, on the ontological imperative these sexual desires must entail.

The success of gayness as a social and communal identity in the West in the last four and a half decades has assured it of a new nonbiological form of kinship that is not necessarily conditioned by biological relations or Oedipal structures. Rather, if biological kinship is ensured through compulsory heterosexuality and compulsory straightness (which also reproduce themselves nonbiologically and non-Oedipally through universalizing their ontological forms), which reproduce children biologically and Oedipally (through the bourgeois nuclear family form) to ensure the future of heteronormative straightness, if not of "society" as a whole, then compulsory gayness reproduces itself strictly through nonbiological and non-Oedipal forms of kinship, by interpellating gays coercively through an imperial order imposed within empire and on the rest of the world, through the law, politics, and the reorganization of

98. Joseph Massad, *Colonial Effects: The Making of National Identity in Jordan* (New York: Columbia University Press, 2001), 278. Saba Mahmood criticizes the Western feminist notion of agency, as one that inherently subverts and resists, on similar grounds. See Mahmood, *Politics of Piety*, 1–39.

99. Joseph Massad, Reply to Ghassan Makarem, published in *Reset DOC* on 14 December 2009, http://www.resetdoc.org/EN/Massad-counter-replies.php (accessed 1 April 2014).

the social (the recent US phenomenon of establishing reproductive gay kinship through white gay and lesbian couples' "adoption" of Chinese babies notwithstanding).[100] Thus universalizing the hetero-homo binary is ultimately a reproductive act, wherein universalizing gayness is as necessary for reproductive homonormativity as universalizing straightness is for reproductive heteronormativity.

My concern here again is not only that an existing "native" culture of sexual desires and subjectivities and a set of corporeal and pleasurable practices are being eliminated and replaced forcefully by an imperial culture, but that this imperial universalization project is also predicated on an insistence that, to become gay, non-European and non-Euro-American subjects with certain sexual desires and practices must unthink and unlearn the ways they understand their desires, sexual practices, and subjectivities, viewing them as false and outmoded forms that are the result of false consciousness, thus rendering them unrecognizable to Westerners, and that their liberation lies in this unlearning *and* in the learning of a new vocabulary of Western identities which *will* render them recognizable to Westerners and therefore free. For their different identities, practices, and desires are not considered variations on or of the identities, practices, and desires of Europeans and Euro-Americans, but decidedly *deviations* from them that must be set right. What is demanded by Gay Internationalists then is nothing less than what Foucault identified as the demand of the modern state in the West since the eighteenth century, namely that the "'modern state' as an entity which was developed above individuals . . . [is] a very sophisticated structure, in which individuals can be integrated, under one condition: that this individuality would be shaped in a new form and submitted to a set of very specific patterns."[101] This is then the price of agency insistently demanded by the Gay International and the purveyors of European and Euro-American sexual identities.

As Talal Asad concludes:

The West has become a vast moral project, an intimidating claim to write and speak for the world, and an unending politicization of power. Becoming Western has meant becoming transformed according to these things, albeit in a variety of historical circumstances and with varying degrees of thoroughness. For conscripts of Western civilization

100. On non-Oedipal forms of kinship and queer liberalism and transnational adoption, see David Eng, *The Feeling of Kinship: Queer Liberalism and the Racialization of Intimacy* (Durham, NC: Duke University Press, 2010).

101. Michel Foucault, "The Subject and Power," *Critical Inquiry* 8, no. 4 (Summer 1982): 783.

this transformation implies that some desires have been forcibly eliminated—even violently—and others put in their place. The modern state, invented in Europe, is the universal condition of that transformation—and of its "higher truth."[102]

This is not unlike the process analyzed by Valentine through which people in the United States have been coerced, cajoled, coaxed, and helped into the identification "transgender" by social service and health organizations established to "help" them, through making them recognizable to the world of NGOs under the rubric of an identity not of their own making and that often fails to describe much of the way through which they understand their own identities and their relationship to questions of desire, gender, and sexuality.[103] These concerns are evidently part of the wider ongoing political and philosophical debates about justice as a problem of *recognition* and/or *redistribution*.[104]

These are not new ideas that question the universalization of homosexuality, a project whose progenitors were mostly white American gay and lesbian anthropologists who wrote ethnographies of homosexualities around the globe in the 1970s and 1980s in an attempt to prove the universality of homosexuality, even if many insisted on placing it in a Social Darwinist grid. In her masterful survey of this literature Weston identified this universalizing problematic:

To say "I am a gay person" assumes the infusion of sexuality into total personhood in a way that might be incomprehensible to someone who touches the genitals of another man or woman in a society without a word for such an action. The experience of going to a gay bar . . . or engaging in lesbian-feminist politics . . . contrasts sharply with the organization of homoeroticism in societies that have not formed "communities" based on sexual identity. To complicate matters, the rise of queer politics in the United States destabilized the concept of a fixed identity (homosexual or otherwise) even for the Western societies that had generated classifications such as lesbian and bisexual, bull-dagger and sodomite. . . . Writing about multiple genders or homosexualities does not extricate researchers from this philosophical dilemma, because these can be nothing more than varieties of something already assumed to be known or recognizable. . . . What is to count as homosexuality, gender, and sexual activity? . . . In whose eyes are such interpretations salient? . . . Yet the move to employ indigenous categories is no more neutral in its effects than the earlier, less reflective application of "homosexuality"

102. Asad, "Conscripts of Western Civilization," 345.
103. See Valentine, *Imagining Transgender*.
104. See Nancy Fraser and Axel Honneth, *Redistribution or Recognition? A Political-Philosophical Exchange* (London: Verso, 2003).

to a multitude of occasions. Although intended as a corrective to ethnocentrism and overgeneralization, the use of "foreign" names constructs the subject of inquiry as always and already Other. Now seemingly without parallel [and in the context of studies of the Middle East, the use of such "foreign" words] becomes implicated in a renewed form of Orientalism in which linguistic terms subtly reify differences and buttress ethnographic authority.[105]

Like Najmabadi, Valerie Traub, however, is unperturbed by any of this. She remains so distressed by scholarship that uncovers the analytic errors of Western academic studies on Arabs and Muslims, not to mention the Orientalist and racist approaches of the Gay International, that she musters a vituperative response defending them against such "allegations" and claiming that such problems do not at all "comprise a dominant pattern among scholars working on Islamicate sexualities or lesbian/gay/queer studies" without offering any evidence or a single academic source to support her righteous indignation, or even a counter-reading of the literature.[106]

US-based Palestinian academic Amal Amireh in turn objects to the tracking of the universalizing efforts and missions of Gay Internationalism. She states that "the desire to defend against orientalism as the dominant paradigm by which the West represents the East has encouraged the privileging of [Said's] *Orientalism* as the main paradigm by which we seek to understand what is happening in the Arab world" and that it is "a misapplication of models drawn from Michel Foucault's *History of Sexuality* and Edward Said's *Orientalism*."[107] Thus, once again, privileging "the small number of [Palestinian] members"[108] who belong to Palestinian NGOs located in Israel and who identify as "gay" or "queer" (the two terms are used interchangeably in Amireh's account) over the much larger number of Palestinians inside and outside Israel who do not and in whose lives and identifications she, like the rest of Gay Internationalists, shows no interest, Amireh wants to insist that everyone else should privilege this "small number" as well: "What I am calling the *Orientalism* paradigm privileges the power of the West's

105. Weston, "Lesbian and Gay Studies in the House of Anthropology," 347–48.
106. Traub, "The Past Is a Foreign Country?" 6. She further volunteers, also without citing a single piece of research that had not already been examined in my article on the Gay International which she engages, that "much recent scholarship on such topics is informed by theoretical perspectives and methodological commitments that would support Massad's contentions about the complex and historically specific configurations of male-male sex in the Arab world" (6).
107. Amal Amireh, "Afterword," *GLQ* 16, no. 4 (2010): 645.
108. Ibid., 644.

discourse to a degree that obscures resistances to this discourse, other competing discourses, and material realities. The inability of Massad to see anticolonial queer Arab activists outside this *Orientalism* paradigm is a case in point."[109] Amireh's joining the posthumous neoliberal and Orientalist attacks on Edward Said's work, notwithstanding, the point of my contribution, which Amireh and other commentators seem to miss, is precisely in demonstrating how much resistance persists outside (and even inside) Euro-America to the imposition of homo-hetero binarization and sexual identifications. That I locate this resistance among those who refuse these identifications and who remain by far the numerical majority across the world, is registered by Amireh as nothing short of seeing the "West" as irresistible to everyone in some Adornoesque fashion.[110]

109. Ibid., 645.

110. This facile position, which ignores my arguments that despite the complicity of many Arab intellectuals writing on the subject with Western taxonomies, most Arabs continue to resist them, is taken up by Sahar Amer, who claims: "Reading Massad's work, one gets the sense that Arabs are passive, always in a reactive position vis-à-vis the West, never actors or in charge of defining their own lives or sexualities." Amer goes further by thinking that *Desiring Arabs* should not be the intellectual history it claims to be but must be a *social* history even though this is not its aim. That the book deals with what Orientalists and Arab intellectuals posited as the central themes that would define the process of recovering the Arab past, a process that included some but not major debates about lesbianism (all references to lesbianism in this debate are cited and discussed in critical detail in *Desiring Arabs*, which also discusses the side-stepping of lesbian desires in literary representations), Amer believes that I should have imposed some nonexistent debates about lesbianism on this intellectual project nonetheless: "Except for an occasional reference or footnote (or the brief analysis in chapter 6 of Hanan al-Shaykh's *Misk al-Ghazal*), very little is said about lesbians in the Arab world." See Sahar Amer, "Joseph Massad and the Alleged Violence of Human Rights," *GLQ* 16, no. 4 (2010): 652–53. Ironically, it is Amer who, while insisting that sexuality is universal and that Western notions of sexuality are applicable to the Arab world—declaring that she disagrees "with scholars (like Joseph Massad, for instance)" who think it is not (in ibid., 394n13)—depicts Arab lesbians as linguistically (and even epistemologically) subservient to and dependent on a Western sexual vocabulary from which she wants to rescue them by providing them with a set of medieval Arabic alternatives. See Sahar Amer, "Naming to Empower: Lesbianism in the Arab Islamicate World Today," *Journal of Lesbian Studies* 16, no. 4 (2012) 381–97. Amer objects strenuously to the Western term "homosexuality": "When Freud used the word Homosexualität over a hundred years ago, he was constructing it as a mental illness, a pathology of deviancy requiring long-term psychoanalysis, aversion therapy, and at times even electroshock in order to be 'cured'—a situation that the U.S. gay rights movement has combated at least since 1924, and with a political edge during the 1969 Stonewall riots" (ibid., 385–86). I should note here that the term "homosexuality" was invented by Karl-Maria Kertbeny in 1869, and not by Freud. Freud resisted the term and mostly used "inversion" instead, especially in his early work. Aside from her inventing a fictional gay movement in the United States in 1924, Amer's account of Freud clearly lacks even basic and elementary knowledge of his oeuvre. In fact, Freud never pathologized homosexuality nor did he ever prescribe any therapy for it whatsoever but rather considered it "a variation of the sexual function." See Sigmund Freud, "Letter 277" (letter to an anonymous American mother), in *The Letters of Sigmund Freud*, ed. Ernst L. Freud (New York: Basic Books, 1960), 423. See also Henry Abelove, "Freud, Homosexuality, and the Americans," in *The Lesbian and Gay Studies Reader*, ed. Henry Abelove, Michèle Aina Barale, and David M. Halperin (London: Routledge, 1993), 381–93, and Kenneth Lewes, *The Psychoanalytic Theory of Male Homosexuality* (Markham, ON: Meridian Books, 1988). The desire that I should have

Amireh, like others who follow the Gay Internationalist paradigm, invokes the fictional claim that my argument about the universalization of gayness posits "queer" Arabs as "inauthentic" and that I "discredit their rootedness, relevance, and loyalties."[111] These fabricated quotations

---

written a social history or even a native informant account of the Arab world, rather than an intellectual history, pervades the literature that criticizes *Desiring Arabs*. Indeed, many of the criticisms leveled by Gay Internationalists treat the book as a social or even anthropological history that they find wanting. This is such an obsession that Wilson C. Jacob is "frustrat[ed]" that, as a putative native informant, I seem to possess native truths about Arab desires but nonetheless refuse to "divulge" these details of the sexual lives of the Arabs to my Western audience. He objects that "the discursive renderings of the Arab and of desire [in *Desiring Arabs*] are cast as historical but they recursively appear as flawed portrayals, evoking the presence of an immanent truth only known to the author but never fully divulged." Wilson C. Jacob, "Other Inscriptions: Sexual Difference and History Writing Between Futures Past and Present," posted on H-net, September 2009, http://www.h-net.org/reviews/showrev.php?id=25004 (accessed 1 April 2014). Jacob also strangely claims that in *Desiring Arabs* I "characterized modern Arab engagements with sexuality as *simply* [emphasis added] adopting Western terms," or that "Arab engagements" with sexuality "appear as a *simple* [emphasis added] case of internalization of an epistemology imposed from elsewhere," in contrast with his approach, which is allegedly "more historically nuanced," in Wilson Chacko Jacob, *Working Out Egypt: Effendi Masculinity and Subject Formation in Colonial Modernity, 1870–1940* (Durham, NC: Duke University Press, 2011), 16, 161. In fact, contra Jacob's distortions, in *Desiring Arabs* I make no such claims about "engagements with sexuality" and the "adoption of Western terms," but rather that a preponderance of modernizing Arab intellectuals "internalized the epistemology by which Europeans came to judge civilizations and cultures along the vector of something called 'sex,' as well as its later derivative, 'sexuality,' and the overall systematization of culture through the statistical concept of 'norms,' often corresponding to the 'natural' and its 'deviant' opposite," which is a different matter altogether (see *Desiring Arabs*, 6), and that, "as in European scholarship," the "new European concepts of civilization, culture, decadence, degradation, degeneration, heritage, sex, and deviance, among others . . . would be internalized" by a good number of "Arab scholars" and "institutionalized as solid scholarly concepts that required little if any questioning" (*Desiring Arabs*, 99). It is in the context of reading shifts in literary representations in the work of Naguib Mahfouz that I say clearly that "Mahfouz's representation of [one of his characters] as a self-declared deviant is intelligible to readers precisely because of the transformation of Arab society since the late nineteenth century, where the epistemic shifts instantiated by the Arab Renaissance project and the simultaneous European colonial project began to seep through to the interstices of society at large, to be internalized by new modern subjects, no longer remaining within the purview of the literati and colonial officers," an internalization which clearly was anything but simple, even for the fictional world of Mahfouz (*Desiring Arabs*, 287–88). If anything, much of *Desiring Arabs* is dedicated to showing how Western sexual identities, norms, and taxonomies *failed* to be internalized by the majority of Arabs, and that, to the extent to which they were internalized by certain classes of urbanites, including a good number of intellectuals, they were so in no "simple" manner at all: "The advent of colonialism and Western capital to the Arab world has transformed most aspects of daily living; however, it has failed to impose a European heterosexual regime on all Arab men, although its efforts were successful in the upper classes and among the increasingly Westernized middle classes" (*Desiring Arabs*, 173). It remains unclear why the realm of "nuance" and non-simplicity fall only within the purview of Gay Internationalists.

111. Amireh, "Afterword," 644–45. It is notable that Amireh insists on misrepresenting my argument even though she cites the very exchange I had with Ghassan Makarem in which I addressed these Gay Internationalist misrepresentations and inventions of quotes that are falsely attributed to me and challenged Makarem and his cohort to produce a single citation from my work where I allegedly make such arguments. While some of these misrepresentations may be based on a misunderstanding of my work by some, Amireh's misrepresentation of my work appears to be the result of a conscious and deliberate act of distortion, and *not* a misunderstanding.

aim at having a cumulative effect that would establish facticity through sheer repetition by Gay Internationalists.[112] Nowhere do I (or any of the other scholars who are critics of Gay Internationalism) ever claim that those who adopt Western identifications of gayness (or straightness, for that matter) among Palestinians (or Arabs or Muslims) are necessarily not anti-Occupation or that they are not part of the Palestinian struggle against Israeli colonialism. These ideologically informed charges betray the inability of those who level them to make distinctions between adopting imperial epistemologies and ontologies on the one hand and remaining anti-imperialist politically on the other, a point I discuss in *Desiring Arabs* with regards to Islamist and secular nationalist Arabs, some of whom are complicit with gay *and* straight internationalism epistemologically but are anti-imperialist in their political stances.[113]

What then informs Al-Kassim's, Najmabadi's, Habib's, Traub's, Kamal's, Amireh's, and others' psychic and political resistance to the resistance of many to the applicability of Anglo-American epistemologies and universalization as another form of imperialism and Anglo-American hegemony that obliterates difference under the banner of a desired and hoped for queer normativity? There is a peculiar misunderstanding here on the part of these scholars of the antinormative move that queerness instantiates. Queer can only exist ipso facto as antinormative, and attempts to disseminate it as a social formation, or as a form of resistance, or as a desired form of social hegemony undercut its very ontological structure and its specific and very recent histories.

Al-Kassim is careful in proposing "translation as a model for this figure of reemergent discipline within the form of power that usurps it. However translation is not only a path of successful transfer, and it does not always subvert. Translation also transfers by leaving something behind or by failing fully to carry over."[114] Al-Kassim however wants to obliterate the resistance to Anglo-American hegemony and imperial-

112. A most recent addition to this accumulation of fabrications is an essay by one Jared McCormick, who quotes the term "authenticity" allegedly from *Desiring Arabs* without page references. See "Hairy Chest, Will Travel: Tourism, Identity, and Sexuality in the Levant," *Journal of Middle East Women's Studies* 7, no. 3 (Fall 2011): 81.

113. See also my interview "L'empire de la sexualité, ou peut-on ne pas être homosexuel (ou hétérosexuel)? Entretien avec Joseph Massad," *Revue des Livres*, Paris, January-February 2013, http://www.revuedeslivres.fr/l'empire-de-«-la-sexualite-»-ou-peut-on-ne-pas-etre-homosexuel-ou-heterosexuel-entretien-avec-joseph-massad/ (accessed 1 April 2014). See also my rseponse to Stéphane Lavignotte and Philippe Colomb, "Débat: L'empire de la sexualité en question," *Revue des Livres*, March-April 2013, http://www.revuedeslivres.fr/debat-l'empire-de-«-la-sexualite-»-en-question-22-par-jospeh-massad/. Translation of the interview to English was published in *Jadaliyya*, March 2013, http://www.jadaliyya.com/pages/index/10461/the-empire-of-sexuality_an-interview-with-joseph-m.

114. Al-Kassim, "Epilogue," *Islamicate Sexualities*, 332.

ism and to "overcom[e] the kinds of caution that foreclose the reading of desire when alterity is allegedly assured, and I seek to trouble that assurance."[115] Unfortunately, what she offers as a troubling of this alleged assurance is the same reductive reading of resistance to European nativism offered by Najmabadi, Traub, and Amireh, namely that resistance is another form of "sexual and epistemological essentialism."[116] Her refusal to understand the varieties of resistance to the institutionalization of the homo-hetero binary as not only epistemological but also as *material* is symptomatic of her objection to the separation between homo/hetero sexual identities and homo/hetero sexual practices. As I have argued in *Desiring Arabs*, this is not to say that there are no operative sexual binaries in societies outside the "West," but that they are not always mappable onto Western binaries:

The human rights advocates are not bringing about the inclusion of the homosexual in a new and redefined human subjectivity, but in fact are bringing about her and his exclusion from this redefined subjectivity altogether while simultaneously destroying existing subjectivities organized around other sets of binaries, including sexual ones.[117]

Al-Kassim participates in the Western liberal production of opponents to Western liberal universalism as nativists or apologists for localism and the authentic and refuses to see European nativism and its apologists as the ones offering a form of nativism and essentialism, which causes much harm in countries with majority Muslim and non-Muslim populations outside Europe. What is significant, however, is that the charge of investing in the authentic applies appropriately, not to critics of Gay Internationalism, but to the arguments of Al-Kassim, Najmabadi, Amireh and their cohort who are the ones who insist, as we saw, on identifying these groups as indeed *authentic*, and that they are products of local and not of imperial developments, and therefore they deserve Western support as representatives of the authentic and the local, which turns out to be coincidentally also universal. Al-Kassim is explicit on this point in another article. Basing herself on two studies of the premodern Ottoman Empire and Iran (the latter by Najmabadi), Al-Kassim (along with her co-author Lara Deeb) rejects the theory of Western imperialism in favor of a universal coeval development of the notion of sexuality and the biopolitical state around the world. She states that the two

115. Ibid., 333.
116. Ibid., 305.
117. *Desiring Arabs*, 41.

studies she consulted "clarify a multivalent conversation between East and West, North and South that cannot be reduced to mere influence or importation of Western science and social attitudes. Rather, these discourses emerge coevally to affect subject constitution, notions of desire and communitarian practice." Indeed, she adds that the two studies "corroborate the dissemination of the discourse of sexuality in the development of the modern biopolitical state in the Middle East." Arguing against the contention that sexual identity travels with colonialism to the Middle East, Al-Kassim concludes unequivocally that "biopolitics is a global affair" and therefore local and authentic, which impels her to call on others to produce "more material studies" as evidence to prove the point that European imperialism is *not* responsible for the institution and dissemination of sexuality globally.[118]

In this context, the recent Ugandan case comes to mind. A draconian law imposing the death penalty on homosexual activity, proposed in Uganda in 2009, as threatening the "African family" was instigated by American evangelicals proselytizing in the country. It was left to the Gay International to launch a campaign against the "Anti-Homosexuality Bill of 2009." Even the *New York Times* had to admit that "Uganda seems to have become a far-flung front line in the American culture wars, with American groups on both sides, the Christian right and gay activists, pouring in support and money as they get involved in the broader debate over homosexuality in Africa."[119] The bill was passed in December 2013, in parliament, but Ugandan president Yoweri Museveni refused to sign it, declaring that it was passed illegally and that homosexuals were "abnormal" and needed to be "rescued."[120] This is hardly an exceptional development; even in Romania, a country often seen within European

118. Lara Deeb and Dina Al-Kassim, "Introduction," *Journal of Middle East Women's Studies* 7, no. 3 (Fall 2011): 2.

119. Jeffrey Gettleman, "Americans' Role Seen in Uganda Anti-Gay Push," *New York Times*, 3 January 2010. On Gay Internationalist propaganda and trumped up charges against Iran as allegedly a place where gay men are executed, see Scott Long, "Unbearable Witness: How Western Activists (Mis)Recognize Sexuality in Iran," *Contemporary Politics* 15, no. 1 (March 2009): 119–36. Long, who seems to have gotten more sensitized in recent years to *some* of the arguments regarding the harm caused by Gay Internationalism and his own principal role in it, exposes how a global campaign against Iran in recent years (in line with the US imperial agenda) was spearheaded by British, American, and other European gay groups and newspapers. Long also exposes the anti-Islam and anti-Muslim rhetoric of much of the campaign. For his earlier reticence to accepting these same arguments, see his "The Trials of Culture: Sex and Security in Egypt," *Middle East Report*, no. 230 (Spring 2004): 12–20, and my critique of his human rights activism in *Desiring Arabs*, 185–87.

120. "Uganda Passes Draconian anti-Gay Law," *Guardian*, 20 December 2013; and Yaslin Mugerwa, "Museveni Blocks Anti-Homosexuality Bill," *Daily Monitor* (Uganda), 17 January 2014, http://www.monitor.co.ug/News/National/Museveni-blocks-Anti-Homosexuality-Bill/-/688334/2148760/-/15lby8fz/-/index.html (accessed 1 April 2014).

Union states as "unruly and 'un-Westernised,'"[121] the first gay organization, ACCEPT, was founded in 1994 "with the help of some foreigners residing in the country."[122] ACCEPT's "twinning with COC [The Federation
of Dutch Associations for the Integration of Homosexualities], which
included a Dutch project coordinator based for a time in Bucharest, not
only assisted with the development of infrastructure, but also provided
a link back to a (liberal) EU member state (and one that had invested
money in an NGO challenging state law in Romania)."[123] Romania, as
an internal European other, would become the template for gay internationalist human rights work that would soon be applied to Europe's
external others. Scott Long, who helped found ACCEPT while living and
teaching in Romania as his first test case, would soon move to defend
the rights of "homosexuals" and "gays" in South Africa and then the
Middle East as a representative of the US-based International Gay and
Lesbian Human Rights Campaign (IGLHRC) and Human Rights Watch
respectively.[124] Here it seems that not only do imperial ideas, epistemologies, laws, practices, and organizations circulate the globe to produce
the desired imperial effects, but so does the same imperial personnel.

The case of South Africa is most telling, especially in its marketing
by white American and European Gay Internationalists as a weapon to
shame nonwhite countries that refuse to follow its example and as evidence that a commitment to sexual citizenship and gayness is not an exclusive Euro-American and West European affair. But the deal concluded
between white South African gays and lesbians and Gay Internationalists
on the one hand and the African National Congress (ANC) on the other
to produce the equality clause in the post-Apartheid South African constitution demonstrates precisely how this imperial white racialized project came to be. The involvement of the International Lesbian and Gay
Association (ILGA) and the (exclusively white) Gay Association of South
Africa (GASA) since the early 1980s, and the subsequent transformations
which led to the self-disbanding of GASA in 1987 and its reemergence
in other organizational forms, have been well documented, as has the
blackmail to which GASA was subject by some elements in ILGA to

121. Carl F. Stychin, *Governing Sexuality: The Changing Politics of Citizenship and Law Reform*
(Oxford: Hart, 2003), 115.
122. Emelia Stere, "ACCEPTing the Future: An Interview with Adrian Coman," *Central Europe
Review* 3, no. 16 (7 May 2001).
123. Carl F. Stychin, *Governing Sexuality*, 121.
124. See Jennifer Tanaka, "Report on the Symposium Homosexuality: A Human Right?"
May 1995, available on http://www.france.qrd.org/assocs/ilga/euroletter/35-Romania.html (accessed 1 April 2014).

couple its struggle for (white) gay rights with the anti-Apartheid struggle and the blackmail to which the ANC was subjected by current and former GASA members in the process—in the form of *we will support your struggle if you support ours*.[125] Two decades after the success of that blackmail, American gay scholars are still complaining that gayness in South Africa, as identity and as a protected form of sexual citizenship, remains mostly within the purview of whiteness, while the majority of black South Africans have not internalized it, and in those cases where they have, cannot access the legal protections provided for them by the law.[126]

Sonya Katyal observes that "gay and lesbian activists in the United States . . . have . . . asserted significant leadership over the global constitution of [homosexuality], exerting enormous power in determining the manner by which individuals define their sexual identities. Gay pride parades have become a global phenomenon; and gay and lesbian activists have made their way around the globe to assist the formation of nascent movements."[127] In the mid 1990s, an American, Tim Wright, arrived in Bolivia and set on to found a gay "Pride" movement there: "He contacted influential lawyers and officials and even helped to organize Drag Queen Elections with police escort. He taught about Stonewall, about the meaning of all the symbols that represent the struggle of gays and lesbians. . . . Wright was the closest thing to a real leader the Movement had ever had."[128] The "Movement" would later receive funds from USAID, which it would keep secret. Wright was assaulted in 1995 by anonymous attackers and returned to the US afterwards, leaving behind increased Bolivian police surveillance and repression in the wake of his efforts.[129] *Homosexuality is not the only thing being universalized here; heterosexuality and homophobia are evidently its constant companions.*

Let us return to Al-Kassim, who resists the claim of epistemological difference in different cultural contexts and attacks it by misrepresenting it as a kind of resistance that reifies transhistorical difference and refuses to see it as *dynamic*. Al-Kassim's strange claims are made even

125. On this history, see the testimonies and documents included in Neville Hoad, Karen Martin, and Graeme Reid, eds., *Sex and Politics in South Africa: The Equality Clause / Gay and Lesbian Movement / the Anti-Apartheid Struggle* (Cape Town: Double Storey, 2005).

126. See Xavier Livermon, "Queer(y)ing Freedom: Black Queer Visibilities in Postapartheid South Africa," *GLQ* 18, nos. 2–3 (2012): 297–323.

127. Katyal, "Exporting Identity," 114.

128. On Tim Wright, see Pedro Albornoz, "Bolivia: Landlocked Country," *Harvard Gay and Lesbian Review* 6, no. 1 (Winter 1999): 17. As is clear, Euro-American gay missionaries are not only active in Arab and Muslim countries but all over the globe. A gay American, to give another example, opened and ran a local "gay bookstore" in Thailand in the 1990s. See Dennis Altman, *Global Sex* (Chicago: University of Chicago Press, 2001), 97.

129. Ibid.

when this resistance to European nativism insists on the dynamism of non-European sexual epistemologies and ontologies but refuses to collapse them into the modern European taxonomy of sexual identities nor to construe their dynamism as one heading in the direction of the telos reached in the United States and Western Europe, which, I fear, Al-Kassim seems to think is the *only* possible dynamism.

The "West" has been normalized as the "West" by a series of ontological and epistemological operations, including its hetero-homo binarization. It is these operations that produce it as *the West* and produce the West's others as opposites or approximations of it. This should be clear to any reader of the Saidian project. But instead of attending to how configurations of desire and investments in corporeal pleasure came to be articulated very differently in the normalized "West" and the yet-to-be normalized "East," and that a certain modern reading of desire and corporeal practices in the binarized "West" seeks to assimilate, often through conscription, all "Western" desires across time in its modern image as well as assimilate all non-Western desires transhistorically and transgeographically into its own forms, Al-Kassim *misunderstands* and resists this *resisting* project as one of "arguing for the clarity of the distinction of the East/West divide in ways that resonate with the very Orientalism [one] critiques."[130]

---

130. Al-Kassim, "Epilogue," 304. In a special issue of the *Journal of Middle East Women's Studies* on "sexuality in Middle East Studies" that she coedited later, Al-Kassim published an ally who repeated her position of claiming to transcend alleged binary oppositions. Thus Paul Amar, a white American scholar, ventriloquizes Al-Kassim without citing her by asserting that what he is offering along with "more nuanced" others (including Wilson Jacob, from whom he borrows the phrase "more nuanced," also without citation) who study sexuality and/in Islam, whom he cites approvingly, also transcend this alleged "binary [which] often reanimates the dualism of West versus East, implying that a realm of sexuality is a driving force of modernity, with some focusing on its power to incite and dominate and others underlining sexuality as a realm of eroticized autonomy and emancipation." Paul Amar, "Middle East Masculinity Studies: Discourses of 'Men in Crisis' Industries of Gender in Revolution," *Journal of Middle East Women's Studies* 7, no. 3 (Fall 2011): 43, 44. Amar makes the strange allegation that critics of the claims of the universality of sexuality (specifically my work) view it "as [a] mechanism of collaboration with coloniality and as training in dependency" (53), thus repeating the allegation made by Samar Habib and Ghassan Makarem (also without citing them) that I call Arab or Muslim gays "dupes" or "agents" of imperialism. But, lack of originality aside, Amar misses the whole point of the historical, geographic, and cultural specificity of sexuality as a mode of subjectivation, which could never render it into a "mechanism" or a "dependent" performance, much less one that elicits "collaboration." Amar's shoddy scholarship is in evidence also in his later book where he alleges that my 2002 article on the Gay International was "originally written as an analysis of the Queen Boat raid in Egypt," when in fact the article was based on a lecture I had delivered at the University of Chicago in February 2000, fifteen months before the Queen Boat raid, and was submitted for publication a year before the Queen Boat raid had even taken place (something which is mentioned in the article itself had Amar bothered to check; see "Re-Orienting Desire: The Gay International and the Arab World," *Public Culture* 14, no. 2 [Spring 2002]: 385). The lecture and the original version of the article were in fact predicting that Gay Internationalism was inciting

juridical and police repression in the Arab world, which the Queen Boat raids would later exemplify. The article was amended in the middle of *Public Culture*'s editorial process with added information to reflect the then recent Queen Boat events. But Amar even goes further by alleging ironically, contra Gay Internationalist critics of *Desiring Arabs* who claim that I deny them "agency," that the article gives Gay Internationalists too much "agentive power," which he believes they lack. He also alleges that I deny such agency to organs of state security in Egypt when I had devoted a whole section of a chapter in *Desiring Arabs* to criminology and police strategies of entrapping "sexual deviants" since the mid 1990s (see *Desiring Arabs*, 246–56). Amar then misattributes this finding and the historicizing of such entrapment to *himself*, offering this appropriated "account" as his own "as opposed to Massad's focus on transnational NGOs" (Amar, *Security Archipelago*, 76). While Amar accuses me of "hypervisibilizing" Gay Internationalists by granting them this "agentive power" which they allegedly lack (when my critique of Gay Internationalism targets precisely their invention of "gays" which they want to "out" to the state and thus to "hypervisibilize"), it is Amar, like the Gay International, who seems invested in "hypervisibilizing" Egyptian "gays" when he claims erroneously and with a smattering of Arabic that the Egyptian Armed Forces allegedly identified protesters in 2011 as "khawaliya" (which he translates as "fags"), a word that he most likely made up (possibly because it rhymes with the other word he cites: "baltagiya" meaning "thugs") but which unfortunately does not exist in Egyptian, or any other form of, Arabic, no matter how much Amar, whose claim to have "acquire[d] fluency in Arabic and Egyptian colloquial" years ago is nowhere evinced, wants it to. Amar must mean "khawalat," a derogatory term that refers to men who take the "passive" position in coitus with other men, which at any rate was never used in any publication or written orders by the Egyptian Armed Forces and no evidence exists that it was used orally either, at least none that Amar cites. Indeed neither of the two sources that Amar provides to support his fabricated claim mentions it or even alludes to it (they both mention the term "thugs" but not "fags" or "khawaliya" or anything remotely connected to it as he falsely claims). See Paul Amar, *The Security Archipelago: Human-Security States, Sexuality Politics, and the Ends of Neoliberalism* (Durham, NC: Duke University Press, 2013), 75, 3. Amar cites a Human Rights Watch Report (http://www.hrw.org /news/2011/04/29/egypt-military-trials-usurp-justice-system) and a news item on the Ahramonline portal (http://english.ahram.org.eg/NewsContent/1/64/17874/Egypt/Politics-/New-batch-of-arrests -in-Tahrir-Aquare-to-add-to-th.aspx) to support this claim even though neither of them mentions it. Amar's baseless citations include his accusation that in my 2002 article I accuse the Gay International of "'penetrating' [note the quotation marks] . . . the embodied identities of the nations of the Arab world," when I have never used the verb to "penetrate" at all against the Gay International (neither in my article nor in my book), let alone "embodied identities of the nations of the Arab world," whatever that means (Amar, *The Security Archipelago*, 75). In his quest to "hypervisibilize" Egyptian "gays" further, Amar shows such poor knowledge of the Egyptian scene (perhaps on account of his evidently poor Arabic) that he makes up another fabrication, namely that those arrested in the Queen Boat raid "self-identified with sexualized global citizenship" when in fact only some of them had signed false confessions under torture and duress that they had had sexual encounters with other men (Amar, *The Security Archipelago*, 74). On their denial of these allegations, see *Desiring Arabs*, 184–85. Most surprising, however, is Amar's coining the term "Moorist transnational" as a presumably clever riposte to the notion of the "Gay International": in the context of discussing the reaction to a United Nations Human Rights Commission resolution introduced by Brazil in 2003 (and cosponsored by 26 European countries and Cyprus and supplemented by the efforts of IGLHRC, Amnesty International's Outfront Project, and Human Rights Watch's Lesbian and Gay Rights Project in support of the resolution, relevant facts that Amar fails to mention) "to ban discrimination based on sexual orientation," Amar states "Pakistan, Saudi Arabia, and the Holy See, along with the US administration of George W. Bush, came together to lead the mobilization against the resolution," which leads him to conclude that "for the moment, the new 'Moorist [*sic*] transnational' had conquered the 'gay international'" (ibid., 63). The racial privileging that leads to an insistence that 28 million Saudi Arabians (who are presumably "Moors") should trump the 300 million Americans and 180 million Pakistanis, let alone the hundreds of Catholic clergy inhabiting the Vatican, by calling the coalition of governments representing them the "Moorist transnational" raises more questions (especially about this racist designation) than it answers. Amar's distortion of facts and false

What is resonant with Orientalism however is *not* the resistance to reproduce the Orient as a copy of the Occident, but Al-Kassim's insistence that European history should unfold in non-Europe in the same way it unfolded in Europe.[131] Al-Kassim may not realize that her critique shares the aims of the European project, which Talal Asad described as one that "requires not the production of a uniform *culture* throughout the world but certain shared modalities of legal-moral behaviour, forms

---

documentation is in evidence also here, as it was in fact Pakistan and the Holy See who opposed the resolution. More opposition came from Sub-Saharan African states also. The Saudis only proposed amendments while the Holy See lobbied Latin American governments to oppose it. The vote was postponed to 2004, with only 4 out of the 23 countries that voted for postponement being Arab or "Moorish," let alone "Moorist," countries! Brazil refused to reintroduce the resolution in 2004 and, when called upon to do so, the European Union and South Africa also refused. All this information is available in the very source that Amar uses as documentation for his factual distortions. See Françoise Girard, "Negotiating Sexual Rights and Sexual Orientation at the UN," in *Sex Politics: Reports from the Front Lines*, ed. Richard Parker, Rosalind Petchesky, and Robert Sember (New York: Sexuality Policy Watch, 2004), 344.

131. Another member of the club of those who insist that resistance to imperialism and to the universalization of sexuality is a form of Orientalism is Howard Chiang, who labels critics of gay internationalism as engaging in "full-blown self- or re-orientalisation, by which I mean an intentional project that continually defers an 'alternative modernity' and essentialises non-westernness (including Chineseness) by assuming the genealogical status of that derivative copy of an 'original' western modernity is somehow always already hermeneutically sealed from the historical apparatus of westernization," in Howard Chiang, "Epistemic Modernity and the Emergence of Homosexuality in China," *Gender & History* 22, no. 3 (November 2010): 634. For Chiang, neither colonialism nor imperialism is of any importance (and neither word makes any appearance in his article); what is important is rather Western "modernity," which, for him, seems unconnected to either. While Chiang explains that the notion of "homosexuality" was introduced to China in the 1920s by Western-educated Chinese Republican intellectuals and scholars who upheld Western modernity as the model for China's future compared to which they considered Chinese culture "deficient," he thinks this was not part of self-Orientalization at all, rather that anyone who thinks it was self-Orientalization is the self-Orientalizer! His argument states that the introduction of the notion of homosexuality to China was carried out through "a discursive apparatus that I call 'epistemic modernity,' in which explicit claims of sexual knowledge were imbricated with implicit claims about cultural indicators of traditionality, authenticity and modernity" (ibid., 647, 650). He defines "epistemic modernity" as "a series of ongoing practices and discourses that could generate new ways of cultural comprehension and conceptual engagement, allowing for possible intersecting transformations in history and epistemology" (ibid., 50). That these new ways are translations and adaptations of what was considered a superior European culture seems to be immaterial to Chiang. One should not have to rehearse for Chiang the voluminous literature on nationalism, especially outside Europe, to explain that this imbrication of tradition, the authentic, and the modern with what he calls "epistemic modernity" is not separable from the superiority and hegemony of European modern culture that was formed through and by direct and indirect European colonialism on a global scale and is therefore not simply a case of an un-"intentional" or co-incidental "intersection." If Homi Bhabha's work, in another register, sought to code racial passing of the colonized as a form of anticolonial resistance, Chiang and his cohort go further by coding (homo)sexual cultural passing as an *equal yet unintentional and coincidental partaking* of the Western modern by Orientals. Chiang and the other members of the club (like Al-Kassim, as we saw above) also insist that anyone who deigns to question their liberal equalization and expose it as one more liberal ruse with which they seek to obscure imperial processes is nothing short of a self-Orientalizer and an essentialist! On Bhabha's coding, see Joseph Massad, "Affiliating with Edward Said," in *Emancipation and Representation: On the Intellectual Meditations of Edward Said*, ed. Hakem Rustom and Adel Iskander (Berkeley: University of California Press, 2010), 40–42.

of national-political structuration, and rhythms of progressive historicity. It invites or seeks to coerce everyone to become the West—to express
their particularities through 'the West' as the measure of universality."[132]

Whence then comes this resistance by Al-Kassim and her cohort to
the resistance to their queering project and their attempt to rewrite it
as another form of essentialism? Could the attraction of metropolitan
theories and the need to identify with them be so strong as to obfus-
cate critiques of their universal applicability? It is after all metropolitan
theories that insist on the conjunction between sexuality *and* Islam as
a viable research project which creates a false parallel between two untranslatable notions as a cover for the anthropological Euro-American
and European impulse, which is in fact a ruse of power, and pre-position
of studying sexuality *in* Islam.

Is this fascination with Western theories a form of Orientalism or
Occidentalism? It is important to note that Occidentalism (or "orientalism in reverse"), in contrast to those, like Ian Buruma, Avishai Margalit, or
Sadik Jalal al-ʿAzm, who use it as the opposite of Orientalism, is no such
thing.[133] *Occidentalism is always already Orientalism.* Occidentalism is the
way the Orientalist always views the West, as a fantastical place (in contrast with the fantasized Orient) of sexual freedom and gender equality, of
social and economic justice, of advancement and progress, of democracy
and liberty, etc. Occidentalism was never the opposite of Orientalism; it
has always been its correlate, informed by it and informing it. Attributing
Occidentalism to critics of Orientalism, as has been done since Said's book
was published, is therefore a spectacular instance of méconnaissance.

Herein lies Al-Kassim's major objection to the resistance to Western
theories, which she misidentifies as static and essentialist. Al-Kassim's
concern seems to be with what she fears is a closing off of international
gay (and straight) solidarity networks with the sexually oppressed in non-
Europe, putting in jeopardy their liberal save-and-rescue missions. She
specifies the debates over the Egyptian Queen Boat arrests when Egyptian
authorities arrested fifty-two men in 2001 over accusations of sexual de-
bauchery, which elicited widespread Euro-American and European condemnation by gay activists whose international solidarity was a key factor
in the police repression. Al-Kassim, in a sleight of hand, alleges that this
repression has not stopped since 2001 and that the "vice raids . . . continue

---

132. Talal Asad, "A Comment on Aijaz Ahmad's *In Theory,*" *Public Culture* 6, no. 1 (Fall 1993): 36.
133. See Ian Buruma and Avishai Margalit, *Occidentalism: The West in the Eyes of Its Enemies* (New York: Penguin Press, 2004). See also Sadik Jalal al-ʿAzm, "Orientalism and Orientalism in Reverse," *Khamsin* 8 (1981): 5–26.

to the present,"[134] in a move that signals the urgency for the continued need of international, read Western, solidarity. Indeed, Al-Kassim's zeal to save the sexually oppressed leads her to argue for the use of psycho-analysis in "Queer" Middle East Studies on the basis that the latter has been an "all[y] in the fight to secure human rights for GLBT people."[135] One is reminded when reading such quasi Christian sermons, calling for rescuing and saving the sexually oppressed, of Foucault's diagnosis of this prevailing discourse in "our" European "civilization," one

in which sex, the revelation of truth, the overturning of global laws, the proclamation of a new day to come, and the promise of a certain felicity are linked together. Today it is sex that serves as a support for the ancient form—so familiar and important in the West—of preaching. A great sexual sermon—which has had its subtle theologians and its popular voices—has swept through our societies over the last decades; it has chastised the old order, denounced hypocrisy, and praised the rights of the immediate and the real; it has made people dream of a New City. The Franciscans are called to mind. And we might wonder how it is possible that the lyricism and religiosity that long accompanied the revolutionary project have, in Western industrial societies, been largely carried over to sex.[136]

It is noteworthy, that the missionary zeal with which these objections are made is manifest in the very scholarship and activism that insist on a relationship between sexuality and Islam rather than *between sexuality and Christianity* from which they in fact issue!

But the objection raised against Euro-American and West European gay solidarity was not an objection against international solidarity *tout court* but against this specific form of solidarity and its unidirectionality, wherein Euro-American and West European gay activists insist on three strategies in their solidarity: (1) of identifying the victims of repression in Egypt and "Islamic" countries as "gay" when the victims have not identified themselves as such nor constituted themselves as groups nor called upon Euro-American or West European gays to come to their rescue; (2) of leading the struggle on behalf of such victims under the pretext that the victims are unable or unfit (the difference between the two is slight) to defend themselves or even to call for help, and indeed go as far as establishing their groups for them in their own countries and then proceed to fund them; (3) and of *teaching* (not learning from) the

134. Al-Kassim, "Epilogue," 304.

135. Dina Al-Kassim, "Psychoanalysis and the Postcolonial Genealogy of Queer Theory," *International Journal of Middle East Studies* 45, no. 2 (2013): 345.

136. Foucault, *The History of Sexuality*, vol. 1: *An Introduction*, 7–8.

victims how to identify and defend themselves. International solidarity is a time-honored form of activism that has not always followed such dubious imperialist strategies.[137]

Gay Internationalist sympathies with the oppressed outside Europe and Euro-America is "not a simple matter of 'sympathy' with another's position," as Judith Butler put it, "since sympathy involves a substitution of oneself for another that may very well be a colonization of the other's position *as* one's own."[138] Criticism and condemnation of the existing types of Euro-American and West European organizational gay solidarity (or of feminist solidarity, as we discussed in the previous chapter) should not be mistaken for a rejection of international solidarity, but rather of its imperial and racial pretensions, let alone its ontological impositions and epistemic violence.[139]

In light of these criticisms, care has been taken by some to refrain from identifying people who engage in same-sex acts outside Euro-America with the new coinage "men who have sex with men" or MSM for short. But this has also been a disingenuous move, as MSM was quickly transformed from a descriptor into an identity formation (or as Talal Asad describes the effect of tabulation, as a "social type")[140] in order to be tabulable in the data collection and analysis of human rights organizations and NGOs and in the discourse of HIV/AIDS prevention.[141] While

137. For an informative article about how IGLHRC and other NGOs negotiate some of these issues in relation to their project of international solidarity, see Ryan Richard Thoreson, "Power, Panics, and Pronouns: The Information Politics of Transnational LGBT NGOs," *Journal of Language and Sexuality* 2, no. 1 (2013): 145–77.

138. Judith Butler, *Bodies that Matter: On the Discursive Limits of Sex* (London: Routledge, 1993), 118.

139. In a detailed review of my book *Desiring Arabs* in *Committee on Lesbian and Gay History* (an organ of the American Historical Association) vol. 22, no. 2, independent scholar Rudy Bleys, who wrote an insightful book on European views of the sexual practices of non-Europeans—see his *The Geography of Perversion: Male-to-Male Sexual Behaviour outside the West and the Ethnographic Imagination, 1750–1918* (New York: New York University Press, 1995)—assures his readers that Massad "reveals himself as committed to the fate of homosexually active men and women in the Arab world, yet is also highly critical of the global campaign for gay rights, which he considers counter-productive in that it advocates a 'Western' model of gay emancipation, and, as a result, provokes intolerant reactions within the Arab world" (7), and that "the material and analysis provided by Massad should not be seen as obstructing the emancipatory struggle of men having sex with men in these countries" (9). He concludes that "the firm political stance against a gay rights approach . . . does leave the reader wondering if Massad can indeed advise us all on how to proceed wisely indeed when it comes to untangling the problem of social stigmatization of homosexually active men, whether gay-identified or not" (9), and recommends that the book be read by international gay and lesbian activists not for its arguments but rather as "intelligence information" (9)!

140. Talal Asad, "Ethnographic Representation, Statistics, and Modern Power," *Social Research* 61, no. 1 (Spring 1994): 63.

141. See Traub, "The Past Is a Foreign Country?" 33n12, where she thinks MSM has resolved the question of the imperialism of gay identity.

MSM started with the insight in HIV prevention efforts that practice rather than identity is the ground for HIV transmission, its ossification into identity was not necessarily obvious or inevitable except under the epistemological pressures I identified above.[142] And just like "Islamicate" is used in the very same way "Islamic" or "Middle Eastern" is used while pretending to offer a different signification, MSM has come to be used in the same way "homosexual" or "gay" was used before to identify and conscript people who inhabit what is perceived as recalcitrant ontological and epistemological formations into becoming subjects of (Western) sexuality. In the words of Talal Asad:

The figures and the categories in terms of which [statistics] were (are) collected, manipulated, and presented belong to projects aimed at determining the values and practices—the souls and bodies—of entire populations. Central to these projects has been the liberal conception of modern society as an aggregate of individual agents choosing freely and yet—in aggregate—predictably. The construction of modern society in this sense is also, of course, the construction of radically new conditions of experience.[143]

Thus if men who have sex with men do not see what they do as identificatory and do not even describe themselves as "men who have sex with men," how then does identifying them as such eschew the imperial problem of endowing them with gay identities in the first place? The attempt to (re)introduce nomenclature that claims to oppose what it replaces, when it reproduces the very same problems it claims to supplant, can perhaps be read as a *repetition compulsion* on the part of these scholars and activists.

Sexuality as a European Category

In his entry on "sexualities and queer studies" in the *Encyclopedia of Women and Islamic Cultures*, Frédéric Lagrange finds queer studies "highly useful in the study of non-European cultures, which in turn could certainly benefit from an academic debate on the construction of

142. For an informative discussion on the differences of the LGBTI versus the MSM strategies of international activism, especially as relates to Africa, see Hakan Seckinelgin, "Global Activism and Sexualities in the time of HIV/AIDS," *Contemporary Politics* 15, no. 1 (March 2009): 103–18. Dennis Altman remarks in this regard: "Ironically the term 'men who have sex with men' was coined to reach men who rejected any sense of identity based upon their sexual practices, but fairly quickly became used in ways which just repeated the odd confusions between behavior and identity" (Altman, *Global Sex*, 74). On the transformation of MSM to an identity, see also Katyal, "Exporting Identity," 156–57.

143. Asad, "Ethnographic Representation, Statistics, and Modern Power," 77.

sexuality in Islamic societies."[144] I find this formulation too committed to the very problematic terms that this chapter has tried to highlight. Indeed, it would be more germane for queer studies to interrogate the way through which European identities are being refashioned, even at the level of law, as encompassing homosexuality as a constituent part and as a defining limit of their nationhood, nay their nationality. This should be contrasted with the redefinition of US notions of Americanness and citizenship after World War II, which began to retreat from racial definitions in favor of sexual ones. In this regard, Joanne Meyerowitz poses the important question "Did heteronormativity in some sense supplant whiteness as an explicit legal attribute of respectable, healthy, and worthy citizens [in the United States]?"[145] And might an assimilated homonormativity be now brought into it to buttress it?

With the redefinition of American and European racialized nationness and identities since the 1970s along the axis of "egalitarian" gender and sexual rights, "inegalitarian" non-European cultures and civilizations become poles of hierarchical contrast and difference. Indeed in a context where the traditional European right wing is now embracing sexual rights and equality as a central part of their anti-Muslim rhetoric and policies, Eric Fassin notes, "sexual democracy—or at least the rhetoric of sexual democracy—may thus be the price that many conservatives are willing to pay so as to provide a modern justification to anti-immigration politics that could otherwise appear merely as reactionary xenophobia."[146]

Leticia Sabsay, in turn, has brilliantly argued that the very notion of sexual citizenship is nothing short of a new form of Orientalism and colonialism, as the former has become "a marker that distinguishes the so-called advanced Western democracies in opposition to their 'undeveloped others.'"[147] She adds that "sexual citizenship has been cast under the framework of political liberalism in order to conceive the subject as entitled to be a claimant of sexual rights" and how this "follow[s] from an orientalist conception of citizenship."[148] It is within this understanding of the universalization and democratization of sexuality that

144. Frédéric Lagrange, "Sexualities and Queer Studies," *Encyclopedia of Women and Islamic Cultures*, ed. Suad Joseph (Leiden: Brill, 2003), 1:419.

145. Joanne Meyerowitz, "Transnational Sex and U.S. History," *American Historical Review* 114, no. 5 (December 2009) 1280.

146. Eric Fassin, "National Identities and Transnational Intimacies: Sexual Democracy and The Politics of Immigration in Europe," *Public Culture* 22 no. 3 (2010): 513.

147. Leticia Sabsay, "The Emergence of the Other Sexual Citizen: Orientalism and the Modernization of Sexuality," *Citizenship Studies* 16, nos. 5–6 (August 2012): 606.

148. Ibid.

"not only determine in advance the ways in which queerness should be performed for queers to be read as such, but also orientalises those who are reluctant to perform their queerness according to these (in fact provincial) standards."[149] I would add that it also orientalizes those who are reluctant to perform any kind of queerness even if their sexual desires are seen as mappable onto Western notions of what is queer. Therein lies the impossibility that any sexual resistance to Western Gay Internationalism and the universalization of sexuality would register on the radar of Euro-American and European sexual universalists as legitimate. Sabsay misreads me in this context, thinking that I do not "believe in the possibility of any queer resistance to sexual imperialism." It is not that I do not believe in such a possibility, it is rather that the constitution of sexual citizenship in Europe and Euro-America as an imperial and Orientalist project does not permit anti-imperialist resistance under the ontological banner of queerness, but rather in opposition to it.[150]

The recent move since March 2006 by the Netherlands to require Muslim immigrants to watch a film, showing two Dutch men kissing in a sexual embrace, in preparation for their immigration exams and to demonstrate thus that their value system is assimilable to Dutch society's "liberal values" is hardly exceptional, as other European countries are following suit.[151] The implication here is that all immigrants from white Christian countries (let alone white Christian non-immigrants and citizens) love homosexuals and support their rights to equality with heterosexuals (which is why they need not be tested to prove such love and tolerance) but not so nationals of "Muslim" countries.[152]

Perhaps the moment that illustrates this best took place in the fall of 2001 during the US bombing of Afghanistan when the National

149. Ibid., 608.

150. Ibid., 614.

151. Gregory Crouch, "Dutch Immigration Kit Offers a Revealing View," *New York Times*, 16 March 2006. Some legal questions have arisen regarding the test since July 2008 but no legal resolution has yet emerged. On the thirty questions Muslim immigrants are required to answer, including their views on homosexuality, to obtain a German passport in the southern German state of Baden-Württemberg , see Sonia Phalnikar "New Rule for Muslims in German State Blasted," *Deutsche Welle*, 5 January, 2006. While a Dutch court decision questioned the legality of the exam on a technicality, Human Rights Watch reported that Denmark, France, and the United Kingdom are also contemplating similar measures. See http://www.hrw.org/en/news/2008/07/16/netherlands-court-rules-pre-entry-integration-exam-unlawful (accessed 1 April 2014).

152. For the recent historical transformation of mainstream Dutch politics from open expression of homophobia to public defense of homosexuality as a pretext for Islamophobia, see Paul Mepschen, Jan Willem Duyvendak, and Evelien H. Tonkens, "Sexual Politics, Orientalism, and Multicultural Citizenship in the Netherlands," *Sociology* 55, no. 5 (October 2010): 962–79.

Coalition of Anti-Violence Programs (a coalition of American gay groups) responded to a reported incident when a bomb being loaded onto the USS Enterprise showed a warhead on which it was written: "Hijack this fags." The Coalition objected that "the message equates gays with the 'enemy,' it places gay, lesbian and bisexual servicemembers, who are serving as honorably as anyone else at this time at risk and dishonors them."[153] Lisa Duggan cites New York activist Bill Dobbs, who objected that while "the graffiti in question is deplorable . . . there is the slight matter of the bomb itself. And what happens when it is armed, dropped from the air and explodes. Does the National Coalition of Anti-Violence Programs . . . speak to such matters?" Instead, Dobbs concludes, the Coalition "sends the message that the bombs and the dropping of same is fine. As long as there is no bad graffiti on them."[154] Dobbs should have added that the bombs were fine precisely because they were being dropped on Muslims. Jasbir Puar has argued effectively that "the Muslim or gay binary mutates from a narrative of incommensurate subject positionings into an 'Islam versus homosexuality' tug of populations war; a mutation that may reveal the contiguous undercurrents of conservative homonormative ideologies and queer liberalism."[155] Puar astutely analyzes much of the active complicity between Euro-American and European gay groups and Islamophobia, "whereby homonormative and queer gay men can enact forms of national, racial, or other belongings by contributing to a collective vilification of Muslims."[156] Indeed, in this sense, what Puar calls "homonationalism" is nothing short of the ex post facto justification for the formation (and the universalization project) of the Gay International, indeed for gay internationalism *tout court*. Unfortunately, Puar herself remains committed to the universalization of the category of sexuality, which she never questions. Her criticisms target the imperial circuits through which the dissemination of sexuality is enacted but not its universalization as a category and as epistemology and ontology, which she seems to think can be universalized through non-imperial channels. Significantly, Puar deploys her radical critique of

153. National Coalition of Anti-Violence Programs (NCAVP), press release, 13 October 2001, cited by Duggan, *The Twilight of Equality*, 46.

154. Ibid.

155. Jasbir K. Puar, *Terrorist Assemblages: Homonationalism in Queer Times* (Durham, NC: Duke University Press, 2007), 19.

156. Ibid., 21. This is not unrelated to the Gay International's campaigns against African, Afro-Caribbean, and African-American "homophobia." As Greg Thomas puts it, citing Inge Blackman: "Black people are grossly overrepresented in [white gay groups'] targeting of homophobia, a targeting that permits the homophobic press of the white ruling class and the gay white middle-class press to coalesce in North America" (Thomas, *The Sexual Demon of Colonial Power*, 138).

US homonationalism in defense of liberal forms of gay internationalist activism (including Western-funded NGOs like the Israel-based alQaws, which Puar insists is not "liberal" at all but rather "radical"),[157] which she actively encourages, especially in the Arab world.[158]

157. Jasbir K. Puar, "Homonationalism as Assemblage: Viral Travels, Affective Sexualities," *Jindal Global Law Review* 4, no. 2 (November 2013): 36–37. alQaws, which means "The Arc" or more precisely "The bow" for "Qaws Quzah," meaning rainbow, following the American Gay and Lesbian movement's adoption of the rainbow flag for its banner, defines itself and its mission as follows: "alQaws for Sexual & Gender Diversity in Palestinian Society is a group of gay, lesbian, bisexual, transgender, questioning and queer (LGBTQ) Palestinian activists who work collaboratively to break down gendered and hetero-normative barriers. alQaws seeks to create an open space for all its members so that they may be engaged and energized in the struggle for equality and inclusion" (http://alqaws.org/q/content/who-are-we, accessed 1 April 2014). These are nothing if not bona fide liberal goals and include nothing radical in them at all. Puar misrepresents alQaws as not seeking these goals of equality for LGBTQ-identified Palestinians in Palestinian society, but rather that "its primary work is about ending the [Israeli] occupation, not about reifying homosexual identity that mirrors an 'Israeli' or 'Western' self-serving form of sexual freedom" ("Homonationalism as Assemblage," 37), even though such a goal or the word "occupation" is not even mentioned once or alluded to in alQaws's definition of itself ("Who we are") on its website. It remains unclear how Puar understands the very name of alQaws as not "mirroring" Western forms of sexual liberation. In its mission statement, alQaws is clear that it is not an organization that seeks to serve a LGBTQ community, but rather one that seeks to create it: "Our mission is to contribute towards building an active Palestinian LGBTQ community that is capable of challenging Palestinian civil society to become more inclusive and respectful" (http://alqaws.org/q/content/mission-goals). alQaws's funders include such liberal luminaries as the Ford Foundation Israel Fund, the US gay internationalist Astraea Lesbian Foundation, and the liberal Zionist organization the New Israel Fund. The director of alQaws went on a fundraising trip to the Netherlands in 2009, which is arguably the most Islamophobic and anti-Palestinian country in Europe, whether at the level of government policy, the press, or civil society and NGO discourse. No radical funders, whatever those may be, are anywhere in sight! See its Annual Report, Strategic Plan for 2009–10, http://alqaws.org/q/sites/default/files/Al-Qaws%20Strategic%20Plan%202009-2010%20%28PDF%29.pdf More recently alQaws's funds have also come from such organizations as the Euro-Mediterranean Foundation of Support to Human Rights Defenders (EMHRF), the Global Fund for Women, the Open Society Foundations, the Heinrich Böll Stiftung, and the Arcus Foundation (http://alqaws.org/q/en/content/our-supporters). Puar's misrepresentation of the group ignores the very speech that she cites as proof that anti-occupation activity is "primary" for alQaws, when the speech clearly outlines how alQaws's director measures success: "The first criterion is that we measure success in our ability, as LGBTQ movements, to change the political and social discourse around sexuality" (http://alqaws.org/q/ar/node/452). As for the second group which Puar mentions, Palestinian Queers for Boycott, Divestment, and Sanctions, or PQBDS, their entire website (http://www.pqbds.com) is in English, which might indicate that the readership that is sought is an "international' one. The group's website does not provide any information or names about the people who founded it, how many of them exist, or whether they have an office, or any funding. There are indeed indications that the group is US-based and not Palestine-based. At any rate, PQBDS seems to have become defunct in the last year. I should note that most of the information that is also available on alQaws's website is in English with the less numerous Arabic webpages sounding for the most part like translations from English than as texts originally written in Arabic.

158. See, for example, Puar, *Terrorist Assemblages*, xiii, 93, 111. For her role in promoting Israel-based Palestinian gay activism, especially the organization alQaws, see the account given by Sarah Schulman, *Israel/Palestine and the Queer International* (Durham, NC: Duke University Press, 2012), 133–35, 152–54. Puar would participate in the recent trend of solidarity tourism to the West Bank that has become fashionable in liberal circles in Europe and the United States in the last decade, including the first American "LGBT delegation to Palestine," which took place in January 2012 (see

But if for a liberal Western Europe and the liberal United States the order of Islam as other is always already the order of difference and the order of sexuality as the self is always the order of sameness (in that the other can only transcend her/his difference and become the same through mimicry, whether voluntary or coerced), then what seems clear from these various approaches and policies is that *the term "Islam" is always already a mode of othering in the logic of reaction formation and the term "sexuality" is always already a mode of assimilation in the logic of narcissistic incorporation.* My argument is not *only* that these imposed identities are exported outside (and within) Europe and Euro-America and therefore they must be opposed in an anti-imperialist and antiracist move, but also that this notwithstanding, they aim to eliminate differing yet existing desires, practices, and identities, which they deem non-European if not un-European, and which they insist on obliterating as false, oppressive, traditional, outdated, nonmodern, and therefore in need of being "liberated" through assimilation into Western modernity and normativity. The subjects of academic and human rights investigations, not to mention of other institutionalizing procedures, including NGO social services among others, are ordered by this very distinction. As Valentine comments in a related register, "such institutionalization is indeed a feature of knowledge production itself, especially in an academic system where the establishment of fields of knowledge is vital for such scholarship (and the scholars who do its work) to be validated."[159]

What is missed by scholars and activists located in Europe and Euro-America in these approaches, caveats, and apparent vigilance, in short, by these alibis, is the resistance to the need to reverse the order of the terms of the conjunction-cum-preposition "sexuality and/in Islam" by refusing the anthropological impulse of studying *sexuality in Islam* to studying how Islam is produced *in sexuality* discourses among activists and academics. It is the production of *Islam in sexuality* that needs to be

---

Schulman, 177). For Puar's subsequent differences with alQaws, see Jasbir Puar and Maya Mikdashi, "Pinkwatching and Pinkwashing: Interpenetration and its Discontents," *Jadaliyya* 9 (August 2012), http://www.jadaliyya.com/pages/index/6774/pinkwatching-and-pinkwashing_interpenetration-and-, and Heike Schotten and Haneen Maikey, "Queers Resisting Zionism: On Authority and Accountability Beyond Homonationalism," *Jadaliyya* 10 (October 2012), http://www.jadaliyya.com/pages/index/7738/queers-resisting-zionism_on-authority-and-accounta. See also Jasbir Puar and Maya Mikdashi, "On Positionality and Not Naming Names: A Rejoinder to the Response of Maikey and Schotten," *Jadaliyya* 10 (October 2012), http://www.jadaliyya.com/pages/index/7792/on-positionality-and-not-naming-names_a-rejoinder- (all accessed 1 April 2014). For a detailed account of how American gay internationalists play a central role in creating, supporting, and marketing Arab gay organizations, see Shulman's account of her own central role in the creation and promotion of alQaws and PQBDS, in Schulman, *Israel/Palestine and the Queer International.*

159. Valentine, *Imagining Transgender,* 171–72.

studied so that we can understand the emergence of a field that seeks and insists on the need to study an object it calls "sexuality in Islam."[160] What is required is a Foucaultian investigation into the conditions of possibility for truth statements about "Islam." Instead of assuming and seeking to uncover the mechanisms by which something called sexuality operates inside the category Islam, scholars must begin with the "positive mechanisms" that generate this Western will to know. Following Foucault, "we must investigate the conditions of their emergence and operation . . . we must define the strategies of power that are immanent in this will to knowledge."[161] The outcome of this kind of approach will reveal much about how Western scholarship on sexuality not only constitutes something it calls "Islam" but also how it constitutes "Europe," the "West," as an always already racialized normativity.[162]

The question to ask then is not what is the nature of "sexuality," its operations, repressions, manifestations, and productions in Islam, but rather in a *specific type of discourse* about *sexuality in Islam* (in the Western academy, NGO activism, Western media representations, Western governments' policy making), "in a specific form of extortion of truth, appearing historically and in specific places," around the place of women and homosexuality in Islam, to name the two privileged axes to be investigated. To echo Foucault one more time, what were "the most immediate, the most local power relations at work? How did they make possible these kinds of discourses, and conversely, how were these discourses used to support power relations? How was the action of these power relations modified by their very exercise, entailing a strengthening of some terms and a weakening of others . . . ?"[163]

While I have tried in this chapter to investigate how this comes to be in those specific projects that declaredly aim to "study" something they call "sexuality in Islam" and their scholarly complicity in assuming and imposing a Euro-American and West European normativity, under the capacious umbrella of liberalism, on the "Muslim" world, a

160. David Valentine asserts in the case of the invention of the category "transgender" that "even as transgender studies critically engages 'transgender,' its very institutionalization and naming presupposes a referent. Simultaneously, for all its critical impulse, transgender studies comes to stand as evidence of such a community for those concerned with representation in the academy and beyond" (Valentine, *Imagining Transgender*, 167).

161. Foucault, *The History of Sexuality*, vol. 1: *An Introduction*, 73.

162. With regards to the emergence of an American "queer liberalism" whose constitutive condition resides in its very failure "to recognize the racial genealogy of exploitation and domination that underwrites the very inclusion of queers and queers of color in this abstract liberal polity," see David Eng, *The Feeling of Kinship*, 45.

163. Foucault, *The History of Sexuality*, vol. 1: *An Introduction*, 97.

comprehensive project that encompasses the field of sexuality studies more generally is indispensable to understanding the very *production* of "sexuality in Islam." Only then will it be possible to identify the conscious and unconscious dynamics of epistemological and political complicity of many scholars with Western normativity and the desire to disseminate it globally as a guiding principle of research.

FOUR

Psychoanalysis, "Islam," and the Other of Liberalism

Historically, psychoanalysis did not take "Islam" as an object of study, as a concern, or as a problem. Except for Freud's passing comments in *Moses and Monotheism* about "the founding of the Mohammedan religion" seeming to be "an abbreviated repetition of the Jewish one, of which it emerged as an imitation," little was written on the topic.[1] Indeed, psychoanalytic studies on religion have been remarkable for the absence of any mention of Islam. This includes, for example, the early study by Erich Fromm on the topic, which makes no mention at all of Islam, while attending to Christianity, Judaism, "Buddhism," and "Hinduism."[2] Psychoanalysts and psychoanalytic thinkers working more recently on the object called "Islam" have, however, become active participants in the process of multiplying its significations, referents, and antonyms with little self-questioning or analysis of what they are doing.

In addition to Arab clinical psychoanalysts trained in France and the United Kingdom, who began to practice and teach in Egyptian universities during the 1930s and after and to translate works of Freud and other psychoanalysts,[3]

1. Sigmund Freud, *Moses and Monotheism*, in *The Standard Edition of the Complete Psychological Works of Sigmund Freud* (hereafter *S.E.*), ed. and trans. James Strachey et al. (London: Hogarth Press, 1953–1974), 23:92.

2. Erich Fromm, *Psychoanalysis and Religion* (New Haven, CT: Yale University Press, 1950).

3. On the history of Egyptian psychoanalysts, see Hussein Abel Kader, "La psychanalyse en Egypt entre un passé ambitieux et un future incertain," *La*

Arab intellectuals showed an early interest in psychoanalytic knowledge, especially in studies of the unconscious.[4] Yet those who employed a psychoanalytic method were not interested in applying it to the Qur'an, or the biography of the Prophet, or "Islam" *tout court*,[5] but used it rather for cultural analyses that took as their subjects secular historical figures such as the medieval poet Abu Nuwas,[6] or modern Arabic literature (especially novels),[7] or the "group neurosis" said to afflict contemporary Arab intellectuals working on the question of culture and modernity.[8] The Moroccan intellectual Abdelkebir Khatibi once noted in this regard that "in short, one could say that Islam is an empty space in the theory of psychoanalysis."[9] While psychoanalytic works, especially those of Freud, were translated into Arabic and engaged with seriously by Arab intellectuals from across the Arab world, those works of Freud's that dealt with religion and civilization (*The Future of an Illusion, Civilization and Its Discontents,* and *Moses and Monotheism*), as their Arabic translator

---

Célibataire, no. 8 (Printemps 2004): 61–73, and Raja Ben Slama, "La psychanalyse en Egypte: Un problème de non-advenue," *La psychanalyse au Maghreb et au Machrek,* a special issue of *Topique: Revue Freudienne,* no. 110 (June 2010): 83–96. On the biography of Mustafa Zaywar (1907–90), the founder of psychoanalysis in Egypt and the first Arab member of the International Psychoanalytical Association, see Husayn ʿAbd al-Qadir, "Atruk Sharayini Fikum," in *Mustafa Zaywar: Fi Dhikra al-ʿAlim wa al-Fannan wa al-Insan,* ed. Usamah Khalil (Paris: Maʿhad al-Lughah wa al-Hadarah al-ʿArabiyyah, 1997), 7–14. On the history of psychoanalysis in Morocco and the involvement of French psychoanalysts during French colonial rule and beyond, see Jalil Bennani, *Psychanalyse en terre d'islam: Introduction à la psychanalyse au Maghreb* (Strasbourg: Éditions Arcanes, 2008), first published in 1996 by Éditions Le Fennec in Casablanca.

4. See Salamah Musa's early book *Al-ʿAql al-Batin wa Maknunat al-Nafs* (The Unconscious and the Soul's Latent Innermost Thoughts) (Cairo: Dar al-Hilal, 1928), and his later book *ʿAqli wa ʿAqluk* (My Mind/Reason and Yours) (Cairo: Salamah Musa Lil-Nashr, 1947).

5. In his 1968 biography of the Prophet, French Orientalist Maxime Rodinson does employ the notion of the unconscious to explain some of the Prophet's experiences, but does not do so in any strict psychoanalytic sense. See Maxime Rodinson, *Muhammad: Prophet of Islam* (London: Tauris Parke Paperbacks, 2002), 77.

6. See Muhammad al-Nuwayhi, *Nafsiyyat Abu Nuwas* (The Psychology of Abu Nuwas) (Cairo: Dar al-Fikr, 1970), first published in 1953, and ʿAbbas Mahmud al-ʿAqqad, *Abu Nuwas, al-Hasan Bin Hani: Dirasah fi al-Tahlil al-Nafsani wa al-Naqd al-Tarikhi* (A Study in Psychoanalysis and Historical Criticism) (Cairo: Kitab al-Hilal, 1960), first published in 1953. For a critical take on the psychoanalytic study as applied to Abu Nuwas, see Husayn Muruwwah, *Dirasat Naqdiyyah, fi Duʾ al-Manhaj al-Waqiʿi* (Critical Studies, in the Light of the Realist Method) (Beirut: Maktabat al-Maʿarif, 1965). For a detailed discussion of these studies, see Joseph Massad, *Desiring Arabs* (Chicago: University of Chicago Press, 2007), 84–92.

7. See Jurj Tarabishi, *ʿUqdat Udib fi al-Riwayah al-ʿArabiyyah* (The Oedipus Complex in the Arabic Novel) (Beirut: Dar al-Taliʿah, 1982), *Al-Rujulah wa Aydiyulujiyyat al-Rujulah fi al-Riwayah al-ʿArabiyyah* (Manliness and the Ideology of Manliness in the Arabic Novel) (Beirut: Dar al-Taliʿah, 1983), and *Untha Didd al-Unuthah: Dirasah fi Adab Nawal al-Saʿdawi* (A Female against Femininity: A Study of the Fiction of Nawal al-Saʿdawi) (Beirut: Dar al-Taliʿah, 1984).

8. See Jurj Tarabishi, *Al-Muthaqaffun al-ʿArab wa al-Turath, al-Tahlil al-Nafsi li-ʿUsab Jamaʿi* (Arab Intellectuals and Heritage: Psychoanalysis of a Group Neurosis) (London: Riyad al-Rayyis lil-Nashr, 1991).

9. Abdelkebir Khatibi, "Frontières," *Cahiers Intersignes,* no. 1 (Spring 1990): 15.

Jurj Tarabishi states, were latecomers to the Arabic library on account of the very topics they discuss.[10] Tarabishi, in his 1974 introduction to the Arabic translation of *The Future of an Illusion*, does add that Freud's Western readers had also failed to appreciate the importance of these works because of the topics they engaged.[11]

More recently, however, there have emerged a number of psychoanalytic attempts to evaluate critically not only Islam as religion, its scriptures, and theological tradition, but also contemporary Islamist movements, often conflated with/as "Islam." While an American-based Indian Muslim psychoanalyst wants to showcase the contributions of Muslim immigrant psychoanalysts to psychoanalysis (which did not include writings on Islam and psychoanalysis), and another speaks of her experience with anti-Muslim analysands in the United States,[12] Arab psychoanalysts and psychoanalytic thinkers—including Moustapha Safouan (Egyptian), Fethi Benslama (Tunisian), Adnan Houbballah (Lebanese), Khatibi (Moroccan), and Tarabishi (Syrian), to name the most prominent, who are without exception male and living in France, and whose psychoanalytic writings (except for Tarabishi, who is the only one writing in Arabic and who writes on Arab intellectuals and Arabic literature)[13] are mostly written in French and focus on "Islam"—started

10. Jurj Tarabishi, "Taqdim," in Sighmund Fruyd, *Mustaqbal Wahm*, trans. Jurj Tarabishi (Beirut: Dar al-Taliʿah, 1974), 5. Tarabishi had also translated *Moses and Monotheism* from the French in 1973 as well as Freud's *Civilization and Its Discontents* in 1977. See Sighmund Fruyd, *Musa wa al-Tawhid*, trans. Jurj Tarabishi (Beirut: Dar al-Taliʿah, 1973), and Sighmund Fruyd, *Qalaq fi al-Hadarah*, trans. Jurj Tarabishi (Beirut: Dar al-Taliʿah, 1977). This is not to say that there was no familiarity in the Arab World with *Moses and Monotheism* prior to its translation. Fethi Benslama mentions the controversy that ensued in Cairo upon the announcement of the publication of the book's English translation, which was noted in the Egyptian newspaper *Al-Ahram* on 10 May 1939 in a report by the newspaper's London correspondent citing the British *News Chronicle*. Several readers (one Mansur Wahbah was a university graduate of the natural sciences, another, Hilal Farhi, was a "doctor") in Cairo objected to Freud's de-judaization of Moses and his attributing to him Egyptian origins, basing themselves on scriptural and other historical evidence (see *Al-Ahram*, 13 May 1939 and 20 May 1939 respectively). The controversy is reproduced in ʿAbd al-Wahhab Najjar, *Qisas al-Anbiya'* (Cairo: Muʾassassat al-Halabi wa Shurakaʾihi lil-Tabʿ wa al-Tawziʿ, 1966), 155–57. The book was initially published circa 1933 with updated later editions. Fethi Benslama refers to it in *La psychanalyse à l'épreuve de l'Islam* (Paris: Flammarion, 2002), 277–78.

11. I should note here that Egyptian psychoanalysts and psychologists published an encyclopedia in 1993 that also contained an English–Arabic glossary of psychoanalytic and psychological terms in order to unify their use in Arabic across the Arab world. See ʿAbd al-Qadir Taha, ed., *Mawsuʿat ʿIlm al-Nafs wa al-Tahlil al-Nafsi* (The Encyclopedia of Psychology and Psychoanalysis) (Kuwait: Dar Suʿad al-Subah, 1993).

12. See Salman Akhtar, "Muslims in the Psychoanalytic World," and Aisha Abbasi, "Whose Side Are You On? Muslim Psychoanalysts Treating Non-Muslim Patients," in *The Crescent and the Couch: Cross-Currents between Islam and Psychoanalysis*, ed. Salman Akhtar (Lanham, MD: Jason Aronson, 2008), 315–33, 335–50.

13. Tarabishi, more recently, started to write on "Islam," and occasionally punctuates his texts with psychoanalytic references, as he does in *Hartaqat 2: ʿan al-ʿIlmaniyyah ka-Ishkaliyyah*

to write on the linkage between Islam and psychoanalysis in the context of the rise of Islamisms, the phenomenon of which seems to have triggered their interventions.[14] Khatibi is the first to have broached the subject, initially in a text he wrote in 1984 (and published in 1988) on the Prophetic Message.[15] He later revisited his article and its conclusions from a more explicitly psychoanalytic angle in a 1987 lecture at a colloquium Benslama and he had organized on "The question of psychoanalysis in the area around [aux abords de] Islam," held at the Collège International de Philosophie in May 1987. Khatibi's paper and the other colloquium papers were published in 1991 in the first issue of the journal Cahiers Intersignes, edited by Benslama. One of Khatibi's more interesting points has to do with the Prophet's "sacrifice" of his "signature" on the Qurʾan as book to God. This sacrifice, Khatibi claims, is the condition of Muhammad becoming a prophet.[16] Khatibi has nothing to say about contemporary Islamisms or Islamists in these texts.[17]

The approach of the other writers, however, as we will see, is characterized by a perception on their part that "Islamism" is a "return of the repressed" of something that should, according to these thinkers, have disappeared long ago. Benslama, for example, states explicitly: "This generation [of Arab and Muslim intellectuals], which opened its

---

Islamiyyah-Islamiyyah (Hereticisms 2: On Secularism as a Muslim-Muslim Problematic) (Beirut: Dar al-Saqi, 2008), where he references Freud's *Moses and Monotheism* and *Totem and Taboo*, speaks of the "return of the repressed" in addressing Shiite–Sunni sectarianism in post-US invasion Iraq, and claims to differ from Freud in considering Christianity and Shiite Islam as "son-religions" rather than "father-religions," as Freud "had interpreted the emergence of monotheistic religions from his illusory scheme of parricide," which Freud, according to Tarabishi, correctly applied to Judaism but which does not apply to "Christianity and Shiite Islam." See *Hartaqat 2*, 11, 15, 17n. This is an odd assertion of difference with Freud on the part of Tarabishi, as Freud was quite clear at the end of *Moses and Monotheism* that "Christianity, having arisen out of a father-religion, became a son-religion" (*S.E.* 23:136).

14. Indeed, Benslama recognizes this clearly, by excepting himself as having shown interest in "Islam" earlier than his colleagues. He states that his initial interest in "Islam" had started due to an encounter with Pierre Fedida after which he published his first book dealing with psychoanalysis and Islam in 1988 "when Islam had not constituted yet a sharp problem in the international public sphere, nor a question for psychoanalytic research." Fethi Benslama, "Une recherche psychanalytique sur l'islam," in a special issue of *La Célibataire* entitled "La psychanalyse et le monde arabe," no. 8 (Printemps 2004): 77. On Benslama's first book on the subject, see Fethi Benslama, *La nuit brisée* (Paris: Éditions Ramsay, 1988). This is an interesting assertion since the more usual dating of the international interest in "Islam" as "Islamism" coincides with the Iranian Revolution of 1978–79.

15. Abdelkebir Khatibi, "Du message prophétique (argument)," in *Par-Dessus l'épaule* (Paris: Aubier, 1988). He writes on page 135 that he had written the text in 1984.

16. Khatibi, "Frontières," 17.

17. There are also others writing on psychoanalytic themes like the Egyptian Karim Jbeili who is based in Canada and whose book *Le psychisme des Orientaux: Différences et déchirures* (Montréal: Liber, 2006) consists of a series of contemplations that rely on strong identitarian essentialisms of what an "Oriental" and "Occidental" are, what their psyches consist of, and how, in pointing this out, Jbeili is simply attending to their particularities and not necessarily engaging in reification.

eyes at the end of colonialism and the beginning of the establishment of the nation-state, thought that it had finished with religion, that it would never again be a question in the organization of society."[18] Algerian anthropologist and psychoanalytic thinker Malek Chebel, who also lives in France and writes in French, states without equivocation that Islamism, as "theological awakening," constitutes the "return of the repressed and what is repressed is always related to childhood and what Islam is experiencing at the moment is a return to the period of childhood."[19] Houbballah speaks of Islam's "waking up" to face possible dangers.[20] What is not thought in these propositions, though, is the possibility that the return of the repressed is a feature of these thinkers' own anxiety and not only, or necessarily, that of other Muslims or Islamists. This "return" reopens the scene of the trauma, for these thinkers, of the persistence of Islam as *not only* "religion" in the life of Arabs and Muslims; and this causes some of our psychoanalytic thinkers "embarrassment" and "shame" before their European counterparts and, more importantly, before their Europeanized selves.[21] Indeed, much of

18. Benslama, *La psychanalyse à l'épreuve de l'Islam* (Paris: Flammarion, 2002), 17. At the time of writing this chapter, an English translation of Benslama's book was still forthcoming; all subsequent translated quotations are my own, while pagination refers to the 2002 French edition. It is noteworthy that the latter part of this sentence "that it would never again be a question in the organization of society" is dropped, without explanation, from the Arabic translation of the book. See Fathi Bin Salamah, *Al-Islam wa al-Tahlil al-Nafsi*, trans. Dr. Raja³ Bin Salamah (Beirut: Dar al-Saqi and Rabitat al-ʿAqlaniyyin al-ʿArab, 2008), 29.

19. See the interview of al-Muʿti Qabbal with Malek Chebel, "al-Islam wa Sahwat al-Tufulah" (Islam and the Awakening of Childhood), in *Al-Tahlil al-Nafsi wa al-Thaqafah al-ʿArabiyyah-al-Islamiyyah* (Psychoanalysis and Arab-Islamic Culture) (Damascus: Dar al-Bidayat, 2008), 77.

20. He describes it thus in a dialogue with Moustapha Safouan in Mustafa Safwan and ʿAdnan Hubbu Allah, *Ishkaliyyat al-Mujtamaʿ al-Arabi: Qiraʾah min Manzur al-Tahlil al-Nafsi* (The Problematics of Arab Society: A Reading from a Psychoanalytic Perspective), with an introduction by Adunis (Beirut: Al-Markaz al-Thaqafi al-Arabi, 2008), 96.

21. In response to a question about the (alleged) rejection of psychoanalysis in Arab-Islamic societies on account of it being "foreign," Malek Chebel states that "this statement reveals an actuality that can cause embarrassment." See al-Muʿti Qabbal's interview with Malek Chebel, "al-Islam wa Sahwat al-Tufulah," 78. In contrast, Moustapha Safouan feels pain not on account of the return of Islam but by what he believes to be the absence of democratic thinking in the Arab world manifested by his mistaken presumption that Alexis de Tocqueville's *Democracy in America* has not been, but should be, translated to Arabic given its pedagogical importance for a people lacking democracy: "it is a painful proof of our backwardness that [Alexis de Tocqueville's *Democracy in America*] is still not translated into Arabic." Moustapha Safouan, *Why Are the Arabs Not Free? The Politics of Writing* (Oxford: Wiley-Blackwell, 2007), 60. Leaving aside what the translation of this book into Arabic could mean or not mean, the book had in fact been translated and published in 1984 (twenty-three years before Safouan felt the pain and expressed it in a 2007 book) by Amin Mursi Qandil, edited by Muhsin Mahdi, and published by Dar Kitabi in Cairo and again by ʿAlam al-Kutub in Cairo in 1991 under the title and exact translation *al-Dimuqratiyyah fi Amrika*. I should note that in July 2006, the American occupation government of Iraq, through its "ambassador" to the country Zalmay Khalilzad, distributed free copies of the book in Arabic to Iraqis on US Independence Day to teach them democracy (Kim Gamel, "Fourth of July Iraqi Style," Associated Press Blog,

their writing on this question displays a deep narcissistic injury suffered by these writers, who as Arabs and Muslims, as *Europeanized* Arabs and Muslims, who grew up in modernizing times and sought Europeanization as the telos of modernity, now found themselves inhabiting an era in which the project of Europeanization had failed as a result of the "return" of Islam in the form of Islamisms. The most ambitious of these thinkers, in terms of dedication, serious attention to detail, depth of thinking, and passion, is Fethi Benslama. Given the importance of his analysis, I will address his work in more detail than that of the others in an attempt to examine the intellectual and psychic mechanisms at work in his thinking on this interesting but uninterrogated conjunction of a reified psychoanalysis *and* a reified Islam.

Benslama's book, *La psychanalyse à l'épreuve de l'Islam*, published in 2002, is perhaps the most serious engagement with one possible relationship that a certain psychoanalysis could have with a certain "Islam," namely, one in which this psychoanalysis is put (or puts itself) to the test of this "Islam," in which it stands before the test or crisis of Islam. Benslama proceeds as if he were writing a corollary to Freud's *Moses and Monotheism* along the lines of *Muhammad and Monotheism*. This is, in fact, his second attempt to do so. His first book to deal with "Islam," *La nuit brisée (The Shattered Night)*, published in 1988, was less explicitly presented as such a project. *La psychanalyse à l'épreuve de l'islam* is a more profound second attempt, a *repetition*, at an engagement with that very same project, and it intensifies Benslama's dependence on *Moses and Monotheism* as the main psychoanalytic and Freudian scripture guiding his project.

One of the more important achievements of Benslama's book is his exploration of the role of Abraham and Ishmael as the grandfather and father of the Arabs, coupled with his argument that the Qurʾan, following the Torah, imposed the figure of non-Arab Ishmael (whose mother is the Egyptian Hagar and whose father is the Mesopotamian Abraham) on Arab lineage—a lineage which was never resisted by post-Islam Arabs, even though neither Abraham nor Ishmael had any presence in their cosmological lore prior to the Qurʾanic moment. Here, Benslama seems to ignore the fact that in contrast to "pagan" Arab tribes, for Jewish and Christian Arab tribes, perhaps not considered Arabs by him, Ishmael and Abraham were indeed present. In fact, and in accordance with post-

---

published in the Washington Post, 4 July 2006, http://www.washingtonpost.com/wp-dyn/content/article/2006/07/04/AR2006070400818_pf.html). Clearly whatever expectations Safouan entertained about the effect of its publication in Arabic have yet to materialize.

Qurʾanic stories about pre-Islamic Mecca, which may be apocryphal, even Arab "pagan" tribes had much knowledge of Abraham, whom they deemed the original builder of the Kaʿbah. Unlike Freud's Moses, who is exposed *contra* the Jewish scriptural and theological tradition as an Egyptian outsider to his chosen people, Benslama's Ishmael, who is not the main prophet of the Muhammadan call, is *not revealed* to be non-Arab, since his non-Arab lineage is clear enough in the Qurʾan and in Islamic theology. Rather, what Benslama aims to do is consider this non-Arabness in relation to the question of identity and maternalism in order to argue that Hagar is "repressed" in "Islam" and Islamic theology in favor of Sarah without much deviation from the Judaic story.

To some extent, Benslama's discussion corresponds to Edward Said's important reading of Freud's Moses as an antinationalist call that rejects essentialism and group homogeneity as necessary founding myths. "In other words," Said concludes his discussion of Freud's Moses, "identity cannot be thought or worked through itself alone; it cannot constitute or even imagine itself without that radical originary break or flaw which will not be repressed, because Moses was Egyptian, and therefore always outside the identity inside which so many have stood and suffered— and later, perhaps, even triumphed."[22] But Benslama, in contrast, wants to read the repression of Hagar as informing "Islam's" views of women and the figure of the mother more generally: "Islam was born from the stranger at the origins of monotheism, and this stranger remained a stranger in Islam."[23]

Benslama does not limit himself to a discussion of paternity and maternity, the question of origins in the Qurʾan, and subsequent theological exegesis, but brings his conclusions to bear on the contemporary situation. It is clear throughout the text that the entire archeological project Benslama is engaged in is an attempt to respond to the claims put forth by many contemporary Islamisms and their enemies about "Islam" and Islamic origins. It is in the context of discussing contemporary Islamisms, however, that Benslama's book shows less engagement with psychoanalytic thought and concepts and moves to liberal critiques concerned with the individual, freedom of thought, tolerance, and the separation of the theological from the political.

Definitionally, Benslama insists that "Islam" is multiple and that it is always already "Islams," yet at key moments in his narrative these

---

22. Edward W. Said, *Freud and the Non-European* (London: Verso, 2003), 54.
23. Benslama, *La psychanalyse*, 171.

multiple "Islams" converge into one which is conflated with a singular "Islamism," as both an utterable name and one that should only be used under erasure ("sous rature"). My concern is the ideological context of these slippages, conscious and unconscious, and the political philosophy and psychic processes that inform them. While he does not define Islam in his book, Benslama provides two meanings in a later article on the subject, in which he claims that the word *Islam* "has been fixed by a theological connotation into 'an abandonment to God' [*un abandon à Dieu*]," and that its etymology designates this act as "having been saved after abandoning itself."[24] The latter, in fact, may be one possible connotation of the word, though not necessarily its immediate one, since the most common meaning of Islam in Arabic is "deliverance [of one's self] to God," and not "abandonment," or the more common Orientalist translation as "submission to God," which Benslama problematically cites as the "theological" meaning of the word in "Islam," even while mentioning its other meaning(s) of "being saved," but curiously not its meaning of "deliverance."[25] While he claims that it is only Islamists who want to render the meaning of Islam as "submission," he participates, if ambivalently, in the same project with his endorsement of the Orientalist meaning of *Islam* as *submission* when he insists that "the Islamism of groups and institutions today is . . . submission [*soumission*] to the religion of submission."[26] The word for *submission* in Arabic, however, is *khuduʿ* (which also means subjection), a word that has no etymological or other connection to the word *Islam*. Perhaps Benslama is here projecting onto Islam his own liberalism, which, after all, is the tradition that speaks oxymoronically of the "freedom of the subject." As Étienne Balibar reminds us, "Why is it that the very name which allows modern philosophy to think and designate the *originary freedom* of the human being—the name of 'subject'—is precisely the name which *historically* meant suppression of freedom, or at least an intrinsic limitation of freedom, i.e. *subjection*?"[27]

Benslama is certainly not alone in his problematic translations. The question of translation and language is essential for psychoanalytic

24. Benslama, "Une recherche psychanalytique sur l'islam," 79. He also enumerates many of the possible meanings of Islam except that of "deliverance" in Fethi Benslama, *Déclaration d'insoumission: À l'usage des musulmans et de ceux qui ne le sont pas* (Paris: Flammarion, 2004), 28–29.

25. Benslama, *La nuit brisée*, 176.

26. Benslama, *Déclaration d'insoumission*, 24.

27. Étienne Balibar, "Subjection and Subjectivation," in *Supposing the Subject*, ed. Joan Copjec (London: Verso, 1994), 8.

thinkers in general.[28] The major thesis of Safouan regarding what he constantly refers to as Arab "backwardness" is that it is a problem of language. Like Benslama, but with less erudition, Safouan often seems to confound Arabic and Latin etymologies in ways that exoticize modern Arabic, as he does, for example, in his discussion of the difference between the Latin-based word "sovereignty" and its Arabic equivalent *siyada*.[29] Safouan objects that the Arabic word, *siyada*, "unlike sovereignty," means mastership, "whereas its true meaning, at least according to Karl [*sic*] Schmitt's definition, is the 'right to take decisions in the last resort.' The translation leaves us only with the primitive, dual relation of master and slave, whereas what is at stake is a political conception of decision."[30] Safouan appears to regard Schmitt as offering a linguistic definition of sovereignty rather than a staking out of a position in a theoretical debate. He also seems not to know the Latin meaning of the term *sovereignty*, which comes from "over above," in Latin "superanus," nor that the traditional English use of the term, according to the Oxford English Dictionary, is "sovereign lord," and "one who has supremacy or rank above, or authority over, others; a superior; a ruler, governor, lord, or master (*of* persons, etc.)" and that "sovereignty" means "supremacy or pre-eminence in respect of excellence or efficacy." It remains unclear whether Safouan would consider the original Latin meaning of *sovereignty*, and the later English one, as "primitive" or if only its Arabic rendering is so.

The answer Safouan discovers in addressing his own question, "Why are the Arabs not free?" is found in what he considers to be the division between literary and vernacular (spoken) Arabic: the former is a "sacred" language and slated for the use of elites, while the latter is the language of the masses. Safouan reifies the two uses of Arabic as completely separate and even splits them into two languages, showing utter unfamiliarity with their actual imbrication in one another. He is under the impression that literary Arabic today is the same Arabic of the Qur'an

---

28. On the various translations of psychoanalytic concepts into Arabic which have created incommensurable uses of psychoanalytic vocabulary, see Raja Ben Slama, "L'arbre qui révèle la forêt: Traductions arabes du vocabulaire freudien," *Transeuropeenes: International Journal of Critical Thought*, 5 November 2009, http://www.transeuropeennes.eu/en/articles/106/The_Tree_that_Reveals_the_Forest (accessed 1 April 2014). Ben Slama borrows most of her information on translations from Egyptian psychoanalyst Husayn ʿAbd al-Qadir, who was critical of Jurj Tarabishi's translations of psychoanalytic concepts and Tarabishi's refusal to use the terms translated by Mustafa Zaywar. See Husayn ʿAbd al-Qadir, "Atruk Sharayini Fikum," in *Mustafa Zaywar: Fi Dhikra al-ʿAlim wa al-Fannan wa al-Insan*, ed. Usamah Khalil (Paris: Maʿhad al-Lughah wa al-Hadarah al-ʿArabiyyah, 1997), 14.

29. See Safouan, *Why Are the Arabs Not Free?* 65.

30. Ibid.

when in fact it is as different from the latter as are the contemporary vernaculars. While contemporary educated Arabic speakers have the ability to read texts from the seventh to the eighteenth century with varying degrees of difficulty (just as contemporary educated English speakers are able to read Marlowe, Chaucer, and Shakespeare with varying degrees of difficulty), it would be next to impossible for seventh-century Arabic readers to read contemporary literary Arabic (since the script itself has changed), much less comprehend it, given the changes in syntax, structure, and vocabulary. This reification of modern literary Arabic as fossilized in the language of the Qur'an is not unique to Safouan but is a common Orientalist claim that has no substantiation in fact. Indeed, neither contemporary literary nor spoken Arabic could exist independently of one another; so integrated are they in their very syntax, structure, and vocabulary that any attempt to disentangle them would require a project of social engineering of the sort that Safouan attributes to the Pharaohs, who, he claims, first instituted the division between the literary and the spoken in order to rule the masses unhindered. Yet it is he who calls for such a project, namely that the state institutionalize the split he thinks already exists between literary and vernacular Arabic and that it teach the vernacular in its schools as a precondition for democracy.[31] This view of literary Arabic, which also equates it with Latin, harkens back to Orientalist assessments and to debates among Arab intellectuals in the colonial times of the 1930s and 1940s.[32] Safouan, however, presents it not only as a sane rational fact but also as one that, if denied by any Arab, would expose an antidemocratic position: "It is often thought and said that Arabic is one language, but in fact the distance between classical Arabic and the Arabic of Egypt, the Gulf States and North Africa is analogous to the relation between Latin and the Romance languages Italian, Spanish, and French. The failure, or rather the refusal, to acknowledge these differences is the refusal to allow the uneducated a full say in their future."[33] Since cultures achieve modernization through language, Safouan wonders: "Who could imagine the destiny of Europe if Latin had remained the language of literature, science, philosophy, and theology?"[34] But one need not spend much time imagining, since

31. Safouan elaborates on these views in a dialogue with ʿAdnan Hubbu Allah in "Al-Tahlil al-Nafsi wa al-Mujtamaʿ al-ʿArabi" (Psychoanalysis and Arab Society), in Mustafa Safwan and ʿAdnan Hubbu Allah, *Ishkaliyyat al-Mujtamaʿ al-ʿArabi*, 137–38.

32. On this debate, see Yasir Suleiman, *The Arabic Language and National Identity: A Study in Ideology* (Washington, DC: Georgetown University Press, 2003).

33. Safouan, *Why Are the Arabs Not Free?* 10.

34. Ibid., 49.

Safouan offers the Arab world as the answer. Indeed, even the Europe that Safouan imagines remains in the grip of the very Latin (and Greek) that he believes had disappeared (and this includes the German Schmitt, who used the Latinate form "souverän" for sovereign and not a German word). In fact, Latin survives in Europe *specifically* as a specialized language of science (including medicine), philosophy, law, and theology whose Latin-based conceptual vocabulary dominates these fields. This is also true for the language of psychoanalysis itself, at least in its English translation, where Freud's ordinary German terms were Latinized to endow them with scientificity. Perhaps the most illustrious example is his book *Das Ich und das Es*, which was rendered in Latinized English as *The Ego and the Id*.[35]

Benslama, like Safouan, locates the "crisis" in Islam in language: "It does not have to do only with a lack of modernity, as is often said, but rather with a modernity that has ignored its subject, one that had to do with a progressivist ideology, in which had to be included the imperative of economic and technical development without taking into account the work of culture . . . or, if you will, a modernization without the linguistic foundations that constitute the work of civilization," something both Christianity and Judaism, in contrast, had obviously done.[36]

It is clear that the two meanings of Islam Benslama posits are not the only ones he employs in *La psychanalyse à l'épreuve de l'islam*. While Benslama explains at the outset that the many "Islams" he posits are diverse, various, and sometimes unconnected, even though they may all hide "behind" the singular name "Islam,"[37] he soon abandons this multiplicity in favor of a singular Islam whose signifieds and referents remain multiple but unspecified even as they are presented consciously and ideologically as singular. It is rarely made clear, for example, when he uses the term *Islam*, whether he is referring to all Islamist movements and individuals or just some of them; whether *Islam* refers to the history of Islamic theology from the seventh century to the present, or to the history or present of states that call themselves Islamic, or even those that call themselves "Muslim"; whether it refers to the Qur'an, the Hadith, the Sunnah, or all combined, and so on and so forth. While Benslama sees the attempt to homogenize "Islams" into Islam as not only an Islamist project but also as a "superficial" European attempt to

35. For a discussion and a critique of the English translations of Freud's works, see Bruno Bettelheim, *Freud and Man's Soul* (New York: Alfred A. Knopf, 1983).

36. Benslama, *Déclaration d'insoumission*, 76–77.

37. Benslama, *La psychanalyse*, 23.

deal with the rise of many "Islamist" movements in different geographic and social contexts, their reduction by a European political sociology to one Islam, Benslama declares, is nothing short of "resistance to the intelligibility of Islam" on the part of Islamologists, a resistance that, he maintains, also applies to European psychoanalysts.[38] It is remarkable that Benslama would insist upon such "intelligibility" even as he insists upon the proliferations and incommensurables of "Islam's" invocations; that he would call upon this intelligibility under the heading of a "resistance" to it by others, thus situating intelligibility negatively, through its failure to register, while making, it would appear, the intelligible uniquely available to him.[39]

Benslama's understanding of the multiplicity of Islams as signifiers—whose signifieds, however, remain obscure in Benslama's own text—falls by the wayside through his constant invoking of "Islam" in the singular as a subject with a self that expresses itself and whose meaning is readily intelligible. Benslama speaks of the "actuality of Islam"[40] that imposes itself on him, of "the tradition of Islam"[41] within which people grow up, and how he had "realized [*je m'apercevais*] simply that, in the majority of cases [he consulted], Islam was always the effect and the cause of subjective and trans-individual structures."[42]

In these telling slippages (and there are many more), what is most interesting is that the perception of the singularity of Islam and its effect on Muslims belongs not to Benslama alone but is shared by many (though not all) Islamist thinkers. Indeed, Benslama identifies the reaction of many Islamists and Muslims to Salman Rushdie's *The Satanic Verses* as occurring within the singular world of Islam. He states that the "shock in the case of Islam came from where we did not expect it, from literary fiction that put on stage the truth of origins as a trick."[43] In doing so, Benslama follows a liberal secular tradition, which often seems to recognize the Islam of some Islamists as the one "Islam," even though he is well aware (and curiously adds a footnote to the Arabic translation of his book clarifying this point) that what is at stake in contemporary debates is the "meaning of Islam," and what is unfolding is indeed "a war of the name," or a nominalist war.[44]

38. Ibid., 24.
39. I thank Lecia Rosenthal for raising this point.
40. Benslama, *La psychanalyse*, 26.
41. Ibid., 27.
42. Ibid.
43. Ibid., 43.
44. Fathi Bin Salamah, *Al-Islam wa al-Tahlil al-Nafsi*, 36n.

In his book, however, and despite his noted vigilance, Benslama opts not only to analyze the terms of this war between the different antagonists, but, and herein lies the contradiction, also to join in as a party to the war. In this light, the battle over the Islamist notion(s) of Islam (which Benslama and many secularists often oppose as the one Islam) is, as many Islamists correctly claim, between those who want to uphold "Islam" and those who want to uphold anti-"Islam." In fact, Benslama ambivalently posits this singular "Islam," whose meaning, as we have seen, he often shares with many Islamists and Orientalists, as the other (or the Other?) of liberalism.[45] He does not do so explicitly, but his invocation of "freedom," "tolerance," and "individualism" as the values or key ingredients, absent from the one Islam but necessary to the Islam he wishes for, structures his polemic against Islamists. Moreover, his insistence that Islam be transformed from a *din* into the Christian *and* secular liberal notion of "religion" ("La religion musulmane")[46] as well as his attack on Islamists who, unlike him, regard "Islam not only as a religion,"[47] commits him to a hegemonic form of liberal epistemology whose aim is the assimilation of the world in its own image.[48] To make his point unequivocal, he titles his more recent pamphlet *Déclaration d'insoumission*, that is, "declaration of rebellion" or more precisely of "insubmission," to "the religion of submission."[49] But if Islam for Benslama means submission, then his declaration is essentially and consciously a "declaration of un-Islam," or, to be more precise, a "declaration of anti-Islam"!

But there is an important ambivalence in Benslama's project. While this Islam seems, according to him, to be opposed to the individual freedoms of writers of the caliber of Rushdie, he also criticizes European Islamologists for not recognizing that another Islam (whose referents again remain multiple—the Qur'an, Islamic theology, Islamic "culture," and so on) upholds individualism. Benslama insists that "Islam rather deploys one of the extremely powerful dimensions of individuality, a

45. See page 45 of *La psychanalyse* on his liberal defense of personal freedom and the individual.
46. Benslama, *La psychanalyse*, 24.
47. Ibid., 25.
48. I should note here that Benslama is aware that one of the meanings of the word *din* in Arabic is "debt" and that the logic of its meaning is different from that of religion but still thinks that it is the word through which the Qur'an "designates the equivalent or the similar term which we call in Christianity 'religion.'" See Benslama, *Déclaration d'insoumission*, 26n. On how the universal definition of "religion" originated in early modern Christianity, see Talal Asad, "The Construction of Religion as an Anthropological Category," in *Genealogies of Religion: Disciplines and Reasons of Power in Christianity and Islam* (Baltimore: Johns Hopkins University Press, 1983), 27–54. See also Tomoko Masuzawa, *The Invention of World Religions: or, How European Universalism was Preserved in the Language of Pluralism* (Chicago: University of Chicago Press, 2005).
49. See Benslama, *Déclaration d'insoumission*, 24.

dimension of great conceptual abundance. This dimension could not have developed without being compatible with the reality of the culture. This is indeed a culture of individuality, but one that is essentially governed by an identification with God."[50] Benslama is very critical of those Western psychoanalytical pronouncements on Islam and Muslim cultures that represent it as the obliterating of the individual, and which see the Western achievement that gave birth to the individual as the ultimate achievement of civilization *tout court*. He declares that those who insist that an alleged absence of individualism in Islam prevents Muslims from being accessible to psychoanalysis are simply "ignorant," adding: "I will not cite anyone's name so as not to privilege those who are in the order of ignorance and carelessness."[51]

The problem of the multiplicity of Islam as Islams, however, is something Benslama does not explain adequately if at all. If Islam should always be seen as plural and multiple, in the form of Islams, and never in the singular form, then what are "Islams" a plural of, what are they multiples of? Since for Benslama this plurality refers to the signifier and the signified, he does not elaborate on whether the signifieds have anything in common other than the signifier. Moreover, if both signifiers and signifieds are plural, would this mean that the term "Islam" is actually and simply a homonym, which in itself is what creates the confusion for religious Muslims and for liberals (including psychoanalysts), whether Muslim or not? But the notion of Islam as plural, as Islams, does not solve the problem that Benslama wishes to solve, namely that Islam in its entirety and in all its forms constitutes the other of liberalism, since even if one accepts the contention that there may be varieties of Islams that are compatible with liberalism, one of those that is not would still be singled out as the other of liberalism, and that is the one Islam that liberalism contests and wants to eliminate, which brings us back to the same troubling question with which Benslama began.

Benslama's ambivalence is not necessarily and only a conscious one, but more likely the effect of an ideological commitment that imagines different audiences differently. The reference to multiple Islams might be said to be an ideological position (the position of political correctness?) and/or an expression of a *wish*, while the references to one singular Islam in the many slips seem to betray what Benslama actually *fears* to be the case. This could indicate his own unconscious resistance to the claim (his own claim) that there are many Islams, or his conscious

50. Benslama, *La psychanalyse*, 302.
51. Ibid.

recognition that his claim is a mere wish and not an acknowledgement of observable reality, and that what he does notice or "realize," as he tells us, is that there actually exists only one Islam and therefore that this Islam must be opposed (hated?) for not pluralizing itself as it must and should. In this regard, he announces at the outset of the book that the origins of his own interest in writing on Islam emerged in the early 1980s (elsewhere, he would tell us that his interest started in the mid 1980s)[52] or "in a critical historical situation marked by a fanatical surge," as a decision to explore "the gap between a terminable Islam and an interminable one."[53] While Benslama cautions us (and perhaps himself) to use a new vocabulary and to adjust to a new epistemology wherein we (he) must "hear Islams when we say Islam," it would seem that he often remains deaf to his own warning.[54] Perhaps then, the singularity of actual Islam is itself the scene of the trauma that one cannot but revisit and whose claims one (or Benslama) is compelled to repeat at the very same moment and in the very same text where he insists that he, and we, must resist.

La psychanalyse repeats many of the same scenes (and discussions) in the biography of the Prophet Muhammad that Benslama had conjured up in *La nuit brisée*. It remains unclear if this act of repetition is merely a self-repetition that revisits his first (inaugural?) text (child?) on "Islam" or a revisiting of the Prophetic scenes themselves as the site of trauma that compels repetition. Indeed, one of the main scenes of *La nuit brisée*, repeated in *La psychanalyse*—the one in which Khadija, the Prophet's wife, reassures Muhammad that the angel Gabriel who had appeared to him was indeed an angel and not a demon—is a scene Benslama borrows, and therefore revisits, from the inaugural article by Khatibi, the very first psychoanalytic visit to that scene.[55] *La psychanalyse* surely is a repetition with a twist. It is a more comprehensive, more elaborated second

52. Benslama, "Une recherche psychanalytique sur l'islam," 77.

53. Benslama, *La psychanalyse*, 20.

54. Ibid., 76.

55. Abdelkebir Khatibi, "Du message prophétique (argument)," 83–84. Benslama does cite the article for Khatibi's views on the question of the Prophet's literacy or illiteracy and on the importance of Khadija to the question of revelation, but does not cite him for introducing him to this important scene, which is not one of the more standard stories about the beginning of revelation and is not usually included in modern narratives of the Prophet's biography, even though Khadija's relationship to the beginning of revelation is extensively discussed in such biographies. See Benslama, *La nuit brisée*, 44, 140–41, 143. On the absence of the story from the Prophet's modern biographies, see for example Safi al-Rahman Mubarakfuri's celebrated *Al-Rahiq al-Makhtum: Bahth fi al-Sirah al-Nabawiyyah ʿala Sahibiha Afdal al-Salah wa al-Salam* (The Sealed Nectar) (Riyad: Maktabat Dar al-Salam, 1995). I thank Ahmad Atif Ahmad for sharing with me some of his extensive knowledge of the classical and contemporary biographies of the Prophet.

attempt by Benslama at producing a psychoanalytic reading of "Islam."
As Benslama's youngest child (and, as we know, books which carry the
names of their authors are always reproductively connected to them, just
as children carry the name of the father), *La psychanalyse* seems more
privileged and more celebrated by critics, just as the younger male child
in the Torah is always more privileged—Abel, Isaac, Jacob, and others. It
is unclear if an unconscious wish on the part of Benslama is at work here,
one of preferring, once again as God and Abraham did, Isaac to Ishmael.

Before I indulge in further speculations, let me cite Benslama's own
statement of his task in his important book: "to translate the Islamic
origin in the language of Freudian deconstruction. . . . Translation is
not application or annexation, but through a signifying displacement,
conveys the very texture of a tradition in its language and its images,
in order to give access to what is unknowingly thought, inside it [*à son
insu*]."[56] I am unpersuaded by this assertion, mostly because translation
of "Islamic" texts into European languages often seems to mean retrieval
of dictionary meanings of words and their etymology without much
attention to the intellectual context and historicity of the uses and
significations of words and how they change over time—the "links" that
Mohammad Arkoun has juxtaposed as "language-history-thought"[57]—
something all contemporary interpretative exercises of the texts of the
past must attend to in order to avoid projecting contemporary meanings and values onto them. It is clear that Benslama is concerned that
translation can be a form of annexation. But he wants to insist that
translation in this case gives access to the unconscious of the tradition
("à son insu"). While this may be so, it does not do away with his initial
concern. Translation in this case is not "annexation" but *assimilation*,
in that Benslama's "Freudian deconstruction," whether it uncovers an
"Islam" that is individualist or anti-individualist, can only do so in relation to a modern liberal European value that Benslama posits as universal, namely, "individualism." This assimilationist move is presented as
useful for psychoanalysis and as useful psychoanalytically to the extent
to which it secures "the intelligibility of the logic of repression, which
subtends the foundation of a symbolic organization."[58] There is some
tension in this assimilationist project, however. On occasion, like the
Orientalists, Benslama insists on *not* translating Arabic words, including

56. Benslama, *La psychanalyse*, 319.
57. Muhammad Arkun, *Tarikhiyyat al-Fikr al-ʿArabi al-Islami* (The Historicity of Arab Islamic
Thought) (Casablanca: Al-Markaz al-Thaqafi al-ʿArabi, 1998), 16.
58. Benslama, *La psychanalyse*, 319.

the one for God, *Allah*, into its French equivalent, *Dieu*, when translating an Islamist text from Arabic, but he seems invested in exoticizing it as the specific and exclusive proper name of the Muslim God, when, and as noted earlier, it is the name that Arab Christians had used for their God before Muhammad and still use after him.[59] On another occasion, he insists on using the Arabic word *'awra*, whose etymology he provides, without translating it into the French (and English) "pudendum" (which has similar etymological origins), which would render its equivalent meaning to his French readers.[60]

Ultimately, however, Benslama wants to present his Islam as assimilable to the liberal notion of the individual, even if it is so with a difference. It is possible here that Benslama is engaged in deploying this Islamic individualism as a way of passing his Islam off as European, and that this passing off is indeed a form of resistance to Orientalist liberal accounts of Islam as lacking in individualism, while simultaneously condemnatory of Islamist resistance to this passing off, which he brands as pathological or as suffering from some form of "group delirium" (*délire collectif*).[61] In another related but earlier text, he makes a policy recommendation for Arab pedagogy by cautioning that if Arabs were to fail to "introduce Kant's *Critique of Pure Reason* into their educational curricula, they would be committing a horrendous error."[62]

Benslama is engaged in a project of simultaneously othering the Islam of the Islamists and identifying his own wished-for Islam with Europeanness. In this vein, he is partly mimicking Freud who, in *Moses and Monotheism*, insists on assimilating European Jews by declaring that they are not "Asiatics of a foreign race, as their enemies maintain, but composed for the most part of remnants of the Mediterranean peoples and heirs of the Mediterranean civilization."[63] Edward Said wondered about Freud's move: "Could it be, perhaps, that the shadow of anti-Semitism spreading so ominously over his world in the last decade of his life caused him protectively to huddle the Jews inside, so to speak, the sheltering realm of the European?"[64] Unlike Freud, Benslama, it seems, is caught between the Scylla of Orientalist hostility to all Islams and the

59. Ibid., 59.
60. Ibid., 197. He uses it again in *Déclaration d'insoumission*, 35.
61. Benslama, *La psychanalyse*, 49.
62. "Shajarat al-Islam, al-Tahlil al-Nafsi, al-Huwiyyah" (The Tree of Islam, Psychoanalysis, Identity), interview conducted by Husayn al-Qubaysi with Fethi Benslama, in *Al-Tahlil al-Nafsi wa al-Thaqafah al-ʿArabiyyah-al-Islamiyyah* (Psychoanalysis and Arab-Islamic Culture) (Damascus: Dar al-Bidayat, 2008), 15.
63. Freud, *Moses and Monotheism*, S.E. 23:91.
64. Said, *Freud and the Non-European*, 40.

Charybdis of his own hostility to the one (Islamist) Islam, which leads him to the (in)decision of identification *and* othering simultaneously.

Herein lies the importance of the discourse of scientism and rationalism—with which Benslama identifies modernity, the West, and psychoanalysis—to which he opposes Islamism (in the singular, despite his own assertions that it is a plural phenomenon) and the one Islam.[65] He consecrates a series of binaries to make this opposition clear:

> This line does not only pass between those who are tolerant and those who are fanatical, between rationalists and believers, between the logic of science and the logic of faith, but also between the position that thinks it can find the truth of origin in the texts of tradition—and this position thinks that this could be done through rational procedures armed with the valid discourse of the historical method—and the position that considers these same texts as a fiction or as a legend.[66]

In this regard, it is perplexing that Benslama discusses some Islamists' attempts to make the Qur'anic text correspond to scientific knowledge as a sort of neurosis or, more precisely, as "interpretative delirium" (*délire interprétatif*), and not part of their rationalization of the Qur'an.[67] He adds that "examining these [Islamist] documents leaves one with the impression of an immense interpretative delirium, ushered in from a destruction anxiety [*angoisse de destruction*] and constituting an attempt to repair from the outside that which has collapsed on the inside."[68] This is ironic, given Benslama's commitment to rationalism and the fact that he chose the *non-ironically* named "Association of Arab Rationalists," of which he is a member, to publish the Arabic translation of his book.[69] Benslama's use of these taxonomies of rationalism and irrationalism, science and faith, knowledge and ignorance, is in fact shared by many Islamist thinkers. If the Islamist thinker, Sayyid Qutb, referred to his contemporary Muslims and non-Muslims as still living in an age of ignorance (echoing the Qur'an's description of the pre-Revelation period), Benslama, aside from using post-Enlightenment descriptions of "darkness" and "obscurantism" to characterize Islamists, insists that Muslim men of religion live "in great ignorance."[70]

65. Benslama, *La psychanalyse*, 24–25.
66. Ibid., 36.
67. Ibid., 70.
68. Ibid.
69. See Fathi Bin Salamah, *Al-Islam wa al-Tahlil al-Nafsi*. Jurj Tarabishi is one of the main founders of this Association.
70. "Shajarat al-Islam, al-Tahlil al-Nafsi, al-Huwiyyah," 18.

The opposition of science to religion, and the correlate characterization of psychoanalysis as a "science" that is opposed by Islam as "religion," is shared among many of Benslama's psychoanalytic colleagues, including Tarabishi, Safouan, and, more recently, Houbballah. Safouan, for example, offers two theories to explain the nature of the relationship between "Islam" and science. On the one hand, he contends that "the Arabs" were open to learning from foreign science and building on it when they were in power, but upon losing power, they henceforth refused to learn from a science that came from colonial powers.[71] On the other hand, he offers an analysis that does not fully cohere with the first, namely that it was the Turks who destroyed science in "Islamic civilization."[72] He also asserts that "Islam was the victim of the nations it invaded, because they themselves were the victims of political regimes and administrative apparatuses whose sole purpose was to ensure the state's domination over all the aspects of life."[73] Yet Safouan makes a sweeping and disconcerting generalization that, in the contemporary period, "the West has accomplished great things on account of this separation [between religion and science], while the Islamic world has produced nothing as a result of their generalization of the idea that scientific discourse is the product of infidels and therefore should not be adopted."[74] The angry and contemptuous tone of this last declaration may be due to the fact that the text is in Arabic, which renders it an address exclusive to Arab Islamist audiences, an auto-critique to which most Europeans would not have access.

Safouan contends that, unlike the church in Christianity, the church in Islam is the State, specifically in the form of a dictatorial monarchy that eliminates the possibility of civil society (and here he is invoking Oriental despotism without naming it). This produces in many Muslims and Islamists an "excessive normopathology" of conformity to practicing religious rituals.[75] Safouan refuses essentialist arguments that privilege Christianity's alleged openness to science and democracy over Islam's. Yet, his materialist analysis leads to the same conclusion, namely, that whether Islam or the Arabs are essentially hostile to science

---

71. Mustafa Safouan, "Pratique analytique dans le monde arabe: Incidences et difficulté," *La Célibataire*, no. 8 (Printemps 2004): 15.

72. Ibid., 16.

73. Safouan, *Why Are the Arabs Not Free?* 43.

74. Safwan in a dialogue with ʿAdnan Hubbu Allah in "Al-Tahlil al-Nafsi wa al-Mujtamaʿ al-ʿArabi" (Psychoanalysis and Arab Society), in Mustafa Safwan and ʿAdnan Hubbu Allah, *Ishkaliyyat al-Mujtamaʿ al-ʿArabi*, 117.

75. Safouan, *Why the Arabs are not Free?* 14.

or democracy, or have become thus on account of socioeconomic reasons and foreign invasions, they are today hostile to them, which accounts for their state of unfreedom.

Houbballah, to take another example, is concerned with the relations among science, religion, and psychoanalysis (a theme around which he and other psychoanalysts convened the third international conference of Arab psychoanalysts in Beirut in 2007), as well as with the "inhospitable" reception that psychoanalysis is said to have received in "Arab intellectual circles."[76] Houbballah is most interested in the lack of democracy in Arab countries, to which he credits this inhospitality to psychoanalysis, as the latter cannot be "imagined" to exist in a repressive country, for "psychoanalysis is the acting out of one's freedom of thought."[77] Houbballah insists that democracy "has failed to conquer Arab thought. The concept of the individual is eclipsed before *el raiiya*, the community, where the power of the shepherd, 'the caliph,' is imposed by divine order, an order to which all the people cannot but be subjected [*être soumis*]."[78] What is remarkable here is Houbballah's understanding that the concepts of the individual and democracy are European concepts, while *raʿiyyah* ("*el raiiya*"), which means "subjects" in Arabic, as in "the king's subjects," becomes an Islamic concept! How *raʿiyyah* becomes essentialized as an Islamic concept that cannot be conquered by democracy and that must eclipse the individual is key to understanding Houbballah's approach, which insists that "the subject of science has not gained an entry into Arab culture."[79]

Houbballah, who uses "Islam" in all the same ways Benslama uses it, without specification, argues in his opening address to the third international conference of Arab psychoanalysts:

---

76. For the proceedings and papers of the conference, see *Al-ʿIlm wa al-Din wa al-Tahlil al-Nafsi: Aʿmal al-Muʾtamar al-Dawli al-Thalith lil-Muhallilin al-Nafsiyyin al-ʿArab, Beirut 17–19 May, 2007* (Science, Religion, and Psychoanalysis: The Proceedings of the Third International Conference for Arab Psychoanalysts) (Beirut: Dar al-Farabi, 2008) in Arabic and French. When I refer to this volume, I will indicate if I am quoting from the Arabic text, which has its own pagination, or the French text, which also has its own separate pagination. On Arab intellectuals' alleged inhospitable response to psychoanalysis, see Houbballah's introduction to Mustafa Safwan and ʿAdnan Hubbu Allah, *Ishkaliyyat al-Mujtamaʿ al-Arabi*, 8. He also discusses this at length in Adnan Houbballah, "La psychanalyse et le monde arabe," *La Célibataire*, no. 8 (Printemps 2004): 19–28. Before his recent concern with Islam and science, Houbballah had written a semi-autobiographical study of the Lebanese civil war in which many of his recent concerns were not present. See Adnan Houbballah, *Le virus de la violence: La guerre civile est en chacun de nous* (Paris: Albin Michel, 1996). His book was translated into Arabic as *Jurthumat al-ʿUnf, al-Harb al-Ahliyyah fi Samim kull Minna* (Beirut: Dar al-Taliʿah, 1998).

77. Houbballah, "La psychanalyse," 20.

78. Ibid., 22.

79. Ibid., 28.

Islam in the Ottoman period remained removed from these scientific developments [that had unfolded in Europe], and social revolutions (the French Revolution) on account of geographic limitations. Now, however, as the gates have loosened and opened wide, Islam no longer has a choice but to confront the scientific wave of postmodernity. In my opinion, the violence exploding everywhere constitutes a primitive phenomenon as a first defensive reaction which will have to be followed later by an intellectual wave that can absorb modernity and interact with it.[80]

The question he poses is "Why did Islam experience modernity as a danger?"[81] The answer he offers is that Arabs/Muslims (who are used interchangeably in the very title of his essay) have not been "subjected to two surgeries since the emergence of Islam, namely, the separation of religion from authority, for there did not occur a revolution like the French Revolution, and the separation of religion from science."[82]

Here, the reification of psychoanalysis as a science and the elision of the important debates within psychoanalysis about its own scientificity, let alone Freud's own overdetermined and ambivalent relationship to science, are never acknowledged or referenced by any of these thinkers. Perhaps Benslama's (as well as Safouan's and Houbballah's) resistance to, or anxiety about, the possibility of many *psychoanalyses* rather than one true psychoanalysis parallels his anxiety about the one Islam and the many. Still, these thinkers differ among themselves in certain respects regarding the nature of the relationship between "Islam" and science. This opposition, which they consecrate, however, is not new but continues a tradition inaugurated by Orientalist Ernest Renan's infamous debate with Jamal al-Din al-Afghani in the nineteenth century about this very question and which we discussed in chapter 1, wherein Islam and the Arabs were castigated as "hostile to science"—a debate which none of these thinkers cites or seems familiar with.[83]

These liberal commitments are not confined only to Arab psychoanalysts. Iranian psychoanalyst Gohar Homayounpour shares many of them, though unlike Houbballah, who thinks psychoanalysis has

---

80. ʿAdnan Hubbu Allah, "al-ʿIlm wa al-Din fi ma baʿd al-Hadathah" (Science and Religion in Postmodernity), in *Al-ʿIlm wa al-Din wa al-Tahlil al-Nafsi*, 15 of the Arabic pagination. It is curious that the paragraph from which this quotation is taken is not included in the French version of the speech contained in the same volume (see 16 of the French pagination).

81. ʿAdnan Hubbu Allah, "Limadha takhallafa al-ʿArab ʿan al-ʿIlm al-Muʿasir: ʿAmaliyyatan Jirahiyyatan lam Yakhdaʿ lahuma al-Muslimun" (Why have Arabs Remained Delayed from Contemporary Science: Two Surgeries to which Muslims have not been Subjected), in *Al-ʿIlm wa al-Din wa al-Tahlil al-Nafsi*, 67 of the Arabic pagination.

82. Ibid., 73.

83. On this important debate, see Massad, *Desiring Arabs*, 11–16.

had difficulty in the Arab world due to the "lack" of democracy, Homay-ounpour seems to think that the Iranian context, which she seems to also believe "lacks" democracy, has not been a hindrance to her in prac-ticing psychoanalysis in Tehran. In a memoir of her practice of psycho-analysis in Tehran after her return from Boston, she informs the reader at the outset that while she takes Edward Said's work on Orientalism seriously, she is quick to echo Western liberal mantras about taking re-sponsibility for one's failures: "I would like to add the responsibility of the 'Orientals' themselves in creating orientalism. . . . We have to stop blaming the West for our condition, for our destiny."[84] Homayounpour's political assessment of postrevolutionary Iran is not distinguishable from Western liberal views, though her ability to practice psychoanalysis there is:

I do not need to play any political games, none whatsoever, in Tehran. Ironically, this privilege has been given to me in a country that at this moment in history is one of the most politicized countries in the world. A country stigmatized by the world for its viola-tions of human rights, its lack of democracy, its nuclear ambitions, and its lack of free-dom of speech. . . . In Tehran, in one of the most controversial countries in the world, I have gotten closer to my rights as a psychoanalyst than I could have anywhere else.[85]

Homayounpour's memoir constantly enacts contrasts between "tradi-tional" Iranian society and ancient Greek society, between the modern West and contemporary Iran, and between Iranian and Oriental cultures on the one hand and American culture on the other. Despite her belief in the "universality of Oedipus," she asserts that "the Iranian collec-tive fantasy is anchored in an anxiety of disobedience that wishes for an absolute obedience," wherein it is the sons who are killed by the fathers and not the other way around: "To avoid being killed, they settle for the fear of castration. I find that this is characteristic of traditional cultures."[86] Therein lies the difference between Islam and Christianity, or at least Catholicism, for Homayounpour:

Islam means submission, and demands absolute obedience to God the father, while in Christianity the demarcation between God the father and Christ the son is not quite as clear. It seems as though religions were socially constructed to fulfill the collective

84. Gohar Homayounpour, *Doing Psychoanalysis in Tehran* (Cambridge, MA: MIT Press, 2012), xviii.
85. Ibid., 4–5.
86. 54–55.

fantasies of these differing cultures. An analysis of Iranian history reveals that it has constantly been a one-man show, while democracy was born within and is the essence of Greek society.[87]

We need not rehearse again how her characterizations reflect Christian and Western, not Muslim, views of Islam. Homayounpour's Iranian nationalism as essence cannot be contained. Though Shiism began as a movement by Arab Muslims in the eighth century and the majority of Iranians did not convert from Sunni to Shiite Islam until the sixteenth century, Homayounpour bestows on Iranians the credit of creating the sect:

We never properly mourned the loss of our glorious past before it was taken over by Islam. Our melancholic response was to create Shiism, which is a culture of mourning, as a way of mourning the symbolic past. . . . One has to bear in mind that in countries like Iran the past is everything, and unfortunately we do indeed breathe the air of regrets.[88]

It is perfectly clear that the "one" who has to bear this "in mind" is Homayounpour's Western reader. Her quest for origins does not only drive her to go back from Boston to Tehran, but she also seeks to find in Tehran the origins of psychoanalysis, of the era of Freud himself, a century ago. Going back to Tehran seems to be for her a way of joining Freud the father, as Iran, for her, is living in the time of Freud. Unlike the contemporary West, where Homayounpour believes sexuality is no longer central to psychoanalysis, when she moved to Tehran, she, like European Orientalists, embarked on time-travel to a time where arrested development can be observed in situ: "I have found sexuality in Tehran. In Tehran, today's sexuality is still Freud's sexuality. . . . In short, in Tehran I have encountered a kind of patient who is very much in line with the kinds of patients Freud was seeing during his time, a kind of patient that reminds me of a time when psychoanalysis was still in its early years."[89]

In the tradition of Western liberalism, which she cherishes (her invocation of Milan Kundera's dissidence from Czechoslovak communism and yearning for West European liberalism is in evidence throughout the book), the psychoanalyst Homayounpour is compelled to value

87. Ibid., 55–56.
88. Ibid., 56–57.
89. Ibid., 129–30.

"freedom instead of happiness, *à la* Simone de Beauvoir."[90] In her description of Iran and Tehran specifically to her English readers, comparisons abound—between Iran and the ancient Greeks, Iran and the United States, Tehran and Paris, upper class and lower class people, and between group A and group B of a 1970s American mental health study, where group A children grew up in "traditional" and "conservative" families and group B grew up in "more open-minded, intellectual" families. It is the latter that seems to instantiate liberal goals that Homayounpour seeks in Tehran, as they allow "for creativity to surface and enabl[e] freedom."[91] In her commitment to liberal concepts rather than psychoanalytic ones, Homayounpour fits neatly in our cohort of Arab psychoanalysts.

Benslama in turn has a major concern with the liberal notion of tolerance, which he finds lacking in the one Islam propagated by the Islamists (all of them?), but which he seems to think is in abundance in European rationalism and secularism (all of it?). Here Benslama's commitment to liberalism is also a commitment to the Freudian equation of individualism with phylogenetic and ontogenetic maturity—to which Freud opposes group solidarity and organicism as primitive and regressive— *and* a commitment to Freud's consideration of tolerance as the highest achievement of liberal politics—which is essentially synonymous with the highest degree of civilization. Freud's accounts of these questions, as Wendy Brown has shown, can be read in two different directions, both as the way men overcome primitive asociality through forms of social life free from strife in a social contractarian manner (*Civilization and Its Discontents* and *Totem and Taboo*), and as the overcoming of primitive solidarity and organicism in the achievement of civilized individuality (*Group Psychology and the Analysis of the Ego*). In contrast, liberal notions insist that civilized individualist liberal tolerance, as Brown put it, "is only available to liberal subjects and liberal orders and constitute the supremacy of both over dangerous alternatives. They also establish organicist orders as a natural limit of liberal tolerance, as intolerable in consequence of their own intolerance."[92] Thus, while Benslama chastises the one Islam and Islamists (always seen as deploying one singular meaning and interpretation of the one Islam) for lacking any rationalism or tolerance (denying them any tolerance on the grounds of their own alleged intolerance), he extends tolerance to the individualist Islam he rescues

90. Ibid., 92.
91. Ibid., 141, 143.
92. Wendy Brown, "Subjects of Tolerance," in *Political Theologies: Public Religions in a Post-Secular World*, ed. Hent De Vries and Lawrence E. Sullivan (New York: Fordham University Press, 2006), 303.

from (all?) the Islamists and from the Orientalists as one that features this important civilized value. In this sense, his liberal values differ little from the general understanding liberalism has of societies that insist on different forms of sociality and which it thus considers other. As Brown maintains, "Organicist orders are not only radically other to liberalism but betoken the 'enemy within' civilization and the enemy to civilization. Most dangerous of all would be transnational formations imagined as organicist from a liberal perspective, which link the two—Judaism in the nineteenth century, communism in the twentieth, and today, of course, Islam."[93] Here the historic links between liberal anti-Semitism and Orientalism and liberal anticommunism are shown to inhabit the very same politics of identity and othering.

International lawyer and Cambridge University professor Clive Parry offered in 1953 a slightly different historiography than Brown, though he would agree with her premise in principle: "We smile now to read how a century ago James Lorimer [the eminent Scottish lawyer who was a founder of the discipline of international law] could argue that an Islamic state ought not to be admitted into the family of nations because of the essentially intolerant character of Islam, because there would be lacking what Professor MacIver has called 'the will for society.' But if we substitute Communism for Mohamemedanism, we may perhaps confess that the problem is as large as it ever was, if not larger."[94] Little did Parry know in midcentury that once the Communist threat would be neutralized, the threat of Islam would take center stage again.

I should note, however, that Judaism, having emerged in the shadow of World War II within the liberal Western dyad identified as "Judeo-Christian" civilization—replacing the earlier prewar formulation, which Freud referred to as "our-present day white Christian civilization"[95]— now mostly escapes such descriptions, except for those Judaisms that resist their inclusion in this liberal order. Indeed, Benslama himself is implicitly so impressed with the Jewish achievement of Western liberalism (that is, Jews having reached and achieved Western liberal individual maturity), which he would have Muslims emulate, that he exaggerates the scientific achievement of Jews by endowing Christian thinkers with Jewish identities. In his rush to demonstrate his defense of the Europeanized and therefore liberal, mature, and Enlightened "Jews" against a

93. Ibid., 310.

94. Clive Parry, "Climate of International Law in Europe," *Proceedings of the American Society of International Law at Its Annual Meeting* 47 (April 23–25, 1953): 40.

95. Freud, *The Future of an Illusion, S.E.* 21:20.

fantasized primitive obscurantist Arab anti-Jewishness that would explain what he sees as an "Arab" or "Muslim" rejection of psychoanalysis
as the "Jewish science" (a European notion which in fact has little resonance among Arab or Muslim thinkers, though some American Jewish
and Zionist scholars formulate it as such),[96] Benslama responds thus:
"I feel some shame when I find myself having to draw attention to the
fact that he who thinks like this must also deny the theory of gravity
or the theory of relativity, which were both the result of the work of
Jewish scientists, Newton and Einstein."[97] It seems Benslama is not only

96. See for example Yosef Haim Yerushalmi, *Freud's Moses: Judaism Terminable and Interminable*
(New Haven, CT: Yale University Press, 1991), 46–50, 96–100.

97. "Shajarat al-Islam, al-Tahlil al-Nafsi, al-Huwiyyah," 14. He returns to this theme later when
he speaks of "the traditional anti-Judaism in the Arab world," and of "the anti-Judaism that has
existed since the origins of Islam," in Benslama, *Déclaration d'insoumission*, 38, 40. In the context
of discussing the Palestinian–Israeli conflict, he shows concern only about the Islamist "religious
readings" of the origins of the "conflict" but not of the Judaization of the Zionist colonial endeavor
since the beginnings of Zionism. While clearly critical of the policies of Israeli governments, he
only praises those Palestinians who are willing to "compromise" by recognizing Israel as he refers
to them as "democrats," without noting that they are willing to recognize an Israel that is racist
and *undemocratic* by law, granting legal privileges and rights to its Jewish citizens that it denies to
non-Jewish citizens. It is curious that Benslama considers the democratic position on the part of
Palestinians as the position of "non-violence" while he deems the position of violent resistance to
a violent occupation undemocratic (see ibid., 44). Benslama's sister and translator Raja Ben Slama,
who is a psychoanalytic scholar, is equally committed to condemning Arab criticisms of Zionism.
For example, she dismisses Mustafa Zaywar's analysis of Israeli Jewish psychology as motivated by
anti-Jewish racism, though not on the same level of the "elementary racism of his disciples who
used to speak of a 'Jewish personality.'" R. Ben Slama concludes that "conspiracy themes and amal-
gamations motivated by the hatred of Jews have led and still lead today to [Arab] scholarly constructions about the relationship between psychoanalysis and Zionism," in Raja Ben Slama, "La
psychanalyse en Egypte," 88. In fact, contrary to R. Ben Slama's allegations, Zaywar was sympathetic
to European Jews in all his writings; see for example his 1952 lecture "Saykulujiyyat al-Taʿassub"
(The Psychology of Chauvinism), reproduced in *Mustafa Zaywar: Fi Dhikra al-ʿAlim wa al-Fannan wa
al-Insan*, ed. Usamah Khalil (Paris: Maʿhad al-Lughah wa al-Hadarah al-ʿArabiyyah, 1997), 59–77.
In the case of Israel, Zaywar diagnosed Israeli Jewish psychology as one of "identification with the
aggressor" and former enemy of Jews, namely the Nazis, and that this identification is what propels
Israeli Jews to oppress the Arabs and the Palestinians. Nowhere in his analysis does Zaywar show any
antipathy towards Jews but he rather proceeds from a Hegelian understanding of identity, showing
how for Israeli Jews their new sense of identity as "masters" is directly related to and dependent
upon their transformation of the identity of the Arabs and Palestinians into "slaves." In exchanging
their former status as Hegelian "slaves" to Nazi "masters," Zaywar invokes Sándor Ferenczi's and
Anna Freud's thesis of the "identification with the aggressor" as well as a study on the surviving
Jewish children of Buchenwald to support his diagnosis. See his "Adwaʾ ʿala al-Mujtamaʿ al-Israʾili:
Jadal al-Sayyid wa al-ʿAbd" (Shedding Light on Israeli Society: The Master-Slave Dialectic), *Al-Ahram*,
8 and 9 September 1968, republished in *Mustafa Zaywar*, 78–92. On Zionist identification with anti-
Semitism and the transformation of Palestinians into Jews, see Joseph Massad, *The Persistence of the
Palestinian Question: Essays on Zionism and the Palestinians* (London: Routledge, 2006), especially
the last chapter of the book. I should note here that the earliest text that accuses psychoanalysis of
Zionist sympathies was written by an Egyptian Christian psychiatrist who had championed Freud in
the 1930s and repudiated him in 1970. See Dr. Sabri Jirjis, *Al-Turath al-Yahudi al-Suhyuni wa al-Fikr al-
Fruydi: Adwaʾ ʿala al-usul al-Suhyuniyyah li-fikr Sighmund Fruyd* (Zionist Jewish Culture and Freudian
Thought: Shedding Light on the Zionist Origins of the Thought of Sigmund Freud) (Cairo: ʿAlam

unfamiliar with the fact that Newton was Christian (perhaps Newton's first name "Isaac" led to Benslama's confusion?) but also with the latter's major exegetical contributions to Christian theology.[98] His exaggeration of Jewish achievements and Arab failures recalls his preference for Isaac over Ishmael noted earlier.[99]

In reading Benslama, one gets the general sense that psychoanalytic studies of Islamists (seen in their entirety as upholding the one illiberal Islam) replicate ego psychology's method of looking for neurotic mechanisms in the childhood of a person to explain his or her inability to accept authority and respond to the call of normativity. Islamist and Muslim resistance to Western secular and liberal (read Christian) normativity is seen as psychic resistance to maturity and adult authority, as a

---

al-Kutub, 1970). Egyptian psychoanalyst Hussein Abdel Kader explains that Jirjis's repudiation of Freud was part of a dispute he had had with Mustafa Zaywar, the doyen of Egyptian psychoanalysts, who was the real target of his attack, "and not Freud." See Hussein Abdel Kader, "La psychanalyse en Egypt," 65. Incidentally, Zaywar edited and introduced Safouan's 1958 translation of Freud's *The Interpretation of Dreams* into Arabic. For the most recent edition of the translation published under the auspices of the Arab Center for Psychological and Psychoanalytic Research (ACPPR) headed by Adnan Houbballah, see Sighmund Fruyd, *Tafsir al-Ahlam*, trans. Mustafa Safwan (Beirut: Dar an Farabi and ACPPR, 2003). ʿAbd al-Munʿim al-Hifni retranslated the book in 1995 in a new edition with a respectful yet critical discussion of Safwan's translation, and republished it with a new introduction in 2004. See Sighmund Fruyd, *Tafsir al-Ahlam*, trans. Abd al-Munʿim al-Hifni (Cairo: Maktabat Madbuli, 2004).

98. I should add here that Newton dabbled in early Protestant Zionism, which may be another reason for Benslama's mistaken presumption that he was Jewish. In his *Observations upon the Prophesies of Daniel and the Apocalypse of St. John*, Newton asserted that the Jews would be restored to Palestine: "The manner I know not. Let time be the interpreter." See Regina Sharif, *Non-Jewish Zionism: Its Roots in Western History* (London: Zed Press, 1983), 36.

99. A vulgar Islamophobic psychoanalytic study is that of the French Zionist writer Daniel Sibony, who wants to psychoanalyze Palestinian resistance to European Jewish colonization of their country. In his book on the topic, which reads more as official Israeli *hasbara* (or propaganda), Sibony alleges that Palestinian resistance is not based on the actual theft of Palestinian land and the expulsion of the Palestinians but is rather related to how the Qurʾan allegedly expelled the Jews who were "indigenous" to the Islamic Message because the Jews refused to accept to "submit" to Islam, that is, to "Islamize themselves." See Daniel Sibony, *Proche-Orient: Psychanalyse d'un conflit* (Paris: Éditions du Seuil, 2003), 16. The "return" of the Jews to Palestine, Sibony alleges, was perceived by the Palestinians (which he represents as Muslims in their entirety, thus eliding the presence of Palestinian Christians who were always and remain prominent in the resistance to Zionism) not as part of a European colonial population taking over a land that previous European Christian Crusaders had colonized with similar religious justifications and arguments a millennium earlier and which European converts to Judaism were emulating through Zionism, but rather as the return "d'une faille dans un Texte qu'il l'a déniée" (16). For Sibony, the problem of the Palestinians is that they thought that the fact that they were born in Palestine was sufficient for them to be in possession of the land, but in doing so, Sibony tells us, they did not see "the nature of the symbolic link [that their country constitutes for Jews] that has come back" (18). Sibony could have added that the Palestinians also do not see the nature of the "symbolic link" that their country constitutes for European Christians either, which the latter justified/justify to conquer them. Statements that allege that the Qurʾan today (though Sibony does claim that it was not always like this) is essentially anti-Jewish, that it is a call for the hatred of Jews—"un appel à les hair" (37)—and that the Palestinians allegedly use it "comme Manifeste de libération," proliferate throughout the book.

rebellion against normativity. Like American imperialism, a liberal civilizational psychoanalysis of the sort Benslama promotes seeks to bring recalcitrant and sick elements back into society and nurse them back to good health.

Jacques Derrida worried about what Freud once termed the "foreign policy" of psychoanalysis, and complained about the silence or equivocation of psychoanalysis, as institution, on the question of torture and violence in the "rest of the world," which he feared was a form of complicity. Derrida maintained:

Psychoanalysis may serve as a conduit for these new forms of violence ["invisible abuses, ones more difficult to detect—whether in Europe or beyond its borders—and perhaps in some sense newer"]; alternatively, it may constitute an irreplaceable means for deciphering them, and hence a prerequisite of their denunciation in specific terms—a necessary precondition, then, of a struggle and a transformation. Inasmuch, indeed, as psychoanalysis does not analyze, does not denounce, does not struggle, does not transform (and does not transform *itself* for these purposes), surely it is in danger of becoming nothing more than a perverse and sophisticated appropriation of violence, or at best merely a new weapon in the symbolic arsenal.[100]

Psychoanalytic interventions, however, in the form of translation in the direct or indirect service of power might also be accomplices of abuse and violence. Benslama does not seem to share Derrida's concern about certain forms of psychoanalysis and the way they approach an object they name "Islam." He fortifies himself behind the liberal language of individualism, freedom, and human rights. But as Derrida maintains, these are not psychoanalytic concepts: "Shelter is taken behind a language with no psychoanalyical nature. . . . What is an 'individual'? What is a 'legitimate freedom' from a psychoanalytical point of view?"[101] Benslama's answer might very well be more "translation." This is not to say that psychoanalysis, since its inception, did not rely on a certain liberal understanding of the individual and the social, as many of its Marxist critics pointed out; it is to say, however, that psychoanalysis undid and undoes the liberal sovereign subject, when it demonstrates time and again that this subject is not sovereign at all and indeed is not always, if ever, in command of her/his actions, let alone her/his choices.

100. Jacques Derrida, "Geopsychoanalysis: '. . . and the rest of the world,'" *American Imago* 48, no. 2 (Summer 1991): 211.
101. Ibid., 215.

In the year 2000 Derrida commented that "what still links psycho-analysis to the history of Greek, Jewish, Christian Europe is not very well known. And if I add—or if I don't add—Muslim to fill out the list of Abrahamic religions, I am already opening the gulf of an immense interrogation."[102] He added "why does psychoanalysis never get a foot-hold in the vast territory of the Arabo-Islamic culture? Not to mention East Asia."[103] Derrida's answer seemed to have to do with the "European-ness" of psychoanalysis above all else, despite its recent attempts at glo-balization. For those who have reiterated Derrida's question, however, an Orientalist answer seemed most apt; for them, like for the Lebanese Christian Mounir Chamoun, it was not the resistance of psychoanalysis to abandoning its European origins and presumptions that prevents it from globalizing itself except in European terms; rather:

The resistance to psychoanalysis in the Arab and Islamic world is due to the closure linked to the fact of religion, the dogmatic fixity of the religious law and the impos-sibility to interpret the text of the law, which leads to the passivization of the subject as freedom. It equally has to do with . . . the fascination of the Muslim peoples with dictatorial and autocratic regimes that are linked to a theocratic conception of society that reduces any prospect of democracy, which is an essential condition for the estab-lishment and practice of psychoanalysis.[104]

It is not clear how or if this answer applies to East Asia as well. Indeed, it is fully in tune with Benslama's, Safouan's, and Houbballah's propositions. But for Derrida, liberal forms of democracy differ little from monarchical structures of authority on questions of cruelty and sovereignty, or even patriarchality: "for who will seriously claim that our [French] republic is not monarchical, and that modern democracy, in the form we know it, does without a monarchical principle and a founding reference to a prince, as to a principle of sovereignty?"[105]

Two trends are juxtaposed in Benslama's text: condemnation of a static Islamic theology, which he sees as "fossilized by centuries of immobility,"[106] and a break with Islamic origins (ushered in by modernity

102. Jacques Derrida, "Psychoanalysis Searches the States of its Soul: The Impossible Beyond of a Sovereign Cruelty" (Address to the States General of Psychoanalysis), in Jacques Derrida, *Without Alibi* (Stanford, CA: Stanford University Press, 2002), 255.

103. Ibid.

104. Mounir Chamoun, "Islam et Psychanalyse dans la culture arabo-musulmane," *Pratiques Psychologiques* 11 (2005): 3. See also pages 6–7.

105. Derrida, "Psychoanalysis Searches the States of its Soul," 260.

106. Benslama, *La psychanalyse*, 43.

via colonialism) which brought about the one Islam in reaction to this break. Based on his research, Benslama diagnoses the situation today as follows: "What has happened in Islam in the last twenty odd years emerges from this conjuncture; it proceeds from a break which cuts through its history and opens inside it another possibility of history."[107] The findings he arrives at while researching "the transformation of the figure of the father and of the paternal function" in a Tunis suburb in the mid 1980s were sufficient for him to recognize that there was a "deeper" and "more longstanding" dis-ease (*malaise*) afflicting "Islamic civilization," and not merely one suburb.[108] It is unclear if this is the result of Benslama's or his Tunisian subjects' symbolic conflation of the father and the paternal function with Islam as one and the same. This is significant because Benslama argues, correctly, that unlike in Christianity, in "Islam" God has no paternal role at all to play; indeed, such a role is explicitly repudiated in the Qurʾan. Benslama blames Arab and Muslim intellectuals and the political elite for the dis-ease from which "Islam" seems to suffer: "an elite that did not know how to translate the modern to the public, nor how to deploy the interpretative and political possibilities to moderate the public's excesses."[109] His conclusion that, in the Arab world, "modernity was nothing but a simulacrum of the modern"[110] betrays a belief that "modernity" in the West is an unmediated fact, rather than an interpretation.

Even though Benslama insists that "~~Islamism~~ [again, seen as a single phenomenon] does not sum up Islam" (but which Islam?),[111] he maintains that analyzing the destructive effects of the break (*césure*) should not serve an essentialist process, which would in turn ignore the contemporary historical and material forces that have led Islam to "be out of joint."[112] The work of culture, he continues, has difficulty thinking through this "deracination" of Muslims from their own history in their encounter with a simulacrum of modernity. It is "this transgression, without words, that has determined here the task of the psychoanalyst."[113] Yet at the end of the book, and after he presents the reasons why Islamism should be read under erasure, we are reminded that "one cannot exoner-

---

107. Ibid., 317.
108. Benslama, "Une recherche psychanalytique sur l'islam," 76.
109. Benslama, *La psychanalyse*, 317–18.
110. Ibid., 318.
111. Benslama, *La psychanalyse*, 319. Bracketed commentaries are mine and do not appear in Benslama's text.
112. Ibid., 319.
113. Ibid.

ate Islam of this ideology," of Islamism![114] This tension between the one Islam and the many informs Benslama's discussion throughout.

There is, however, a resolution to this tension. Believing that the only way out of the one Islam is the way into liberal secularism, Benslama has more recently co-founded "The Association of the Manifesto of Freedoms" and is signatory (author of?) to its founding declaration.[115] It is noteworthy that the vocabulary that informs the declaration, including the alleged "totalitarian" nature of Islamism, is borrowed wholesale from French, West European, and American cold-war anticommunism. The declaration affirms that its members who are "holders of the values of secularism and of sharing a common world . . . [are] linked by our own individual histories, and in different ways, to Islam," which the declaration defines "as a place where many of the dangers of a globalized world crystallize: identitarian fascism and a totalitarian hold, civil and colonial wars, despotisms and dictatorships, inequality and injustice, self hatred and hatred of others, amidst political, religious, and economic extremes."[116] Islamists (all of them?) are said to constitute "forces of destruction" that must be opposed through democracy and the institution of the political, which cannot be imposed militarily but must "target the internal structures of Islam and modify its relations to its geopolitical borders."[117] It is not clear which structures Benslama wants to target. While a singular Islam (which seems to be the only state in which "Islam" can exist at present, according to Benslama's reading) is being singled out in the declaration for this transformation, the signatories insist that they will fight and resist what they call "totalitarian Islamism."[118] This cold-war language is sometimes ironically compounded with Christian anti-Judaism, wherein the "loving" and "forgiving" God of Christianity has always been compared to the "angry" and "vengeful" God of Judaism. Benslama (unconsciously?) adopts the same description. What Islamists offer to the "subjected" Muslims of today, he tells us, is nothing short of "a vengeful and rewarding God [*un Dieu vengeur et rémunérateur*]."[119] The latter term, *rémunérateur*, mainly

114. Ibid., 318.

115. Jurj Tarabishi is also a signatory to the manifesto, but not Safouan or Houbballah. See http://www.manifeste.org/signatures.php3?id_article=1&alpha=T (accessed 1 April 2014). Tarabishi was also consulted on the translation of Benslama's *La Psychanalyse* into Arabic. See the translator's introduction in Benslama, *Al-Islam wa al-Tahlil al-Nafsi*, 18.

116. "Déclaration de fondation de l'Association du Manifeste des libertés," in Fethi Benslama, *Déclaration d'insoumission*, 91–92.

117. Ibid., 92.

118. Ibid., 93.

119. Benslama, *Déclaration d'insoumission*, 48–49.

a business term, implies further that Islam's God is "profitable" in a financial sense, suggesting more connections to anti-Semitic notions of Jews and money.

The connections between anti-Islam and anti-Judaism are not just co-incidental here but also productive of the coupling of Islamophobia and anti-Semitism. The two are picked up from Benslama and put to use by flamboyant Slovenian psychoanalytic thinker Slavoj Žižek, who affirms that "the difference between Judaism and Islam is thus ultimately not substantial, but purely formal: they are the SAME religion in a different formal mode." He adds that "we usually speak of the Jewish-Christian civilization—perhaps, the time has come, especially with regard to the Middle East conflict, to talk about the *Jewish-Muslim civilization* as an axis opposed to Christianity."[120]

Ironically, and contra Benslama, not all Islamists oppose psychoanal-ysis, and some of them are in fact open to it.[121] Unlike Benslama's full scale rejection of Islam as Islamism (both seen as singular, as signifiers and signifieds), Ahmad al-Sayyid ʿAli Ramadan, an Egyptian professor of psychology teaching in Saudi Arabia, is not only tolerant of Freud-ian psychoanalysis but offers an Islamist assessment of the "positive" and "negative" aspects of it from an "Islamic" perspective. After review-ing and commenting on the oeuvre of Freud and the psychoanalytic method, as well as the history of Western critiques of psychoanalysis and the history of its practice in Egypt, Ramadan concludes with a list of the "positive" contributions of psychoanalysis, including Freud's con-cept of the "unconscious," the method of "free association," "releasing the patient's anxieties," "giving confidence [to the patient]," "bringing unconscious struggles to the surface of consciousness," "reducing the resistance" of the patient, the discovery of the Oedipus complex, and more.[122] Ramadan takes psychoanalysis so seriously that he compares it

120. Žižek's quotes are taken from Slavoj Žižek, "A Glance into the Archives of Islam," http://www.lacan.com/zizarchives.htm (accessed 1 April 2014). As for the question of Islam and women, for Žižek, who praises and relies on the work of Benslama, "Islam itself is grounded on a disavowed femininity, trying to get rid of the umbilical cord that links it to the feminine." For a scathing critique of Žižek and his views of Muslims and Islam, see Anne Norton, *On the Muslim Question* (Princeton, NJ: Princeton University Press, 2013); 7–8, 45–46, 174.

121. For an Islamist misapprehension of Freud's theories and their dismissal as "pornographic" in nature, see Saʿd al-Din Sayyid Salih, *Nazariyyat al-Tahlil al-Nafsi ʿind Fruyd fi Mizan al-Islam* (Freud's Theory of Psychoanalysis [weighed] on the scales of Islam) (Jiddah: Maktabat al-Sahabah, 1993). The association of Freud's thought with Zionism and Jewishness in this book is hardly an Islamist innovation. As cited earlier in the footnotes, it was a Christian Egyptian psychiatrist who had first elaborated on these themes.

122. Ahmad al-Sayyid ʿAli Ramadan, *Al-Islam wa al-Tahlil al-Nafsi ʿind Fruyd* (Islam and Freud's Psychoanalysis) (al-Mansurah, Egypt: Maktabat al-Iman, 2000), 227–28.

to the Qurʾanic notions of the psyche and shows where they converge and diverge.[123] My point here is not only to cite the openness of Ramadan to Freudian psychoanalysis but also to show that Benslama seems not only intolerant of the "intolerance" of Islamism(s), but also of its *tolerance*.

Benslama, then, like some of the Islamists he decries, but certainly not like others who do not exist in his epistemological framework, wants to fix the many Islams he identifies in one form. For him the only tolerable Islam is a liberal form of Islam that upholds all the liberal values of European maturity and is intolerant of the Islam of the Islamists whose values are said to oppose liberal values even *when they do not*. This seems to be the Islam that is "intelligible" to him but not to others. He also wants to fix the meaning of Islamism as one that upholds the illiberal Islam, which he cannot tolerate. In Benslama's work, psychoanalysis becomes a handmaiden of European liberalism and demonstrates neither internal ambivalence nor ambivalence toward its projected other. On the contrary, the certainty with which "Islam" is christened *the other of liberalism* and the West aligns it with the figure of the primitive and the pre-oedipal child in the cosmology of Freudian psychoanalysis. Benslama is not alone in effecting this transformation but is rather part of a large group of European and Arab and Muslim thinkers who are insistent on these representations. While he has brilliantly analyzed the figures of Abraham and Ishmael in the Qurʾan and, along with Hagar, in the Islamic theological tradition (neither Hagar nor Sarah are in fact named in the Qurʾan at all), when he deals with contemporary Islamists his psychoanalytic insights are transformed into invocations (shall we call them incantations?) of liberalism.

Showing an ongoing concern with the horrors that are committed "in the name of Islam," Benslama is much less worried about the greater horrors that are committed in the name of *anti*-Islam.[124] In fact, as I have shown earlier, he is an ambivalent participant in the discourse of anti-Islam as his consciously chosen title *Déclaration d'insoumission* clearly illustrates. But the problem of the name could be more complicated than I have hitherto allowed. In the context of writing on the Prophetic Message, Khatibi investigates the reasons for his decision to write on it, and cites his brother's name, Muhammad, his father's name, Ahmad (one of the names by which the Prophet is also known), and his own

123. Ibid., 269–327.
124. Benslama, *Déclaration d'insoumission*, 69.

name, Abdelkebir (as he was born on the day of *al-ʿId al-Kabir*, the major Muslim feast of Abraham's sacrifice of his son), as reasons that might have led him to write on these themes.[125] In contrast, Benslama, instead of reading his own name into his desire to work on psychoanalysis and Islam, shifts the blame onto "Islam." He tells us that "it is because Islam began to concern itself with us that I decided to be concerned with it."[126] Reading his name into this equation, which Benslama himself does not do (though he is remarkably playful in his books when dealing with words, names, their Arabic etymologies and three-letter roots, and their relationship to the unconscious), produces an interesting psychoanalytic interpretation of his discoveries. Benslama—or "bin Salamah," as his name is written in Arabic, as two separate words, meaning "son of Salamah" (not unlike the formulations of English last names, such as Johnson, meaning "son of John," or more relevantly "Christianson" and "Christopherson")—shares his patronym with Islam, since both are based on the three-letter radical *s-l-m*. Salamah means peacefulness and safety, which Benslama recognizes as two of the meanings of Islam.[127] In this sense, one might consider that Benslama speaks also in the name of Salamah, his patronym, the name of the symbolic father who imposes the law and who says no (Lacan's "le nom/non du père"), which is also the name of Islam, but he speaks in its/his name to produce a declaration against it/him, against his own name and his own "father," Salamah-Islam. His entire project is in fact to fight this Islam ("pour combattre partout"),[128] the one Islam, the Islamist Islam, indeed, to kill it and replace it with a kinder, gentler father who does not lay down the law, namely, a liberal Islam, which Benslama spends considerable time wishing into existence. This contingent reading of Benslama's name and his relationship to "Islam" would address the Oedipal rebellion (*insoumission*) that he stages against Islam *as* the symbolic father who regulates desire, and this might be read in relation to Benslama's ongoing and impressive attempts to rescue Hagar, the (grand)mother of the Arabs, from "Islam's" marginalization of her.

Benslama's political and geographical location in France, like others of his cohort, seems to account consciously for his liberal commitments, as does the time period in which he is writing, beginning in the late 1980s, coinciding with the weakening and later collapse of the Soviet

125. Khatibi, "Du message prophétique (argument)," 88–89.
126. Benslama, *La psychanalyse*, 17.
127. Benslama, *La nuit brisée*, 176.
128. Benslama, *Déclaration d'insoumission*, 93.

Union and the globalization of imperial capital; it certainly explains his sense of "shame" for belonging to a group of Muslims with a questionable relationship to psychoanalysis and also his ambivalent rejection of his own patronym and, more generally, his paternal lineage, in favor of a European (French) liberal psychoanalysis. It also contextualizes the kinds of critiques with which he wants to engage and in which he wants to *insert* his own. He himself pauses to assert that the issuing of his declaration "here in France, on this European continent that is being reorganized, obligates us especially and in many ways. Primarily, by the opportunity of being in a democratic space that wonders about its future and appeals to a democracy to come."[129] This unwavering commitment to the liberal values of individualism, freedom, tolerance, and separation of the theological from the political[130] begins increasingly to function like religious doctrine for those intellectuals who uphold

129. Ibid., 59–60.
130. A shorter version of this chapter was presented at the London Freud Museum as a keynote address on November 29, 2008 at the conference, "Psychoanalysis, Fascism, and Fundamentalism," sponsored by the London Freud Museum, Middlesex University, and the French Société Internationale d'Histoire de la Psychiatrie et de la Psychanalyse. Unfortunately, I could not deliver the keynote in person because the British embassy delayed my British visa while checking my fingerprints. Professor Glenn Bowman graciously read the address on my behalf. I was able to join in by telephone at the end of the session to answer audience questions. In response to my lecture, Elisabeth Roudinesco, who was a member of the audience, stood up and declared that Fethi Benslama was her friend, proceeded to give an extensive list of his other friends, including Jacques Derrida and Etienne Balibar, and insisted that Benslama was not a "neoliberal" as my lecture supposedly claimed, when in fact no such claim had been advanced. She demanded in conclusion that I should inform the audience of whether I "support terrorism or not." Roudinesco is a signatory to Benslama's Manifesto of Freedom, which, interestingly, she did not mention in her comments. See http://www.manifeste .org/signatures.php3?id_article=1&alpha=R. In a different context, Roudinesco, who is a declared enemy of Islam and French Muslims and who was/is one of the most vocal supporters of the French racist ban of the hijab (dubbed "veil"), had labeled French feminists who opposed the ban in 2003 as supporters of "fundamentalism" and as "partisans of the veil." On her views, see Joan Wallach Scott, *The Politics of the Veil* (Princeton, NJ: Princeton University Press, 2007), 105, 132, 157–58, 166–67. Indeed, at a conference on "psychoanalysis in the Arab and Islamic world" held in May 2005 at the Université Saint-Joseph in Beirut and co-organized by Roudinesco and financed "directly" by the French foreign ministry and under the aegis of the French ambassador to Lebanon and in which Fethi Benslama participated (see the address by the French ambassador to the conference, where he underscores the interest of the ministry of foreign affairs in financing the conference "directly" in "Mot de S.E.M. Bernard Emié, ambassadeur de France," in *La psychanalyse dans le monde arabe et islamique* [Beirut: Presses de l'université Saint-Joseph, 2005], 23), Roudinesco, in a classic Orientalist way that also endorses sectarian right-wing Christian claims in Lebanon, identified the city of Beirut in her opening address as lying "on the border between the Orient and the Occident," and saw no irony in speaking about the relationship between psychoanalysis and democracy and freedom, but not colonialism, at a conference hosted by a Jesuit university set up initially as a French colonial institution and under the aegis of the French government, the former colonial and current neocolonial master of Lebanon. Roudineso expressed the hope in her remarks that psychoanalysis would inaugurate a "new sovereignty" in Lebanon as it had done in Europe. See Elisabeth Roudinesco, "Mot d'ouverture," in *La psychanalyse dans le monde arabe et islamique*, 19–20. It is noteworthy that Adnan Houbballah did not participate in this conference.

them, and, insofar as they do, can be likened to obsessional neurosis, just as religion was by Freud. Indeed, Freud articulates objections to his commitments to science by ventriloquizing critics who would state: "If you want to expel religion from our European civilization, you can only do it by means of another system of doctrines; and such a system would from the outset take over all the psychological characteristics of religion—the same sanctity, rigidity and intolerance, the same prohibition of thought—for its own defence."[131] Freud's feeble retort to this criticism is that "my illusions are not, like religious ones, incapable of correction."[132] As liberal doctrine's prejudice against Islam proves less open to correction than the very Islamist doctrines it wants to criticize, its "illusions" are indeed more "religious" than those of Islamisms. In this light, and as Freud described followers of religions, devout followers of liberal doctrine "are safeguarded in a high degree against the risk of certain neurotic illnesses; their acceptance of the universal neurosis spares them the task of constructing a personal one."[133] Arab and Muslim intellectual migrants to Europe (and the US), in the geographical and/or political sense, who are converted to liberal doctrine have the added and difficult task of self-othering, of repudiating Islam as *not only* "religion," in order to integrate a version of it into the liberal Christian and secular notion of *only* a "religion," which would make it tolerable to devout liberals.

This liberal identity and the mechanisms through which it produces its others are taken as uninterrogable referents in Benslama's work and that of others like him. This constitutes a serious limitation of Benslama's oeuvre generally and can be productively read in a psychoanalytic way. Indeed, this might be useful for psychoanalysis at present, namely to study the processes through which the liberal self is constituted by Europeans and by Muslim and non-Muslim intellectual migrants from non-European postcolonies. A more curious psychoanalysis would perhaps do well to undertake a study of the group psychology of liberal and secular thinkers more generally on the question of "Islam" in order to uncover the unconscious processes and mechanisms at play in the formation of their liberal ego, which in turn privileges this liberal reading of something they insist on othering as "Islam." In the words of British scholar Roger Ballard:

131. Freud, *The Future of an Illusion*, S.E. 21:51.
132. Ibid., 53.
133. Ibid., 44.

The most urgent priority is not for Europe to understand its *alters* better, but rather itself and its own history—for it is within Europe's own longstanding structures of self-definition that pluralism in general, and the Islamic presence in particular, have been rendered into nightmares. If so, it is Europe itself which stands in urgent need of therapy. But as yet the patient is still in denial, and as any psychotherapist would confirm, those who refuse to acknowledge the seriousness of their self-generated plight find it far easier to engage in a process of transference. Rather than confronting the illusory character of their own mental constructions, they prefer to ascribe the very behavior which they refuse to acknowledge in themselves to those whom they believe are harassing them.[134]

In the meantime, the important question Benslama and Khatibi posed in the call for papers for their inaugural 1987 colloquium on psychoanalysis and Islam—namely, "from which foundations and in relation to which specific problems can psychoanalysis enter into a relationship with this other civilization without doing so in the mode of a cultural psychology or a pure transposition that would reproduce the avatars of colonial thought with regards to the matter of the psychic being?"—is still in search of an answer and thus remains an open challenge.[135]

134. Roger Ballard, "Islam and the Construction of Europe," in *Muslims in the Margin: Political Responses to the Presence of Islam in Western Europe*, ed. Wasif Shadid and Sjoerd von Koningsveld (Kampen, Netherlands: Kok Pharos, 1996), 49.

135. Khatibi, "Argument," *Cahiers Intersignes*, no. 1 (Spring 1990): 11.

FIVE

Forget Semitism!

Memory occupies a significant position in nineteenth- and twentieth-century theories of origins, whether of the species, of the races, of cultures, of civilizations, of religions, of nationalities, or of the psyche. Racial, cultural, and civilizational memories at the level of the group or the individual would indeed become crucial for many of these sciences and systems of knowledge, not least of which was psychoanalysis. Hence Freud's insistence that "ontogeny recapitulates phylogeny" in the development of the human psyche was not merely a continuation of Social Darwinist thought but also symptomatic of how the group and the individual came to be seen as related, through memory.

Nationalist movements' attempts to "retrieve" the memory of the "nation" were analogized by Freud to a person's childhood memories. "This is often the way in which childhood memories originate. Quite unlike conscious memories from the time of maturity, they are not fixed at the moment of being experienced and afterwards repeated, but are only elicited at a later age when childhood is already past; in the process they are altered and falsified, and are put in the service of later trends, so that generally speaking they cannot be sharply distinguished from phantasies." Freud proceeds to explain how nations come to write their histories:

Historical writing, which had begun to keep a continuous record of the present, now also cast a glance back to the past, gathered traditions and legends, interpreted the traces of antiquity that survived in customs and usages, and in this way created a history of the past. It was inevitable that this early history should have been an expression of present beliefs and wishes rather than a true picture of the past; for many things had been dropped from the nation's memory, while others were distorted, and some remains of the past were given the wrong interpretation in order to fit in with contemporary ideas. Moreover people's motive in writing history was not objective curiosity but a desire to influence their contemporaries, to encourage and inspire them, *or to hold a mirror up before them* [emphasis added].[1]

In the formation of identities, memory is not only invented, conjured up, or reawakened, but it is also purposely suppressed, erased, and deleted. As identities are elaborated and predicated on the dualism of self and other, identity formation requires of the carriers of identity that they not only remember and forget certain memories about the self but also about the other, whose history and present have to undergo a series of operations to guarantee what is to be remembered and what is to be forgotten. Freud's *Moses and Monotheism*, as we saw in the last chapter, is the most illustrative text in this regard.

This is particularly important for European thought as regards Hebrews and Jews and Arabs and Muslims, given their importance as central others used in consolidating European identity if not in the consolidation of the very collectivity called Europe, a process that, as we saw earlier, started during the Crusades through the othering discourse of religion and more so since the eighteenth and nineteenth centuries when philology and scientific racism supplemented religion as the primary othering discourse. Whereas modern Europe is produced by the industrial revolution and massive proletarianization in an important relation to colonial adventures, its identitarian ideology retrieves the Crusades as a differentiating moment that sets Jews and Muslims as other. Instrumental for this was not only the new system of knowledge that was grouped under the heading Orientalism but also that of philological and racial thinking that was grouped under the heading Semitism. Both Orientalism and Semitism were dependent on and productive of many of the assumptions of eighteenth- and nineteenth-century knowledge, including racialism, biologism, nationalism, and most of all Social Darwinism.

Yet, there is an increasing academic and political trend in the past few years that tells us that we must forget certain formative discourses in order to proceed with politics. Although some have suggested that

1. Sigmund Freud, *Leonardo da Vinci and a Memory of His Childhood* (1927), in *The Standard Edition of the Complete Psychological Works of Sigmund Freud* (London: Hogarth Press, 1953–74), 11:83–84.

we must forget feminism in order to have new forms of sexual politics,[2] others insist that we must forget Orientalism and Semitism and only remember *anti-Semitism* in order to abide by the new forms of international politics. In the case of feminism, the proposition famously and recently made by Janet Halley is that the feminist theoretical and political agenda be bracketed but remain accessible when considering other theories of sexuality to which a prescriptive feminism has been an obstacle. In the case of Orientalism, the claim is often made that Said's and the Saidean-derived analysis produce a politically correct straitjacket and/ or that Said got it all wrong and that his analysis needs to be thrown out in order for politics, or even cross-racial forms of sexual pleasure, to proceed, as a recent critic of *Desiring Arabs* put it.[3] Of course, there is a difference between feminism, which is both a movement and a theory, and "anti-Orientalism," which is a theoretical critique but not a movement. But for the bulk of the critics of Said's and Saidean analysis, this is immaterial. Many among them, who emerged with books attacking him, assail the central place he gave to Orientalism in understanding the production of Europe and its relationship to a produced Orient, and misread Said as a demonizer of Orientalists, whom Robert Irwin, for one, wants to show as benevolent seekers of knowledge. Other critics include Zionist apologists who insist that the only thing to be considered when assessing the Palestinian encounter with Zionist colonial settlement is not Orientalism or colonialism but rather, and exclusively, anti-Semitism.[4]

Another memory that has recently been emphasized is that of Abraham through the invocation of "Abrahamic religions," or the "Abrahamic," ostensibly as a stand in for the monotheistic. The Abrahamic is said to bring together Jews, Muslims, and Christians, as emerging from a similar tradition and addressing themselves to similar ends. Jacques Derrida deploys the term in his writings on religion in a most productive way. The Derridean Abrahamic, in contrast with the Semitic, purports to

2. See for example Janet Halley, *Split Decisions: How and Why to Take a Break from Feminism* (Princeton, NJ: Princeton University Press, 2008). On the critique of *Desiring Arabs*, see Amr Shalakany, "On a Certain Queer Discomfort with Orientalism," *Proceedings of the Annual Meeting (American Society of International Law)* 101 (28–31 March 2007): 125–29.

3. Joseph Massad, *Desiring Arabs* (Chicago: University of Chicago Press, 2007).

4. See Robert Irwin, *For Lust of Knowing: The Orientalists and Their Enemies* (London: Penguin Books, 2007). As for Zionists, see the post by Martin Kramer about the conference "Orientalism from the Standpoint of its Victims," held at Columbia University, on 7–8 November 2008. Kramer insists that anti-Semitism is the main reason for Palestinian suffering, something shared according to him from the "Mufti [al-Husayni] to [Joseph] Massad." Martin Kramer, "Muftis of Morningside Heights," 13 October 2008, posted on http://www.martinkramer.org/sandbox/2008/10/muftis-of-morningside-heights (accessed 12 February 2014).

eliminate the hierarchy not only among the Semites themselves, and between the Semites and the Aryans which Orientalism and Semitism consecrated, but also between all three groups in the name of an equalizing gesture. In its elision and forgetting of the Semitic, for Derrida the memory of the Abrahamic, as we will see later, is instrumental for this gesture owing to its emphasis on "religion" rather than race.

I will argue that engaging the politics of memory in the case of Semitism is crucial for our understanding of the lives of those whom Semitism has interpellated and interpellates as Semites to this day. This will bring us to the Jewish Question and to the Palestinian Question, or to the Palestinian Question *as* the Jewish Question. The Palestinian Question in the last thirty years has come to be seen in the West as an essential part of the Muslim Question, if not the very Question of Islam.[5] As both Palestinians and Jews inhabit the taxonomy "Semite," I want to discuss the way their question(s) constitutes the Semitic Question— indeed how the Semite became a Question, *for Europe.*

Semites and Orientals

But, what exactly is Semitism and what does it have to do with the Palestinians? We know much about *anti*-Semitism and how in popular European and American understanding it has much to do with Jews as victims of it. Increasingly the Euro-American and European depiction has it that Muslims, Arabs, and often Palestinians are perpetrators of it. But what is this Semitism that anti-Semitism is opposed to, that it wants to persecute, to oppress? Why have recent accounts—or memories?—of anti-Semitism forgotten the history of Semitism? Why do they often fail to remember the Semites in their historiography? Are Muslims, or specifically Palestinians as a metonym for them, in these memories opposed to Semitism, to the Semites, and if so, why would they oppose them? Are they in fact victims or perpetrators of Semitism, or of anti-Semitism? The crucial question that I want to pose is whether anti-Semitism is indeed the enemy of Semitism at all, or if their relationship is of a different order altogether.

When Edward Said embarked on his study of Orientalism, he explained that "by almost an inescapable logic, I have found myself writing the history of a strange, secret sharer of Western anti-Semitism. That

5. See Anne Norton, *On the Muslim Question* (Princeton, NJ: Princeton University Press, 2013).

anti-Semitism . . . and Orientalism resemble each other very closely is a historical, cultural, and political truth that needs only to be mentioned to an Arab Palestinian for its irony to be perfectly understood."[6] Here I must remind us that the time the Semite became a question was a time when many of the questions Europe had to consider from the late eighteenth century onwards had to do with the Orient; not least among them was the question of the Oriental Ottoman Empire whose presence in Europe and the necessity to evict it from Europe, as we saw in chapter 1, was coded the "Eastern Question." The almost contemporaneous emergence of the "Jewish Question" dealt with the presence of another people, also identified as "Orientals," who had been present for millennia in the heart of Europe. Said's invoking of anti-Semitism as the "secret sharer" of Orientalism, a term he borrows from Joseph Conrad,[7] is instructive. In his famous short story, Conrad identifies his "secret sharer" as a "second self," "my other self," a "double" or, as Said himself put it, as a "mirror."[8] The Oriental and the Semite, the Orientalist and the anti-Semite, Orientalism and anti-Semitism are therefore second selves to one another, doubles, and mirror reflections that must always be read and seen in tandem.

The category of the Semite was invented by European philologists in the eighteenth century and was transformed in the nineteenth from a linguistic into a racial category. Ernest Renan was perhaps one of the most illustrious Orientalists who helped bring about this transformation. For Renan, the "Semitic spirit" had two forms: "The Hebraic or Mosaic form, and the Arabic or Islamic form."[9] Indeed, according to such representations, as Said summarizes them, "The Semites are rabid monotheists who produced no mythology, no art, no commerce, no civilization; their consciousness is a narrow and rigid one; all in all they represent 'an inferior combination of human nature.'"[10] For Renan (1823–92), as for Semitic studies, or Semitics, as it was called, "'The Jew is like the Arab' and vice versa."[11] In this regard, the fact that medieval Christians, including the Crusaders, referred to Arabs as "Saracens," as

6. Edward W. Said, *Orientalism* (New York: Vantage, 1978), 27–28.

7. I thank Andrew Ruben for alerting me to this.

8. See Joseph Conrad, *The Secret Sharer*, in Conrad's *The Nigger of the "Narcissus" and Other Stories* (New York: Penguin Books, 2007), 171–214. See also Edward W. Said, *Conrad and the Fiction of Autobiography* (1966; New York: Columbia University Press, 2008), 127.

9. Quoted in Gil Anidjar, *Semites: Race, Religion, Literature* (Stanford, CA: Stanford University Press, 2008), 32.

10. Said, *Orientalism*, 142.

11. Quoted in Anidjar, *Semites*, 32.

in the descendants of Sarah, prefigures this modern identity between the two groups.[12]

The construction of the Semite was of course a ruse for the invention of the Indo-European, not only in philological terms but also specifically in racial terms, when the Indo-European becomes the Aryan. Semitism, therefore, is always relational to Europeanism as Aryanism. Hannah Arendt was clear on this in relation to Jews.

Whether the Jews are a religion or a nation, a people or a race, a state or a tribe, depends on the special opinion non-Jews—in whose midst Jews live—have about themselves, but it certainly has no connection whatever with any germinal knowledge about the Jews. As the people of Europe became nations, the Jews became "a nation within a nation"; as the Germans began to see in the state something more than their political representation, that is, as their fundamental "essence," the Jews became a state within a state . . . and since the end of the last century, when the Germans transformed themselves into Aryans, we have been wandering through world history as Semites.[13]

Arendt's astute understanding of the historicity of the category "Semites" is based on her insistent memory that at least, in her case, Jews existed before becoming Semites. Still, however, she does not question the accepted wisdom that anti-Semitism exists *in opposition* to the Semite. This is an important problematic we must elaborate in order to understand what is required of "our" memory in relation to the Semite. How are we to forget or remember this key Enlightenment and Romantic figure?

Indeed hegemonic ideas about the Semite would be elaborated further in the nineteenth century through the influence of Social Darwinian and evolutionist criteria. The Arab and the Jew were seen in these accounts as manifestations of evolutionary arrest. Said describes how Semiticists represented both groups:

In no people more than in the Oriental Semites was it possible to see the present and the origin together. The Jews and the Muslims, as subjects of Orientalist study, were readily understandable in view of their primitive origins: this was (and to a certain extent still is) the cornerstone of modern Orientalism. Renan had called the Semites an instance of arrested development and functionally speaking this came to mean that

---

12. My interest here is not in whether this is a necessarily correct etymology of "Saracens," but rather that many see it as such (see footnote 54). Another proposed etymology has it that "Saracens" derives from the Arabic word "Sharqiyyin" meaning "Easterners" or "Orientals."

13. Hannah Arendt, "Antisemitism," in *The Jewish Writings*, ed. Jerome Kohn and Ron H. Feldman (New York: Schocken Books, 2007), 69.

for the Orientalist, no modern Semite, however much he may have believed himself to be modern, could ever outdistance the organizing claims on him of his origins.[14]

This identity between Jews and Muslims was not only made by Europeans hostile to the two groups or even by those hostile to one of them, but also by people and thinkers who thought it an objective racial criterion to be traced back to a biblical and Qurʾanic genealogy. Orientalist Louis Massignon, who supported the Palestinian struggle against Zionism, would identify the colonial situation on the ground in 1960 with reference to Semitism: "I think that for the problem of the future of the Arabs, it must be found in Semitism. I think that at the base of the Arab difficulties there is this dramatic conflict, this fratricidal hatred between Israel and Ishmael. . . . The Arabs find themselves in collision with it in the claim of exclusivity among the Semites, the privileged Semites of the right. They, on the contrary, are the outlaws, the excluded."[15] The development of the Semitic idea was such that Jews and Arabs came to identify themselves as "Semites," thereby distancing themselves from their pre-Semitic existence. This would even be put to political use quickly. Indeed, Zionist intelligence, which set up front organizations in Palestine as early as the 1920s between Jews and Arabs under the guise of Arab-Jewish friendship (but which in fact operated as a cover for Palestinian collaborators with Zionism), termed one such organization "The Semitic Union."[16]

Semites and Anti-Semites

If the designation of people as Semites was precisely a ruse for the designation of their superior other as Aryan, Semitism then begins to look indistinguishable from anti-Semitism. The act of inventing the Semite is the very act of inventing the carrier of that identity as other. It is indeed the act of creating the anti-Semite. In this light, *Semitism has always been anti-Semitism*. The ruse of anti-Semitism is in having us believe that there was a historical gap, a conceptual chronology of sorts, wherein there existed a Semite before Semitism, and that there was Semitism before

14. Said, *Orientalism*, 234.
15. Louis Massignon, 1960, cited in Anouar Abdel-Malek, "Orientalism in Crisis," in A. L. Macfir, *Orientalism: A Reader* (New York: New York University Press, 2001), 51. See Said on Massignon and Berque in *Orientalism*, 270.
16. See Hillel Cohen, *Army of Shadows: Palestinian Collaboration with Zionism, 1917–1948* (Berkeley: University of California Press, 2008), 25.

anti-Semitism. What I am proposing here is that this historicization is itself an *effect* of the very discourse of Semitism. This is indeed what Arendt had missed in her historiography of anti-Semitism.

Let us consider how Semitism relates to the Jews as an entry point to understanding how Palestinians would figure in this history. In the light of Semitics and based on its taxonomies, anti-Jewish sentiment clustered in the nineteenth century in a full-fledged othering ideological edifice that called itself anti-Semitism. In contrast to Semitism, which was invented by a certain class of intellectuals, who were scholars and philologists, anti-Semitism was invented by intellectuals in the political and journalistic professions. The term was coined in 1879 by a minor Viennese journalist by the name of Wilhelm Marr and would first appear as a political program titled *The Victory of Judaism over Germanism*. Marr was careful to decouple anti-Semitism from the history of Christian hatred of Jews on the basis of religion, emphasizing in line with Semitics and racial theories current at the time that the distinction to be made between Jews and Aryans was strictly racial.[17]

In the European world and its American extension where racial theories became the arbiter of rights and privileges by the second half of the nineteenth century, many Jews embraced the Semitic origin story "as a way of establishing the positive impact of their group on world history." In the United States, Jewish philanthropists would endow Semitics departments at universities to "insure proper recognition."[18] According to the historian Eric Goldstein, "during the nineteenth century the claim of 'Semitic' origin had become something of a badge of honor for American Jews, allowing them to trace their heritage back to the dawn of civilization and take credit for laying the ethical foundations of Western Society."[19] Remembering the Semitic origin, therefore, was part of the process of forgetting the active operation of inventing this origin by philologists.

This however would change considerably in the twentieth century, especially after scientists began to attribute an African origin to the Semites. While this theory was first proposed in 1890 in the United States by the archaeologist and language specialist Daniel Brinton, within a decade it became so orthodox that when race scientist William Z. Ripley published *The Races of Europe* in 1899, he adopted it and "helped spread

17. See Bernard Lewis, *Semites and anti-Semites: An Inquiry into Conflict and Prejudice* (New York: W. W. Norton, 1986), 94.

18. Eric Goldstein, *The Price of Whiteness: Jews, Race, and American Identity* (Princeton, NJ: Princeton University Press, 2006), 20.

19. Ibid., 108.

it to a large audience."[20] The connection of modern Jews to the ancient Hebrews (insistently made by Catholic Christianity and more so the Protestant Reformation) remained part of an unresolved academic debate at the time, but the question of the origin of the Semites seemed to have been resolved. Indeed, with the increasing identification of Semites with Africa, some Jews seeking full assimilation into whiteness began to retreat from the claim, forgetting it altogether in favor of another memory. Martin A. Meyer, a Reform rabbi in San Francisco and a scholar of Semitic studies, felt it necessary in 1909 to declare that American Jews shared more with non-Jewish white Americans than they did with "the Arab of the desert, the true representative of the Semitic world of yore," or even with the Jews of the Middle East.[21] Meyer claimed that although the ancient Jews who came out of the desert were Semites like the Arabs, their blood was "rapidly diluted." He concluded that "today, but little of that original Semitic blood will be found in the veins of any of us."[22] Another Reform rabbi, Samuel Sale, added that "we can not get away from the bald fact, based on anatomical measurements, that only about five percent of all the Jews bear the characteristic mark of their Semitic origin on their body."[23] Here the act of disavowal is not only a psychic one but decidedly physiological, when bodies are said to forget their origins except for a few remaining traces.

Another strategy to disavow the African origin hypothesis was to continue to embrace the Semitic identity but to argue that Semites were in fact white, having originated in the Caucasus and not in Africa, as some Jewish anthropologists and some Zionists argued.[24] The predominant Zionist explanation, however, for the condition of Jews in Europe would differ from that in the United States, insofar as the European Zionists (unlike their US counterparts, who rejected anti-Semitic descriptions of Jews as prejudiced mischaracterizations) accepted (anti-)Semitic descriptions of Jews, which, however, unlike the anti-Semites, they explained by recourse to the Jewish history of persecution that they claimed caused these traits, and not necessarily to innate racial characteristics.

Zionism was predicated on the double operation of remembering and forgetting: for Zionism stipulated on the one hand that modern Jews must remember their peoplehood, that the Hebrews were their ancestors, and that Hebrew culture had always been their heritage which

20. Ibid., 108.
21. Cited in ibid., 109.
22. Ibid.
23. Cited in ibid.
24. See ibid., 111, 179.

they could now access through the European Enlightenment, and that Palestine was their ancient homeland to which they must return, while on the other hand it insisted that modern Jews must forget their European Jewish identities and cultures as the historical predecessors of their current identity and that they forget that Palestine had continued to have a living non-Jewish and non-Hebrew population to the present. Although Zionism espoused the goals of the maskilim and other Jewish assimilationists in its understanding that the mark of Jewish otherness had to be removed, it differed from both in affirming that Jews could become Europeans only in Asia. It is in adopting nationalism as the solution—or, more precisely *dissolution*—of the Jewish Question that Zionism assimilated the most important form of political life unleashed by the French Revolution. If Semitism and anti-Semitism insisted that the Jews were not Aryan or European, that they were a separate race and a separate nation, Zionism could not agree more. Its transformative project would also include the Palestinians whom it sought to transform into Jews in a displaced geography of anti-Semitism.[25] This move would also guarantee that the figure of the Semite, as always already a negative value, would be preserved but would be identified solely with and displaced onto the Arab.

Here, Arendt, who grasped better than most the structural position of Jews in European Christian societies, would still muddle the position of Palestinians and Jews in relation to European Christians more generally. Her insistence on the national principle in defining Jews as a people dominated much of her discussions.[26] She states that

since the days when Polish nobles invited Jews into their country to act as tax collectors, buffering them from the peasants they hoped to suck dry, there has never been such an ideal coordination of interests, such ideal cooperation. In those days, Jews arrived rejoicing in the convergence of so many interests and unaware of their future role. They knew no more about Polish farmers than Zionist officials did about Arabs prior to the Balfour Declaration. In those days the Jews of Central Europe were fleeing from the pogroms of the late Middle Ages to an Eastern paradise of converging interests, and we are still fleeing the consequences of that today.[27]

25. I elaborate on this process in Joseph Massad, "The Persistence of the Palestinian Question," *Cultural Critique*, no. 59 (Winter 2005): 1–23.

26. On Arendt's complex relationship with Zionism, see Richard J. Bernstein, "Hannah Arendt's Zionism?," in *Hannah Arendt in Jerusalem*, ed. Steven E. Aschheim (Berkeley: University of California Press, 2001), 194–202.

27. Hannah Arendt, "Antisemitism," in Arendt, *The Jewish Writings*, 58–59.

Arendt's placing Palestinians in the same structural position as Polish peasants is both instructive and mishandled: her description of "Jews" as tax collectors betrays her nationalist historiographical perspective just as her allegation of the ignorance of Zionist officials of the Palestinian Arabs betrays an ignorance of Zionist history. The major conceptual limitation in Arendt's writings on Jews and Zionism, however, is her persistent belief that Zionism and assimilationism are opposed rather than complementary. Despite her incisive criticisms of Zionist practices, her major failure was one of insisting on remembering the Hebrews as the ancestors of the Jews and of reifying European Jews as a people trans-historically. That Zionism sought to normalize Jews was a project that Arendt zealously supported; she would even invoke Kafka's *The Castle* to bolster her argument.[28] Her enthusiasm for Zionism's quintessential racially separatist institution, the kibbutz (what Domenico Losurdo refers to, citing an earlier anti-Zionist Arendt, as "master race socialism"),[29] was on account of the kibbutz acting as a transformative institution of Jews from Semites with a negative value into normalized Europeans with a positive one. She celebrates this as Zionism's "greatest achievement," namely its "creation of a new type of man and a new social elite, the birth of a new aristocracy which differed greatly from the Jewish masses in and outside of Palestine in its habits, manners, values, and way of life, and whose claim to leadership in moral and social questions was clearly recognized by the [Jewish] population [in Palestine]."[30] That Zionism transformed the Jew into what the Israeli psychologist Benyamin Beit-Hallahmi called the "anti-Jew," and the Palestinian into the Jew did not deter Arendt from supporting this central Zionist idea.

But how was this transformation of Palestinians effected? It is at the juncture of Semitism that Edward Said locates his intervention. He asserts that "what has not been sufficiently stressed in histories of modern anti-Semitism has been the legitimation of such atavistic designations by Orientalism, and . . . the way this academic and intellectual legitimation has persisted right through the modern age in discussions of Islam, the Arabs, or the Near Orient."[31]

In his book *Semites and anti-Semites*, Bernard Lewis states that "the argument is sometimes put forward that the Arabs cannot be anti-Semitic because they themselves are Semites. Such a statement is self-evidently

---

28. Arendt, "The Jew as Pariah," in Arendt, *The Jewish Writings*, 291–95.

29. Domenico Losurdo, *Liberalism: A Counter-History*, trans. Gregory Elliott (London: Verso, 2011), 180.

30. Arendt, "Peace of Armistice in the Near East?" in Arendt, *The Jewish Writings*, 443.

31. Said, *Orientalism*, 262.

absurd, and the argument that supports it doubly-flawed. First the term 'Semite' has no meaning as applied to groups as heterogeneous as the Arabs or the Jews, and indeed it could be argued that the use of such terms is in itself a sign of racism and certainly either of ignorance or bad faith." I am in full agreement with Lewis and I add that something similar can be said about the Jews. Indeed to echo Lewis, the argument that is sometimes made that the Jews cannot be anti-Semitic because they themselves are Semites is refuted on the same grounds of the meaninglessness of the term Semite when applied to a heterogeneous group like the Jews, as Lewis himself argues.

Lewis, however, adds a qualifier to make the use I have just made of his argument untenable. He maintains that the second reason the argument is flawed is that "anti-Semitism has never anywhere been concerned with anyone but Jews, and is therefore available to Arabs as to other people as an option should they choose it."[32] But, as histories of Zionism have revealed, anti-Semitism has always been made available to those Jews who seek to other themselves and assimilate into European Protestant Christian normativity by repudiating the Semite within, namely, their perceived Jewishness—and the Semite without, namely the Arab Oriental as elaborated by Orientalism. Here, let me recall the function of Freud's mirror. If assimilationist anti-Semitism is the mirror being held up by Zionism before European gentiles, it is merely, as Freud insists, "to encourage and inspire them" to see themselves reflected in the figure of the assimilated nationalist (anti-)Jew. As such, anti-Semitism is also available to the Jews as it is available to the Arabs should they choose to use it.

Freud's own views of the Semites were discordant with his intellectual milieu. As Said notes,

Freud had his own ideas about European outsiders, most notably Moses and Hannibal. Both were Semites, of course, and both (especially Hannibal) were heroes for Freud because of their audacity, persistence and courage. Reading *Moses and Monotheism*, one is struck by Freud's almost casual assumption (which also applies to Hannibal) that Semites were most certainly not European . . . and, at the same time, were somehow assimilable to its culture as former outsiders. This is quite different from theories about Semites propounded by Orientalists like Renan.[33]

32. Bernard Lewis, *Semites and anti-Semites*, 117.
33. Edward W. Said, *Freud and the Non-European* (London: Verso, 2003), 16–17.

Late in his life, Freud, as we saw in the last chapter, went as far as attempting to rescue modern Jews from Semitism. He insisted that European Jews were not "Asiatics of a foreign race, as their enemies maintain, but composed for the most part of remnants of the Mediterranean peoples and heirs of the Mediterranean civilization."[34]

In the first half of the twentieth century, anti-Semitism would continue to focus on the figure of the Jew while its double, colonial Orientalism, would focus on the Arab and the Muslim, often conflated as one, as the Semite of choice. In the wake of the Nazi holocaust and the end of colonialism, both would retreat but only temporarily. Soon anti-Semitism and Orientalism would reemerge with one main racialized Semitic object, the Arab and the Muslim, both seen as one in this racialist economy. This transformative moment in Europe and America, which was consolidated during and after the 1967 war, would gain momentum quickly, so much so that in the wake of the 1973 war and the oil embargo, Arabs, as Said observed, came to be represented in the West as having "clearly 'Semitic' features: sharply hooked noses, the evil mustachioed leer on their faces, were obvious reminders (to a largely non-Semitic population) that 'Semites' were at the bottom of all 'our' troubles, which in this case is principally a gasoline shortage. The transference of popular anti-Semitic animus from a Jewish to an Arab target was made smoothly, since the figure was essentially the same."[35] Here, Said deploys the history of anti-Semitism to illustrate his findings about the history of the Arab, and specifically the Palestinian. To clarify what he means, Said states that in depicting the Arab as a "negative value" and as "a disrupter of Israel's and the West's existence . . . as a surmountable obstacle to Israel's creation in 1948," what Orientalist and anti-Semitic representations produce is a certain conception of the Arab that is ontologically linked to the Jew: "The Arab is conceived of now as a shadow that dogs the Jew. In that shadow—because Arabs and Jews are Oriental Semites—can be placed whatever traditional, latent mistrust a Westerner feels towards the Oriental. For the Jew of pre-Nazi Europe has bifurcated: What we have now is a Jewish hero, constructed out of a reconstructed cult of the adventurer-pioneer-Orientalist . . . , and his creeping, mysteriously fearsome shadow, the Arab Oriental."[36]

34. Sigmund Freud, *Moses and Monotheism*, in *The Standard Edition of the Complete Psychological Works of Sigmund Freud* (London: Hogarth Press, 1953–74), 23:90.
35. Said, *Orientalism*, 286.
36. Ibid.

Said's analysis urges us not to remember or forget Orientalism, the Muslim, the Arab, and ultimately the Palestinian without remembering the forgetting of European Jewish history and the history of European anti-Semitism in the context of European colonialism, which made and makes all these historical transformations possible and mobilizes the very discourses that produce them as facts. Increasingly, especially following the events of September 11 and the rise of "Islamophobia," this readily available archive of representing Arabs and Palestinians as the quintessential Muslims would be expanded to encompass Muslims worldwide.

The Abrahamic and the Semitic

Freud, perhaps, had the most original hypothesis on the relation between the origins of monotheism's God and the Semites. If the chronological story has it that the Arabs, through Islam, recapitulated the Jewish and Christian God as their own, Freud posits that the Jewish God was in fact not only an extrapolation of the Egyptian Aton but also of the god Jahwe whom the Jewish tribes "took over . . . probably from the neighbouring Arabian tribe of Midianites," in the country "south of Palestine, between the eastern exit from the Sinai Peninsula and the western border of Arabia."[37] This also seems to apply to Moses, whom Freud identifies not only as Egyptian but, as there was another Moses, also as an Arab Midianite—who together with the Egyptian Moses, constituted what would become the biblical prophet.[38] Either way it seems the Semites, their prophets, and their gods/God were connected since time immemorial.

But if the Semitic Question brings together Jews, Arabs, and increasingly Muslims (the majority of whom would not be considered Semites at all by eighteenth- and nineteenth-century European philology and racialism) hierarchically in relation to Aryanism, Semitic monotheism, bringing together Jews, Christians, and Muslims, began to be coded recently as part of the neologism "Abrahamic religions." Although the contemporaneous "Judeo-Christian," emphasized around and especially after World War II, sought to exclude Muslims from the new alliance,

37. Freud, *Moses and Monotheism*, 33.
38. Ibid., 35. On Freud's intellectual precursors on the question of Moses and monotheism, see Jan Assmann, *Moses the Egyptian: The Memory of Egypt in Western Monotheism* (Cambridge, MA: Harvard University Press, 1997).

the contemporaneous but less hegemonic "Abrahamic" sought their inclusion.

Let us remember that Shem, which means "name" and from which the term Semite is derived, is the biblical son of Noah, and that Abraham is a direct descendant of Shem through his son Arpachshad. Shem and Abraham are biblical figures that have been ambivalently secularized by the Enlightenment tradition. It might have been Gotthold Ephraim Lessing who in 1779 in *Nathan the Wise* started a Christian (or should I call it "Enlightened" or even "liberal"?) trend that he did not name, of insisting on the commonality of monotheisms, but it was left to the Orientalist Massignon to christen it "les trois cultes Abrahamiques" in his 1949 essay "Three Prayers of Abraham."[39] If the Semites and Aryans were grouped as radically other synchronically in racial theories, the Abrahamic was going to link them genealogically as one and the same, or, at least, so hoped Lessing.

In contrast to Semitism which revolved around language and race as an ontological effect, the Abrahamic would link what was separate under the sign of monotheism as *religion*, literally as that which links, or what Orientalist H.A.R. Gibb, in reference to Massignon's efforts, referred to as "the community of Abrahamanic origins."[40] Massignon's interest was to remind Christians to claim an Abrahamic heritage that they had forgotten. He invokes Abraham as the common ancestor for the sake of erasing difference and asserting, if not identity, then at least commonality:

At that moment when the terror which conceals from us the approach of our final end makes us turn inwards, to return to our origins, when the toxic malice of our disagreements forces us to seek out once again our common ancestors, it is wise to take up once again the links in the spiritual chain of pure witnesses upon which we depend . . . and which leads us back to Abraham, all the more boldly the more desperate our situation.[41]

Massignon affirms that "Abraham continues to be invoked as their father, by twelve million circumcised Jews, who aspire to take possession for themselves alone of that Holy Land which was long ago promised

---

39. Louis Massignon, "Trois prières d'Abraham, père de tous les croyants," in *Parole Donnée* (Paris: Julliard, 1962), 261. See Jacques Derrida, "Hostipitality," in *Jacques Derrida: Acts of Religion*, ed. Gil Anidjar (New York: Routledge, 2002), 369.

40. Said, *Orientalism*, 265.

41. Massignon, "Three Prayers of Abraham," in *Testimonies and Reflections: Essays of Louis Massignon*, selected and introduced by Herbert Mason (Notre Dame, IN: University of Notre Dame Press, 1989), 6.

to him, and by four hundred million Muslims who trust patiently in his God through the practice of their five daily prayers, their betrothals, their funerals, and their pilgrimage. The Jews have no more than a hope, but it is Abrahamic. The Muslims have no more than a faith, but it is Abraham's faith in the justice of God (beyond all human illusions)."[42]

The role of the uncircumcised Christians, that is, those who have not kept the covenant with Abraham's God, as Jews, Muslims, and "Eastern" Christians had done, is a historic one, namely, that of love, which they can impart to their brothers in Abraham (let us remember here one of Freud's explanations for anti-Semitism, namely, that it results from the horror felt by Christian boys when they hear of the circumcision of Jewish boys, which they interpret as castration, and which explains the contempt they feel for Jewish men).[43] The context of Massignon's call for a Christian pedagogy of love that could have prevented, but due to its absence failed to prevent, hatred between the Jews and the Muslims, was the "horrible war" of 1948. However, this Christian historic role remains necessary because of geography. Massignon maintains:

Like history, the geography of today brings us closer to Abraham by focusing our attention on the high place of humanity which began with his own. . . . Here is the physical return of the two inimical brothers to the chosen places of their resurrection (the al-Aqsa Mosque for the Muslims, the Temple for the Jews, only 150 meters apart on the same *Haram*); and only 350 meters from the Anastasis or *Qiyama* (the Holy Sepulcher) of the Christians, who, because they have not developed sufficient consciousness of their 'Abrahamic adoption' are not yet concerned about returning to Jerusalem to await the Parousia of the Lord. Nevertheless, there in Jerusalem the Christians have Arab witnesses of their faith and the geographical convergence of the pilgrims of the three Abrahamic faiths in one and the same Holy Land, trying to find there that justice which Abraham through his threefold trial found in his God, led a year ago to a horrible war. Why? Because the Christians have not yet fulfilled their complete responsibility towards their brothers in Abraham. Because they have not yet explained to them how to love the Holy Land which is one of the two terms of the promise to Abraham.[44]

Note here that Massignon portrays everyone as external to Jerusalem and that everyone wants to return to it. Palestinian Jerusalemites,

42. Ibid., 7.
43. Sigmund Freud, "Analysis of a Phobia in a Five-Year-Old Boy," in *The Standard Edition*, 10:36n. Freud repeats this hypothesis in *Moses and Monotheism*, 90.
44. Ibid., 8.

Muslims and Christians alike, are presented as foreign to their native city, as much outsiders as the colonizing (European) Jews.

More recently, the notion of "Abrahamic religions" has been posited as having a prior Islamicness. Jonathan Z. Smith argued that it was "adopt[ed] . . . from Muslim discourse," a contention that would be adopted in turn by those who have more recently sought to theorize the Abrahamic as that which *links* and *delinks* Jews, Christians, and Muslims.[45] In his introduction to Derrida's work on religion, Gil Anidjar relies on Smith's claim that "the notion of the Abrahamic, like the notion of 'The People of the Book,' is of Islamic origin. It is an ancient notion which, as Derrida notes, was on occasion revived in Europe (Kierkegaard, of course), perhaps most recently by the important Islamicist Louis Massignon."[46] Massignon, to my knowledge, spoke only of "Abrahamic faiths" or "worship," "cultes" not religions, even though Derrida, in a discussion of Massignon's work, renders the latter's use of "cultes" as "religions."[47] This is a strange rendering given Derrida's knowledge of and engagement with the history of the concept "religion." The French *culte*, like the English cult, is derived from the Latin *cultus*, and *colere*, as in to cultivate, the very same root of the term culture. But the Qurʾan (or "Islam" as it is posited metonymically to refer to the "Qurʾan") makes no mention of "Abrahamic" faiths or religions, or "Abrahamanic religions," as Edward Said used the term in *Orientalism*,[48] at all, and the Qurʾan's invoking of "millat Ibrahim," where *milla* refers to the "traditions," "ways," and "path" of Abraham (there is no "*din Ibrahim*" in the Qurʾan),[49] to encompass all the prophets from Abraham to Moses to Jesus and Muhammad, which is often invoked as evidence of the notion of "Abrahamic *religions*," was not necessarily or at all a gesture toward the inclusion of Christianity and Judaism qua *religions* (even though the Qurʾanic text was always inclusive of the traditions and prophets of Judaism and Christianity whose extant scriptures it considered distorted versions of the same word of God), but rather to assert an originary Islam which Abraham, Moses, and Jesus preached and

45. See Jonathan Z. Smith, "Religion, Religions, Religious," in Mark C. Taylor, *Critical Terms for Religious Studies* (Chicago: University of Chicago Press, 1998), 276.
46. Gil Anidjar, "Introduction: 'Once More, Once More': Derrida, the Arab, the Jew," in *Jacques Derrida:, Acts of Religion*, 3.
47. Jacques Derrida, "Hostipitality," 369.
48. Said, *Orientalism*, 268.
49. Indeed the Qurʾan is explicit on this in *The Holy Qurʾan*, Sura 6:161, "Say, my Lord has guided me to the straight path, to an upright *din*, in the ways of [*millat*] Abraham, the Hanif, and he associated no one with God." According to the Qurʾan, the word *hanif* refers to the earliest form of monotheistic worship, which the Qurʾan recognizes by the name "Islam."

to which they belonged and from which Jews and Christians had deviated (the Qur'an announces that "Abraham was neither Jew nor Christian but was a Hanif, a Muslim, and he did not associate anyone with God").[50] In fact, the Qur'an never uses the word *din* in the plural at all, restricting it to the singular throughout. For "*indeed, din, for God, is Islam,*"[51] which is not to mean that for nonbelievers (that is polytheists and idol worshippers who are not Christians or Jews) in God, there is not another *din*. Indeed there is, as the Qur'an declares to the unbelievers: "For you have your *din* and I have mine."[52] While the Qur'an sublates Judaism's and Christianity's scriptures, it does not call upon Muslims to sublate Jews and Christians, but rather to *include* them as "people of the book."

Whether to cultivate or to link, as the etymology of *cult* and *religion* reveal respectively, "Islam" has no notion of Abrahamic "cultivation" or "linking" in its scriptural or theological history, but more importantly maintains in its very identification in the Qur'an and in its etymology the notion of judgment, accounting, and a continuing debt as *din/dayn* and one of "deliverance to God" as *Islam* (often Orientalistically translated, as we saw in the last chapter, as "surrender" or "submission" rather than as "deliverance"). The predominant understanding in Islamic theology, as far as the God of Muslims and (the Qur'anic) Abraham are concerned, is that there cannot exist but one *din*, that which delivers humans to God. This is not to say that Abraham is not important in the Qur'an or in Islamic theological traditions and prophetic literature; on the contrary, a huge importance attaches to him in them. The point is simply that neither the notion of "religion" (let alone "religions") nor "din" is attributed or attributable to Abraham, even while he is recognized as the first prophet to worship the one God by heeding His call.[53]

So what then of the Abrahamic? Why is the Abrahamic, or at least "Abrahamic religions," which, it turns out, have an Orientalist and *not*

---

50. *The Holy Qur'an*, Sura 3:67.

51. *The Holy Qur'an*, Sura 3:19. To bolster his claim that "Abrahamic *religions*" (in the plural, no less) has an "Islamic," rather than an Orientalist, provenance, and that the words *milla* and *din* have the very same meaning and significance in Arabic, which he (mis)translates into English as "religion," Anidjar cites the authority of a short inconclusive study by Gerald Hawting, a Bernard Lewis-trained British Orientalist scholar (and Guy Stroumsa, an Israeli scholar of Judaism from Hebrew University). See Gil Anidjar, "Yet Another Abraham," paper presented at Columbia University, Middle Eastern, South Asian, and African Studies Departmental colloquium, Fall 2011, 8 December 2011, 3n.

52. *The Holy Qur'an*, Sura 109: 6.

53. For an informative study of the place of Abraham in Islamic theological literature, see Tuhami al-ʿAbduli, *Al-Nabiyy Ibrahim fi al-Thaqafah al-ʿArabiyyah al-Islamiyyah* (The Prophet Abraham in Islamic Arab Culture) (Damascus: Dar al-Mada lil-Thaqafah wa al-Nashr, 2001).

an Islamic provenance, projected onto "Islam"?[54] I argue that the notion of "Abrahamic religions" is one more ruse of an untenable inclusivity that consolidates and maintains the exclusion of the Semite, while at the same time huddling Muslims in their entirety, and not only the Arabs amongst them, under the sign of the Semitic. It is certainly not a case of "where religion has emerged, race has all but disappeared."[55] On the contrary, Massignon, expectedly links the Abrahamic and the Semitic *a priori*:

The discoveries of Semitic archeology are bringing us closer and closer to a continuity in the steps which 'external' history had to traverse in order to overtake the Abrahamic milieu and emphasize more and more the exceptional character and monolithic permanence of the two circumcised groups, the Jews and the Arabs, in the face of the Christian apostolate.[56]

In analyzing the notion of the Abrahamic, Anidjar tells us that

this ancient notion . . . has been considered either the original and gathering root of the three major monotheistic faiths or, more pervasively, as the (three) branches of one single faith. It suggests the reclaiming of territorialized roots, the reoccupation and gathering of a site of welcoming togetherness, where old fallen branches can come back to life. . . . This return may promise, minimally, the resurrected togetherness and enabling of "religion," but it also institutes the possibility of comparison under the allegedly unified figure of Abraham, whose name appears in the three scriptural traditions. The modern discourse of comparative religion, which rendered the incommensurable comparable, could hardly have emerged independently of Jewish, Christian, and Muslim medieval disputations that stage the one/three faith(s) in different and complex ways. However, the Abrahamic is not simply a figure that can be subsumed as one theme among many. The Abrahamic is the very condition of "religion."[57]

This conditionality, for Anidjar, is on account of the Abrahamic's separating and linking the theologico-political simultaneously. Indeed Anidjar adds that the Abrahamic, for Derrida, "dissociates and breaks the

54. This is not unlike how the European Christian appellation "Saracens," which refers to Arabs, was projected onto the Arabs themselves who are said to have made the claim of descent from Sarah. Indeed, "St. Jerome (Ezek. VIII.xxv) identifies the Saracens with the *Agareni* (Hagarens, descendants of Hagar) 'who are now called Saracens, taking to themselves the name of Sara'" (OED, *s.v.* "Saracen").

55. Anidjar, *Semites*, 21.

56. Massignon, "Three Prayers," 7.

57. Anidjar, "Introduction," in *Jacques Derrida: Acts of Religion*, 3.

dividing movement around which 'Europe'—and religion—constitutes itself."[58]

Regardless of whether it has an Islamic or an Orientalist origin, the terms Abrahamic and Abrahamic religions would also carry much currency outside academic theory, and in the heart of international relations. Jimmy Carter, one of those enamored of the brotherhood of the children of Abraham, as he refers to Jews and Muslims, understands Abrahamic descent in racial terms, and along the lines of Massignon, he believes that Christians can access Abraham through faith. He explains this in a 2006 interview in the light of attacks on him as an anti-Semite based on his critical views of Israeli policies:

I've always looked upon Israel as a people that was blessed by God through his covenant by Abraham. I taught this last Sunday as a matter of fact. I reminded people that Abraham's first child from [Hagar] was a founder of the Arab nations in general. His second child obviously, by his wife Sarah was a founder of the Jewish people and then after the early Christian church was founded Saint Paul explained that those blessings from God for his children were based not on their race but on their faith. Since Christians believe, have faith, in God, to have faith in Jesus Christ, then we are also children of Abraham. So Christians, Muslims and Jews all are children of Abraham, and I think that's one of the factors that many people outside this country don't understand.[59]

The notion of the children of Abraham, however, was not a reactive notion used by Carter to fend off the anti-Semitic label. It was something central to his policies from the 1970s, when the same forces that now accused him of anti-Semitism considered him to be a philo-Semite. When he spoke in 1979 at the signing of the Camp David Accords between Anwar Sadat and Menachem Begin, President Carter declared in the name of the United States: "Let us now lay aside war. Let us now reward all the children of Abraham who hunger for a comprehensive peace in the Middle East. Let us now enjoy the adventure of becoming fully human, fully neighbors, even brothers and sisters."[60] Indeed since the early 1980s, a large number of books about an inclusive notion of the children of Abraham has been published in English, most likely to

58. Ibid., 7.
59. Riz Khan, "An Interview with Jimmy Carter," transcript of 12 December 2006 interview on Al-Jazeera, *Counterpunch*, 14 December 2006, http://www.counterpunch.org/khan12142006.html (accessed 14 February 2014).
60. "Remarks by President Jimmy Carter at the Signing of the Peace Treaty between Egypt and Israel," 26 March 1979, http://www.historyplace.com/specials/calendar/docs-pix/mar-carter-cdavid .htm (accessed 14 February 2014).

bring about this fuller humanity that Carter insisted on. Although I am sympathetic to Carter's, Derrida's, and Massignon's projects of seeking to eliminate oppression, or what they might call "conflict" or "violence," I am troubled by what their positing of the Abrahamic as the filiative and affiliative link between the three monotheistic communities must forget to bring that about, namely how the deployment of the Abrahamic is linked to the Semitic, to the Semite.

Perhaps a return to Massignon is in order. Massignon's neologism might have been an outcome of his Catholic faith, which defined much of his life, or an outcome of some other Orientalist passion, or a combination of both. In his discussion of Massignon's notion of the Abrahamic, which he couples with a discussion of Emmanuel Levinas's work, Derrida expresses a need "to answer a concern that you might share with me, I imagine, regarding the ellipsis, if not the exclusion, in any case the active silence with which [Massignon's project of Badalya, which included Arab Christians] suppresses, walls in, chokes all fraternity with those who have, after all some right to figure in an Abrahamic prayer front—to wit, the Jews."[61] Although, on the one hand, Derrida wants to reference Massignon's concern for the Palestinian refugees of the 1948 war (a concern that Derrida himself does not seem to share) by quoting his journal entry from 1949 (while claiming mistakenly that "the three prayers" were written in 1923), at the same time, he wants to remind his readers of clues to Massignon's position on Jews. Derrida concludes that Massignon's bourgeois French Catholicism "to which one could add other characteristics, leaves us with the feeling of some probability of anti-Semitism."[62] Here Derrida wants to insist that the Abrahamic must be inclusive by demonstrating how for Massignon, it, on occasion, slips into an exclusive realm, one that excludes the Jews.

Although Massignon's motive in conjuring up the Abrahamic was one of self-declared Christian love for the rest of the children of Abraham that was punctuated by racialist criteria, Levinas's views on Palestinians were also troubling. But Derrida does not seem to pay similar attention to Levinas's anti-Palestinian ethics, which exclude Palestinians (as Muslims) from the Abrahamic, as he did to Massignon's probable anti-Semitism, though he is careful to remind us that "Levinas declares nothing but the greatest respect for Islam."[63]

61. Derrida, "Hostipitality," 418.
62. Ibid.
63. Ibid., 367.

Levinas's views on Zionism are important in this regard, as he represents Zionism as a movement geared toward an ethical politics, or what he terms "monotheistic politics."[64] Asked by Shlomo Malka in a radio broadcast following the Sabra and Shatila massacres of 1982, "Isn't history, isn't politics the very site of the encounter with the 'other,' and for the Israeli, isn't the 'other' above all the Palestinian?" Levinas replied:

> My definition of the other is completely different. The other is the neighbor, who is not necessarily kin, but who can be. And in that sense, if you're for the other, you're for the neighbor. But if your neighbor attacks another neighbor or treats him unjustly, what can you do? Then alterity takes on another character, in alterity we find an enemy, or at least then we are faced with the problem of knowing who is right and who is wrong, who is just and who is unjust. There are people who are wrong.[65]

This subtle exclusion of the Palestinians as Muslims from the Abrahamic through an endorsement of Israeli terror in support of a Maronite Christian neighbor against the Palestinians was justified by Levinas on ethical grounds, even though Said, in a generous move, believed that Levinas's stance, like that of Martin Buber's before him, simply lacked "ethical dimensions."[66] Derrida also did not seem to want to say much, if at all, about the massacres at Sabra and Shatila, although Anidjar, in an astute reading of Derrida's silence, wants to force him to say what he must but cannot (or refuses to) say.[67]

But, I pose the question once again: what kind of labor does the Abrahamic perform in relation to the Semitic? Before I can offer a possible answer, let me recall what Said said about the Semite. Understanding that Zionist ideology emerged as a particular brand of Orientalism and therefore of (anti-)Semitism in the context of Europe's colonial project, Said maintained that "by a concatenation of events and circumstances the Semitic myth bifurcated in the Zionist movement; one Semite went the way of Orientalism, the other, the Arab, was forced to go the way

---

64. Emmanuel Levinas, "The State of Caesar and the State of David," in *Beyond the Verse: Talmudic Readings and Lectures*, trans. Gary D. Mole (London: Athlone Press, 1982).

65. Leora Batnitzky, *Leo Strauss and Emmanuel Levinas: Philosophy and the Politics of Revelation*, (Cambridge: Cambridge University Press, 2002), 153.

66. Edward W. Said, *The End of the Peace Process: Oslo and After* (New York: Pantheon, 2000), 208. I should note here that three years later and while recalling a conversation with Levinas that had taken place at a conference in 1965, Derrida expressed a passing concern that Levinas had identified himself as a Catholic and André Neher as a Protestant, absenting the "Islamo-Abrahamic." See Jacques Derrida, "Avowing the Impossible," in Elisabeth Weber, *Living Together: Jacques Derrida's Communities of Violence and Peace* (New York: Fordham University Press, 2013), 21.

67. See Anidjar, "Introduction," in *Jacques Derrida: Acts of Religion*, 25–26.

of the Oriental."[68] The journey that the Semite has traveled from its eighteenth-century philological origins was one of setting the Arab and the Jew apart from the Aryan until Zionism split the Semite into two kinds in the twentieth century, setting one in alliance with, and the other in opposition to, the Aryan.

For those who have realized the untenability of the Jewish position through Zionism as the Semite who went the way of Orientalism, deploying the notion of the Abrahamic is ambivalently useful in leveling the field between the two Semites. Anidjar is more nuanced about this in relation to Derrida than Derrida himself seems to be. Anidjar concludes:

This trait of the primal father (Abraham) that splits his offsprings, disseminates his sperm, into already politicized entities, factionalized ethnicities, and "religions" grafted and cut off from one another, testifies to the consistently split origin that in Derrida's text fails to gather while inscribing itself in world historical, political explosions. "Religion" as the Abrahamic, while we claim it as "our own" can only disown us.[69]

Derrida's interest in the Abrahamic can be located at this moment of the splitting and might be inspired by an egalitarian impulse to distribute his notion of Jewish messianism seen through a Zionist optic across all three "Abrahamic religions," to which he refers as "Abrahamic messianism."[70] This is most apparent when he strangely calls Zionist occupation and colonization of Jerusalem (which he always calls by its Latinized Hebrew version and never in its Arabic name "al-Quds," the name by which its inhabitants have known it for a millennium and a half) and the resistance to that conquest as "the war for 'the appropriation of Jerusalem.'"[71] Such a descriptor, echoing Massignon, represents the Palestinians' anticolonial struggle to hold onto their lands and homes in al-Quds against Zionist colonial-settler theft as much of an "appropriation" of their own city as is the Zionist theft. Indeed, Derrida is even forgiving of the foundational violence of Israel that visited the Catastrophe/Nakba on the Palestinians, for it was not unique, as "no state has ever been founded without this violence, whatever form and whatever time it might have taken."[72] Derrida recalls how as a child he had asked himself "whether the founding of the modern state of Israel— with all the politics and policies that have followed and confirmed

---

68. Said, *Orientalism*, 307.
69. Anidjar, "Introduction," 20.
70. Jacques Derrida, *Specters of Marx* (London: Routledge, 1994), 210.
71. Ibid., 73.
72. Derrida, "Avowing the Impossible," 29–30.

it—could be no more than an example among others of this originary violence from which no state can escape, or whether, because this modern state intended not to be a state like others, it had to appear before another law and appeal to another justice."[73] Derrida seems to have opted for normalizing Israel among the nations, which was of course the explicit goal of Zionism. In this democratic, liberal, and egalitarian spirit, Derrida refuses to pose *the Palestinian question as the Jewish question* and refuses to see it as an anticolonial struggle over land, but rather and instead as the "unleashing of messianic eschatologies" by the three "Abrahamic religions," or what he calls the eschatological "triangle."[74] In this, he does not deviate much from the position of Bernard Lewis, who had identified the Palestinian struggle against Zionist colonialism as "the return of Islam," although Derrida would object to the notion of "return." In rendering Islamic "messianism" or "Islam" the culprit in opposing Zionism, there seems to be an insistence on glossing over the fact that the struggle against Zionism has always been shared by Palestinian and Arab Muslims *and* Christians, and that it is not necessarily supported by all non-Arab Muslims. Said's response to Lewis may also be an apt riposte to Derrida. For Lewis and Orientalists more generally, concludes Said, positing Islam, or any force that speaks in its name, as the motivation of anticolonial Arab struggles simply means that "history, politics, and economics do not matter."[75]

The most radical position that Derrida had expressed on Zionist colonialism and the Palestinian question did not deviate much from the "international consensus" of the great (Christian) powers, namely: "Palestinians and Israelis will truly live together only on the day when peace (not only armistice, cease-fire, or the peace process) comes into the bodies and souls, when what is necessary will have been done by those who have the power or who have simply the most power, state power, economic, military, national or international power, to take the initiative for peace in a manner that is first of all wisely unilateral."[76]

When Derrida speaks of opposing certain Israeli policies, it is with the tormented twists and turns of a tortured man fearing excommunication

73. Ibid, 30. In *Specters of Marx*, Derrida maintains that "one would have to analyze . . . in particular since the founding of the State of Israel, the violence that preceded, constituted, accompanied and followed it on every side, *at the same time* in conformity with *and* in disregard of an international law that therefore appears today to be at the same time more contradictory, imperfect, and thus more perfectible and necessary than ever" (72–73).

74. Derrida, *Specters of Marx*, 73. See also Christopher Wise, "Deconstruction and Zionism: Jacques Derrida's *Specters of Marx*," *Diacritics* 31, no. 1 (Spring 2001): 61–62.

75. Said, *Orientalism*, 207.

76. Derrida, "Avowing the Impossible," 23.

by the community of believers. Having voiced a criticism of Israel, he tells us that he must "hasten to immediately add . . . that one can remain radically critical in this regard without implying from it any threatening or disrespectful consequences for the present, the future and the existence of Israel, on the contrary."[77] This is an ongoing sentiment on the part of Derrida that precedes his manifest interest in the Abrahamic. When he lectured in occupied al-Quds in 1988, during the first Palestinian uprising against Israeli occupation across the Occupied Territories, he declared his "anxiety" that Palestinians and Arab scholars were not "officially invited" to participate in the conference! It is unclear to what notion of hos(ti)pitality Derrida was appealing when he expressed his wish for an "invitation" to be extended "officially" by the racially privileged citizens of a conquering and racially discriminatory state to their conquered racially inferior victims.[78] Yet Derrida seemed to grasp the situation on the ground as one of mutual "violence," equalizing once again the violent acts of the conqueror with those of the resisting conquered:

I wish to state right away my solidarity with all those, in this land, who advocate an end to violence, condemn the crimes of terrorism and of the military and police repression, and advocate the withdrawal of Israeli troops from the occupied territories as well as the recognition of the Palestinians' right to choose their own representatives to negotiations, now more indispensable than ever.[79]

Derrida, however, felt it necessary to assert in his speech that the Israeli State's "existence, it goes without saying, must henceforth be recognized by all and definitively guaranteed" not least of course, by the Palestinians it conquered and continues to conquer.[80]

Despite Derrida's opposition to white supremacist South Africa in the mid-1980s, he believed that Israel—which defines itself as a Jewish state for all the Jews of the world rather than an Israeli state for all Israeli citizens and guarantees that definition by laws that grant differential rights and privileges to Jews (whether citizens or not) over non-Jewish

---

77. Ibid., 29. On the question of Derrida's ambivalence regarding the necessary courage required for him to speak in defense of the Palestinians, see Caroline Rooney, "Derrida and Said: Ships That Pass in the Night," in *Edward Said and the Literary, Social, and Political World*, ed. Ranjan Ghosh (London: Routledge, 2009), 45–46.
78. Jacques Derrida, "Interpretations at War, Kant, the Jew, The German," in Anidjar, ed., *Acts of Religion*, 137.
79. Ibid., 138.
80. Ibid.

Israeli citizens—should be recognized by all. His refusal and resistance to see that Israeli colonialism and racism operate with the same force, albeit with different means, inside the Jewish state as they do in the territories Israel occupies seems to be a reflection of an emotional attachment to this Israel, which Derrida expresses openly as the motive for his statement: "As is evident by my presence right here, this declaration is inspired not only by my concern for justice and by my friendship toward both the Palestinians and the Israelis. It is meant as an expression of respect for a certain image of Israel and as an expression of hope for its future." Here, it is not an Aristotelian or a Marxist notion of justice—wherein justice means treating equal people equally and unequal people unequally—which Derrida is invoking, but rather a bourgeois liberal notion of justice—wherein equal and unequal people must be treated equally—to which he seems committed.

The tension between bringing the Semites together for Massignon and Derrida through the filiation and affiliation of the Abrahamic (and here we should remember, as Derrida reminds us twice, that one of his two grandfathers was indeed named Abraham)[81] as a Christian or Zionist position projected onto "Islam," or of separating them through Levinasian Othering and conceptualization of justice, characterizes much of the ongoing discourse on the Palestinian Question *as* the Jewish Question. The problem with the current deployment of the Abrahamic, however, is that it (mis)places religion, eschatological messianism, and, finally, theory over and against, or at the expense of, the political.

Here I want to consider the appeal to the Abrahamic one last time on its own terms. Let us suppose that those thinkers who appeal to it in the context of the Palestinian Question aim to make an ecumenical move, of integrating religions in the "Middle East" under the capacious umbrella of Abrahamic commonality, hoping to provide a theme of unity in the midst of a conflict in which religion has tended to overlay the political aspects. Setting aside for a moment this depoliticizing move, which distracts from the colonial past and present in which the "conflict" lies and in which it is carried out, and avoids the whole question of justice and decolonization for the Palestinians, the Abrahamic move seems to falter on its own terms and not just because of this depoliticizing effect. For even if integrating, ecumenizing appeals to unity among "religions" were not to distract from the political aspects of the conflict in this way, such appeals can only really be meaningful if this presupposed unity

81. Jacques Derrida, *Archive Fever: A Freudian Impression* (Chicago: University of Chicago Press, 1996), 78, 89. I thank Nasser Abourahmeh for alerting me to this.

and the presumed integrating elements are syncretic, that is, if the unities and integrations among the religions that are in conflict are part of the lived life of quotidian practice, ritual, festival, custom, community. In such a scenario, then appealing to these integrating factors may have the effect of demonstrating that the conflict between these "religions" is part of a false and trumped up political manipulation. But in the appeal to the Abrahamic, the opposite is true. The lived reality of the colonial past and the colonial present is that of the deep ongoing and quotidian brutalization of a people by another. In the case of Israeli Jews and Palestinians, there was/is no commonality of living outside the conquest of the land by European Jewish colonists, anymore than there was in the lives of white and black South Africans during Apartheid. As for the Arab Jews, whatever memories still survive of a commonality of life between Arab Jewish, Muslim, and Christian neighbors in those Arab countries from which Arab Jews came, they are separated from and contrasted with the conquering relationship that Arab Jews, like their European counterparts (mutatis mutandis), also have to Palestinians. The appeal to the Abrahamic is not therefore an appeal to a lived reality but an appeal to something purely abstract, scriptural, normative.[82]

Here, I want to remind you that the Abrahamic does have a political life of its own in Palestinian history and geography, specifically in the name of one major Palestinian city, al-Khalil, which is the city of Abraham, the friend of God ("Khalilu Allah"). Al-Khalil's Palestinians, known as Khalilites (in Arabic *khalaylah*), have been enduring some of the worst forms of Jewish settler colonialism in the heart of their city and in their Abrahamic Sanctuary, where Abraham is said to be buried. Their Abrahamic name is erased in English and other European languages, which insist on using the dead Hebrew name of their city, "Hebron," and not the living name that has identified it for almost a millennium and a half: al-Khalil (the same process also applies to other Palestinian cities). In 1994, when Baruch Goldstein, a Jewish colonial settler from Brooklyn, massacred twenty-nine Muslim Palestinians while they were praying in the Abrahamic Sanctuary Mosque, Derrida paid attention and referred to them in the context of his discussion of "wars of religion, open war over the appropriation of Jerusalem." Derrida offers the massacre as an example of such wars: "Yesterday (yes, yesterday, truly, just a few days ago), there was the massacre of Hebron at the Tomb of the Patriarchs, a place held in common and symbolic trench of the

---

82. I thank Akeel Bilgrami for his engagement with me on this point.

religions called 'Abrahamic.'"[83] Derrida's insistence on the use of the dead name of al-Khalil, on calling the *Abrahamic Sanctuary* by its Jewish colonial terminology ("Tomb of the Patriarchs"), on claiming the massacre as part of a religious and not a colonial war and contextualizing all of this in the "religions called 'Abrahamic'" reveals the explanatory potential of the Abrahamic and what it can and cannot include. For a philosopher like Derrida, so invested in the proper name, to refuse to call Palestinian geography and holy places by their proper Abrahamic names opens him to the *probability* of a similar charge like the one he leveled against Massignon.

As Abrahamic Palestinians, Khalilites emblematize the bifurcation of which Said spoke, when they have to live under the terror of armed colonial settlers from Brooklyn in their midst. Palestine's Abrahamic city today is indeed inhabited by 400 Semites who went the way of Orientalism and 180,000 Semites who were forced to go the way of the Oriental. Semitism continues to define their lives precisely because of this bifurcation and the slippage the term experiences with every pronouncement.

But despite the persistence of the Palestinian Question, Derrida did not worry about the survival of the Palestinian people but remained more concerned about the "interminable Jewish Question," as he called it, and worried, as late as 1995, about the disappearance of the Jewish people. The context in which European Jews lived as *Oriental* Semites in Europe and live as *Orientalist* Semites in the Middle East is one that he forgets. He affirms unhesitatingly that Europe and the Middle East are places "in which the Jewish people had such great difficulty surviving and bearing witness to its faith."[84] In March 2000, while visiting Egypt to deliver a series of lectures, Derrida reinvoked his continued opposition to Israeli occupation of the West Bank and Gaza (but not of the whole of Palestine) while echoing his continued concern for *Jews*: "I am also not on the side of anti-Jewish tendencies," he declared, im(ex?)plicitly connecting Palestinian resistance against Israeli Jewish racist violence to "anti-Jewish tendencies," and thus equalizing the anti-Palestinian Israeli occupation with what he (mis)names as "anti-Jewish tendencies" in Palestinian resistance to Israel.[85] The shuttling and oscillation of the

83. Jacques Derrida, "Faith and Knowledge: The Two Sources of Religion and the Limits of Reason Alone," in Anidjar, *Jacques Derrida: Acts of Religion*, 45.

84. Ibid., 91.

85. Muna Tulbah, "Jak Drida: Thaqafat 'al-Tafkik' takhtalif min balad ila akhar wa laysa kul naqid adabi muhayya' l'imtilakiha" (Jacques Derrida: The Culture of 'Deconstruction' differs from one country to another and not every literary critic is ready to acquire it), *Al-Hayat*, 3 March 2000, 16.

Abrahamic in Derrida's work, evidently, can do very little to level the field between Oriental and Orientalist Semites, much as he would have liked it to do.

Here, the invocation of the Abrahamic demonstrates most clearly its Orientalist origins and functions, no matter how hard it tries to invent an Islamic pedigree for itself. The deployment of the Abrahamic ultimately proves itself to be a liberal move that wants to equate the powerful and the powerless, the Aryan Orientalist, the Semite who went the way of the Orientalist, and the Semite who was forced to go the way of the Oriental. The elimination of hierarchy in this recent deployment of the Abrahamic and its commitment to an equalization of the three groups is precisely what is most depoliticizing about the term. Derrida is explicit on this: "three other messianic eschatologies," he tells us, "mobilize [in the Middle East] all the forces of the world and the whole 'world order' in the ruthless war they are waging against each other, directly or indirectly."[86] The Abrahamic is indeed an antihistorical notion that wants to return us to a nineteenth- and early twentieth-century discourse on Semitism, forgetting the Zionist bifurcation. Like those who insist that when considering Israel, anti-Semitism is all that need be remembered, Derrida declares in the context of a rush by European powers to confess and avow their colonial and genocidal sins that "this globalization of avowal is therefore not thinkable in its inaugural emergence without what happened to the Jews of Europe, in this century, nor is it any more separable from the international recognition of the state of Israel, a legitimation I would also interpret as one of the first moments of this avowal and of this world's bad conscience."[87] Derrida's account of international support for Israel as motivated by guilt flies in the face of all available histories that have demonstrated beyond any doubt that international (read Christian powers) support for the establishment of Israel was the result of geopolitical reasons that involved no sense of guilt over the holocaust whatsoever. Indeed the very same Western (Christian) countries that voted to partition Palestine on 29 November 1947 had voted against or abstained from voting on a UN resolution (introduced by the Arab states) calling on them to take in the Jewish holocaust refugees, shortly before.[88] That Derrida has become a patron saint for many theorists who are critical of liberalism is ironic given that

86. Derrida, *Specters of Marx*, 72.
87. Derrida, "Avowing the Impossible," 32.
88. See Evyatar Friesel, "The Holocaust and the Birth of Israel," *Wiener Library Bulletin* 32, nos. 49/50 (1979), and Joseph Massad, "Palestinians and Jewish History: Recognition or Submission?" *Journal of Palestine Studies* 30, no. 1 (Fall 2000): 52–67.

Derrida's invocation of the "Abrahamic" can be seen as nothing short of an attempt at producing a *liberalism with a human face* with regards to the question of monotheistic religions, including Islam.

Today, as Arabs, as Muslims, Palestinians have become the quintessential Semites. That Muslims worldwide have been huddled by this European taxonomy under the umbrella of the Semitic, whose inferiority to the Aryan must always be reasserted, makes the Palestinian Question one of the main battlefields where former Semites who have joined Europe are battling those Semites who refuse to join Europe and cannot be allowed to join it even if they so wished. In forgetting Semitism and Orientalism, *and Zionism*, and in urging us to remember only anti-Semitism, Derrida and the Abrahamic readvance the claim that anti-Semitism, rather than Semitism, is what opposes the Semite. That Aryanism and Semitism can only exist as parts of the same discourse of European racial and religious supremacy, which the Abrahamic forgets at its own peril, demonstrates that the Jewish and the Palestinian Questions have never been other than the Aryan and the Semitic Questions, which are globalized today as the question of *liberalism and Islam* rather than the question of *Islam in liberalism*. The lesson that Said wanted to commit to Palestinian memory was therefore simple: To forget Semitism, to forget the Semites, we must *always* remember them.

Works Cited

"1 1/2 Cheers for Indonesia," Editorial, *Chicago Tribune*, 12 October 1965.

Aaftaab, Gina Naheed. "(Re)Defining Public Spaces through Developmental Education for Afghan Women." In *Geographies of Muslim Women: Gender, Religion, and Space,* edited by Ghazi-Walid Falah and Caroline Nagel, 44–67. New York: Guilford Press, 2005.

Abaza, Mona. "ʿAda/Custom in the Middle East and Southeast Asia," in *Words in Motion: Towards a Global Lexicon*, ed. Carol Gluck and Anna Lowenhaupt Tsing, 67–82. Durham, NC: Duke University Press, 2009.

Abbasi, Aisha. "Whose Side Are You On? Muslim Psychoanalysts Treating Non-Muslim Patients." In *The Crescent and the Couch: Cross-Currents between Islam and Psychoanalysis,* edited by Salman Akhtar, 335–50. Lanham, MD: Jason Aronson, 2008.

Abdel-Malek, Anouar. "Orientalism in Crisis." In *Orientalism: A Reader,* edited by A. L. Macfir, 45–78. New York: New York University Press, 2001.

ʿAbduh, Muhammad. *Al-Radd ʿala al-Dahriyyin* (Response to the Materialists). Cairo: Al-Salam al-ʿalamiyyah lil-Tabʿ wa al-Nashr wa al-Tawziʿ, 1983.

ʿAbduli, Tuhami, al-. *Al-Nabiyy Ibrahim fi al-Thaqafah al-ʿArabiyyah al-Islamiyyah* (The Prophet Abraham in Islamic Arab Culture). Damascus: Dar al-Mada lil-Thaqafah wa al-Nashr, 2001.

Abelove, Henry. "Freud, Homosexuality, and the Americans." In *The Lesbian and Gay Studies Reader,* edited by Henry Abelove, Michèle Aina Barale, and David M. Halperin, 381–93. London: Routledge, 1993.

Abu-Lughod, Lila. "The Active Social Life of 'Muslim Women's Rights': A Plea for Ethnography, Not Polemic, with Cases from

Egypt and Palestine." *Journal of Middle East Women's Studies* 6, no. 1 (2010): 1–45.

———. "Anthropology's Orient: The Boundaries of Theory on the Arab World." In *Theory, Politics, and the Arab World: Critical Responses*, edited by Hisham Sharabi, 81–131. London: Routledge, 1990.

———. "Dialects of Women's Empowerment: The International Circuitry of the Arab Human Development Report 2005." *International Journal of Middle East Studies* 41, no. 1 (2009): 83–103.

———. "Do Muslim Women Really Need Saving? Anthropological Reflections on Cultural Relativism and Its Others." *American Anthropologist*, n.s., 104, no. 3 (2002): 783–90.

———. *Do Muslim Women Need Saving?* Cambridge, MA: Harvard University Press, 2013.

———. "Seductions of the 'Honor Crime.'" *Differences: A Journal of Feminist Cultural Studies* 22, no. 1 (2011): 17–63.

Abu-Odeh, Lama. "Crimes of Honour and Constructions of Gender in Arab Societies." In *Feminism and Islam: Legal and Literary Perspectives,* edited by May Yamani, 141–94. Beirut: Ithaca Press, 1996.

———. "Crimes of Honor and Constructions of Gender in Arab Societies." *Comparative Law Review* 2, no. 1 (2011): 3–47.

Adely, Fida. "Educating Women for Development: *The Arab Human Development Report 2005* and the Problem with Women's Choices." *International Journal of Middle East Studies* 41 (2009): 105–22.

Afghani, Jamal Al-Din al-. *Réfutation des matérialistes.* Translated by A. M. Goichon. Paris: Paul Geuthner, 1942.

Afkhami, Mahnaz, and Erika Friedl, eds. *Muslim Women and the Politics of Participation: Implementing the Beijing Platform.* Syracuse, NY: Syracuse University Press, 1997.

Ahmad, Aziz. *Islamic Modernism in India and Pakistan, 1857–1964.* Oxford: Oxford University Press, 1967.

Ahmed, Leila. "Western Ethnocentrism and Perceptions of the Harem." *Feminist Studies* 8, no. 3 (1982): 521–34.

———. *Women and Gender in Islam: Historical Roots of a Modern Debate.* New Haven, CT: Yale University Press, 1992.

Ahmed-Ghosh, Huma, ed. "Lesbians, Sexuality, and Islam." Special issue of the *Journal of Lesbian Studies* 16, no. 4 (2012): 377–80.

Akhtar, Salman. "Muslims in the Psychoanalytic World." In *The Crescent and the Couch: Cross-Currents between Islam and Psychoanalysis,* edited by Salman Akhtar, 315–33. Lanham, MD: Jason Aronson, 2008.

Albornoz, Pedro. "Bolivia: Landlocked Country." *Harvard Gay and Lesbian Review* 6, no. 1 (1999): 16–17.

Alexander, Michelle. *The New Jim Crow: Mass Incarceration in the Age of Colorblindness,* rev. ed. New York: New Press, 2012.

Alexiev, Alex. Soviet Nationalities in Nazi Wartime Strategy, 1941–1945: Report Prepared for the Net Assessment, Office of the Secretary of Defense. Rand Foundation, Rand Publication Series. Santa Monica, CA: Rand, 1982.

Ali, Shaheen Sardar. Conceptualizing Islamic Law, CEDAW and Women's Human Rights in Plural Legal Settings: A Comparative Analysis of Application of CEDAW in Bangladesh, India and Pakistan. In *Islamic Law through the CEDAW Lens*, a publication of UN Women, South Asia, United Nations Entity for Gender Equality and the Empowerment of Women, 2006, http://www.unwomensouthasia.org/assets/complete-study.pdf.

Almond, Gabriel A. "The Intellectual History of the Civic Culture Concept." In *The Civic Culture Revisited*, edited by Gabriel A. Almond and Sydney Verba, 1–36. Boston: Little, Brown, 1980.

Almond, Gabriel A., and Sydney Verba. *The Civic Culture: Political Attitudes and Democracy in Five Nations*. Princeton, NJ: Princeton University Press, 1963.

Althusser, Louis. *Montesquieu, Rousseau, Marx*. London; Verso, 1972.

Altman, Dennis. "Global Gaze/Global Gays," *GLQ* 3, no. 4 (1997): 417–36.

———. *Global Sex*. Chicago: University of Chicago Press, 2001.

———. "On Global Queering." *Australian Humanities Review*, http://www.australianhumanitiesreview.org/archive/Issue-July-1996/altman.html#2 (accessed 1 April 2014).

———. "Rupture or Continuity? The Internationalization of Gay Identities." *Social Text*, no. 48 (1996): 77–94.

Alvarez, Sonia E. "Latin American Feminisms 'Go Global': Trends of the 1990s and Challenges for the New Millennium." In *Cultures of Politics/Politics of Cultures: Revisioning Latin American Social Movements*, edited by Sonia E. Alvarez, Evelina Dagnino, and Arturo Escobar, 62–85. Boulder, CO: Westview Press, 1998.

Amar, Paul. "Middle East Masculinity Studies: Discourses of 'Men in Crisis' Industries of Gender in Revolution." *Journal of Middle East Women's Studies* 7, no. 3 (2011): 36–70.

———. *The Security Archipelago: Human-Security States, Sexuality Politics, and the Ends of Neoliberalism*. Durham, NC: Duke University Press, 2013.

Amer, Sahar. "Joseph Massad and the Alleged Violence of Human Rights." *GLQ* 16, no. 4 (2010): 649–53.

———. "Naming to Empower: Lesbianism in the Arab Islamicate World Today." *Journal of Lesbian Studies* 16, no. 4 (2012): 381–97.

Amin, Ahmad. *Zuʿamaʾ al-Islah fi al-ʿAhd al-Hadith* (The Leaders of Reform in the Modern Era). Cairo: Maktabat al-Nahdah al-Misriyyah, 1948.

Amin, Qasim. *Tahrir al-Marʾah* (The Liberation of Woman). In *Qasim Amin: Al-ʿAʿmal al-Kamilah* (Qasim Amin: The Collected Works), edited by Muhammad ʿImarah. Cairo: Dar al-Shuruq, 1989.

Amin, Samir. *Accumulation on a World Scale: A Critique of the Theory of Underdevelopment*. New York: Monthly Review Press, 1974.

Amireh, Amal. "Afterword." *GLQ* 16, no. 4 (2010): 635–47.

"Amnesty International Says Soviet Has Detained 400 Dissidents; Abuse of Psychiatry Reported." *New York Times*, 30 April 1980.

Anderson, Lisa. "Arab Democracy: Dismal Prospects." *World Policy Journal* 18, no. 3 (2001): 53–60.

———. "Policy-Making and Theory Building: American Political Science and the Islamic Middle East." In *Theory, Politics and the Arab World: Critical Responses*, edited by Hisham Sharabi, 52–80. New York: Routledge, 1990.

Andrea, Bernadette. "Islam, Women, and Western Responses: The Contemporary Relevance of Early Modern Investigations." *Women's Studies* 38 (2009): 273–92.

Anidjar, Gil. "Introduction: 'Once More, Once More': Derrida, the Arab, the Jew." In *Jacques Derrida: Acts of Religion*, edited by Gil Anidjar, 1–39. New York: Routledge, 2002.

———. *Semites: Race, Religion, Literature*. Stanford, CA: Stanford University Press, 2008.

———. "Yet Another Abraham." Paper presented at Columbia University, Middle Eastern, South Asian, and African Studies Departmental Colloquium, 8 December 2011.

Arendt, Hannah. *The Jewish Writings*, edited by Jerome Kohn and Ron H. Feldman. New York: Schocken Books, 2007.

Arguelles, Lourdes, and Ruby B. Rich. "Homosexuality, Homophobia, and Revolution: Notes toward an Understanding of the Cuban Lesbian and Gay Male Experience." Part 1, *Signs* 9, no. 4 (Summer 1984): 683–99, and part 2, *Signs* 11, no. 1 (Fall 1985): 120–35.

Arkun, Muhammad. *Tarikhiyyat al-Fikr al-Arabi al-Islami* (The Historicity of Arab Islamic Thought). Casablanca: Al-Markaz al-Thaqafi al-ʿArabi, 1998.

Arnold, Matthew. *Culture and Anarchy*. Edited by Samuel Lipman. New Haven, CT: Yale University Press, 1994.

Arnold, Thomas. *The Caliphate*. Oxford: Clarendon Press, 1924.

Asad, Muhammad. *Islam at the Crossroads*. Lahore: Arafat Publications, 1947.

Asad, Talal. "A Comment on Aijaz Ahmad's *In Theory*." *Public Culture* 6, no. 1 (1993): 31–39.

———. "Conscripts of Western Civilization." In *Dialectical Anthropology: Essays in Honor of Stanley Diamond*, vol. 1: *Civilization in Crisis: Anthropological Perspectives*, edited by Christine Ward Gailey, 333–51. Tallahassee: University Press of Florida, 1992.

———. "The Construction of Religion as an Anthropological Category." In *Genealogies of Religion: Disciplines and Reasons of Power in Christianity and Islam*, 114–29. Baltimore: Johns Hopkins University Press, 1983.

———. "Cultural Translation in British Social Anthropology." In *Genealogies of Religion: Discipline and Reasons for Power in Christianity and Islam*, 171–99. Baltimore: Johns Hopkins University Press, 1993.

———. "Ethnographic Representation, Statistics, and Modern Powers" *Social Research* 61, no. 1 (1994): 55–88.

———. "Europe against Islam: Islam in Europe." *Muslim World* 87, no. 2 (1997): 183–95.

———. *Formations of the Secular: Christianity, Islam, Modernity*. Stanford, CA: Stanford University Press, 2003.

———. *Genealogies of Religion: Discipline and Reasons of Power in Christianity and Islam*. Baltimore: Johns Hopkins University Press, 1993.

Asad, Talal, and John Dixon. "Translating Europe's Others." In *Europe and Its Others*, vol. I, edited by Francis Barker, Peter Hulme, Margaret Iversen, and Diana Loxley, 120–40. Colchester: University of Essex Press, 1985.

Assmann, Jan. *Moses the Egyptian: The Memory of Egypt in Western Monotheism*. Cambridge, MA: Harvard University Press, 1997.

ʿAqqad, ʿAbbas Mahmud al-. *ʿAbd al-Rahman al-Kawakibi, Al-Rahhalah Kaf*. (The Traveler K) Beirut: Dar al-Kitab al-Arabi, 1969.

———. *Abu Nuwas, al-Hasan Bin Hani: Dirasah fi al-Tahlil al-Nafsani wa al-Naqd al-Tarikhi* (A Study in Psychoanalysis and Historical Criticism). Cairo: Kitab al-Hilal, 1960.

———. *Al-Dimuqratiyyah fi al-Islam* (Democracy in Islam). Cairo: Dar al-Maʿarif bi-Misr, 1964.

ʿAzm, Sadik Jalal al-. "Orientalism and Orientalism in Reverse." *Khamsin* 8 (1981): 5–26.

Babayan, Kathryn, and Afsaneh Najmabadi. *Islamicate Sexualities: Translations across Temporal Geographies of Desire*. Cambridge, MA: Harvard Center for Middle East Studies, 2008.

Balibar, Étienne. "Subjection and Subjectivation." In *Supposing the Subject*, edited by Joan Copjec, 1–15. London: Verso, 1994.

Ballard, Roger. "Islam and the Construction of Europe." In *Muslims in the Margin: Political Responses to the Presence of Islam in Western Europe*, edited by Wasif Shadid and Sjoerd von Koningsveld, 15–51. Kampen, Netherlands: Kok Pharos, 1996.

Bartlett, Robert. *The Making of Europe: Conquest, Colonization, Cultural Change, 950–1350*. London: Allen Lane, Penguin Press, 1993.

Basu, Amrita. "Globalization of the Local/Localization of the Global: Mapping Transnational Women's Movements." *Meridians: Feminism, Race, Transnationalism*, no. 1 (2000): 68–84.

Batnitzky, Leora. *Leo Strauss and Emmanuel Levinas: Philosophy and the Politics of Revelation*. West Nyack, NY: Cambridge University Press, 2002.

Beinin, Joel, and Zachary Lockman. *Workers on the Nile: Nationalism, Communism, Islam and the Egyptian Working Class, 1882–1954*. Princeton, NJ: Princeton University Press, 1987.

Benard, Cheryl. *Civil Democratic Islam: Partners, Resources, and Strategies*. Santa Monica: Rand, 2003.

Bennani, Jalil. *Psychanalyse en terre d'islam: Introduction à la psychanalyse au Maghreb*. Strasbourg: Éditions Arcanes, 2008.

Benslama, Fethi. *Déclaration d'insoumission: À l'usage des musulmans et de ceux qui ne le sont pas.* Paris: Flammarion, 2004.

———. [Bin Salamah, Fathi]. *Al-Islam wa al-Tahlil al-Nafsi* (Islam and Psychoanalysis). Translated by Dr. Raja' Bin Salamah. Beirut: Dar al-Saqi and Rabitat al-ʿAqlaniyyin al-ʿArab, 2008.

———. *La nuit brisée.* Paris: Éditions Ramsay, 1988.

———. *La psychanalyse à l'épreuve de l'Islam.* Paris: Flammarion, 2002.

———. "Une recherche psychanalytique sur l'islam." *La Célibataire,* no. 8 (2004): 75–84.

———. "Shajarat al-Islam, al-Tahlil al-Nafsi, al-Huwiyyah" (The Tree of Islam, Psychoanalysis, Identity), interview conducted by Husayn al-Qubaysi with Fethi Benslama, in *Al-Tahlil al-Nafsi wa al-Thaqafah al-ʿArabiyyah-al-Islamiyyah* (Psychoanalysis and Arab-Islamic Culture). Damascus: Dar al-Bidayat, 2008.

Bernstein, Richard J. "Hannah Arendt's Zionism?" In *Hannah Arendt in Jerusalem,* edited by Steven E. Aschheim, 194–204. Berkeley: University of California Press, 2001.

Bettelheim, Bruno. *Freud and Man's Soul.* New York: Alfred A. Knopf, 1983.

Bhabha, Homi. "Identities on Parade: A Conversation." *Marxism Today,* June 1989, 2–5.

Bilici, Mucahit. *Finding Mecca in America: How Islam Is Becoming an American Religion.* Chicago: University of Chicago Press, 2012.

Binder, Leonard. *Islamic Liberalism.* Chicago: University of Chicago Press, 1988.

Binnie, Jon. *The Globalization of Sexuality.* London: Sage, 2004.

Blackburn, Robin. *The Overthrow of Colonial Slavery, 1776–1848.* London: Verso, 1988.

Blackmore, Josiah, and Gregory S. Hutcheson. *Queer Iberia: Sexualities, Cultures, and Crossings from the Middle Ages to the Renaissance.* Durham, NC: Duke University Press, 1999.

Bleys, Rudy. *The Geography of Perversion: Male-to-Male Sexual Behaviour outside the West and the Ethnographic Imagination, 1750–1918.* New York: New York University Press, 1995.

Blunt, Wilfred Scawen. *The Future of Islam.* 1882. Rpt., Charleston, SC: Bibliobazaar, 2007.

Boellstorff, Tom. *The Gay Archipelago: Sexuality and Nation in Indonesia.* Princeton, NJ: Princeton University Press, 2005.

———. "Queer Studies in the House of Anthropology." *Annual Review of Anthropology* 36 (2007): 17–35.

———. "Queer Trajectories of the Postcolonial." *Postcolonial Studies* 11, no. 1 (2008): 113–17.

Bonaparte, Napoleon. "Proclamation of Bonaparte to the Egyptians. Muharram 1213 A.H." In *The Journals of Bonaparte in Egypt, 1798–1801,* edited by Saladin Boustany. Cairo: Dar Al-Maaref, 1971.

Bouhdiba, Abdelwahab. *La sexualité en Islam.* Paris: Presses universitaires de France, 1975.

Brown, Wendy. "Civilizational Delusions: Secularism, Tolerance, Equality." *Theory and Event* 15, no. 2 (2012).

———. "Sovereign Hesitations." In *Derrida and the Time of the Political*, edited by Cheah Pheng and Suzanne Guerlac, 114–30. Durham, NC: Duke University Press, 2009.

———. "Subjects of Tolerance." In *Political Theologies: Public Religions in a Post-Secular World*, edited by Hent De Vries and Lawrence E. Sullivan, 298–317. New York: Fordham University Press, 2006.

Buheiry, Marwan. "Colonial Scholarship and Muslim Revivalism in 1900." *Arab Studies Quarterly* 4, nos. 1–2 (1982): 1–16.

———. "Islam and the Foreign Office: An Investigation of Religious and Political Revival in 1873." In *Studia Arabica et Islamica: Festschrift for Ihsan Abbas on His Sixtieth Birthday*, edited by Wadad al-Qadi, 47–59. Beirut: American University of Beirut, 1981.

Burke, Edmund. "Speech in Opening the Impeachment." Fourth Day, Saturday, February 16, 1788, in Speeches in the Impeachment of Warren Hastings, Esquire, Late Governor-General of Bengal, February 1788, in *The Works of The Right Honourable Edmund Burke*, 12 vols., vol. 9. London: John C. Nimmo, 1887. Retrieved from http://www.gutenberg.org/files/13968/13968 -h/13968-h.htm#ARTICLES_OF_CHARGE (accessed 1 April 2014).

Burton, Antoinette. *Burdens of History: British Feminists, Indian Women, and Imperial Culture, 1865–1915*. Chapel Hill: University of North Carolina Press, 1994.

Buruma, Ian and Avishai Margalit. *Occidentalism: The West in the Eyes of Its Enemies*. New York: Penguin Press, 2004.

Butler, Judith. *Bodies That Matter: On the Discursive Limits of Sex*. London: Routledge, 1993.

———. *Gender Trouble: Feminism and the Subversion of Identity*. London: Routledge, 1990.

———. "Restaging the Universal: Hegemony and the Limits of Formalism." In *Contingency, Hegemony, Universality: Contemporary Dialogues on the Left*, edited by Judith Butler, Ernesto Laclau, and Slavoj Žižek, 11–43. London: Verso, 2000.

Buzpinar, Tufan. "Opposition to the Ottoman Caliphate in the Early Years of Abdülhamid II: 1877–1882." *Die Welt des Islams* 36, no. 1 (1996): 59–89.

Carl, Michael. "Decorated General: Shariah Is Here Now." *World Net Daily*, 13 July 2012. Retrieved from http://www.wnd.com/2012/07/decorated-general -shariah-is-here-now/ (accessed 1 April 2014).

Carter, Jimmy. Remarks at the signing of the peace treaty between Egypt and Israel, March 26, 1979. Retrieved from http://www.historyplace.com/specials /calendar/docs-pix/mar-carter-cdavid.htm (accessed 1 April 2014).

———. "Those Who Call Me an Anti-Semite Are a Small Fringe of Radical People in My Country: An Interview with Jimmy Carter," 12 December 2006, interview with Al-Jazeera, reproduced on *Counterpunch*, 14 December 2006, http:// www.counterpunch.org/khan12142006.html (accessed 1 April 2014).

Casale, Giancarlo. *The Ottoman Age of Exploration*. Oxford: Oxford University Press, 2010.

Casanova, Pascale. *The World Republic of Letters*. Cambridge, MA: Harvard University Press, 2007.

Chamoun, Mounir. "Islam et Psychanalyse dans la culture arabo-musulmane." *Pratiques Psychologiques* 11 (2005): 3–13.

Chandler, David. "The Road to Military Humanitarianism: How the Human Rights NGOs Shaped a New Humanitarian Agenda." *Human Rights Quarterly*, no. 23 (2001): 678–700.

Chaudhuri, Nupur, and Margaret Strobel, eds. *Western Women and Imperialism: Complicity and Resistance*. Bloomington: Indiana University Press, 1992.

Chauncey, George. *Gay New York: Gender, Urban Culture, and the Making of the Gay Male World, 1890–1940*. New York: Basic Books, 1994.

———. "The Queer History and Politics of Lesbian and Gay Studies." In *Queer Frontiers: Millennial Geographies, Genders, and Generations*, edited by Joseph A. Boone, Martin Dupuis, Martin Meeker, Karin Quimby, Cindy Sarver, Debra Silverman, and Rosemary Weatherston, 298–315. Madison: University of Wisconsin Press, 2000.

Chiang, Howard. "Epistemic Modernity and the Emergence of Homosexuality in China." *Gender & History* 22, no. 3 (November 2010): 629–57.

Christelow, Allan. *Muslim Law Courts and the French Colonial State in Algeria*. Princeton, NJ: Princeton University Press, 1985.

Clinton, Hillary Rodham. Interview with Shahira Amin. *Nile TV Channel*, 16 March 2011.

Cohen, Hillel. *Army of Shadows: Palestinian Collaboration with Zionism, 1917–1948*. Berkeley: University of California Press, 2008.

Conrad, Joseph. *The Secret Sharer, in Conrad's The Nigger of the 'Narcissus' and Other Stories*. New York: Penguin Books, 2007.

Cooley, John. *Unholy Wars: Afghanistan, America, and International Terrorism*, 3rd ed. London: Pluto Press, 2002.

Crouch, Gregory. "Dutch Immigration Kit Offers a Revealing View." *New York Times*, 16 March 2006.

Curtis, Mark. *Secret Affairs: Britain's Collusion with Radical Islam*. London: Serpent's Tail, 2010.

Curtis, Michael. *Orientalism and Islam: European Thinkers on Oriental Despotism in the Middle East and India*. Cambridge: Cambridge University Press, 2009.

D'Emilio, John. "Capitalism and Gay Identity." In *The Lesbian and Gay Studies Reader*, edited by Henry Abelove, Michèle Aina Barale, and David M. Halperin, 467–78. New York: Routledge, 1993.

Dainotto, Roberto M. *Europe (In Theory)*. Durham, NC: Duke University Press, 2007.

Davis, Angela. *Women, Culture, and Politics*. New York: Random House, 1984.

———. *Women, Race, & Class*. New York: Vintage, 1983.

Deeb, Lara, and Dina Al-Kassim. "Introduction." *Journal of Middle East Women's Studies* 7, no. 3 (2011): 1–15.

Derrida, Jacques. *Archive Fever: A Freudian Impression*. Chicago: University of Chicago Press, 1996.

———. "Geopsychoanalysis: '. . . and the rest of the world.'" *American Imago* 48, no. 2 (1991): 199–231.

———. "Psychoanalysis Searches the States of Its Soul: The Impossible Beyond of a Sovereign Cruelty" (Address to the States General of Psychoanalysis). In *Without Alibi*, 238–80. Stanford, CA: Stanford University Press, 2002.

———. *Rogues: Two Essays on Reason*. Stanford, CA: Stanford University Press, 2005.

———. *Specters of Marx*. London: Routledge, 1994.

Dorill, Stephen. *MI6*. London: Simon and Schuster, 2002.

Dreyfus, Robert. "Cold War, Holy Warrior." *Mother Jones*, January/February 2006.

———. *Devil's Game: How the United States Helped Unleash Fundamentalist Islam*. New York: Metropolitan Books, 2005.

Duggan, Lisa. *The Twilight of Equality? Neoliberalism, Cultural Politics, and the Attack on Democracy*. Boston: Beacon Press, 2003.

Eddy Melissa. "In Germany, Ruling over Circumcision Sows Anxiety and Confusion." *New York Times*, 13 July 2012.

Edelman, Lee. *No Future: Queer Theory and the Death Drive*. Durham, NC: Duke University Press, 2004.

Eickelman, Dale F., and James Piscatori. *Muslim Politics*. Princeton, NJ: Princeton University Press, 1996.

Eisenhower, Dwight. Speech made on January 5, 1957, available at http://miller center.org/scripps/archive/speeches/detail/3360 (accessed 1 April 2014).

Eisenstein, Zillah. *Sexual Decoys: Gender, Race and War in Imperial Democracy*. London: Zed Books, 2007.

Emié, Bernard. "Mot de S.E.M. Bernard Emié, ambassadeur de France." In *La psychanalyse dans le monde arabe et islamique*, 21–24. Beirut: Presses de l'université Saint-Joseph, 2005.

Enayat, Hamid. *Modern Islamic Political Thought*. Austin: University of Texas Press, 1982.

Eng, David. *The Feeling of Kinship: Queer Liberalism and the Racialization of Intimacy*. Durham, NC: Duke University Press, 2010.

Ezzat, Heba Raouf. "Secularism, the State, and the Social Bond: The Withering Away of the Family." In *Islam and Secularism in the Middle East*, edited by Azzam Tamimi and John Esposito, 124–38. London: Hurst, 2000.

Faludi, Susan. *The Terror Dream: Fear and Fantasy in Post-9/11 America*. New York: Metropolitan Books, 2007.

Farah, Caesar. "Great Britain, Germany, and the Ottoman Caliphate." *Der Islam* 66 (1989): 264–88.

Farrell, Amy, and Patrice McDermott. "The Challenge of Human Rights Discourse for Transnational Feminism." In *Just Advocacy: Women's Human Rights, Transnational Feminisms, and the Politics of Representation*, edited by Wendy S. Hesford and Wendy Kozol, 33–55. New Brunswick, NJ: Rutgers University Press, 2005.

Farris, Sarah R. "Femonationalism and the 'Regular' Army of Labor Called Migrant Women." *History of the Present* 2, no. 2 (2012): 184–99.

Faruqi, Isma'il Raji al-. *Toward Islamic English*. Hernden, VA: International Institute of Islamic Thought, 1986.

Fasseur, C. "Colonial Dilemma: Van Vallenhoven and the Struggle between Adat Law and Western Law in Indonesia." In *European Expansion and Law in 19th Century Africa and Asia,* edited by W. J. Mommsen and J. A. De Moor, 237–56. Oxford: Berg, 1992.

Fassin, Eric. "National Identities and Transnational Intimacies: Sexual Democracy and the Politics of Immigration in Europe." *Public Culture* 22, no. 3 (2010): 507–29.

Fazy, Edmond, ed. "L'Avenir de l'islam." *Questions diplômatiques et coloniales* 11 (1901).

Fessenden, Tracey. "Disappearances: Race, Religion, and the Progress Narrative of US Feminism." In *Secularisms*, edited by Janet R. Jakobsen and Ann Pelligrini, 139–61. Durham, NC: Duke University Press, 2008.

Finkelstein, Louis, J. Elliot Ross, and William Adams Brown. *The Religions of Democracy: Judaism, Catholicism, Protestantism in Creed and Life*. New York: Devin-Adair, 1941.

Firjani, Nader. "Sirat Taqrir al-Tanmiyyah al-Insaniyyah al-Arabiyyah: Al-Nash'ah, al-Risalah, al-Manhajiyyah, Wa Rudud al-Fi'l" (The Biography of the Arab Human Development Report: Its Beginnings, Its Message, Its Methodology, and the Reactions to It). *Majallat Idafat*, no. 1 (2008): 83–113.

Foner, Eric. *The Story of American Freedom*. New York: W. W. Norton, 1998.

Foucault, Michel. *The Birth of Biopolitics: Lectures at the College de France 1978–1979*. Edited by Michael Senellart. New York: Picador, 2010.

———. *The History of Sexuality,* vol. 1: *An Introduction*. Translated by Robert Hurley. London: Allen Lane, 1979.

———. *The History of Sexuality*, vol. 2: *The Uses of Pleasure*. Translated by Robert Hurley. New York: Vintage, 1984.

———. "The Subject and Power." *Critical Inquiry* 8, no. 4 (Summer 1982): 777–95.

Fraser, Nancy, and Axel Honneth. *Redistribution or Recognition? A Political-Philosophical Exchange*. London: Verso, 2003.

Freud, Sigmund. "Analysis of a Phobia in a Five-Year-Old Boy." In *The Standard Edition of the Complete Psychological Works of Sigmund Freud,* edited and translated by James Strachey et al., vol. 5. London: Hogarth Press, 1953–74.

———. *Leonardo da Vinci and a Memory of His Childhood*. In *The Standard Edition of the Complete Psychological Works of Sigmund Freud*, edited and translated by James Strachey et al., vol. 11. London: Hogarth Press, 1953–74.

———. *The Letters of Sigmund Freud*. Edited by Ernst L. Freud. New York: Basic Books, 1960.

———. *Moses and Monotheism*. In *The Standard Edition of the Complete Psychological Works of Sigmund Freud,* edited and translated by James Strachey et al., vol. 23. London: Hogarth Press, 1953–74.

Friesel, Evyatar. "The Holocaust and the Birth of Israel." *Wiener Library Bulletin* 32, nos. 49–50 (1979): 51–60.

Fromm, Erich. *Psychoanalysis and Religion*. New Haven, CT: Yale University Press, 1950.

Fruyd, Sighmund. *Musa wa al-Tawhid*. Translated by Jurj Tarabishi. Beirut: Dar al-Taliʿah, 1973.

———. *Qalaq fi al-Hadarah*. Translated by Jurj Tarabishi. Beirut: Dar al-Taliʿah, 1977.

———. *Tafsir al-Ahlam*. Translated by Abd al-Munʿim al-Hifni. Cairo: Maktabat Madbuli, 2004.

———. *Tafsir al-Ahlam*. Translated by Mustafa Safwan. Beirut: Dar an Farabi and ACPPR, 2003.

Frye, Richard N., ed. *Islam and the West: Proceedings of the Harvard Summer School Conference on the Middle East, July 25–27, 1955*. The Hague: Mouton, 1956.

Fuchs, Barbara. *Mimesis and Empire: The New World, Islam, and European Identities*. Cambridge: Cambridge University Press, 2001.

Gauss, Gerald. *Value and Justifications: The Foundations of Liberal Theory*. Cambridge: Cambridge University Press, 1990.

Gettleman, Jeffrey. "Americans' Role Seen in Uganda Anti-Gay Push." *New York Times*, 3 January 2010.

Ghazzoul, Ferial. "Gender and Knowledge: Contribution of Gender Perspectives to Intellectual Formations." *Alif* 19 (1999): 210–30.

Ghoussoub, May. "Feminism—or the Eternal Masculine-in the Arab World." *New Left Review* 167 (1987): 1–18.

Gibb, H. A. R. *Area Studies Reconsidered*. London: School of African and Oriental Studies, 1963.

Gilmore, Gerry J. "Bulk of Iraq Monies 'Will Come from Iraqis,' Rumsfeld Says." *American Forces Press Service*, 2 October 2003, http://www.defense.gov/News/NewsArticle.aspx?ID=28388 (accessed 1 April 2014).

Gilroy, Paul. *Postcolonial Melancholia*. New York: Columbia University Press, 2006.

Gingrich, Newt. "I'd Support a Muslim Running for President Only If They'd Commit to Give Up Sharia." *Huffington Post*, 17 January 2012.

Girard, Françoise. "Negotiating Sexual Rights and Sexual Orientation at the UN." In *Sex Politics: Reports from the Front Lines,* edited by Richard Parker, Rosalind Petchesky, and Robert Sember, 311–58. New York: Sexuality Policy Watch, 2004.

Glasser, Susan. "Qatar Reshapes Its Schools, Putting English over Islam." *Washington Post*, 2 February 2003.

Goldstein, Eric. *The Price of Whiteness: Jews, Race, and American Identity*. Princeton, NJ: Princeton University Press, 2006.

Gran, Peter. *Islamic Roots of Capitalism; Egypt, 1760–1840*. Syracuse, NY: Syracuse University Press, 1998.

———. "Studies of Anglo-American Political Economy: Democracy, Orientalism, and the Left." In *Theory and Politics and the Arab World: Critical Responses*, edited by Hisham Sharabi, 228–54. New York: Routledge, 1990.

Great Britain, Foreign Office 881. Confidential Print no. 2621, *Correspondence Respecting the Religious and Political Revival among Mussulmans, 1873–1874*. London, July 1875, Item 4, "Circular Addressed to H.M. Consuls in the East and also to Mr. Wade and to Consuls and Vice-Consuls in China," Granville, 22 August 1873.

Greenfeld, Lawrence, et al., eds. *Violence by Intimates: Analysis of Data on Crimes by Current or Former Spouses, Boyfriends, and Girlfriends* (Publication NCJ167237). Washington, DC: US Department of Justice, Office of Justice Programs, Bureau of Justice Statistics, 1988.

Grewal, Inderpal. "Outsourcing Patriarchy: Feminist Encounters: Transnational Mediations and the Crime of 'Honor Killings.'" *International Feminist Journal of Politics* 15, no. 1 (2013): 1–19.

———. *Transnational America* (Durham, NC: Duke University Press, 2005.

Grosrichard, Alain. *The Sultan's Court: European Fantasies of the East*. Translated by Liz Heron. London: Verso, 1998.

Habib, Samar. *Islam and Homosexuality*. 2 vols. Santa Barbara, CA: Praeger, 2010.

Haim, Sylvia G. "Blunt and al-Kawakibi." *Oriente Moderno* 35, no. 3 (1955): 132–43.

Hallaq, Wael B. *The Impossible State: Islam, Politics, and Modernity's Moral Predicament*. New York: Columbia University Press, 2012.

———. *Shariʿa: Theory, Practice, Transformations*. Cambridge: Cambridge University Press, 2009.

Halley, Janet. *Split Decisions: How and Why to Take a Break from Feminism*. Princeton, NJ: Princeton University Press, 2008.

———. "What Is Family Law? A Genealogy, Part I." *Yale Journal of Law and the Humanities* 23, no. 1 (2011): 1–109.

Hamami, Rema, and Martina Reiker. "Feminist Orientalism and Orientalist Marxism." *New Left Review* (1988), http://newleftreview.org/I/170/reza-hammami-martina-rieker-feminist-orientalism-and-orientalist-marxism (accessed 1 April 2014).

Harrison, Christian. *France and Islam in West Africa, 1860–1960*. Cambridge: Cambridge University Press, 1988.

Harsono, Andreas. "No Model for Muslim Democracy." *New York Times*, 21 May 2012.

Hasso, Frances. "Empowering Governmentalities rather than Women: The Arab Human Development Report 2005 and Western Development Logics." *International Journal of Middle East Studies* 41 (2009): 63–82.

Hatem, Mervat. "Class and Patriarchy as Competing Paradigms for the Study of Middle Eastern Women." *Comparative Studies in Society and History* 29, no. 4 (1987): 811–18.

———. "Islamic Societies and Muslim Women in Globalization Discourses." *Comparative Studies of South Asia, Africa, and the Middle East* 26, no. 1 (2006): 22–35.

Hayes, Jarrod. *Queer Nations: Marginal Sexualities in the Maghreb*. Chicago: University of Chicago Press, 2000.

Hélie-Lucas, Marie-Aimée.."Bound and Gagged by the Family Code." Interview with Sophie Laws. In *Third World, Second Sex*, vol. 2, edited by Miranda Davis, 3–15. London: Zed Books, 1987.

Hernandez, Miguel J. "Kris vs. Krag." *Military History* 23, no. 4 (2006): 58–65.

Heschel, Susannah. "German-Jewish Scholarship on Islam as a Tool for De-Orientalizing Judaism." *New German Critique* 36, no. 1 (2012): 91–107.

Hoad, Neville. *African Intimacies: Race, Homosexuality, and Globalization*. Minneapolis: University of Minnesota Press, 2007.

———. "Arrested Development, or The Queerness of Savages: Resisting Evolutionary Narratives of Difference." *Postcolonial Studies* 3, no. 2 (2000): 133–58.

Hoad, Neville, Karen Martin, and Graeme Reid, eds. *Sex and Politics in South Africa: The Equality Clause/Gay and Lesbian Movement/the Anti-Apartheid Struggle*. Cape Town: Double Storey, 2005.

Hochberg, Gil. *In Spite of Partition: Jews, Arabs, and the Limits of Separatist Imagination*. Princeton, NJ: Princeton University Press, 2007.

———. "Introduction: Israelis, Palestinians, Queers: Points of Departure." *GLQ* 16, no. 4 (2010): 493–516.

Hodgson, Marshall G. S. *The Venture of Islam: Conscience of History in a World Civilization*, vol. 1: *The Classical Age of Islam*. Chicago: University of Chicago Press, 1974.

Homayounpour, Gohar. *Doing Psychoanalysis in Tehran*. Cambridge, MA: MIT Press, 2012.

hooks, bell. *Ain't I a Woman: Black Women and Feminism*. Boston: South End Press, 1981.

———. *Feminist Theory: From Margin to Center*. Boston: South End Press, 1984.

Houbballah, Adnan. "La psychanalyse et le monde arabe." *La Célibataire,* no. 8 (2004): 19–28.

———. Le virus de la violence: La guerre civile est en chacun de nous. Paris: Albin Michel, 1996.

Hunt, Margaret R. "Women in Ottoman and Western European Law Courts: Were Western European Women Really the Luckiest Women in the World?" In *Structures and Subjectivities: Attending to Early Modern Women,* edited by Joan E. Hartman and Adele Seeff, 176–99. Newark, DE: University of Delaware Press, 2007.

Huntington, Samuel P. "Democracy's Third Wave." *Journal of Democracy* 2, no. 2 (1991): 12–34.

———. "The Clash of Civilizations." *Foreign Affairs* (1993): 29–30.

———. *Political Order in Changing Societies*. New Haven, CT: Yale University Press, 1968.

———. "The United States." In *The Crisis of Democracy: Report on the Governability of Democracy to the Trilateral Commission*, edited by Michael Crozler, Samuel P. Huntington, and Joji Watanuki, 59–118. New York: New York University Press, 1975.

———. *Who Are We? The Challenges to American National Identity*. New York: Simon and Schuster, 2004.

———. "Will More Countries Become Democratic?" *Political Science Quarterly* 99, no. 2 (1984): 193–218.

Hutcheson, Gregory S. "Return to Queer Iberia." *La Corónica* (2001), http://college .holycross.edu/lacoronica/qi/2-Hutcheson.htm (accessed 1 April 2014).

Ibiwoye, Dotun. "Gay Right Controversy: A Gathering Storm over Cameron's Comments." *Vanguard* (Nigeria), 23 November 2011, http://www.vanguardngr .com/2011/11/gay-right-controversy-a-gathering-storm-over-camerons -comments/ (accessed 1 April 2014).

Al-ʿIlm wa al-Din wa al-Tahlil al-Nafsi: Aʿmal al-Muʾtamar al-Dawli al-Thalith lil-Muhallilin al-Nafsiyyin al-ʿArab, Beirut, 17–19 May, 2007 (Science, Religion, and Psychoanalysis: The Proceedings of the Third International Conference for Arab Psychoanalysts). Beirut: Dar al-Farabi, 2008.

ʿImarah, Muhammad. *ʿAbd al-Rahman al-Kawakibi: Shahid al-Hurriyyah wa Mujaddid al-Islam* (Abd al-Rahman al-Kawakibi: The Martyr of Freedom and the Renewer of Islam). Beirut: Dar al-Wihdah, 1984.

———. *Al-Islam wa Usul al-Hukm li-ʿAli ʿAbd al-Raziq: Dirasah wa Wathaʾiq* (Islam and the Bases of Governance by Ali Abd al-Raziq: A Study Accompanied with Documents). Beirut: Al-Muʾassassah al-ʿArabiyyah Lil-Dirasah wa al-Nashr, 2000.

Imber, Colin. *Ebu's Suʿud: The Islamic Legal Tradition*. Stanford, CA: Stanford University Press, 2009.

Irwin, Robert. *For Lust of Knowing: The Orientalists and Their Enemies*. London: Penguin Books, 2007.

Isin, Engin F. "Citizenship after Orientalism: Ottoman Citizenship." In *Citizenship in a Global World: European Questions and Turkish Experiences*, edited by Fuat Keyman and Ahmet Icduygu, 31–51. London: Routledge, 2005.

"Islam against Nationalism." *Economist*, 2 June 1962.

"Islam and the Arab Spring: Bring the Islamists In." *Economist*, 6 August 2011.

"Islam and Democracy: Uneasy Companions." *Economist*, 6 August 2011.

"Islam's Philosophical Divide: Dreaming of a Caliphate." *Economist*, 6 August 2011.

Jacob, Wilson C. "Other Inscriptions: Sexual Difference and History Writing between Futures Past and Present." Posted on H-net, September 2009, http:// www.h-net.org/reviews/showrev.php?id=25004 (accessed 1 April 2014).

Jacquemond, Richard. "Translation Policies in the Arab World: Representations, Discourse, and Realities." *Translator* 15, no. 1 (2009): 15–35.

Jad, Islah. "Comments from an Author: Engaging the *Arab Human Development Report 2005* on Women." *International Journal of Middle East Studies* 41 (2009): 61–62.

———. "The Demobilization of the Palestinian Women's Movement." In *Women's Movements in the Global Era*, edited by Amrita Basu, 329–58. Philadelphia: Westview Press, 2010.

———. "Islamist Women of Hamas: A New Women's Movement." In *On Shifting Ground: Muslim Women in a Global Era*, edited by Nouraine-Simone, 172–202. New York: Feminist Press at CUNY, 2005.

Jayawardena, Kumari. *Feminism and Nationalism in the Third World*. London: Zed Books, 1986.

Jbeili, Karim. *Le psychisme des Orientaux: Différences et déchirures*. Montréal: Liber, 2006.

Jirjis, Sabri. *Al-Turath al-Yahudi al-Suhyuni wa al-Fikr al-Fruydi: Adwaʾ ʿala al-usul al-Suhyuniyyah li-fikr Sighmund Fruyd* (Zionist Jewish Culture and Freudian Thought: Shedding Light on the Zionist Origins of the Thought of Sigmund Freud). Cairo: ʿAlam al-Kutub, 1970.

Johnson, Ian. *A Mosque in Munich: Nazis, the CIA, and the Muslim Brotherhood in the West*. New York: Houghton Mifflin Harcourt, 2010.

Kader, Hussein Abel. "La psychanalyse en Égypte entre un passé ambitieux et un future incertain." *La Célibataire*, no. 8 (Printemps 2004): 61–73.

Kahn, Paul W. *Putting Liberalism in Its Place*. Princeton, NJ: Princeton University Press, 2008.

Kaiser, Thomas. "The Evil Empire: The Debate on Turkish Despotism in Eighteenth-Century French Political Culture." *Journal of Modern History* 72, no. 1 (2000): 6–34.

Kamal, Hala. "Translating Women and Gender: The Experience of Translating *The Encyclopedia of Women and Islamic Cultures* into Arabic." *Women Studies Quarterly* 36, nos. 3–4 (2008): 254–68.

Kandiyoti, Deniz. "Islam and Patriarchy: A Comparative Perspective." In *Women in Middle Eastern History*, edited by Nikki R. Keddie and Beth Baron, 23–42. New Haven, CT: Yale University Press, 1991.

Kapur, Ratna. "The Tragedy of Victimization Rhetoric: Resurrecting the Native Subject in International/PostColonial Feminist Legal Politics." *Harvard Human Rights Journal* 15, no. 1 (2002): 1–38.

Al-Kassim, Dina. "Epilogue." In *Islamicate Sexualities: Translations across Temporal Geographies of Desire*, edited by Kathryn Babayan and Afsaneh Najmabadi, 297–339. Cambridge, MA: Harvard Center for Middle East Studies, 2008.

———. "Psychoanalysis and the Postcolonial Genealogy of Queer Theory." *International Journal of Middle East Studies* 45, no. 2 (2013): 343–46.

Katyal, Sonya. "Exporting Identity." *Yale Journal of Law and Feminism* 14, no. 1 (2002): 97–157.

Katz, Jonathan Ned. *The Invention of Heterosexuality*. New York: Dutton, 1995.

Kawakibi, ʿAbd al-Rahman al-. *Tabaʾiʿ al-Istibdad wa Masariʿ al-Istiʿbad*, in ʿAbd al-Rahman al-Kawakibi, *Al-Aʿmal al-Kamilah lil-Kawakibi*, edited by Muhammad Jamal Tahhan. Beirut: Markaz Dirasat al-Wihdah al-ʿArabiyyah.

———. *Umm al-Qura*, in ʿAbd al-Rahman al-Kawakibi, *Al-Aʿmal al-Kamilah lil-Kawakibi*, edited by Muhammad Jamal Tahhan. Beirut: Markaz Dirasat al-Wihdah al-ʿArabiyyah.

Keck, Margaret E., and Kathryn Sikkinik. *Activists beyond Borders: Advocacy Networks in International Politics*. Ithaca, NY: Cornell University Press, 1998.

Kedourie, Elie. *Democracy and Arab Political Culture*. Washington, DC: Washington Institute for Near East Policy, 1992.

Khalafallah, Muhammad. *Al-Qurʾan wa al-Dawlah* (The Qurʾan and the State). Cairo: Maktabat Al-Anjlo al-Misriyyah, 1973.

Khalil, Usamah, ed. *Mustafa Zaywar: fi Dhikra al-ʿAlim wa al-Fannan wa al-Insan* (Mustafa Zaywar: In Memory of the Scholar, the Artist, and the Man). Paris: Maʿhad al-Lughah wa al-Hadarah al-ʿArabiyyah, 1997.

Khatibi, Abdelkebir. "Argument." *Cahiers Intersignes*, no. 1 (1990).

———. "Du message prophétique (argument)." In *Par-Dessus l'épaule,* edited by Abdelkebir Khatibi, 77–89. Paris: Aubier, 1988.

———. "Frontières." *Cahiers Intersignes*, no. 1 (1990).

King-Irani, Laurie. "Imperiled Pioneer: An Assessment of the Institute for Women's Studies in the Arab World." In *Muslim Women and the Politics of Participation*, edited by Afkhami and Friedl, 101–8. Syracuse, NY: Syracuse University Press, 1997.

———. "Women's Rights Are Human Rights." *Al-Raida* 13, nos. 74–75 (1996): 11–12.

Klein, Naomi. *The Shock Doctrine: The Rise of Disaster Capitalism*. New York: Picador, 2008.

Korey, William. *Taking on the World's Repressive Regimes: The Ford Foundation's International Human Rights Policies and Practices*. New York: Palgrave Macmillan, 2007.

Kra, Pauline. "The Role of the Harem in Imitations of Montesquieu's *Lettres Persanes*." *Studies on Voltaire and the Eighteenth Century* 182 (1979): 273–83.

Kramer, Martin. "Muftis of Morningside Heights," blog post on 13 October 2008, http://www.martinkramer.org/sandbox/blog/page/14/.

Kroebner, R. "Despot and Despotism: Vicissitudes of a Political Term." *Journal of the Warburg and Courtauld Institutes* 14 (1951): 275–302.

Kugle, Scott. *Homosexuality in Islam: Critical Reflection on Gay, Lesbian, and Transgender Muslims*. Oxford: Oneworld Publications, 2010.

Kuhn, Annette, and Ann Marie Wolpe, eds. *Feminism and Materialism: Women and Modes of Production*. London: Routledge and Kegan Paul, 1978.

Kuhn, Thomas. *The Structure of Scientific Revolutions*. Chicago: University of Chicago Press, 1962.

Kurzman, Charles, ed. *Liberal Islam: A Sourcebook*. Oxford: Oxford University Press, 1998.

———. *Modernist Islam: A Sourcebook*. Oxford: Oxford University Press, 2002.

Landau, Jacob M. *The Politics of Pan-Islam: Ideology and Organization*. Oxford: Clarendon Press, 1990.

———. "Saint Priest and His *Mémoire sur les Turcs*." In *L'Empire Ottoman: La République de Turquie et la France,* edited by Hâmit Batu and Jean-Louis Bacqué-Grammont, 127–49. Istanbul: L'institut Français d'études Anatoliennes d'Istanbul, 1986.

Landler, Mark. "Clinton Praises Indonesian Democracy." *New York Times*, 18 February 2009.

Laub, Katin. "Hamas Hard-Liners Edge toward Cease-Fire." Associated Press, 22 June 2003.

Lazreg, Marnia. *The Eloquence of Silence: Algerian Women in Question*. New York: Routledge, 1994.

———. "Feminism and Difference: The Perils of Writing as a Woman on Women in Algeria." In *Feminist Studies* 14, no. 1 (1988): 81–107.

Lees, James Cameron. "Mohamedanism." In *The Faiths of the World*, St. Giles Lectures 331, 361–96. New York: Scribners, 1882.

Lenin, Vladimir Ilyich. "Preliminary Draft of Theses on the National and Colonial Questions." In *Lenin on the National and Colonial Questions, Three Articles* by Vladimir Lenin, 20–29. Peking: Foreign Languages Press, 1967.

Lerner, Daniel. *The Passing of Traditional Society: Modernizing the Middle East*. New York: Free Press, 1958.

Levinas, Emmanuel. "The State of Caesar and the State of David." In Emmanuel Levinas, *Beyond the Verse: Talmudic Readings and Lectures*, 177–87. Translated by Gary D. Mole. London: Athlone Press, 1982.

Lewes, Kenneth. *The Psychoanalytic Theory of Male Homosexuality*. Markham, ON: Meridian Books, 1988.

Lewis, Bernard. "Communism and Islam." *International Affairs* 30, no. 1 (1954): 1–12.

———. "The Roots of Muslim Rage." *Atlantic Monthly* 266 (1990): 47–60.

———. *Semites and Anti-Semites: An Inquiry into Conflict and Prejudice*. New York: W. W. Norton, 1986.

Lewis, Hope. "Between Irua and 'Female Genital Mutilation': Feminist Human Rights Discourse and the Cultural Divide." *Harvard Human Rights Journal* 8 (1995): 1–55.

Lewis, Hope, and Isabel Gunning. "Cleaning Our Own House: 'Exotic' and Familial Human Rights Violations." *Buffalo Human Rights Law Review* 4 (1998): 123–40.

Livermon, Xavier. "Queer(y)ing Freedom: Black Queer Visibilities in Postapartheid South Africa" *GLQ* 18, nos. 2–3 (2012): 297–323.

Lockman, Zachary. *Contending Visions of the Middle East: The History and Politics of Orientalism*. Cambridge: Cambridge University Press, 2004.

Long, Scott. "The Trials of Culture: Sex and Security in Egypt." *Middle East Report*, no. 230 (2004): 12–20.

———. "Unbearable Witness: How Western Activists (Mis)Recognize Sexuality in Iran." *Contemporary Politics* 15, no. 1 (2009): 119–36.

Losurdo, Domenico. *Liberalism: A Counter-History.* Translated by Gregory Elliott. London: Verso, 2011.

Lugard, Frederick. *The Dual Mandate in British Tropical Africa.* 5th ed. Hamden, CT: Archon Books, 1965.

Mahmood, Saba. "Feminism, Democracy, and Empire: Islam and the War on Terror." In *Women's Studies on the Edge,* edited by Joan Wallach Scott, 81–114. Durham, NC: Duke University Press, 2008.

———. "Feminist Theory, Embodiment, and the Docile Agent: Some Reflections on the Egyptian Islamic Revival." *Cultural Anthropology* 16, no. 2 (2001): 224–25.

———. *Politics of Piety: The Islamic Revival and the Feminist Subject.* Princeton, NJ: Princeton University Press, 2005.

———. "Secularism, Hermeneutics, and Empire: The Politics of Islamic Reformation." *Public Culture* 18, no. 2 (2006): 323–47.

Makarem, Ghassan. "The Story of Helem." *Journal of Middle East Women's Studies* 7, no. 3 (2011): 98–113.

———. "We Are Not Agents of the West." *Reset DOC,* 10 December 2009, http://www.resetdoc.org/EN/Helem-replies-Massad.php (accessed 1 April 2014).

Malcolm X. "Malcolm X: Human Rights and the United Nations." In *Malcolm X: A Historical Reader,* edited by James L. Conyers Jr. and Andre P. Smallwood, 125–30. Durham, NC: Carolina Academic Press, 2008.

Mamdani, Mahmood. *Citizen and Subject: Contemporary Africa and the Legacy of Late Colonialism.* Princeton, NJ: Princeton University Press, 1996.

Marchand, Susanne E. *German Orientalism in the Age of Empire: Religion, Race and Scholarship.* Washington, DC, and Cambridge: German Historical Institute and Cambridge University Press, 2009.

Margoliouth, D. S. *Mohammedanism.* London: Williams and Norgate, 1896.

Marx, Karl. *The Communist Manifesto.* In *The Marx-Engels Reader,* edited by Robert Tucker, 469–500. New York: W. W. Norton, 1978.

———. *The Eastern Question.* Edited by Eleanor Marx Aveling and Edward Aveling. London: Swab Sonnenschein, 1897.

———. "Letter from Marx to Engels, 2 June 1853." In *K. Marx and F. Engels on Religion,* 120–22. Moscow: Foreign Languages Publishing House, 1957.

Massad, Joseph. "Affiliating with Edward Said." In *Emancipation and Representation: On the Intellectual Meditations of Edward Said,* edited by Hakem Rustom and Adel Iskander, 23–49. Berkeley: University of California Press, 2010.

———. "Arab Instability and US Strategy." *Al-Jazeera English Web,* 17 July 2012, http://www.aljazeera.com/indepth/opinion/2012/07/201271511521721772.html (accessed 1 April 2014).

———. *Colonial Effects: The Making of National Identity in Jordan.* New York: Columbia University Press, 2001.

———. "Conceiving the Masculine: Gender and Palestinian Nationalism." *Middle East Journal* 49, no. 3 (1995): 467–83.

———. "Débat: L'empire de la sexualité en question." *Revue Des Livres*, March– April 2013, http://www.revuedeslivres.fr/debat-l'empire-de-«-la-sexualite -»-en-question-22-par-jospeh-massad/ (accessed 1 April 2014).

———. *Desiring Arabs.* Chicago: University of Chicago Press, 2007.

———. "L'empire de la Sexualité, ou peut-on ne pas être homosexuel (ou hé-térosexuel)? Entretien avec Joseph Massad." *Revue Des Livres*, January– February 2013, http://www.revuedeslivres.fr/l'empire-de-«-la-sexualite -»-ou-peut-on-ne-pas-etre-homosexuel-ou-heterosexuel-entretien-avec-joseph -massad/ (accessed 1 April 2014).

———. "Love, Fear, and the Arab Spring." *Public Culture* 26, no. 1 (2014): 129–54.

———. "Palestinians and Jewish History: Recognition or Submission?" *Journal of Palestine Studies* 30, no. 1 (2000): 52–67.

———. "The Persistence of the Palestinian Question." *Cultural Critique*, no. 59 (2005): 1–23.

———. *The Persistence of the Palestinian Question: Essays on Zionism and the Palestinians.* London: Routledge, 2006.

———. "Re-Orienting Desire: The Gay International and the Arab World." *Public Culture* 14, no. 2 (2002): 361–85.

———. Reply to Ghassan Makarem, published in Reset Doc on December 14, 2009, http://www.resetdoc.org/EN/Massad-counter-replies.php (accessed 1 April 2014).

———. "Sexuality, Literature, and Human Rights in Translation." In *Teaching World Literature,* edited David Damrosch, 246–57. New York: Modern Language Association, 2009.

Massell, Gregory J. *The Surrogate Proletariat: Moslem Women and Revolutionary Strategies in Soviet Central Asia, 1919–1929.* Princeton, NJ: Princeton University Press, 1974.

Massignon, Louis. "Introduction à l'étude des revendications musulmanes." *Revue du monde Musulman* 39 (1920): 1–26.

———. "Three Prayers of Abraham." In *Testimonies and Reflections: Essays of Louis Massignon,* edited by Herbert Mason, 257–72. Notre Dame, IN: University of Notre Dame Press, 1989.

———. "Trois prières d'Abraham, père de tous les croyants." In *Parole Donnée,* 19– 49. Paris: Julliard, 1962.

Masuzawa, Tomoko. *The Invention of World Religions: Or, How European Uni-versalism was Preserved in the Language of Pluralism.* Chicago: University of Chicago Press, 2005.

Mavelli, Luca. *Europe's Encounter with Islam: The Secular and the Postsecular.* Lon-don: Routledge, 2012.

McCormick, Jared. "Hairy Chest, Will Travel: Tourism, Identity, and Sexuality in the Levant." *Journal of Middle East Women's Studies* 7, no. 3 (2011): 71–97.

Mehrez, Samia. *Egypt's Culture Wars: Politics and Practice*. London: Routledge, 2008.

Mehta, Uday Singh. *Liberalism and Empire: A Study in Nineteenth-Century British Liberal Thought*. Chicago: University of Chicago Press, 1999.

Mejcher, Helmut. *Imperial Quest for Oil: Iraq, 1910–1928*. London: Ithaca Press, 1976.

Menocal, María Rosa. "Pride and Prejudice in Medieval Studies: European and Oriental." *Hispanic Review* 53, no. 1 (Winter 1985): 61–78.

———. *The Arabic Role in Medieval Literary History: A Forgotten Heritage* (Philadelphia: University of Pennsylvania Press, 1987).

Mepschen, Paul, Jan Willem Duyvendak, and Evelien H. Tonkens. "Sexual Politics, Orientalism, and Multicultural Citizenship in the Netherlands." *Sociology* 55, no. 5 (2010): 962–79.

Mercer, Kobena, and Isaac Julien. "Race, Sexual Politics and Black Masculinity: A Dossier." In *Male Order, Unwrapping Masculinity*, edited by Rowena Chapman and Jonathan Rutherford, 97–164. London: Lawrence and Wishart, 1988.

Mernissi, Fatima. *Beyond the Veil: Male-Female Dynamics in Modern Muslim Society*. Cambridge: Schenkman, 1975.

Meyerowitz, Joanne. "Transnational Sex and U.S. History." *American Historical Review* 114, no. 5 (2009): 1273–86.

Mill, John Stuart. *On Liberty*. In *On Liberty and Other Essays*. Oxford: Oxford University Press, 1991.

Mir-Hosseini, Ziba. *The Religious Debate in Contemporary Iran*. Princeton, NJ: Princeton University Press, 1999.

Mitchell, Juliet. *Psychoanalysis and Feminism*. New York: Pantheon Books, 1974.

Mitchell, Richard P. *The Society of the Muslim Brothers*. Oxford: Oxford University Press, 1969.

Mitchell, Timothy. *Carbon Democracy: Political Power in the Age of Oil*. London: Verso, 2011.

———. "The Middle East in the Past and Future of Social Science." In *The Politics of Knowledge: Area Studies and the Disciplines*, edited by David Szanton, 74–118. Berkeley: University of California Press, 2002.

Moghadam, Valentine M. "Feminist Networks North and South: DAWN, WIDE and WLUML." *Journal of International Communication* 3, no. 1 (1996): 111–25.

Mohanty, Chandra Talpade, Ann Russo, and Lourdes Torres, eds. *Third World Women and the Politics of Feminism*. Bloomington: Indiana University Press, 1991.

Montesquieu, Charles-Louis de Secondat, Baron de. *The Spirit of the Laws*. Translated by Thomas Nugent. New York: Hafner, 1949.

Morgan, Robin. *Sisterhood Is Global: The International Women's Movement Anthology*. New York: Anchor Press/Doubleday, 1984.

Morris, Rosalind. "All Made Up: Performance Theory and the Anthropology of Sex and Gender." *Annual Review of Anthropology* 24 (1995): 567–92.

———. "Theses on the Question of War: History, Media, Terror." *Social Text* 20, no. 3 (2002): 149–75.

Moyn, Samuel. *The Last Utopia: Human Rights in History*. Cambridge, MA: Belknap Press of Harvard University Press, 2010.

Mubarakfuri, Rahman. *Al-Rahiq al-Makhtum: Bahth fi al-Sirah al-Nabawiyyah ʿala Sahibiha Afdal al-Salah wa al-Salam* (The Sealed Nectar: A Query into the Biography of the Prophet). Riyad: Maktabat Dar al-Salam, 1995.

Murray, Stephen O., and Will Roscoe, eds. *Islamic Homosexualities: Culture, History, and Literature*. New York: New York University Press, 1997.

Muruwwah, Husayn. *Dirasat Naqdiyyah, fi Duʾ al-Manhaj al-Waqiʿi* (Critical Studies, in the Light of the Realist Method). Beirut: Maktabat al-Maʿarif, 1965.

Musa, Salamah. *Al-ʿAql al-Batin wa Maknunat al-Nafs* (The Unconscious and the Soul's Latent Innermost Thoughts). Cairo: Dar al-Hilal, 1928.

———. *ʿAqli wa ʿAqluk* (My Mind/Reason and Yours). Cairo: Salamah Musa Lil-Nashr, 1947.

Musallam, B. F. *Sex and Society in Islam: Birth Control before the Nineteenth Century*. Cambridge: Cambridge University Press, 1983.

Mutiʿi, Muhammad Bakhit al-. *Haqiqat al-Islam wa Usul al-Hukm* (The Truth of Islam and the Bases of Governance). Cairo: n.p, 1926?

Najjar, ʿAbd al-Wahhab. *Qisas al-Anbiyaʾ* (The Biographies of the Prophets). Cairo: Muʾassassat al-Halabi wa Shurakaʾihi lil-Tabʿ wa al-Tawziʿ, 1966.

Najmabadi, Afsaneh. "Said's War on the Intellectuals." Letter to the editor. *Middle East Report* (1991): 42–44.

———. "Transing and Transpassing across Sex-Gender Walls in Iran." *Women's Studies Quarterly* 36, nos. 3–4 (2008): 23–42.

———. *Women with Mustaches and Men without Beards*. Berkeley: University of California Press, 2005.

———. "Wrong Regardless." Letter to the editor. *Iranian*, 18 September 2001, http://iranian.com/Opinion/2001/September/Wrong/index.html.

Newman, Louise. *White Women's Rights: The Racial Origins of Feminism in the United States*. Oxford: Oxford University Press, 1999.

Nicolacopoulos, Toula. *The Radical Critique of Liberalism: In Memory of a Vision*. Melbourne: re.press, 2008.

Norman, Daniel. *The Arabs and Medieval Europe*. London: Longman, 1975.

Northrop, Douglas. *Veiled Empire: Gender and Power in Stalinist Central Asia*. Ithaca, NY: Cornell University Press, 2004.

Norton, Anne. *Alternative Americas: A Reading of Antebellum Political Culture*. Chicago: University of Chicago Press, 1986.

———. "On the Muslim Question." In *Democracy, Religious Pluralism and the Liberal Dilemma of Accommodation*, edited by M. Mookherjee, 65–76. Vol. 7 of Studies in Global Justice. New York: Springer, 2011.

———. *On the Muslim Question*. Princeton, NJ: Princeton University Press, 2013.

Nuwayhi, Muhammad al-. *Nafsiyyat Abu Nuwas* (The Psychology of Abu Nuwas). (Cairo: Dar al-Fikr, 1970.

Obama, Barack. "Text: Obama's Speech in Cairo." *New York Times*, 4 June 2009.

Okin, Susan Moller, et al. *Is Multiculturalism Bad for Women?* Princeton, NJ: Princeton University Press, 1999.

Oliver-Dee, Sean. *The Caliphate Question: The British Government and Islamic Governance*. Plymouth, England: Lexington Books, 2009.

Owen, Roger. *Lord Cromer: Victorian Imperialist, Edwardian Proconsul*. Oxford: Oxford University Press, 2005.

Padmore, George. *How Britain Rules Africa*. London: Wishart Books, 1936.

Paidar, Parvin. *Women and the Political Process in Twentieth-Century Iran*. Cambridge: Cambridge University Press, 1995.

Parry, Clive. "Climate of International Law in Europe." *Proceedings of the American Society of International Law at Its Annual Meeting* 47 (23–25 April 1953): 37–44.

Pierce, Leslie. "Writing Histories of Sexuality in the Middle East." *American Historical Review* 114, no. 5 (2009): 1325–39.

Pirenne, Henri. *Mohammed and Charlemagne*. Translated by Bernard Miall. New York: Barnes and Noble Books, 1992.

Povoledo, Elisabetta. "A Call for Aid, Not Laws, to Help Women in Italy." *New York Times*, 18 August 2013.

Puar, Jasbir K. "Circuits of Queer Mobility: Tourism, Travel, and Globalization." *GLQ* 8, nos. 1–2 (2002): 101–37.

———. "Homonationalism as Assemblage: Viral Travels, Affective Sexualities." *Jindal Global Law Review* 4, no. 2 (November 2013): 23–43.

———. *Terrorist Assemblages: Homonationalism in Queer Times*. Durham, NC: Duke University Press, 2007.

Puar, Jasbir K., and Maya Mikdashi. "On Positionality and Not Naming Names: A Rejoinder to the Response of Maikey and Schotten." *Jadaliyya*, 10 October 2012, http://www.jadaliyya.com/pages/index/7792/on-positionality-and-not-naming-names_a-rejoinder- (accessed 1 April 2014).

———. "Pinkwatching and Pinkwashing: Interpenetration and Its Discontents." *Jadaliyya*, 9 August 2012, http://www.jadaliyya.com/pages/index/6774/pinkwatching-and-pinkwashing_interpenetration-and- (accessed 1 April 2014).

Qabbal, Al-Mu'ti. "Al-Islam wa Sahwat al-Tufulah" (Islam and the Awakening of Childhood), Hiwar ma' Malik Shibl (interview with Malek Chebel). In *Al-Tahlil al-Nafsi wa al-Thaqafah al-'Arabiyyah-al-Islamiyyah* (Psychoanalysis and Arab-Islamic Culture), 73–82. Damascus: Dar al-Bidayat, 2008.

Qadir, Husayn 'Abd al-. "Atruk Sharayini Fikum" ("I leave my arteries within you"). In *Mustafa Zaywar: fi Dhikra al-'Alim wa al-Fannan wa al-Insan*, edited by Usamah Khalil, 7–14. Paris: Ma'had al-Lughah wa al-Hadarah al-'Arabiyyah, 1997.

Quinet, Edgar. *Le Christianisme et la Révolution française*. Paris: Fayard, 1984.

Qutb, Sayyid. *Al-Islam wa Mushkilat al-Hadarah* (Islam and the Problems of Civilization). Cairo: Dar al-Shuruq, 2005.

Ramadan, Ahmad al-Sayyid 'Ali. *Al-Islam wa al-Tahlil al-Nafsi 'ind Fruyd* (Islam and Freud's Psychoanalysis). Al-Mansura, Egypt: Maktabat al-Iman, 2000.

Ramusack, Barbara N. "Cultural Missionaries, Maternal Imperialists, Feminist Allies: British Women Activists in India, 1865–1945." In *Western Women and Imperialism: Complicity and Resistance*, edited by Nupur Chaudhuri and Margaret Strobel, 119–36. Bloomington: Indiana University Press, 1992.

Rancière, Jacques. *Hatred of Democracy*. Translated by Steve Corcoran. London: Verso, 2006.

Al-Rasheed, Madawi. *A Most Masculine State: Gender, Politics, and Religion in Saudi Arabia*. Cambridge: Cambridge University Press, 2013.

Raziq, ʿAli ʿAbd al-. *Al-Islam wa Usul al-Hukm: Bahth fi al-Khilafah wa al-Hukumah fil Islam* (Islam and the Bases for Governance: A Query into the Caliphate and Government in Islam). Edited by Mamduh Haqqi. Beirut: Dar Maktabat al-Nahar, 1966).

Reid, Donald Malcolm. *Cairo University and the Making of Modern Egypt*. Cambridge: Cambridge University Press, 1990.

Renan, Ernest. "Islamism and Science." In *Orientalism: Early Sources*, vol. 1, *Readings in Orientalism*, edited by Bryan S. Turner, 199–217. London: Routledge, 2000.

Rodinson, Maxime. *Islam and Capitalism*. Translated by Brain Pierce. Austin: University of Texas Press, 1981.

———. *Muhammad: Prophet of Islam*. London: Tauris Parke Paperbacks, 2002.

Rooney, Caroline. "Derrida and Said: Ships That Pass in the Night." In *Edward Said and the Literary, Social, and Political World*, edited by Ranjan Ghosh, 36–52. London: Routledge, 2009.

Rossi, Ettore. "Una traduzione Turca dell'opera 'Della Tirannide' di V. Alfieri probabilmente conosciuta da al-Kawakibi" (A Turkish Translation of the Work "Of Tyranny" by V. Alfieri, Probably Known to al-Kawakibi). *Oriente Moderno* 34, no. 7 (1954): 335–37.

Sabsay, Leticia. "The Emergence of the Other Sexual Citizen: Orientalism and the Modernization of Sexuality." *Citizenship Studies* 16, nos. 5–6 (2012): 605–23.

Saʿdawi, Nawal al-. *Dirasat ʿan al-Marʾah wa al-Rajul fi al-Mujtamaʿ al-ʿArabi* (Studies about Women and Men in Arab Society). Beirut: al-Muʾassassah al-ʿArabiyyah lil Dirasat wa al-Nashr, 1986.

Sadowski, Yahya. "The New Orientalism and the Democracy Debate." In *Political Islam: Essays from Middle East Report*, edited by Joel Beinin and Joe Stork, 33–50. Berkeley: University of California Press, 1997.

Safouan, Mustafa. "Pratique analytique dans le monde arabe: Incidences et difficulté." *La Célibataire*, no. 8 (2004): 11–18.

———. *Why Are the Arabs Not Free? The Politics of Writing*. Oxford: Wiley-Blackwell, 2007.

Safwan, Mustafa, and ʿAdnan Hubbu Allah. *Ishkaliyyat al-Mujtamaʿ al-ʿArabi, Qiraʾah min Manzur al-Tahlil al-Nafsi* (The Problematics of Arab Society: A Reading from a Psychoanalytic Perspective). Beirut: Al-Markaz al-Thaqafi al-Arabi, 2008.

Said, Edward W. *Conrad and the Fiction of Autobiography*. New York: Columbia University Press, 2008.

———. *Covering Islam: How the Media and the Experts Determine How We See the World.* Rev. ed. New York: Vintage Books, 1997.

———. *Culture and Imperialism.* New York: Knopf, 1993.

———. *The End of the Peace Process: Oslo and After.* New York: Pantheon, 2000.

———. *Freud and the Non-European.* London: Verso, 2003.

———. *On Late Style: Music and Literature against the Grain.* New York: Pantheon Books, 2006.

———. *Orientalism.* New York: Pantheon Books, 1978.

———. "Orientalism: An Exchange." *New York Review of Books,* 12 August 1982.

Saliba, George. *Islamic Science and the Making of the European Renaissance.* Cambridge, MA: MIT Press, 2011.

Salih, Saʿd al-Din Sayyid. *Nazariyyat al-Tahlil al-Nafsi ʿind Fruyd fi Mizan al-Islam* (Freud's Theory of Psychoanalysis [weighed] on the scales of Islam). Jiddah, Saudi Arabia: Maktabat al-Sahabah, 1993.

Sargent, Lydia, ed. *Women and Revolution: A Discussion of the Unhappy Marriage of Marxism and Feminism.* Boston: South End Press, 1981.

Saunders, Frances Stoner. *The Cultural Cold War: The CIA and the World of Arts and Letters.* New York: New Press, 2001.

Savage, Charlie. "Senators Say Patriot Act Is Being Misinterpreted." *New York Times,* 26 May 2011.

Schotten, Heike, and Haneen Maikey. "Queers Resisting Zionism: On Authority and Accountability beyond Homonationalism." *Jadaliyya,* 10 October 2012, http://www.jadaliyya.com/pages/index/7738/queers-resisting-zionism_on -authority-and-accounta (accessed 1 April 2014).

Schulman, Sarah. *Israel/Palestine and the Queer International.* Durham, NC: Duke University Press, 2012.

Schulze, Reinhard. *A Modern History of the Islamic World.* New York: New York University Press, 2002.

Schwanitz, Wolfgang G. "The German Middle Eastern Policy, 1871–1945." In *Germany and the Middle East, 1871–1945,* edited by Wolfgang G. Schwanitz, 1–23. Princeton, NJ: Markus Wiener Publishers, 2004.

Scott, David, and Charles Hirschkind, eds. "The Trouble of Thinking: An Interview with Talal Asad." In *Powers of the Secular Modern: Talal Asad and his Interlocutors,* 243–303. Stanford, CA: Stanford University Press, 2006.

Scott, Joan Wallach. *The Fantasy of Feminist History.* Durham, NC: Duke University Press, 2011.

———. *The Politics of the Veil.* Princeton, NJ: Princeton University Press, 2007.

Seckinelgin, Hakan: "Global Activism and Sexualities in the Time of HIV/AIDS." *Contemporary Politics* 15, no. 1 (2009): 103–18.

Sedgwick, Eve Kosofsky. *Epistemology of the Closet.* Berkeley: University of California Press, 1990.

Shakir, Mahmud Muhammad. *Risalah fi al-Tariq ila Thaqafatina* (A Message on the Path to Our Culture). Cairo: Muʾassassat al-Risalah, 1992.

Shalakany, Amr. "On a Certain Queer Discomfort with Orientalism." *Proceedings of the Annual Meeting (American Society of International Law)* 101 (28–31 March 2007): 125–29.

Sharafuddin, Mohammed. *Islam and Romantic Orientalism: Literary Encounters with the Orient.* London: I. B. Tauris, 1994.

Sharif, Regina. *Non-Jewish Zionism: Its Roots in Western History.* London: Zed Press, 1983.

Sibony, Daniel. *Proche-Orient: Psychanalyse d'un conflit.* Paris: Éditions du Seuil, 2003.

Simpson, Bradley R. *Economists with Guns: Authoritarian Development and US–Indonesian Relations, 1960–1968.* Stanford, CA: Stanford University Press, 2008.

Sindi, Abdullah M. "King Faisal and Pan-Islamism." In *King Faisal and the Modernisation of Saudi Arabia*, edited by Willard A. Beling, 184–201. London: Croom Helm, 1980.

Slama, Raja Ben. "L'arbre qui révèle la forêt: Traductions arabes du vocabulaire freudien." *Transeuropeenes: International Journal of Critical Thought*, 5 November 2009, http://www.transeuropeennes.eu/en/articles/106/The_Tree _that_Reveals_the_Forest (accessed 1 April 2014).

———. "La psychanalyse en Égypte: Un problème de non-advenue." *La psychanalyse au Maghreb et au Machrek*, a special issue of *Topique: Revue Freudienne*, no. 110 (2010): 83–96.

Smith, Jonathan Z. "Religion, Religions, Religious." In *Critical Terms for Religious Studies*, ed. Mark C. Taylor, 269–83. Chicago: University of Chicago Press, 1998.

Spivak, Gayatri Chakravorty. *An Aesthetic Education in the Era of Globalization.* Cambridge, MA: Harvard University Press, 2012.

———. *A Critique of Postcolonial Reason: Toward a History of the Vanishing Present.* Cambridge, MA: Harvard University Press, 1999.

———. *Outside in the Teaching Machine.* New York: Routledge, 1993.

———. "The Politics of Translation." In *Outside in the Teaching Machine*, 200–225. New York: Routledge, 1993.

Springborg, Patricia. *Western Republicanism and the Oriental Prince.* Cambridge: Polity Press, 1992.

Stere, Emelia. "ACCEPTing the future: An Interview with Adrian Coman." *Central Europe Review* 3, no. 16 (2001), http://www.ce-review.org/01/16/stere16.html.

Stoler, Ann Laura. *Race and the Education of Desire: Foucault's History of Sexuality and the Colonial Order of Things.* Durham, NC: Duke University Press, 1995.

Stychin, Carl F. *Governing Sexuality: The Changing Politics of Citizenship and Law Reform.* Oxford: Hart, 2003.

Sukarieh, Mayssoun. "The Hope Crusades: Culturalism and Reform in the Arab World." *Political and Legal Anthropology Review* 35, no. 1 (2012): 115–34.

Suleiman, Yasir. *The Arabic Language and National Identity: A Study in Ideology*. Washington, DC: Georgetown University Press, 2003.

Sullivan, Winifred Fallers. "Comparing Religions, Legally." *The Washington and Lee Law Review* 63, no. 1 (2006): 913–28.

Szymanski, Albert. *Human Rights in the Soviet Union: Including Comparisons with the USA*. London: Zed Books, 1984.

Taha, ʿAbd al-Qadir, ed. *Mawsuʿat ʿIlm al-Nafs wa al-Tahlil al-Nafsi* (The Encyclopaedia of Psychology and Psychoanalysis). Kuwait: Dar Suʿad al-Subah, 1993.

Tanaka, Jennifer. "Report on the Symposium Homosexuality: A Human Right?" 1995, http://www.france.qrd.org/assocs/ilga/euroletter/35-Romania.html (accessed 1 April 2014).

Tarabishi, Jurj. *Hartaqat 2: ʿAn al-ʿIlmaniyyah ka-Ishkaliyyah Islamiyyah-Islamiyyah* (Hereticisms 2: On Secularism as a Muslim-Muslim Problematic). Beirut: Dar al-Saqi, 2008.

———. *Al-Muthaqaffun al-ʿArab wa al-Turath: Al-Tahlil al-Nafsi li-ʿUsab Jamaʿi* (Arab Intellectuals and Heritage: Psychoanalysis of a Group Neurosis). London: Riyad al-Rayyis lil-Nashr, 1991.

———. *ʿAl-Rujulah wa Aydiyulujiyyat al-Rujulah fi al-Riwayah al-ʿArabiyyah* (Manliness and the Ideology of Manliness in the Arabic Novel). Beirut: Dar al-Taliʿah, 1983.

———. "Taqdim." In Sighmund Fruyd, *Mustaqbal Wahm*, trans. Jurj Tarabishi, 5–6. Beirut: Dar al-Taliʿah, 1974.

———. *ʿUntha Didd al-Unuthah: Dirasah fi Adab Nawal al-Saʿdawi* (A Female against Femininity: A Study of the Fiction of Nawal al-Saʿdawi). Beirut: Dar al-Taliʿah, 1984.

———. *ʿUqdat Udib fi al-Riwayah al-ʿArabiyyah* (The Oedipus Complex in the Arabic Novel). Beirut: Dar al-Taliʿah, 1982.

Taylor, Charles. *A Secular Age*. Cambridge, MA: Harvard University Press, 2007.

Tessler, Mark, and Amaney Jamal. "Political Attitude Research in the Arab World: Emerging Opportunities." *PS: Political Science and Politics* 39, no. 3 (2006): 434–35.

Thomas, Greg. *The Sexual Demon of Colonial Power: Pan-African Embodiment and Erotic Schemes of Empire*. Bloomington: Indiana University Press, 2007.

Thoreson, Ryan Richard. "Power, Panics, and Pronouns: The Information Politics of Transnational LGBT NGOs." *Journal of Language and Sexuality* 2, no. 1 (2013): 145–77.

Tilly, Charles, ed. "The Emergence of Citizenship in France and Elsewhere." In *Citizenship, Identity and Social History*, 223–37. Melbourne: University of Cambridge Press Syndicate, 1996.

Tolan, John, Gilles Veinstein, and Henry Laurens. *Europe and the Islamic World: A History*. Oxford: Oxford University Press, 2013.

Tocqueville, Alexis de. *Democracy in America*. 2 vols. New York: Adlard and Saunders, 1838.

————. *Oeuvres complètes*. Edited by Jacob-Peter Mayer. Paris: Gallimard, 1951.

Trotsky, Leon. "Perspectives and Tasks in the East." Speech delivered on the third anniversary of the Communist University for Toilers in the East in the USSR, 21 April 1924. London: Index Books, 1973. Available at http://www.marxists .org/archive/trotsky/1924/04/perspectives.htm (accessed 1 April 2014).

Trumpener, Ulrich. *Germany and the Ottoman Empire, 1914–1918*. Princeton, NJ: Princeton University Press, 1968.

Tucker, Judith. *In the House of the Law: Gender and Islamic Law in Ottoman Syria and Palestine*. Berkeley: University of California Press, 1998.

"The Turkish Model: A Hard Act to Follow." *Economist*, 6 August 2011.

Turner, Bryan. "Orientalism and the Problem of Civil Society in Islam." In *Orientalism, Islam, and Islamists*, edited by Asaf Hussain, Robert Olson, and Jamil Qureshi, 20–35. Brattleboro, VT: Amana Books, 1984.

UNAIDS. *HELEM: A Case Study of the First Legal, Above-Ground LGBT Organization in the MENA Region*. Report published 21 October 2008.

United Nations Development Program. *Arab Human Development Report 2003: Building a Knowledge Society*. New York: UNDP, 2003.

————. *The Arab Human Development Report 2005: Towards the Rise of Women in the Arab World*. New York: UNDP, 2003.

Valensi, Lucette. *The Birth of the Despot: Venice and the Sublime Porte*. Ithaca, NY: Cornell University Press, 1993.

Valentine, David. *Imagining Transgender: An Ethnography of a Category*. Durham, NC: Duke University Press, 2007.

Van Sommer, Annie. *Our Muslim Sisters: A Cry of Need from Lands of Darkness Interpreted by Those Who Heard It*. New York: F. H. Revell, 1907. Available at http://archive.org/stream/ourmoslemsisters30178gut/30178-8.txt (accessed 1 April 2014).

Vance, Carole. "Anthropology Rediscovers Sexuality: A Theoretical Comment." *Social Science and Medicine* 33, no. 8 (1991): 875–84.

Venturi, Franco. "Oriental Despotism." *Journal of the History of Ideas* 24, no. 1 (1963): 133–42.

"Violence against Women: A National Crime Victimization Survey Report." US Department of Justice, Washington, DC, January 1994.

Vitalis, Robert. *America's Kingdom: Mythmaking on the Saudi Oil Frontier*. Stanford. CA: Stanford University Press, 2007.

Voloshinov, V. N. *Freudianism: A Marxist Critique*. London: Verso, 2012.

Volpp, Leti. "Blaming Culture for Bad Behavior." *Yale Journal of Law and Humanities* 12 (2000): 89–117.

————. "(Mis)Identifying Culture: Asian Women and the 'Cultural Defenses.'" *Harvard Women's Law Journal* 57 (1994): 91–93.

von Grunebaum, G. E. *Islam: Essays in the Nature and Growth of a Cultural Tradition*. London: Routledge and Kegan Paul, 1955.

Waltz, Susan Eileen. "Universal Human Rights: The Contribution of Muslim States." *Human Rights Quarterly* 26, no. 4 (2004): 799–844.

Warner, Michael. "Something Queer about the Nation-State." In *After Political Correctness: The Humanities in the 1990s,* edited by Christopher Newfield and Ronald Strickland, 361–71. Boulder, CO: Westview Press, 1995.

Waterbury, John. "Democracy without Democrats: The Potential for Political Liberalization in the Middle East." In *Democracy without Democrats? The Renewal of Policy in the Muslim World,* edited by Ghassan Salamé, 23–47. London: I. B. Tauris, 2001.

Waterbury, John, and Alan Richards. *A Political Economy of the Middle East.* Boulder, CO: Westview Press, 1990.

Watt, Nicholas. "Cameron Calls on Islam to Embrace Democracy and Reject Extremism." *Guardian,* 12 April 2012.

Weber, Elisabeth. *Living Together: Jacques Derrida's Communities of Violence and Peace.* New York: Fordham University Press, 2013.

Weeks, John. *Among Congo Cannibals.* Philadelphia: J. B. Lippincott, 1913.

Weston, Kath. "Lesbian/Gay Studies in the House of Anthropology." *Annual Review of Anthropology* 22 (1993): 339–67.

The White House Office of the Press Secretary. "Memorandum for the Heads of Executive Departments and Agencies: International Initiatives to Advance the Human Rights of Lesbian, Gay, Bisexual, and Transgender Persons," 6 December 2011.

Wilde, Oscar. *Two Plays by Oscar Wilde:* An Ideal Husband *and* A Woman of No Importance. New York: Signet Classics, 1997.

Williams, Raymond. *Culture and Society, 1780–1950.* New York: Columbia University Press, 1983.

———. *Keywords: Vocabulary of Culture and Society.* Rev. ed. Oxford: Oxford University Press, 1983.

Wise, Christopher. "Deconstruction and Zionism: Jacques Derrida's *Specters of Marx.*" *Diacritics* 31, no. 1 (2001): 56–72.

Wittfogel, Karl A. *Oriental Despotism: A Comparative Study of Total Power.* New Haven, CT: Yale University Press, 1957.

Wollstonecraft, Mary. *A Vindication of the Rights of Woman.* 1792. New York: Dover, 1996.

Wood, Elizabeth A. *The Baba and the Comrade: Gender and Politics in Revolutionary Russia.* Bloomington: Indiana University Press, 1997.

Yerushalmi, Yosef Haim. *Freud's Moses: Judaism Terminable and Interminable.* New Haven, CT: Yale University Press, 1991.

Yildiz, Yasemin. "Governing European Subjects: Tolerance and Guilt in the Discourse of 'Muslim Women.'" *Cultural Critique* 77 (2011): 70–101.

Zaywar, Mustafa. "Adwaʾ ʿala al-Mujtamaʿ al-Israʾili: Jadal al-Sayyid wa al-ʿAbd" (Shedding Light on Israeli Society: The Slave-Master Dialectic). In *Mustafa Zaywar: fi Dhikra al-ʿAlim wa al-Fannan wa al-Insan* (In Memory of the Scholar, the Artist, and the Man), edited by Usamah Khalil, 78–92. Paris: Maʿhad al-Lughah wa al-Hadarah al-ʿArabiyyah, 1997.

————. "Saykulujiyyat al-Taᶜassub" (The Psychology of Chauvinism). In *Mustafa Zaywar: fi Dhikra al-ᶜAlim wa al-Fannan wa al-Insan* (In Memory of the Scholar, the Artist, and the Man), edited by Usamah Khalil, 59–77. Paris: Maᶜhad al-Lughah wa al-Hadarah al-ᶜArabiyyah, 1997.

Žižek, Slavoj. "Against Human Rights." *New Left Review* 34 (2005): 115–16.

————. "A Glance into the Archives of Islam," http://www.lacan.com/zizarchives .htm (accessed 1 April 2014).

Zolondek, L. "Sabunji in England, 1876–1891: His Role in Arabic Journalism." *Middle Eastern Studies* 14, no. 1 (1978): 102–15.

Zonana, Joyce. "The Sultan and the Slave: Feminist Orientalism and the Structure of 'Jane Eyre.'" *Signs* 18, no. 3 (1993): 592–617.

Index

'Abd al-Majid I, Ottoman Sultan, 85
'Abd al-Nasir, Jamal, 76, 81–82;
    coup against, 80
'Abd al-Raziq, 'Ali, 95
'Abduh, Muhammad, 25, 65, 86
Abdülhamid II, Ottoman Sultan,
    63–64, 64n160, 66, 69–70, 84–
    85, 89, 92
Abraham (prophet), 280–81, 307–
    8, 326–28, 330, 334, 338; as
    Muslim, 329
Abrahamic religions, 314, 325–26,
    329–30, 334–35; appeal to,
    as abstract, 338; Arab Jews,
    338; commonality of, 337–38;
    deployment of, 340; Islamicness
    of, 328; Israeli Jews and, 338;
    Palestinians and, 338; Semitic,
    linked to, 332
Abrahamic Sanctuary, 338–39
Abu-Lughod, Lila, 139–41, 174–75,
    175n216, 175n217, 176, 182,
    195
Abunimah, Ali, 237–38n57
Abu Nuwas, 229, 276
Abu-Odeh, Lama, 172n206
ACCEPT, 259
Accumulation on a World Scale
    (Amin), 40
Aceh (Indonesia), 60, 61n150, 70
Activists beyond Borders (Keck and
    Sikkinik), 164
Adely, Fida, 177
Afghani, Jamal al-Din al-, 40–41,
    86, 295

Afghanistan, 45, 76, 83, 94, 104–5,
    111, 139–40, 202, 206n305, 269
Afkhami, Mahnaz, 133–35
Africa, 10, 15, 22, 24, 26–27, 38–39,
    44, 47–48, 56, 67, 91, 116, 118,
    137, 144, 148, 150, 239, 320;
    active and passive citizenship
    in, 24; bifurcated citizenship in,
    27; as colonial subjects in, 27;
    decentralized despotism in, 27;
    indirect rule in, 53
African Americans, 116, 131
African National Congress (ANC),
    259–60
agency, 11, 235, 245; as anti-
    colonial, 250; sexual, 248–51,
    262n130; universalism, 248,
    250
Age of Enlightenment, 50
Agha Khan, 92, 117
Ahmad, Ahmad Atif, 289n55
Ahmed, Leila, 118–19, 154
Ajami, Fouad, 228
Akhter, Farida, 160
Al-Ahram (newspaper), 277
Albania, 68
Aleppo (Syria), 61
Alexandria (Egypt), 84
Alfieri, Vittorio, 86
Algeria, 65, 72, 111, 149–50, 156,
    192
Al-Hiwar (magazine), 83
Alif (journal), 159–60
Al-Ittihad (newspaper), 64
Al-Jazeera television, 209

Eastern Question (*cont.*)
Christianity, 17; Western Europe, 15; as Western Question, 16; as Woman Question, 122–23

East India Company, 26

East Timor, 100

Ebu's Suʿud, 62

Economic and Social Commission for Western Asia (ESCWA), 201

Edelman, Lee, 233

The Ego and the Id (Freud), 285

Egypt, 34, 50, 61–62, 64, 65, 70, 85–86, 90, 92, 101, 105, 111, 118, 134, 139, 164, 185, 190, 192, 203, 261–63n130, 339; Asian and African Islam, as barrier between, 68; "Culture of Optimism" campaign in, 167; Napoleonic invasion of, 84; Queen Boat raid in, 261–63n130, 264–65; women in, 118

Egypt Air flight 990, 8

Egyptian Feminist Union, 122

Egyptian National Party (al-Hizb al-Watani), 102

Egyptian Society of the Muslim Brothers, 76, 78–81

Egyptian University, 101. *See also* Cairo University

Einstein, Albert, 300

Eisenhower, Dwight D., 77–78, 97

Eisenhower Doctrine, 81, 163; Middle East alliance, with United States, 96–97

Eisenstein, Zillah, 119

Eickelman, Dale F., 5n12

El-Taller, 146

Emié, Bernard, 309n130

Encyclopedia of Women and Islamic Cultures (Lagrange), 267

England, 87, 91, 118, 152, 186–87, 190. *See also* Great Britain

Enlightened despotism, 52–53

Enlightenment, 3, 11, 17, 22, 26, 37, 44, 53, 105, 108, 123, 200, 321, 326

Enver Pasha, 91

Equality Now, 147

Equal Rights Amendment (ERA), 125

An Essay in Defence of the Female Sex . . . Written by a Lady, 114

Essay on the Inequality of the Human Races (Gobineau), 56–57

Euro-America, 39, 153, 217, 245, 248, 254, 272; gay solidarity in, 265–66; sexual citizenship in, 269; sexuality, as term in, 219

Eurocentrism, 158, 242

Euro-Mediterranean Foundation of Support to Human Rights Defenders (EMHRF), 271–72n157

Europe, 11, 17, 19, 20, 20n18, 39, 51–52, 58–59, 69, 71, 83, 99, 106–7, 112, 120, 124, 129, 135, 137–38, 148, 153, 173, 175, 207, 209, 212, 217, 225, 232, 234, 237, 246, 249–50, 252, 263, 272–73, 295, 302–3, 309n130, 310, 315–16, 320, 324, 328, 331, 339, 341; ancient Greece, as democratic origins of, 28; Arabo-Islamic origins, suppression of, 16; and coal, 99; colonial settlers, defending of, 111; democracy in, 24, 27, 56; as "democratic," 13; despotic colonial rule, 57; despotism, 23; external others of, 1, 12; fascism, 29; and gender, 200; Hellenism and Hebraism, dual tradition of in, 28; identitarian ideology of, 313; identity crisis of, 123–24; imperialism, 21, 233; industrialization in, 99; internal others of, 1, 11–12; invention of, 15; Latin in, 285; liberalism in, 1–3, 24, 96, 110, 158; liberal thought in, 21–22, 109; missionizing democracy of, 13; multiculturalism, 154; as multicultural laboratory, 124; and Orient, 1–2, 316; Orientalism, theory of, 15; others in, 54; pluralism, and Islamic presence in, 311; Protestant Reformation, 41; sexual citizenship in, 269; sexuality, as term, in, 218–19; as transcendental idea, 15; women's equality in, 124

European Assembly of the Council of Europe, 204n299

Europeanism: Aryanism, 317; Semitism, 317

European Union, 123, 204n299, 259, 261–63n130

Evans, Trefor, 80

Farhi, Hilal, 277n10

Farrell, Amy, 141

Farris, Sarah R., 124

Faruq, King, 95

Faruqi, Ismaʿil Raji al-, 9

fascism, 29, 44

Fassin, Eric, 268

Faysal, Prince, 82

INDEX

De Gids (journal), 91
Gilroy, Paul, 56–57
Gingrich, Newt, 58
global feminism, 148
Global Fund for Women, 271–72n157
globalization, 18, 145, 167, 178
Gobineau, Arthur de, 56–57
Goldstein, Baruch, 338
Goldstein, Eric, 319
Goldziher, Ignác, 69
Gorbachev, Mikhail, 132
governmentality, 167
Gran, Peter, 43n88
Granville, Minister, 61
Great Britain, 14, 21, 61–62, 64–65, 77, 83, 85, 90, 92, 94–95, 99, 116, 118, 143, 189, 210, 216, 275; culturalist arguments against, lack of, 57; Muslims in, 107. *See also* England
Greece, 20n18, 28, 32, 48, 161–62
Grewal, Inderpal, 137, 141, 145, 171, 174
Group Psychology and the Analysis of the Ego (Freud), 298
Guignard, François-Emmanuel, comte de Saint-Priest, 62
Guizot, François, 41
Gulf states, 167, 202
Gunning, Isabelle, 138–40
Guzmán, San Domenico de, 36

Habib, Samar, 215, 238, 239n60, 247, 256, 261–63n130
Hagar, 280–81, 307–8, 331
Hallaq, Wael, 9, 26–28, 60, 156–57, 188
Halley, Janet, 314
Hamas, 8
Hannibal, 323
Hapsburgs, 62
Hariri financial empire, 167
Hartmann, M. Martin, 69, 71, 91
Hartz, Louis, 46
Hashemites, 81
Hasso, Frances, 181
Hastings, Warren, 50
Hatt-I Hümayun Decree, 61
Hawting, Gerald, 329n51
Hayes, Jarrod, 244–45
Heartland Alliance, 224
Hebron (West Bank), 338–39. *See also* al-Khalil (Palestine)
Heinrich Böll Foundation, 224, 271–72n157

Helem organization, 223–24, 224n23, 226–27; acronym of, 223n18
Hélie-Lucas, Marie-Aimée, 149–51, 151n144, 153, 156
Helsinki Watch, 136. *See also* Human Rights Watch
Hibri, Aziza al-, 155
Hijaz, 62, 64–65, 89, 92
Hilmi, ʿAbbas, 65, 67, 86, 89–90, 102
Hinduism, 35, 275
History of Sexuality (Foucault), 253
Hoad, Neville, 221n16, 231
Hoagland, Richard, 227
Hochberg, Gil, 235–36n53
Hodgson, Marshall, 215; Islamdom, as term, 214
Holland. *See* Netherlands
holocaust, 324, 340
Holy Land, 15, 326, 327
Holy See, 261–63n130
Homayounpour, Gohar, 295–98
homonationalism, 270–71
homosexuality: in China, 263n131; essentialist claims about, 246; imperialism, 220n14; and Islam, 239; as term, invention of, 254–55n110; universalization of, 252. *See also* gay and lesbian identities; gayness
Homosexuality in Islam (Kugle), 215, 239
honor crimes, 172, 172n206, 175, 207n306, 208; in Arab countries, 129; and hijab, 201; in Italy, 207n306; as Orientalist category, 171, and women, 205
Houbballah, Adnan, 277, 279, 293–95, 300–301n97, 303, 305n115
Hrawi, Muna al-, 146
Hudaybi, Hasan Ismaʾil al, 80
Hu Jintao, 33
human rights, 126, 130–32; of Arab women, 146–47; as Christian idea, 142–43; internationalist dimension of, as crucial, 143; law of, as Euro-American cultural system, 128; neoliberal global capitalism, 133; as US imperial policy, 143
human rights internationalism, 143, 174, 176
human rights movement: and culture, 127–29; gender-based violence, 127–28; gender essentialism, 129; modernity, international culture of, 127–28; violence against women, campaign to end,